D0578421

Edited by Don Zahner and the staff of Fly Fisherman magazine.

Book design by James Sulham.

ISBN: 0-87165-013-4
Library of Congress Catalog Card Number: 78-53591

Published in the United States of America in 1978 by Ziff-Davis
Publishing Company, One Park Avenue, New York, New York 10016, U. S. A.

First Edition

Printed by Judd & Detweiler, Inc. • Printers Washington, D.C. 20002, U. S. A.

FLY FISHERMAN'S Complete Guide to . . .

FISHING with the FLY ROD

Cordes • Kreh • Lyons • Merwin • Niemeyer • Richards
Schwiebert • Sosin • Swisher • Traver • The Wulffs • Zahner
and the staff of Fly Fisherman Magazine

CONTENTS

CONTRIBUTORS

RON CORDES *(Lake Fishing for Trout)* is the West Coast Field Editor of FLY FISHERMAN magazine. This is a region of the country in which fly-rodding for stillwater trout is becoming increasingly popular.

JIM ENGER *(Casting About: Canada)* is FLY FISHERMAN'S Midwestern Field Editor who often forsakes the fine fishing in his native Michigan for the lure of the North Woods.

LEFTY KREH *(Fly-Fishing for Bass and Panfish)* is widely acknowledged to be among the world's most proficient anglers and is also an excellent instructor.

ART LEE *(Casting About)* is the Northeastern Field Editor of FLY FISHERMAN magazine, but that hasn't kept him from swimming a fly in most of America's productive waters from Connecticut to California.

ERIC LEISER *(Fly-Tying Materials)* is the author of the book, *Fly-Tying Materials* (Crown), and a frequent contributor to FLY FISHERMAN.

NICK LYONS *(Building a Fly-Fishing Library)* is a prominent editor of angling books, and is also the author of several books, including the recently published *Bright Rivers* (Lippincott). He is a Contributing Editor of FLY FISHERMAN magazine, in which his regular column, "The Seasonable Angler," appears.

JOHN MERWIN *(Stream Fishing for Trout)* is the Managing Editor of FLY FISHERMAN. He has fly-fished long enough to have been frustrated by most of the situations that confront stream anglers, and has fished around enough to have found solutions to a few of them.

TED NIEMEYER *(Tying Your Own Flies)* is often mentioned as being one of the foremost fly tiers in the field. He is also a Contributing Editor of FLY FISHERMAN, whose regular assignment includes the magazine's Fly-Tier's Bench department.

CARL RICHARDS *(What Trout Eat)* achieved national prominence with the publication of *Selective Trout* (Crown), which he co-authored with Doug Swisher in 1971, and which was a path-finding book in the field of angling entomology.

ERNEST SCHWIEBERT *(The History and Lore of Fly-Fishing)* is a name that has become synonymous with the finest in fly-fishing, both in his writing and in his angling. He is FLY FISHERMAN magazine's Editor-at-Large.

MARK SOSIN *(Fly-Fishing in Salt Water)* is a widely known and respected outdoor writer who specializes in fishing topics, and who is one of the true authorities on saltwater fly-fishing. He is also a Contributing Editor of FLY FISHERMAN magazine.

DOUG SWISHER *(Reading the Water)* has become best known in recent years as a fly-fishing writer *(Selective Trout* and *Fly-Fishing Strategy*, Crown, both co-authored with Carl Richards) and instructor who offers an extensive series of fly-fishing schools around the country each year.

ROBERT TRAVER *(Foreword)* is the pen name of a former Michigan State Supreme Court Justice who wrote the best-selling novel, *Anatomy of a Murder*, during the 1950's. He then retired and wrote several angling books, including the well-known *Trout Madness*. He presently lives and fishes in northern Michigan.

CRAIG WOODS *(Fly-Tackle Directory)* is FLY FISHERMAN'S Associate Editor.

LEE AND JOAN WULFF *(Casting with the Fly Rod* and *Choosing Your Fly)* are probably fly-fishing's best-known couple. Joan is a former tournament caster who has held both national and international titles, and who now devotes much of her time to teaching casting. Lee has been filming and writing about fly-fishing for nearly 50 years, and has done much to make the sport almost a household word.

DON ZAHNER *(Getting Started in Fly-Fishing)* is the Editor and Publisher of FLY FISHERMAN magazine.

EDITOR'S PREFACE

WHEN WE AT FLY FISHERMAN MAGAZINE conceived the idea for *Fishing with the Fly Rod,* it was to be a book directed primarily at the beginning angler. Then we thought that over a bit.

If a *beginning* angler is one that isn't *finished,* which the word suggests, then the scope of this book is considerably broadened. Any fly fisherman who thinks he has learned everything about his craft hasn't learned much. We know anglers in their 80's, still spry and eager, who will go gracefully to their rest still looking for that perfect presentation to the perfect rise of the perfect fish.

We would like to think that there's something in this book that would even help them. Primarily, however, we have tried to bring together fly-fishing authorities of impeccable credential to guide and counsel anyone—rank beginner, novice or experienced—who might have a problem catching a fish on every cast.

We promise *not* to solve *that* problem. But we will show the "incompleat angler" why it isn't all that important, and that there is more to fishing than the fish.

Don Zahner
Editor and Publisher
Fly Fisherman Magazine

Now, here's a man . . .
who deserves an introduction, even if he doesn't need one.

FEW OUTDOOR RECREATIONS can boast a living, ready-to-worship folk myth. Fly-fishing has one.

Truthfully, however, before making his presence generally known to the angling multitudes, Robert Traver was long a legend to those hale and hardies who people that most loose-hung and distant of U.S. protectorates, the Upper Peninsula of Michigan.

From boyhood street-tough to lawyer, from district attorney to Michigan Supreme Court Justice, Traver nurtured his love for the brook trout and the places they live. He even paused in his career occasionally to write several books, including *Trout Madness*, of which he is both the author and the first clinically recorded case.

Then came the biggie. *Anatomy of a Murder* became an instant best-seller, and Traver proved he was a best-selling author by selling the movie rights to Otto Preminger. He then played on-location host and technical director to Preminger's cast, including Jimmy Stewart, Lee Remick, George C. Scott and, in a brilliant casting move, Joe Welch as the judge (the Boston lawyer who settled so many people's hash during the Army-McCarthy hearings in the 1950's).

Traver quickly but gracefully retired from the court to return permanently to the Upper Peninsula and pursue the more important things in life, such as fishing, writing and the other miscellaneous things the citizens of that 51st State do to ward off the pellagra and exorcise evil demons.

By-products of this sabbatical, besides an unspeakably modest number of fish, have been *Trout Magic*—after *Trout Madness* he had mellowed a bit in his aberrations—and the classic *Anatomy of a Fisherman.* The latter work resulted from the visit to the U. P. by *Life* photographer Robert W. Kelley to do a picture story on "another best-selling author," a routine assignment until Kelley fell under the Traver spell and ended up using most of the out-takes to co-author the book with Traver.

The highest moment of this delightful labor of love was Traver's eloquently simple statement of why he fishes, "Testament of A Fisherman." This fragile fragment is reprinted, by permission of the author, on the first color plate following page 32.

But Kelley and I are not the only ones to fall under the spell of Robert Traver and his newest of testaments. CBS News personality Charles (On the Road) Kuralt visited Traver to do a 30-minute television special, became converted, both to Traver and trout, and proceeded to recite the litany of "Testament of A Fisherman" voice-over as counterpoint to Traver's deft casts (which finally produced on-camera a trout, a full nine inches).

If TV viewers suspect that Kuralt is "On the Road" less these days, they can assume that he is more often "on the stream," for he is now one of Traver's "wild-eyed, mosquito-crazed characters," ready, upon hearing "of a place where they splash waves in your face," to "zoom to the moon, gaily negotiating seven cedar swamps on the way."

This is vintage Traver, but a more recent harvest lies ahead for the many readers of *Fishing with the Fly Rod* who have not previously met up with The Judge. He speaks only the truth, and if you read only his words in the "Foreword" to this book and nothing else—for shame—you will understand the strange malady to which you have been exposed.

For his love affair with words and the people who read them, and with trout and the people who fish for them, is worn on the sleeve of his smelly old fishing jacket, along with his little bottle of fly dope and those tiny #28 flies, the very existence of which requires a total and willing suspension of disbelief.

Speaking of which, his name isn't "Robert Traver" at all. It's John Voelker. The man lies through his teeth—but not about important things.

Donald D. Zahner
Editor and Publisher
Fly Fisherman Magazine

Foreword

FLY-FISHING is one of the more amiable forms of an incurable madness that confines its victims to crowded prison cells along with all their precious gear—thus often adding Santa Claustrophobia to their woes. To prevent escape these cells have bars from six to nine feet long, cunningly contrived of strips of split bamboo costing upwards of five dollars an inch. Or of fiberglass. Or of graphite. Or, in advanced cases, of a crazy mixture of all three.

I was born in the heart of the Lake Superior bush country of northern Michigan around the turn of the century—though of late years I sometimes get turned around about precisely which century. But however foggy my centuries may be getting, I'll never forget the plight of a youngster raised in a land of many lakes and streams all crammed with wild native brook trout. For back in those days the brook trout was just about the only gamefish there was around.

Alas, I still bear the psychic scars of that deprived childhood. Imagine, if you can, a poor lad day after day being forced to fish for the same old thing and day after day trudging home with just another creelful of those same plump old brookies. I can still feel the pangs of shame and ignominy over it all, the frustration and the monotony, the sense of desolation and denial.

Still another bitter price I paid for those vanished days was that the fishing was so incredibly easy that virtually nobody thought of stooping to fish for our trout with a fly. *That* was an expensive and highfalutin affectation reserved for a few local eccentrics one shunned like lepers. Consequently I became just one of the many forsaken local lads who had no one to set them upon the paths of fishing virtue. For most of our fathers shunned fly-fishing just as they did those few pariahs lucky enough to have found that golden path.

I've told this sad story elsewhere (surely this is no place to plug *Trout Magic*, is it?), so I'll not repeat it here. Doing so might also pain its anonymous publisher (Crown, N.Y, 1974)—wups, it just slipped out—so I'll merely say I was well out of college before I seriously took up fly-fishing, incredible as that may seem. And I'm still gnawed by all those wasted years I went without that sweet obsession and the comfort of nestling in my very own cell made of split bamboo. Or fiberglass. Or graphite. Or all three.

So I am naturally filled with wonder and envy over the vast good fortune once denied me but now given to the beginning fly fishermen of our day. For he or she may now for a pittance claim such a treasure as *Fishing with the Fly Rod* to ease their transition to the magical and—let's face it—only civilized way to take *any* gamefish *anywhere.*

Imagine the soul-wounds I might have been spared had I as a lad been able to own and read such a book, one in which some of the savviest and most battle-scarred fly-fishing hands in the country break down and reveal the secrets of a lifetime. Dark hard-won secrets such as, to name but a few, how to get started fly-fishing; how to cast a fly and where and what to do it with; how to tie your own; the background and the fascinating lore; the books to buy and others to use as door stops; all about rods and lines and the endless gear and, oh yes, so much about reels until the mind inclines to do likewise.

Imagine, too, all the poor trout that might have been spared during those barbaric years when I was derricking up countless trout on those ice-tong hooks I heaved out with a rusty steel girder strung with an old frayed hawser. Imagine also that I once might have actually learned to tie a decent fly instead of having to confess, which I recently did in a certain book that shall remain absolutely nameless (since once ought to be enough, anyway), that far from ever learning to tie a fly I'm still barely able to unzip one.

So get, read, and covet this fabled book, you lucky lads and lassies out there poised on the brink of piscatorial paradise.

Robert Traver
Somewhere on the Upper Peninsula, Michigan
January 31, 1978
(3 months till fishing!)

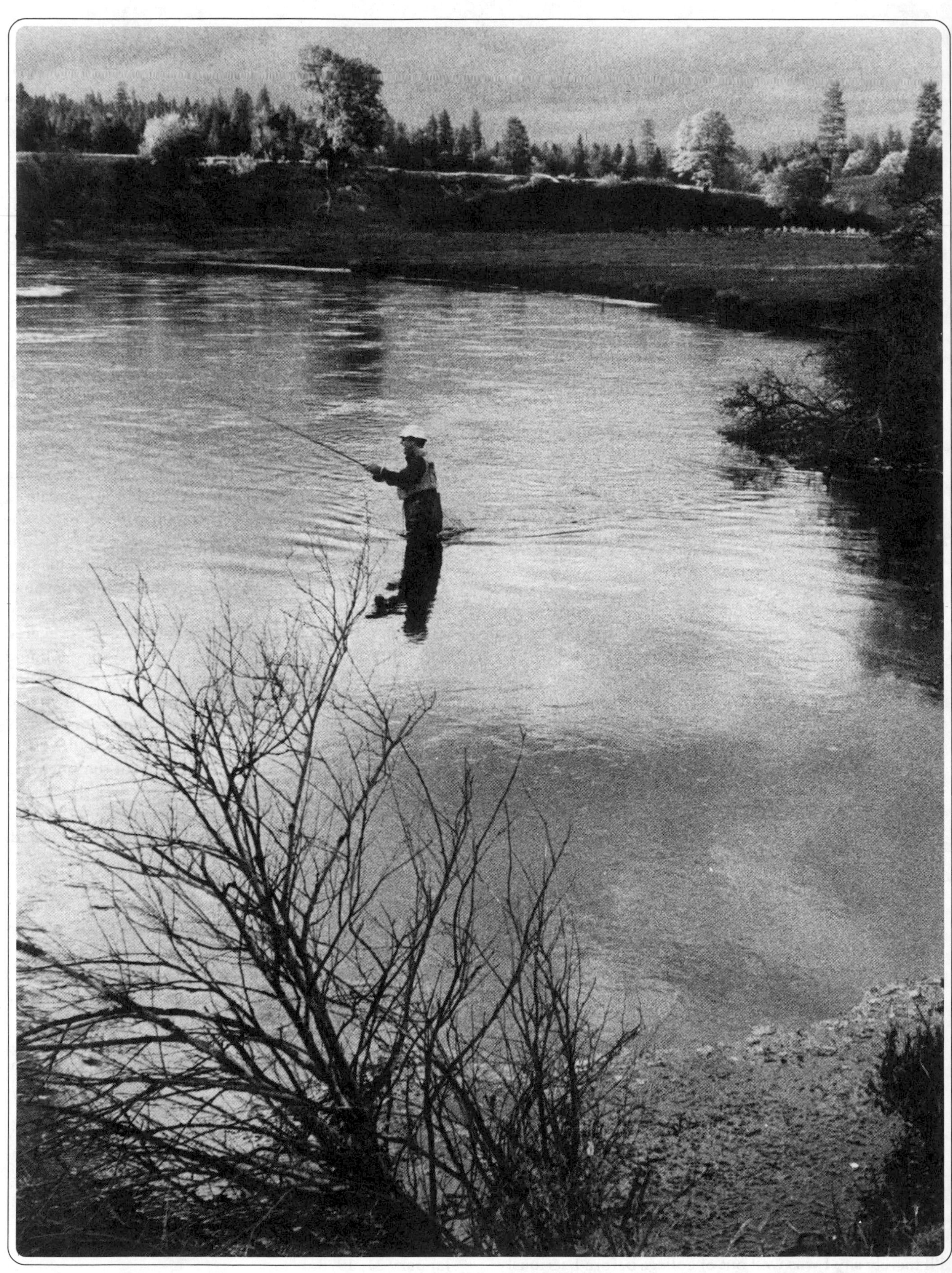

Photo by Valentine Atkinson.

THE EVENING WAS AS WARM AND SOFT as one could ask of early summer. The shaded banks of the stream were already places of dark mystery, but the quick flow of midstream seemed to hold a life of its own, still sparkling and silvery in the graying dusk. There had been a hint of rain, just enough to round off the corners of nightfall, just enough to cause faint mists downstream, just enough to let the overhanging willow wands seem to drip, drip, drip incessantly, almost rhythmically, soft plinks of moisture into the dark pools below. You could even see, if your eyes were as clear and sharp as a 12-year-old boy's, the little rippled circles that the drops made before they were wiped away by the gentle bankside current.

Then there was the sudden sound of riffled water downstream, and a dark shape began to take form in the mists below the sheltering willows. It moved silently along, its wake barely disturbing the water, until it became the figure of a man. It was the Old Geezer who had been walking along the bank earlier that afternoon: at least 50, the studied judgment of 12 years reckoned. Suddenly the Old Geezer's arm, the one that didn't hold the long, slim fishing rod, reached out and plucked at what seemed to be a piece of the gathering mists. He uncupped his hand, then reached out and up again in a mysterious ballet and finally pulled in a gossamer something that seemed to satisfy him.

The Old Geezer tensed, and his eyes focused on the dark pool beneath the willow, on the widening circles beneath the overhanging limbs. Then it happened. So gracefully, so smoothly, so silently, the Geezer lifted his right arm and, with the glint of the wispy rod in the twilight to signal his action, the white line that had been coiled at his side like a limp lariat suddenly sailed back, far behind him in a long and gentle bowing arc. As quickly, the arching line moved forward in a mirror image of itself, then straightened out to drop lightly just above one of the spreading rings beneath the willows and forming a tiny ring of its own.

But this ring had a short life. It had scarcely begun to make itself known when the quiet of the dark was broken by a sparkling splash of light and sound. The Old Geezer's rod began to twitch, then bend, and the line, once loose and drifting, now was taut as the fish—what else could it be?—drew it down into the deep. Once, then twice, the fish—which now it certainly was—twisted upward into the night air as it sought to free itself from the flimsy but firm bond that had lured it from its element into a new and unfamiliar world.

And now a third leap, then nothing. The arched rod straightened, the water quieted, and only the muffled curse of the Old Geezer remained. The boy had heard worse than that in his time, but to him it was the curse of Merlin himself as the old sorcerer stood, in his dotage, above the rocks of Tintagel and struggled to conjure his final and master spell. For the boy had never seen such earthly magic as this, and he knew that, even if he lived to be 50 years old, he would never be able to do such a thing as he had just seen done here before him by the Old Geezer. This magic act, dark and occult. This private, mysterious art of the fly fisherman.

Chapter 1

Getting Started in Fly-Fishing

The Ultimate in Angling

DON ZAHNER

THERE ARE THOSE, like that young boy you just watched, who still believe that fly-fishing is an act of magic, an illusory bit of prestidigitation beyond the ken of mortal man. They have certainly been assisted in this illusion by a few stalwarts of our clan who, after taking their solemn vows of purity and serving out their novitiate years astream, like to give the impression that they have, as fly fishers, been called to some higher order of endeavor. Some even give the impression that they really don't need those waders while they're fishing—that they could just as easily walk *on* the water as in it. (But confidentially, they sink!)

But to be quite truthful, the young boy was not totally wrong. I can speak with some authority here, for I was the young 12-year-old-boy back in my native Missouri Ozarks, and now, unsteadily approaching Old

Geezerhood, the magic is still there. It's just that the magic is in me now, and not so much in the fishing.

It took exactly 25 years for me to get things in gear and start fly-fishing. As a kid, and like any kid, I found fishing to be a natural attraction, but like any kid, you have to catch fish to keep at it, and I found myself, again and again, matched up with a $3.00 bait-casting reel with a cunningly built-in backlash guaranteed to send any 12-year-old reeling back to his Erector set for rest and recuperation.

My dad was a city boy born and bred and never willingly ventured beyond the city limits. I've always wondered what dark secrets Mother held over his head to get him out into the countryside on those rare Sundays. Not that I was neglected—Dad was a sports fanatic, and by the time I reached my teens I had attended practically all scheduled baseball, football, and basketball games of that era, as well as prize fights, wrestling matches and bowling tournaments. All this prepared me, if not for life as we know it, at least to sneer knowledgeably at Howard Cosell, but until my adult years I was still a babe in the woods and a fumbling idiot on the stream.

So, conscious of my father's piscatorial benign neglect, when two sons of my own magically appeared on the scene—there were other things he didn't teach me, too—I felt it my duty to take them hunting and fishing as part of their education. Besides, it turned out to be easier to explain about the trout and the mayflies than the birds and the bees.

The boys were well into fishing when the first fly rod arrived on the scene, but I proved an inept instructor. I still remember those graceful figure eights my line made in the air before dumping the fly and leader in a majestic lump at my feet. One son sneered, the other giggled, and life ebbed low for the lonely angler.

But as someone so succinctly put it, it's always darkest before the dawn, and dawns of the next few years found me flailing away on ponds, lakes, streams, any body of water that I suspected might hold fish. I was even catching some.

I'll not bore you with the details of my major embarrassments and minor triumphs along the way to becoming a gut-hooked fly rodder, except to tell you that a new world soon opened up for me. I had become a believer. Fly-fishing requires that. If not an act of magic, fly-fishing *is* an act of faith. You've got to believe there are fish out there with a suicidal bent, ready and willing to impale themselves, at your bidding, on a flimsy construction of wire and thread and wool and fur.

Of course, you *won't* believe this, not really, until you actually pull it off. Then there'll be no stopping you. I know from experience. Within five years of the time I made my first glumpy cast, I left the security of a ten-year position with a large corporation, took my modest savings and rushed out to start a magazine for fly fishermen. There's no one more evangelistic than a converted sinner.

What Fly-Fishing Is—and Isn't

Fly-fishing is merely a way to catch fish. It is not just fishing for trout, though trout are traditionally a prime target for the fly rod. Any fish that feed on smaller baitfish or on insects are fair game for the fly fisher. Some fish do this more readily, at various times and in various places, than others, of course, and if I were to list the most consistent fly rod gamefish I would have to include, besides the brook, rainbow and brown trout, those smashing largemouth bass, the fighting smallmouth, the river-running shad, the spawning Atlantic salmon and his West Coast brethren, and last but certainly not least, those ubiquitous little "God-must-have-loved-'em" devils, the bluegill and their panfish cousins. And this doesn't begin to cover some of the more exotic types of freshwater gamefish and, of course, dozens of saltwater fish that inhabit the river estuaries, bays, reefs, surf, flats and even the ocean deeps.

Almost all of the freshwater gamefish listed above are available in nearly every state of the Union. The few states that don't have some type of trout population have so many other fly-rod targets that they never miss them. And those denizens of the salt lurk along every shoreline in the country. Fly-fishing is what you want to make it—where you want to take it.

Fly-fishing is not a "snob" sport. However, it offers such a challenge, such an escape through total involvement that it attracts the type of person who is looking for something different, who wants to go beyond the norm, who wants to go all the way to the ultimate in angling—which fly-fishing is.

Fly-fishing attracts people who love the places where quality fish live—the untarnished waters of isolated ponds, clear mountain streams, tinkling brooks, and wilderness lakes. They want to become a participant in all this, not just a spectator, and they find that fly-fishing offers the one natural way in which they can become an active part of the environment without destroying it. They know they have the option of releasing their catch without harming it, allowing it to fight again another day.

People like this come from all walks of life, but they move with a brighter step, a livelier eye, and often with deeper thoughts.

If these are snobs, then God love them!

Fly-fishing's earlier image of an elitist recreation for the privileged few did have some basis in fact. The fly fisher's roots sprang from the chalkstream seepages of southern England, where fly-fishing had its beginnings in the clear, chalk-bottomed, vegetation-rich waters of streams such as the Dove (Walton's home water), the Avon, the Test and the Itchen. All choice trout streams, as well as the salmon rivers to the north, were owned by

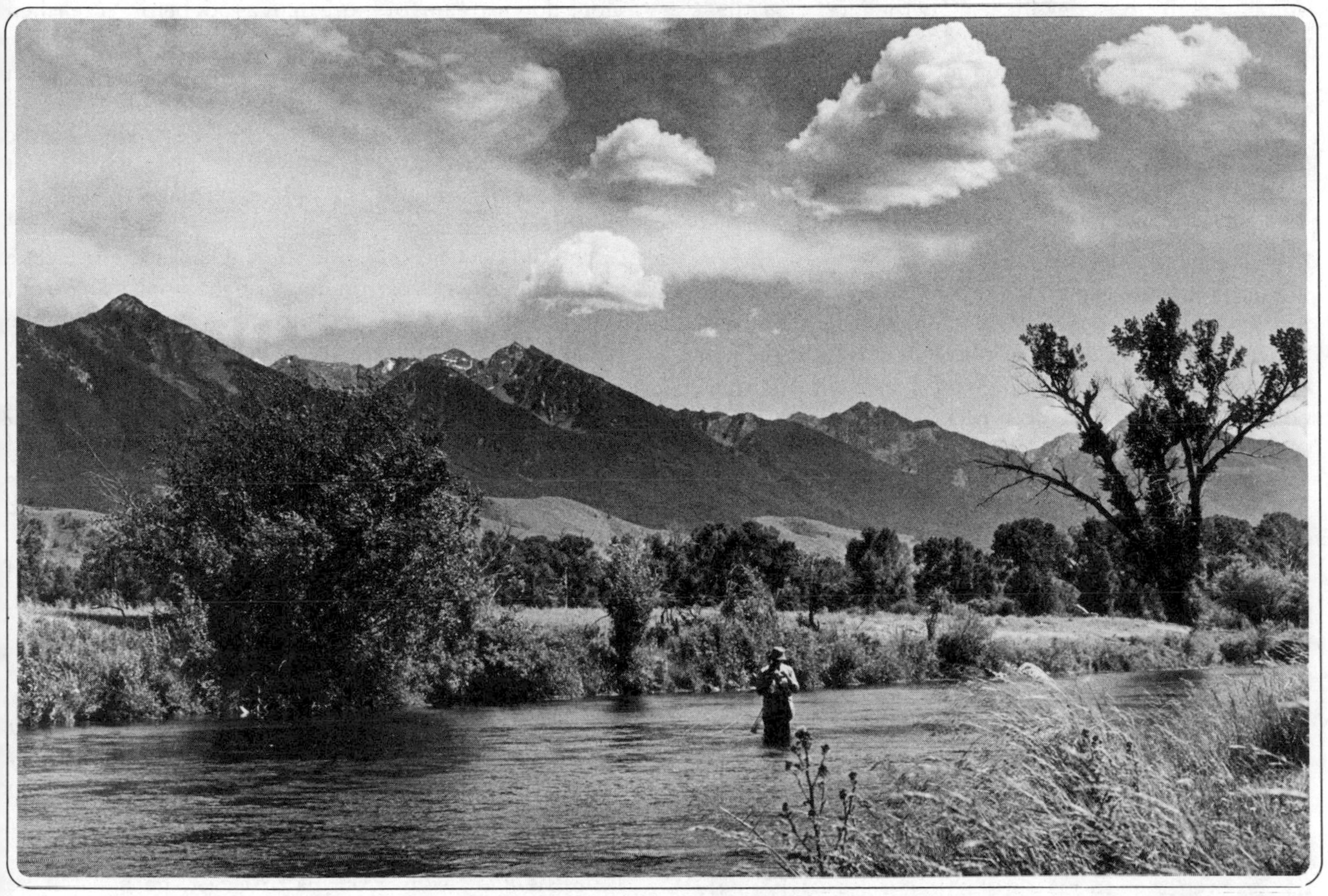

Armstrong's Spring Creek, Montana. Photo by Dave Engerbretson.

individuals, syndicates and other landowners, strictly the preserve of the landed gentry and their guests. To a degree, such is still the case today in Britain.

While most waters in this country are public, access is another matter, and in the early days of fly-fishing and proper equipment. The British heritage was cherished by the wealthy classes of the large Eastern cities, for they had the time, the money and the mobility, first by carriage, then trains, and finally the motor car, to reach the coldwater fisheries of the Catskills, the Poconos, the Adirondacks and the salmon rivers of Maine, Quebec and the Maritime Provinces of Canada.

They formed their clubs, posted their lands, wrote their articles and books, and in essence preserved the status quo of fly-fishing. And trout and salmon continued to be taken with regularity and taken for granted. But then the great leveler, the Depression, followed by World War II and the ensuing years of prosperity and upward mobility changed the social structure a bit, and expendable income, two-car families and the 40-hour work week released millions of people for sports, hobbies and recreation, and fishing was one of the major pursuits. Even so, fly-fishing fell into the shadows cast by the post-war "Spinning Occupation," as the new casting device and its spawn, the push-button spincasting reel, captured the imaginations of most anglers and brought millions of new anglers into the fold. A bit mechanical, true, but the spinning reel made it easy for these new anglers, men, women and children, to enjoy the sport of fishing.

And from these millions, each year a few thousand anglers were drawn toward the art of fly-fishing, then tens of thousands, until today the annual sales of fly rods number in the many hundreds of thousands. Fly rodders will probably always remain in the minority, though, because not everyone wants to devote the time and effort to develop their angling skills to the degree the fly fisherman needs.

But now comes the question: Why fly-fishing? There are times and places where more and bigger fish can be taken with other techniques. Why do they fish with the fly?

Before we answer this, let's define our terms. We at *Fly Fisherman* Magazine consider a fly fisherman to be someone who would *rather* fish with a fly than any other angling equipment. We made a reader survey several years ago and found, not to our complete surprise, that less than one out of five of these "purist" types fished *only* with the fly rod. They've merely chosen the fly rod because it's often the most effective, sometimes the most deadly, usually the most versatile—and always the most satisfying.

To complete our answer to that very logical question, we have to return to our stream, but this time as viewed through the eyes of the Old Geezer.

The Act of Fly-Fishing

EVEN BEFORE HE MOVED into the tail of the pool, the angler knew he was right. The hatch of mayflies was moving upstream like clockwork. In the distance they appeared to be clumping into misty clouds, but he chalked that off to myopia and continued his quiet glide through the knee-deep riffles until he entered the spillway of the Evening Pool.

Slowly now, he moved into the deepening slot. The water riffled around his wader seat now, but his eyes were intent on the darker water ahead under the sheltering willows. He had never had success during the daylight hours here, even in the morning hatch, but the dusk fell early in the deep, shaded pool that lay ahead and his hopes were high.

Almost within casting distance of the pool he stopped for a moment to survey the stretch ahead. Flies were heavy on the water now, and the warm, moist air seemed to melt around him. The soaring then dropping mayflies were thick about him, and he reached out, came back empty-handed, then captured one in a lightly clenched fist, examined it to his satisfaction, released it to fly away. "Dark Hendrickson," he muttered. "Size sixteen." Then he smiled softly. "How inbred we anglers are," he mused. "We name the insects after the flies we tie to catch the fish that feed on them. Even measure them by the hook size."

A muffled "slurp" broke into his thoughts. His eyes flashed upstream just in time to see the last ripples of the trout's quiet rise beneath the willow frond. Watching intently, he reflexively pulled a few extra feet of line into his left hand, looping the smooth, loose strands onto his fingers. As he tossed off a loose belly of fly line into the water behind him, he caught the sight and sound of a second rise. He was beginning to catch the rhythm of the rises, and he rolled the line into the air in front of him, then pulled back into a long, low backcast.

Just as it began to drop, he subconciously felt the nagging tug of heavy line started to cock his rod, loading it to the point that the long, slim taper of the rod seemed to bow to the breaking point. But at the proper moment the angler's forearm slid forward, straightening out the backcast only to send it forward in a tight, ever-lengthening loop of flashing fly line. As the line seemed to reach its farthest limits, the angler let a few more feet of running line pull from his left hand. The line rolled out, then seemed to hover for a moment over the water before it dropped lightly to the surface with a slight curl of its gossamer tippet. The fly at the end of the tippet wafted delicately onto the slight current, riding cockily along downstream for more than a foot before it reached the point of repeated rises.

The rise repeated once more, then turned into a flash of silver as the rainbow took the fly. The Old Geezer's rod rose as his left hand pulled the line down sharply. The trout turned quickly against the tautening line, but the fly held firmly in the liplike cartilage toward the rear of its mouth.

The rod bent fiercely, and the angler let the fish take some line as it ran for the head of the pool. The trout was into the reel now, and the angler liked to hear the rising shrill of the buzzing reel-clicks.

Then the jump, several feet in the air, the fish shaking its jaw as it launched itself upward. Out of respect, tradition—and fear of losing it—the Old Geezer bowed to the fish and slacked his line for a moment. As quickly he pulled line back through the rod guides as the fish turned and broke downstream.

The long leader was nearly into the tip-top of the rod and the fish was just below the angler when it happened. It caught the Geezer off guard, that last jump, and his reflexes weren't as sharp as his adversary's. His former adversary.

He muttered a mild condemnation, not of the fish, but of himself. He had missed the full satisfaction of bringing the fish to heel for a moment and that sharp twist of the wrist that would slip the fly from the fish and send it back down into the depths of the pool.

But he *had* taken it on his first cast, he *had* felt its surge of life transfer itself to his line, back to the limber rod, down to his hand and arm. For a moment the trout had given him a few extra seconds of life—and then had taken it away. Who had been in control?

But his moment of philosophizing passed quickly. Suddenly he was just another broken-down, broken-off angler with a twisted strand of nothing dangling from his rod tip—and a limp ego to match. The Old Geezer glanced back over his shoulder for an instant, then headed for the bank. Rest the pool, rest the angler. He was glad no one had been watching.

WE CAN ONLY HELP YOU *take* fish on a fly rod—you'll have to learn how to lose them yourself, and we're certain you'll do as good a job as we've done over the years.

However, we can talk a bit about the equipment used in fly-fishing, for in the next chapter Joan and Lee Wulff will spend some time discussing its use in the act of casting. How unfortunate it is that the various aspects of deluding the fish cannot be brought together all at once, nicely integrated and orchestrated as if in a symphony. Although we have suggested that fly-casting can be so absorbing that it can easily become a satisfying end in itself, this just will not do if we are to take our fish.

We must learn to seek the proper spots in our waters, whether they be stream, brook, pond, lake or bay. We

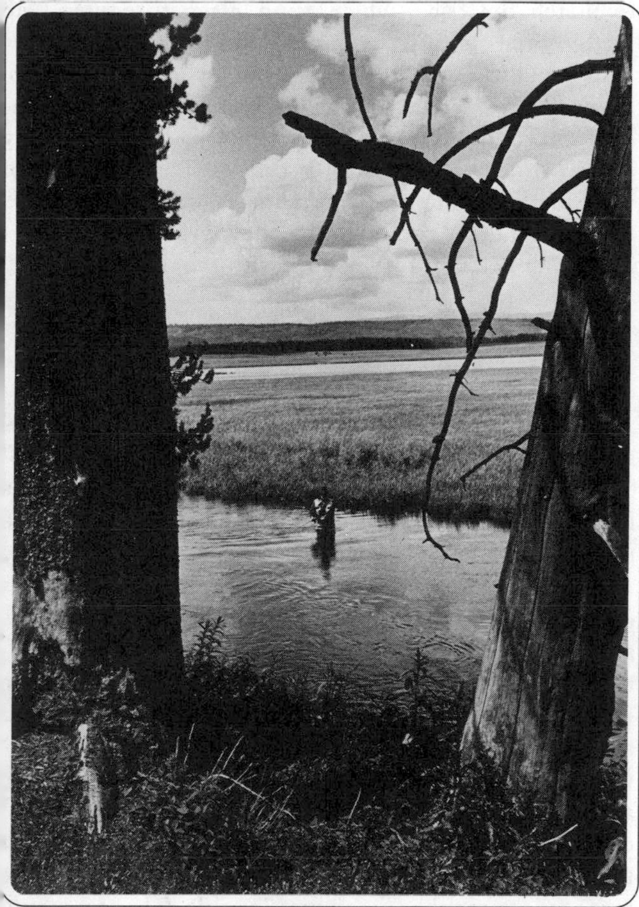

Railroad Ranch, Henrys Fork of the Snake, Idaho. Photo by Dave Engerbretson.

must then spot the fish itself, or at least the most likely place it might be lying. When this is accomplished, we then have to find—or make an educated guess about it—just what the trout is feeding on—if such it is doing. Then, of course, we proceed to that ultimate illusion—the selection of a man-made construction designed to suggest that particular *plat du jour* to the fish. And finally, it must be served up in the style to which the fish is accustomed.

While all this is done, to continue our musical metaphor, in concert, it cannot be revealed that way. We must begin at the beginning—with the fly rod and its associated paraphernalia—if we are to reach the end. For the rod is the medium which we use to deliver the fly to the fish, usually across some 30 to 60 feet of intervening water. The fly rod is the alpha and the omega—the remainder of the alphabet will be filled in in later chapters. We'll now focus on the fly rod and the act of casting the fly.

PART OF THE CHALLENGE and charm of fly-fishing lies in the fact that there are less intervening mechanical contrivances between the cast and the catch than in any other form of fishing. In bait-, plug- or lure-casting, the angler only flips his wrist; after this, the rod is in control, setting in motion a rather large piece of metal or bait, which drags behind it a length of line. To varying degrees, the rod and the technical design of the reel are primarily responsible for delivering the missile to ground zero. The fisherman himself is merely a middleman.

This is not true of the fly fisherman. If he had a long enough arm, with long, tapered fingers and translucent fingernails, he could merely reach out and dip his fly onto the water. Practicably, such a scheme is "inoperative," but in effect this is what he is doing when he casts to his quarry.

With his body, his arm and his eye, he is in almost total control from beginning to end. The long and limber *rod* becomes an extension of his arm. The *line* continues this chain of dynamic events as it flows forward and gradually unrolls its subtle taper. As it does, the energy is transmitted, without a break, to the butt of the *leader*. In turn, the leader continues the unfolding as its tapering profile diminishes the force until the *tippet end* of the leader is almost totally extended. At this point, the wind resistance built into the hackled *fly* itself takes over, allowing the fly to drop soundlessly to the surface—where the fish, totally mystified and beguiled, completes the chain in quick and brisk fashion.

The purity in the dynamics of the fly-rodder's cast has attracted the attentions of both poet and scientist—happily, neither has done lasting violence to the act. It is still the most direct and natural route to the fish, and there is no need to draw up equations to explain it. It balances out beautifully, with a lovely fish at one end and a pixilated fool at the other who believes all this can happen.

The combination is also coldly efficient. Other fishermen, after completing their cast, must draw upon their miniaturized derricks to return the lure to rod tip for the next cast. The fly fisher, on the other hand, can complete a cast in a matter of seconds, and then make another and another while the hardware caster is still grinding away in the recovery of the lure to the rod-tip position of his next cast. A fly-rodder can work a stretch of water five times as quickly as a plug- or spin-fisherman.

Probably the hardest thing for the novice caster to realize is the basic difference between the fly rod and the other types of casting rods and reels. With a spinning or plug-casting rod, the angler is throwing the weight of the lure, often a weight of several ounces. In fly-casting, the angler is throwing the weight of the line itself, as the Wulffs will detail in the pages just ahead.

In fly-casting the "lure" has no appreciable weight; it's the weight of the line that cocks the rod and eventually sends the fly to its destination. In other types of casting, the reverse holds—the monofilament line has little weight, and the lure drags the line along behind it.

In spin-casting, the cast is almost instantaneous; the fisherman suddenly cocks his wrist, snaps it forward, and the lure is on its way. But in fly-casting, the angler's participation continues throughout the cast, at once a demanding task and a satisfying involvement giving him total control in his presentation of the fly to the fish. Directly or indirectly, the fly-caster is throwing a line which has different accelerations and conformations at every point along its length, and it is under his control. It is a high art, performed partly by the caster and partly by the fly rod. Neither should get in the other's way.

IN THE FINAL PAGES OF THIS BOOK, we have included detailed descriptions of most of the fly rods, reels, lines, leaders and other accessories available on today's market. The abundance is appalling, especially to someone who began fly-fishing 20 or 30 years ago. We've tried to give some guidelines at the beginning of these sections to aid the novice in selecting his equipment, but it might be well to touch on some of the basic design features of fly rods and lines in particular at this point—before turning you over to Joan and Lee Wulff and our other contributors, for they will be referring to various aspects of these items of equipment as they discuss their specialized topics. It should also aid the beginner in selecting his initial equipment.

FROM BEGINNING TO END, the casting of a fly is a continuing taper—a diminution of size, weight and force. The caster's body itself is the base for the cast, then the arm muscles and a bit of wrist at the proper moment.

After that, the rod takes over. From the rod butt, deep in the cork handle, the rod gradually tapers to what might seem an impossible flimsiness at the tip. Considerable planning has gone into that taper, however, even programmed computer expertise in some cases. It's designed to give a progressive acceleration to the line, a line of a specific weight for that rod, and a line which itself carries a gradual taper throughout its working length.

This taper, as we mentioned earlier, allows the looping, curling line to unfold in an optimum manner at the proper time. As the fly line begins to straighten out over the water on the forward cast, its momentum is continued by the leader. And the leader, as we know, is also tapered to continue the dynamic flow which began with the caster himself.

The leader is made of monofilament, one long nine- to 12-foot segment in its simplest form, but frequently compounded of two or more knotted sections of varying lengths, diameters, and relative stiffnesses. All this is done to bring about the gradual diminution of force and acceleration so that the entire line and leader unfold and in effect straighten out over the water and the fish below it.

And deliver the fly. In fact, if fly rodders could have caddies, the fly rod, line and leader could be selected to match the fly itself. And the fly, of course, is selected to match the fish—which is in ultimate control, no matter what fantasies we may build in our minds.

In actual fact, however, it is the fly rod itself which is selected to match the type of fishing to be done. The line, leader and, to some extent, the fly, all follow along in that order. Thus, the fly rod itself is the heart of what matters to the fly fisherman. A few words toward the selection of a rod might be appropriate before moving on in our quest for "fishing with the fly rod."

Selecting a Fly Rod

AS YOU'VE ALREADY SUSPECTED, the selection of the ultimate fly rod is a "consummation devoutly to be wished," but possibly never to be totally realized. The fly angler's horizons have expanded beyond the capabilities of one rod.

Some ten years ago, partly in reaction to the long rods of the earlier days of the century—nine to ten feet was average—the "midge" rod hurtled into a frenzied notoriety. Measuring around six feet in length, the midge seemed to carry a reverse "macho mystique," and no angler worth his weight in waders was "compleat" without one. They were certainly a challenge to use, and they did serve the purpose of demonstrating most dramatically that the fly rod is merely an extension of the angler's forearm, but the suggestion that they were more "sportsmanlike" was questionable. They were fun, and good exercise if you couldn't book time on the squash court, but it was rather like playing football without a helmet. There are few of us who don't need all the help we can get in outwitting our common foe, and such is not in the midge.

Now, in happy reaction to the passing of the midge and because of advances in rod design and fabrication we find a varied array of fly rods available to cover many requirements. Without suggesting that the rank beginner will require the more specialized rods, we can briefly cover some of the general rod types now on the market.

For fishing the *dry fly*, the angler needs a fairly *light* rod with a *quick-return action* to allow him to dry his fly between casts with the fewest false-casts possible. In the case of constantly repeated casting, such as in working a hatch, or covering considerable suspected lies, the lightness of a dry-fly rod becomes even more important, and the advent of graphite has been a giant step, especially for the fly rodder who doesn't fish regularly and whose wrist and hand muscles are not in shape.

The *nymph* fisherman likes to have a *longer* and *more supple* rod, because he often needs considerable follow-up line control after his cast to mend and adjust the free float of his sunken fly. In fact, this could be said of the *wet fly* fisherman as well. Suppleness—not limpness, however—becomes a factor in delicacy of presentation, but is especially important in the often-required delicate setting of the nymph hook when the fly is taken by a trout.

The *bass fisherman* will usually use a heavier line to carry the heavier and more air-resistant bass bug or popper, and as a result will need a *heavier* rod. The bass rod is also a *longer* rod (8½ to 9 feet), much for the same reason as above—for line control both before and after the take, especially when fishing among lily pads and other vegetation and drowned trees common to the largemouth's habitat.

The *salmon* and *steelhead* fisherman fishes big flies for big fish in big waters, and normally requires a *big rod* to match his quarry, both before and after the take. The same factor applies to the saltwater fly rodder, of course, but with the added factor of hardware impervious to the effects of exposure to the salt. Happily, however, there has been a tendency toward shorter and lighter rods for much of this type of fishing, with 9- and 9½-footers replacing the ten- to 12-foot fly rods still seen on many salmon streams.

But for the first-rod fly fisher, rather specific recommendations can be made. Many of us use rods of 7 to 7½ feet in length for our normal small-stream angling, and such a rod would not unduly handicap the rank novice. However, the shorter the rod the shorter the travel of the rod tip. As a result, the timing of the back-cast and the forward cast becomes slightly more critical, with a longer rod giving the beginner a bit more time to make his judgments.

Nor would the beginner want his first rod to be especially *stiff* in action (though hardly a word to describe the delicacy of response in a good dry-fly rod). The action should be soft enough to initiate him into the subtleties of *feel*, the soft warning tug that will soon trigger reflexes and set the caster's arm, wrist and hand for the next casting motion forward.

Eight to 8½ feet would be a sound recommendation for a first, or all-around, rod, with an action neither stiff and fast nor soft and slow. (We can only use words here, but think of the fun you'll have in making your own definitions—and of the later frustrations of trying to pass *these* on to others.)

When bamboo and glass rods were the only choices, rod *weight*, coupled with rod *length*, usually gave a suggestion of the type of *action* a rod might offer. However, with the advent of graphite on the scene quite recently—rod designers are still learning how to use it to best advantage in various types of rods—such a simple combination is no longer valid. And even before graphite, designers were learning new ways to use fiberglass, especially through varying tube-wall thickness, to lighten glass rods or to give them specific actions. Even the lovely and living bamboo allows for subtle variations in the weight/length/action combination.

The typical graphite fly rod is some 50% lighter than a fiberglass or bamboo rod designed to carry the same weight of line, so the old factor of rod weight vs length does not apply. This is not really a problem, though, because length and recommended line-weight should be sufficient indication of a graphite rod's built-in action and end-purpose.

The angler's rather personal involvement with his fly rod does not allow him to overlook the cosmetics of his rod. In most instances, the coloration will be understated, with wrappings of fairly subdued hues. However, the fittings of a rod are definitely not cosmetic.

The *ferrules* joining the two or more sections of the rod must fit each other flawlessly; these are turned on a lathe and frequently "lapped in" with jeweler's rouge for a perfect fit. Equally important, they must be firmly snugged to the rod sections themselves to prevent any play and to minimize the possibility of breakage under strain.

Almost all glass and graphite fly rods have ferrules made of the reinforced tubular structure of the rods themselves to act as male and female parts. Such design is built in to minimize "flatness," or interruption in action, at the joint-sections when a rod is flexed. This cannot be done with bamboo rods.

Both the positioning and the composition of the snake and line guides are quite critical. The snake guides, usually twisted wire fittings, keep the line as straight as possible as it slides freely through them. Snake guides are usually positioned at gradually decreasing distances from each other as the rod tapers from butt to tip. They are made of metal alloys (some have ceramic inserts) which resist abrasion, lest such defects be transferred to the swiftly gliding line and interfere with its acceleration in casting or render it prematurely worn.

Especially important in this function is the stripping guide, the larger ring-shaped guide nearest the butt, which receives a considerable "sawing" effect from line held by the angler's rod hand, and the tip-top, the elongated line guide at the tip of the rod, which receives an equal amount of line wear on the forward and backward casts, as well as on line pick-up from the water. Both of these are made of special metal alloys, although the stripping guide is often lined inside with agate or space-age plastics.

However, we may be telling you more than you need or want to know at this time about fly rods. You now know a bit of the work that goes into designing them, something of the selection of them, and as much as you should about the general theory behind using them.

In fly-fishing, as in many other pursuits, there is a great difference between theory and practice. Let's begin to bridge that gap now, beginning with Joan and Lee Wulff. We'll wander along with you, at a respectful distance, basking in the illumination of our stellar array of fly-angling talent. We expect to learn quite a bit ourselves.

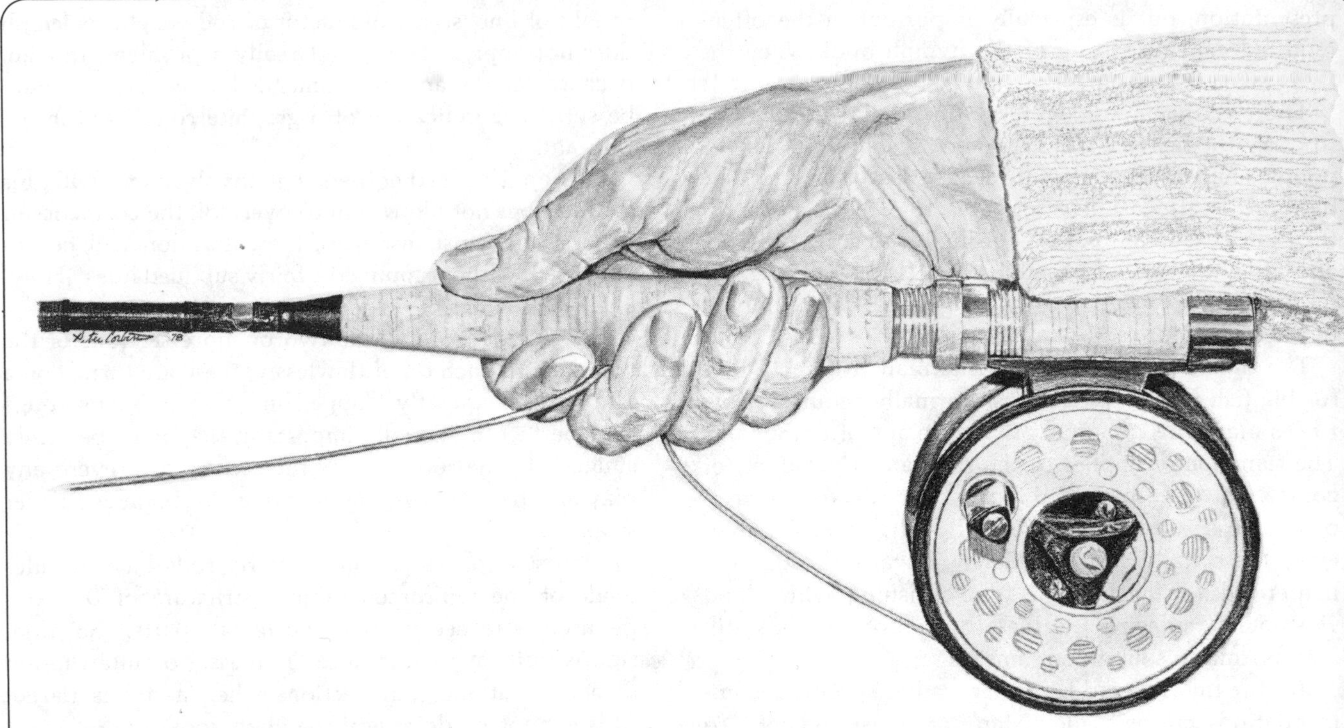

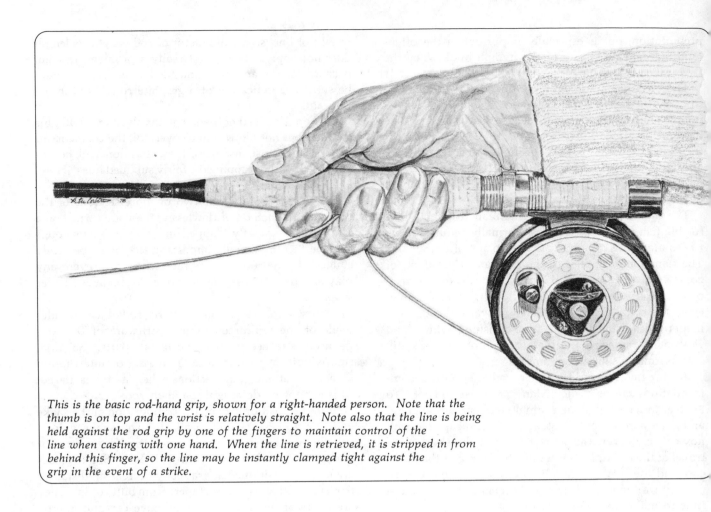

This is the basic rod-hand grip, shown for a right-handed person. Note that the thumb is on top and the wrist is relatively straight. Note also that the line is being held against the rod grip by one of the fingers to maintain control of the line when casting with one hand. When the line is retrieved, it is stripped in from behind this finger, so the line may be instantly clamped tight against the grip in the event of a strike.

Some Notes on Tackle

THE BEGINNER will find fly rods from 8 to 9 feet long the simplest with which to learn to fly-cast. Short rods, 7½ feet or less, are more difficult to cast; they require longer strokes and more precise timing than longer rods do. Your first rod should not be too heavy to handle, yet long enough to keep the line well above your head while learning to cast.

The distance that a cast travels depends upon the weight of the line and the speed that can be given to it. Lines that are lighter than six-weight do not have the mass (weight) to be cast long distances easily, nor do they give the beginner a feeling of recognizable weight that's so important in the first stages of learning to cast. Fly lines of from 6- to 8-weight are best for the beginner. They require less line speed to cast a reasonable distance. Floating lines are easier to handle than sinking lines and should be a part of your first outfit.

The smaller and lighter the fly, the easier it is to cast. Heavy flies tend to have an inertia (and sometimes air resistance) that conflicts with the smooth turnover of the line when the loops straighten out. Being heavier than the line and leader, they tend to fall below the level of the path that the line and leader follow. In practice casting, use a piece of brightly colored yarn at the end of your leader in place of a fly, so your eyes can follow its flight.

Leaders are designed to make the fish think there is no connection between the artificial fly and the bulky and visible line. The butt of the leader should be matched, in size and stiffness, to the forward end of the line to which it is attached. From that point, it should taper on down to its finest point where the fly is attached. The leader, in essence, is a nearly invisible continuation of the fly line. Commercial leaders range in length from 7½ feet to 12 feet or more, and some at their finest point are only a few thousandths of an inch in diameter.

The beginner's fly-casting outfit should consist of a glass, graphite or bamboo rod that is 8 to 9 feet in length and handles a 6-, 7- or 8-weight line. (A seven-weight will be easiest for most people.) The line should be a weight-forward (preferably long belly) floating type in a light, easily seen color. The leader should be 7½ to 9 feet long, with a butt diameter of at least .023 inch. Attach orange or red yarn to the end of the leader for easy visibility.

JOAN WULFF

It's probably presumptuous to tell you more than we have already about casting with the fly rod, because you're about to be taken in hand by two of the best casters fly-fishing has produced—Joan and Lee Wulff. Lee, of course, is one of the world's ultimate anglers, and his wife Joan has spent most of her last fifteen years instructing in the art of casting. Fly-casting is an art, and Joan, a former dance and ballet teacher, makes it even more so, both in her own casting and in her instruction. The Wulff-pack combination is a lethal one, but even they realize that words, and even pictures, can only guide you in your first casts. However, those first casts are the hardest, and Joan and Lee should be able to get you over the hump quickly. After that, it's between you and the fish.

Chapter 2

Casting with the Fly Rod

The Natural Way to Go

JOAN and LEE WULFF

Illustrations of Joan Wulff by Peter Corbin

HAVE YOU EVER TRIED to throw a feather? Throwing a feather is sheer magic. A spinning lure can be thrown almost as far by hand as by the use of rod and reel, but an artificial fly, which, like a feather, has essentially no weight, cannot be thrown any significant distance. It can only be "carried along for the ride" at the end of a tapered leader and a bulky, pliable fly line and attached to a delicate but powerful rod.

The fly cast is accomplished by moving the line through the air in a back-and-forth motion. This motion causes the line to form an unrolling, open-ended loop on the backcast and on the forward cast—and it is on the forward cast that the line delivers the leader and fly to its destination. The loop unrolls in time for the fly to land softly on the water.

Fly-casting is fun! The physical feeling of the fly line and rod as they move through the air is a satisfying, even exciting experience that grows in depth as the caster becomes familiar with his tackle and fly-casting techniques. A fly fisherman can enjoy even a fishless day if he executes his casts well, presenting his fly to the right spot and in the most delicate manner, regardless of distance or obstacles.

In fly-casting the forearm and wrist may be considered an extension of the fly rod, and the elbow becomes the pivot. The hand holding the rod does the basic job of casting and is called the rod hand. The handling of line, from stripping it off the reel to making retrieves of the fly and coiling excess line between casts, is done with the other free, or line, hand.

To get the feeling of fly-casting, pull some line out of the rod tip (about 10 feet or so plus leader) and focus your attention on the *tip* of the rod. Using your elbow as the pivot and keeping your wrist static but not stiff, make patterns in the air that you can see in their entirety—circles, ovals, zigzags; make them large and small. Try writing your name. Feel the very light weight of the line. Notice that the tip of the rod is delicate compared to the butt and bends very easily.

At the end of one of these maneuvers, let the line fall to the ground to your left. Keeping the rod parallel to the ground, move your hand and the rod horizontally to the right a foot or so and stop it *suddenly!* Observe what happens. (The rod tip will flip over after you stop the motion of your hand and the line will fall to the right.) Reverse the procedure and move the rod to the left, again stopping suddenly. This sudden *stop* lets the rod do *its* work, that of transferring its power to the line and forming the loop. This is the "instant of turnover" — when the line moves from one side of the rod tip to the other. This motion, moving then stopping, can be done in any plane and, when it's done vertically, is the basis of conventional fly-casting.

While the rod's length moves through an arc, the *tip*, under the pressure and weight of the line, moves in a *straight line* between those "instants" of turnover. Those straight lines, if illustrated, would indicate the path of the line, for *where the rod tip leads, the line will follow.* The line has the weight — you give it acceleration and guide its trajectory in making the cast.

The Roll Cast

Now that you have watched the way a rod and line work together and have experienced the feeling of making patterns in the air, we'll introduce you to the roll cast — which takes the action to a different plane. The simplest of all casting techniques and one of the most valuable, the roll cast is the standard cast to use when there is no room for a conventional backcast, such as when you are backed up against high bushes, a wall, or even under trees. Beyond these special uses, the roll cast can actually get the beginner fishing with a fly in the shortest time possible.

Stroking out line.

First, let's get some line out (a clean floating line works best). Pull the leader and two or three feet of line out through the rod tip. Let it fall on the water. Keeping the rod tip pointed toward the water and a bit below the horizontal, strip line from the reel (15 or 20 feet) to the ground beside you. Now *stroke* the rod tip back and forth parallel to the water. Your rod hand will travel six inches or so while the rod tip will move two or three feet to the stroke. Meanwhile, your line hand is feeding the line out through the guides to pile up on the water in front of you. When all the line is out of the rod, on the water, put the line coming from the reel under your rod hand, holding the line at the grip.

Roll-casting is a matter of getting the rod and line into a position that is, in effect, a substitute for a backcast. Then a forward motion is made that rolls the line out onto the water to its complete extension. The fly is then in a fishable position.

1. Keeping the fly on the water, slowly bring your forearm and the rod back and up to a vertical position. Make sure your hand, with your arm in flexed position, is a little higher than your eye level. Keep your arm directly in front of your shoulder, *not* to the side. This position will give you good leverage and make the forward-casting motion easy.
2. Tilt the rod tip a few degrees away from you (to the right, if you are right-handed). This puts the line and rod in different vertical planes so they won't collide during the forward cast.
3. The line, in a position two or three feet to the side, should be hanging even with your shoulder. If it goes back any farther, the line will be forced to go *up* first, instead of *forward*, on the roll, which will waste the energy you put into the cast and give you a wide, sloppy roll.
4. Let the line come to rest. *As soon as it does,* make a forward and downward motion, applying power with a wrist-snap and ending with the rod tip pointed where the fly is expected to land. The line should roll out straight on the surface of the water, carrying your leader and fly with it. If the piled-up line has sunk below the surface of the water, it may take two or three rolls to get it to the surface where it can straighten out; keep trying until it does.

As a beginner you can roll-cast a fly 25 feet or more with a minimum of energy. Later, depending on the

At the start of the roll cast, the rod is brought up to a point at which the line hangs even with the rod-hand's shoulder.

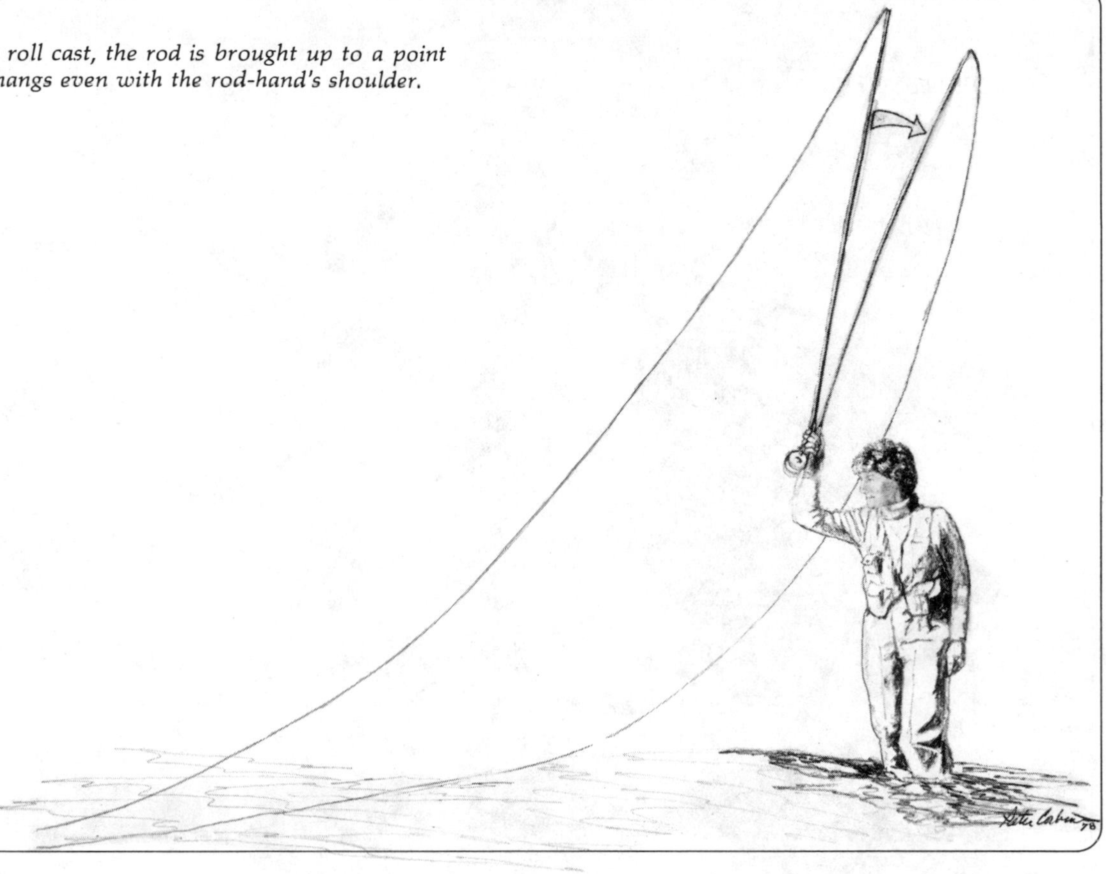

Power is delivered in a downward direction as indicated by the arrow, and the line will roll out straight on the water.

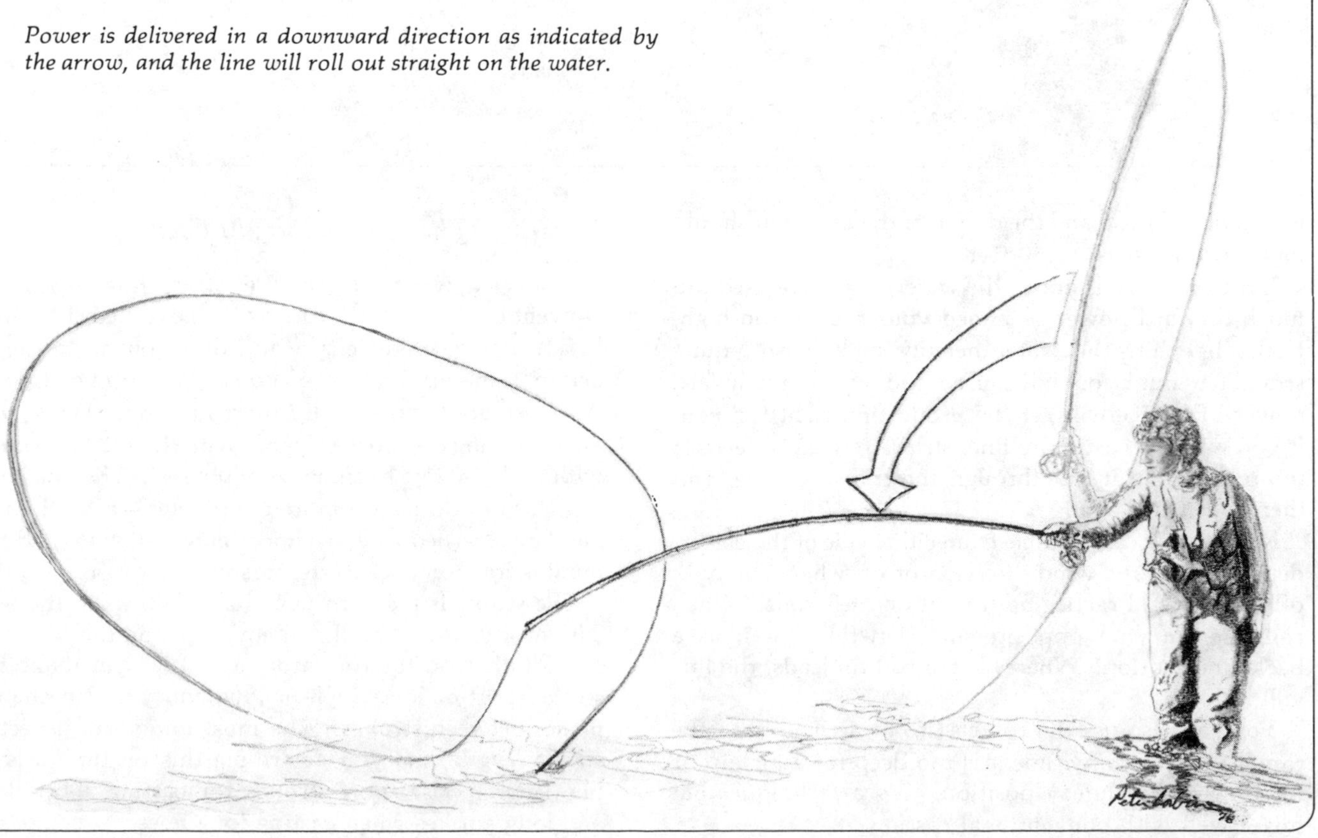

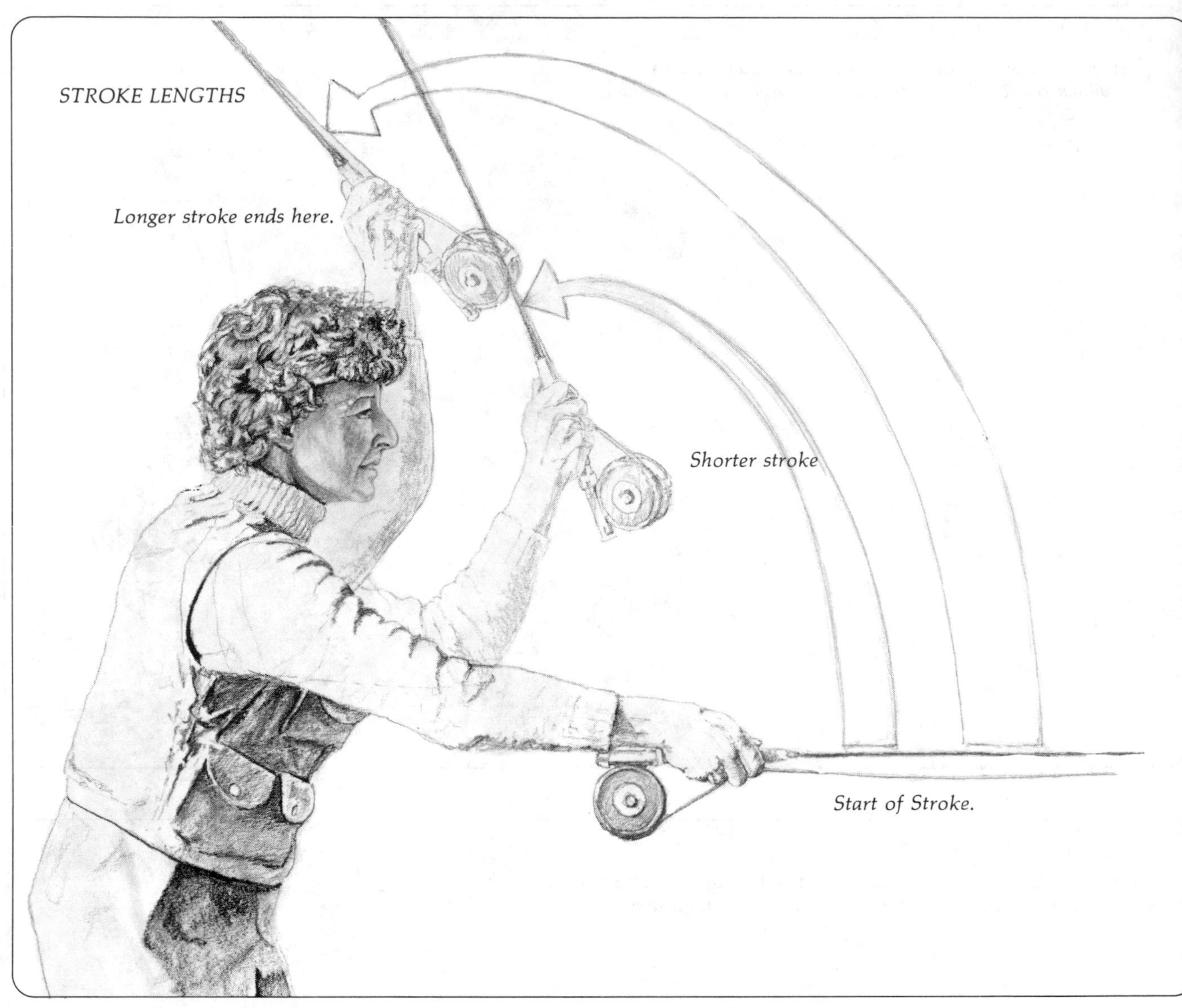

length of your rod and the design of the line, you should be able to roll-cast to 50 feet.

If the line unrolls above the water, you have used too much forward power or aimed your rod tip too high. If the line hits the water heavily and doesn't quite straighten out, you have used too much downward power. Practice will get the proportion right for you. If you want to cast more line, strip a few more feet off the reel, stroke it out through the rod as before, and then roll it out again.

Roll-casting can be done from either side of the caster, depending on the wind direction or on where the bulk of the line is. Practice both right and left rolls. When rolling from your opposite shoulder, think of it as a backhand motion. Wherever the rod tip leads, the line will follow.

You can also use the roll cast to bring line up to the top of the water any time it is too deep for a pickup or in some other clumsy position. It's a technique that mixes well with conventional casting.

The Basics of Fly-Casting

No matter whether you are roll-casting or casting conventionally, all fly-casting is governed by three basics: *stroke* (both length and direction or "plane of action"), the application of *power*, and proper *timing*. All three are controlled by the rod hand. While you are mastering these basics, work with the rod hand only, with no loose line hanging from the reel. The line hand can learn to do its job more easily later—after the rod hand has learned to cast almost automatically, and the mind is free to concentrate on something else.

The *stroke* is the path your hand follows in the execution of a cast. You'll make a stroke on the backcast and another on the forward cast. You can make the stroke short or long, high or low, and you can change planes between strokes. The most important aspect is *stroke length*, and you determine this on the basis of line length. Use short strokes for casting short lines and long strokes when casting long lines.

The controlled application of *power* changes a limp, supple fly line into something that has a definite form and sufficient force to carry the fly to a predetermined spot. This power is generated by the forearm muscles, and its journey to the line takes it through the wrist and hand of the caster and finally through the rod. Though power is built up during the moving of the rod on the *stroke*, its *release* to the line occurs at the "instant of turnover," when the line starts to pass from one side of the rod tip to the other and the new loop is formed. This power release is comparable to the instant a bat hits a baseball; the power is transferred in that instant, and more can be subsequently added. In fly-casting, the transfer takes place through a wrist-flick with a split-second stopping of the rod hand's motion at the end of that wrist-flick. (The secret of stopping suddenly is to *squeeze* the rod grip.)

During the rest of the casting motion, the wrist is static. At the "instant of turnover"—the *power release*—the wrist does its only job and does it as quickly and in as short a distance as possible. This wrist-flick over a short, rather than long, distance will produce a desirable narrow loop in the cast.

Your power should be varied in its force and in its timing according to line length, but it must always be applied as smoothly as possible for maximum casting efficiency. Take note of your casting visually; watch your line at all times. Look for humps in the line as it unrolls in the air; these are signs of poorly applied power. When it *looks* right and when it *feels* right, it usually *is* right.

The third basic is *timing.* Perfect timing turns the right stroke length and power application into a *beautiful* fly cast. Perfect timing is a matter of feeling. It's inside you. Words can't give it to you, but casting varying lengths of line through thousands of casts in fair wind and foul *will* give it to you. Forever.

The key to perfect timing is "constant pressure," a feeling of the line on the rod tip that is always there. If you have ever waved a pennant or a banner, you have experienced the feeling of constant pressure. Without constant pressure, the timing falters, the pennant collapses, and so does the fly line, leaving the caster with a disconnected, "Where did it go?" feeling. It usually happens on the backcast and occurs when the caster waits too long before starting his forward cast. If the forward cast is made too late, the line falls limply below the horizontal and the energy for the forward cast cannot be generated smoothly—the line will start forward with a jerk. If the forward cast is made too soon, there is no pressure (or load) against which the rod can work. The easiest way to determine when the forward cast should be started is to use your eyes. Turn and look at it. Standing sideways, make the backcast, and just *before* the line straightens, while there is still a "hook" in it, start the forward cast. Notice that the line straightens beautifully at a horizontal level without dipping down and gives perfect line control on the forward cast. Of course, you can't watch your line *and* fish effectively, so once you've seen the perfect backcast position a few times, face forward again and try to feel it—with constant pressure as your key.

You could determine perfect timing mentally, with your brain going through this kind of exercise: "Let's see. I let out a little over three feet of line on that cast, making the total of line and leader forty-seven and a quarter feet. Therefore it will take about two-and-a-half milliseconds longer for the line to reach the turnaround point on this backcast than it did on the last one. That will be just about . . . . NOW!!!"

Even with the new pocket calculators—what a chore! Think of the years it would take to learn to do it that way. Instead, trust your physical self, your muscles, to tell you when to start your forward cast—using *constant pressure* as the key.

Timing changes according to the length of line being cast, of course, but also according to any wind (whether it's helping you or hindering), and whether you are just extending line in the air (false-casting) or making final delivery of the fly. These points will be covered in their appropriate areas. Now let's *do it*—make a conventional overhead cast.

The Conventional Overhead Cast

THIS IS THE BASIC CAST in which the extended line is taken off the water, turned over in the air above and behind the caster, and then returned to the water ahead of the caster. When you're first starting to practice, the length of the rod, extended line and leader should equal about 30 feet. If you are practicing on water, use the roll cast to extend the line first. If you are on grass, put the rod down in front of you, then walk ahead to pull out sufficient line.

Casting on water is preferable to casting on grass. Water will give you a better understanding and feeling of the cast because of the surface tension against which you will move the line on the pickup. Remember to use the rod hand *only* as you learn; hold any loose line under your rod hand against the grip.

The basic cast is divided into two parts: the *backcast* and the *forward cast.*

Backcast

1. *Load* the rod. This means that as you start the pickup stroke, the rod bends under the weight of the line. The continuing stroke slides the line off the water and into the air.

2. *Transfer power* with a wrist flick and *sudden stop* of the rod butt. (Don't forget the *squeeze.*) Maximum power goes through the rod to the line

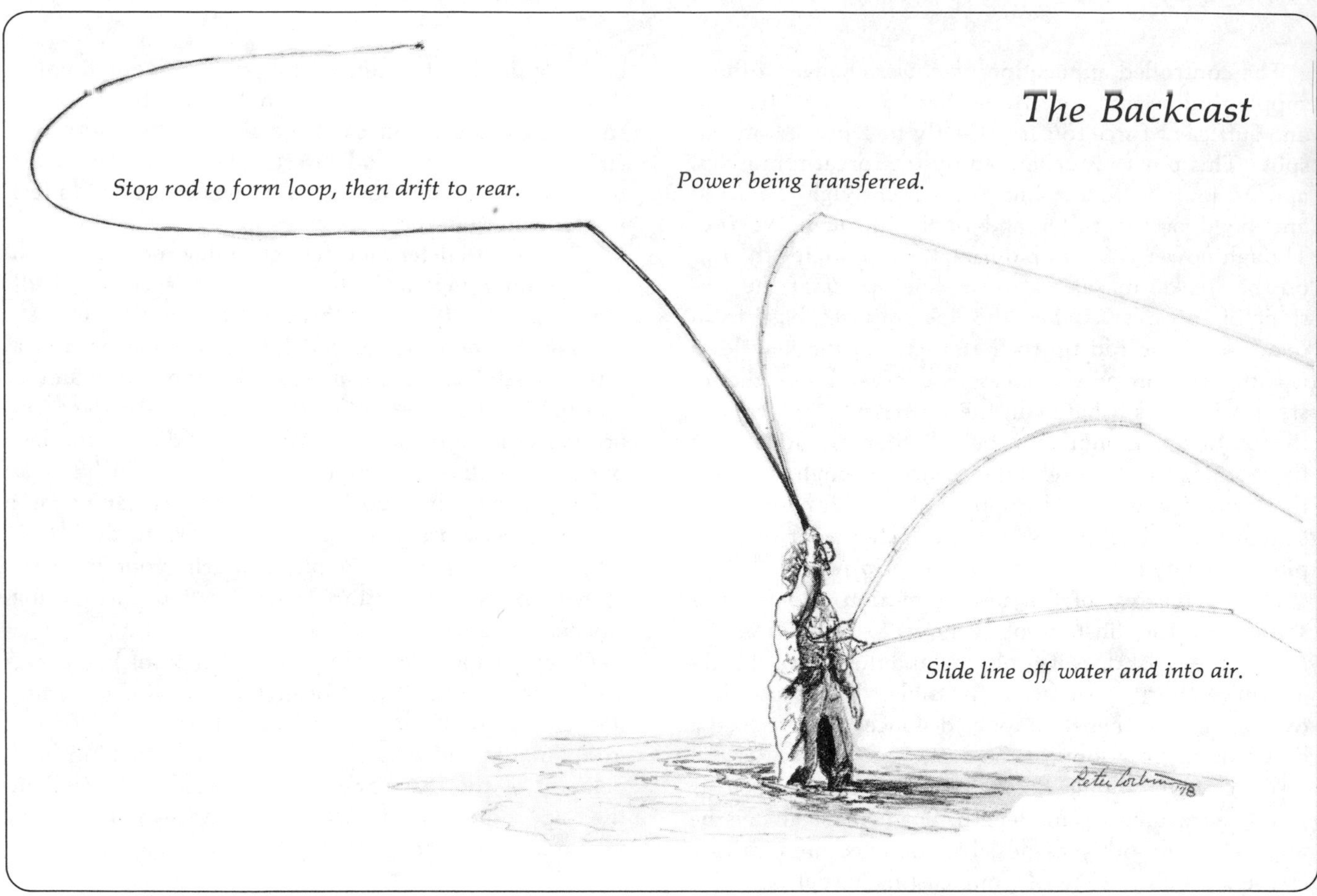

at the instant of turnover (when the line switches from one side of the rod tip to the other).

3. *Drift.* Without applying any power, the rod hand follows the direction of the rod tip as the line loop is unrolling in the air behind you. You should feel the *constant pressure* of the line on the rod tip and drift to the perfect position for the start of the forward cast. There is no change in the rod/wrist attitude during the drift.

Forward Cast

1. As the forward cast is started (while the back-cast still has a "hook" in it), the rod is again under load, which builds up power to the point of the power release.

2. *Power* is released at the instant of turnover. The shorter the arc through which the wrist and rod tip travel at this point, the narrower will be the loop formed in the line when it travels forward through the air.

3. *Follow through* by pointing the rod tip where the fly should go and by lowering your arm and rod as the line unrolls and lands gently on the water. If done properly, every inch of line and leader will straighten just above the water, and line, leader and fly will land as one unit.

Body Position

Your body position should be comfortable. Stand with the foot that's on the same side as your casting arm slightly behind the other. Keep your body facing forward; your casting arm should move within that framework. Don't take the arm to the side, but do take the hand up to eye level or above (as long as your arm is flexed). This is a position of strength and leverage, similar to that from which one could wield a hammer.

Looking at the illustrations of conventional casting, note that, on the backcast, *stroke length* includes the lifting and loading of the rod up to and including the instant of turnover and transfer of *power.* After that, the arm's motion is called *drift.* On the forward cast, stroke length again includes the loading and power release, but *not* the follow through.

The old idea that all casting, as shown on a clock face, was done properly between the 9 and 1 o'clock positions fostered the one-length stroke. Only poor casters make the same motion regardless of whether they are casting 15 feet or 50. The proper stroke length will vary from a few inches for a very short cast to a full swing of the arm, which may be three feet or more.

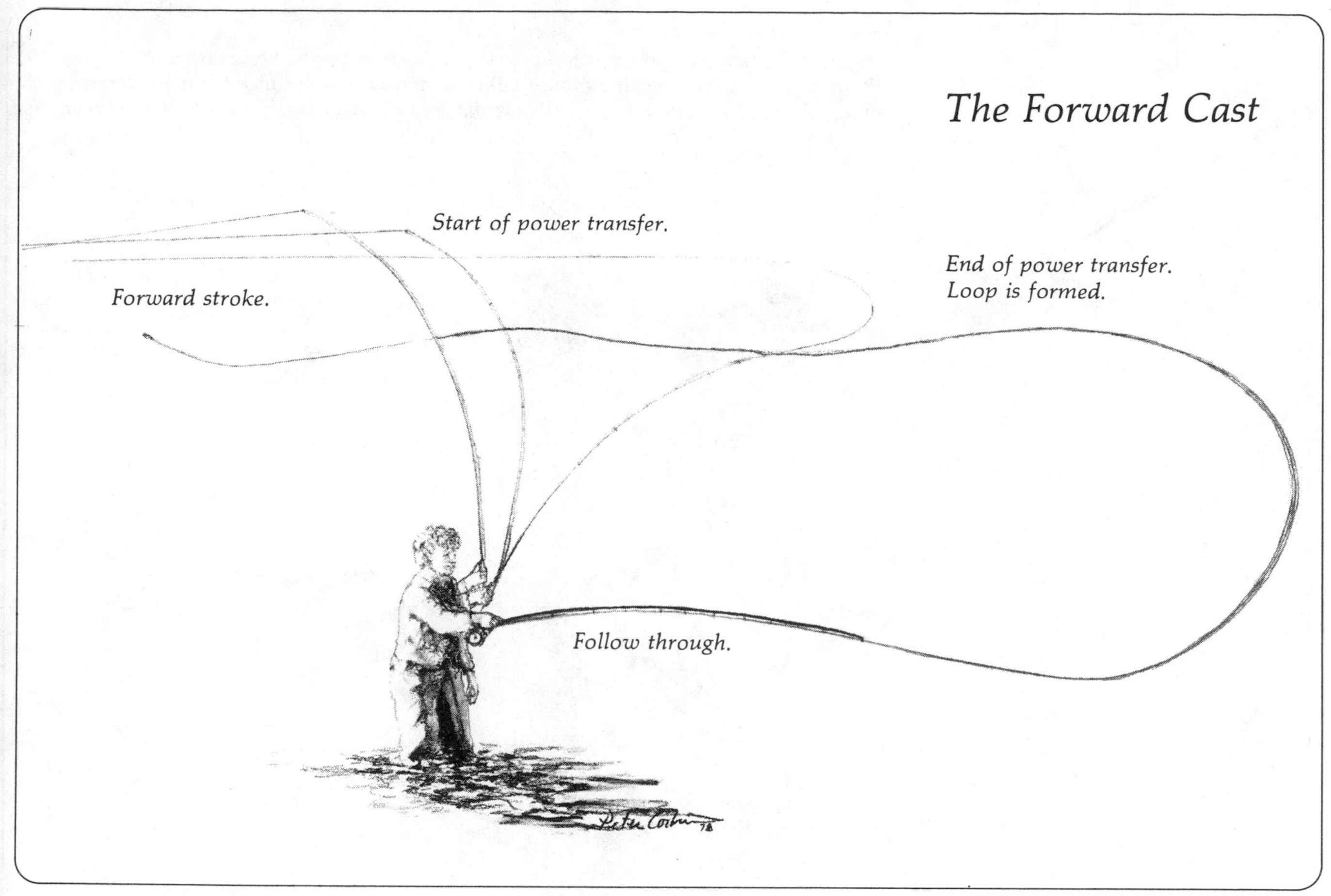

The stroke should always be minimal, no longer than necessary for any length line. If the stroke length is too long on the backcast, for instance, the energy will pass through the line and be expended before the stroke is finished, causing the line to drop before the caster can make the forward cast. There will be a loss of control. If the stroke is *too* short on the backcast, the line will not completely unroll its backward loop due to lack of momentum and will collapse on itself. Again there will be a loss of control, and a probable result will be a knot tied in the line or leader and a failure of the forward cast to straighten out on the water.

Rod length also affects stroke length. For a given length of line, a shorter rod will require a longer stroke and vice versa.

The *rod-tip position* at the end of the stroke (and power release) will determine where the line will go and, of course, the direction of drift in a conventional cast. Always be sure your rod-tip position is *above* a horizontal line on the backcast, even if it's only a fraction of an inch above, no matter how long a stroke is needed or in which plane it is made. Along with the *sudden stop* of the hand at the end of the wrist flick (power transfer), this is the secret of a perfect backcast.

Regardless of how long or short the stroke may be, the drift that follows keeps the feeling of *constant pressure* that assures perfect timing and gives an opportunity for the repositioning of the rod hand preparatory to making the forward cast. It is during this drift that the caster can change planes or direction. Between the backcasts and forward casts, the rod hand can be lowered or raised, moved inward or outward. It can be taken from one side of the head to the other or wherever is necessary to put the casting hand in its best position for the forward stroke.

In a headwind, the caster can make a high backcast, drift his hand to a lower position and drive the forward cast inches above the water. If wind is coming from a right-hander's right side, he can make a high backcast on that side, drift his hand toward the top of his head, angling the rod tip to his left side at the same time and make a backhand stroke on the downwind side. Once the caster realizes he has a *full sphere* of motion in which to cast and is not limited by any clock face, his casting prowess can grow for the rest of his fishing life.

Stroke length is limited in an overhead plane. Once you make the rod pass through an arc of more than 90 degrees vertically, the rod tip and, consequently, the line will be thrown *down* behind you and spoil your backcast. When you reach this point in overhead casting, you will have to change body position and casting plane to get the longer stroke you need.

The solution starts with the position of your feet. As suggested earlier, don't stand with your feet next

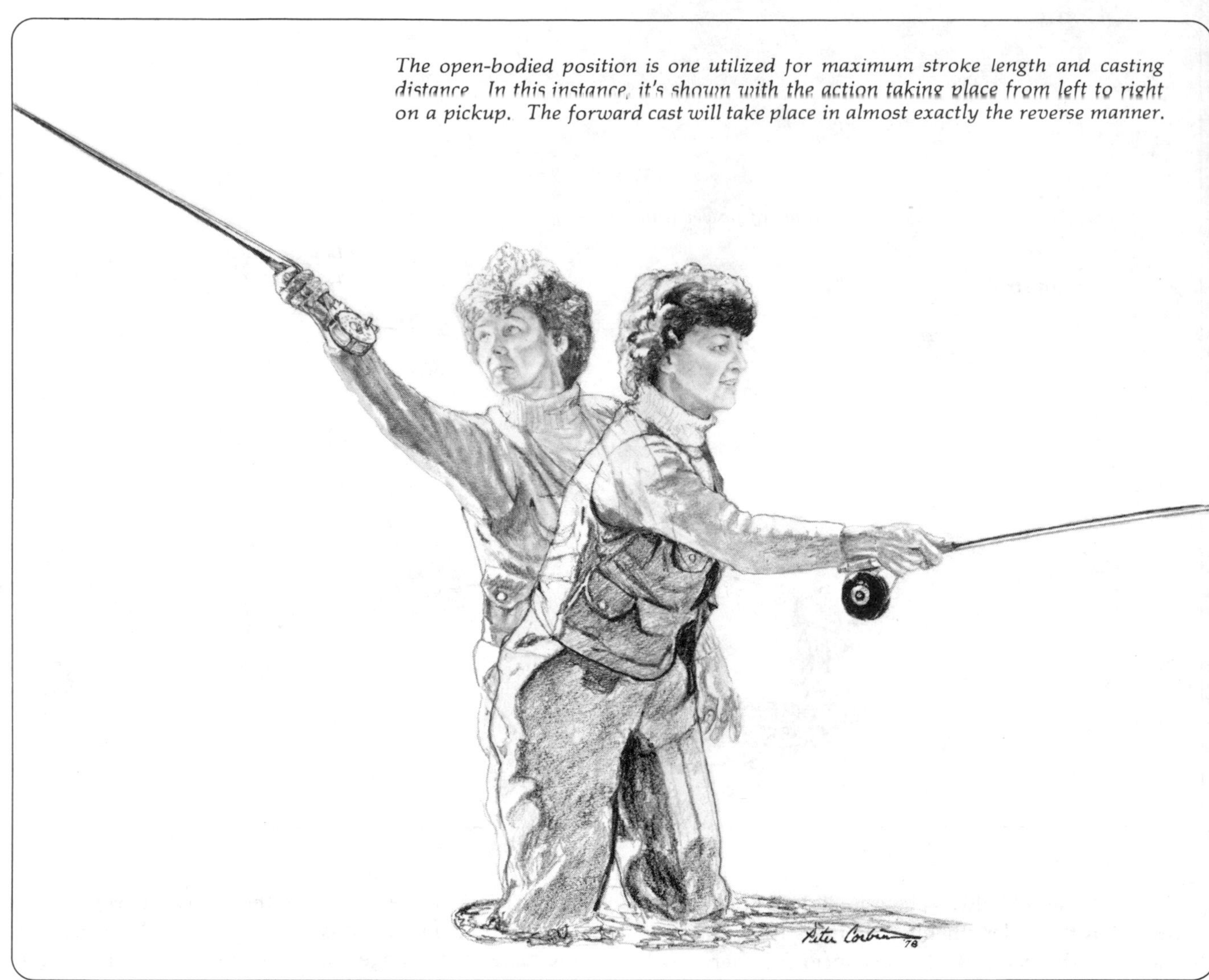

The open-bodied position is one utilized for maximum stroke length and casting distance. In this instance, it's shown with the action taking place from left to right on a pickup. The forward cast will take place in almost exactly the reverse manner.

to each other facing forward. Stand with your left foot ahead of your right (if you are casting right-handed), with your right at a 90-degree angle and a foot or so to the rear. This facilitates opening your shoulder and upper body rearward to what we'll call an open-bodied position.

The second change is to take the rod out of the vertical plane and drop it to a 45-degree off-vertical position. Without allowing the rod and reel to *rotate* in your hand, turn your hand so that your palm faces upward at the *end* of the backcast stroke when casting in this plane. Start the forward cast with palm up, but rotate the hand and forearm 90 degrees back again to your normal casting position at the end of the forward cast. This slight rotation on both forward casts and backcasts is necessary for you to make the stroke in a straight line. This open-bodied position and off-vertical plane will enable you to make your longest strokes and your longest casts.

Be careful that you don't swing the rod in a rounded motion that exceeds 180 degrees in this position. To check it, look at your backcast. It's not truly *back*, it's ideally a position from which you could throw a good punch (so the arm must be flexed). Your shoulders, arm, hand, rod and most of the line will be in a generally straight line. If the rod tip disappears around behind you, out of your vision, it has gone too far and you are trying to do the impossible: moving your rod tip in a curve and expecting it to give you a straight cast.

Loop Size

We mentioned earlier that during the power release the distance over which the wrist flick occurs will determine the width of the loop.

While tight, narrow loops *are* desirable, because they move through the air with less resistance and therefore produce more control for the caster, the beginner must not be carried away with the idea that narrow loops are the only acceptable ones. This is not true. Under certain conditions wide ones may be better (certain winds, or when using large flies, for instance), and it takes time to develop the muscles and techniques that will give a narrow loop. A wider loop (while you are learning) will keep you from tangling or hitting your leader against the line on the forward cast. If you work on applying your power *smoothly*, your muscles will improve at their job over a period of time and you will be able to control the width of your loops.

False-Casting

Up until now, we've been talking about a basic cast: taking the line up and behind the caster in a backcast, and then making a forward cast that extends the line on the water. If that forward cast is, instead, made *parallel* to the water and not allowed to land before the next backcast is begun, it is a *false cast*, which calls for a forward drift rather than a follow-through. The mechanics of the backcast change only in that, to compensate for a higher plane on the forward cast, the backcast drift position may take the rod tip to a slightly lower spot than on a basic cast. Otherwise, use high backcasts for short distances and gradually change the angle of *trajectory* of the *line* from low in front and high in back on short casts to slightly lower in back and higher in front for the longest casts and greatest distances.

False casts are used when extending line so that it is not necessary to put the line on the water and possibly disturb fish. It's a faster way to get the line out. In dry-fly fishing, extra false casts may be taken to dry a fly in the air. It will become a basic part of your casting when you are completely familiar with your tackle and the technique. It is the goal of the experienced caster to get the line out through the rod and the fly on the water with a *minimum* number of false casts, shooting line on both the front and backcasts. A fly in the air doesn't catch a fish.

A word about timing on false casts: When you are extending line, the line should be started on its reverse course *before* it has completely extended, as described earlier. When the time comes to shoot line on the final delivery of the fly, *then* let the line straighten completely behind you and catch it, through the feeling of *constant pressure*, at the exact instant it reaches its terminal extension. This will load the rod a little more heavily and give you a better capability to shoot line—a technique we'll explain right now.

Shooting Line

To increase the distance that you can cast, you must be able to shoot line; that is, to extend line while in the process of casting.

To do this, start with the line held firmly *under* the rod hand at the grip, hook the thumb of your line hand in the line at the reel and pull down and away toward your left thigh (if you are right-handed). The line comes off the reel doubled and you should be able to strip five feet of line easily. Drop this loose line at your thigh, and grasp the line again where it goes *under* your rod hand. Holding the line about a foot to the side of the reel in a firm grip, make the backcast normally. Make a forward cast *up to and through* the instant of turnover and power release. Then, as the loop forms in front of you, release the tension of your line hand and let the line slide through your fingers. Your forward cast should be aimed a little higher (aim the rod tip higher) than with the previous amount of line, to allow extra time for the longer line to unroll before settling to the water. A little extra power is in order on the forward cast only. To put it simply, *shoot line after the power transfer* (whether you are doing the basic cast or false-casting).

Line can be "shot" on the backcast as well as on the forward cast when there's enough line weight outside the rod tip to facilitate this. Shoot line on the follow-through of the forward cast and during the drift of the backcast. The line hand should maintain a position of control after the release of the line on the forward cast so that the line won't wrap around the rod above the grip if you overpower it. One way to do this is to cup your line hand loosely around the shooting line.

There *are* times when letting it shoot freely, without hand control, is a better technique, such as on very long casts with no obstructions around for the line to catch on. The caster will come to recognize those times with experience.

Line Handling

After you have made your cast and the fly is moving through the fishing pattern, the line should be held under your rod hand's second or third finger. Hold any extra line in your line hand, and on a strike you'll have two points of tension to help in setting the hook.

Retrieving the line between casts, either to give motion to the fly or to bring in the line to workable casting length, can be handled well by coiling the line in the line hand. To make loops of line in your hand as you retrieve, grasp the line just below the rod hand and pull it back toward your left thigh (if you are right-handed). Cup your hand, palm upward, and let the line lie across your fingers. Move the line hand back up to the rod hand (which continues to hold the line), and make another strip down toward your thigh. Make this second loop a little smaller than the first. It should be on top of or forward of the first loop across your fingers. Continue stripping from your rod hand to your left side, decreasing the size of the loops. When you are ready to shoot the line out again, controlling the release with the fingers of your line hand, the smaller loops that went on last will come off first and there should be no tangles.

This method may be varied according to the length of line you have to coil. The first loop may be made with two or three strips in order to make it a very big one, and some line may lie on the water before you actually make the first loop. Some fishermen make all

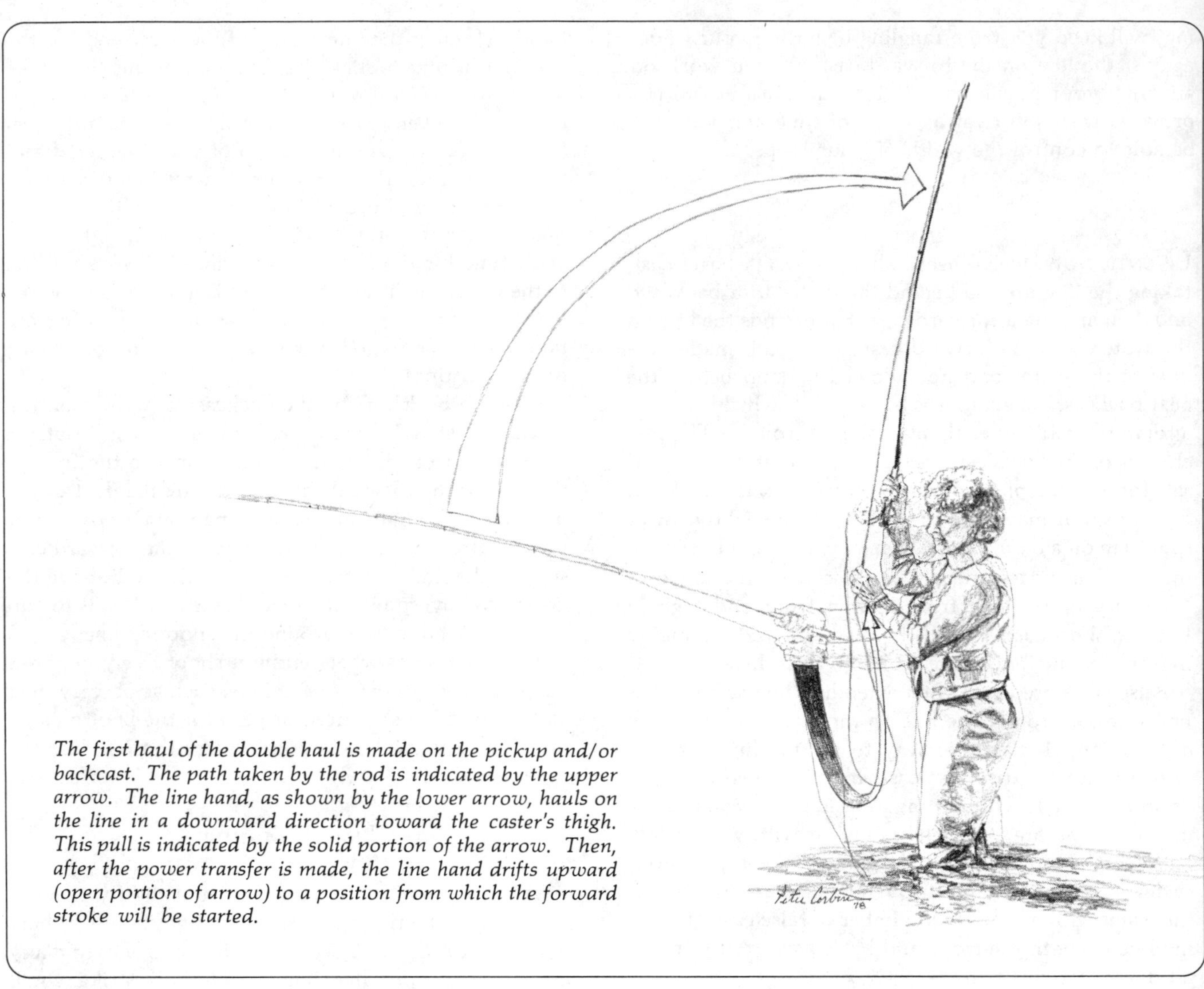

The first haul of the double haul is made on the pickup and/or backcast. The path taken by the rod is indicated by the upper arrow. The line hand, as shown by the lower arrow, hauls on the line in a downward direction toward the caster's thigh. This pull is indicated by the solid portion of the arrow. Then, after the power transfer is made, the line hand drifts upward (open portion of arrow) to a position from which the forward stroke will be started.

of the loops starting from forward of the rod grip in order to get a longer length to the strip, and in this case, the line must be *released* from the rod hand and then led *back under* one of its fingers on each strip.

Increased Distance

THE TECHNIQUES you have learned thus far, when assimilated over a period of time, will enable you to enjoy fly-fishing up to a point. That point may be enough for some fishermen, but as in all worthwhile endeavors requiring muscle skills and good reflexes, there is more to fly-casting than the basics. Your ultimate goal should be to cast as accurately as possible under calm or windy weather conditions at any distance within your physical limitations. If you want to be *really good,* you must eventually master the following techniques, from the single and double hauls through the sections on fishing techniques and wind conditions. We think the satisfaction gained will be well worth the effort.

Single and double hauls are techniques that were developed by tournament casters to increase the distance that an angler can cast a fly line. Many people think that doing a double haul is like patting your head and rubbing your tummy at the same time, but it's within your capabilities if you have understood the mechanics of the basic cast. The hauls will add speed to your line so that it will shoot farther. They will also allow you to shorten some of your longest strokes so you won't have to work as hard.

Increased line speed will help you cast into a wind, make narrower loops and give you better control over your casts. Once you have mastered the single and double hauls, you'll fit them into your casting repertoire and use them as often as you fish.

The Single Haul

HAULING IS DONE by the line hand, the hand that pulls the line through the rod guides as the stroke is made with the rod hand. A single haul is usually used on the

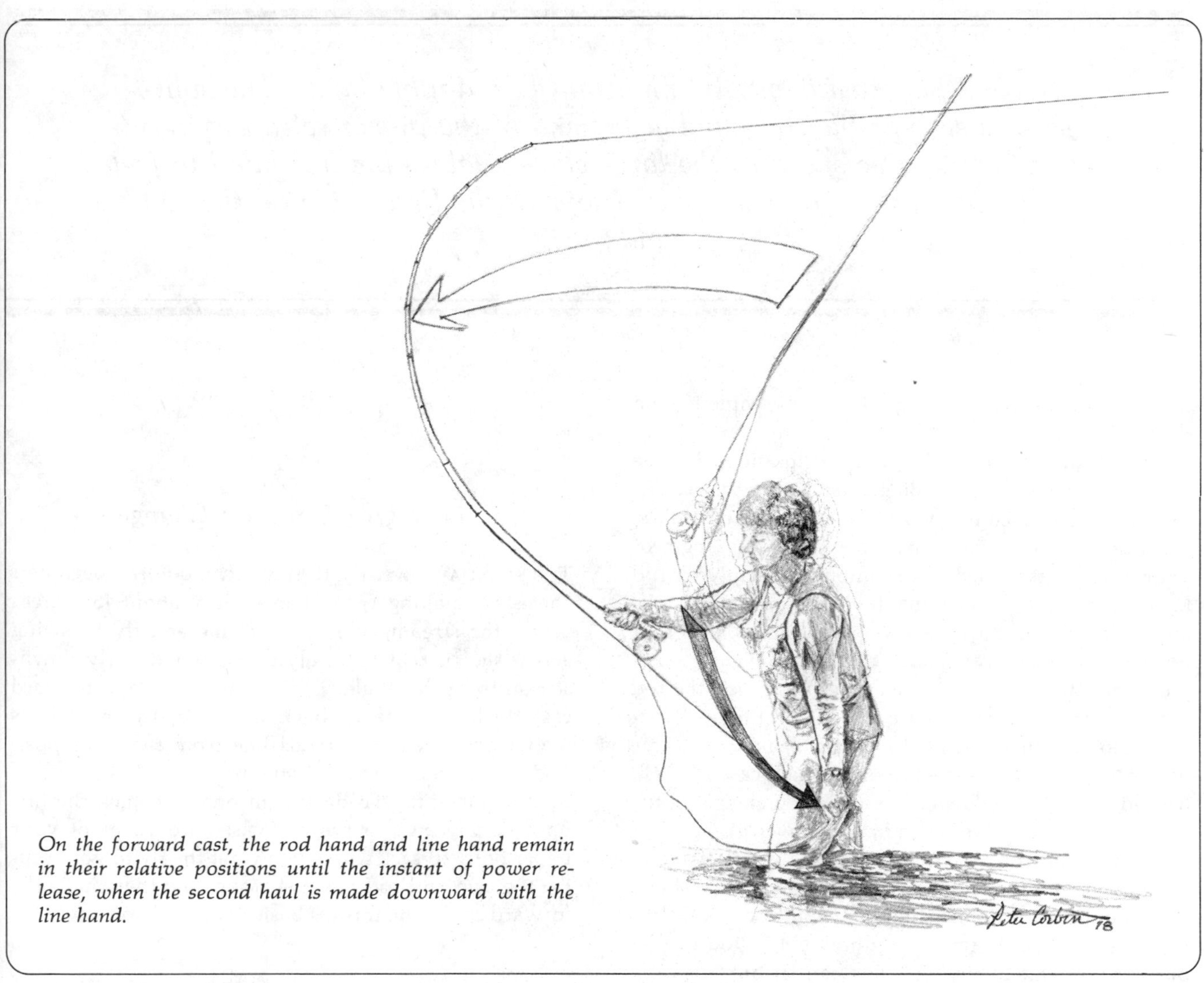

On the forward cast, the rod hand and line hand remain in their relative positions until the instant of power release, when the second haul is made downward with the line hand.

backcast, so we'll concern ourselves with this, although after you learn the principles you can try it on the forward cast, too.

The line hand pulls the line in and away from the first guide as the rod is *lifted* and *loaded* on the pickup stroke. The finish of that pull and the instant of turnover and power release should coincide *exactly*. The line hand makes a *sudden stop*, just as is done with the wrist flick of the rod hand, and the work is done. While the rod hand drifts up and back with the rod, the line hand *keeps tension* on the line and continues to do so through the forward *loading* and *power release*. Then it releases the line, as described earlier in shooting line.

Keeping tension on the line means that the line hand may have to change its position, moving forward or backward a few inches, depending on the length of the stroke and drift; but the key to that position is simple. Keep the line pulled away from the first guide so as not to allow it to catch on the body of the caster. Single hauls work very well with bulky bass bugs and large flies and when there is wind behind you. A little experimenting will tell you when to use it in place of the double haul.

The Double Haul

As in the single haul, pull the line away from the first guide with the line hand while the *stroke* is being made; end the haul abruptly to coincide with the *power release* at the instant of turnover and then, while the rod hand and rod drift upward and backward, the line hand floats up toward the first guide (still holding the line tightly). No *pushing* here, it moves at the speed of the unrolling line.

The rod hand's *drift* ends and the forward *stroke* is started as the line hand reaches the *up* position. The line hand stays there until, at the instant of turnover and power release, the second haul is made.

The second haul is made, again, at the instant of turnover and power release. If the fly is to be delivered to a target, the line is released after the second haul has been completed. If it's only a false-cast, the line hand

A good backcast is vitally important to a double haul. The split-second stop of the rod hand at the end of the power release is very necessary to give speed to the line, which enables the line hand to feel the tension as it follows upward toward the first guide on the rod hand's drift.

will float toward the first guide after completion on the second haul.

The length of the haul will be determined by the amount of line you are hauling. Remember that stroke length is determined by the same factor — short strokes, short lines; long strokes, long lines — and the length of your haul is determined by the amount of help your rod hand needs. A haul can cut the length of your stroke almost in half, so it can be a couple of inches, or a foot or even more. If you make a *one-foot* pickup haul, your line hand will move upward a *foot* during the rod hand's drift as the line goes back out on the backcast. The second haul will be a foot long again *unless* line has been "shot" on the backcast, in which case the help needed to move the longer line will be greater and the second haul will be longer and more powerful.

To shoot line on the backcast during a double haul, let the line slip through your fingers as the line hand moves up toward the first guide. Count on the feeling of constant pressure to tell you how much you can let out; it's a matter of timing. You can let out line *only* after the power release and *during the drift* of your rod hand. When it's over, it's over; constant pressure will tell you when.

A good backcast is vitally important to a double haul. The split-second stop of the rod hand at the end of the power release is very necessary to give speed to the line, which enables the line hand to feel the tension as it follows upward toward the first guide on the rod hand's drift. The backcast also needs to be as high as possible, providing a cushion of time and space as the speeding line unrolls, and allowing you to reposition the rod hand for the perfect forward trajectory.

It's sometimes helpful to learn the double haul in two sections, separating the backcast from the forward cast. Follow the directions for the backcast through the rod hand's *stroke* and *drift* and the line hand's *haul* and *float* upward. Allow the line to fall to the ground behind you (do this on a lawn). Then start the forward cast and do the second haul. You'll find it coming together after a half-dozen of these. Practice the double haul with the basic cast, in overhead and 45-degree off-vertical positions, and while false-casting in either of those planes.

ON THE STREAM

45-Degree Direction Change

THE STANDARD wet-fly fishing technique for beginners consists of making a cast at an angle of about 45 degrees across the stream, allowing the line and fly to swing across the current naturally to a point directly downstream from the angler. In one backcast and forward cast, the line can be put back at that 45-degree angle as the fisherman either extends line from the same position or moves a step downstream and makes a cast of the same length. To do this in one cast, pick the line up normally and, as the backcast unfolds, pivot your upper body to face where you want the fly to go, keeping the arm and rod position static, and then make the forward cast. The form is basically a V shape.

90-Degree Direction Change

THIS CHANGE OF DIRECTION can be made in a V shape if the line is short, but other techniques are better. Move the rod tip in a plane parallel to the water from downstream to upstream, ending with a sweep upward to a vertical position for your backcast. The stroke starts horizontally, but the power release and wrist flick are made vertically.

The position at the end of the sweep upward should allow you to make a *standard* forward cast to the point of aim, 90 degrees from where you started.

Another way to change direction, from downstream to up, is to make a rounded backcast in the form of a wide-open U, taking the rod tip and line behind you (overhead) from downstream to upstream. It will be in a generally horizontal, off-vertical plane with the beginning of the stroke rounded, but the wrist flick and power release will be in a straight back-to-front line to the point of aim. A rounded motion such as this is also good when a short backcast is needed; it won't use as much room to the rear as will a standard V-shaped direction change.

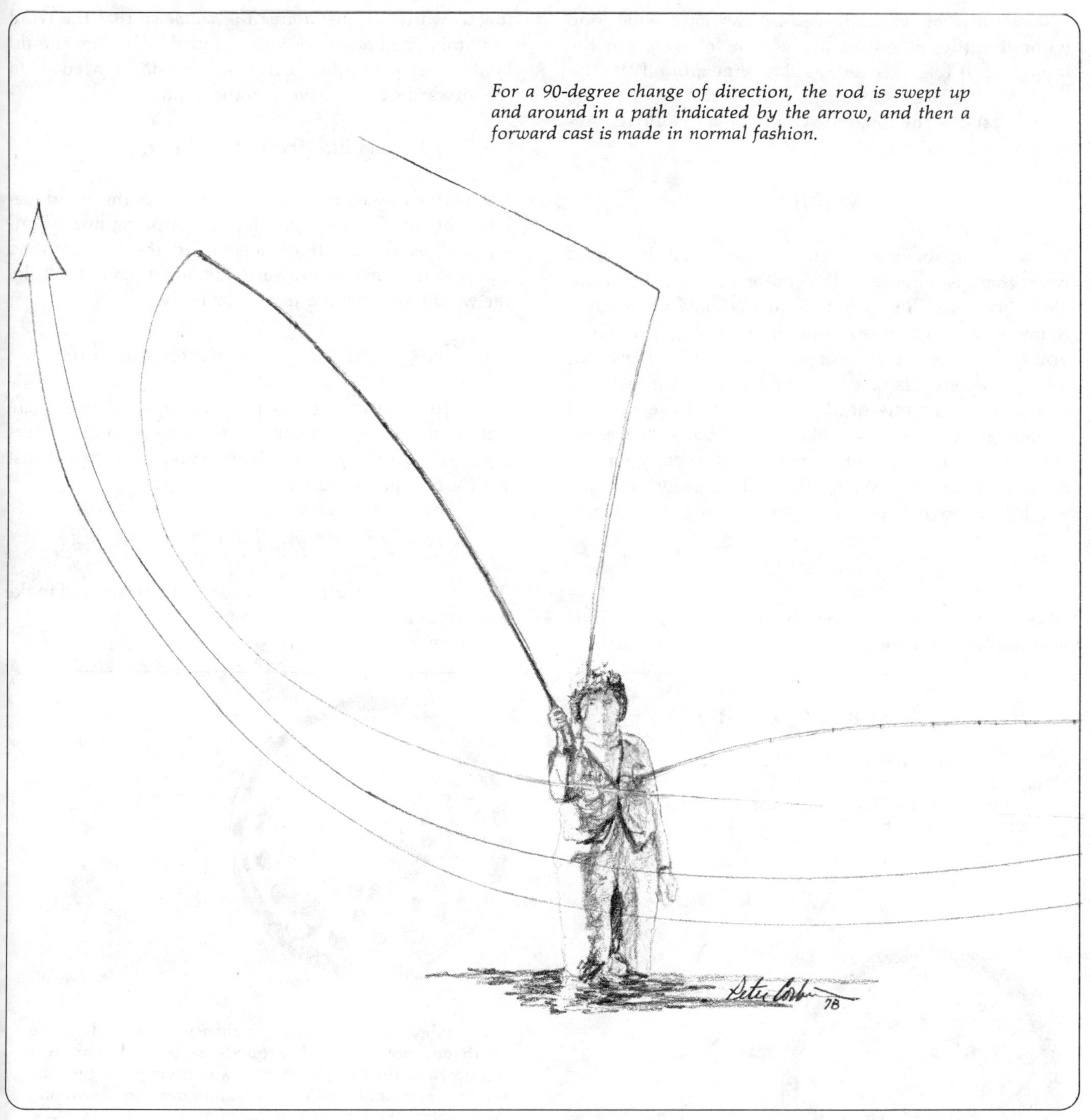
For a 90-degree change of direction, the rod is swept up and around in a path indicated by the arrow, and then a forward cast is made in normal fashion.

Roll Pickup Cast

THIS CAST CAN BE USED when the fly line has sunk or has too much slack in it to be picked up conventionally.

Start in a roll-cast position as described earlier, but instead of rolling the line *on* the water on the forward cast, roll it *above* the water (by pointing the rod tip higher and making the cast parallel to the water). Just before it straightens in the air, make a regular backcast. Then continue as you would normally in the presentation of the fly. This takes less time than a conventional roll cast (putting line on water) followed by a conventional overhead cast (picking it up again).

The Dry-Fly Slack Cast

HAVING LEARNED to stretch a cast out straight, it may come as a shock to find that for some types of fishing, a perfectly straight line is not the answer. Instead, in the dry-fly slack cast, the important thing is to put *slack* in the line and leader so that the fly will float for the longest possible period with a free drift before the current, which is pulling on the line, starts to affect the way in which the fly's drifting.

Slack can be put into a cast by straightening it out above the water and then giving a backward yank to put curves of slack in the line as it falls to the water.

It can also be accomplished by casting a wide loop without sufficient power in the cast to straighten the loop out. It falls, instead, as slack line around the fly.

This is the preferred method, since the closer to the fly the slack is, the longer it will have a free float. Accuracy comes with practice.

WIND

WIND SCARES beginning anglers and well it should when there is a hook on the end of the line. Most anglers have been hit with a fly at one time or another. Remember not to set the hook, if you can help it, when you feel the fly hit you (or a companion!). However, a simple awareness of where the wind is coming from, and where your line needs to travel to have the best advantage, can usually make a potentially dangerous situation workable. *Feel* the wind; *feel* where your line is, and be careful. Where the rod tip leads, the line will follow, except, perhaps, in the strongest of winds.

Headwind

MAKE THE BACKCAST normally, but drop the casting arm and rod downward during the drift, and make a low forward cast *just above the water* so that the wind can't take the line out of your control. The line should land just as it unrolls. Extra power will be needed on the forward cast to drive into the wind.

Wind from the Rear

USE EXTRA POWER to *drive* the line into the wind behind you, as it will be fighting the unrolling line. Timing will be shorter than normal on the backcast, so trust your constant-pressure judgment and don't let the wind blow the line into your body.

Crosswind from the Rod-hand Side

BRING THE ROD TIP and line *in* on the upwind side high. Rotate the rod tip and hand to the downwind side during the drift (over your head) and make the forward cast with a backhand motion.

Crosswind from the Line-hand Side

TAKE THE ROD TIP off-vertical for best control and make the cast in a 45-degree or lower plane on the downwind side.

Tying Backing to a Flyreel

THE KNOT THAT YOU USE should be easy to tie and reasonably strong. If a fish has stripped all of your line, there's not much you can do with a light leader tippet to hold your quarry. This basic tie will be sufficient.

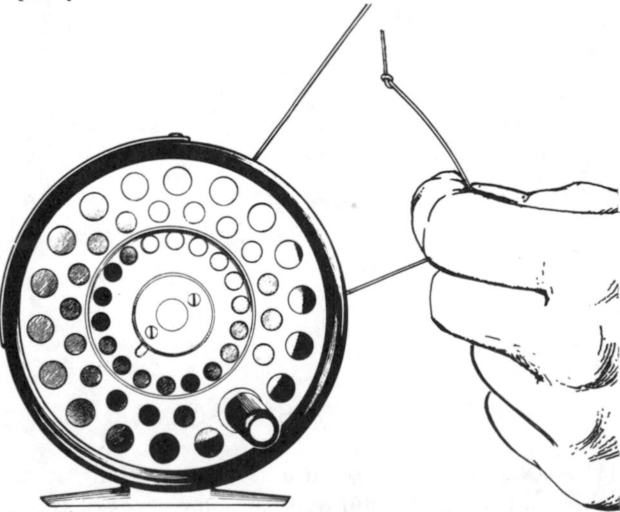

Tie an overhand knot in the tag end of the backing and trim reasonably close to the knot. If there is a line guide on the reel, start the tag end of the backing within the confines of the guide and pass it around the spool. Bring it back out the same way it went in.

Hold the tag end against the standing part, and tie an overhand knot around the standing part with the tag end.

Pull on the tag end (while holding the standing part) to tighten the overhand knot.

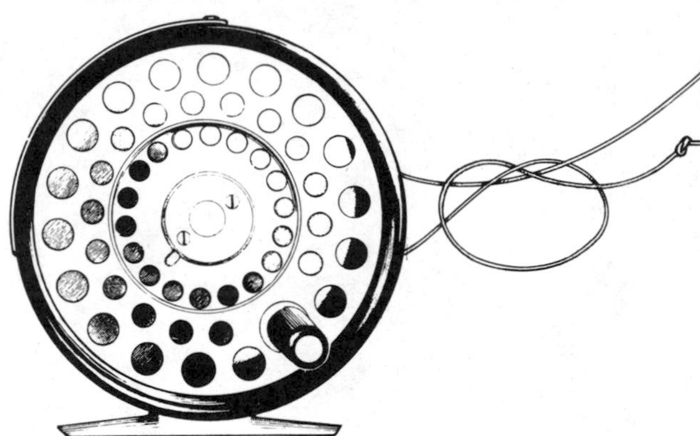

By pulling steadily on the standing part of the line, the overhand knot you made around the standing part will slip down to the hub of the reel. Continue pulling on the standing part until the first overhand knot slips down and jams against the second one.

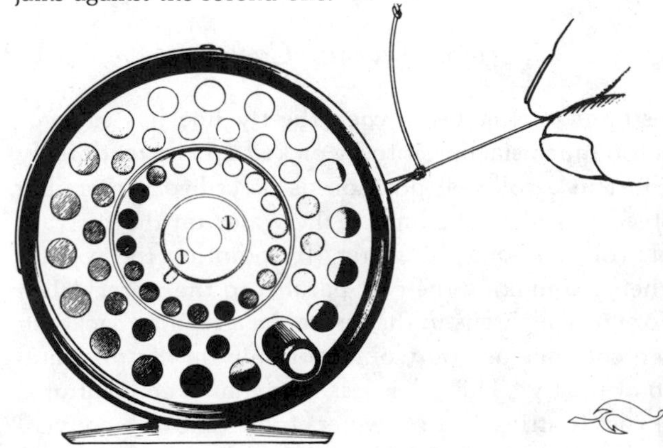

Testament of a Fisherman
I fish because I love to; because I love the environs where trout are found, which are invariably beautiful, and hate the environs where crowds of people are found, which are invariably ugly; because of all the television commercials, cocktail parties, and assorted social posturing I thus escape; because, in a world where most men seem to spend their lives doing things they hate, my fishing is at once an endless source of delight and an act of small rebellion; because trout do not lie or cheat and cannot be bought or bribed or impressed by power, but respond only to quietude and humility and endless patience; because I suspect that men are going along this way for the last time, and I for one don't want to waste the trip; because mercifully there are no telephones on trout waters; because only in the woods can I find solitude without loneliness; because bourbon out of an old tin cup always tastes better out there; because maybe one day I will catch a mermaid; and, finally, not because I regard fishing as being so terribly important but because I suspect that so many of the other concerns of men are equally unimportant — and not nearly so much fun.
ROBERT TRAVER

Photo by John Merwin.

Plate 2

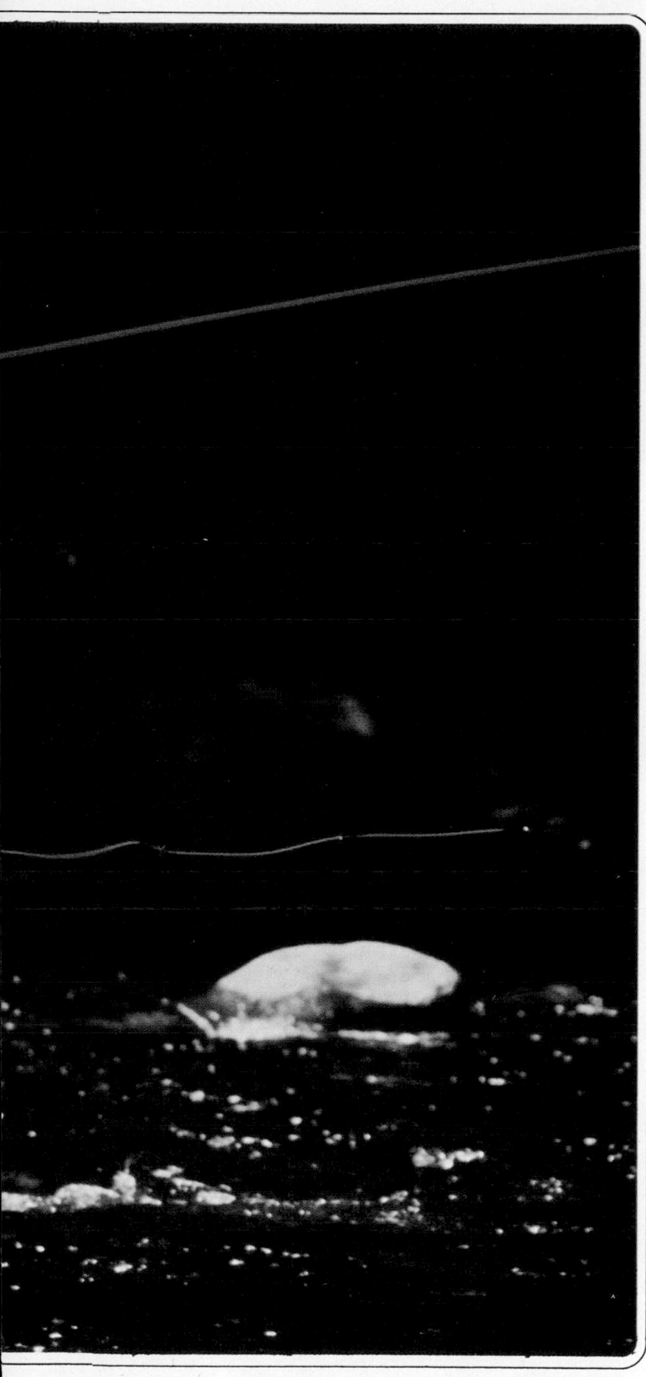

Joan Wulff following through after a double-haul while fishing a New Hampshire stream. She describes this technique in detail on page 29.

Lee Wulff gathering loops of slack fly line in his left hand prior to making another cast. Note that each loop is smaller than the previous, which enables the line to be shot on a forward cast without tangling. Photos by John Merwin.

This scene is almost a reading-the-water parlor game because of the vast number of good holding places for trout that are shown. The caverns under the beds of trailing weeds hold fish, as do the pockets above, below and around the rock. That's one reason why this portion of Montana's Madison River is such a fine fishery. Photo by John Merwin.

Plate 5

Finding out what this fish has taken may be the first step in catching him. Photo by Carl Richards.

Plate 6

These photos illustrate the stages of the life cycle of the mayfly that are of importance to fly fishermen. Above: the subaquatic stage, or nymph.

Directly above: the adult stage, or dun. Below: the spinner. Note the translucent quality of the spinner's wings when compared to those of the dun.

Two stages of the life cycle of the caddisfly with which anglers should be familiar: above, a caddis larva just before it pupates into an adult.

Directly above: a caddis adult viewed from below—note the tentlike configuration of the wings. Bottom: an adult caddis imitation.

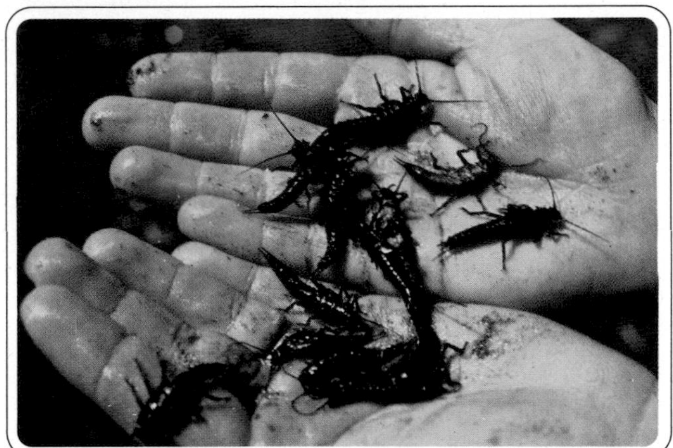

In the photo at upper left is an imitation of an emerging adult midge. Below that is a handful of stonefly nymphs, collected in the spring when they become active before emerging to become adults such as the one shown at lower left, a Western salmon fly. A smaller yellow stonefly is shown at upper right, and a variety of stonefly imitations (drys) are shown directly above. Photos at left and lower left by Ron Cordes; others this plate by Carl Richards.

You can't be taught to read the water — you have to learn. The frivolous currents, the deep pools, the submerged rocks, and the fish themselves — or the lack of them, at first — will eventually train your eye and your reflexes. First, you'll learn where the fish aren't. You'll remember those places well, because you'll have fished so many of them. Then you'll learn where they should *be, and sometimes are. Finally, when you find out where they really are, phone us collect at* FLY FISHERMAN *— we'd like you to do a ten-year series of articles for us. But as a guide until that day comes, we can't think of a better person to take you down to the stream than Doug Swisher. He'll take you beneath the water's surface, down to where the action is, showing you that a trout stream has three dimensions — and sometimes even a fourth. After learning to cast, this could be the most important step you'll take before actually wading in yourself.*

Chapter 3

Reading the Water

From Top to Bottom

DOUG SWISHER

AS AN ANGLING INSTRUCTOR, I'm faced daily with the problem of teaching my students where to cast their flies so they will have the best possible chance of catching a trout. After all, if you continually cast your fly into dead water — even though you may be a superb caster and have excellent patterns — you simply don't have any chance of being successful.

Attempting to determine where the fish are is called *reading the water* — must reading for a fly fisher. I say "attempting," because we can never be positive that fish are where we judge them to be. Literally, we have to "read between the lines." There are simply too many variables. So we must come up with certain guidelines that tell us where the trout *should* be under normal conditions.

The hitch here is the word *normal.* It seems that the waters we fish are either too high or too low, too warm or too cold, too clear or too murky. To read the water properly, then, one must learn what the guidelines are, make adjustments for specific conditions and, finally, add the ingredient of experience. Of course, that last element usually, but not always, varies with the amount of stream time each individual has logged. Some anglers have greater ability to catalog each stream experience into their memory banks than others. Developing that ability, which can be called learning from experience, is one of the most important, if not *the* most important factor in reading the water.

First Glances

TROUT, NOT UNLIKE HUMAN BEINGS, have two very important requirements in life: They must have shelter, and they must have food. Those basic requirements are of primary importance to the angler who attempts to read the water. Shelter is a twofold problem for the trout. It must find an area that will provide protection from enemies and refuge from the heavy currents of the stream. The trout also must find a location where it can easily intercept food that comes drifting by. Some trout have a single location that meets all three requirements — shelter from predators, refuge from heavy current flow and an adequate food supply. We call such a spot a *prime lie*, and quite often we will find larger fish there. Other trout, usually smaller ones, have both *sheltering lies* and *feeding lies*. They spend part of their day at a location where they can easily gather a good supply of food, and the rest of the time they are in a well-protected area.

Numerous creatures continually prey on a trout. Diving birds, water animals, larger fish and especially man pose constant threats to its survival. The trout's first concern, then, is to *find cover* that will shelter him from enemies. A trout will search out the best protection available in its underwater world. In order of preference, it will first seek *overhead* cover; then, if overhead cover is not available, it will seek *side* cover; and finally, if neither overhead nor side cover is available, a trout will seek *depth* for protection. That statement is undoubtedly the most important thing to keep in mind when it comes down to the nitty-gritty of reading a stream under normal conditions.

In my fly-fishing instruction, the primary point that I try to drive into my students is to *look for overhead cover*. All blue-ribbon trout streams provide such protection. Some kinds of overhead cover are quite obvious and easy to identify. They would include objects that project out from the stream bank, such as overhanging trees, tag alders, bushes, grass, docks, bridges, log sweepers and brush piles. Others are less obvious and much more difficult to locate visually — undercut banks, rock ledges, logs along the bank, underwater shelves, weed beds and sunken logs. Close examination of those various types of cover will quickly reveal that the majority of the best action in most streams is likely to be *along the bank*, because most of the prime cover is located there.

One of the biggest mistakes made by the neophyte fly fisherman is that he spends most of his time fishing the midstream currents. One of the reasons, of course, for fishing the middle of the river is that the casting is easier. Pinpoint accuracy usually is not critical, drag-free floats are much easier to come by, and overhanging obstacles, such as tree limbs, are not a problem. The beginner, then, takes the path of least resistance and fishes where most of the more difficult casting situations are eliminated. Unfortunately, the better fish are rarely in midstream, but are near or under the bank. And there, of course, is where most of the overhead cover is found. That is why many fly fishermen never catch large fish; they simply do not fish where big trout are located.

If overhead cover is not available to a trout, it will, as a second choice, look for *side cover*. By positioning itself alongside a rock or some obstacle in the stream, a trout is automatically protected on one side, which gives a greater feeling of security than being out in open water and exposed for a full 360 degrees to his enemies. The trout has to look to only one side to check for danger. Besides rocks and boulders, other objects that provide good side cover are logs, rock ledges, stumps, weed beds and shoals. And stream banks, especially those with tall grass, provide some of the best side cover of all.

In the absence of both overhead cover and side cover, trout will seek out *depth* for protection as a last resort. Streams with only depth for protection are not very productive. Only small fish are normally found in water that is devoid of cover. In blue-ribbon trout streams good fish can be found in the deep pools and runs, but that is not because of depth alone. There are always rocks, ledges or depressions that combine with the depth to make for a good sheltering lie. In fact, the very best lies are made up of a combination of overhead cover, either overhanging branches or undercut banks, or both. Almost all have held tight to the stream edge, which, of course, provides side cover. And most of them, especially if they were in a sheltering lie, have been in a fairly substantial depth of water.

Shelter is a two-part situation for the trout. It must find shelter that will offer protection not only from enemies, but also from the heavy currents of the stream. If a trout had to fight a fast current flow all day, its strength would quickly be sapped, and it would not have enough energy to survive. The main currents of many of our rivers, especially the large free-stone variety, are simply too fast and too strong for trout to hold in. Fish in those types of rivers must find shelter from the heavy flow, and such protection is found in basically the same locations that provide shelter from predators — next to the banks, around obstacles and along the bottom of the stream.

Anywhere you find water flowing next to or around an object, whether it be a rock, a weed bed or the river bottom, there is a reduction in current speed due to friction. The water closest to the object will be moving at a much slower pace than the water farther away.

Think of it this way: Picture water as being made up of many layers, sort of like a deck of cards. The bottom layer and the river bottom will have much more friction between them than the layers at the stream surface. That phenomenon works in both the vertical and horizontal planes. When you start to think of the stream in such a manner (as being made up of many layers of varying speeds), then you'll start doing a better job of reading the water. You'll be thinking like a trout, which is what you have to do to be successful.

Current in a vertical plane. Illustrations by Robert Seaman.

Getting to the Bottom of Things

Now, LET'S CARRY OUR THINKING a step further by varying the type, or configuration, of the stream bottom. If we first consider a stream that has a relatively smooth bottom, let's say a typical mixture of sand and fine gravel, we find the variance in speed between the top and bottom currents is minimal. If the bottom changes to rocks and coarse gravel, the variance is greater, and if we add boulders and depressions to the stream profile, the change in current speed from top to bottom is greater yet. We have progressively increased the friction, which in turn reduces the flow along the lower layers and creates excellent sheltering lies for the trout.

Surface Currents

Now, LET'S SEE WHAT WE CAN LEARN from studying the currents at the surface of the stream, working in the horizontal plane. Again, let's imagine the water as being made up of many layers with minimal friction between each layer but maximum friction between the layers and the immovable objects of the stream. If you observe closely right at the edge of the stream, you'll see a layer of current moving very slowly in comparison to the current a foot or so farther out. The width of this slow-moving layer is largely dependent on the contour of the stream edge. A rough or irregular stream edge has more friction and therefore creates a wider lane. That lane, of course, provides a great hiding place where trout can rest without expending excess energy and where they also can be in position to grab an easy meal.

In addition to the bank and bottom areas just discussed, midstream obstacles, such as rocks and boulders, provide excellent relief from the heavy currents. Such objects, especially if they reach to or protrude above the stream surface, give us a good visual picture of the varying currents. Their effect is normally quite obvious compared to the more subtle variances created along the bank of the stream. As the current approaches a midstream obstacle, such as a large rock, pressure builds up on the front side. At the point where that pressure, or frictional buildup, is the greatest, the current splits. The exact spot at which the current divides can be anywhere from a few inches to a few feet upstream from the rock — the point is determined basically by the size and shape of the rock and the speed of the current.

The larger and flatter the front edge of the rock and the faster the current, the farther upstream we'll find that point. In the roughly triangular area directly ahead of the obstacle, the currents are compressed, creating a high-pressure area. If sizable enough, such a space can provide an excellent sheltering lie for one or

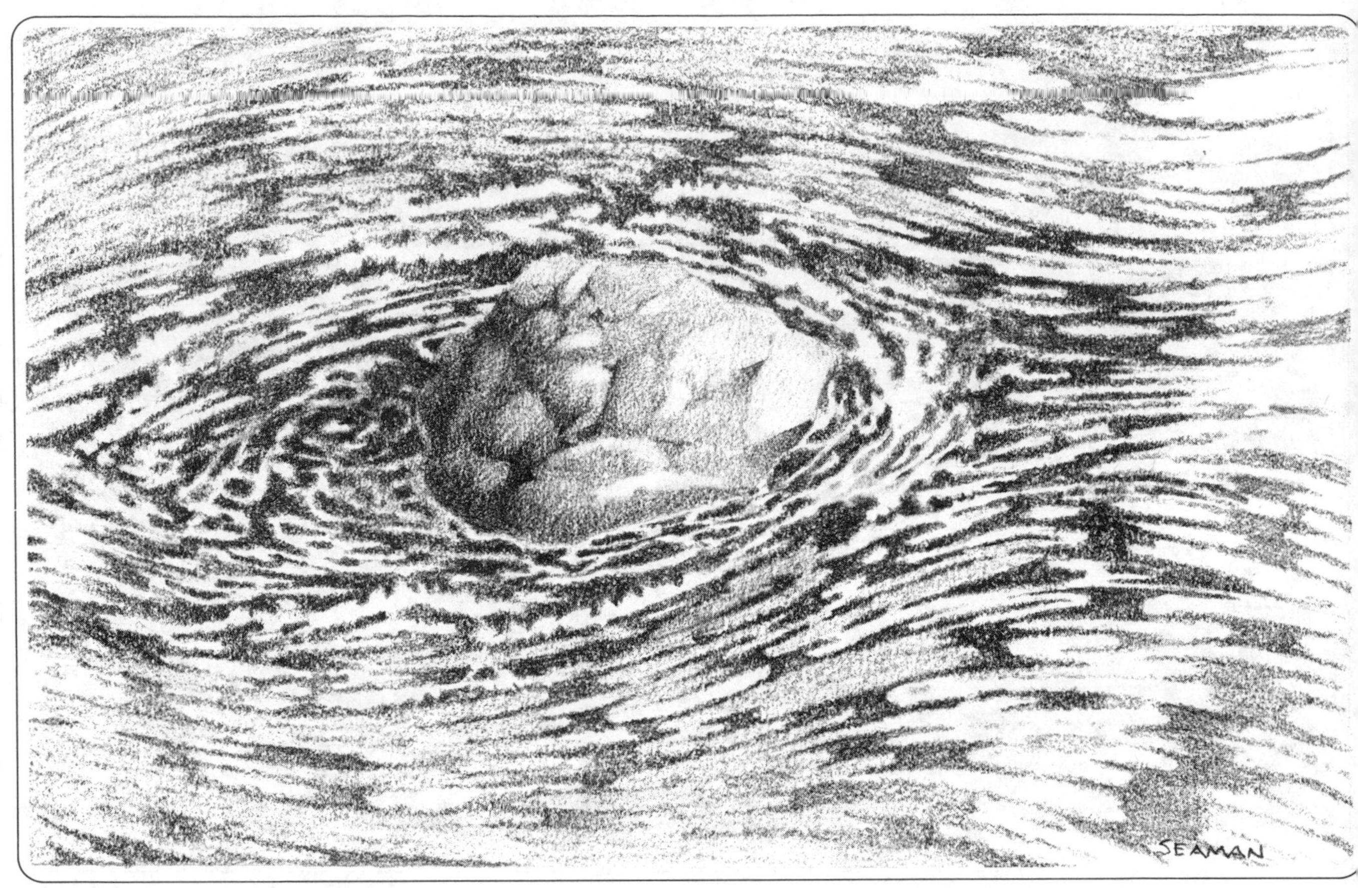

Midstream obstructions, such as rocks, offer an opportunity to observe current in a horizontal plane. The current compresses on the upstream edge of the rock until it splits; the currents then rejoin below the rock. Areas above and below the rock may offer excellent holding lies for trout.

more fish. The rock gives good side or rear cover, and the current is minimal, making it easy for trout to hold their position without wasting valuable energy. It is also a good feeding lie. The faster moving current splits right up in front of the fish, where they can quickly dart in either direction to pick up an easy meal. Such movement from dead water into swift water is an easy maneuver for the trout.

Hydrodynamic principles are at work in that situation. A differential in speed between two currents is accompanied by a corresponding differential in pressure. Faster current flow has lower pressure than slower current flow. The trout, resting in relatively dead water, is literally pushed from his high-pressure lie into the low-pressure line of drift with only the slightest help from his fins. The phenomenon is a great aid to the trout in his feeding activity, especially in streams that have heavy currents.

Let's continue to follow the flow of the current as it goes around the rock. After splitting, each current segment is diverted at an angle, which is determined basically by the size and shape of the rock. Larger and blunter configurations cause the diverted currents to strike the main current flow at a greater angle, which in turn creates a compressed current area along each side of our obstacle. Anywhere you have compressed currents, you have an increase in current speed. Again, if you apply the principle of dividing up the total stream flow into many small increments, you can better understand what happens.

In areas where layers are pushed together or compressed, there must be an increase in speed to allow the same volume of water to pass by. It's like an adjustable nozzle on a garden hose. Reduce the size of the hole, which compresses the layers, and the water really squirts out fast. Open up the nozzle, which expands the layers, and the water no longer squirts but instead comes out at a much more leisurely pace. The same thing happens in a trout stream. Currents flowing around the sides of rocks, or any other obstacles, tend to increase their speed (similar to the nozzle being closed down). Likewise, the same segment of current that moved faster as it went around the rock will slow down when it arrives at the downstream edge of the rock (similar to the nozzle being opened).

Such information is extremely important to the fly fisherman when it comes to reading the water. First of all, it's not likely that we'll find fish, at least good ones, lying right to the sides of rocks and boulders where all of that fast water is flowing. An exception could exist if there were definite undercuts, relatively large indentations or other irregularities in the structure. If that were the case, the fast flow would probably not be tight to the edge of the rock or boulder. Instead, there would be a telltale lane of slow water.

The area behind or downstream from an obstacle presents an entirely different situation, one that can offer jackpot possibilities to the angler. Once the current passes the downstream extremities of the rock, the area to be occupied by the flowing water immediately increases in the pocket left by the divided current. The sudden expansion of space forces current into the pocket from both sides. Of similar strength and traveling a collision course, the currents negate each other, thus creating an area of almost still water. Trout love to lie in these triangular locations, where they have not only excellent refuge from strong currents, but also have their own built-in delicatessen. Food drifts in, quite often from both the right- and left-hand expansion currents, and is held for long periods of time at the tip of the trout's nose. All the trout has to do is tip up and sip in the morsel. Sometimes the rising forms of fish feeding in the quiet water behind rocks and boulders are almost undetectable, especially if small spinners or tiny duns are on the water.

To the fly fisher who is trying to figure out where trout might be holding in a given piece of water, those midstream objects become important landmarks and demand careful attention. Rocks, logs, boulders, stumps, brush piles and bridge abutments are all likely locations that may harbor fish. Each is characterized by triangular-shaped areas of relatively dead water immediately fore and aft, with the downstream area normally being the most productive. Area size and differentials in current flow are the two main keys to success. Generally speaking, large objects create larger triangles and greater changes in flow velocities. You've probably heard the saying that large rocks produce large fish. Nothing is iron-clad, but that statement is certainly worthy of your attention.

Finding Holding Water and Lies

TROUT ARE CAUTIOUS CREATURES — most of the time, that is. Good trout, especially, spend a great portion of their day in sheltering lies, hiding from predators and staying out of the heavy current flow. Quite often, however, when it's time to put the feed bag on, they throw caution to the wind. Even fish that have a prime lie — great cover and good food supply — will move into some seemingly unexplainable places to feed. The reason for such movements is really quite obvious: if the food isn't coming to the trout, the trout must go to the food.

Most of the time, stream fish do not have to wander in search of a meal. The majority of their diet floats by and passes directly overhead, which is one of the main reasons trout select a lie that provides easy access to their daily menu. Once they have decided that a certain location will provide them with protection from predators and shelter from heavy currents, they must evaluate the food supply. Obviously, a sheltering lie that averages a hundred units of food drifting past it each day is much more enticing than one that averages only ten units.

If we could install in our favorite stream a "food intensity meter," a device that would measure the amount of food that drifts by each square foot of water surface, we'd see vast differences from one area to another. Those variances would be pretty much proportional to the variety of water found in the area being metered. It makes sense, then, that fish would select a type of water that had a high rating on the meter. To find a high concentration of drifting food, I look for two basic kinds of water, a *funnel system* or a *collection area.*

The first variety of water is a location where *currents converge.* They tend to funnel the food into heavy concentrations, which is typical of what happens at the head of a pool. The lead-in riffle is normally made up of many converging currents, which come together and act as a funnel system, literally pouring food of all types into the pool. We invariably find great numbers of fish, although not always the biggest ones, feeding here. Shelter for the fish is supplied mainly by water depth and side cover from rocks, boulders and depressions in the bottom of the pool.

An even better funnel system — certainly better if you're looking for larger fish — is an area where currents converge along the bank of the stream. Such a situation commonly is created along the deep side of pools, especially pools located on the bend of a river or pools with a lead-in riffle that is angled off to one side. Under those circumstances, the main food-bearing current is directed against the bank. Its force deepens that side of the pool and frequently forms undercut banks. Its direction conveys maximum amounts of food to the trout's location. Those conditions combine to create possibly the prime lie of all. We find overhead cover, side cover, depth, relief from the heavy currents and a great food supply all wrapped up in one location — a real jackpot for any angler.

Funnel systems, as we have just discussed, are made up of converging currents, which originate from the flow of water around and against various obstacles in the stream. After passing those objects, however, a reverse phenomenon takes place. Increased flow allows the currents to expand and pour into the pockets behind each object. It was pointed out earlier that such a condition creates a relatively dead, triangular area that affords the trout shelter from the heavy currents. It also is a *collection area* where food can accumulate and rates as a first-class feeding lie.

Large obstacles located along the bank form even greater collection areas. Boulders tight to the stream edge and logs extending out from the shore allow the main current to pass on *one* side only, as compared to midstream rocks, which split the current and allow segments to pass on *each* side. With the heavy flow pass-

Above, a funnel area, where currents converge. Below, a collection area, where currents may concentrate available food forms. These areas warrant particular attention from the angler.

ing on one side only, a sort of swirling effect, or eddy, is produced. Food is collected in great quantities and held in the backwater for long periods of time. As a feeding lie, that type of water is tops. As a sheltering lie, some are good, some are not. It all depends on the amount of overhead or side cover present. Individual logs and boulders are usually not too effective. Log jams and brush piles are excellent.

Special Problems

So far, we've covered basic guidelines of reading the water when conditions are normal. But quite often conditions are not normal, and we must learn how to make adjustments.

Let's start at the beginning of the season when the water is invariably *high and cold.* With such conditions, the trout's metabolism will be very low, and no fish will be in the mood to chase your fly all over the stream. In fact, you'll almost have to put it right in the trout's mouth. If the water is not too high, fish the normal lies, but right on the bottom. Extremely high water, on the other hand, creates an enormous increase in current force, which forces the trout to seek other shelter. They usually find refuge along the stream edge, especially in and around overhanging logs and bushes.

If the Opening-Day problem is only one of cold weather, you have two possibilities: fish the bottom in the normal places, as previously mentioned, or seek out shallow, slow-moving water. Even in the low temperatures of early season, the streams warm somewhat by early afternoon. Shallow water will obviously warm more quickly and becomes your best bet for dry-fly action. Each April when I open the season on Michigan's Au Sable, my method of attack is to cover as much water as possible and concentrate on the quiet, knee-deep runs.

Murky, dirty water is another problem and is often associated with high water. The approach is pretty much the same—fish the shallow runs along the banks and cover lots of water. Also, be on the lookout for springs and small feeder streams. Their influx improves clarity and adds oxygen to the water. Fish will move into those areas under such conditions.

As we progress into the *warmer part of the season,* the hatches of aquatic insects become heavier and more varied. While we are dealing mainly with those periods when the water is devoid of rises, it's obviously rather easy to read the water when the fish are feeding on top. However, the hatches *can* have an effect on how we read a stream when there are no visible rises. That is why it pays to study the habits of the more important aquatic insects. If, for example, you know that the nymph of a certain species becomes active an hour before its actual emergence, and you also know the water type required, you have some valuable information. When the trout migrate from their normal lies into the hatch area, you can be ready for them.

During the *late season,* the water level of many of our streams drops drastically. Areas that provided good sheltering and feeding lies earlier in the year become devoid of water, and the fish must move elsewhere. Rivers like the Firehole and Madison usually afford excellent cover for the trout with their undercut banks, but when the water is very low, most of the undercuts are barren, and the big fish have to move out into the weed beds and deep holes.

Temperature and oxygen can also be problems late in the year. In many of our Eastern streams elevated temperatures drive fish from their normal lies. They simply move into the coolest water they can find, usually near springs or feeder streams, and into deep, shaded holes. Oxygen levels also drop late in the season, just at the time when trout actually require more oxygen. During late August and September it is not uncommon to find trout in riffles so shallow that their backs are almost out of the water.

Some anglers feel that it's very important to know which species of trout prefer which type of lie. (Frankly, I don't feel it's that critical.) Generally, browns are most concerned about having overhead cover, rainbows are more apt to be out in the mainstream and brookies will be almost anywhere. It's difficult to come up with hard, fast rules; they'll fool you every time.

As I said in the beginning of this chapter, the ability to read water can partially be taught, but the rest must be learned through experience. I've attempted to cover the teaching aspect by putting down some basics. Learn to look for cover and a food supply. The very first thing I do on a strange stream is to try to identify overhead cover. If it's a good stream, it almost *has* to have it. Then I try to read the currents, looking mainly for side-by-side currents of different velocities. I call those areas "seams," and if I find one next to a good cover, that is where I concentrate my casts.

A great aid in learning to identify cover and reading currents is to don a scuba or snorkel outfit and spend a few hours diving in your favorite stream. You'll learn much more than you would from reading ten books on the subject. Also, when you fish new water, it pays to walk up and down each side of the stretch you're going to fish before you make your first cast.

Along with the basics of cover and food, you must be able to adapt to any abnormal conditions affecting temperature, water level and clarity. And finally, you must add the ingredient of experience. That, of course, is difficult for the beginner, but you should learn to catalog every stream experience, so you can refer to it again when a similar situation arises—which is really one of the most important aspects of reading the water.

Photo by Michael Fong.

Trout get hungry. If they didn't, you'd have to use what the folks in the Pennsylvania coal country used to call "Lithuanian fly rods." We would call it "dynamite." But because trout do have the same instincts we have, there are times when they relegate their instincts for survival to second place. This, of course, is proved by the rather exotic items of hardware they can sometimes be persuaded to take in their fits of hunger pangs; we fly fishers would like to think that trout snap at such constructions in a fit of pique, anger and personal insult. We like trout too much to insult them, so we play their game, learn what they are eating, then try to match it with, if not an exact imitation, at least a logical impression of what they are feeding on at the moment. This is not as easy as it sounds, and Carl Richards, Doug Swisher's long-time accomplice in reading the trout's water, menu and mind, will show you that most of this goes on under the water, not on top.

Chapter 4

What Trout Eat

Take a Trout to Lunch

CARL RICHARDS

IN MY TRAVELS AROUND THE COUNTRY I find that many anglers, and even some veterans, know little about basic trout-stream insects. This limits their fish-taking ability drastically. To me, the study of aquatic entomology is at least half the fun of fly-fishing. I admit it is not necessary for an angler to be able to differentiate between a male *Siphlonurus occidentalis* subimago and a female *Siphlonurus quebecensis* imago to be successful, but he should at least know the difference between a mayfly and a stonefly. He should also know the difference between a mayfly dun and a mayfly spinner, be able to recognize what is on the water at a given time, and select an appropriate imitation that will fool some fish. So, though you don't need to become a Latin scholar, you do need to become a practical entomologist.

Let me illustrate how helpful a little familiarity with the hatches can be. I was fishing Michigan's incredibly rich Au Sable on a warm June evening. It was about an hour before dusk, a small caddis hatch was in progress, and the fish were taking a size 18 Henryville Special with splashy enthusiasm. I noticed a young fellow downstream who appeared to be casting fairly well but was not hooking any fish. As I waded closer to his position, he asked what the fish were taking and I told him. He was obviously a beginner and had no notion of the correct fly to use to imitate a caddis hatch, so I presented him with a Henryville Special. I explained that a little later on the hatch would switch to a small, yellow stonefly, and then, just at dark, a size 16 Pale Evening Dun would appear. I picked out two suitable patterns from his fly box and proceeded on my way. After dark, as I waded back to the car, I encountered the young angler, who made up in enthusiasm what he lacked in experience. He was astounded that I was able to predict which insects would hatch and what patterns would take fish at such a precise time. He had been camped in the area for three days and until then had been unable to hook even one fish. He had been casting over hundreds of risers for three evenings without taking any of them.

It was easy for me because I had been there before. However, if he had only known the difference between an adult caddis, an adult stonefly, and a mayfly spinner, he could have easily captured a specimen, matched the size and color with the correct kind of fly, and he would have been catching fish from the first day. That is what I am going to explain here: how to recognize the basic orders of aquatic and terrestrial insects, how to capture one when the fish are feeding (both adult and immature forms) and how to pick an imitation that is the correct size, color and shape.

Certain basic types of aquatic insects make up the major portion of the trout's diet. The four main insect orders that emerge from our trout streams and lakes (listed by degree of their importance) are: mayflies *(Ephemeroptera)*, caddisflies *(Trichoptera)*, midges *(Diptera)*, and stoneflies *(Plecoptera)*.

All four orders belong to the class *Insecta*. The practical entomologist should understand basic biological classification. All living things are classified as plant or animal. All members of the plant or animal kingdom are classified under categories that progress from the general to the specific. An example would be the famous Brown Drake, found in both the East and the West:

Kingdom:	Animal
Subkingdom:	Invertebrate (all animals without backbones)
Phylum:	*Arthropoda* (all animals with bilateral symmetry, external skeletons, and jointed legs)
Class:	*Insecta* (all true insects)
Order:	*Ephemeroptera* (all mayflies)
Family:	*Ephemeridae* (all burrowing mayflies)
Genus:	*Ephemera* (a group of related burrowing mayflies)
Species:	*simulans* (a particular kind of burrowing mayfly)

To be an effective hatch-matcher you must at least be able to differentiate between adult mayflies, caddisflies, midges, stoneflies, and all the immature stages of each of these orders and do so rather quickly. Many hatches and most spinner falls do not last very long. You do not have time to try four or five patterns on a trial-and-error basis. Rather, you should be able to choose the right fly at the right time, only then will you be suitably equipped to hook your share of fish.

Mayflies

THE MAYFLY *(Ephemeroptera)* is the single most important order of trout-stream insect. All mayflies have two large, upright wings, two or three tails, and most have two very small hind wings. They look like little sailboats floating in the current and are the *only* trout-stream insects with upright wings. The life cycle is: egg, nymph, dun (subimago), spinner (imago).

The Nymph. The eggs hatch into an underwater form called a nymph, which usually lasts about a year but may last two months to two years or more, depending on the species. They range in size from 3 mm. to 36 mm. or more and have three tails (rarely two) and gills emanating from the sides of the middle segments of the abdomen. The nymphs grow from a very small size through progressively larger stages, each stage, called an instar, is accompanied by a molt. They vary greatly in shape, depending on the ecosystem they have become adapted to, such as fast or slow water. Most are dirty tan to brown in color with a lighter underside, but they can vary from cream to olive to black.

The Emergence. When the nymph is fully grown, it swims to the surface and changes into a winged fly called a dun (subimago) by splitting its nymphal skin and emerging from it. The dun rests on the surface, drying its wings, and then flies away to nearby trees or meadows. This entire procedure is called the hatch. At this time the nymphs and the duns are extremely vulnerable. Before and during the hatch a standard fur-bodied type of mayfly nymph of the correct size and color fished wet is a good imitation. During the hatch a mayfly-dun imitation such as a Sidewinder No-Hackle Dun is my personal choice.

A standard hackle pattern can be fairly effective if tied sparsely, that is, with the hackle very short (one half the length of the body) and two or three turns only, although it presents an inferior outline. The fur body is what really floats both the No-Hackle Dun and the sparse standard pattern. I always use fine-wire hooks, which are a great help in flotation.

One of the most deadly patterns of all during an emergence is the floating nymph. A few years ago I purchased a stomach pump so I could see what the fish were eating without damaging them. I learned, to my great surprise, how ignorant I was about how trout feed during a rise. During my first sessions with the pump, I selected a good fish that was feeding regularly on the surface and that I believed to be taking only duns. On examining the stomach contents I found these trout invariably took two or three nymphs for each floating dun. It was not nymphs at the beginning of the hatch

Mayflies are an important food source for trout. Trout may feed on these insects at any stage in their lifecycle: nymph, dun or spinner. Illustrations by Bill Elliott.

and duns toward the end, as we had all been taught. It is my belief that trout prefer the floating nymphs because they have more time to capture the nymph. The dun, after all, can fly away at any time, but the nymph cannot.

The Spinner Fall. After the dun has dried its wings and flown to the trees, it rests for a period of a few hours to a few days and then undergoes a final molt into a spinner (imago). *Ephemeroptera* is the only one of the four important orders that undergoes a molt after attaining the winged stage. The dun is a drab insect with dull, opaque wings, and tails approximately equal in length to the body. The spinner is, by contrast, bright and shiny, with long tails (twice as long as the body) and clear transparent wings. The spinners return to the river, mate in a swarm (usually over riffles), and fall spent into the stream after egg-laying. At this time (the spinner fall), the correct imitation is a one-half-spent or full-spent mayfly spinner imitation. My personal choice is a Hen Spinner in the correct size and shape.

Spinner falls occur more often in the evening or at dark but can also happen during the morning hours, depending again upon the species and, of course, the weather. There are approximately 120 *Ephemeroptera* species of major importance to the fly fisherman in the United States, and with a little observation, you will quickly become familiar with the important ones in your area. Usually one stream or geographic area has only about ten to fifteen species that are of great interest to the average fly fisher.

As a general rule, early-season mayflies (March-May) tend to be dark in color: dark gray wings and dark brown or olive bodies. Later, as the lighter yellows and greens appear, the prevalent insects are lighter in color, most likely to blend in with the background and escape their many predators. The wings become pale gray and the bodies yellow and pale buff or olive. Then in September and October, emerging flies are darker again. As the autumn leaves turn dark, so do the insects.

Caddisflies

Caddisflies are also very important trout-stream insects, and in some locations they are even more numerous than mayflies. They can easily be distinguished by their four wings of nearly equal length, which are covered with tiny hairs and, when at rest, are carried in an inverted V or tent over the back. They are usually medium to small in size (#14-24) and have no tails. There are over one thousand known species on this continent.

The life cycle of a caddis differs from the mayfly and follows this order: egg, larva, pupa, adult. The eggs are deposited in or near the water, eventually hatching into a worm, which may or may not build a case, depending on the species. Two large groups of caddis

In many locations, caddisflies are more important than mayflies as trout-stream insects. Unlike mayflies, caddisflies have no nymphal stage in their lifecycles; they emerge from their protective larval encasements and rise directly to the water's surface as pupae to emerge.

larvae exist. One group builds a case or house (evidently for protection and camouflage) in which the larva lives. These cases may be constructed of practically any material such as twigs, stones, and bits of leaf or bark. The other caddis are free-living, meaning they range about the bottom of the stream without cases. When matured the larva makes a cocoon (much like a caterpillar) in which it changes into a pupa. When the pupa is fully developed, it cuts its way out of the cocoon and migrates to the surface. Some species crawl out of the water to emerge, and some drift in the film until the pupal skin is broken and the adult flies away. The adult caddis are able to live much longer than mayflies, as they can absorb water. Most species mate at rest, so the females are the ones taken by trout at egg-laying time. The eggs are deposited on the water, on vegetation overhanging the water, or underwater by diving females.

During a caddis hatch three imitations are effective. Due to the drifting of the pupa in the film before emergence, a pupal imitation fished wet is often deadly. The stillborn adult, which is a pattern tied to imitate a fly stuck halfway out of the shuck on the surface, is, in my experience, the most deadly of all the patterns during an emergence. The dry Henryville Special is good at hatch time and during the egg-laying flight. A spent caddis is effective at the end of the fall of spent adults.

Of course, the angler must match the size and color of the natural with the artificial. As with all flies, this cannot be done by observing the natural on the wing; a specimen must be captured and examined in the hand. Adult caddisflies are jumpy and wary, thus rather difficult to capture. Often a net is required. Caddisflies are attracted to bright lights, however, and during the evening your car lights can be a good collecting spot. With so many species existing, most anglers do not bother to identify this order precisely as to species. It is enough to be aware of the five main colors — tan, gray, olive, cream, dark brown — and to have reasonable imitations in sizes from 14-20.

Midges

THESE FLIES HAVE ONLY two short wings (shorter than the body), which lie flat along the top of the body, usually slightly to the side in a V, and possess no tails. Most are small, sizes 22-28 and even smaller. The life cycle is: egg, larva, pupa, adult. At hatch time the pupa ascends to the surface where it drifts for a time; the winged insect then emerges and flies away.

During the hatch a pupa or stillborn artificial is usually effective; a hackled adult type can be used later during the emergence or at the egg-laying flight.

These flies are especially important to trout in slower-moving water such as spring creeks and limestone streams. Some lake species are fairly large. They are rarely of much importance in faster currents. This is a very large and diverse group; they can be almost any color, but black and olive are common. When trout are feeding on midges, they can be extremely selective. Exact size in the artificial is often critical. An error of a single size (20 instead of 22) can mean a discrepancy of over 30 percent, and almost always this is perceived by the critical eye of a brown trout. To be effective, close imitations are necessary!

Midge fishing is often considered the ultimate challenge in fly-fishing, because the imitations are very tiny and leaders must therefore be extremely long and fine. Leaders of 10 to 14 feet with tippets of 6x-7x-8x are the most effective sizes. Light rods with fine tips are required to protect the fine tippets when striking and fighting a hefty fish. Many neophytes shun this interesting and satisfying type of fly-fishing because the extremely fine tackle frightens them away. It is really not that difficult and you owe to yourself the exhilarating experience of landing a fine trout on such tackle. Of course, there are very small mayflies (*Tricorythodes, Baetis, Pseudocloeon*), caddis and terrestrials that require the same light tackle, and while they are not technically midges, they are generally lumped together under the term midge fishing.

Stoneflies

THIS RATHER SMALL ORDER of flies is of very little importance in slow waters, yet in turbulent, rocky streams, such as the Madison and the Big Hole in Montana, they provide the largest flies and the most spectacular fishing of the season. In certain Oregon streams they are the second most important trout food. Stoneflies vary in size from very large to very small (#2-20). Adults have four long wings, which are hard, shiny, heavily veined, and held flat over the back when at rest.

The life cycle is: egg, nymph, adult. The generally flatish nymphs are readily distinguished from mayfly nymphs since they have only two short tails with rather long antennae, no gills on the abdomen, and two equal wing cases. When the nymph is mature, most species (but by no means all) crawl to land and emerge. They mate at rest and return to the water a few days to a few weeks later to lay their eggs.

The emergence is important only in those species that emerge in water, and they are best imitated by a combination latex-and-fur stonefly nymph or a down-hair-wing dry imitation. The egg-layers are well imitated by an adult stonefly artificial with a lot of hackle to simulate moving wings. Many of the medium and small stones are yellow with a few showing olive, tan, and dark brown. Usually the underside of the nymph is much lighter than the top.

Other Food Items

TROUT, OF COURSE, FEED on many other food items besides the four major orders listed above. Although these other orders are normally of lesser importance, when they *are* numerous, fish will feed on them selectively, so a few representative imitations should be carried for the other aquatic, semi-aquatic or terrestrial forms, such as dragonflies and damselflies (order *Odonata*), grasshoppers and crickets (order *Orthoptera*), leafhoppers, true bugs (order *Hemiptera*), spongilla flies (order *Neuroptera*), Dobsonflies, fish flies, alderflies (order *Megaloptera*), aquatic moths (order *Lepidoptera*), beetles (order *Coleoptera*), true flies (order *Diptera*) and aquatic wasps (order *Hymenoptera*).

As you can see, this is a pretty diverse group of insects available for fish to feed upon, and furthermore, they have adapted to every type of ecosystem imaginable, from lotic (running waters) to lentic (standing waters) and everything in between. Some aquatic insects actually survive and flourish in streams that periodically dry up completely.

A new book is available entitled *An Introduction to the Aquatic Insects of North America*, edited by Professor Richard W. Merrit of Michigan State University. It will probably become the standard reference on the subject.

In addition to aquatic insects, some crustaceans are heavily fed upon by trout. Thus wet flies, fished deep to represent scuds, sowbugs, shrimp, crayfish and the like, are often very effective when no surface activity is apparent.

If all those weren't enough for the fly angler to imitate, quite often terrestrial insects get blown onto the water's surface. These are not normally as important as the aquatic insects, but at times, when large numbers appear on the surface, they can provide some very exciting fishing. Grasshoppers provide a large juicy meal and large fish will be on the lookout for them in season (late July, August and September). Trout seem to relish ants, and in the fall, large flights of winged ants often appear in numbers. At these times the fish are very selective and antlike body imitations are essential.

Other terrestrial forms such as green oak worms, jassids, large beetles and spiders, when they are in season are also important. Most fly-fishing to terrestrials is done with the dry fly.

Selecting an Artificial

NOW ASSUME WE HAVE the preceding firmly in mind, can distinguish between all the stages of all the naturals, and know what pattern types to tie on to imitate the various stages of the four major orders of aquatic insects. How do we translate this knowledge into a fishing situation? Imagine you are in the middle of a pool with fish rising all around, flies buzzing in the air and drifting on the currents. How do you select the correct imitation? That's the meat of this discussion—how to pick an artificial at the right time that will take fish when trout are feeding. It can be easy if you are

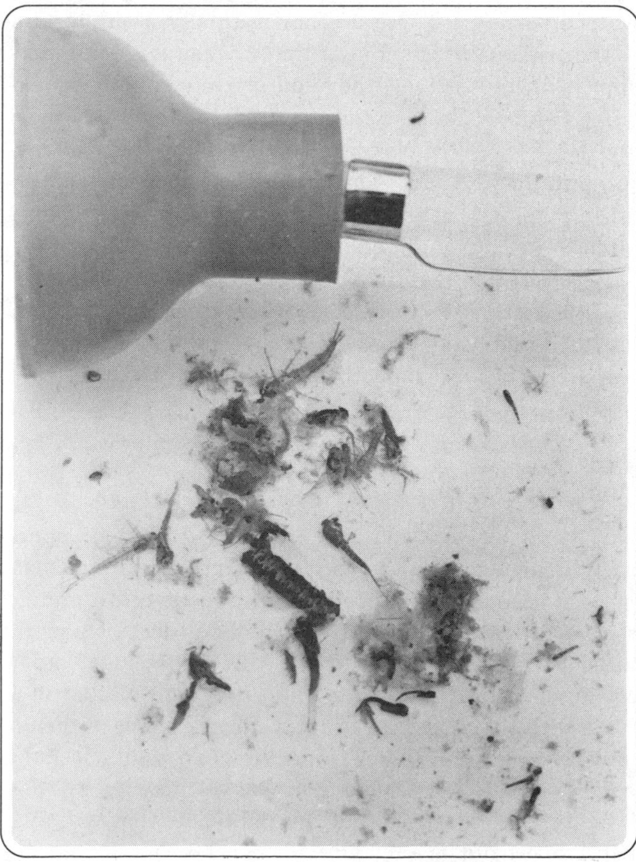

Above, a stomach pump designed for trout is an effective way of discovering what the fish is feeding on without harming it. At left, the stomach contents of a trout, including, mainly, mayfly nymphs, but also the encasement of a caddis larva. Photos by Michael Fong.

not rattled by the feeding fish. The first thing to do is find out what type or order of insect is on the water, and this is done by capturing one and examining it closely in the hand, preferably with an 8x or a 10x glass. If the flies are on the water, a simple tropical-fish aquarium net can be dipped onto the flow, and the current will carry the specimen into the net. If the fly is in the air, a simple net can be fixed to the tip of the fly rod and used in the fashion of a butterfly net.

If fish are observed feeding underwater, two methods can be used to discover what they are feeding on. The best way is to catch a fish (usually *one* dummy can be taken using an attractor, fished wet, such as a Coachman) and pump his stomach with a simple stomach pump. These are available at better fly shops. You then have proof positive of the fish's preference. If landing a fish is impossible, a simple wire seine can be held in the current while gravel and vegetation is dislodged upstream. Whatever is present will be washed into the seine and can be examined closely.

Once the specimen is in the hand, the order and stage is determined (e.g., wet fly, nymph, dun, or spinner).

Then an artificial of the correct size, shape, coloration and type is selected from the fly box, and you should be in business quickly and logically. This whole process takes place in the heat of battle, however, and a certain calm deduction is required. Most people get so excited by splashing trout that they take a wild guess as to the correct pattern and immediately begin to flail the water. They normally end up exhausted, frustrated and fishless. To be successful you must remain calm, patiently obtain a specimen, and know a mayfly has upright wings, a caddis has tent-shaped wings, a stone has flat wings over the body, and a midge has flat, V-shaped wings (flat but to the side of the body), and you must know which artificial type works when each natural is on the water. If you are thoroughly familiar with these facts, you will be light-years ahead of the majority of anglers and much more effective!

The Multiple Hatch

I HAVE JUST DESCRIBED a simple hatch where only one or at the most two types of insects are hatching at a time. Any observant fly fisher with a little knowledge of practical entomology should be able to choose his pattern and do well. A much more difficult experience will be had during a multiple hatch. At times, especially on rich streams, many different types of insects can be on the water at the same time. On the lime-rich Rogue near my Michigan home, I have seen midges, caddis, stones, craneflies, and four mayfly species, both duns and spinners, simultaneously. During a multiple hatch such as this, trout usually feed selectively on one of the types.

How do we select the right fly? This is a difficult problem even for the veteran anglers; the answer is never simple. Experience, knowledge and close observation are required. A few bits of information should be of help. First, trout will usually feed on the insect present in the greatest numbers. Quite often a small fly will be present in company with a large fly but in much greater number; the fish will feed on the smaller fly exclusively, though the inexperienced angler usually tries the larger fly first. Try to decide which natural is most numerous. If a suitable imitation does not work within five minutes, look again and try another idea. Do not keep casting uselessly with the same pattern.

Next, try to identify the riseform and relate that to a fly type. Trout will rise very quietly and deliberately to insect forms that are smaller and cannot escape, such as medium to small mayfly spinners. The larger and more escape-prone the insect, the more hurried and splashy the rise. Therefore, if you observe that size 12 Green Drake duns and size 18 Baetis spinners are both on the water, and the riseforms are quiet dimples, the obvious choice would be size 18 Hen Spinner in the correct color. Conversely, a violent riseform would indicate a size 12 Sidewinder Dun to imitate the Green Drake.

At times when no hatch is in progress, and especially just before a hatch, fish will feed on the bottom as the immature insect forms become active prior to hatching. Seine the river and discover which nymphs are the most numerous and more mature (these will have the darkest wing pads). Often, you will find that the fish have a preference for smaller but more numerous forms over the larger but less prevalent species.

These multiple hatches can be mystifying, so don't be discouraged by a few failures. One of the most pleasing aspects of fly-fishing is its complexity. I, for one, would soon tire of constant success, and multiple hatches certainly insure against that. However, the practical entomologist will have a fighting chance at a solution to the problem; the uninformed will be all but helpless. A thorough study of practical aquatic entomology will pay huge dividends before, during and after hatch time!

Photo by Michael Fong.

If you now expect to be led into one of the fly fisherman's major vices, you will be disappointed. Lee Wulff knows full well that you can handle such excesses on your own later without any help from him. But hats, vests and stock boxes brimming with flies do not a fly fisherman make. As an angler and artist, Lee sees with the eyes of both. He sees shape, size, silhouette and hue. He designs and ties his flies for the water and the fish, not for the tackle counter. It is ironic, however, that the Wulff series of flies (which he does not tie commercially or have a financial interest in) has for decades been among the most used and most successful of any basic fly patterns. You'll soon find out why this is so.

Chapter 5

Choosing Your Fly

Let the Trout Help

LEE WULFF

HAD I BEEN ASKED for a list of suitable basic trout flies fifty years ago the task would have been simple, the list short. It would have consisted of half a dozen accepted patterns that every trout fisherman knew. It might have read: Royal Coachman, Hare's Ear, Black Gnat, Professor, Silver Doctor and Beaverkill. Some wet, some dry, in sizes 8 to 12.

Fifty years ago Ed Hewitt was just experimenting with his flat nymphs (bodies of plastic wood) and skaters and bivisibles. The Wulff series, which first brought animal hair to dry flies, was still two years away in the future. The Mickey Finn was six years off. Don Gapen's Muddler Minnow was a generation away. The coming of age of trout fishing was just beginning.

The flies listed above all fell into two basic categories, one for wet flies, one for dry. Hold them up to the light in silhouette and it's almost impossible to tell one from another in either category. Only the colors are different.

In those days the streams were carrying a rather full complement of trout. They were using the stream's food supply to its capacity, and normally, they were pretty hungry. Now our streams are carrying a lesser complement of trout and their food needs are usually well supplied by the food in the stream. They are not so competitively hungry as they were then—and they are far, far wiser. Today the knowledgeable fly fisherman often carries hundreds of flies in many categories. What I can list here are just a few flies in those categories—the ones without which I would feel naked on the stream.

Wet Flies and Nymphs

The first and most important group of flies for the pursuit and taking of trout is the wet fly/nymph group. I personally do not differentiate between wet flies and nymphs. To me, a wet fly is an old-fashioned nymph. The old-timers made up artificial flying insects, *with wings*, and *swam* them under the water. It was quite unrealistic but it worked. Some of the patterns of antiquity still work today because they are either close to reality in nymph imitation (Hare's Ear) or startling enough (Royal Coachman) to tease trout into striking.

In the last fifty years we have come to understand the stream life and recognize nymphs as the basic food for most trout. We now imitate the aquatic insect forms well enough to fool trout with them on a free drift—or we give them movement on the retrieve and draw strikes because they look both living and lovely to a trout.

I prefer imitations that are not necessarily perfect but are soft in makeup, which lets the fly itself have some movement in the water. When I was young we had rubber crickets that were perfect imitations of the real thing. They were never as effective as the feathered imitations we made up—not true imitations but ones that had more life in the water. It is important, I believe, that even though a fly is not moving through the water, the small currents that surround it be allowed to create a little movement within the fibers of the fly itself.

First in this category I would choose a stonefly nymph imitation. I like them fairly large, on long-shanked size 8-10 hooks in medium to very dark gray. I would want a general mayfly nymph imitation, too. Something smaller than the stonefly, off-gray with a reddish or brownish tint, in size 12.

Woolly Worms, like the old-time winged wet flies that swam, are sort of incongruous "aquatic" caterpillars. They catch trout even though there's nothing quite like them in the stream. Give me Woolly Worms on 4X long hooks in sizes 6-10, and even a couple of size 4's. Choose your own colors: I like olive and I like black. The size 4, if you can crawl it slowly across a deep pool near the bottom, may well surprise you (as well as the fish).

All three of these patterns can be weighted or unweighted, as you choose. My recommendation is to get them unweighted or lightly weighted. If you want to fish them very deep, place enough weight on your leader (lead wire wrapped on at the tippet knots) to take them down where you want them. A heavily weighted nymph is a "feathered sinker," which will never respond as naturally to the stream currents as an unweighted or lightly weighted one will. Several wrappings of lead wire on the leader are better than split-shot, which concentrate too much weight at one point; this can make casting much less pleasant and may have enough bulk to put a wary trout off.

Because I can remember well the fine fish I've caught on them, I'd want to have some clipped-wing Hare's Ears in sizes 12 and 14 and some Royal Coachmen in 10 and 12. I might even put one of these on as a dropper ahead of a stonefly nymph.

While we're still fishing beneath the surface, let's add a few streamers. Pick two kinds, the kind that looks most like a minnow to you . . . and then the wildest, most exotic attractor you can find. To me that would mean something like a Black-Nose Dace for reality and a Mickey Finn for a startler. They should be on 4X long hooks in sizes 8, 6 and 4, with one almighty big one of the attractor pattern in size 1 or 2 that you save for high water or for those times when you've really given up but want to keep on going through the motions of fishing.

Carry a couple of Muddler Minnows (size 6). I don't worry too much whether or not they're Don Gapen's original pattern. Any other streamer pattern with a Muddler-type head will do very well. The clipped-hair head makes up a special category that has little to do with the color of the fly. Any Muddler is a teaser and a good one.

Dry Flies

Now let's go to the surface—where the fishing is more fun but where the fish feed far, far less than they do underwater. To simplify your needs you'll want flies that look a bit like many insects, rather than definite patterns that look like one and only one. For the imitation, carry the Adams in size 16, 14 and 12. It will look like a bug not only to you but to a militant majority of trout.

Carry some Royal Wulffs in sizes 14, 12 and 10. These look like strawberries-and-cream in a bowl to a lot of trout that seem to have been waiting all their lives for just such a fly. They will sometimes take a Royal right in the middle of a hatch they're working, and I think it's the best exploratory fly to use when the trout aren't surfacing.

To cover the midge category, get some sizes 18 and 20—Adams again, plus some Pale Watery Duns or Light Cahills to have something in a lighter shade. When you need something smaller to sink into the surfac

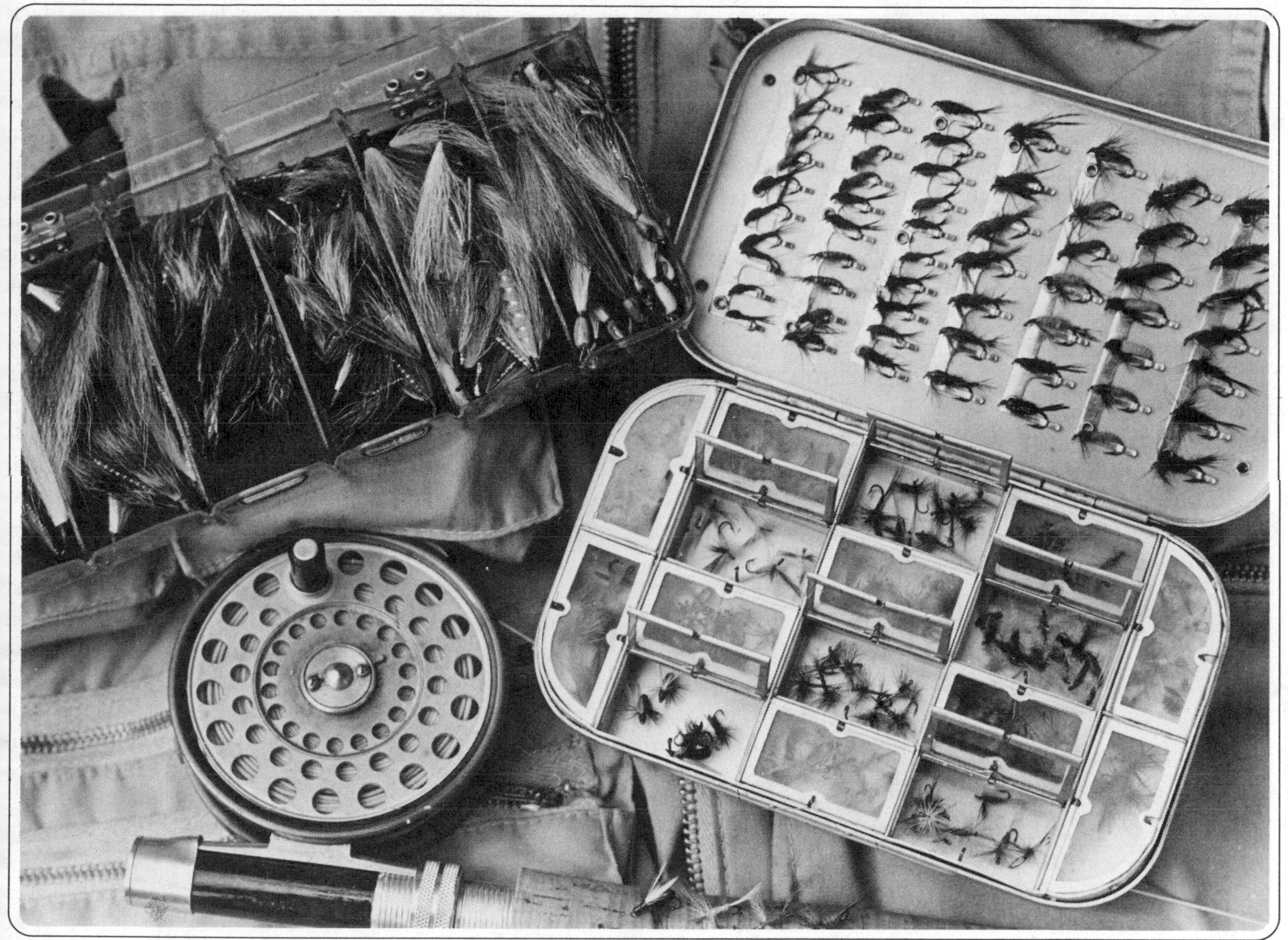

A well-rounded fly selection should include a variety of patterns, including nymphs, wet flies, dry flies and streamers. Photos by Michael Fong.

film, trim them down, a bit at a time, until they're not much more than the body left. If that doesn't do it, put on a big Royal Wulff or a Mickey Finn.

A good trick to broaden your fly coverage is to carry a few non-water-soluble Magic Marker pens. Black, green and red give a good range. Applying them to a light-colored fly such as a Pale Watery Dun can be carried through a variety of color phases.

Terrestrials

THE TERRESTRIALS COME NEXT. Carry a good-looking Grasshopper in sizes 8 and 10. You may also want an ant imitation in sizes 12 and 14, but the times of the ant falls and most of the other specific terrestrials are short and few, and certainly not as important as the long, hot time of the hopper.

The Grasshopper, of course, works best in late summer when the real thing is most prevalent. Hoppers get into the stream a good deal on windy days, and at such times, a hopper imitation can be plopped down hard on the surface, just as a real one would fall. Hopper fishing is rarely delicate but it can be tricky. The most effective use of the hopper is to cast it into the grass of an overhanging meadow bank, and then, with a twitch, coax it from the grass to drop into the water as a real hopper might fall.

When the various-size *beetles* come floating down, half sunken, and you find a lot of them in the stomach of a trout that accidentally took your Hare's Ear, find some matching thread from a sock or shirt and wind a fat body over the regular body of the proper-size Adams and drift that over those slurping fish.

One more surface fly I'd hate to be without is the long-hackled Spider or Skater. You can float it free-drift or you can dance it crazily across the water behind a fine, well-greased leader. The trout may miss it as often as they connect, but if they come at all, it will be with a rush. The size 16 Skater can pull up a fish that nothing else will and put new life in dead days on the stream. The Spider is a great fly in tough times because it can be the raw material for a wide variety of shapes on a small hook. I tie my own; they're very easy to make and inexpensive, so they're particularly expendable. I trim them to meet the needs of the situation.

When the fish are rising to something small and difficult to imitate, I'm likely to put on a size 16 or 18 Spider. Sometimes it will work just as it is. On some of our Western streams, when cottonwood down that looks much like a spider was blowing onto the streams, I've had little hope that this fly would work—but the trout could tell the difference and were willing to take it. Who's to argue?

When they refused a standard Spider quite often, I knew I had to change the fly's silhouette. Out came the scissors. The first step is to cut the hackles off the bottom of the fly, leaving about a 1/16-inch of fibers next to the shank. That brings the body down to the surface and sometimes that will work. If it doesn't, the top hackles can be cut off in similar fashion, leaving full whiskers out to both sides. If that doesn't deliver, trim the side whiskers until only one or two long fibers remain on either side. The fly will still float and now it's getting down to midge size. This can be an excellent midge imitation from a trout's point of view. Finally, the Spider can be trimmed until it's just a fuzzy body that will sink but be held just under the surface by the floating tippet it is attached to.

Spiders made with badger hackles will give a dark body when trimmed severely. Those made with barred-rock hackles will give a lighter, mottled effect. Don't ever underestimate the scope of the Spider.

For the fly fisher who traditionally carries more than five hundred flies in his fishing vest, it is hard to limit himself to a relative few. There'll be times when the green worms drop down from the overhanging bushes and he'll find himself right back in the same frustrating situation he was in when he first encountered those conditions.

More complete lists of regionally effective patterns are included in this book's fly-tying section. If I were to go afield with the fly types I've suggested, I know I'd miss a lot of the other flies I now carry, but with this list as a bare minimum, I'd figure that I could catch trout, most of the time, on practically any of this nation's trout streams.

The beginner will need to improvise with the flies he does carry. Perhaps he'll learn to squash the wings of an Adams flat and trim the hackles to a minimum when the spentwing flies start floating down. He'll find the need to trim a Woolly Worm to change its shape and then grease it for a drift in the surface film. He'll sculpture a wet fly into a slim shape when the one he has is too fluffy. And each time he does he'll make a note to

Improved Turle Knot

To start the Turle Knot, insert the tag end of the leader through the hook eye. Allow almost a foot of leader to tie the knot; most will be recovered when the knot is tightened. Pass the tag end of the leader around the standing part to form a loop.

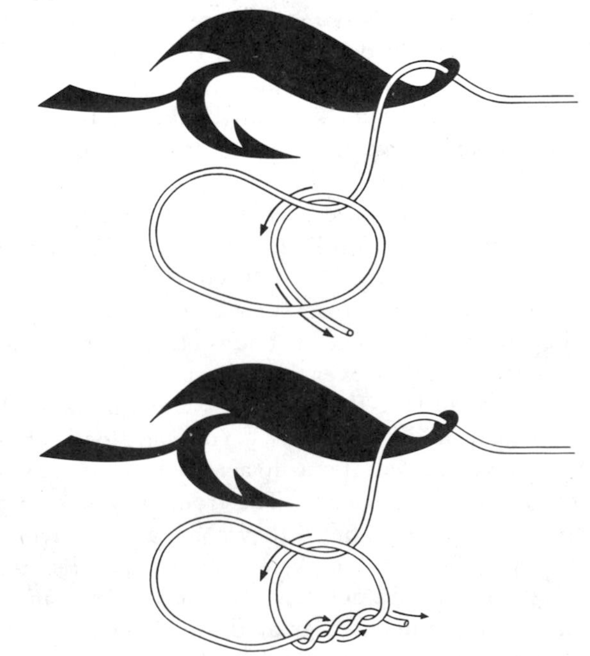

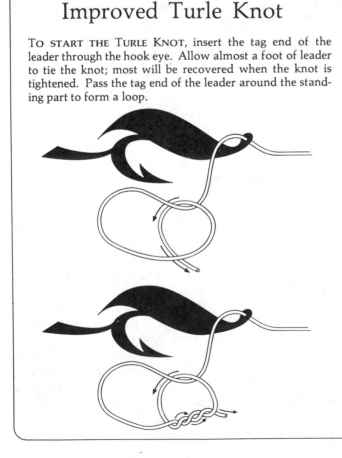

Insert the tag end of the leader through the small loop just created, and then insert it a second time. Hold the tag end of the leader in one hand and one leg of the loop in the other and pull them apart. This will tighten the slip knot that you just made.

Carefully pass the big loop over the fly, working from the tail toward the eye. As the loop clears the fly, take one turn around a leg of the loop with the tag end of the leader. This adds a bit of strength to the knot.

The Turle Knot must be drawn up carefully by pulling slowly on the standing part. The loop must clear the hackles or hair on the fly. The slip-knot portion then jams in the eye of the hook, and the loop seats across the eye, giving a straight angle of pull between the leader and the hook shank. Trim off the tag end to finish the knot.

The fly is designed to appeal to the trout, who doesn't know or care whether the fly feathers came from a gamecock in Spain or a dyed rooster in Brooklyn.

buy or make such an imitation and carry it with him from that point on.

As he continues to fish, his stock of flies will gradually grow. And his understanding of the purpose of the fly will grow, too. The fly is designed to appeal to the trout, who doesn't know or care whether the fly feathers came from a gamecock in Spain or a dyed rooster in Brooklyn. Patterns are not sacred. Think in terms of sizes and shapes and colors. Let the trout be the judge.

Thinking Like a Fish

THE SELECTION OF FLIES YOU CARRY should reflect your knowledge of the fish and the water you'll be working. You should consciously develop a sense of the fish's feeding habits and choose flies to match them. Think of yourself as a fish just for a moment. Assume, if you can, that you have to scrounge around for natural foods in order to live and that these foods cannot be larger than an average-size trout's mouth.

You'll consider caterpillars, grasshoppers, wasps, bumblebees and other insects. As your thoughts expand you'll realize that, because you're cold-blooded, you'll be immune to the sting of a wasp, a bee or a mosquito. You'll leave your human tendencies behind and think like a voracious, low-grade animal.

You'll expect the things you eat to have a substantial body, and you'll reflexively recognize the various body shapes, varying from mayfly to worm to ant; they may be fat and round or long and segmented, but in every case they'll house the insect's power center and energy-storing complex. That's where the energy will come from when you eat it.

A body, therefore, is the essence of a trout's attraction to any floating food-form. That body can range from a simple worm or slug to a centipede or a spider, and it also can have some frills in the way of legs and wings or gills and stingers. It will have something to give it the power to swim or crawl or fly so it can itself feed or prey on something else. Those frills can be very enticing — legs that wave in the water or wings that buzz in the air. Now you're thinking like a trout.

But let's start thinking like an angler again. Concentrate for a moment on caterpillars. You've seen a lot of them and recognize them readily. Unless you're particularly squeamish, you've picked them up and let them crawl across your hand. If you saw something that *looked* like a caterpillar, you might be tempted to pick it up for a closer look. The trout looks that way at your fly. If it looks like a bug, he'll be tempted to pick it up in his mouth, his only way of inspecting it for taste and feel.

If you were a caterpillar eater, you'd eventually develop certain preferences. You'd find that the brown ones tasted better than the green ones or vice versa. You'd find that the bugs with black wings might taste better than those with white ones. The longer you fish, the more certain you become that special color combinations are particularly attractive to the trout of the waters you fish. Even if you're not too sure of yourself, you may suspect that a trout would prefer a green-bodied insect to a white one — and choose a fly accordingly.

When you put your own preferences into the choice of your flies, you gain a deeper involvement in your fishing. Your choices may start with mere whims, but gradually your experiences on the stream will help you establish mental pictures of what trout like to eat. A certain fly will "look" good to you in a specific situation. It may be because of the full shape of the body, the texture of its wings, or for some other reason — but the pleasure of finding out that the trout will think as you do on occasions and take the fly *you* select will give you a thrill. As your choices become more and more attractive to the trout, your fishing pleasure will increase. The object of this technique is to help you develop a sense of the right flies rather than depend on the written words of "experts."

Trout are hungry for everything from midges to mice. You'll learn to see shapes like a potbellied sculpin or a pollywog as a particularly attractive trout food. You'll see bits of yarn and feather as insect legs or bodies or as minnow shapes and fins. Your flies will come to life for you.

Meanwhile you'll be learning about particular trout streams and the food that lives in or near them. You'll combine this knowledge with your own feelings of what a fly should look like. You'll pick particular flies for particular times and streams, and you'll be deep in the heart of fly-fishing and all its problems and satisfaction.

When you join me in this happy state, you'll be able to pass the word on to the newcomers. You'll say, "That's a good-looking fly," and you won't be looking so much at the neatness of the tie as at the bugginess it suggests to you — and hopefully will convey to the trout.

When a certain fly catches your eye and you start muttering under your breath, "I'd like to drift *this* one over that wise old brownie in Bridge Pool," you're well on your way to becoming a *fisher* of flies, not just a dunker.

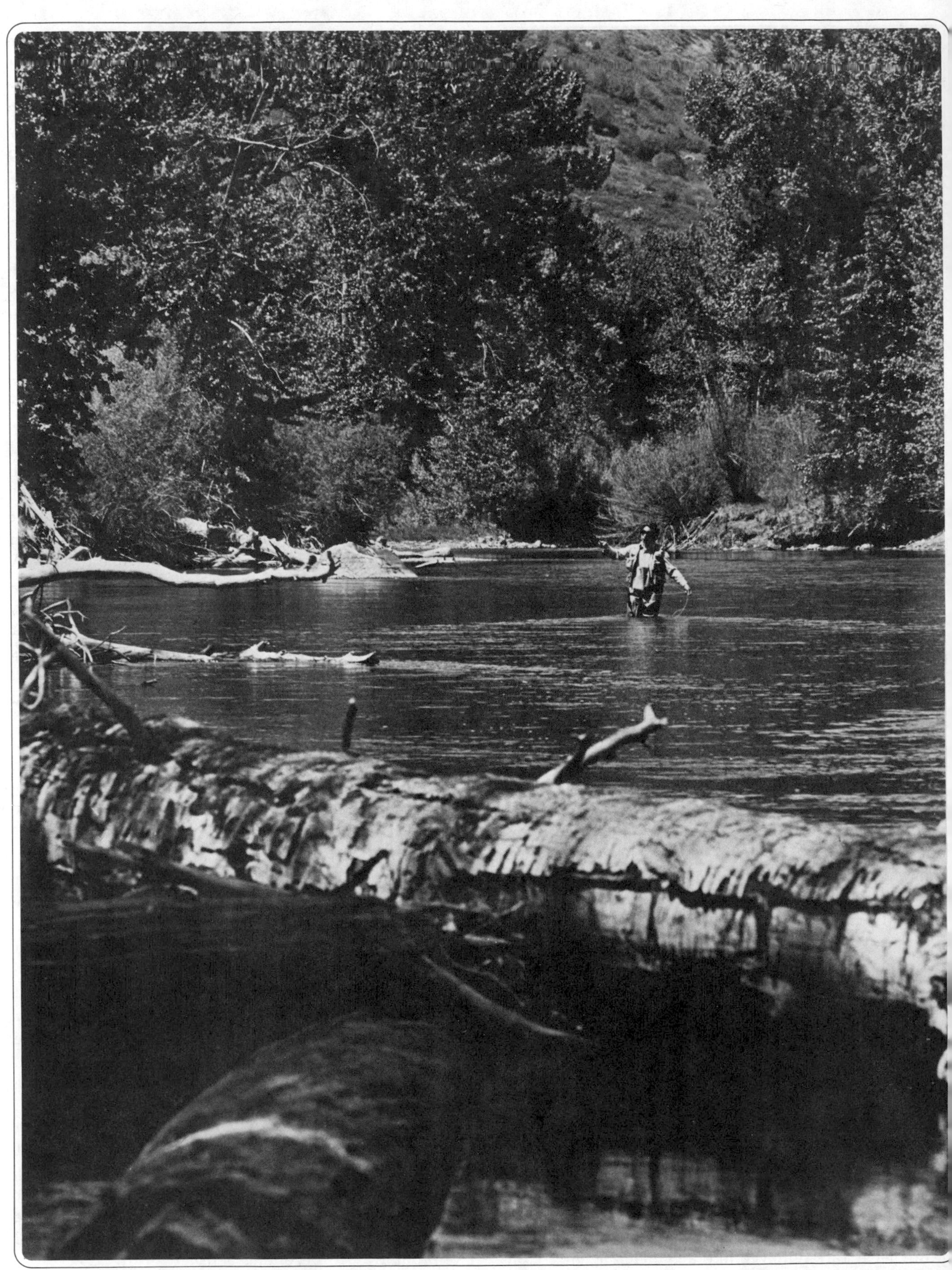

Photo by Christine Fong.

Now we're putting it all together. It just might turn out to be a fish! This frequently happens—after you've located the trout's lie, determined what it's feeding on, decided on the proper fly, and then presented it in the most natural way. All that remains is to strike, play the fish and then net it. FFM Managing Editor John Merwin seems to do this with sickening frequency. Even though we sometimes think that he fishes too much for an editor, his knowledge of what the beginning fly fisherman needs to know gives a special authority to his succinct words of advice as revealed in this chapter. He'll put you into the water and, hopefully, into a fish.

Chapter 6

Stream-Fishing for Trout

Waters that Move, Fish that Don't

JOHN MERWIN

THE GENTLE MUSIC of the early-morning riffles on the North Fork of Arkansas' White River was shattered by a yell from the head of the pool. "What do I do now? You didn't tell me what to do when I got to this part!" I looked up to see Angie, a reconstructed fishing widow whose fly-fishing career was now an hour old, holding a deeply bowed rod and watching a two-pound rainbow cartwheel over the surface of the pool with the fly in its jaw.

I waded over to her side and talked her through the process of playing, landing and releasing her fish—something we hadn't discussed earlier because I frankly didn't think the occasion would arise. I should have known better.

She had gotten, through lengthy conversations and demonstrations on the lawn, most of the instructional information that's been presented in the earlier chapters of this book. She had, however, never actually fished.

We had walked quietly upstream shortly after dawn, looking for a spot she might fish without having to cope with a complex casting situation. Finally, we stopped to look at a riffle that shelved into a long flat. "Didn't you tell me that rainbows like the faster water at the head of a pool? Well, here's a situation like that. What do I do with it?" she asked.

"Fish it if you like," I answered, "but you'll have to roll-cast because the trees are so close to where you'll be fishing."

We walked out onto a low ledge that bordered the spot where the riffling current started to slow down. Chuck Davidson, a fly-fishing friend who has the good fortune to live along the North Fork, had given us some small nymph patterns that were generally representative of a wide variety of light-colored mayfly nymphs—patterns that will appeal to trout in many different situations. Since there were no trout rising, Angie decided the nymph was the fly of the hour.

"All you have to do," I explained, "is to make a short cast diagonally across the stream and then let the current swing the fly and line around below you. The current isn't too fast here, so the fly will drift slowly and look like the real thing. Follow the drift of the fly with your rod tip until the line and fly are hanging straight below you in the current. Then you can raise your rod, flip the line and fly back across the current with a roll cast and repeat the whole thing."

"That's easy. How do I know when I've got one?"

"You'll know," I called over my shoulder as I walked down the bank. "I'll fish downstream."

I like to think that I'm not always that dumb. Her fly pattern was right, her fishing position was good, the presentation wasn't difficult — of course she'd catch fish. Which she did. I expect to spend the rest of my life living that incident down, but it did hammer home a couple of lessons of considerable value.

If you are relatively new to fly-fishing — or if you're an old hand who is teaching a beginner — make every attempt to get your early lessons in stream tactics at a place that is relatively easy to fish. You are, after all, going fly-fishing for the fun of it, and much of that fun comes from catching something once in awhile. The mysteries of the brawling Madison River in Montana or the intricacies of a number of famous spring creeks and limestone streams have made experienced anglers sit on the bank and sob with frustration; they can destroy the spirit of a neophyte angler. There are waters all over the country that are less demanding, that hold plenty of fish and that offer the angler relatively easy wading and few casting obstructions—these are the places to learn. You find these places by asking other fishermen, most of whom are usually flattered by a request for advice.

It's also a matter of common sense on your part. A long, calm flat on the Battenkill in Vermont, for example, that's bordered by high brush on both sides will obviously be more difficult than an open riffle with no obstructions on the Beaverkill in New York's Catskills. Since both hold a good quantity of fish, your choice as a beginner should be an obvious one.

Finally, since most of us are limited by time and money to most often fishing waters close to home, at least try to choose a stretch on those waters that will offer the best chance at taking fish with the least amount of physical difficulty. Make your initial forays to the open riffle leading into a pool rather than to that stretch of calm water in a brushy reach of the same stream. Once again, you'll get more from the lessons on stream tactics in this chapter if you fish in an area where you can practice them most easily.

Principles of Stream Strategy

In terms of stream tactics, and disregarding effective imitation, trout take artificial flies for one of two reasons: The fly has been presented in a natural manner or it has been presented in a way that elicits a reflexive, predatory response — or sometimes both at once.

Trout are creatures of habit, accustomed to having their food presented to them in a certain manner within and by the currents of the stream. The physical laws that govern the characteristics of flowing water are immutable, and the stream trout must deal with these characteristics in an efficient manner in order to survive. Those same stream currents also govern the behavior of everything in a stream upon which trout naturally feed — the way a minnow swims, the way a dislodged nymph bounces along the bottom, the way an ant drifts when it falls on the surface — and so a trout becomes programmed to take that food available to it in a manner consistent with the currents in which it is feeding. These fish have developed feeding patterns that enable them to do this in the most efficient manner possible; feeding at the tail of a pool where converging currents concentrate a number of hatching insects is a basic example.

It then follows that a trout will be most likely to accept an artificial fly if that fly is generally imitative of a familiar food form and if that fly *behaves* like that food form in the currents of the stream. A streamer fly designed to imitate a baitfish must also be made to *behave* like a baitfish. A dry fly designed to look like a particular mayfly must also *behave* like that mayfly when floating on the surface. Presenting your fly in a manner naturally consistent with the currents of the stream is the keystone to your stream tactics for trout.

There's one other behavioral aspect of trout in general that will, at times, govern the tactics you use on the stream. Trout are predators, and although that may seem to be an unkind word to use on a jewellike brookie, that aspect does govern its behavior dramatically in certain instances.

A predator will often single out the cripple in a group for its prey, whether it's a lion choosing a disabled antelope from among a healthy herd or a big brown trout attacking a wounded minnow in a school of hundreds. The principle is the same; the prey will be caught with less effort.

One other aspect of trout behavior derives from a basic predatory response, the fact that the fish will sometimes violently pursue a baitfish or insect which appears to be trying to escape. Let's use baitfish as an example.

If a minnow that's been lingering next to a trout suddenly darts away, it calls attention to itself. The trout, in effect, is forced into a snap decision, no longer having the luxury of contemplating its rapidly disappearing quarry. Often enough to be of considerable significance to the angler, the fish's response will be to attack the quarry before it disappears.

So in general, the way in which you fish your fly will be governed by two basic factors: the trout's relationship to the currents of the stream and that same fish's basic instincts as a predator. The remaining portion of this chapter will be divided into specific tactics that are appropriate to the four basic types of flies you'll be using: dry, wet, streamer and nymph. It should be clear to you by the time we've finished our fishing in this chapter that those two basic considerations are the things to which you'll be adapting your techniques.

FISHING THE DRY FLY

Dry flies are, in most respects, easier to fish than other types of flies simply because you can see what you're doing — and not doing — as the fly floats on the currents of the stream. Subsurface flies — wets, nymphs and streamers — are often out of sight when they are being fished, and the angler's control over their behavior is based largely on intuition and educated guesswork. There are times, to be sure, when a floating fly is virtually invisible in poor light or when extremely small patterns are being fished at some distance, but these are exceptions.

One of the most popular dry flies in the West is the Royal Wulff. It does work well on Western waters (and elsewhere), but in the opinion of several major purveyors of flies in the West to whom I've put the question, one reason that so many flies of this pattern are sold is because it's an easy fly for anglers to see. Trout like the fly also and so the combination is a happy one.

If a dry fly is dropped on the surface of a stream with no leader or line attached, its behavior will be totally controlled by the stream currents, and our goal of a naturally behaving imitation will have been achieved. The leader, line, rod, reel and angler, however, are connected in sequence to the fly, and in order to make the fly drift naturally, the cast must be made and manipulated in such a way that the effects of all these components on the floating fly are minimized.

Let's work through a basic dry-fly situation on a typical stream to see what problems arise and how they might be handled. Remember that your goal is to float a fly over a fish in the most natural manner possible without, of course, scaring the fish by your presence.

The best way to approach any stream you're intending to fish is — quietly. Walk slowly and deliberately up to a position from which you can stand and watch the water for signs of fish. This is the time to read the water, to decide what you're going to do before you start fishing. Most of the fish that are caught by more experienced anglers are really caught at this point, before any fishing is actually done.

Our hypothetical stream has a gravel bottom and is about 70 feet across. The water at our bank is about two feet deep. The bottom gently slopes to a depth of three feet at midstream and slopes more abruptly to a depth of about six feet against the far bank. Our side of the stream is bordered by a meadow; against the far bank are piles of dead stumps and branches that form the actual border of the stream in the area of the deeper water. The deeper main channel against the logs on the far bank looks like an obvious home for trout — there's plenty of cover there and the current will carry drifting food close by.

A small dimple appears on the surface about two feet out from one of the logs. We watch that spot now, waiting for the fish to rise again.

Another dimple in the same spot, and now we can see the fish, a brown trout about a foot long, his yellow-brown back and his black spots clearly visible in the late-afternoon sun, even at this distance. As we watch, he holds just a few inches below the surface in the gentle current, swimming only hard enough to maintain his position. His body tips upward and he takes from the surface what appears to us as a light-colored speck.

A small mayfly flutters by on our side of the stream, and a lucky grab catches it in midair. Its size and coloration closely resemble the #16 Light Cahill dry flies we bought yesterday at the tackle shop in town, where the owner told us that these were hatching late in the day at this time of year.

We'll be using one of the small Light Cahill drys, so let's make sure that the tippet material at the end of the leader is appropriate for a #16 dry fly. A simple way to remember this is to divide the fly size by the number four and add one to the result. For our #16 dry fly, this would suggest a 5x tippet. There's a nine-foot knotless tapered leader on our line already, and to its 4x tip we'll add about 40 inches of 5x tippet material. The long length of tippet is stretchy and will act as a shock absorber if and when we get to hooking and playing this fish.

The most important thing that remains is the decision as to where we should stand to cast to the fish in the most successful manner.

Since we want the fly to float over the fish in the most natural manner possible, we could wade to a position below the fish, cast above him and then let the fly float back over his head. But in this case, the leader and possibly the fly line would be cast over the fish as well and the fish would probably be frightened off.

We could wade above the fish and cast down to it, in which case the fly would float downstream to the fish and would be the first thing he saw. That's a better idea, but another problem arises. If and when the fish took the fly in this instance, when we tightened up on the line to set the hook in the fish's mouth, we would be likely to pull the hook right out of his mouth without ever getting a secure hold.

When the hook is to be set in the mouth of a striking fish, the most desirable angle of pull on the angler's part is one which will pull the fly into the corner of the fish's jaw. This is best achieved from a position across- and perhaps slightly downstream from the fish. Whenever possible, this is the single best position from which to work to a rising trout. The hooking percentage on a strike is the highest, and there are other important advantages as well, as you'll see shortly.

Having concluded that much, we wade out to within about 30 feet — no closer — of the rising fish. Wading should be done cautiously without a lot of splashing or grinding of the river gravel. Take your time or you won't take your fish.

Before you cast, study the surface currents between you and the fish. Luckily, the current speed is constant and we won't have to complicate our setup right now with the problem of conflicting current speeds that we'll be encountering later. You should now cast so that the fly lands about four feet upstream from the fish and a few inches toward our side.

The first attempt is a couple of feet short, but don't yank the line off the water to try again, because if you do there won't be anything to try for—such a disturbance so near the fish will probably put him down. Let the line float well beyond the fish before you try a pickup.

You should be following the line of drift with your rod tip. If you don't, one end of the line (your end) remains stationary while the rest of the line is pulled around by the current. This will pull the fly along the surface—a problem known as drag—a decidedly unnatural act for the natural insect we're trying to imitate and one that offers a sure signal to the trout that your fly is a phony.

Make your pickup and cast again. A much better shot; now the fly is drifting right in line with the fish. The fly is about a foot upstream of the fish and he starts to tilt upward. Suddenly your fly is right in front of him. His nose is less than an inch below it.

The fly disappears in a small dimple just like the others. A slight tightening on the line accomplished by a gentle raising of the rod tip sets the hook. The fish pulls hard for deeper water. Let him take the line from the reel. If you try to snub him, the hook may pull free or the leader may break. You can gradually increase the pressure as the fish tires, taking in line with the reel as necessary to keep the pressure on the fish.

The fish will soon become tired enough to be brought to the net. Don't continue to play the fish beyond this point; that amounts to beating him when he's down, no matter how much you might enjoy the act of playing him.

Grasp the fish gently in the mesh of the net and remove the hook. Now you can gently support him in the water, his head facing upstream, for a few moments while his strength comes back. Shortly, he'll swim out of your hands—to grow and to be caught once again.

LET'S LOOK BACK OVER some of the more important points that came up in the previous basic example, because most of them apply in the more complex situations that follow.

- Approach the stream slowly and carefully.
- Don't jump in and start flailing; look over the water first and formulate a plan.
- Make sure that your gear and fly are in order before you start fishing.
- Wade carefully to avoid scaring fish.
- Try to cast from a position that will enable you to show the fish the fly before it sees the line or leader and, at the same time, give you the best chance of hooking the fish if it hits your fly.
- Study the surface currents between you and a fish before you start casting. The current will dictate the manner in which you must manipulate your line and leader to avoid a dragging fly.

That first example of a stream dry-fly situation was rather lengthy because a lot of very basic information was introduced. The remaining examples will be adding information to those basic points already covered. Don't forget them as you go through some of the more complicated situations that can confront the dry-fly angler.

Conflicting Current Speeds

IT SEEMS BASIC to the perverse nature of trout that they will almost always be rising on the far side of a series of different currents, each of which is flowing at a different speed. The currents pull and tug at the line every which way and would seem at first glace to make a drag-free float over the fish an impossibility. And here is a basic example of the problem and a couple of common solutions.

You're standing in midstream, fishing to a trout that's rising only inches from the bank. Most of the current between you and the bank is flowing much more quickly than the flow immediately adjacent to the bank. The trout, of course, is feeding in the slower current, although not really from a sense of perversity; it's just less work for the fish to collect its food in slower water.

If you cast straight across-stream to the bank, the intervening current will immediately catch your line and pull the fly away from the fish. Even worse, the wake of the dragging fly may spook the fish completely.

The first of two possible solutions is a technique known as mending the line, a basic tactic with which you should be familiar.

In this situation, it would be done in this manner: Make a direct across-stream cast, dropping the fly a couple of feet above the fish. As soon as the line settles to the water, move the rod tip with a sharp semicircular motion that will throw the line upstream in a U-shaped curve. If everything works right, it will take the faster current the same amount of time to straighten the upstream line curve as it takes the slower current to carry your fly to the fish.

That's the principle involved in line mending. It may be necessary to repeat this line manipulation several times in the course of fishing out a single cast in order to get a long enough float in the slower bankside current.

If you are starting to feel more confident in your casting, try making your first line-mend in the air before the line hits the water. Simply make the same sharp rod-tip motion while the airborne line is straightening out on its way to delivering the fly to the target, and the line will be mended when it hits the water.

The second possibility is what Doug Swisher calls a "reach cast," and although it was he who first showed me the technique, I've since seen it called by a variety of other names, both in print and along the stream.

This technique is really the best way for a dry-fly man to have his cake and eat it too in terms of getting the hooking advantage of an across-stream approach coupled with a drag-free float.

In its simplest form, the technique is performed as follows: Start to make an across-stream cast in the normal manner. Immediately after the forward power-

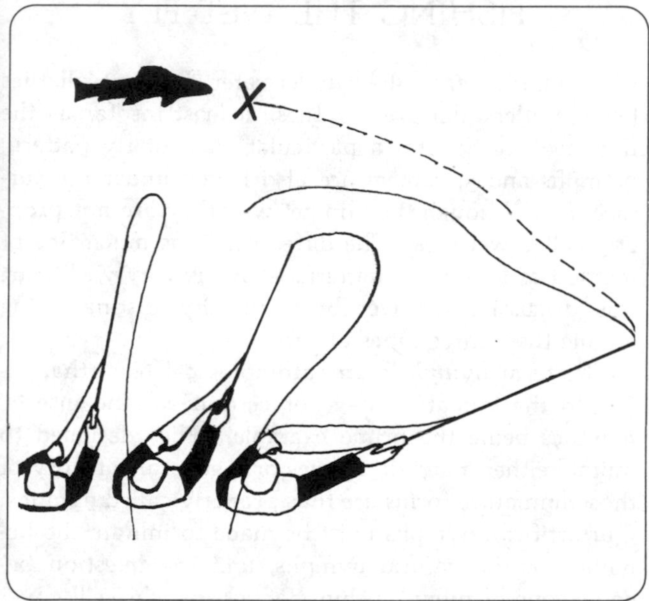

A schematic representation of the reach cast. An upstream reach (to the right) is made with body, arm and rod before the line hits the water.

stroke is completed, lean with your body and reach with your rod hand in an upstream direction. The fly will land on target, but the line will have followed the reach of your extended rod and will fall *upstream*, angling down toward the target to a degree dictated by the length of your reach (see illustration). You may find it necessary to release some additional slack line after the power stroke and while you are reaching in order to avoid pulling the fly off target.

Now follow the drift of the line with your rod tip. The line (and your rod tip) may travel 15 feet or more downstream before drag sets in on the more slowly floating fly next to the bank. If everything else is right, the fly will have been solidly hit before that happens. Often the line and your rod tip will be slightly downstream of the fish by the time the fly is taken, giving you the advantage of a good hooking angle, as well. (For a very detailed discussion of this technique and some further refinements, see *Fly Fishing Strategy* by Doug Swisher and Carl Richards (Crown).

There is one additional factor that applies to the problem of conflicting current speeds and to other situations as well. Not only does the long, fine tippet we use in the first example act as a shock absorber when playing fish, but it can also provide some extra insurance against premature drag.

If your cast is made with somewhat more force than usual and stopped sharply in the air, the leader will "kick back" and the long, flexible tippet will fall in serpentine waves in the surface. As the fly floats downstream, the tippet will straighten out behind it, insuring a longer float without drag than would be possible if the leader landed on the water perfectly straight. There is a danger, however, that goes with great amounts of slack in either the line or leader—if a fish hits prematurely there may be so much slack in the line or leader that you'll be unable to set the hook quickly enough. With time and experience, you'll be able to judge just how much slack is enough.

In a more complex situation, you may wish to combine all three techniques within a single cast. I'm about to give a rather extreme example to make the point, but don't choke up—it doesn't happen that often and when it does, it's an intriguing problem.

Occasionally, a long, narrow eddy—as little as a foot wide—will exist next to a productive bank. If there's a rising trout in that spot, the fish will be facing downstream. On an across-stream cast, the fly must be made to float upstream toward the fish in the current of the eddy while the main current is taking the fly line downstream.

Once you've tried the techniques described previously and gained some proficiency, try combining them. Make an across-stream cast, stop the rod abruptly with the line high in the air. Before the line hits the water, make as long an upstream reach as possible with the rod. The tippet will pile up in the eddy. The line will be upstream of your position. The piled-up tippet in the eddy will allow the fly to float upstream, but to get the most out of it, you'll have to follow through your reach-cast with a series of line-mends. These line-mends will keep the current from pulling on your line and thus pulling the piled-up tippet out of the eddy before the leader has a chance to straighten. When the leader finally becomes straight, you've had it. Hopefully, you will have gotten the fish first.

That was, as I warned you, a rather extreme example, but it does serve to illustrate one of the innumerable ways in which a variety of tactics can be combined.

The Downstream Dry Fly

Sometimes you are going to have to present a dry fly *downstream* because the physical characteristics of that stream prohibit any other approach. Your first cast will be your best chance, especially to a rising fish, because when the float ends, you'll often have to pick your fly line up directly over the fish. Here's how to make that first cast count.

After the forward power-stroke, stop your rod high. Before the line settles to the water, wave the rod tip from side to side several times. As you know, the line goes where the rod tip goes, and that movement will cause the whole line to fall to the water in a series of S curves. The extent and number of the curves will depend on the degree of rod-tip movement.

The line will gradually straighten as the fly drifts downstream without drag. When the line becomes straight — end of float. If the fish didn't hit, try twitching the fly back upstream past the fish. Sometimes this will produce a strike.

The Twitch

Your dry fly has floated to within view of a trout. The trout isn't responding. On your next cast, when the fly gets fairly close to the fish, twitch the fly slightly — no more than an inch or two. Although mayflies don't flop about on the surface very much, most other insects do — notably caddisflies — and the movement of your artificial will accomplish a couple of things.

First, the movement will get the fish's attention. As a predator, if you'll recall our earlier discussion, the fish is attracted by the movement.

Second, the movement may actually simulate the actions of the insects upon which the fish is feeding. Be very careful not to overdo it, however. This is very definitely a case in which too much is worse than none at all.

Pocket Water

Working pocket water with a dry fly almost always means fishing blind, casting to likely looking spots without having daintily rising trout as visual targets. Pocket water means fast water, flicking a buoyant fly behind a boulder, getting a two-foot float, dropping it next to a log, getting a three-foot float — taking another couple of steps upstream and then hitting another couple of targets.

Trout in such waters don't have the luxury of their flat-water brethren, in that pocket-water trout have to grab a morsel fast or it's gone in the churning currents; there's little time for prolonged inspection of an offering. Tippets can generally be heavier, fly patterns more heavily tied. This is the place for the high floaters — the Royal Wulffs, the Bivisibles. This is the place for short, quick casts, of hard, slashing strikes. It's also the time for demanding wading, upstream against the heavy currents weaving among the rocks.

But the novice can get away with more errors here. Pocket water is more forgiving. If you don't have the patience for flat-water trout, try their pocket-water neighbors — those fish don't have any patience either.

In the following sections on wet flies, nymphs and streamers, you'll be encountering some of the principles we've already applied to dry-fly fishing. As both a reminder of what we've covered and as an explanation, remember that our development of stream tactics for *all* flies derives from the same two principles: The fly must be presented in a manner *naturally consistent* with the stream currents, and trout have certain *predatory instincts* that can work to the angler's advantage.

FISHING THE WET FLY

All wet flies are fished underwater, but not all flies fished underwater are wet flies, at least insofar as the term *wet fly* denotes a particular class of fly pattern. Nymphs and streamers are also fished under the surface, and although they do get wet, they are not properly called wet flies. The difference is as much one of method as it is of fly pattern, which is why we'll start this discussion of wet-fly tactics by distinguishing among these three types of flies.

The term *nymph* is an entomological term that refers to the immature stage of certain aquatic insects, mayflies being the prime example. Flies designed to imitate either a certain species or a general category of those immature forms are thus properly called nymphs. Our artificial nymphs must be made to imitate the behavior of the natural nymphs, and the question becomes one of nymph-fishing tactics, which we'll cover in a subsequent section.

Streamers are virtually always imitative of some type of baitfish in form and action, even if not always in color. The angler seeks to make the streamer that he's fishing behave as a baitfish does in the currents of the stream. The stream tactics involved are thus quite different from those used in fishing nymphs, and we'll deal with streamers in a subsequent section as well.

In every trout stream, there is a smorgasbord of trout food carried below the surface by the currents that is neither nymph nor baitfish. The drowned forms of terrestrial insects, shrimp, sowbugs, the adult forms of mayflies and caddis that have been recaptured by the stream, and various living aquatic forms that are not true nymphs — all of these are imitated by wet flies of one sort or another. The fly may be a conscious imitation of a freshwater shrimp, for example, or just a generally buggy pattern such as a Woolly Worm; it's a wet fly none the less.

Many of those life-forms imitated by wet flies behave in a manner unique to themselves in the currents of the stream; and most proficient anglers will vary their wet-fly tactics to suit both their pattern and the behavior of the natural, but always within the confines set by the need for a natural presentation within the currents of the stream.

Thus the wet fly is perhaps the most diverse class of fly among the four we're considering. On the other hand, it can also be the most simple. Let's see first how the latter applies.

Fishing Down-and-Across

THIS IS A TRADITIONAL WET-FLY METHOD that's too often obscured by the difficult fly patterns and complex casts that we evolve to entertain and confound ourselves. More than 100 years ago, when anglers fished almost exclusively with patterns with such colorful and unscientific names as the Professor, the Montreal and countless others, they were talking about wet flies and they were almost always fishing in this manner. It worked well then and it works well now.

It's a simple matter of casting across- and downstream with a floating line and then letting the current swing your line, leader and fly around to a point directly below your rod tip. When the fly swing is completed, the fly is usually retrieved upstream in a series of short darts, in imitation of something struggling against the current.

The rod should be held at an angle of about 30-45 degrees above the surface of the stream, in which position the rod tip will be able to absorb the shock of a sudden strike. The line, leader and fly will be taut in the current, and when a fish hits, you'll feel it instantly. Don't rear back on the rod; you'll pull the fly out of the fish's mouth. In this down-and-across situation, the best way to strike is not to strike at all, but rather to just let the fish hook itself against the tight line.

In this situation, your leader tippet must be carefully correlated to the size of the fish you expect and the condition of the water. If the water is relatively high and fast and the fish are running to a pound or more, your tippet should be relatively heavy to absorb a hard strike — say 2x or 3x. If the water is low and clear and small flies are in order, you'll have to go to a finer tippet — 4x or 5x, sometimes smaller — to get a natural and delicate presentation. You'll have to do this, by the way, even though you may be breaking off a higher percentage of fish on the strike, because if your leader is too heavy in this instance, you'll be getting few hits.

The down-and-across wet fly is one of the most pleasant ways in which to work a stream. You will be, first of all, wading with the current instead of fighting it. Casting to the bank and letting the fly swing out into the stream allows you to fall into an almost lazy pattern, a reverie interrupted occasionally by the hard pulse of a strike. It can also be a trap, because that lazy rhythm of down-and-across can cause an angler to stop thinking about the water he's fishing, and when that happens the number of fish that you'll bring to a fly will also drop considerably.

In a typical down-and-across wet-fly situation, the current is usually fast enough to cause the fly to swing fairly rapidly across the current. As the fly moves quickly over holding water, it may draw that reflexive predatory response of a trout that attacks something it thinks is escaping.

When the fly-swing is completed, the rapidly traveling fly will stop dead in the current. For the trout whose attention has been drawn by the fly's movement, this is the time to hit — the target has become more vulnerable. Also, if the fly has been traveling across the current at some depth below the surface, it will be carried to the surface at the end of the fly-swing. To the trout, it may well appear that his food is about to escape the confines of the stream, and the fish's response is often both startling and vicious.

Except in very slow currents, in which the fly's rate of across-stream travel is slow enough to allow the fish to get a good look at it, the down-and-across method as commonly practiced depends largely on a trout's predatory reflexes.

Slowing the Fly Down

AS WAS DISCUSSED EARLIER in this section, most wet-fly fishing centers around imitating something within that toothsome spread of trout food that's carried in the current. So now we're concerned with making our wet fly drift or otherwise behave in a manner consistent with the currents of the stream. In contrast to the often rapid fly-swing developed in the traditional down-and-across method, this most often is a matter of slowing the fly down, often with the goal of making it drift in the current without drag. In essence, the same techniques we used for dry-fly fishing when we wished to avoid drag apply to many wet-fly situations as well.

The stream's currents diminish in rate of flow as the depth increases, most often being the slowest near the bottom. In our earlier discussion of down-and-across with a floating line, the fly-swing was taking place in the fastest current near the surface. One way in which the speed of the fly-swing can be reduced is by the use of a sinking-tip or full-sinking line. Even when fished down-and-across, the line will carry the leader and fly into the realm of slower current where the trout are more apt to be holding. Let's fish through such a situation and see how it works.

We're standing in the slower currents near shore and facing a deep, fast run in the center of the stream. The bottom of that run is a promising lie for trout; the problem is to get our wet fly drifting naturally in the deeper, slower currents in a fashion that's imitative of the way current-born insects will be sinking from the faster surface waters into the deeper, slower currents below.

We're using a full-sinking line and a short, about 5-foot, leader, so the currents won't carry the fly to the surface. Cast across the run, or across and slightly upstream, and immediately — before the line starts to sink — make an upstream line-mend. If the current is tugging on the line, the line will be held near the surface. By throwing slack in the line with a mend, we are permitting it to sink. As the line drifts downstream by our position, it will be approaching the bottom. Follow its drift carefully with your rod tip close to the surface; ready for a hit.

As the line starts to swing, drag will set in, the rate of the fly's travel will accelerate, and it will start to be pulled toward the surface. We still wish to keep the fly traveling slowly and deep, so, when you feel the fly-swing start to speed up, start feeding slack line in a controlled fashion through the guides to slow it down, giving you a few extra feet of productive drift.

You can often feed 10 feet or more of extra line in this situation before the fly swing starts to pick up speed beyond your control. At the instant the fly-swing starts to speed up, get ready — this is the same prime instant for a hit that we encountered when fishing wet flies nearer to the surface. If you're unlucky this time, let the fly complete its swing, retrieve the fly, and work your way down the run, repeating the whole process every few steps.

It should be apparent now that the rate of the fly's travel through the water is a key. You can control it by mending upstream to slow it down, by mending downstream to speed it up, by taking in some line to speed it up, and by feeding out line to slow it down. It's entirely possible to use all four tactics in a single cast, especially when fishing to a specific lie.

Fishing to a Target

THE ANGLER WHO HAS BECOME PROFICIENT at reading the water will often spot a promising lie in the stream's currents and will view it with the absolute conviction that there's a trout there that can be caught. Let's examine two of those situations — one in deep and the other in shallow water — that place the greatest demands for finesse on the wet-fly angler.

Suppose at the end of the deep run we fished in the previous example that there's a large rock, the end of which is barely above water and the mass of which apparently extends to the stream bottom. The stream's currents will have scoured out one or more pockets around the bottom of the rock, making it a fine lie for trout (or stream smallmouth, for that matter) and an ideal place for a deeply drifted wet fly.

In looking over the situation, we realize that we'll have to drop the fly some distance upstream of the rock to give our sinking line time enough to carry the fly to the bottom before the current carries it beyond the rock.

The procedure is essentially the same that we used to fish the upstream portion of the run. Slightly upstream cast, quick mend, drift and sink, drift and sink . . . now the fly ticks bottom, so take in a little line to speed it up and to keep it just over the gravel. We sense now that the fly is about a foot upstream of the rock, so we feed a couple of feet of line to slow the fly down again. It drifts well, unseen by us, but we have faith bred by practice on the stream. The rod suddenly dips — hard — and a rainbow cartwheels through the air, headed for the riffle at the end of the pool.

Late-Season Wet-Fly Techniques

SUPPOSE NOW THAT THE HISS of high, early-season water has faded to the murmur of late summer and fall. We elect to fish with a small Hare's Ear wet, a #16 should be about right, on a long 6x tippet. We'll wade down the center of the stream (it's about 60 feet wide), working the fly through promising lies along the bank.

This is a very common fishing situation all over the country at various times of the year. The key to success in this instance is to remember that your small wet fly should be fished in exactly the same manner as a dry fly in the same stream conditions, except, of course, that the wet fly will be underwater.

A log along the bank has a deep pocket at its edge. An across-stream cast drops the little wet fly just above the pocket, and a series of line-mends keeps the fly drifting slowly and parallel to the log. A tap is transmitted to our fingers by the line and we tighten up. A bulge in the water, and then we see a large brown streaking downstream, pulling out the slack line accumulated at our feet. A tangle in the line catches in the stripping guide, the rod bends deeper and the leader snaps. Such a fish had no business in such a small hold, but it happens. A hard lesson; next time we'll start by keeping better track of *everything*.

Are Two Better Than One?

IT ONCE WAS COMMON PRACTICE to fish two, three or even more wet flies at once, attached at intervals along one's leader. Two flies will cover more water on a single drift than will one, and it's still a viable method. More than two flies are difficult to cast, however.

One fly is tied to the end of the leader in normal fashion. The second is tied in about three feet above the first. If you've tied in three feet of tippet material, you should have left about eight inches of the heavier strand sticking out from the side of your blood knot. (Directions for this knot appear on page 76.) The second fly will be tied to this as a "dropper" fly.

The combination can often be fished through a natural drift with greater effectiveness than a single fly. Also, when the combination is being retrieved at the end of a fly-swing, it sometimes pays to hold your rod tip high, making the dropper fly dance along the surface, while the fly at the end of the leader swims in normal fashion. Watching your dropper dance along the surface of the stream can be a refreshing change from the more exacting process of fishing blind and deep, and the fly's action, as in some previous instances, will often convince a trout that it's time to strike before your fly can escape.

THIS HAS BEEN ONLY a basic introduction to the art of the wet fly, and yet I think you've seen that by using both the stream currents and a trout's predatory instincts to your advantage, your wet flies can be made to work.

Remember the four basic ways in which you can control the rate at which your fly swims in the stream:

- Mend upstream to slow it down.
- Mend downstream to speed it up.
- Feed slack line to slow it down.
- Take in line to speed it up.

Don't be afraid to try all of these in combination at various times to get the kind of drift you feel you need. And as you fish these subsurface flies, have the confidence in yourself to really believe that you know where your fly is at all times during the drift; you'll be amazed at the number of times you'll be right.

FISHING THE NYMPH

A DORSAL FIN BROKE THE SURFACE, followed by a broad spotted tail that came all the way out of the water and waved as the trout slipped back down to the currents at mid-depth. Idaho's Snake River broadened into a long meadow flat where I stood, and trout — big trout — were feeding everywhere.

A hatch of mayflies was just beginning, and their pale gray upright wings gave the impression of a sailboat race in progress on the smoothly flowing water. I bent over to look, and sure enough, these were Pale Morning Duns hatching right on schedule, as I'd been told earlier at the fly shop in town. I continued to watch and finally realized that none of the trout were taking the floating flies. Fish were rolling right next to the duns, but those adult flies floated downstream unmolested.

I bent over once more to look into the waist-deep water. Literally hundreds of struggling nymphs and empty nymphal shucks were sweeping by my knees below the surface. Here and there, individual nymphs had almost made it, wriggling violently just under the surface in their fight to escape the stream as adult mayflies. They had to be what the fish were taking.

I picked a fish that seemed to have established a steady rhythm of rolling takes. His dorsal and tail fins were coming out of the water every 20 seconds or so, and although I couldn't see him under the surface, he was easy to keep track of. I waded to a position directly across stream and about 35 feet from the fish and stopped to watch again; his feeding pattern continued without interruption.

The nymphs appeared to be about halfway in size between a #16 and #18, so I chose the smaller size in a color that approximated the naturals. I dried the leader with a handkerchief and then coated all but the last two feet with dry-fly dressing, which would cause the nymph to ride just under the surface.

I held the fly between my thumb and forefinger and squeezed it underwater a few times, making sure that it was thoroughly soaked and would sink immediately when fished.

I used a reach-cast to drop the fly a few feet above the fish, mended the line once, and then bent at the waist, following the drifting nymph with my rod tip and concentrating. The fish rolled and I struck gently — nothing. He'd taken a natural near my fly. I cast again. The drift was perfect as far as I could tell, but there was no response. The fly had drifted some distance beyond the fish when he rolled again, taking another natural.

I started to get a bad case of buck fever and stopped casting, calming myself down, telling myself that it was only a trout. I spent the time watching the nymphs floating by just under the surface, more of them close to the top now, and all wiggling like mad. Then I had an idea.

My fish — and by this time I really had a proprietary interest in him — was still rolling in the same pattern as before. I cast as before, and when I judged the fly to be about two feet upstream from his position, I twitched the rod tip enough to move the fly a couple of inches.

Another twitch, as lightly as I could accomplish it. Another. Then a dorsal breaking the surface. I tightened on the line, and the rainbow wallowed on the surface, my fly in the corner of his jaw, throwing spray half the distance between us and then shooting downstream.

The fish were feeding on nymphs that were behaving in a particular fashion. I made a reasonable imitation of those nymphs behave in the same manner. In nymph fishing, as with other types of flies, that combination is essential.

Big Flies on the Bottom

THE PREVIOUS EXAMPLE may have reminded many of you of some of the instances I used to describe both dry- and wet-fly fishing, and in many ways, nymph fishing resembles them both. Successfully fishing nymphs does depend on how well you manipulate your rod, line and leader to present the fly properly. This is the case with dry and wet flies as well.

Let's look at another style of nymph fishing that's quite different from the previous examples. Note that the difference arises because of what had to be done to get the fly to the fish in a manner consistent with the currents of the stream.

The Lower Madison River in southwestern Montana is absolutely frightening. It's big. It's faster than it is big. And it's more slippery than it is wide *or* fast.

Usually by the end of June in this stream, and in others like it in the West, thousands of big stonefly nymphs are starting to crawl along the stream bottom toward shore where they will crawl out onto rocks and twigs before emerging as adults. When the nymphs become active, they become more exposed, and the trout feed on them avidly.

The nymphs are on the bottom under a sheltering blanket of very fast water, and for the wading angler who has to contend with bad footing in fast water, it's tough to get a fly to the fish.

I stood in the water a few feet out from the bank, wondering if I was silly enough to wade out any farther. There was a narrow slick where a shallow pell-mell riffle shelved into a slightly deeper run, and I decided to fish it. It took me all of ten minutes to wade the next 20 feet and I was still only up to midthigh in water.

I tied a heavily weighted stonefly nymph to a short leader backed by a sinking-tip line and dropped it about 30 feet straight across stream. I started mending line, but before I'd really gotten into action, the fly had been swept around and was dangling on the surface downstream. I tried casting upstream at a greater angle and was then able to mend line fast enough to fish the fly to a certain degree, but not without some drag still holding the fly off the bottom.

I finally reeled in about 10 feet of excess line and cast the remaining 20 feet of my working line almost straight upstream. As soon as the fly hit the water, I mended some line directly upstream, keeping any line belly from getting caught by the current.

By the time the fly was going by me — about eight feet out from where I stood — I had stripped in some slack line and could feel the big nymph ticking on the rocks. My next sensation was as if someone had jumped on the end of the rod. I grunted and then gaped as a rainbow of about two pounds tried to jump in my lap before heading downstream in the current.

When you have to fish on the bottom — during cold-water periods or at any other time — don't try to do so with any more line than you can easily control. If you can't control your line precisely, the currents will usually pull your fly away from the fish.

At this point, let me add that entomological expertise is not essential for you to enjoy productive fishing with nymphs. It's entirely possible to start nymph fishing with only three general patterns — light, medium and dark — in a variety of sizes. Fish these patterns as water conditions and the behavior of the fish demand. In time, you'll learn more about the inhabitants of your favorite waters and their characteristic behavior patterns. Then you'll be able to gradually develop both your fly patterns and your nymphing methods to more closely match them.

If you're just starting out, however, simplify things for yourself as much as possible — keep the number of patterns to a minimum and concentrate on your technique. Try to determine, either by seining or by just picking up and examining rocks, the general size and coloration of the prevalent nymphs in your stream. Try to determine in what *areas* of the stream those nymphs are the most common. Then fish those areas with a pattern that approximates those nymphs.

All of the basic techniques that have been presented in these three sections are appropriate to nymph fishing. Experiment with them, singly and in combination. They aren't gospel, but rather a composite that I continue to develop for my own fishing by reading, talking, asking questions and, most of all, by giving some thought to my fishing — before, during and after. Don't be afraid to alter any of the methods that I suggest to suit your *own* needs.

Caddisflies

Both caddisflies and midges aren't true nymphs, but the tactics needed to fish their imitations successfully are appropriate to this section and so I've included them.

You've already picked up some information about the life cycle of the caddisfly from Carl Richards in an earlier chapter. Let's put that information to work on the stream.

Caddis are bottom dwellers as a rule, and that's where imitations of their larval forms should be fished. Once again, try to determine the types of caddis in your favorite waters. Select an appropriate imitation. Try to imagine how a relatively helpless caddis larva will tumble in the slow bottom currents, and then fish your fly in the same manner — slowly, with a dead drift — and with absolutely no drag. The key to fishing in this manner is a short line, certainly no more than you're confident about being able to control.

More exciting fishing will come when the caddis start to emerge. The caddis pupae rise rapidly from the bottom to the surface in a flurry of activity during a major hatch, and the trout respond by pursuing the ascending pupae at all depths of the river.

Cast your imitation a considerable distance above a bulging fish, and allow the fly to sink without drag as it drifts downstream. Just before your fly reaches the fish, tighten up on the line, causing the fly to start a swing toward the surface. This action mimics perfectly

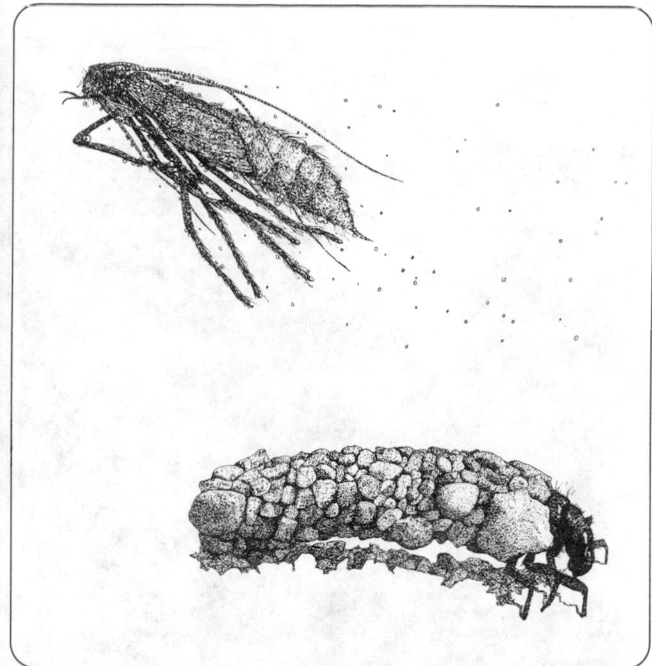

A cased, bottom-dwelling caddis larva (lower) and an ascending pupa, the stage that produces the most excitement on the stream. Illustrations by Victor Ichioka.

the action of a caddis pupa rising to the surface in the current, and the strike is apt to be hard. Because small flies (down to #20) are sometimes needed in this fishing, correspondingly light tippets will be used. You may sometimes find that it's much harder to avoid breaking off fish than it is to get a hit in the first place. Use a gentle hand.

Although this is most easily done when fishing straight downstream, you'll lose far fewer fish and still get an effective drift if you work to a fish in a down-and-across manner. This, as was the case with other types of flies, is closer to your ideal striking position, one in which your control of the situation exceeds that of the fish.

Midges

STREAM FISHERMEN occasionally encounter hatches of midges, especially in the summer and early fall months when these hatches aren't masked by larger hatches of other insects. Such hatches are typically encountered in the evening, when water temperature is dropping, and often occur most obviously on flat-water stretches.

This order of flies includes craneflies, mosquitoes and the notorious blackfly of the North Woods, but by far the greatest number of insects in this order fall within the family *Tendipedidae*, or true midges. Almost all of the approximately 3,000 species in this family are less than 3/8 of an inch long; most are smaller. Forget the technicalities if you like, but do remember that these flies are *very* small. Pupal imitations are commonly used in sizes down to #28 on 8x tippets.

During an emergence, the pupae hang in the surface tension where the adult emerges from the pupal shuck. Trout often become selective feeders on the pupae at the surface, which are easier to catch than the emerged adults.

The flies are apt to emerge in substantial quantities, and trout typically hold near the surface, tipping up and down in a rapid rhythm to take the drifting pupae.

Suppose it's late evening, and you've spotted a group of trout dimpling in a long flat. Their gentle rises suggest a mayfly spinner fall, but you check the surface and find no spinners. If it's summer or early fall, you have probably been blessed (you may not agree) with a midge hatch.

By seeing some flying adults, you should be able to get some idea of their size and color. Let's assume that a #24 black pupa seems to be about the right choice. Tie on a long (40 inches, or even more) 7x tippet, and then tie on the fly. Dress the leader to within an inch of the fly with dry-fly dressing. Then moisten the fly so that it will sink just below the surface, prevented from sinking farther by the floating leader.

Pick a working fish and wade to within 30-35 feet, in position for a directly across-stream cast. Now stop to consider two things. If the hatch is heavy, the fish will not move to one side or the other to chase your fly; he can get all he wants without moving. The trout may also be feeding with a distinct rhythm, and you should count off the time between rises. Cast the fly so that it will drift in a *direct* line to the fish, and cast it upstream from the fish so that it will reach him when he's due to rise again according to his measured feeding rhythm.

If it's late in the evening, you won't be able to see the fly. If you see a rise where you think your fly is, set the hook *very* gently.

If the fish ignores your offering, as a last resort try the twitch trick we've used in other situations. It works well enough some of the time to be worth trying.

This is very fussy fishing; many of you won't bother with it. Those of you who do will eventually get the immense satisfaction that comes from having dealt successfully with a difficult angling situation.

Nymphing for trout is, as you should now realize, a tremendously varied facet of fly-fishing. It includes many of the tactics appropriate to the dry fly, all of the tactics appropriate to the wet fly, and adds a few twists of its own.

I've continued to hammer away at the two tactical principles that I stated at the start of this chapter: (1) your fly must be presented to a trout in a manner consistent with the stream currents, and (2) trout have certain predatory instincts that can work to the angler's advantage. All of the examples we've been through since then have related directly to one or both of those precepts. Your ability to relate them to your fishing is even more important when fishing with streamers, as you'll see in this fourth and final section.

FISHING THE STREAMER

THE FLY WAS A HORRENDOUS CREATION; I hate now to think that I ever tied such a thing, but I was then 12, had just learned to tie flies and was admiring the bright green saddle hackles that went askew as I knotted the streamer to my leader. I cast the fly into the current at the head of the pool below the falls and watched it drift toward some overhanging bushes.

I twitched it aimlessly, enjoying the sight of my fly darting in the current. It was a pleasant morning, and I really didn't mind that nothing was happening; it usually didn't anyway. Eventually, my clumsy casting caused the leader to become fouled under the fly's wing hackles. As I gently twitched the fly across the current, it spun slowly and erratically. A big brown came at full tilt from somewhere in the depths of the pool and literally erupted into the air over my fly. He missed it—or so I thought at the time; now I think he refused it—and I fished hard there for an hour afterward. He wouldn't come again.

The fishing of streamer flies can be relatively simple, but at the most refined state of the art, they are the most difficult of all flies to master. We'll be exploring both of those aspects—and some in between—in this section, but first let's take a look at the flies themselves.

At one time, the term "streamer" referred to a baitfish imitation made with hackle-feather wings. The other popular group of baitfish imitations were called "bucktails" and featured wings made of the long hair from a deer's tail. Eventually, bucktails came to include any minnow imitation made with a hair wing. Then along came flies with wings made of a combination of hair and hackle. Now the numbers and styles of patterns have become so diverse that any attempt to distinguish between "streamers" and "bucktails" is meaningless. For purposes of this discussion, any fly designed to imitate a baitfish will be called a streamer.

If you don't know what the baitfish in your stream look like and how they behave, you can't fish streamers there effectively. On virtually any stream, there are eddies and backwaters close to shore where baitfish can be observed. Set your rod against a tree, get in a comfortable position and invest some time in watching them. This is the first and *most important step* in learning to fish streamer flies.

Dace, for example, are a common Eastern baitfish. They often hang close to the surface near the banks of a stream. They occupy trout-holding water—but in miniature; an eddy behind a small branch is typical. These fish will dart upstream a few inches, then drop back in the current without moving. Then dart. Then drift. Swim up; swim to the side. Most importantly, they usually stay in about the same place. A successful imitation must usually be made to do the same.

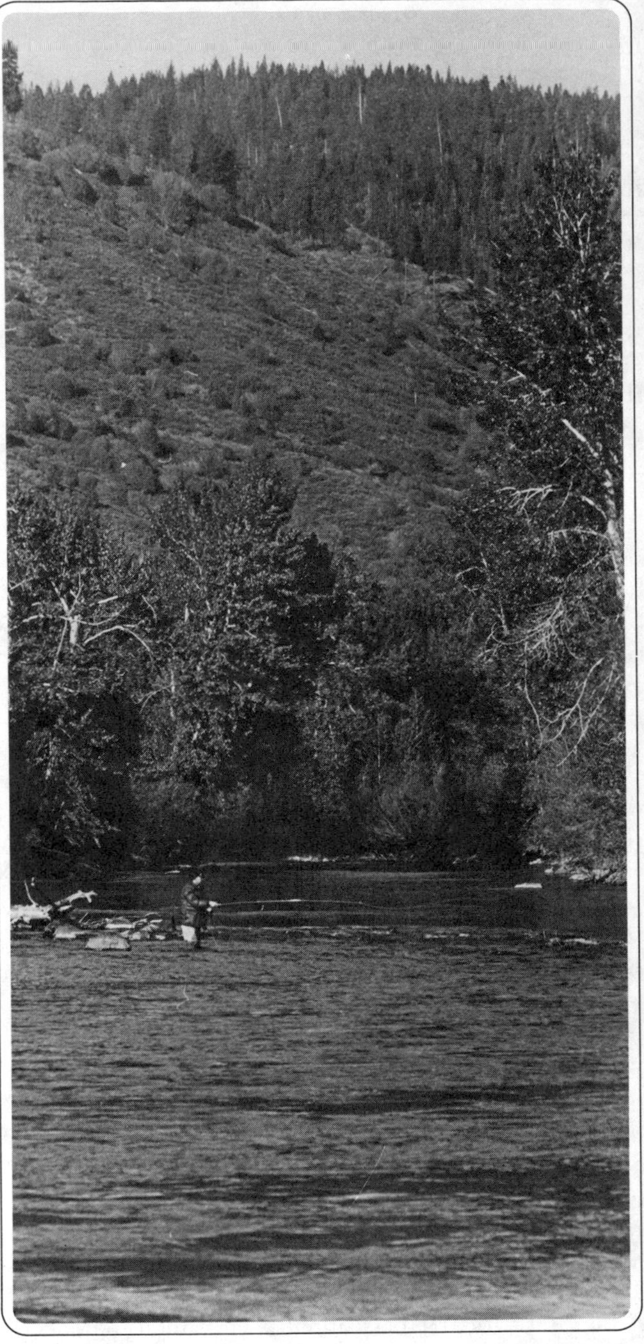

Drifting and dropping an across-stream streamer can be an effective way to work a riffle such as this. Photo by Christine Fong.

The sculpin is another baitfish common to most streams around the country. These squat little fish spend almost all of their time on the bottom; partly swimming, partly hopping about on their oversize pectoral fins, and darting rapidly for cover when startled. A successful imitation should be made to emulate all of these characteristics at various times and should be fished where the naturals live — on the bottom.

Having observed the baitfish, you may now have realized that there's something unique about the way in which their imitations must be fished. Most dry flies are fished without any constantly added motion. The same applies to wets and nymphs. Forage fish, however, are always moving and your fly will require constant attention and manipulation to keep it behaving naturally. It is in this type of fishing more than any other that the behavior of the fly in the water is a real extension of the angler through his rod and line. The dry-fly fisher is concerned with fly form and a dead drift. The streamer fisherman must endow his fly-form with life.

Attractors and Imitators

STREAMER-FLY TYPES fall within two general classifications. Those flies, which by virtue of their extreme action or by their color are designed to draw the fish's attention, are called *attractors*. Examples of these are the White Marabou, the wing of which pulsates dramatically when fished, and the Mickey Finn, which has a bright yellow-and-red wing.

The other category covers those flies designed and fished as actual *imitations* of specific kinds of baitfish. The famous Gray Ghost, for example, was designed as a smelt imitation, and the Whitlock Sculpin, by Dave Whitlock, was designed to imitate sculpin and to be fished as such.

You'll find that as you fish more and more in conscious imitation of a particular baitfish, your use of attractor patterns may decrease. That's a common trap; these flies are too effective to be neglected. The best way to limit your success when streamer fishing — and this really applies to all flies — is to fall into a repetitive fishing pattern; a one-fly, one-method habit that will *never* work all of the time.

Down-and-Across

THIS IS THE EASIEST and most common method of streamer fishing. Essentially, it's the same technique described under a similar heading for wet-fly fishing. The fly is cast across-and-downstream and allowed to swing across the current. You may wish to twitch it as it swings, giving it a more minnowlike action. When the fly-swing is completed, the fly is retrieved upstream and the process is repeated. A fish may slash at the fly at any point in the process.

This is the easy method, and if you're generally without experience, it's the way to start out. But there are some problems inherent here. Since you're fishing downstream, you'll be setting the hook at the worst possible angle when a fish hits. Also, you're not really *fishing* the fly; you're dragging it through the water in a fashion that's not imitative of any baitfish.

As you gain a little practice, you should start modifying your down-and-across technique by manipulating the speed of the fly, just as was described in the section on wet-fly fishing. Both the fly's speed in the current and the depth at which it's being fished can be established, as with wet flies, by:

- Mending line upstream to slow it down.
- Mending line downstream to speed it up.
- Feeding slack to slow it down.
- Taking in line to speed it up.

Once you're using all of these methods in conjunction with fishing down-and-across, you'll find that your fly can be made to behave in a much more lifelike manner. As the streamer swings by a likely looking spot, you can suddenly slow it down with a line mend, making it pause and flutter over a downstream hole before it takes off again in the current. Working the fly in this manner should make a marked difference in your results.

Now you're fishing the fly in a manner that's much more in keeping with the stream currents, and in a manner that may elicit a predatory response on the part of a trout or bass. As has been the case in other sections, however, there are some specific tactics that can be adopted to increase the odds on the side of the angler.

Escaping Baitfish

THE WATER DROPPED ABOUT SIX FEET over the spillway, creating a plunge pool with a large eddy on either side against the face of the dam. It was possible to sit on the dam during a sunny afternoon and watch a few brown trout cruising the eddy on the near side of the spillway.

There was invariably a small school of silver shiners near the surface of the eddy, drifting in the current as a group and occasionally dimpling the surface. The trout cruised below them and the mouth of a larger fish sometimes showed white as it took a drifting nymph that had been dislodged by the falls.

It was a tranquil scene that sometimes erupted into violence — shiners skittering along the surface, bouncing off the face of the dam and disappearing in a vicious swirl. When one trout started chasing shiners, the baitfish scattered, skipping along the surface, often leaping from the water in attempting to escape. This seemed to wildly excite the other trout in the eddy, and for a few seconds the eddy would be a turmoil. Then calm again. The shiners would regroup placidly, and the trout would return to their mid-depth cruising.

Watching this happen a number of times gave me the idea of trying to simulate a fleeing baitfish with a streamer. I waded to one end of the eddy and knotted on a small Black Ghost. I cast the fly to the base of the dam and, before the fly actually landed, started sweeping it back toward me in rapid, foot-long twitches. Because the retrieve started before the fly landed, it was coming toward me when it hit the water. I kept the rod tip fairly high and so the fly skipped along the surface, much like those panic-stricken shiners.

Nothing happened on the first cast. On the second to the same spot, a foot-long brown leaped out of the water and over the fly. On the third try, it didn't miss.

In that same location, which I've fished on and off for the last 20 years, that technique has continued to work and in exactly the same way. It's also proved applicable to a variety of other situations and is one of the best examples I've seen in which a trout's reflexive predatory response overcame the fish's normal caution. Let's look at a slightly more complicated one-two punch that depends partly on this response and that you can use with streamer flies to bring a strike when the water seems dead.

Switch-Hitting with Streamers

It was a small stream, but with enough pockets and eddies along the banks to provide plenty of holding water next to the generally swift and shallow currents at midstream. I stood in the middle, trying to decide what fly to fish through the eddy behind a stump about 20 feet distant. It had been a slow morning, one small brown coming to a Muskrat Nymph, and no fish rising anywhere in the stream.

I picked an old friend, a White Marabou streamer, often called a "locater" because the seductive action of the marabou feathers in the water will often cause a logy fish to at least flash at the fly. I soaked the fly well before fishing it and then cast across-stream into the eddy, mending line upstream to buy some time, and then twitching the fly gently through the backwater. On the third cast, there was a golden-yellow flash deep in the eddy below the fly; a brown had been teased into making a false move.

I didn't cast again, but instead stripped in line to change flies. The fish's interest had been aroused by the attractor fly, but the more I showed it to him, the more evident would become the fact that it was an imitation and not a baitfish on which the trout was accustomed to feeding. I then tied on a slightly smaller Badger Matuka, an excellent imitation of the black-nosed dace that I knew to be prevalent in the stream. Again a cast into the eddy, a line mend, and a gentle series of twitches over the trout's lie; this time a sudden swirl and a solid take on the first cast.

If a fish comes in a false rise to your streamer fly—and most especially if you're using an attractor pattern—don't put the same fly over him again. At least not in the same manner. Either he didn't like the fly or he didn't like your retrieve, or both. Let's separate those two factors and look at each of them briefly.

An attractor pattern will often stir a fish's interest, but not always enough to make that fish strike. But once the fish's interest is aroused—as most often evidenced by a false rise—that same fish is looking for something to eat or attack. A quick follow-up with an imitative pattern offers the trout a chance to react to a familiar target.

If you get a false rise to a slowly retrieved streamer and don't feel that changing flies is the answer, change the speed of your retrieve—the trout may respond to a fly that is apparently fleeing. Conversely, if you get a false rise to a rapidly retrieved fly, slow it down on the next cast. A fish that only tried half-heartedly for a fast-moving fly, may smash one that goes by in a series of slow, seductive twitches.

Variations on a Slow Retrieve

One key to using streamers for trout in moving water lies in getting the fly in the vicinity of a fish and keeping it there with the appearance of a natural. If we're using a pattern that's imitative of a baitfish, that fly must be fished in an imitative manner as well. There are a variety of ways in which this can be accomplished, depending on the baitfish you're imitating and the water conditions that exist at the spot you're fishing. All of the various tactical suggestions that I've mentioned in this and previous sections can come into play at one time or another. Let's work through an example to illustrate what I mean.

You're rigged up with a small Blue-Dun Matuka, generally imitative of a wide variety of minnows and shiners. Straight across-stream from your position is a large rock, behind which is a deep eddy about four feet in diameter, through which a side current turns before heading downstream. That old feeling in your stomach tells you with no uncertainty that there's a good trout in that dark hole.

Keeping your fly near the fish means that you'll have to keep the main current from pulling your line—and the fly—out of the neighborhood. You *must* be able to control your line. The less line you have out, the better you can control it, so get as close as you comfortably can to that eddy without scaring whatever may be in there. Twenty-five to thirty feet away should be fine, with the eddy directly across-stream to give you the optimum hooking angle on the strike.

Soak your fly in the water so that it will sink instantly on the first cast. Make your false casts both sparingly and gently to avoid drying out the fly. If you have to tug and yank the fly line to get the fly to sink when you should be fishing it, you're wasting your time.

Aim your cast so that the fly will land in the downstream portion of the eddy. While the line is straightening out in the air, make an upstream mend so that the line will be mended when it hits the water. The fly, having landed in the lower portion of the eddy, will be carried upstream. Your upstream mend will give you time to get your rod tip up and to hold the line belly above the conflicting currents near your position. Twitch the rod tip gently. A little twitch makes the fly's hackles pulsate and your imitation comes alive. You stop; it stops. It rests and drifts a few inches. Twitch again, gently. The fly swims a few inches and then rests.

By now you're probably holding the rod tip as high as you comfortably can, and the currents are threatening to grab the line belly, pulling the fly out of productive water. Now make an *underpowered* roll cast back into the eddy—this will throw some line and leader back into the eddy without actually lifting the fly from the water. Once again, you can resume your gentle twitching of the fly, with your rod tip up but still ready for a strike.

You may have to repeat this cycle several times before you get a hit, or it may not work at all. In that case, the fish needs a little something extra to tease him into striking. If you're using a Matuka-style streamer, try tying it on with a riffling hitch. If you're using a standard hair- or feather-wing pattern, loop the leader under the wing behind the head. The object in either case is to make the fly spin or vibrate unnaturally as it *slowly* passes through the eddy. That, sometimes, is more than a poor trout can stand. Be careful, though, because after a few tries this may start to twist your leader.

Drifting and Dropping

This is the last technique I'm going to describe in this section, and it's one that combines the subtleties of dead-drifting a nymph or wet fly with the equally precise control that's needed in most types of streamer fishing. It amounts to the same thing as fishing with live bait in terms of technique. (There are also some "purists" who limit themselves to surface flies and who would extend the analogy even further, which is unfortunate because they're missing a real challenge.)

In times of low water, this works well with unweighted flies and a floating line. At other times, you have to use whatever method you prefer—split-shot, sinking line or sinking shooting-taper with weighted fly—to get the fly deep. In both instances, the object is to keep the fly floating broadside to the current, dropping downstream with a dead drift occasionally interrupted by a subtle twitch. This works well with sculpin imitations that must be fished near the bottom, or with any other imitative pattern. Attractor patterns have always produced better for me when fished with more action than this technique provides.

Once again, an across-stream cast will most often provide an optimum combination of line control and hooking percentage. Cover the holding water carefully, mending your line as necessary to keep your fly at right angles to the current flow but drifting naturally with it. As the fly approaches the area where you anticipate a hit, punctuate the drift with a *very gentle* twitch at randomly spaced intervals. An injured baitfish caught by the current can no longer hold itself in its normal upstream-facing position. It behaves abnormally and is a prime target for a trout. So is your fly when manipulated in this manner. There's something of all the techniques we've covered so far in this method, and it's one of the most productive ways of covering a stream when the fish aren't obviously feeding on a hatch or something else that would make another method more appropriate.

PUTTING IT ALL TOGETHER

Stream tactics aren't conducted on the basis of rule or formula; the best tacticians are good improvisers, adapting their techniques to the situations at hand. Granted, there are some traditional techniques for one kind of fly or another that work well some of the time. These are generally the methods most easily learned and are the ones that you should try first if you're relatively new to the sport.

Sooner or later, however, you'll find that you'll have to modify one standard technique or another to adapt to a particular stream situation. As soon as you understand why that adaptation is necessary, you're on your way to really extending your fly-fishing horizons. After all, your stream tactics are really based on two things, either singly or in combination. Once again:

- Your fly must behave in a manner naturally consistent with the currents of the stream.

- Trout sometimes react in a reflexive predatory fashion that can be made to work for you.

These are the foundations of stream tactics and should be the basis of whatever methods you develop on your own. Don't be afraid to experiment; the tactical examples given in this chapter are just that—examples, *not* rules. We've discussed the traditional methods used with drys, wets, nymphs and streamers, but we've also gone beyond that, into the realm of improvisation on the stream. No two streams are identical; each one places some unique demands on the angler who seeks to understand and fish it. Your imagination will often be the key to your success.

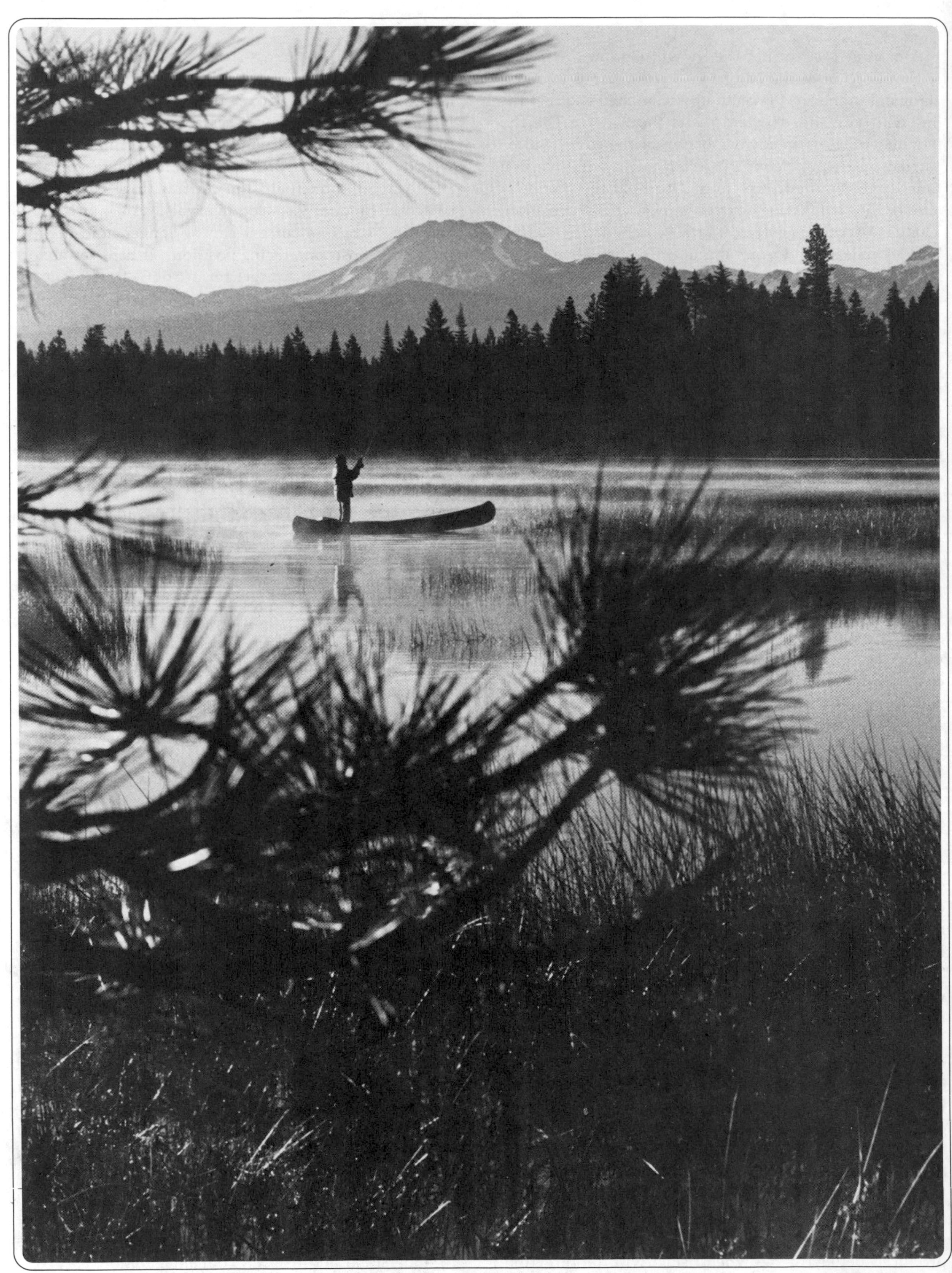

Photo by Christine Fong.

Nothing can be as disconcerting to the stream-bred fly rodder than to face, for the first time, the glasslike surface of a lake. He sees the reflection of the trees on the other side and little more. All the rules are suddenly changed — or so it seems. The water stays still. And the fish move. From the shallows of shore to the far-out deeps, from unseen shoals to hidden weed beds. FFM Field Editor Ron Cordes confesses to such confrontations and frustrations until he learned to fish up and down. And sometimes upside down, because lakes turn over! But lakes are also a real challenge to the fly rodder, for they are often less heavily fished and are always ready to give up a bonanza of fishing to the savvy angler.

Chapter 7

Lake-Fishing for Trout

Trout that Move, Water that Doesn't

RON CORDES

I WINCE WHENEVER I RECALL THE FIRST TIME I stood alone and bewildered alongside a quiet lake, desperately changing flies by the glow of a fast-fading twilight. In front of me was a mosaic of widening rings spreading across the lake, and beneath each ring lay an actively feeding trout — but not once was I able to entice a fish to one of my flies.

An experience such as this early one quickly taught me that lake fishing has its own set of potentially rewarding challenges, each equally as difficult as those of the most demanding chalkstream or spring creek. Yet in spite of this opportunity, many anglers — perhaps afraid to test their abilities — have wrongly written off lake fishing as an unworthy pursuit.

Unlike many streams, with their familiar pools, lies, currents and riffles, a lake may extend out of sight without so much as a clue as to its character. Where does the angler begin? How does he develop the necessary insight? There are no slicks, no runs, no current-breaking rocks or boulders. There is no fast water, no holding water, no eddies. In fact, there are no clues — or so it seems at first glance.

Unfortunately, it is often this very sort of first confrontation with the seemingly faceless water of a lake that has sometimes discouraged anglers and ends up depriving them of some unusual and exciting fishing experiences. They don't realize that frequently they would be likely to catch more trout of a much larger average size in lakes than in rivers—if they would just give themselves a chance to develop their understanding of lake fishing.

Despite the broad physical differences between lake and stream environments, the same fundamental factors govern where the trout may be found, which fly patterns should be used, and how the patterns should be presented. These factors can be considered under the broad categories of the *food preferences* of trout, the *location* of this food, and its *availability*. Once the fly angler understands which varieties of food the trout is looking for, where this food is found in lakes, and then how the trout expect to see their menu served up, the mystery of lake fishing starts to unravel.

Looking at a Lake

EVERY LAKE HAS A CHARACTER as revealing as that of any river. Instead of the familiar pools and riffles, the significant areas in a lake are the weedy regions, the jutting points of land, and those sudden drop-offs, sand bars or shoals that can all be cruising areas for feeding trout at various times of the season and the day.

If we observe flashing baitfish on a lake shoal, for example, we fish there in the morning or evening when trout will be moving in from deeper water to feed, just as we would fish a riffle in a given stream, knowing that trout will move into that riffle in response to hatching mayflies. In a stream or a lake, the fly fisherman probes those areas where he expects trout to be actively feeding, with the item the trout are feeding on dictating the basic choice of imitation.

While there may not be as many exposed rocks or boulders in a lake as in a stream, there are many target areas of equal importance in lakes. *Weed* and *moss beds* are both sources of concentrated nymphal activity—action to which trout are quick to respond. *Underwater springs* also attract vast numbers of fish by creating a cool oasis, especially as the season progresses and water temperatures in other regions of the lake increase. In addition, *river mouths* and *inlets* are also sources of feeding activity, since the oftentimes subtle, cooler currents will invariably carry entrapped aquatic and terrestrial insects. Like a river, each lake does indeed have its distinguishing characteristics, extensive knowledge of which comes only with angling experience. And as these characteristics become better defined, angling success becomes more assured.

Lakes—A Trout Supermarket

ALL FRESH WATERS CONTAIN an extremely diverse assembly of trout food, and lakes often harbor a more extensive variety than rivers. These foods may range from tiny microscopic organisms of little concern to the angler to large dragonfly nymphs, small forage fish, and even the purely terrestrial insects that accidentally become part of a lake's food supply.

The number of possible food sources is amazing in its length and diversity. A partial list might include midges, mosquitoes, caddisflies, dragonflies, damselflies, mayflies, stoneflies, water bugs, aquatic worms, shrimp, snails, leeches, alderflies, beetles, small fish, and such terrestrial insects as wasps, ants, moths, spiders and grasshoppers.

The most abundant and diverse of these food sources are without doubt the insects, some of which spend their entire lives in the lake water, while others are aquatic only during their immature stages, eventually becoming terrestrial adults. In order to continue growing toward this terrestrial adult form, some insects, such as the dragonflies, the damselflies, mayflies and stoneflies, undergo a gradual metamorphosis, during which their brittle outer shell is molted. With each molt the wings develop and grow within the external pads along the back of the immature insect, which at this stage in its life is referred to as a "nymph."

Other insects, such as the caddisflies, midges, mosquitoes, beetles, moths, and alderflies, undergo a complete metamorphosis during which the wing pads develop internally in the early larval stages. The wing pads then revert to the outside in the pre-adult "pupal" stage.

Among virtually all of the aquatic insects that are important food sources for trout, only the immature stages live in the water. Upon completing the metamorphosis, the adult becomes terrestrial, returning to the lake—or stream—either casually or during the egg-laying process. In the case of a lake, the *nymph* and the *pupa* are more sought-after by trout than any other potential food items, either aquatic or terrestrial.

Although feeding periods do occur when the *terrestrial* adult form of an aquatic insect tops the trout's list, the aspiring lake fisherman should first focus his attention on the nymph and pupa.

In spite of this smorgasbord of potential food supply available to the trout, studies of lakes in North America, Great Britain, and Scandinavia have demonstrated that only a relatively few types predominate. Midges (primarily the pupal stage), caddisflies (primarily the pupal and adult stages), mayflies (the nymphal and adult stages), and freshwater shrimp appear over and over again as the food sources most sought after by trout.

In a majority of lakes it is the *midge* in particular that exists in the greatest numbers and makes itself available to the trout more frequently than any other aquatic insect. It also adapts to a much wider variety of aquatic conditions, and as a result the larval stage invariably may be found at depths and locations in a lake that most other organisms avoid. Consequently, the emerging pupae and the adults appear throughout a greater portion of deep lakes than do other organisms.

The *caddisfly,* with its beautifully intricate case, is another favorite food source. Trout take it both in the pupal stage, as it makes its frantic swim for the lake's surface where it can emerge into the adult form and fly to the sanctuary of the wooded shoreline, and in the adult stage, as it flutters and skitters across the surface in its haste to escape its watery environs.

The *mayfly,* also a key food, is pursued in its nymphal form prior to emerging, as it moves about in its weedy, aquatic environment, as well as in its adult form, either after emerging or when returning to lay its eggs.

However, in some lakes, the population of *freshwater shrimp* dominates all other food sources and frequently forms the main staple in the trout's diet throughout the entire year. Henrys Lake in Idaho is a classic example of this sort of occurrence. In past years, during the month of July, shrimp have comprised over one-third of the diet of cutthroat trout—and in the month of August over half!

Belly boats are becoming increasingly popular on many lakes. Photo by Michael Fong.

In many lakes, during periods of the particular abundance of one food type, the trout will focus on that organism during the relatively short period when it is available in such great numbers. At this time food items such as damselflies, leeches, small threadfin shad, or even snails may be sought after to the exclusion of other food sources, even though in general they are not as frequently consumed as other items. The angler must watch for such periods of "selective feeding," since they occur periodically throughout the season.

Where the Trout Meet to Eat

Once the stillwater fly rodder knows what basic food varieties the trout prefer in a lake, he then must locate just where these items may be found, since this is precisely where hungry trout will be lunching.

Some organisms spend their entire existence within the bottom deposits of a lake, others only a short time. Some are extremely active, while others are sluggish. Many construct cases or shelters, although even more dwell unprotected on the weeds and in the soft mud. The environment they choose to inhabit can range from sand, clay, rubble, gravel, rock and weeds to the seemingly suspended ooze so frequently found in the deeper lake waters.

The ever-present midges, although most abundant in soft mud, have demonstrated their ability to survive regardless of the type of bottom or water depth. It is this very adaptability that explains in part their widespread and large populations, and the angler should be prepared to present the appropriate midge pupa or adult imitations in any one of a number of locations in a lake, depending upon where the insect activity is occurring at the time.

Mayfly nymphs, like the midges, occupy a wide variety of substrata, although not the deeper, weedless waters. Some species are mud dwellers, such as the *Hexagenia,* a burrowing form, while others such as *Caenis* prefer gravel, and *Callibaetis,* which prefer weeds. Still others prefer protected rock.

Different species of caddisflies also prefer a wide variety of habitats including open sediments, rocks and weeds. Various species of freshwater shrimp may also be found under rocks and in the weeds. In Utah's fertile Fish Lake, biologists estimated that from 200 to 500 shrimp occupied each square foot of the weedy lake bottom!

Other important lake organisms, including damselflies, leeches and water bugs, are also found in various spots, but the single most important habitat is weed beds. Depending upon the water clarity and the maximum depth to which a significant amount of light is able to penetrate, the lowest depth at which the ever-important weeds will grow may vary from only ten to perhaps thirty feet. In some lakes the weeds may be restricted to a narrow band, particularly along steep shorelines, while in other lakes the entire bottom may be covered with weeds.

In either case, however, the weedy zones of lakes must be thoroughly probed, because they will generally provide the best angling. The angler need not necessarily look out upon a vast expanse of water for some distant location to begin his casting, but instead may look to the shallower shoreline areas for weed beds where browsing trout may be found.

Lake bottoms frequently consist of coarse materials in shallow water and finer materials as the water gets deeper, and certain aquatic growth is more prone to exist and thrive in specific bottom environments. As a result, one feature of the larger aquatic plants is their tendency to be arranged in essentially "parallel zones" along the shorelines. The more protected a particular segment of shoreline is, the more likely that distinct "zoning" will occur. This fact is of great value to the lake fisherman, especially if he is also aware of the preferences shown by certain insects for weeds having specific characteristics. If, for example, the angler recognizes the type of weeds that certain mayfly nymphs prefer to inhabit, he should position himself where he could continually present his imitation over that zone. Not only is this an area where free-swimming nymphs may be available to the trout, but during an emergence period this region could be a hotbed of cruising trout. To either side of the zone the action would be less substantial.

During one of my first experiences fishing out of a float tube, still somewhat reluctant to venture too far from the safety of the shore and the shallow water, I noticed that, although I was surrounded by rising trout, my companion, Hal Janssen, seemed in the midst of even greater activity. Hal is one of the West Coast's most knowledgeable lake fishermen, and when he launched himself into the lake, he had immediately paddled his "belly boat" to the deepest water. When I finally got my nerve up and joined him, I noticed that there was a particular weed growing in large quantities in the deeper water that simply did not grow in the shallower water. In this case, however, the zonation occurred in part because of yearly water level fluctuations. And it was from this type of weed that the greatest number of mayfly nymphs were emerging that morning! The fishing activity proved, of course, to be substantially more productive above those weed beds than elsewhere, and until I joined Hal my strikes were disturbingly few.

As mentioned earlier, certain weeds flourish in specific zones within a lake, and insects in turn inhabit certain weeds more so than they do others. The zone of submerged aquatic plants is generally the most desirable to locate, since the emergence of insects will occur above them where the angler can effectively present his imitation. Furthermore, it's here where trout can be found cruising in search of free-swimming organisms.

The weeds most attractive to aquatic insects are those that provide protection from predators and the opportunity to forage for food, weeds that have nooks and crannies within which to hide. Trout foraging through such weeds find an abundance of food, either by literally picking the insects off the weeds or by knocking them loose by random movements as they cruise.

Because trout become accustomed to seeing certain immature insect forms moving in certain ways when they become dislodged from their weedy homes, presenting imitations of those insect forms with appropriate movements is an extremely effective fishing technique. As a matter of fact, unless there is some reason to employ a different technique, such as during a hatch, this would be one with which the angler should commence his lake fishing each day.

As a general rule, the luxuriant plant growths with the greatest insect populations occur in the quiet, shallow waters of small lakes or in well-protected bays free from water disturbances caused by wave action or the presence of outboard motors. Anglers should seek out such areas as one of their first steps in analyzing a lake fishery. Once found, a sample of aquatic vegetation should be obtained to determine what organisms, and insects in particular, inhabit that area. This information in turn gives the angler an excellent indication of the fly patterns with which he may choose to begin the pursuit.

This weedy region of the lake, generally from the lake's edge itself outward to the lakeward limit of the rooted aquatic vegetation, is referred to as the *littoral zone*. This zone is without doubt the region of the lake that is most important to the angler, since it contains a much greater number of food sources for the trout to feed on than any other region of the lake. It is here that not only a wide variety of food organisms coexist, but where the foraging trout will be found, where the great hatches of insects will occur and where fishing activity will most frequently be of the highest quality.

Availability—and Vulnerability

KNOWING WHICH FOOD ITEMS the trout are interested in and where such items may be found, it remains for the lake fisherman to determine how each of these key food sources become available. Knowledge of availability is of critical importance in determining both where to present a convincing imitation of that item and what constitutes a proper presentation.

Damselflies, for example, are most available when migrating at various depths toward shore to emerge. In Henrys Lake, during the annual migration, which takes place from late June through early July, as many as 1,445 damselflies have been consumed by a single trout in one day! In migrating, the damselflies do not move rapidly, but swim instead in a slow, undulating fashion, stopping occasionally to rest. As with other organisms, this characteristic motion dictates the retrieve to be used by the angler.

Shrimp invariably remain within the sanctuary of rocks and weeds, becoming available as they move throughout their domain in an erratic, jerky fashion. And the well-camouflaged dragonflies when disturbed from their hiding places also become available, but they respond, not by slowly crawling away, but instead by darting for safety in a quick, jetlike fashion.

So intricately interwoven is the characteristic movement of an aquatic animal with the way in which it becomes available that to speak of availability is inherently to speak of mobility. It is imperative that the angler know how and where aquatic feed becomes available, but unless he can impart to his imitation the *characteristic motion* that the trout expect to see, his imitation, no matter how well conceived, will probably be rejected. Unlike fishing a fast-moving river where the angler can successfully "dead-drift" a pattern, more often than not in lake fishing, success is measured in great part by the angler's ability to properly imitate the movements of food organisms.

Small forage fish and many of the leeches available to trout on a continual basis as they move in random fashion through their chosen habitats in search of food are always alert and ready, however, to escape the threat of predators.

Caddisfly pupae become available immediately prior to emerging, when the pupae leave their cases and swim rapidly to the surface, where they must eventually break through the surface film in order to emerge. During their frantic swim and their subsequent struggle at the surface, the caddisfly pupae are conspicuously available.

Some of the newly hatched adult caddisflies do not always escape quickly to the sanctuary of the shore. Many of the newly emerged adults are unable to expand their wings during emergence and must resign themselves to an unexpectedly brief life. Even those that do emerge successfully first rest upon the surface or flutter about ineffectually, often for several minutes, before taking flight. Once again they are readily available as a food source, and depending on the interests of the fish, the angler should either imitate the adult on the surface or first imitate the rising pupa.

In many respects mayfly nymphs are not nearly as conspicuous as the caddisfly larvae, even though in general they are more mobile. Some species inhabit rocks, some weeds, and others burrow into whatever substratum they can utilize. Those nymphs that live among the weeds and rocks can be startled from their sanctuary and subsequently expose themselves to the browsing trout while darting to a new location. Each nymph, regardless of its habitat, does become available as it swims to the surface or toward nearby vegetation prior to emerging. Even the burrowing nymphs, which are consumed infrequently, become highly available when they emerge. The burrower *Ephemera simulans* is an interesting example. The average number of *simulans* once found in the stomachs of trout during an emergence was 507, with a high in one 18-inch trout of 789!

The newly emerged mayfly adult is, of course, available as it rests on the surface prior to taking flight. Later, however, when the female spinner falls to the surface after having deposited her eggs, the adult mayfly is the most readily available. The female lies there helpless, exhausted, unable to resume flight. The trout at this time are quite ready to cruise beneath the surface and in random fashion consume massive quantities of these spent spinners.

The midges, just as with the mayflies and the caddisflies, are most vulnerable during the emergence process. Some larvae are free-swimming and thus readily available, but it is primarily the pupae upon which the trout have the greatest opportunity to prey. During their ascent to the surface and their brief period of emergence, the pupae are totally unprotected. They wriggle and twitch and pause frequently to rest.

Once they arrive at the surface, the pupae will expend considerable effort in positioning themselves. They twist and turn, then hang vertically before lying in the surface film itself, only to resume the process again. Eventually the pupae lie within the film, and the adult emerges onto the surface from a split in the pupal skin. Occasionally the pupae actually accumulate at the surface of the lake, unable to emerge for many hours, thus providing trout with easy, prolonged feeding.

Aquatic organisms are generally well camouflaged, and unless they betray their presence by moving or attempting to swim away from browsing trout, they can often be difficult for trout to find. Obvious aquatic animals like snails frequently stand out as they grasp a

Stillwater food forms for trout: above a damselfly nymph; below a dragonfly nymph.

contrasting piece of vegetation. The same holds true for larger caddisfly larvae with their cases waving in the pulsing lake water. But in general it is when an insect emerges that he becomes most available, not merely in terms of numbers, but in terms of vulnerability as well. And it is these moments of extreme vulnerability that can provide the angler with incredible fishing experiences.

In addition to the process of emergence, there is one other extremely important means by which food items become available to trout—the fall of airborne *terrestrial insects* onto the lake's surface. If one defines these terrestrial insects as including the adult forms of aquatic insects, such as adult midges, mayflies and caddisflies, in addition to the purely terrestrial insects such as ants, bees, spiders, grasshoppers and beetles, then terrestrial insects are one of the most important food sources throughout the entire angling season. It remains for the angler to use his powers of observation to determine when and where the terrestrial insects are becoming available. In addition to the more obvious hatch of aquatic insects or even the return of adult aquatic insects to lay eggs, perhaps a fall of winged ants or a sudden increase in the ladybug population might also result in the appearance of terrestrial insects on the lake's surface.

Late in the angling season, when many of the aquatic organisms that emerge have already done so, the population of this somewhat temporary source of food is at its minimum. The newly hatched insects are too small to be of value to the trout, who must await their growth before once again utilizing them as a food source. Thus the presence of the purely terrestrial insects on the water can be of particular importance to the trout whose food supplies may well be dwindling as the season progresses. In some lakes this does not happen, primarily because of the abundance of permanent bottom-food items such as shrimp, but in most it does.

In some instances terrestrial food sources have been known to account for at least half of the trout's diet during one or more months of the season, and nearly all of its daily food consumption during sporadic occasions of superabundance of terrestrial organisms!

Although purely terrestrial insects may be washed into a lake, the primary means by which they are introduced into the surface layers of the water is from the air. When air masses stabilize and the cold air sinks, the insects fall onto whatever lies below them. This generally occurs at night above areas that are cooler than their surroundings, such as cold trout lakes.

If wind and waves come up on a lake, the different insects are mixed so that there are no longer significant differences between the different sections of the lake. The drifting insects are not distributed uniformly across the lake's surface, however. In very exposed lakes the breaking waves will create foam, which has a tendency to form streaks. The drifting insects are then caught in the streaks and move with these foam lines. Eventually the insects will be swept to the windward shore where they can be washed onto the land if the shoreline is flat and shallow; if the shore is steep they will accumulate until they sink. Amazingly, some insects can stay afloat in the surface film for five days or longer.

Along steep shorelines a phenomenon occurs that anglers can readily capitalize on. The drifting insects in this case do not actually become pressed along the bank, but instead remain along a surface stretch called a drift line, usually some distance from shore. When incoming waves strike the shore, "echo waves" are formed, which are propelled back out into the lake. A

Connecting Leader Material

THE BLOOD KNOT has become the most commonly used means of connecting pieces of monofilament leader material, either to construct an entire leader or to add pieces of tippet to an otherwise knotless leader. It has the advantages of producing a small, neat connection, and allowing the leader material to extend in a straight line from each side of the knot. Here's how it's done.

Cross the tag ends of the two lines to be joined, thus forming an X. Allow about eight inches of each line to extend beyond the point at which they cross.

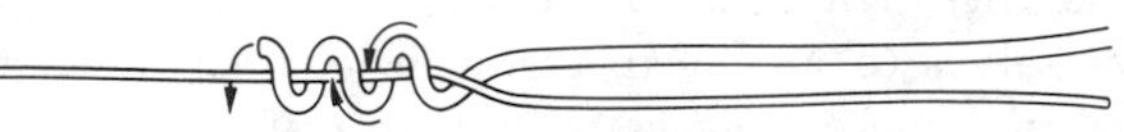

Hold the lines firmly together with your thumb and forefinger at the point at which they cross. Wrap the tag end of one line five times around the standing part of the

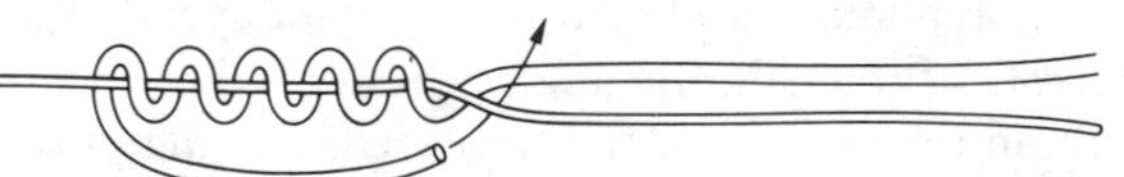

other. Then pass the same tag end between the two lines on the other side of the X formed in the first step.

Reverse your grip and use your other hand to wrap the other tag end five times around the other standing line.

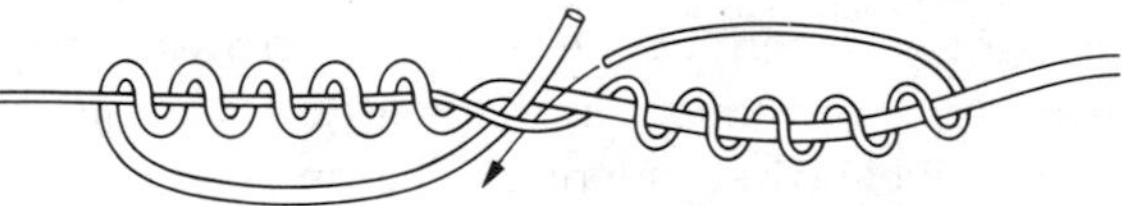

Insert the second tag end through the same opening in the twists that holds the first tag end. One tag end will be going through from top to bottom; the other tag end should pass through in the opposite direction.

Moisten the wraps with your mouth, then grip the standing part of one line in your left hand and the standing part of the other line in your right hand. Unless the lines are extremely light, the knot should be seated by jerking the

two standing parts away from each other. In the case of lighter lines (less than ten-pound test), you will have to pull steadily to avoid snapping them. When the knot is correctly seated, trim the tag ends close to the knot.

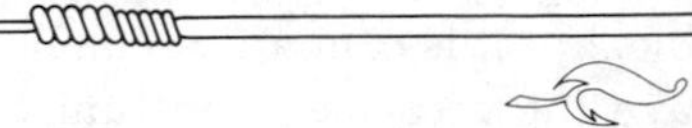

point out from the shoreline is established where the drifting insects are being pushed equally from both sides, so there they remain. Fish in search of food will find this situation highly attractive. No doubt some of these insects, being buffeted from both sides, sink beneath the surface, thus enabling the trout to feed upon them without actually rising all the way to the surface. Dead-drifting a wet-fly pattern beneath such a foam line can be very productive on those windy days that often prevent the use of other techniques.

Lake-Fishing Techniques

THE TECHNIQUES EMPLOYED in lake fishing revolve around the fundamental philosophy that the imitation must be presented where the fish expect to see it and with the characteristic motion of the natural organism itself. If these two basic considerations are mastered, then successful angling is virtually assured. Of course, the angler must also use a good, well-designed imitation of the appropriate size, shape and color.

Freshwater shrimp abound in many lakes that hold trout, and they are an important food source for the fish.

Leaders should vary in length from 9 feet to perhaps over 20 feet, with 18-foot leaders being quite common, particularly when fishing at or somewhat beneath a calm, quiet surface. Delicate tippets as small as 7x can be necessary with smaller mayfly nymphs in general and midge pupae patterns in particular. Tippets of this small size do not restrict the natural movements of the pattern during the retrieve, as can larger, heavier tippets. Unless the angler is fishing with large, heavy patterns, or in dangerously weedy water, tippet size will seldom be thicker than 5x.

The choice of fly line is governed primarily by what may be required to assure that the pattern is presented at the necessary depth. Presenting a shrimp pattern deep among the weeds may require a high-density line, while presentation of that same pattern in moderately deep water may require only a sinking-tip or sinking-belly line.

Always keep in mind that the rate at which a fly line sinks must be balanced against the rate at which it is pulled back toward the surface. In this way the pattern can be kept at the desired depth. When fishing emerging nymph or pupa patterns, however, a floating line and a long leader, or in some instances a sinking-tip line, would be appropriate to lift the pattern off the lake bottom and slowly retrieve it back toward the surface.

Fishing at or slightly below the surface, of course, requires a floating line. And in order to avoid an unnecessarily pronounced disturbance at the lake's surface, as light a fly line as is convenient should be used. Unless too strong a wind comes up or the fly pattern is too heavy, a four-weight line is a good choice for fishing the surface of lakes.

I hope you realize by now that a lake is not just a smooth bowl of clear water, quietly waiting for a surface-feeding trout to break the stillness during a mayfly hatch. It's a multilevel, many-splendored thing for the savvy fly fisher who will take the time to break through the surface mirror and plumb the underwater world of the trout of sylvan lakes. For the stream angler, it's another world—for many lake fly rodders, it's the only world.

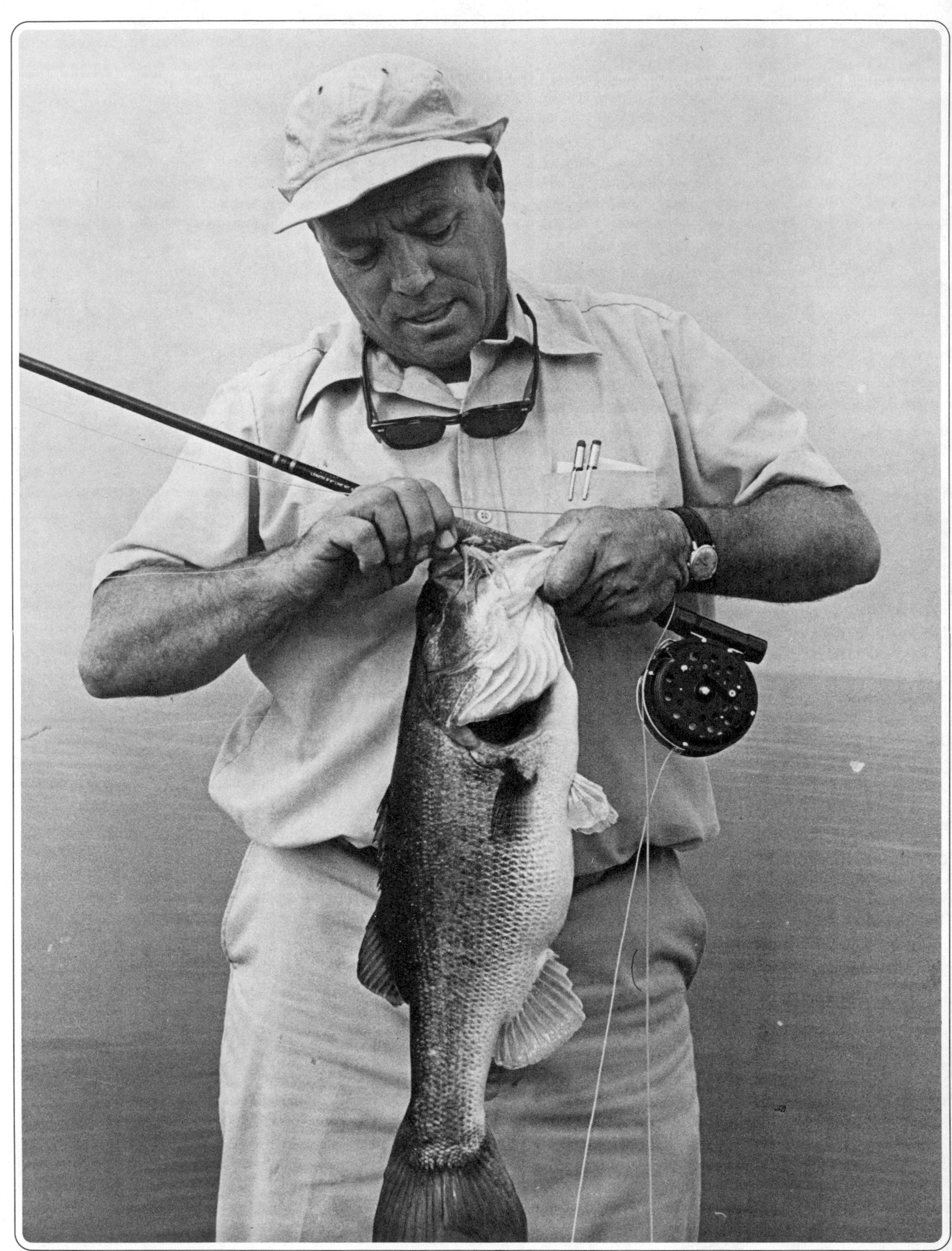

Photo by Lefty Kreh.

Many angling writers still tend to introduce fly-rodding for bass and panfish in the same manner as they might purvey risque French postcards—a bit freaky, even kinky, but something to make-do until the real thing comes along. Utter nonsense. Nearly a century ago anglers were already discovering the delights of bassing with the fly rod, thanks in part to the unfettered flackery of one Dr. James Alexander Henshall, advance agent for the resident bass population of America and author of the much-quoted ode to the bass— "inch for inch, pound for pound . . . the gamest fish that swims." Any fly fisherman who has popped a lunker largemouth in the weeds of a bass lake or outwitted the deep-bodied native smallmouth in a cool Ozark stream quickly becomes a believer—at least, while he's into one on the long rod. The fly rod is especially efficient for bassing because of the repeated casts which can be made with such accuracy and rapidity, and because its length is of considerable utility in negotiating the hazardous beds of weeds, lily pads and brambles usually indigenous to the bass's environment. Bugging for bass or popping for panfish, it's "action central" for the free-wheeling fly rodder.

Chapter 8

Fly-Rodding for Bass and Panfish

Hot Fishing in Warmer Waters

LEFTY KREH

FOR MANY NEWCOMERS to our sport, fly-fishing is synonymous with trout. But not after they finish his chapter! Long before the spinning and spin-casting eels revolutionized angling, the long rod was a familiar ight along bass rivers and lakes in all parts of the coun-ry—especially in the South.

There are times when spin-type equipment and the ssociated spoons, plugs and other paraphernalia do the ob, but for fast and furious fun, and cold efficiency, he fly rod is king. When bass are feeding in extra clear vater or dining on insects or nymphal life, the fly rod is supreme, and for bass in small streams a popping bug or a realistic minnow imitation is deadly.

The fly rod is ideal, too, when pin-point casting is called for—no other tackle can drop a lure so delicately and accurately in the middle of the dimpling surface-rise of a smallmouth sipping mayflies or drifting ants. A fly rod can also throw a popper behind a stump with a left or right curve or skip a bug up to six feet back under an overhanging branch.

Thanks to the variety of fly lines available today, the angler can fish for bass with a fly rod in almost any type of water, from a small farm pond to a broad river. Floating lines are very effective in shallow water up to five feet deep and can be used with moderate success in water as deep as eight feet. In depths greater than that, floating lines will usually produce poorly.

Unless the current is very strong, you can fish to ten feet with a sinking-tip line; and with a lead-core head or a fast-sinking line, you can fish in lakes 25 or 30 feet deep with ease by using the countdown method, which I will explain later.

Rivers as big as the Susquehanna, which measures almost a mile wide on many of its stretches, are as well suited to fly-rodding for bass as the tiny streams that crisscross the East and Midwest. Weedy waters — Currituck Sound or Lake Okeechobee — are especially suited to fishing with the proper fly tackle, and both Southern and Northern waters fall within the realm of fly-casting. I've taken bass in Canada and as far south as Cuba and Mexico, so the bass fisherman can depend upon the fly rod for results.

Before we discuss how to use fly-fishing gear for bass and where to go, let's examine what kind of fly tackle is available and where it should be used.

Fly Rods for Bass

Bass can be taken on fly rods made from bamboo, fiberglass or graphite. For many years the standard bass rod was made of bamboo, measured 8 to 9½ feet long, and tossed one of the old GBF or GAF weight-forward lines. Such a rod was powerful and would do the job in most situations for the person skilled in using it, but it was also heavy and tiring to cast. Yet even today, some anglers prefer bamboo over the synthetics.
the synthetics.

For most bass anglers, the arrival of the lighter fiberglass rods was a welcome change and probably helped convert many fishermen who could neither afford bamboo nor tolerate its weight. Fiberglass had a number of attributes for bassing that bamboo did not possess. Glass rods could be used all day in the rain and forgotten come evening — a careless fisherman could take one home and stash it in a closet or locker without harming the rod. Rods in a boat get banged around frequently and fiberglass was able to take such punishment. Bamboo would have suffered greatly from such treatment.

And day-long casting with glass required less effort, which many fly fishermen found more enjoyable. Today, fiberglass rods are even better, and a well-designed one will do a superb job for the bass-bugger.

Graphite, which has emerged over the past few years, is especially well suited to most bass-fishing situations. First of all, it's light. Also, because the strong tip can turn over line so rapidly, a graphite rod develops a tighter loop for the average angler, which reduces air resistance and results in a longer cast than the same effort would produce when using either bamboo or glass And that tight loop helps drive a bug or fly in along the bank when overhanging tree limbs interfere.

The bass fisherman must constantly pick up between 20 and 40 feet of line and leader. That repeated motion is tiring, especially if one uses a soft-action rod that bends deeply before loading enough line to raise the fly or bug from the surface. The quick, powerful stiffness of graphite, however, makes the pick-up effortless and results in a better performance by most casters.

Graphite has one liability that must be recognized it requires as much or more care than bamboo. The fibers are easily damaged if the rod is slapped sharply against a sharp edge, such as a boat seat, a gunwale or a rock. Still, I believe if most fishermen had their choice of a fly rod for bass fishing, in most situations they would select a well-designed graphite over the bamboo or fiberglass.

The angler should give serious consideration to the length of a bass rod. I can think of no fishing situation where a rod of less than 8 feet would be advantageous so I'd recommend that as a minimum length. For general use a 9-footer is about right. If you intend to purchase a well-designed graphite rod, you may want to select one longer than 9 feet — even as long as 10 feet

There are several outstanding advantages to the longer rods; especially those made of graphite, in which the wall diameter is relatively small and does not create the air resistance inherent in rods made of the other materials. If you wade, you'll be able to lift more line off the water for the backcast with less effort with a long rod You'll also be able to keep the backcast up better. If you fish from a sitting position in a boat or canoe, the longer rods — those 9 feet or more in length — will work for you equally as well.

Longer rods also permit better manipulation of the fly For example, if you fish the Everglades or Okeechobee' pasture fields where the surface is grass with pockets of open water scattered about, you'll be able to drop the fly in those open pockets and move it right or left with the long rod. And you can flip it out easier for the backcast. If you wade for smallmouths, you can manipulate a streamer better with a long rod so that it travels into those places you feel a fish may be lurking. There are other advantages to longer rods, but it should be obvious that short rods will hamper the angler in most fishing areas.

In my estimation, the color of a fly rod is important When trout fishing, I've determined that keeping chrome plated hemostats, spring-wound retrievers and other bright objects hidden underneath my wading jacket results in more strikes. I also feel that yellow, white or brightly finished rods with a high gloss, such as some of the new epoxy finishes, are a handicap.

On a bright day stand some distance from an angler who has such a rod, and before you notice anything

Continued on page 8

Under favorable conditions, and especially when insects are hatching from the weeds, large trout such as this may be encountered over weed beds. Your ability to catch them in such situations may depend on your ability to analyze the lake you're fishing, and you can get a good start right now by checking Ron Cordes' chapter on lake fishing, starting on page 70. Lake-fishing has a certain appeal that's unique to still waters; a set of different challenges with their own great rewards. You'll find some examples of the mysterious moods of stillwater on the following pages. The above photo is by Don Blegen.

Plate 10

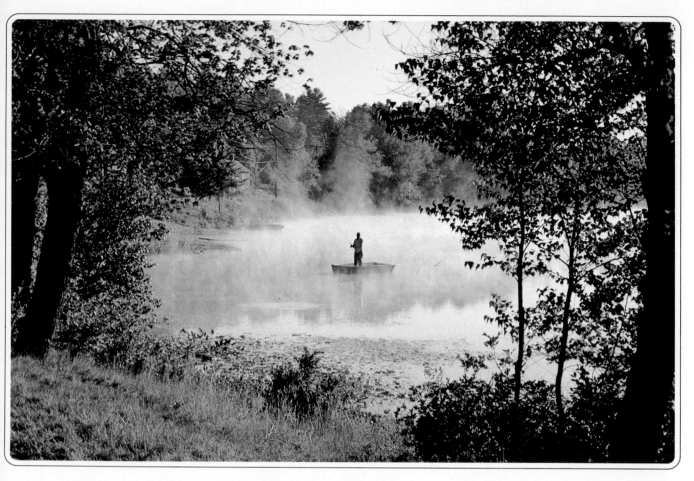

Photos at left and below by Christine Fong. Photo above by Robert L. Peck.

A Snake River bass.

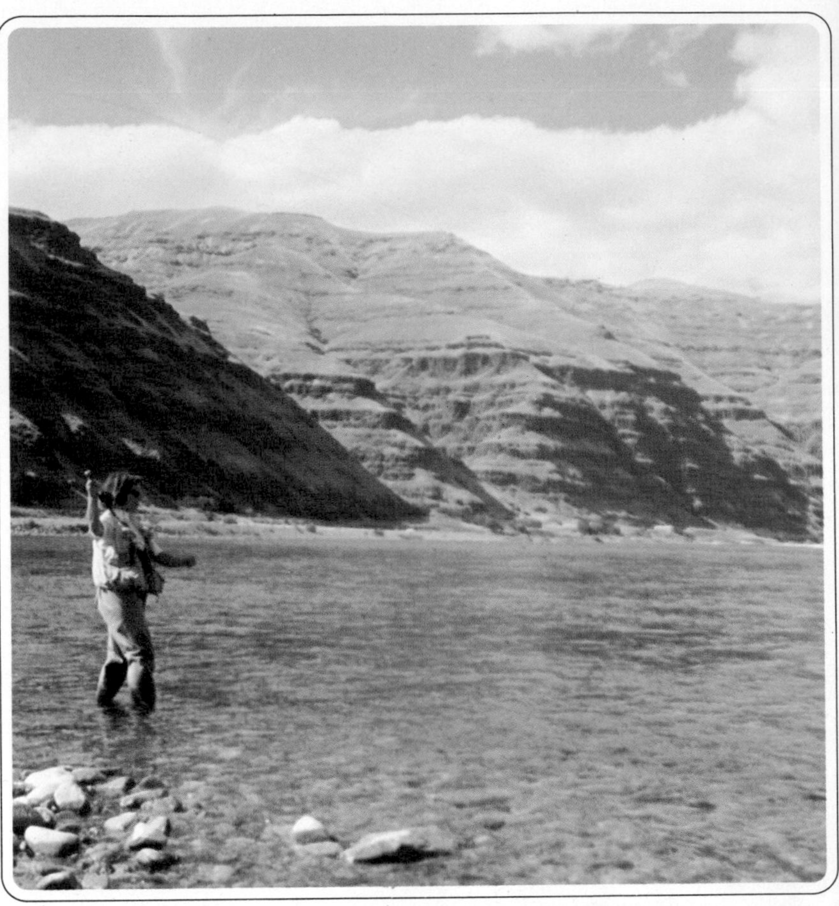

Smallmouth bass water along on the Snake River in Idaho.

Classic bass water.

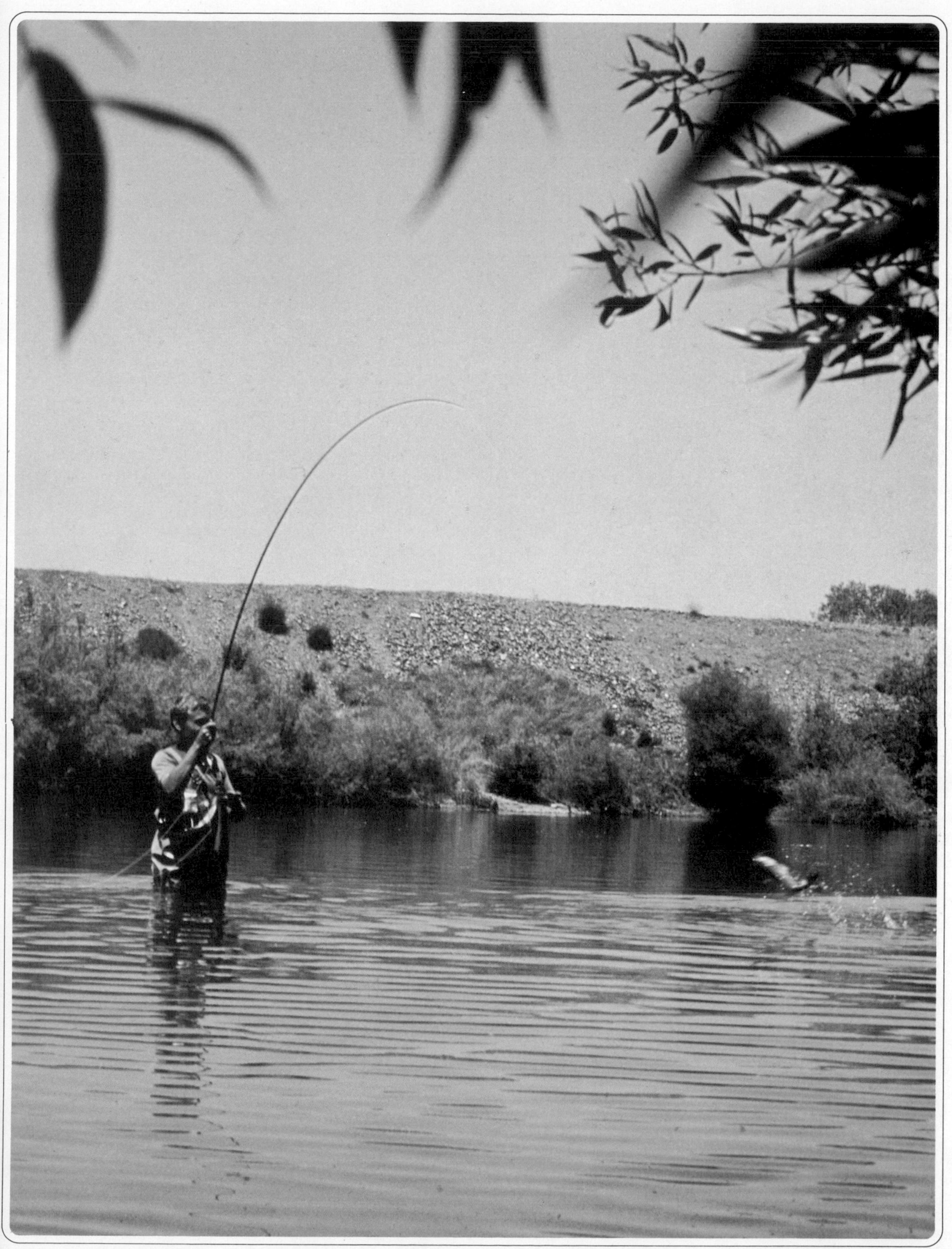

An angler wrestles with a smallmouth that took a surface bug. Photo by Michael Fong.

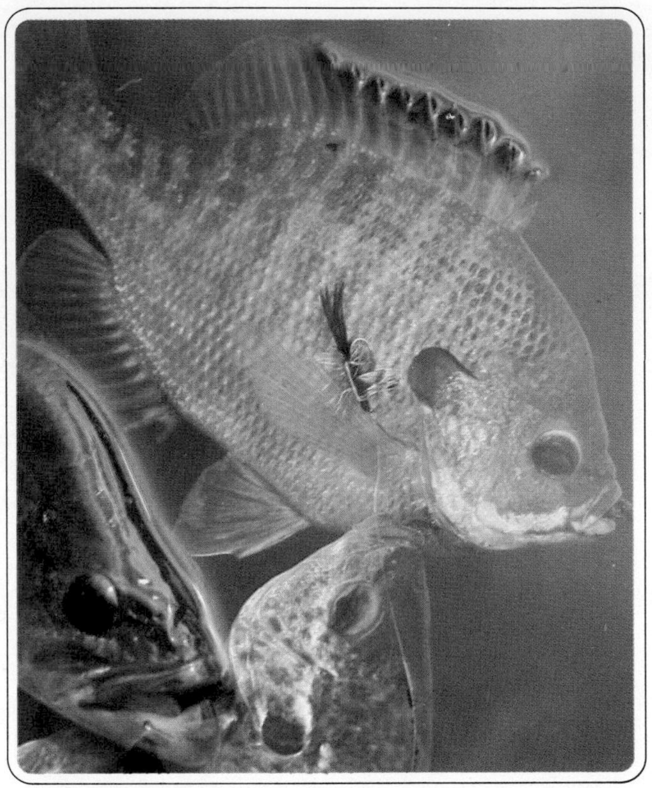

Bluegill and bass taken on a deeply fished nymph, ample evidence that your bass and panfishing can be as sophisticated as you want to make it. Above photo by Dan Blanton. The photo below shows a sculpin, about twice lifesize. These are a baitfish common to many smallmouth streams that can be imitated by a variety of fly patterns, but most commonly a Muddler Minnow. Sculpin photo by Thomas Taylor.

In the photo at right, we're in still another realm of the fly-rodder's world—on the bonefish flats—and looking back from the bow of the skiff to watch the guide poling the boat. This shot is by Lefty Kreh, who also took the inset photo of the bonefish, one of the fly fisherman's ultimate quarries.

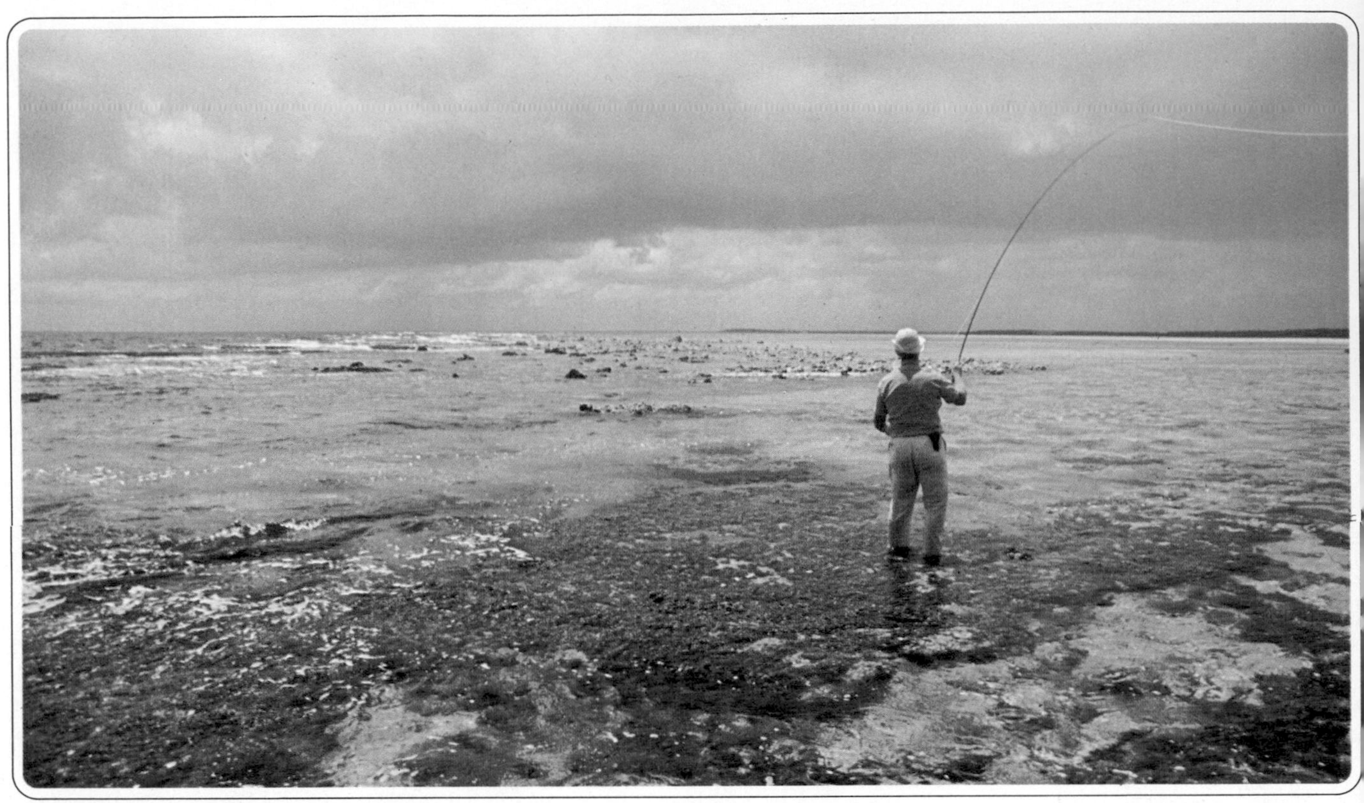

The shallower areas of saltwater coves and estuaries are all prime spots for the fly rodder. Photo by Lefty Kreh. Below is a representative sample of saltwater streamers, most of which are simple ties. Also shown are two reels suitable for saltwater that represent extremes of cost: the relatively inexpensive Scientific Anglers reel at left, and the relatively costly Seamaster at right. Photo below by Mark Sosin.

else, you'll see that rod. Even a dark brown or black rod with a high gloss will flash alarmingly. Perhaps the best colors for rods are those that are dark and have subdued finishes.

The reel seat on a fly rod is important: it holds your reel for casting and fighting the fish. The locking rings on most reel seats slowly loosen and have to be constantly tightened. Most bass anglers I know slip their hand down toward the reel as they cast, and their fingers come in contact with the locking rings to make certain they are tight.

I used to think the answer was a set of locking rings with left-hand threads — but they came loose as quickly as the standard threads. Then I got smart. I pulled off the reel seat and reversed it so the rings were behind the reel, and my problems were solved.

You can reverse the existing reel seat on almost all modern rods. Heat the seat with a propane torch which will soften the glue enabling you to pull the reel seat free with a pair of pliers. (Best to first check with the manufacturer of your rod to see if heat will loosen the seat — he'll be able to tell you.) Add more glue to the rod and slide the seat on in reverse.

Anodized aluminum seats are perhaps the best; they are both strong and light. Chrome-plated brass works fine and will last forever with moderate care, but it is heavier than aluminum and usually more expensive.

There should be as many guides on a fly rod as there are feet of rod; that is, a 9-foot rod should have a minimum of nine guides, plus a tip-top. I prefer ceramic bridge guides on the butt section of a bass rod. Carbide steel guides do crack occasionally, and under certain conditions, such as brackish-water fishing, that hard metal will develop line-cutting pores. Ceramic material is subject to cracking under punishment, too, but the guides are mounted in shock-absorbing rings and should last a lifetime if properly handled.

I like a stripper guide (the first guide after the reel on the butt section) that is a minimum of 10 millimeters in diameter, and on larger rods I prefer that it be 12 millimeters. On the entire butt section I suggest bridge guides, simply because they are strong and don't wear quickly.

The tip section should have snake guides. Triple-plated-chrome stainless steel snake guides are best. Some snakes are plated only once and the slick, silvery finish will quickly wear through, so it pays to buy the best available. The size of the snake guides is important, too. They should be large enough to allow the line to flow through them freely when the angler makes his cast.

There is some discussion that single-foot ceramic guides offer more distance. I've experimented considerably with them and have found that ceramics only add distance and reduce line wear if they are used as the tip-top and the butt stripper, where the line makes sharp turns during casting. Tournament casters, who won't give up a foot in distance if they can help it, have come to the same conclusion and use snake guides on the tip section; some, however, do use a ceramic tip-top.

You can check snake guides for wear and look for cracks in ceramic or carbide by pulling a short section of panty hose through each guide. Any woman can tell you how quickly they snag, and they will catch on almost any burr or crack in your guides. (I suggest you do this at home, not on the stream.)

Lines

Fly fishermen of old had one line available to them, a silk line, which would either slowly sink or could be dressed in the hope it would float. Such a line prevented them from taking bass from waters that the modern fisherman can work effectively.

Today the problem is almost the reverse; manufacturers of lines make such a variety of lines that the average angler simply doesn't know which one to use.

Nontapered level lines are used for bass by some anglers in the southern part of the country. Those fishermen scull or use an electric motor to move their boats slowly along a shoreline at a specific distance from the bank. They pick up, make a backcast, drop the rod down, manipulate the bug for a few feet, then repeat the operation. They fish with one hand and manage the boat with the other. Shooting the line for distance is of no interest to them, and for such an effort the level line, which is much less expensive, is actually a good choice.

Double-taper lines were designed primarily for trout and salmon fishing and have little use in bass fishing. However, few anglers realize that the taper of the first 30 feet of a double-taper line is almost identical to that of a weight-forward line.

The weight-forward line is the most useful in bassing, and there are two basic tapers: bug taper and conventional weight-forward. The belly, or heavy portion of line just behind the front taper, is shorter, fatter and heavier in a bug taper than in a conventional weight-forward taper. The bug taper does not cast or turn over in flight as well, and presentation is a little more difficult. But, if you work waters where you retrieve the fly or popping bug very close to the canoe, the bug taper is best, because it requires that less line be extended beyond the rod tip to effectively pick up and shoot a heavy bass bug to the next target. For most bass fishing situations, however, I would suggest the conventional weight-forward line.

Sink Rates of Lines

There are basically six different densities, or sinking rates, available in lines: floating, sinking-tip, slow sinking, fast sinking and lead-core. In most cases the bass fisherman can get by with two or three.

If you fish rivers, farm ponds and shallow lakes, a floating line will be the one used most of the time, and it's the only line to use with popping bugs.

If you fish a deep lake, you'll need a floater for shoreline work, especially in spring and fall and night fishing with poppers, but a sinking-tip line comes in handy to drive a streamer deeper when fish are holding near the bottom.

You will find that an extra-fast-sinking line or even a lead-core shooting-taper may be necessary to drive your lure 10 to 25 feet below the surface where the bass lurk in warmer periods of the year or when you are fishing over deep underwater structures.

Floating lines are easier to cast than the other lines; they lift from the water well and flow smoothly through the air. Sinking-tips don't turn over as nicely, and the faster-sinking lines are tough to get out of the water and keep aloft, as well as being even more difficult to turn over.

Here is a rough guide that may help you select the lines you need for your bass fishing.

Floating lines are best for fishing poppers, flies or streamers in water less than eight feet deep; for taking bass that are feeding on insects floating on the surface, or on dragonflies, damselflies and grasshoppers, and for most fishing in rivers.

Sinking-tip lines are coated for the ten feet or so with a substance that causes the line to sink. The rest of the head and the running portion of line float. That coating permits the fly to be fished deeper, and the rear floating portion aids in lifting the line from the water on the backcast. A sinking-tip line is best for working streamers, nymphs or underwater flies that won't get down with a floating line in shallow lakes or rivers up to ten feet deep.

Fast-sinking line first appeared on the market as Hi-D, a trademarked line developed and sold by Scientific Anglers. (Today, several manufacturers make similar lines under other names.) Until Super Hi-D came along, fast-sinking line went down more quickly than any line but lead-core. It is most useful in deep-water bass fishing. Super Hi-D was developed recently by Scientific Anglers. It sinks almost as fast as lead-core and much better than the fast-sinking line. It also casts well, handles like a regular fly line and will bomb a fly to great depths.

A lead-core fly line is a length of level lead wire, covered with a braided nylon sheath which gives the line great strength. This section, often up to 30-feet long, is attached to a running line of either monofilament or small-diameter level fly line. The lead-core portion is held outside the guides during the false-casting sequence, and when released it drags the thin running-line to the target. It sinks like an anvil and is the best method known to get a fly deep.

With any sinking line it is important to know the depth at which you are fishing your fly. In lakes and deep, calm waters, bass tend to hold at specific depths, depending on temperature, light and other factors. It is especially effective to know that "hovering depth." If your leader is short (and it should be—bass are not leader-shy underwater), and you use the countdown method described below, you can lower your fly to the same working depth on successive casts.

Make your cast, and as the line hits the water, begin a count: "One-thousand-one, one-thousand-two, etc." If your first strike comes on count 14, for example, then repeat that countdown on every cast and you'll be working your fly to almost the same depth each time.

As a guideline to help you unravel the mystery of sinking lines, I'd suggest that for water more than four or five feet deep you may want to use a fast-sinking line; for water 10 to 20 feet with little or no current, the extra-fast-sinking line would be best; and for depths of 20 feet or more, the lead-core is the best answer.

Bass-Rod Reels

ALTHOUGH THERE IS NO particular fly reel required for bass fishing, some types and sizes work better than others for most bass-angling situations. Both the standard single-action and the automatic fly reels can be used, and though these have been described elsewhere, a few points pertinent to the pursuit of bass should be mentioned here.

Single-action reels are lightweight, simple in design and operation, and by far the most popular for most types of fly-fishing.

However, when fishing from a boat, even an experienced caster can get his loose line hung up on the deck, duckboards, gunwales or his own feet. Recently, geared single-action reels have become popular for any type of casting where loose line must frequently be retrieved; the spool turns on a roughly 2-to-1 ratio with each turn of the handle, speeding up loose-line pickup.

Automatic fly reels accomplish this rather efficiently through a spring-operated spool that winds on line when activated by a trigger mechanism. Whether fishing from a boat or from a weedy shoreline, an automatic can be a convenience. However, they're heavier than similar-size single-action reels—an important consideration if you're planning a long day of continuous casting. Also, there's no real drag-mechanism on most automatics, just the heavy spring. And finally, on most automatics there is room on the reel only for the line itself, with no space for backing. As discussed earlier, backing attached to a fly line not only allows a fish to run beyond the length of the line, it further serves the purpose of giving the line a wider "core" to wrap around, thus minimizing the tight "curls" that a fly line's "memory" builds up when it's wound onto a small-diameter spool.

All in all, a single-action reel large enough to take the heavier line often used for bass-fishing, plus some backing, should do the job for most fly rodders.

Leaders

The nearly invisible connection between the fly line and the fly is the nylon monofilament leader. Effective bass leaders are fairly simple and easy for anyone to tie, certainly far less complex than tapered leaders for trout.

Bass are not leader shy and, except when the water is calm and extremely clear, they rarely notice a fly line falling on the surface. Therefore, I feel that leaders should be kept relatively short. For floating lines, a leader should never be longer than nine feet, and usually a six- to seven-foot leader is better. On all my sinking lines, where I am not casting directly over spooky fish, I use a three-foot leader, never more than four feet, which keeps the fly close to the sinking line and drives it deeper. Longer leaders buoy the fly too far above the line.

If you must cast a bug beneath overhanging brush, a short leader is infinitely easier to tuck low and will drop a bug yards back under a leafy shelf. A long leader tends to stand up as it turns over at the end of the cast, and the fly may hit in the brush.

In the wind, the final moments of the cast can cause a long leader to fold back on itself. It is also easier to roll pickup for the backcast with a sinking line if the leader is short—you simply have less line and leader to remove from the water when readying for the backcast. In almost all situations shorter leaders will let you work more effectively, and the bass don't seem to mind.

Monofilament comes in all colors, and some anglers prefer one over another. An important factor in successful fishing is to have confidence in your tackle—and if you think a certain shade of leader is vital, then that's the color you should be using. However, I've caught bass on all shades of leaders, from brilliant yellow and orange through brown, green, black and clear, and I'm convinced that bass and panfish see all leaders, but ignore them. I think the color of your leader means little; it's how the fly acts on the end of the leader that's important.

There are two types of monofilaments that you can use to build leaders—limp and stiff. There are still some fishermen who cling to the belief that a stiff butt section and a limp tippet is the right combination, but most modern anglers feel that a continuously limp leader will permit better transmission of energy through the unrolling line so that the force of the cast may pass through the leader and turn over the fly properly.

Drag in the water is not a factor as it is in trout fishing. In fact, a fly dragging on the surface often encourages a bass or panfish to strike, so the care needed in leader construction for trout can be pretty much ignored for bass and panfish.

For almost any bass-fishing situation, a butt section that tests 25 pounds is more than enough, and most of the time a butt of 20 pounds will turn over better, even with a heavy bug. Once you've determined what strength you want for the butt section, then add sections, making each one shorter than the previous one until you have arrived at the total length of leader you want. This simple method will allow you to build good bass and panfish leaders.

If you fish in weedy waters, where pockets of open areas are surrounded by heavy vegetation, or near lily pads and line-catching growth, a tapered leader with knots will collect debris and spoil many casts. In such situations I use a very short leader, say four feet, even with a floating line, and make the entire leader from a single strand of 12- to 20-pound-test monofilament, depending on the size of the fish and the conditions.

Check your leader constantly. A nick in the leader can reduce the strength of monofilament by as much as 90 percent. If you feel any nicks or abrasions, it's wise to simply replace that section.

And I sharpen each hook before I put it in my vise and check the point after each fish I catch.

Hooks

With the exception of a few brackish coastal waters, all bass- and panfishing is done in fresh water, so bronzed hooks are okay.

For popping bugs I prefer 3XL (or even 4XL) hooks with a hump shank, which are special bug hooks available from tackle stores or through catalogs. That hump prevents the bug body from twisting on the shank.

Wright and McGill makes dandy Keel Hooks—designed to ride with the hook *up*—for flies that are to be fished in weedy places, and every serious bass fisherman should have a few patterns tied on them. For streamers I prefer Mustad's #9672 3XL or 3906B, and for nymphs and wet flies I like the Mustad #3906B. And I sharpen each hook before I put it in my vise and check the point after each fish I catch.

Knots

You'll need only a few knots to fish well for bass and panfish, and you'll find illustrations of them throughout this book. I'll suggest a few which are especially important for handling those big bass.

A nail knot (page 86) is almost always used to attach the monofilament butt section of the leader to the fly line, however, I prefer to attach the butt section to the fly line with the needle knot, in which the monofilament enters the hollow core of the line point and is secured with a nail knot about a half inch from the line's end. This eliminates knots hanging up in line-guides or grass. The nail knot can also be used to tie the backing to the end of the fly line.

Epoxy splices can be okay — if they are strong enough. I've checked many on my line-testing machine and have found that only one or two types are as strong as a nail knot, so if you do use an epoxy splice to connect leader to line, be sure and test the final connection.

I use a surgeon's knot to connect the various sections of monofilament to form a tapered leader, but the improved blood knot is also excellent.

You'll only need to know one other knot — to tie the tippet to the fly — and any one of several will do the job: the improved clinch knot, Palomar, Jansik Special, and the Crawford or Maxima are all good choices.

Before you tighten any knot, lubricate the line to make the job easier and the knot more secure. Then carefully draw the knot up tight.

Bass Bugs

Popping bugs for bass and panfish, which usually are made from balsawood, cork or plastic, must be attractive to the fish, make a good noise and be easy enough to cast so the angler can place them where he desires. Some poppers fail to meet those specifications, and perhaps the worst drawback to commercially tied bugs is that they are grossly overdressed — so much so that they are tough to cast, won't float well and miss fish on the strike.

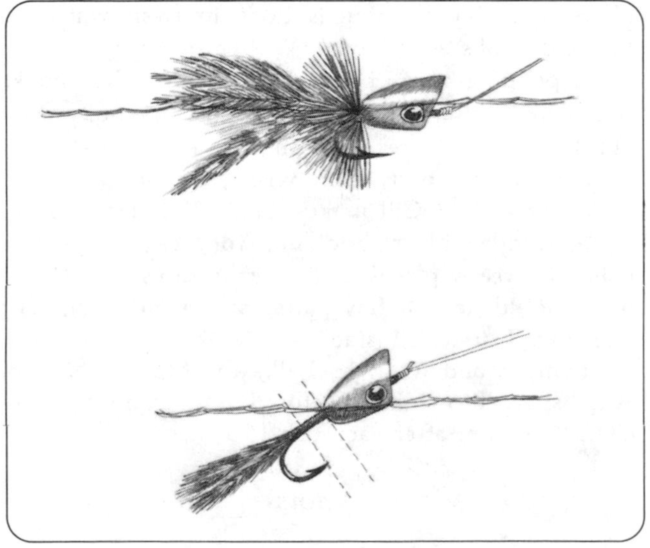

Closed- vs. open-gap bug designs. Illustration by James Sulham.

The bug's functions are basically determined by the design of the front of the face. There are three fundamental designs and all can be useful.

The most popular is the concave, or cup-face, bug in which the front of the bug is indented. When the angler jerks on the line, the cup gathers in water and causes an unusually loud sound for such a small lure. When extra noise is needed the cup-face is a good one, and it can be manipulated to produce more noise with less motion than the other two types. (Making noise with a popper is often overrated, anyway. Bass and panfish take things from the surface that they assume are good to eat. Such foods make very little noise, and a noisy bug is only an asset when you need to "call" bass that may be some distance away, under an obstruction or back in the brush during high water.)

If you fish in a strong current, such as in a river, the cup-face bug is much more difficult to lift from the surface for the backcast, especially if you have much line out. The cup-face bug frequently makes a loud "whooshing" sound, too, when lifted from the water on the cast — a sound that can frighten fish for some distance. It is a poor design for general-purpose bass fishing.

The straight or flat-face bug is a design with a straight front, usually tapering a bit from the top toward the rear. It can be manipulated so it makes almost as much noise as a cup-face type but will perform better in fast currents. And making a good pickup with a flat-face bug on a long line usually is not a problem.

On a slanted flat-face bug it is vital that the face be at right angles to the hook. If it is canted to one side, the bug will twist in the air and spoil the presentation.

The other type of popper design is the slider, which is a bullet-shaped bug that makes little noise when worked on the surface. It is a wonderful imitation of a struggling minnow, and when fished over bass that are in extremely clear water or are normally very wary, a quiet-working slider is often the most effective bug to use.

There is another bass bug that is totally different — the deerhair bug — and many people feel that such hair bugs increase their chances for hooking onto a bass, for the softer material fools the fish into holding on long enough for the angler to strike.

Hair bugs, however, have their faults. When they start to soak up water (and all do sooner or later) they become very heavy and tough to cast — and they are less buoyant on the water and perform poorly.

I don't think hair bugs are a great advantage, and I rarely use them, but there are a few places where they will out-perform other types of lures.

If frogs are prevalent in your area and bass feed on them, a hair frog with wires in the legs to give a swimming action is a deadly lure. And if you fish waters where boat docks exist (a favorite place for bass to hide in ambush) and you drop a hard bug on the dock before pulling it in the water, you alert the fish. The hair bug, however, can be lightly placed on the dock and pulled off without alarming the fish.

Sometimes you'll need a large bug, one that really packs water and makes lots of noise—the trouble is that a big bug is hard to cast. You can solve that problem and several others by making your own bugs. To build a big bug that is easy to cast, make the face portion large, then immediately taper the rear of the bug to a point, which eliminates much weight but retains the big noise-making face.

A good popper must sit on the water properly. Many commercial models have short hooks, and the points hang directly under the body. A fish must swallow the entire bug to be impaled on the hook.

It is much better to build a bug with an extra-long hook shank (3XL or 4XL) which places the bend and point of the hook well behind the body. Such a bug will sit in the water with the hook lower than the bug and regardless of the angle at which the fish approaches, it will contact the hook point first, increasing your chances on the strike.

The tail of a popper is extremely important. Overdressed tails make casting difficult, and such lures plop heavily when they hit the surface and don't work well in the water. Extra frills tend to underwrap the hook, too, spoiling the presentation.

Tails should be simple, sleek in flight with little wound hackle. My favorite material for bass and panfish bugs is squirrel tail. It fluffs out in the water but comes together on the cast. I tie the squirrel tail in at the rear of the bug body, then wrap down the hook shank to the bend, finishing it off with a whip finish. To the angler it may appear too sparse, but bass have given it their approval for years. Such a bug lifts from the water well on the backcast, flows through the air with minimum resistance, and works fine on the surface.

You'll often find leglike segments of rubber bands dangling from a popping bug. If you fish slack waters where the bug will be resting for some time after it has been popped, the rubber bands continue to work and encourage strikes. But don't use bugs that have very heavy rubber legs. They are too stiff for good casting and work poorly in the water. I never use rubber bands on bugs unless fishing in a slack-water situation.

One trick I've learned over the years that I think is important is to paint the faces of *all* your bugs bright yellow. That bright spot allows you to see the bug on overcast days, or back under overhanging brush, or near dusk, one of the best times to use a bug.

The best color for a bug, I believe, is simply whatever color the angler thinks is important. I often have run out of painted bugs and have been forced to build a few in the evening to take with me the next day. I often won't have time to paint those bugs, but the bass grab them as eagerly as the nicely colored ones. I just don't think that bass care what color a bug is; and eyes on bugs make no difference at all, for they lie on top of the body, and a bass never gets to see them. I do believe, however, that a bright yellow face helps you keep track of your lure.

In some weed-filled waters a bug that will not foul in the vegetation is a great asset. Some anglers use Keel Hooks for bugs, and while I am a staunch advocate of Keel Hooks for underwater flies, I have not been able to build a popping bug on a Keel Hook with which I could hook fish well.

You can make weedless bugs in many ways. If you are building your own bugs, one of the easiest methods is to tie in a loop of 15-pound-test monofilament so it protrudes around the point, and the monofilament pushes the bug away from weeds. You also can place two stiff wires in the bug body which project back on either side of the hook to brush away weeds, but you may miss strikes with that rig.

My favorite weedless popper is one designed by Norman Bartlett of Baltimore, who uses a commercial weedless hook with a simple "U" of light, stiff wire which can be purchased in most tackle shops. The weedless hook is installed in a Gerbubble Bug-type popper (popularized by Joe Brooks). As an extra bonus, Norm uses marabou feathers instead of hackle around the rim of the Gerbubble bugs. The marabou continues to wave and swim long after rubber bands would have ceased moving.

Streamers

BASS AND PANFISH are most frequently taken by fly rodders with popping bugs, but underwater flies are gaining in popularity. As more trout fishermen bring their skills with wets, streamers and nymphs to bass and panfishing waters, other anglers are realizing that they have been missing a bet.

Where wary bass are spooked by a popper "thunking" onto the surface, a silent streamer can be extremely effective, and if a specific type of baitfish lives in your bass waters, a realistic imitation of that baitfish will guarantee strikes. The streamer, too, can be moved rather swiftly through the water, and a great area can be searched with the fly, while bass bugs have to be worked slowly, limiting to some degree the amount of water you can cover.

Most streamers are easier to cast than poppers, and if the angler can cast more easily, he will enjoy himself more and be able to fish longer and harder. And weedless streamers are often better designed than weedless poppers, so in many waters you can operate more efficiently with streamer flies than you can with bugs. Of course, the major asset to the streamer is that it can be used to search out fish down deep.

A good streamer, first of all, should be fairly easy to cast. If you can't get it to the fish, the fly has little value.

The Speed Nail Knot

THIS IS THE BASIC KNOT for attaching the butt-section of a leader to the fly line. Hold a small sewing needle in your left hand and hold the tag end of the fly line so it is about

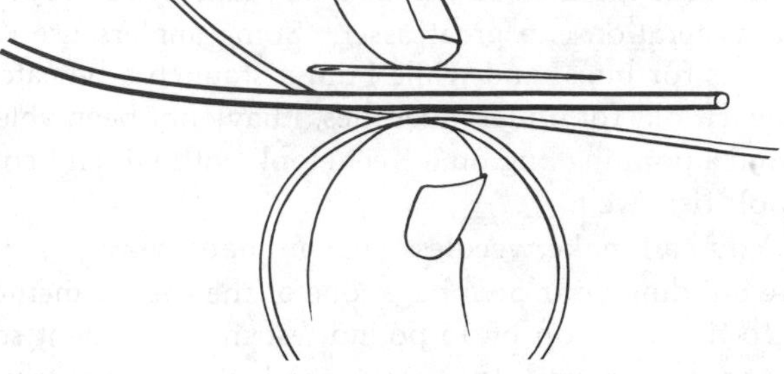

even with the end of the needle. The tag end of the butt section of the leader extends about an inch or so behind the needle while the tag end of the tippet section of the leader

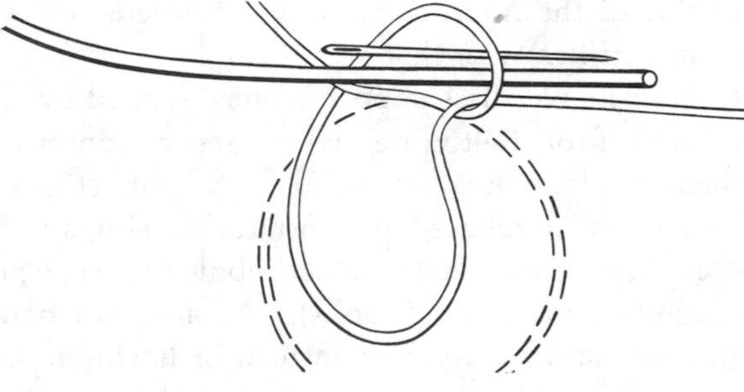

is about an inch or so beyond the tag end of the fly line. The standing part of the leader forms a large loop under the needle.

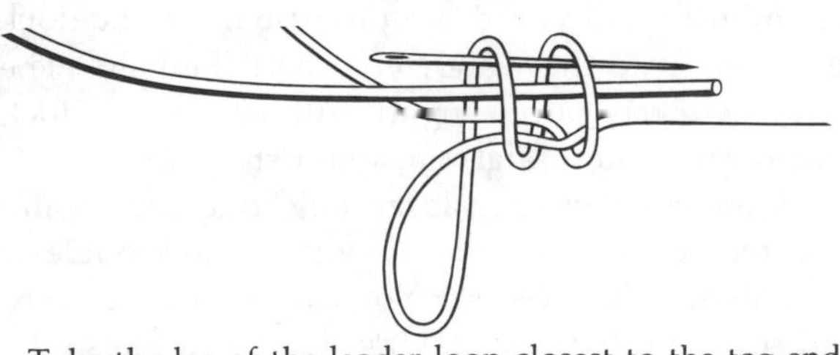

Take the leg of the leader loop closest to the tag end of the fly line in your right hand. Wrap it over the needle, fly line, and leader, working from right to left. Note that the first wrap must cross itself.

After six or seven wraps of the leader around the needle, fly line, and standing part of the leader, grip the wraps securely with the thumb and forefinger of your left hand. Grip the tag end of the leader extending beyond the tag end of the fly line with the thumb and forefinger of your

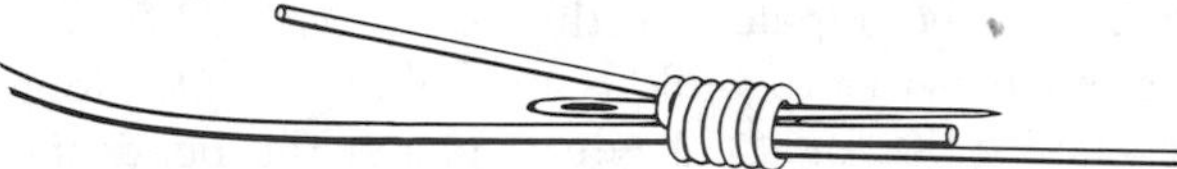

right hand and pull it out smoothly. The entire loop of leader hanging below the needle will feed through the center of the wraps.

Use pliers to grip the heavy tag end of the leader and hold the standing part of the leader firmly in your other hand. Pull both ends until the knot tightens on the needle.

Then slide the needle out from under the wraps and continue the same tightening procedure. Trim the tag ends; the knot can be finished with rubber-based cement if desired.

Generally, commercial streamers are too bulky — people won't buy them if they don't carry a lot of materials. Yet overdressed patterns won't come alive in the water, and fish refuse them.

A wing that underwraps and fouls on the hook will result in a refusal, so well-designed streamers that move through the air without tangling are a must. There are several methods of obtaining that desired characteristic. For example, on a Mickey Finn — a pattern almost all fishermen know, with its yellow, red, and yellow wing — you can reduce fouling in flight by placing the first yellow on the underside of the hook (like an extended beard or throat hackle) and then positioning the red directly above the shank and the yellow on top of that.

Tying a streamer in the Joe Brooks' Blonde style is another answer: the underwing is attached at the rear of the hook, and the top wing or color is placed at the eye, ending about at the rear of the hook. Such a tie eliminates most fouling on the cast.

Examine all the streamers you enjoy using. If there is a way of tying them to reduce fouling, you'll catch more fish. Fouling occurs particularly when you change the direction of your casts a number of times. Remember, too, that long, stiff wings work poorly in the water and cast even worse. Most streamers should be made with hair, feathers or synthetics that undulate with little manipulation.

The sink rate of a streamer is important. You'll need a fly that will barely submerge if you are fishing shallow streams or along a shoreline in spring and fall when big fish cruise the shallows. There a deep-running fly would be on the bottom most of the time. A shallow-working fly can be obtained by adding extra hackling or other buoyant materials, or by using lighter hooks.

In a swift river or a deep-water lake, naturally, you'll want sleek flies that bomb down where the fish are. Weighting the flies can do the job, and proper materials or heavier hooks get the desired results. Whatever you use, consciously think about the sink rates.

There are two basic types of streamers: realistic imitations and attractors. No one can explain why a combination of red and white or red and yellow produce so many bass, but the fish go for both. Another attractor color, long disregarded by all but a few experienced bass anglers, is black. It can be deadly. An orange-and-yellow combination is another attractor pattern that bass go for.

Patterns such as the Black-Nose Dace (an imitation of a small baitfish) are extremely effective if there are baitfish in the water that can be matched with a fly.

Like a good trout fisherman, a competent bass angler will determine the prevalent — and favored — local foods and then tie imitations that realistically suggest those foods to bass. Most of the time, realistic patterns will out-produce attractors, but you should always have some of both.

Bass Characteristics

LARGEMOUTH AND SMALLMOUTH BASS are in the same family, but like brown trout and rainbows, they have individual characteristics that are important to know. The following guidelines are generalized and have exceptions, but they'll prove useful to the beginning fisherman.

•Largemouth bass prefer larger lures than smallmouths; they will attack a hulking six-inch streamer that smallmouths would turn down.

•Largemouths attack brighter-colored attractors more frequently than smallmouths.

•Splayed-wing streamers and flies that move through the water in wide undulations appeal to largemouths; smallmouths prefer smaller flies with a quicker wiggle.

•Largemouths can tolerate waters with a higher average temperature and turbidity than smallmouths, which need clear, rather cool waters. When you find smallmouth populations being replaced by their cousins, the water quality is probably on the downturn.

•In the same environment the smallmouth seems to be able to jump more and give a tougher fight than the largemouth.

•One of the most important factors in smallmouth fishing is to realize they hang around rocks — especially in rivers. Locate a rocky point or drop-off in a lake or find a boulder in a river with current swirling around it, and you will have located the habitat of the smallmouth. Smallmouths are best taken underwater by flies that realistically imitate local foods. Flies that imitate crayfish, small minnows and sculpins are effective.

FISHING SITUATIONS AND TECHNIQUES

Bassing the Streams

THOUSANDS OF SMALL STREAMS crisscross the Eastern and Midwestern portions of the country. Most harbor bass and panfish, and fly-rodding is one of the most effective methods of fishing for them. Most people wade such streams, since they are often too shallow for a boat. Try not to wade downstream when possible, for you take the risk of carrying debris and cloudy water to the quarry and alerting it to your arrival. You'll catch many more fish with slow, careful stalking and by wading against the current. Wet flies and streamers have their place on small streams, but small poppers dressed on #8-12 hooks are your best weapon.

Fishing on large rivers requires a different technique than fishing on a lake. A popping bug on a river should be cast and then worked almost constantly for maximum results. On a lake you might allow the bug to sit for a full minute before bringing it back to life.

Streamers in lakes must be manipulated more than streamers on rivers, where active currents will work the fly to some degree. For river bassing the best retrieve with a streamer is across, and as the fly is swept downstream, a gentle bobbing of the rod tip up and down imparts a swimming motion to the streamer. Recover any slack that accumulates during the drift so you can strike properly, and at the end of each cast let the fly hang for a few moments before lifting it out of the water — often that's when the strike will occur.

On rivers you will discover small areas that will consistently hold larger fish — many of those locations will be no larger than a bathtub. But such pockets will produce repeatedly, and you should remember exactly where you take each fish. While knowing where you have taken fish is vital on rivers, it also is nearly as important on lakes, although you must then relate the hot spot to time and conditions. A sure place on a lake for a monster bass in early spring is not going to be much good in the dead of summer but might be great in the fall when waters cool.

Riffles and their edges are always hot spots on rivers — they are the feeding lanes that bring the minnows and other food to the bass. Be sure to work those spots. Often the best cast there is made at the very upstream top of the riffle, where the funneling effect begins.

Whether you fish running or still water, constantly check your fly to be certain that it has not collected debris or vegetation, which will spoil the presentation. And if the front portion of a popper begins to sink, it will be impossible to manipulate. Look for that problem, and as soon as it begins to occur, either clean the tip section of the line or dress the popper so it will float.

Bassing the Lakes

IN LAKES THE FLY ANGLER should fish the same way that experienced plug fishermen go after bass. They work structures and different water levels and learn the daily feeding patterns of bass.

What works for them will work fo‹ you. In the spring when the water temperature is in the high 50's, lake bass move to the shallows to spawn. They remain there until the temperature reaches the high 60's, at which point you should start looking for them in waters adjacent to the depths. As summer heats the lakes, the bass hover above the thermocline (that layer separating the deeper cold water from the warmer water above), which may be from depths of 15 to 25 feet. Then is the time to switch to Super Hi-D or lead-core shooting-tapers and work rocky points that drop off into the deep. Use a depth finder and locate underwater structure, too. Then swim your streamer or crayfish imitations around those areas with the lead-core or faster-sinking lines and you'll often be rewarded.

Regardless of the type of bug you use and the type of water you fish, you will catch more fish if you retrieve properly. The common tendency is to manipulate the bug by flipping the tip of the rod, which causes slack to form in the line after each rod motion. If the bass strikes then, you often miss the fish. But if you keep the tip low, pointing the rod toward the fish, and strip the line with your hand, each motion you give to the line is imparted to the bug. When that type of retrieve is mastered, the line will remain taut from the rod tip to the lure, and you'll miss few strikes.

Fishing the Farm Ponds

THOUSANDS OF FARM PONDS across the country have been stocked with largemouth bass and panfish, and there are several good rules that will help you fish such water more effectively. Bass roam the shallows early and late in the day and at night, retreating to the depths during midday, so fish for them at the right places at the right time.

In very hot and cold weather bass and bluegill often seek the deepest portion of a pond. If there is a standpipe in the pond for draining off excess water, it is generally located in the deepest hole—and it is also an underwater structure. Fish streamers and nymphs near it.

During the warmer months the bluegills act the reverse of bass, moving to the shallows during the day and going to the depths at night.

In almost all parts of the country bluegills spawn twice a season, and in some areas even a third spawning occurs. Locate their round, white, saucer-shaped beds and drop a small wet fly or nymph there, and you'll be rewarded with an instant strike.

Night-fishing with flies is almost always useless for panfish, but it can be deadly for bass. Night-fishing is most productive during the warmer months, and experienced anglers agree that those dark-of-the-moon nights are best. While it is difficult to predict what part of the night will be best, just before dawn is generally tops in the very warmest periods, simply because the water has cooled off during the night.

Popping bugs will take bass at night, but bulky wet flies that "push" the water are much better, and darker colors seem to out-fish lighter ones—at least I think they do. Know the area you'll fish at night, and instead of working a large section, be content to stay in a familiar, limited stretch where you know every rock and stump. Covering too much water means you're probably fishing too fast.

On a pond, night or day, you'll encounter fewer casting problems if you walk the bank and keep your backcast over the water. For example, if you are right-handed, walk the shoreline so the water is on your right and those line-catching weeds on your left are out of the way.

There are several casts that are particularly suited to bass and panfishing. Because you are frequently working your fly or bug close to shoreline obstructions—logs, rock and fallen trees—you will occasionally hang up your fly. Often you can free it by making a high roll-cast so that the complete line is lifted from the water as it moves toward the fly. When the rolling loop passes *behind* the fly, make a sharp backcast. Because the line and leader are now behind the obstruction holding the fly, it will usually pull free on your backcast.

Many times you'll want to put a fly well back under overhanging limbs—a spot the spin- or plug-caster will rarely be able to reach. For that, use a "grasshopper," or skip-cast, an old and proved technique. Make an extra-hard cast, directing it so that the lure will strike the water about where the outer limbs are above the surface. Be sure to tilt the rod to the side so that it is almost parallel to the water. Because the line is traveling so low and fast, the fly will hit outside the limbs on the surface and skip back under the brush as far as 15 feet.

There are some narrow, tight places we want to throw flies, such as under cypress stumps or between firs on a northern lake. It pays to learn to make a tight-loop cast for such spots.

Speed casting is associated with salt water, but when bass and panfish are chasing minnows, or rising to take emerging nymphs, only a hasty and accurate cast will take them. If you can hit the ring of a rise as soon as it appears, or drop that streamer in front of a bass chasing minnows, you will be rewarded. But it requires practice to be able to cast quickly—and accurately.

Shooting line on the backcast and forward cast is another tool that bass-buggers should learn. Many times you'll work a fly or bug almost to the boat, and then you need to make a hasty, long cast. Make a strong haul on the backcast and let line extend behind you to give you additional weight. Then as you come forward, make another haul and shoot. In that manner you can often pick up a bug that is only 20 feet away and with one cast put it 50 feet or more from you.

Most of the emphasis in this chapter has been on bass, but in general it all applies to panfish as well. Bluegills, crappie and perch live in the same waters as bass and feed on the same basic foods. Scaled-down tackle and bugs that take bass will work for them, too. For panfish a four-, five- or six-weight fly outfit is generally all that is needed.

At first it was just stunting, they said. A place for everything and everything in its place—and the salt seas were certainly not the place for the delicate little fly rod. But why then, year after year, were more and more fly rodders going down to the sea in shorts to wade the flats, fish the jetties, skiff over the reefs, and generally ply their arcane craft in such vast and unfriendly waters?

Was this really fly-fishing's "last frontier," as so many were claiming, and if so, why?

Fly anglers were discovering that the fly rod was a terribly efficient tool for big water and big fish, whether it was striped bass in San Francisco Bay, foraging schools of bluefish off Cape Cod or bonefish in the Florida Keys. For the quick, repeated casts often necessary to intercept a bonefish or a surf-scrounging striper, the long rod soon proved its inherent value. And for the play and fight that stir the blood, the lethal, built-in leverage of the fly rod quickly made believers of the harbor docksters waiting to scoff at the returning fly rodder—when they saw hundred-pound-plus tarpon in the skiff's dry-well.

Matching the far horizons beyond, saltwater fly-rodding is certainly on a larger scale—part of its glamour, we say—but it still comes back to the lone angler and his target fish, with little contrivance in between to mechanize their duel in the sun. Saltwater fly-fishing has come of age, an exciting change-of-pace pursuit that is now firmlv fixed as a part of the fly fisherman's art.

Chapter 9

Fly Fishing in Saltwater

The Fly Rodder's Third World

MARK SOSIN

SALTWATER FLY-FISHING was in its infancy only 20 years ago, but now the word is getting around. It can be inexpensive, easily accessible, and, most of all, exciting fishing—as anyone who's wrestled a powerful striped bass or cast to a skittish bonefish can tell you. In recent years, increasing numbers of fly fishermen have begun to explore the angling potential of our coastlines, and you can too.

Learning to fish a fly in salt water not only adds a new and challenging dimension to the sport, but it can also make you a better all-around fly fisherman in the process. The reason is simple. Light-wand enthusiasts on the marine scene have developed their own set of techniques; they don't have to trip over traditions that sometimes limit the thinking and performance of their brethren who focus their attention solely on trout and salmon and other freshwater species. When you blend the best of both worlds, the total effect is much more rewarding.

There are differences. When you work over a fish in a stream, you usually have ample time to change flies, figure out the best approach, and contemplate the situation. Even a bank-hugging largemouth in a lake or pond has laid claim to a stationary feeding station near a log or under the lip of a lily pad. But saltwater critters are usually on the move. If you happen to see the fish, you often only have seconds to get a fly in front of it. If you are casting blind, you must learn to read a different type of water and look for another set of signals.

Then there are the tides. Predators have a rhythm for feeding and, in salt water, part of this rhythm is often tied directly to the stage of the tide. Fish may concentrate in one area during a certain stage of the tidal pattern and then suddenly disappear until the conditions have run full cycle and the tide returns. Since most tidewater is not confined by narrow banks, the fish can be anywhere not restricted to a few deep pools or the tail end of a run as in the case of stream fish.

Wind can be another problem. Trees along the banks of a stream or next to the shoreline of a pond reduce the effect of strong winds, but aboard a skiff in open water, there is no escape. That doesn't mean that the wind blows constantly, but it is a factor that must be countered when it does occur.

Casting in salt water demands a bit more distance than it does in many freshwater situations. The Western steelheader has an advantage because he already knows how to glean maximum distance. The trout angler who survives with 30-foot casts on tree-canopied Eastern streams must learn to reach out, not only for added distance, but also to buck a sometimes powerful headwind.

Since the fish are on the move, false-casting is a handicap. There simply isn't time to admire the tight loops and match the distance precisely before gently dropping a fly on the skin of the water. Nobody keeps score of your casts in salt water. The idea is to get the fly to the fish; how you achieve this is up to you.

The saltwater fly rodder can find his sport at virtually any spot along America's coastlines, and the way to begin is to pick a time and place in your own backyard where you can be almost instantly successful. It is much easier to toss a streamer, for example, into a wolfpack of prowling bluefish than it is to drop a fly next to a tailing bonefish. In Chesapeake Bay and other East Coast estuaries, one can often find small striped bass that can be taken on trout tackle. Mackerel are frequently overlooked as a fly-rod fish, and the whiting and pollack of colder waters will also take a fly.

Moving across the nation to San Francisco Bay, the basic steelhead outfit with a lead-core or a fast-sinking shooting head can be used to fool huskier stripers. In the Pacific Northwest, coho salmon and sea-run cutthroat trout are primary saltwater targets.

Down South, you can start with ladyfish, jack crevalle, mackerel, and even bluefish. Warm-water weakfish and their related species, the sea trout, both take flies readily.

There are lots of fly-rod fish in the oceans, so let's go after some. You'll have to take a slightly different perspective on this type of angling — both in the selection of equipment and in reading and fishing these waters.

There are, for example, certain types of tackle and fly patterns that are especially appropriate for fly-fishing in the brine. Also, just as the stream fisherman must deal with pools and riffles by varying his technique, the saltwater fly rodder must deal with the shallow flats, the tidal rips, the offshore reefs and the other common situations on both coasts that require adaptability on the part of the angler. Let's start, however, by looking at the tackle you'll need, and understanding why it's often different from that which you may use on your favorite trout stream.

Tackle for the Salt

Rods

A DECADE AGO, MOST WRITERS who had never tried saltwater fly-fishing automatically recommended a 9-foot fly rod with a 9- or 10-weight line and a reel with at least 200 yards of backing. They emphatically stated that, unlike freshwater fishing where several outfits were required, the saltwater devotee could get by with a single rod and reel. Time has proven these people wrong. Today's serious saltwater angler will have an array of rods, starting with a model which would be suitable for trout and moving through the middle ranges to a powerful fish-fighting tool that can cast a 13-weight fly line (and probably a 15-weight, if such was readily available).

If you decide to start with the smaller species and select relatively calm days, you can certainly begin with the same freshwater fly rods you now own. Light trout and bass tackle are frequently the ideal tools for many of the smaller species. A one-pound mackerel will put a trout of the same weight to shame when it comes to a tug-of-war.

If you want to choose a fly rod for a particular type of fishing, start by analyzing the size of the flies you will be casting. In salt water, you can forget dry flies, wet flies and nymphs. You'll be casting bucktails and streamers, plus an occasional popper in certain situations. Because they are often heavily dressed, marine flies are bulky and wind-resistant, requiring more power to get them to the target.

Once you have decided on the fly size you'll be using, you must next determine the line size that will carry these flies to the target. Then, it's a simple matter to match the rod with the line size you need. There is an exception. Some of the saltwater denizens grow to tremendous proportions, and the fighting characteristics of a rod become the primary consideration. Most fly rods in use for fish over 50 pounds; for example, will probably handle a 12-weight line or even a 13-weight; with a rod of that power, there is seldom a problem casting any fly you want to throw.

Buy the best fly rod you can afford. In spite of what some cane manufacturers insist, you will find that glass or graphite rods hold up better than cane in a corrosive atmosphere and require much less care. An extension butt is handy to have when playing a fair-size fish, but many anglers make the mistake of using one that is

A striped bass, one of numerous saltwater species that provide excellent sport for the saltwater fly fisherman. The striped bass is widely distributed along the East Coast; on the West Coast the species is largely concentrated in the San Francisco Bay area. Photo by Mark Sosin.

more than two inches in length. They also subscribe to the removable feature. Veteran saltwater fishermen use a two-inch extension that is either permanently fitted in the rod or, in the case of removable butts, they just leave it in. That way, it's there when it's needed and the shorter butt does not snag the line on a cast.

If you decide to buy a rod for big fish, be sure to check its reserve power. With about six inches of line extending past the tip-top, the rod you select should be able to lift at least a five-pound weight off the floor and still have something left in the butt for even more power. Without a fish-fighting tool of this dimension, you would be handicapped in trying to boat a big fish using a 12-pound-test tippet.

Just the opposite is true when an angler fishes six-pound-test tippets. In that situation, it takes a lighter and more flexible rod to cushion the strain on the lighter tippet. Even for big fish, one must use a rod tailored for an 8- or 9-weight line with six-pound-test leader tippets. Heavier rods could cause the leader to part early in the battle.

Reels

SALTWATER FISH RUN LONGER DISTANCES than their freshwater counterparts, making line capacity on a reel a more significant factor. It becomes a matter of judgment. If a fish can take 200 yards of backing before stopping, then you had better plan on spooling more than that on the reel you select. Most species won't run that far and you can get by with smaller reels and less capacity.

There is another consideration, however. You will be playing most fish directly from the reel, and almost all the standard fly reels are "single-action" (one revolution of the handle produces one revolution of the spool). A large amount of backing in effect increases the diameter of the reel-spool core, and more line can be recovered for every revolution of the handle. That can be an advantage in playing a fish.

Some saltwater fly reels are extremely sophisticated pieces of machinery, handcrafted out of bar-stock aluminum and built with a drag system that is superb. Other reels don't offer all this, but they are also less expensive. It becomes a matter of judgment and need. No one can argue that there is pride of ownership in the best. On the other hand, not every saltwater fly rodder needs a reel that costs between $150 and $300. There have been countless fish caught on these more moderately priced reels. If you intend to do a lot of fishing for big fish, one of the "super reels" may be a worthwhile investment.

Dacron is the preferred backing on a fly reel, because it doesn't stretch very much. Although a lot of fishermen use 18-pound-test backing, some of the veterans still prefer 27-pound test when they are chasing fish over 50 pounds. The margin is just too close between a tippet of 12- or 15-pound test and backing of 18-pound test. For small fish and corresponding fly reels, it's possible to use 12-pound-test Dacron backing.

Fly Lines

THE WEIGHT-FORWARD FLY LINE has become the standard in salt water; level lines and double tapers can be a handicap. Some fly lines are labeled "saltwater taper," and this usually indicates that the weight of the line is concentrated in the first 25 feet instead of the first 30 feet, which is the standard for other weight-forward fly lines. This line was developed for fishermen who spot their quarry before they cast and have to get off a fast but accurate presentation. Actually, a standard weight-forward is superior for long casts. Shooting-heads are also used, especially on the West Coast, where many fly rodders are skilled in their use through big-water steelhead angling.

A floating line is still the standard for most saltwater work, but specialists are taking a long and hard look at fast-sinking lines. Hand-tailored lead-core fly lines, although not essential for the novice, are showing up more and more in the salt, because fishermen recognize that fly-rodding has been needlessly limited to the upper layers of the water. With some of the lead-core modifications, it's possible for a caster to let his line sink as deep as 100 feet. Line manufacturers are aware of this trend and, in the very near future, you'll see several extra-high-density and/or lead-core innovations introduced to the market.

Fly lines are available in a variety of colors, ranging from subtle grays to white and even a blaze orange. In the majority of saltwater situations, fly-line color doesn't really make a difference. There are times, however, when it does. Well-versed shallow-water anglers prefer a matte gray, medium-green, or basic brown line in preference to white or other light shades. You have to see those moments when a fish is spooked by an airborne fly line to appreciate the difference. Change to a subtly colored fly line (gray or tan) and the fish will be much less apt to panic. No one really knows whether this applies to deep water, but it is a matter of fact in the shallows.

Leaders

WHILE THE FRESHWATER FLY FISHERMAN may take a somewhat complex approach to the construction and taper of leaders, the marine angler can move toward total simplicity, because delicacy of presentation is less a factor in most saltwater situations. The butt section is usually 60 percent of the leader length, and is often either 30- or 40-pound test, depending on line size. Consider a 9-weight line as the pivotal size, using the heavier butt with larger lines. For big fish, a double surgeon's loop is tied in the end of the butt section, making it possible to change leaders quickly. The remainder of the leader is the class (middle) section, usually 12- or 15-pound test, followed by a heavier shock tippet to prevent the leader from being cut by sharp teeth or gill covers. (Class section refers to line-test record categories established by the Salt Water Fly Rodders of America.)

The shock tippet is generally less than 12 inches long; the class section is usually around 18 inches. Length of the leader's class section should, however, vary with its breaking strength. Twelve-pound-test sections should be 18-24 inches, while six-pound-test sections should be almost 36 inches.

Fly Patterns

FLY PATTERNS FOR SALT WATER are generally simple. There have been repeated attempts to duplicate common baitfish, but the typical streamer fly still does the job. Hook sizes start at about 6 for bonefish flies, and move sequentially up to a 5/0 or possibly a 6/0. It's difficult to set a hook larger than 4/0, and 5/0 is considered marginal by many in the know. Bigger sizes can be an exercise in frustration. In fact, many of the top anglers use smaller hooks on even the big flies because it facilitates penetration in the fish's mouth. It goes without saying that every hook should be sharpened. Saltwater critters often have hard and bony mouths and, unless a hook point has cutting edges, you are going to miss a lot of fish.

General Techniques

SALTWATER TECHNIQUES are not difficult to learn. The key to casting is to reduce the number of false casts to a minimum. You will want to learn to double-haul if you haven't already mastered the method (See p. 29). This will give you both added distance and the ability to buck a headwind. Unless you are fishing the tropical flats, where you see your quarry first (spot-casting), most of your efforts will be blind-casting. It can be done effortlessly with a weight-forward line if you pick up 30 feet and then shoot another 30 feet without repeated false-casting. This can be done if you are willing to practice. Eventually, you'll also learn to cast farther and to cover a greater area. These techniques are covered in depth by Lee and Joan Wulff in the earlier chapter on casting.

Even expert casters have problems when they first attempt to spot-cast to a cruising bonefish, tarpon or permit. One reason is that they have very little time to make the presentation, but even more important, they must start with the fly in their hand. For a 60-foot cast, you'll have about 15 feet of fly line extending past the rod's tip-top and dragging in the water behind the boat. The fly is in your fingers. When you see a fish, you should be able to make a high forward-roll cast in the air (releasing the fly from your fingers), shoot line on the backcast, and go to the target on the first forward cast. With a little practice, the technique can be mastered, but the time to practice is before you ever step aboard the boat.

When cast to a specific fish, the fly must land beyond the quarry and be moved across its line of vision. If you cast too close, even the gentle splat of a fly landing on the water may spook the fish and, if you cast too far, the fish will never see the fly.

The strip method of retrieve is the most popular in salt water. Put the butt of the rod at your belt buckle and point the tip directly at the fly. The rod is not used to impart action to the fly, because then you would not be in position to strike the fish when the fly was taken, and because you can't pick up and make another cast unless the rod is in front of you.

The fly line is held under the first or second finger of the casting hand and allowed to slip between the rod grip and the fingers. The other hand strips in the fly line from behind the rod hand. It is a simple method and can be used to create erratic motions or short jerks and darts, depending on the timing and length of the pulls. Since the line is always in your left hand and the rod is pointing directly at the fly, you are constantly in a position to pick up line for another cast and ready to double-haul.

Fishing the Water

It should now be apparent to you from the earlier chapters of this book that, as a fly fisherman, you'll have to adapt your techniques to suit the various types of water that you'll be fishing. This applies to salt water as well as fresh, and, just as the stream fisherman must learn to read the water and to vary his approach accordingly, so the saltwater fly rodder must learn to read a seemingly endless ocean.

That's actually much easier than it may sound. There are five common angling situations that confront saltwater fly fishermen everywhere. Each of these situations occurs in both northern and southern waters on both coasts. One might fish a tide rip in Puget Sound for coho salmon; an identical tide rip off Cape Cod might yield bluefish. Once you've learned how to fish such a tide rip, you should be able to do equally well in either location. The same basic reasoning applies to the rest of the situations that I'm about to describe.

One/Fishing the Flats

WHETHER YOU CHOOSE TO WADE or use a skiff to probe the shallows, a stealthy approach is the key to success. Fish in extremely shallow water are apt to be very skittish. If they become alerted to your presence or exhibit nervousness for any reason, they can be exceptionally difficult to fool with a fly.

Locating your quarry is another problem. Stages of the tide can be critical in determining where the fish will be. Some flats produce on an incoming tide, while other shallow-water areas may only come to life when the tide peaks and begins to fall. In some areas, you must also calculate the effects of spring tides (when the moon is new or full), since the amounts of rise and fall will increase and the fish may not follow traditional feeding patterns.

Floating lines are standard for most shallow-water situations, but veteran anglers often use full-sinking or sinking-tip lines to get the fly down quickly.

A fish hooked on a flat will usually run for deep water, no matter how far away it might be. For that reason, it makes sense to have a reel with adequate line capacity; 200 yards of backing is usually sufficient, as I mentioned earlier.

In tropical situations where the water is apt to be clear, you must learn to present a fly quickly and accurately the instant the quarry is spotted. That technique takes practice, and the place to learn it is back on your home waters. If you are working the shallows where you cannot see the fish, develop a systematic approach. Limit your casting to a comfortable distance, and keep the fly in the water as much as possible. Learn to cover an area thoroughly as you move, by putting each cast an established distance from the last.

Changes in water depth are often overlooked by anglers fishing the shallows, but even a few inches or a foot can be critical. As you search for fish, keep varying the depth of the water in which you're fishing until you locate the species you seek. Continue fishing that depth of water until you can't score. When the fish become scarce, resort to a zigzag depth-searching pattern again until you locate the correct depth.

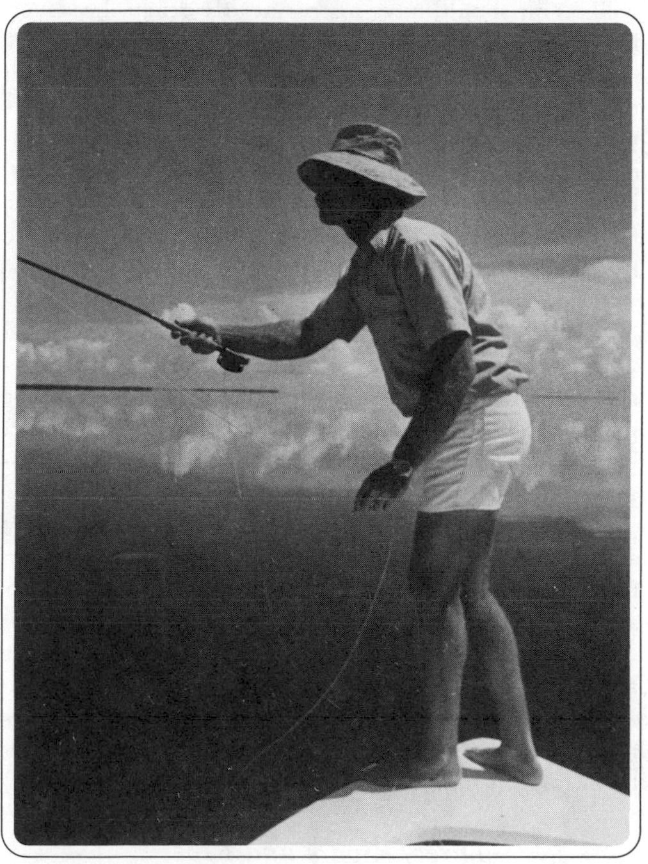

One of the most exciting experiences in fly-fishing is to glide silently over glassy flats stalking bonefish or tarpon. It requires a stealthy approach and accurate casting for success. Photo by Mark Sosin.

Two/Breaking Fish

NOTHING IS MORE EXCITING than the sight of some husky gamefish exploding across the surface of the water in pursuit of schools of baitfish. You know instinctively that if you can get a fly in the midst of the melee a strike is almost certain. It's tough to resist the temptation to power the boat directly into the middle of the school, but that technique may only bring short-term results because you will likely scatter the fish and put them down. A better approach is to work the fringes of the school, keeping the boat clear and casting toward the fish. In any given instance, there are probably many more fish in the school than those you see on the surface.

Determine the direction in which the fish are traveling and try to get ahead of them. It's often possible to work out in front and cut the engine, letting the boat drift toward the fish. The cast should be made toward the main school and then retrieved. Fish must isolate their prey to attack it, and once your fly moves out of the school of baitfish, it's easier for a predator to spot.

The fly you select should approximate the size and shape of the bait. Anglers after surface strikes resort to topwater poppers in this situation and sometimes do well. You should have a streamer fly ready, however, in case the popper is refused.

Feeding fish will not hesitate to strike a fly. If you don't get a strike almost immediately, something is wrong. This is not trout fishing, in which you typically have time to change pattern and presentation. The action is *now* and you must score quickly. If your first cast doesn't bring results, start to vary the retrieve by speeding it up or slowing it down.

A floating line is usually best when working to breaking fish, but if you have a second outfit, keep it rigged with a sinking line. Even though you may see substantial activity on top, there is likely to be even more going on a bit deeper. With a sinking line, you can start the retrieve as soon as the fly hits the water, thus keeping it shallow, or you can let the fly sink.

There are times when the surface activity is sporadic; swirls and boils may appear only infrequently. When this happens, you can often catch fish by waiting for signs of action and then dropping a fly on the spot very quickly. You almost have to keep the line in the air until you see the boil.

When the school finally sounds, take a few minutes to probe the area with a sinking line. You can sometimes take an extra fish or two in the process.

Three/ Rivers and Rips

TRYING TO GET A SINKING LINE DOWN in a fast current can be a problem. You'll need extra-heavy lead-core or one of the new extra-fast-sinking lines to do the job, and even then you'll have to figure out each situation separately. In many cases, you will be forced to make a very long cast upcurrent, perhaps shaking out additional running line after the cast to get the needed depth.

Part of the act is timing the retrieve. This takes experience, but you can master it if you follow your line carefully. If you wait too long, the line will begin to float back up toward the surface, riding the strong currents. Monitoring the line throughout the cast and retrieve is important, because a fish could pick up the fly as it is being carried by the current. Watch the line near the rod tip, just as you would in fishing a nymph in fresh water. If you see the line tug or pause, take in the slack and strike.

Saltwater streamers can also be fished by casting the fly quartering downcurrent and letting it swing around in the same way that a streamer may be fished in fresh water. This can be particularly effective when the fish are congregated at a narrow neck on an outgoing tide, waiting for baitfish to be carried past them in the current.

Unlike a river where the current is steady, rips offer a more difficult challenge because the direction of flow of the water where tidal currents intersect is often confusing. The trick is to determine the direction of the current and then use it to your advantage. Fish often work along the edges of rips, and it's important to keep the fly along the interface of the rip and the adjacent still water.

Four/Structure and Shoreline

CERTAIN SPECIES OF MARINE GAMEFISH will take advantage of undercut banks in rivers and estuaries, while others will prowl around markers, buoys and other structures. In those instances where there is cover along a shoreline, the casts must be made with extreme accuracy. Striped bass, for example, will often hang under the banks in Chesapeake Bay, and the only way to elicit a strike is to drop the fly at the very edge. Look for pockets and points along the bank; pick your casting targets carefully.

In southern or tropical areas, mangrove shorelines are another fish haven. Casts must have a low trajectory to carry the fly back under the overhanging limbs. It can require precision casting, but accuracy pays dividends in fish. The strike can be explosive and the tough job is to get a snook or tarpon coming your way before it crochets the line in a tangle of roots.

Markers and structures should be approached as quietly as possible and the first cast should be a long one. Veterans often approach upcurrent so that they have a better control of the boat, and so that a hooked fish may come back downcurrent toward them. The casts should cover the sides of the structure as well as the center. You must also consider where to place the fly in terms of a strike. If you cast beyond the target, a hooked fish will probably cut you off. Therefore, you want the strike to occur off one corner or in the center of the downcurrent side.

Structures are an excellent place to tease fish with either a live bait or a hookless chugger. Resident fish will stay deep until the surface commotion brings them topside in a hurry. Once you see the fish, casting is simplified.

Five/ Surf Fishing

THE FLY ROD WAS NOT DESIGNED for surf fishing, but it can be used effectively in the breakers if you pick the right locations. The ideal surf location will have a

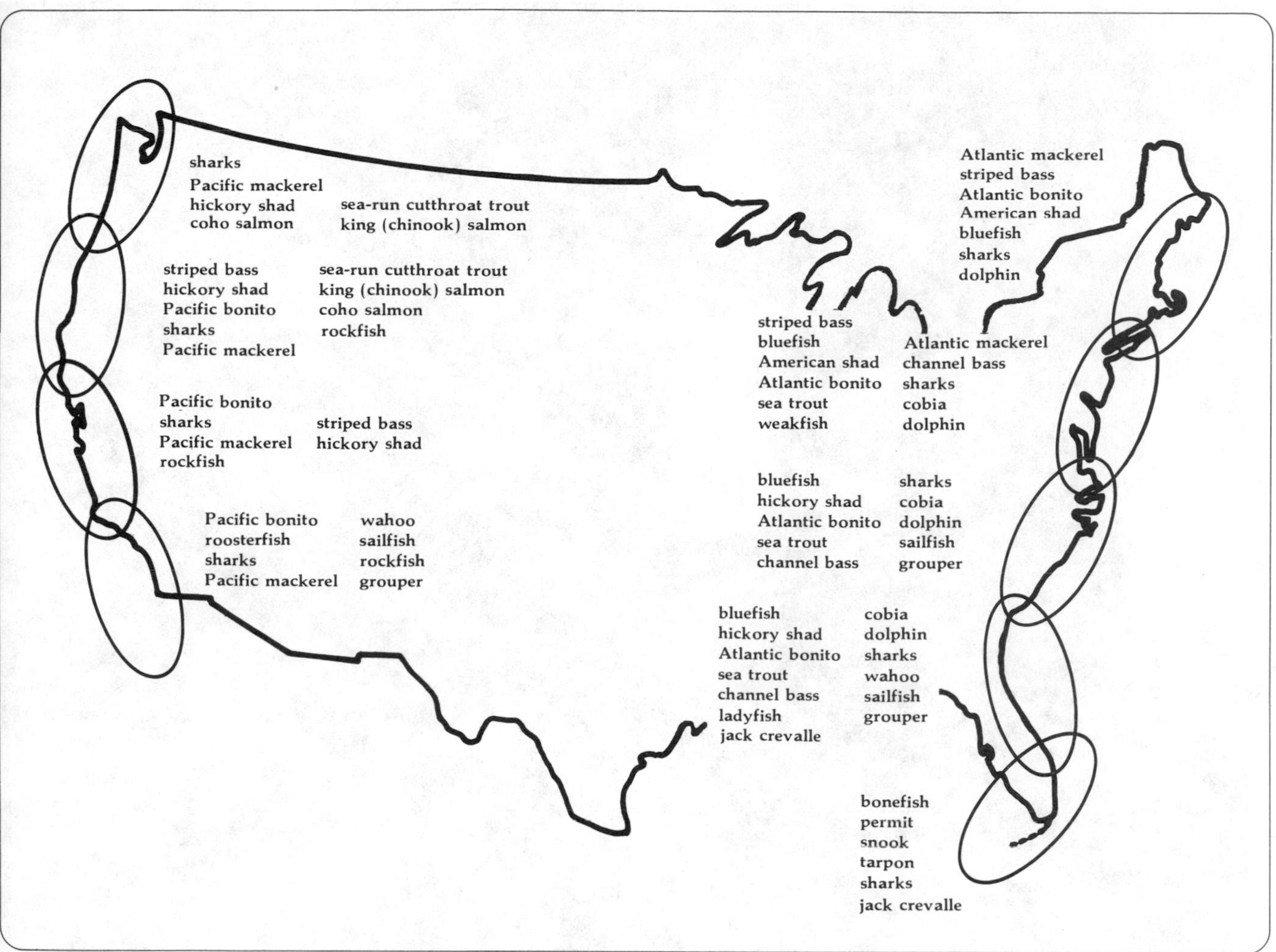

slough (a relatively deep trough), either near the beach or next to a bar that is wadable. Casts should be short, because trying to handle a long line with waves breaking around you is a difficult task.

Blind casting can prove to be an exercise in futility and simply give you hours of casting practice. A better approach is to keep the fly rod handy and to use it only on those occasions when the fish are in that slough.

Along some parts of both coasts, rocky jetties stretch seaward to protect the beaches from erosion. These can be perfect locations for fly rodders because the baitfish congregate near the rocks and the predators are right there looking for food. Although surf fishermen with conventional gear often make long casts away from the jetties, a better technique for the fly rodder is to fish close to the rocks. The fly will hang in the pockets and work effectively.

Try to select times when fish are being caught and you know that the species you seek is in the area. Fly patterns should imitate local baitfish, and floating lines are preferred, since sinking lines could hang up in the rocks.

Fighting and landing a fish from a rockpile on a fly rod is tricky business. You'll need a gaff in the final stages, and luck as well as skill in between. If you are near the beach, get off the jetty and walk the fish around to a position that will allow you to land it on the beach.

Saltwater fly-fishing is really an opportunity sport. For some species, it can be the best technique, but for others, it only works when conditions are right. You cannot catch fish on a fly rod, however, if you leave it home; it pays to take the light wand with you if and when you go saltwater fishing. More important, it makes sense to plan specific trips to catch marine gamefish on a fly. Start with smaller fish and those that are easiest to catch. As you try to gain experience in fighting larger fish on a fly, don't overlook the shark. Nature's greatest predator is found wherever there is salt water and, if you can't chase sharks on the flats, you can often attract them with chum. A well-placed fly should do the rest.

Finally, a word of caution is in order. Saltwater fly-fishing has been known to have addictive qualities, even for those anglers who once considered themselves trout-and-salmon purists and who viewed the marine bunch as second-class citizens. It is fun to hear them now as they extol the virtues of fly-rodding in the briny, and if you have never tried it, you can certainly join their ranks.

Photo by John Merwin.

The perfect fly has yet to be tied. Hopefully, it may be tied by you! Despite the abundance of expertly conceived and beautifully constructed artificial flies available today in tackle shops and mail-order catalogs—all of them "guaranteed" to catch anglers, if not fish—the greatest fly you'll ever use is that first one you've whomped up yourself. You'll always remember that magic moment in history when you cast your scruffy "first-born" over a lurking fish, watched it plop onto the water and then disappear in a sudden swirl. It's a once-in-a-lifetime experience, but one which never quite loses its sharp edge, no matter how often repeated. It's the finishing touch for "the compleat angler."

The fly itself is "bomb zero" in the fly rodder's strategy, and you're only halfway into fly-fishing if you haven't tied at least a few of your own. The rod, line, leader and tippet are really just a natural way of delivering the fly to the fish—where the real action begins. By tying your own, you'll learn how the fly is designed to do what it's supposed to do—sink slowly or quickly, float low in the surface film, or ride lightly and enticingly on top. You'll soon understand the subtle impressionism involving color and silhouette and size that's built into a successful fly. And, whether or not you continue to tie your own, you'll certainly know how to select and present the flies you use.

So dig into this chapter, then tie up a few. No matter how hideous those first attempts may appear to you, try one on the fish for size. They may have a different viewpoint. And after a few takes, you may, too.

Chapter 10

Tying Your Own Flies

The Fly Angler's Ultimate Thrill

TED NIEMEYER

GETTING INTO FLY-TYING is not at all difficult, and it can become a uniquely rewarding hobby. I have found it so, and seldom do I hear of anyone giving up the hobby because it is uninteresting or lacks sufficient challenge for a talented pair of hands. Some patience is required, but it is an established fact that individuals who contend that they lack even a minimum of talent and can't even thread a needle, *can and do* turn out to be fly tiers of considerable ability. Certainly these persons can produce artificial flies that will deceive fish as well as bring admiring glances from fellow fly fishers.

Don't be misled by anyone into believing that you can approach this intriguing hobby without making some investment in quality tools and materials. That may be a slightly jarring note on which to start, but it's better to accept this fact with an open mind so you don't flinch when you make that first purchase of a fine-quality dun neck or that new vise that "does it all."

On the other side of the coin, don't be alarmed when some stranger that you meet along the stream later sends you a fine mess of feathers for which you had been silently wishing. Fly tiers are a friendly bunch, and the exchange of materials often takes place freely.

The happy note where investment is concerned is that it need not occur all at once. Any long-term tier will tell you that he has amassed his vast collection over many years of searching, plus careful planning for the purchase of only quality merchandise. To my way of thinking, that's the only sensible way to approach equipment purchases, and I strongly suggest that you adopt it. I know many tiers who can spin tales of money wasted because of impulse buying.

Don't overlook the very sensible idea of getting your spouse involved in the hobby. Even if she or he has no desire to tie, you can at least present the opportunity for your partner to purchase tools and materials for you. The holidays, when gift giving is practiced in your household, are an excellent time to set your investment plans in motion. A word of caution, however — do *not* offer any suggestions about tools and materials without collateral material to hand out! In other words, don't give the giver the option of inferior or cheap merchandise. Locate a responsible seller, get a copy of his catalog, and mark in bright red pen the exact items that you'd like to add to your collection. Better yet, fill out the mail-order form provided with each catalog and place it in a very conspicuous location, such as under her pillow or around his shaving-cream can, as the case may be.

I have often said that the beginning fly tier should *not* purchase tools or materials without first taking lessons from a competent instructor or, at the minimum, only after seeking some advice from an experienced tier. Most competent instruction will include the use of adequate tools, thus allowing you time to survey the products available and then to ultimately make a much wiser judgment as to the kind and quality of your purchases.

Obviously, not all will have access to structured classes. Some will not even know of a competent tier in their immediate community. Don't be discouraged, however, if you fall into the latter category. In this chapter, I'll take the position of your neighborhood fly tier, and as you look over my shoulder, we'll work together at getting you started. Pay attention, however, even if you're already into tying, because I expect to be offering some ideas that will be new to many experienced tiers as well.

THE PREPARATION OF YOUR WORK AREA is akin to the designing of an artist's studio or a photographer's lab. Properly designed, the fly tier's "home" is a functional, uncluttered domain where some very pleasant hours may be spent. Locate your work space in a warm and comfortable area of the house with pleasant surroundings. Do not, as so many have done, seclude yourself in the basement, attic or a dark corner of the least-used room in the house. Sufficient storage and ease of movement are also important to protect your patience and sanity while you develop your skills.

Good lighting is more essential than all the tools and materials combined. Most fly-tying supply houses carry a fine list of quality lights designed to supplement the normal lighting in most households. Consult catalogs for the supplemental lighting you may require. Pay particular attention to any eye fatigue that may manifest itself when you tie for prolonged periods, and consult your ophthamologist immediately to correct any such problems.

Tools and Materials

THE QUALITY OF THE TOOLS and materials that you use will have a direct relationship to the quality of the flies that you tie; buy the best you can. Don't forget, however, that one of the main ingredients of a good fly will be the care you devote to tying it. Too many tiers tend to blame faulty tools or materials for a poor fly when the fault actually lies with the tier.

To get you oriented at this point, let me explain what will be taking place in the next few pages. First, I'll give you some guidance as to exactly what tools you'll need to get started. Then, I'll briefly discuss materials, and suggest a list of things to buy, beg or borrow. Next, you'll be getting detailed instructions for the tying of four fly patterns — the first will be relatively easy for any beginner; the last, I hope, will be a challenge for any expert. Finally, and because fly-tying materials are of such importance and so often confusing, we have included a section by Eric Leiser and John Merwin devoted exclusively to materials that should serve as a standard reference of a complex subject.

Now that you've gotten a sneak preview of the rest of this fly-tying section, let's take a look at the basic tools you'll need — a vise, a bobbin, scissors, hackle pliers and a dubbing needle.

Vises

The number of different vises available has grown to astounding proportions compared to the handful of a few years ago. A quick check of my files shows a current total of more than 20 of varying quality and practical value. You probably won't have an opportunity to try them all before making a purchase, so here is a list of ten vises that, in my judgment, are all excellent and deserve your consideration:

Roost Vise	Orvis Vise
Sunrise AA Vise	Orvis 2-in-1 Vise

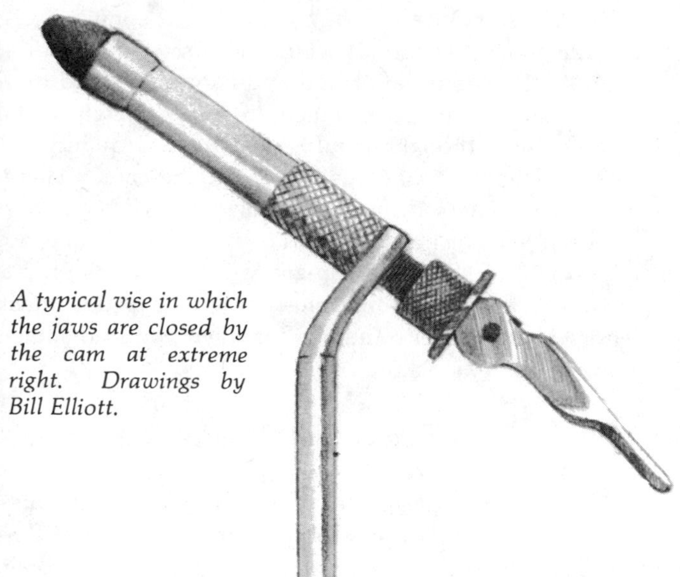

A typical vise in which the jaws are closed by the cam at extreme right. Drawings by Bill Elliott.

Price Vise
Thompson Non-Glare Pro Vise
HMH Premium Vise
Thompson Ultra Vise
HMH Standard Vise
Thompson Model A Vise

Make sure that you check whatever vise you buy for any flaws in workmanship. This shouldn't be the case with any of the products that I've listed, but do look for the following: smoothly working cam, lever or screw-type jaw lock; absence of any metal burrs or filings; a light film of oil on all moving parts; and there should also be a non-glare finish to the jaws.

Scissors

Scissors are extremely important to the fly tier, and for your delicate work, you should obtain the best available. Those for precision work should have long (about 2-inch), thin and extremely sharp blades. The finger holes should be large enough to be comfortable.

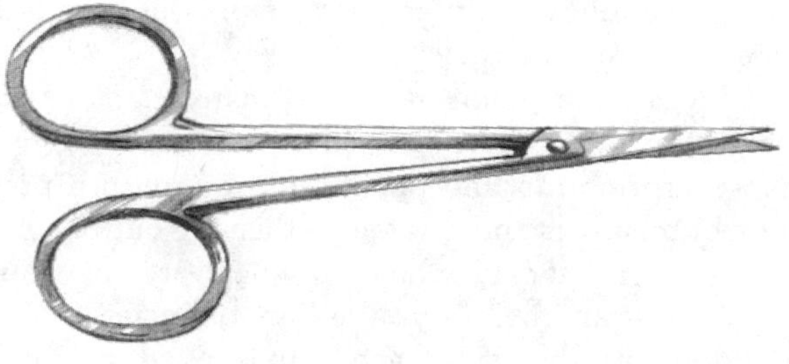

I've had a jeweler enlarge the finger holes on most pairs of scissors that I've used over the years so that they will slide on and off my thumb with ease. Some newer brands of scissors feature enlarged finger holes, eliminating the need for any alteration. Here are five brands or general types of scissors you should consider. The names are those under which they are sold in most catalogs, and any one of the following will do the job well:

Swiss-type Scissors
Solingen Scissors
Thompson Adjustable Scissors
Sunrise Adjustable Scissors
Iris Scissors (designed for eye surgery)

Some of the fly-tying tasks you'll be performing will require the use of heavy-duty scissors. Any of those listed as such in the supply-house catalogs will do nicely. I don't recommend that you confiscate a pair from the household sewing basket. They generally aren't very good for fly-tying work.

Bobbins

Working with a bobbin to hold the tying thread or relying solely on your fingers is a matter of personal taste, although most beginners will find the use of a bobbin easier. Your ability to control the placement and tension of the tying thread is paramount to good results, and that is best achieved by hand without the mechanical assistance of a bobbin. A fly tied with a bob-

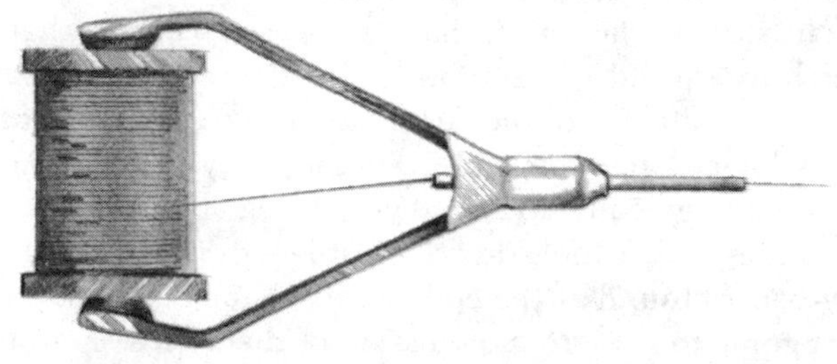

bin looks no different, however, and I defy anyone to tell me which of my flies were tied with or without one.

Most of the tiers that I've observed do use a bobbin and obviously feel comfortable with one. Of the dozens that I've tried, I suggest that you choose from among the following:

S & M Bobbin
Matarelli Bobbin
Sunrise Bobbin
Chase Bobbin
Custom Bobbin

Hackle Pliers

There have been developed over the years about as many different types of hackle pliers as there are supply houses selling them. Most of these pliers do not perform as well as they should, and I'll limit my purchase suggestions to the three I feel perform the best:

E-Z Mini Pliers
Herb Howard Pliers
Sunrise Classic English Pliers

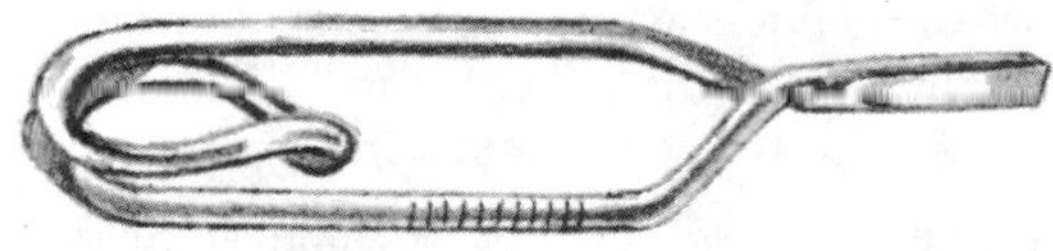

Choose your hackle pliers by closely inspecting all surfaces. Reject any that have uneven jaws, a poor spring action, or jaws that do not mirror each other. I have always found it necessary to lightly hone the burrs and sharp edges from the gripping faces of the pliers that I've purchased, and I suggest that you do the same.

Dubbing Needle

A good dubbing needle is both inexpensive and indispensable. You need only select the one that feels comfortable in your hand. You may see this tool called a bodkin in some catalogs.

THAT CONCLUDES MY LIST of essential tools. Others—such as whip-finishers, dubbing twisters, bobbin threaders and cleaners, floss bobbins, tweezers, hackle guards, material clips, hair stackers, scalpels, half-hitch tools, and more—can be selected and purchased from the catalogs of the larger supply houses. As most tiers have done, you will eventually buy them all just to see if they really do add to your tying abilities. You'll find these other tools described at length in most of the references found at the end of this chapter, and so I'm not going to get into a discussion of them here. For our immediate purpose of getting you started at the tying bench, you don't need them anyway.

There are some other things that you will need though, and let's consider them in the order of hooks, threads and tinsels, and materials.

Hooks

There are as many answers to the question of what makes a superior hook as there are fly fishermen. Tiers who have been around since the 1940's swear by their stock of English Allcock hooks, a brand no longer available. Mustad has, over the long haul, produced the most consistent quality and does manufacture the largest selection in terms of hook-wire weight and hook design.

Despite all the claims from various other manufacturers, the Mustad Company enjoys the largest following among tiers, and you would be well advised to follow that concensus.

I should add right now that, as you progress as a tier, your personal preferences and loyalties to certain items will change. Don't purchase large quantities of anything at first. Once you have established some priorities and some favorites, it would be wise to purchase a good stock. Many favorite brand-name tools and materials have been discontinued in favor of what the manufacturer thought would be improved quality or design. Happily, that's usually been the case. There have been some sad instances, however, when the tier has been left out in the cold. I'd love, for example, to have 2,000 of Allcock's top-grade dry-fly hooks right now, and there are some old-timers who'd give their left leg for a meager hundred. So when you find something you like, stock up.

Threads and Tinsels

Threads and tinsels, along with waxes, cements, flosses and chenilles, can be purchased from any fly-tying supply house and selected at random according to your needs. Most of these items are of fine quality, and you need have little fear on that score. Beware, however, when any old material of this nature goes on special sale, because some of these synthetic materials will deteriorate with age.

Fly-Tying Materials

The materials used in constructing artificial flies fill pages upon pages in supply-house catalogs. Not only can a novice tier become confused, he can also have some understandable concerns about ordering materials from mail-order firms not known to him. This is a difficult question with no certain answers.

Almost every established fly-material supplier places ads in FLY FISHERMAN magazine. While the publisher can't police every advertiser—and has seldom found the need to—there is healthy competition among them, so if one defaults on an order, misrepresents an item, delays in processing of an order, or makes a serious error in fulfilling one, the word will get around. There's a tight little "jungle telegraph" among fly anglers, and sloppy handling of orders or misrepresentation of items doesn't go unnoticed.

I suggest that you send for as many catalogs as you can, look them over, see which ones seem to give the most information and put the most care into preparation of their lists and catalogs—then try out one or two. You'll learn quickly which suppliers are the most dependable—and before you're hurt financially.

I don't, by the way, mean to imply that any fly-tying supply house is in any way disreputable. Virtually all of them do a good job of handling the thousands of orders they get each year. But there's no substitute for actually seeing the items you want before you buy them, and that means visiting one or more supply houses or well-stocked retail tackle shops to get what you want. If that's not possible—and for many it won't be — at least examine the section on materials at the end of this chapter so that you'll be able to fully understand the catalog descriptions of what you'll be ordering.

I keep a list of those items that I need or would like to have in my collection, and I suggest you do the same. Then when you do have the opportunity to visit a store where fly-tying materials are sold, you can look over your want list and pick up a few items.

Basic to any fly tier's collection of materials are some of those items that head the list of every supplier's catalog. If you're just getting into fly-tying, the following should serve as your basic materials list.

Rooster Necks

Grizzly (black-and-white barred)
Red Game (brown)
Black
Light Ginger (pale honey)
Blue Dun (a medium gray)

Animal Hair

Muskrat	Gray Fox
Woodchuck	Red Fox
Black Bear	Calf Tail
Bucktail	Deer-Body Hair
Porcupine	Badger
Beaver	Hare's Mask
Otter	Australian Opossum
Mink Tail	Gray Squirrel Tail
Red Fox-Squirrel Tail	

Feathers

Mallard Skin	Partridge Skin
Peacock Tail Feathers	Turkey Wings
Ostrich Plumes	Canada Goose Wings
Ringneck Pheasant Skin	Turkey Tail Feathers
Marabou Plumes (asst. colors)	Wood-duck Skin

Hooks

Mustad #94840; sizes 8, 10, 12, 14, and 16
Mustad #94833; sizes 10, 12, 14, 16, and 18
Mustad #94859; sizes 20 and 22
Mustad #9575; sizes 6, 8, 10, 12, and 14

This selection of hooks will enable you to tie most of the basic wet flies, nymphs, dry flies, midges and streamers. There is a wide variety of specialty hooks that should be purchased only when you're duplicating a unique pattern, or tying for bass, salmon and other fish that require a hook of unusual wire-weight or configuration. Specialty hooks in most catalogs are usually described as such, and you shouldn't have any difficulty in finding them when you need them.

Threads

Herb Howard prewaxed nylon thread in assorted colors. Silk thread in sizes 2/0, 4/0 and 6/0 in both black and white.

Floss

Four-ply rayon in various colors, including some fluorescent shades.

Chenille

Get the medium size in an assortment of colors.

Tinsels

Flat mylar in fine, medium and wide, each in silver and gold.
Oval mylar in fine, medium and wide, in both silver and gold.

Silks and Synthetics

It is a mistake to assume that one thread can be used for all styles and sizes of flies, and taking into consideration the factors for and against synthetics and silk, here are some simple guidelines for choosing the appropriate thread.

Use synthetic tying thread if:

- You are tying small patterns (#18 through 32).
- You wish to use a bobbin.
- You will be using numerous colors.
- You plan to use your flies in salt or brackish water.

Use silk tying thread if:

- You find that stretch and torque affect your tying.
- You like to tie without a bobbin.
- You choose to apply varnish at critical points.
- You are using brittle or fragile materials (synthetics have a tendency to cut or bite into tying materials).

It is important for tiers to be able to work with silk *and* synthetic threads, so make yourself a more complete tier by learning the capacities of each.

Ted Niemeyer

There are many questions posed by beginners and experts alike — that center around fly-tying materials. Because materials are so important — and because the definition of one material or another is often very vague — the following section by Eric Leiser is presented to give you some further guidance before you start to tie. Eric is a recognized authority in the field, and has written two books and numerous articles dealing with the various attributes of the furs and feathers used for tying flies.

Fly-Tying Materials

ERIC LEISER

One of the most magic — and most meaningless — terms in a fly tier's vocabulary is blue dun. A number of classic patterns call for the use of blue-dun (or dun) hackle; it's been a fly tier's favorite for several hundred years. Since this is such a traditional material, duplicating someone else's dry-fly pattern that requires dun hackle should be easy.

It isn't. The difficulty — and it's one common to many fly-tying materials — is that dun is not a single color; the term refers instead to a family of gray shades ranging from almost white to almost black. There is, incidentally, almost never any blue shading present. The "bronze" duns are some shade of gray with a brownish cast, and there may also be some dun necks with subtle olive undertones. Thus, duplicating someone else's pattern without actually *seeing* the hackle that was used originally may be next to impossible if the only color description given was the word "dun."

The finest vise and tools obtainable are really worthless unless the tier has some knowledge of the materials going into his flies. In addition to color, a given material's physical properties will determine whether or not it's suitable for a particular pattern. A fly-tier may have a choice of tying a clipped-body Rat-Faced McDougall dry fly with either antelope or caribou body hair. The choice will be made on the basis of the color and texture of the two hairs, and without knowing that, the fly tier is headed for trouble. (That fly, by the way, is generally tied with caribou. Antelope is too coarse to be easily worked for the body of a small dry.)

The problem of color becomes severe in three instances, all of which are quite common. First, vast quantities of materials are sold at retail by mail-order, and buyers generally have to rely on verbal or written descriptions of the materials. Descriptions of color are subjective; what's light gray to one may be very pale gray to another. You really have to *know* the color typically associated with the material you're ordering or you may be wasting money.

Second, pattern descriptions are also a problem because of the subjectivity of the color descriptions for the required materials. If you *know*, for example, the color of a cree hackle, your problem will be solved.

Finally, suppose you dye some feathers, or buy them already dyed, to imitate the increasingly scarce wood-duck flank feather. If you've never actually seen a wood-duck flank and don't *know* what color it is, you've got no basis for evaluating the substitute.

In selecting materials to be photographed, we searched several extensive private collections to obtain samples that are most typical in color for a given material. Along with the photographs, you'll find on the following pages my descriptions of the colors, properties and uses of the materials illustrated. That combination should serve as a precise guide to the most important properties of a series of fly-tying materials that are traditional and basic to the needs of contemporary tiers.

FEATHERS

Rooster Necks — The skin and feathers from the head and neck area of any rooster, whether raised in this country or imported. Because there are a variety of important shades, I'll deal with the use of each type individually. In general, however, the hackle feathers from a rooster neck are often used for the hackle collar and/or tail of dry and wet flies. Those rooster hackles having stiffer fibers are used for dry flies, while the softer hackles are used for wet flies. For some patterns, the hackle tips are used for wings without any modification; they may also be cut and shaped for the same purpose. The following are general descriptions of the basic types of necks.

White — Most necks that were originally white are sold after being dyed to shades of gray (dun), olive, yellow, claret, insect green, and red, since very few patterns call for a white hackle as such. Among those that do call for white hackles are the Bivisibles and the Renegade. An off-white to dark-cream neck is closely related. The dark cream is used primarily for the Light Cahill pattern.

Golden Ginger — Sometimes referred to as light ginger or pale ginger, this neck has a buff, golden color.

Some patterns requiring it are the Gray Fox (in a mix with dark ginger and grizzly) and the Ginger Quill.

Dark Ginger—A light reddish-brown neck, sometimes also called red game. It is used for such patterns as the Dark Cahill and Red Fox.

Brown—A medium-brown neck used in countless patterns, often in a mix with grizzly. The Adams is probably the best-known fly using the grizzly-and-brown combination. A Henryville Special, the most widely used caddis pattern, also carries both brown and grizzly hackles, although the latter is palmered along the body, and the brown is used for the front collar. A dark mahogany-brown neck is usually called a "Coachman" brown and is primarily used for the Royal Coachman series of flies. The quality of this hackle is generally on the poor side; it's better to use a good brown hackle instead.

Black—A true black is almost never attained by a natural rooster hackle. A solid black is generally obtained by dyeing. Necks of this color are used for such patterns as the Black Gnat, Black Ant and Black Wulff.

Badger—A neck on which the feathers are cream- to light-ginger, each feather having a black center stripe. White badger is very rare. Some examples of use include the Badger Bivisible and the popular White Wulff.

Furnace—A neck with brown feathers, each with a black center stripe. Very few contemporary patterns use this hackle.

Red Grizzly—A dark-ginger or brown neck with light-ginger barring, commonly used for variant drys.

Ginger Grizzly—Like the red grizzly, also a variant but with reverse barring; primarily cream- to buff-ginger with reddish-brown barring. Both the red and the ginger grizzly are used for a mottled effect in variant-style flies. They also mix well with grizzly since they give an additional break-up effect to the color of any pattern tied with the combination.

Cree—A red- or ginger-variant neck barred additionally with black; in other words, a neck with tricolored hackles. Sometimes called "instant Adams" since all the shades for the pattern are found in one hackle.

Grizzly—Sometimes known as barred rock, it has black hackles with white stripes. In addition to the Adams, the Mosquito and the Hornberg are two favorites among the many patterns calling for this hackle.

Hackles other than those from a rooster neck are also commonly used. Both hen necks and hackles from a rooster's "saddle" (upper back) follow the same color schemes I just outlined for rooster necks, but their physical characteristics are different and so, consequently, are their uses.

The hackles from a hen neck differ from those of a rooster in that the hen hackles have a more rounded shape and are almost fully webbed, thus softer in texture. The primary use of hen hackle is for hackle collars or for imitating the legs of a nymph.

Saddle hackles tied in for a streamer wing. In this case the pattern is a Matuka, for which tinsel will be wound through the wing. Photo by John Merwin.

Saddle hackle is occasionally sold "on the skin," but most of it sold commercially is available in strung or loose form. Saddle-hackle feathers are much longer and generally narrower than either rooster- or hen-neck hackle. The primary use of saddle hackle is for the wings of streamer flies such as the Black Ghost, Gray Ghost and the Supervisor.

Although hackle from roosters and hens constitutes the largest category of feathers used by most tiers, there are numerous others of considerable importance and varied application. The ones that I've included in the following list are those I consider most basic to any tier's arsenal.

Duck Quills—These are available in natural colors of gray (from a mallard or other wild duck) or white (domestic ducks). For the winging of dry and wet flies, you'll need a matched pair of primary quills—one from the bird's left wing, and one from the right. If you can purchase or otherwise obtain a matched set of mallard wings, you'll get the valued primary quills plus some other useful feathers as well. A pair of wings also contains white-tipped secondary feathers (used for such patterns as the McGinty) and a large quantity of small shoulder feathers that will vary in color from brown to gray. These feathers are used for flies of all types, for wings, wingcases, bearding hackle, legs and tails. The list is almost endless. The white primary quills from domestic ducks are used for winging both wet and dry Royal Coachmen and are dyed a variety of colors for other patterns.

Mallard Flank—These feathers are found along both flanks of a mallard drake. The color is a finely barred pearl gray, and the fibers are used for wings on such flies as the Gray Fox. More often than not, the feathers are dyed a lemon-brown to imitate the more scarce wood-duck flank feather. In this dyed shade, mallard flank is used for the wings of such classics as the Quill Gordon, Hendrickson and Light Cahill, all patterns originally calling for wood-duck flank. On wet flies, it is also used as a tailing material and as imitation legs for nymphs.

Goose Quills—These are available in gray and white as natural colors. The white quills are often dyed red, green, yellow or black. Natural gray is occasionally used for wing cases on nymphs. The quill from the center stem can also be stripped to make quill bodies. White or dyed goose is used for wings on larger flies.

Marabou—Generally only available in white as a natural color, since this feather comes from the domestic turkey. These feathers are commonly dyed a multitude of colors. The fibers are used primarily for wings on streamer flies such as the White Marabou, Yellow Marabou and Black Marabou.

Golden Pheasant Neck—When sold as such, this material includes the tippet portion and the crest (top knot). The tippets are a rich orange with black bars. The crest is a brilliant golden yellow. The two portions are sometimes sold separately.

The tippets are used for the tail of the Royal Coachman, both wet and dry. They are also used for numerous salmon patterns, such as the Green Highlander and General Practitioner. The crest feathers are often used for topping or tailing many salmon-fly patterns. A popular streamer pattern calling for its use is the Gray Ghost.

Guinea Hen—The natural feather is a very dark gray, almost black, with white spots. It is also dyed other colors and is used for beard hackle or legs of wet flies and nymphs.

Ostrich Herl—In its natural state, it's available in white, black, chinchilla or gray. The white is also dyed to brighter colors. It's commonly used for collaring nymphs and pupal imitations and is occasionally used for the wings of streamer flies.

Peacock Eyed-Tail—One of the most beautiful and useful feathers in fly-tying. Iridescent blues, golds, greens and bronzes radiate symmetrically from the center of the eyed portion. The fibers below the eye are dark green, with an occasional hint of bronze.

The heavily flued herl fibers are used for the bodies of such famous patterns as the Leadwing Coachman, Royal Coachman, Zug Bug and Gray Hackle. The quill from the "eyed" portion may be stripped of its flues and wound for the body of many dry- and wet-fly patterns, among them the Quill Gordon. Peacock-herl fibers are also used as topping for many salmon and streamer patterns.

Peacock Sword—One of the side feathers from the peafowl with a swordlike shape. The herled fibers near the tip are shorter than those of the "eyed" tail and have a broken, staggered effect. The fibers are generally used for tails on nymphs; the Zug Bug is a good example.

Ringneck Pheasant—The cock bird offers almost all the colors needed for most fly-tying. The feathers themselves also vary in shape and length. Its uses are really too numerous to mention. Many patterns can be tied from the feathers of this bird alone.

Ringneck Pheasant Tail—A reddish-brown with a hint of lavender, the barred tail-feather from a mature bird can be almost two feet long. The individual fibers of this feather are used for tails on nymphs such as the March Brown, and for fly bodies as well, such as the Pheasant Tail.

Silver Pheasant Body Feathers—These feathers are predominantly the same over the entire body—white with black barring. They're used for cheeks on salmon and streamer flies. Again, the Gray Ghost is the foremost example.

Mottled-Brown Turkey Wing Quills—Collect all of these that you can; they're becoming scarce and will soon be collectors' items. Their color is light- to medium-dark brown with darker mottling and speckling throughout. They are used for the wings of such flies as grasshopper imitations and, of course, the ever-popular Muddler Minnow. Also used for wing cases of nymphs.

White-Tipped Turkey Tail—A very dark mottled-brown with a white or cream-white tip. These aren't quite as scarce (yet) as the lighter mottled-brown turkey wing quills and are used for the same purpose.

Turkey Body Feathers—Naturally white, they are dyed various shades. The feather itself is approximately three inches long with a squared-off tip. These feathers are used for fan wings or clump-style No-Hackle wings.

Jungle Cock—A neck skin carrying waxlike black feathers with orange and yellow "eyes." Its importation has been prohibited for several years, and it's scarce. Yet it's so highly traditional that many imitations have appeared. It's used for cheeks of salmon and streamer flies, such as the Green Highlander and Black Ghost. It's also used as a wing for the Jassid patterns.

FURS, HIDES and TAILS

Furs for Dubbing

Beaver—A medium-gray fur, silky and soft, that dubs easily and floats well. It's used for the bodies of dry flies requiring a shade of gray, such as the Blue Dun. The guard hairs are long enough to be used for winging and tailing.

Fitch—The soft texture of its cream to tan fur makes for easy dubbing. It's excellent for Light Cahills and

Soft materials, such as this partridge breast feather, are appropriate to nymphs and other subsurface patterns in which the materials should breathe with the action of the current. Photo by John Merwin.

other patterns of that shade. The dark-brown guard hairs are useful for both wings and tails.

Red Fox—A soft and easily dubbed fur with color ranging from off-white to cream, and fawny tan to gray. Both male and female foxes are also sought for the belly portion, which is sometimes urine-stained to a pale pink. Mostly used for dry-fly patterns, but occasionally wet flies and nymphs also. The famous Art Flick Hendrickson utilizes urine-stained fox belly for the dubbed body.

Hare's Mask—Tan-and-gray speckled in color; both soft and coarse in texture. All colors and textures are mixed when used as dubbing, thus making rough, buggy bodies for both wet flies and nymphs. It's used for a variety of patterns, but most commonly spun onto thread to make the bodies of the popular Gold-Ribbed Hare's Ear wet fly and nymph.

Muskrat—Soft blue-gray fur that dubs easily. The tips of the underfur fibers have a brownish cast to them. It's used for the bodies of dry flies such as the Adams, Dark Cahill and Dark Hendrickson. Also used for wet flies and nymphs.

Nutria—Brownish to dark gray in color; silky soft in texture. Useful for bodies of drys, wets and nymphs.

Mink—The available natural colors include white, cream, tan, blue-gray, brown, and black, thus making it one of the most desirable furs for blending and dyeing. The underfur is smooth and high-floating. The short guard hairs cause a minor problem in removal prior to dubbing the underfur. It can be used for the body of almost any pattern.

Australian Opossum—Color ranges from a rich, creamy yellow on the underside to a soft gray on the back. The fur appears to be kinked slightly but it dubs well. The creamy underfur is excellent for Light Cahills. Both shades are highly suitable for numerous dry flies, wets and nymphs.

Otter—A short-furred animal, brownish gray in color. The guard hairs are very short and are sometimes mixed and dubbed with the underfur for a rough effect. The Otter Nymph is a favorite pattern.

Rabbit—A highly versatile fur. Natural colors include white, blue-gray, brown, and black. Since it can be easily dyed, any shade can be obtained. It also blends extremely well with any other natural fur. The bodies of all wets, drys and nymphs can be made from rabbit. The guard hairs on rabbits can also be used for winging and tailing. Complete strips of rabbit fur (still attached to the skin) can be cut in order to be tied as a Matuka-style streamer.

Hairs for Winging

Badger—The barred cream-and-white guard hairs are usually more than an inch long and may be used for wings and tails on drys, wets and streamers. The Little Brook Trout Bucktail is one example.

Black Bear—Ranging in shade from dark brown to black, the hair when prime is very shiny. Fiber length is generally 1½ to 3 inches. It's used for wings on streamers and bucktails, such as the Black-Nose Dace.

Bucktail—The tail from either a male or female deer. The Eastern whitetail is preferred, since its hair is usually much longer and finer than that of other species, although blacktail deer is also very good. Mule deer is too short and stiff-fibered. The color of the Eastern whitetail is brown on top and white on the underside. It is also available dyed in numerous colors. The hair is used for wings of streamers and bucktails, occasionally also for winging and tailing drys. The Mickey Finn pattern is a popular example of its use.

Calf Tail—Available in the natural colors of white, brown, and black, and in numerous dyed colors as well. The hair is much finer, although somewhat shorter, than deer tail, and is preferred over the latter for some applications. It's used for wings on streamers and bucktails, in addition to the winging and tailing of dry flies. The Wulff series of patterns utilizes calf tail. (White Wulff, Black Wulff, Royal Wulff and so on.)

Elk Hair—Tannish-brown hair fibers similar to deer-body hair, but usually longer and more manageable. Used as outrigger-type tails for various mayfly imitations, and also as a winging material for various Western drys designed to imitate adult stoneflies.

Fitch Tail—The dark-brown guard hairs are 1 inch to 1½ inches long, firm and yet easily worked. They're used for the winging of salmon flies primarily, but don't overlook their use for winging of conventional dry flies.

Gray Fox—This animal's guard hairs are approximately one inch long, black with a white tip. Useful for the winging and tailing of all flies, and essential for some salmon patterns, such as the Rat series.

Mink Tail—As with the body fur, the natural shades of this material include white, cream, tan, brown, and black. The guard hairs are about one inch long and are used for the winging and tailing of dry flies, especially for the wings of such caddis imitations as Len Wright's Fluttering Caddis.

Gray-Squirrel Tail—Commonly sold as full tails with hair that's speckled gray, barred black, and terminating in a white tip. The fibers are 1½ inches long on a prime animal. Some California "grays" carry hair up to two inches long. This hair is used for the winging of streamer and bucktail patterns; one pattern carries the same name as the animal.

Red Fox-Squirrel Tail—A hair of length similar to the gray squirrel's, but a reddish-brown, barred with black and reddish-brown. It is used in the same fashion as Gray-Squirrel Tail.

Woodchuck—The guard hairs change in color from base to tip in sequence of black, tan, black, and white. The hair is soft yet firm; smooth, yet easy to work with. It's one of the finest, although most underrated of materials for the winging and tailing of dry flies (it floats extremely well); and for winging of streamer and salmon flies. Some patterns include the Ausable Wulff (dry), Llama (bucktail) and Woodchuck Caddis (dry).

Hairs for Special Uses

Antelope—A very coarse, hollow, brown-and-gray hair used for bass bugs and other clipped-hair patterns such as the Spuddler and the Whitlock Sculpin.

Caribou—This is also hollow and somewhat coarse, yet finer than antelope or deerhair. It's light gray in color and used mostly for smaller clipped-body patterns such as the Rat-Faced McDougall.

Moose Mane—The fibers from the mane are either dark gray or pale gray and are three to five inches long. For fly bodies, a light and a dark fiber are wound together on the hook for a segmented effect. The Mosquito is a pattern that sometimes uses moose mane for its body.

Peccary—Fairly long (1½ to 4 inches) and fairly stiff fibers, the color of each alternating between black and cream or brown and cream. It's used for the tails and feelers of nymphs, especially stonefly nymphs.

Porcupine—Both quills and bristles are used for various purposes. The quills are white or cream, generally with a black tip. The bristles are predominately brown to black, although occasional white or cream ones are found. Both usually have white tips. The quills are used for the Coffin Fly pattern. The bristles are used for tails and feelers of nymphs.

Other Materials

In addition to feathers and furs, many other materials are used in fly-tying. The scope is endless. Even as this is being written, I'm sure a fly tier somewhere has found a use for fibers from the filter of a cigarette butt after the cigarette has been smoked. (In case he hasn't, I can report here that it makes a good body for a Cahill wet.) Certain materials, however, have been with us a long time and are basic. Here are some of them.

Floss—The most commonly available is made from rayon, although the more-easily worked silk is still preferred whenever it can be obtained. Floss may be purchased in a wide variety of colors, including fluorescent shades, and is used primarily for the bodies of wet flies, salmon and streamer patterns.

Wool—This is a yarn made from sheep's fur. Various sizes are available, and the color range from many manufacturers is almost infinite. It's used for the bodies of numerous flies designed to be fished below the surface.

Tinsel—Available in gold or silver, flat, oval, and embossed, in various widths. Metallic tinsels are the traditional standard, but mylar tinsel is now available, which, though not quite as strong, does not tarnish. Either one may be used for the bodies of wet flies, salmon and streamer patterns, or as ribbing.

Chenille—Manufactured by spinning either rayon or cotton fibers onto a cotton core. Various colors and sizes are available. Chenille is most commonly used for the bodies of wet flies and nymphs. The Woolly Worm series of patterns is a prominent example.

Thread—This is not a material as such, but is certainly necessary to hold them all together. Most threads today are made from nylon, including the popular Herb Howard Flymaster brand. Silk, though generally available only in black and white, is still preferred by many tiers, partly because it doesn't stretch. Threads are available in many sizes and colors.

Having gotten your tools and materials together in a suitable location, it's time to start tying. Now we're back with Ted Niemeyer, who is going to take us through the procedure for starting the thread on the hook, tying the whip-finish knot, and then through a series of four fly patterns of increasing complexity—even the experts among you may find his last fly to be a real challenge!

Starting the Thread

The thread is held across the shank as shown. The bobbin is in my right hand; the other end of the thread is being held with my left. Without moving my left hand, I'm about to bring the bobbin up and over the shank to bind the thread upon itself.

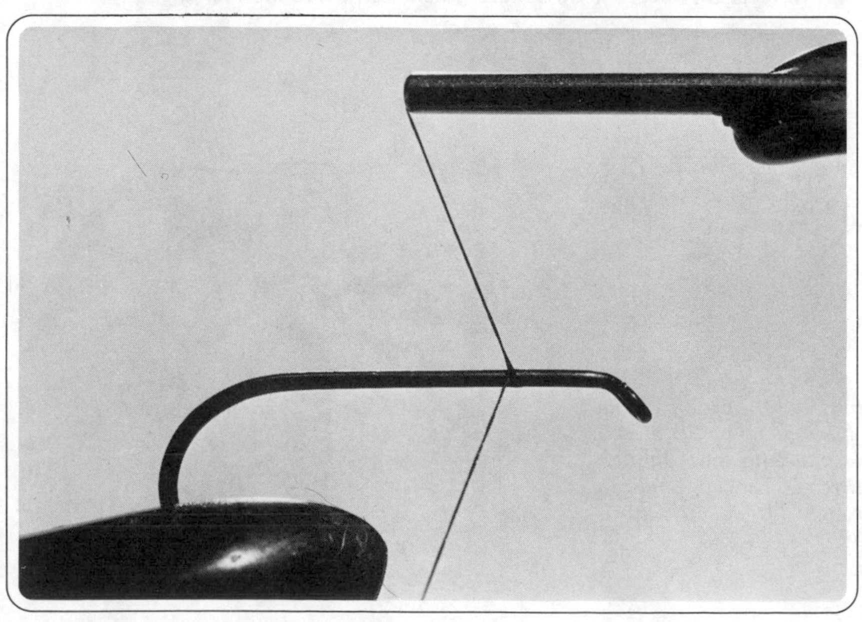

Now the thread has been caught. I'll make another turn toward the left before releasing any tension. Then, holding the left-hand thread parallel to the hook shank, I'll take two more tight turns to the left. The thread will then be locked to the shank and the excess on the left side can be trimmed away.

Tying the Whip-Finish Knot

Illustrated by Robert Seaman

The whip-finish knot is used to tie off the thread when the fly is finished. There are a variety of mechanical aids available for tying this knot, but you're much better off in the long run if you learn to do it with your hands alone. The secret is to maintain constant tension on the thread coming off the hook shank. Start, as shown at right, by holding the fingers of your right hand over the thread at a diagonal.

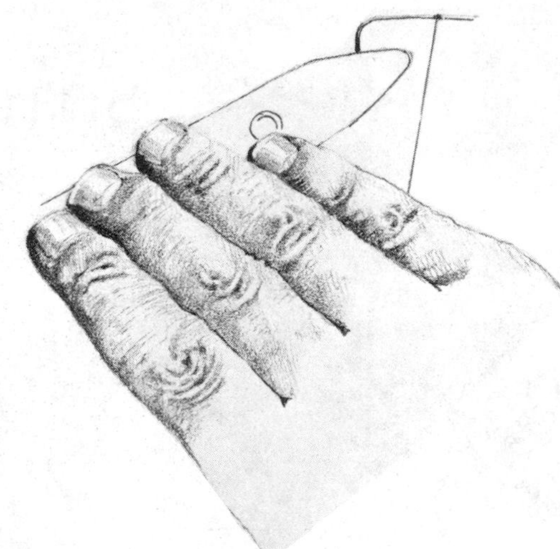

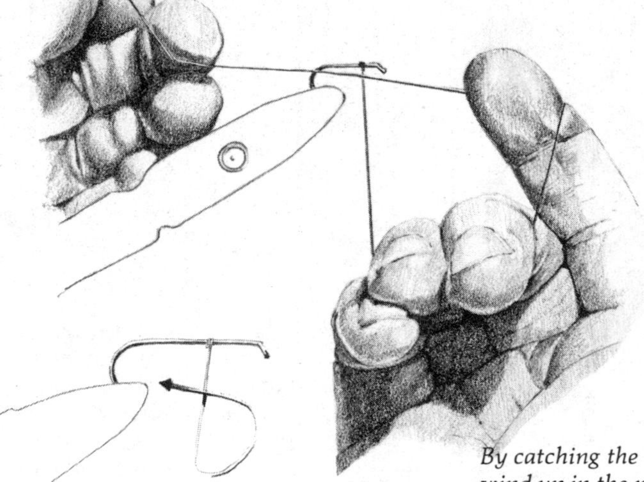

By catching the thread under your fingers as you rotate your hand clockwise, you'll wind up in the position shown above. Remember to maintain tension on the thread coming off the hook shank. The thread coming down from the hook shank is now going to be wound over the thread being held parallel to the shank.

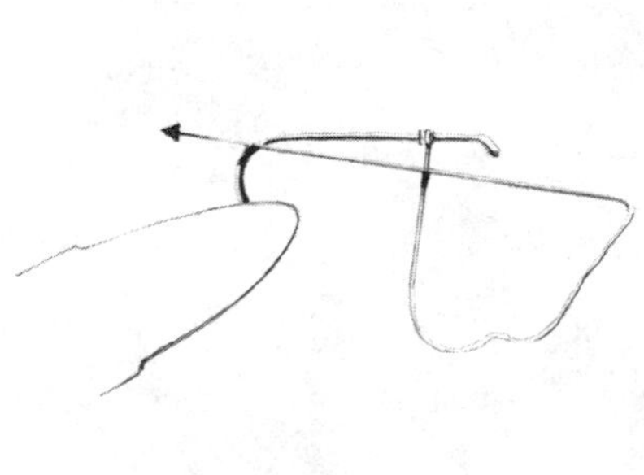

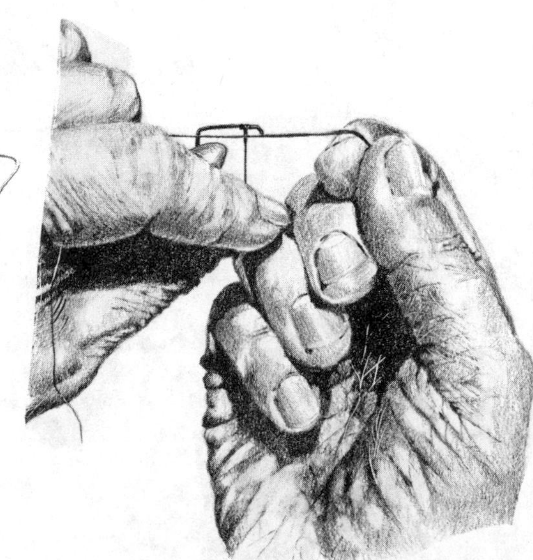

Study the drawing at right carefully. The horizontal portion of the thread is being held by the rear fingers of the left hand and by the thumb and index finger of the right. The thumb and index finger of the left hand have grasped the vertical portion of the thread. The left hand can now be rotated; the vertical thread will be brought up while the horizontal thread will remain in the same position.

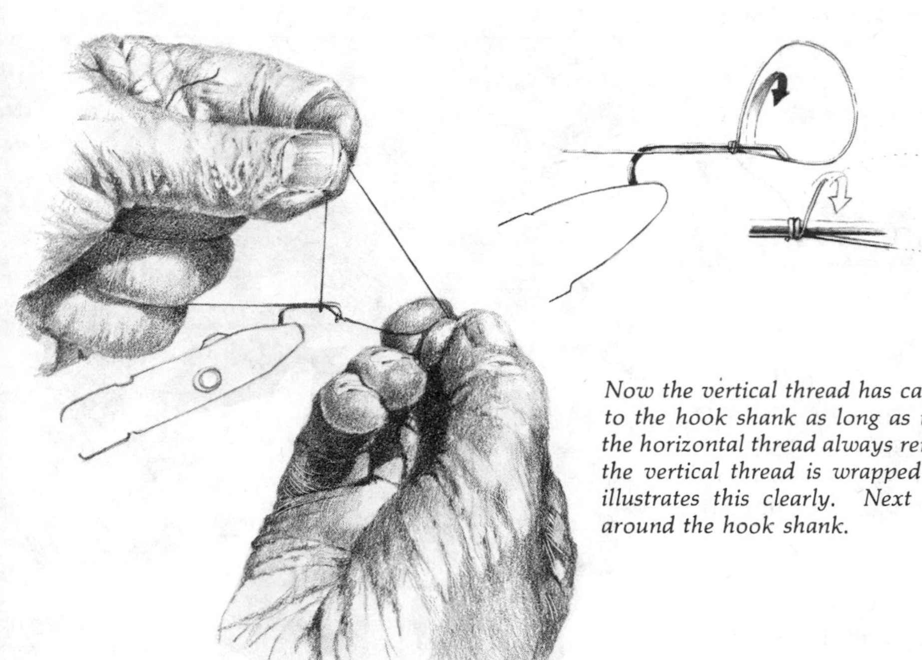

Now the vertical thread has captured the horizontal thread, binding it to the hook shank as long as tension is maintained. Remember that the horizontal thread always remains in about the same position while the vertical thread is wrapped around it. The close-up view above illustrates this clearly. Next the vertical thread will be continued around the hook shank.

Take the vertical thread down on the far side of the shank with your left hand. Then catch it with the thumb and index finger of your right hand. Be careful that tension on the vertical thread is maintained. One wrap has now been completed. Repeat the process twice more, making a total of three complete wraps, each just to the right of the previous.

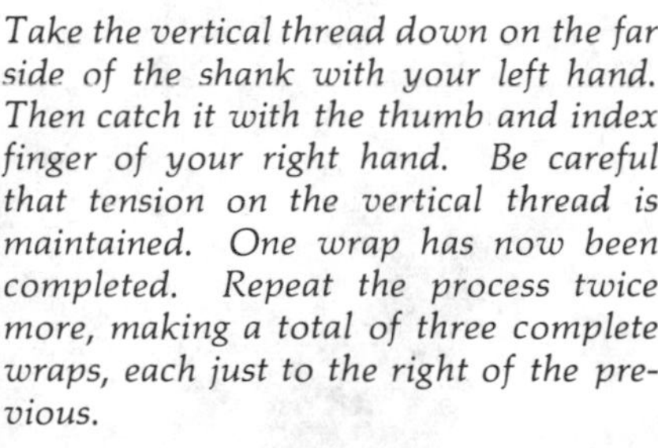

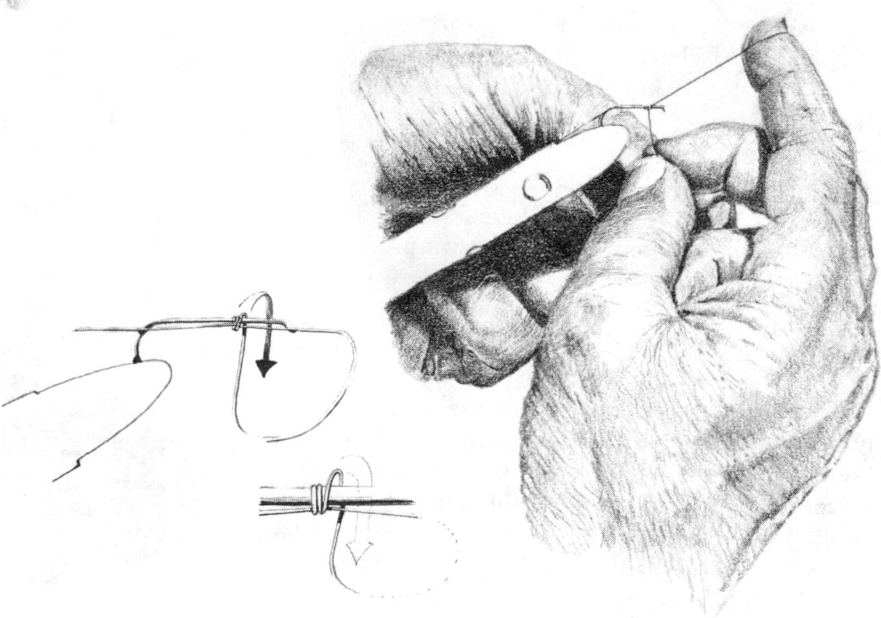

After three complete wraps, pinch the wraps between your right thumb and index finger. Then slip your right-hand fingers out of the loop and pull the end of the thread with your left hand. As shown in the close-up below, the loop will be pulled under the wraps. Pull the free end of the thread firmly to tighten the knot, then trim closely.

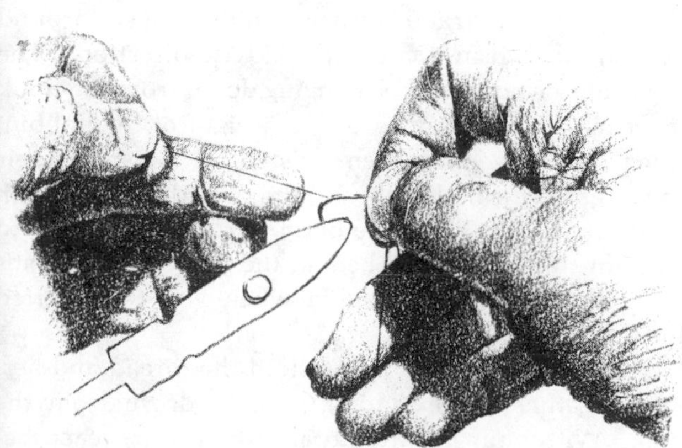

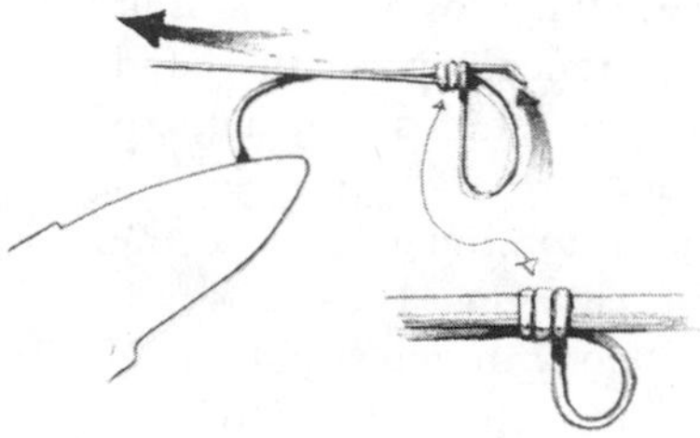

Tying the Isonychia Nymph

THERE SEEMS TO BE a common misconception that the tying and the fishing of artificial nymphs are both difficult. As you learned in the earlier chapter on stream fishing for trout, nymphs aren't difficult to fish. Now you'll see that they aren't always a tier's nightmare either.

This mayfly-nymph imitation is both easy to tie and effective. It is generally representative of the very widely distributed *Isonychia* nymphs, but its effectiveness is enhanced by its resemblance to many of the caddis and dark stoneflies that inhabit trout streams across the country. No wonder it works so well!

You'll need the following materials, all of which were listed earlier in the materials section of this chapter.

HOOK: Mustad 9575, #12
TAILS: Two small dark blue-dun hackle tips
BODY: Four long strands bronze peacock herl
WING: None
HACKLE: Medium blue-dun rooster
THREAD: Black Herb Howard Prewaxed Nylon

Place the hook securely in the vise, and as previously illustrated, lock in the tying thread 1/8" behind the hook eye. Cover the hook shank with a layer of thread by taking tight even turns to the left (toward rear of hook) until you reach a point directly above the hook point.

Pick up the four strands of peacock herl, and while holding them all together near one set of ends as shown, catch them with a loose turn of thread, which is then pulled tight to bind them to the hook. Without letting go of the herl strands, make two more tight turns to the left, each turn of thread butting against the previous one. The herls are solidly tied in now, and you can let go of them.

Hold the two hackle tips so that their ends are even and so they curve away from each other. Hold them in your right hand directly over the hook shank so that their tips extend the proper distance beyond the bend of the hook. The accompanying photos will help to establish the correct proportion.

With your left thumb and forefinger, grasp the hackles by the tips without changing their position relative to the hook shank. Let go with your right hand, and use that hand to take three tight turns of thread

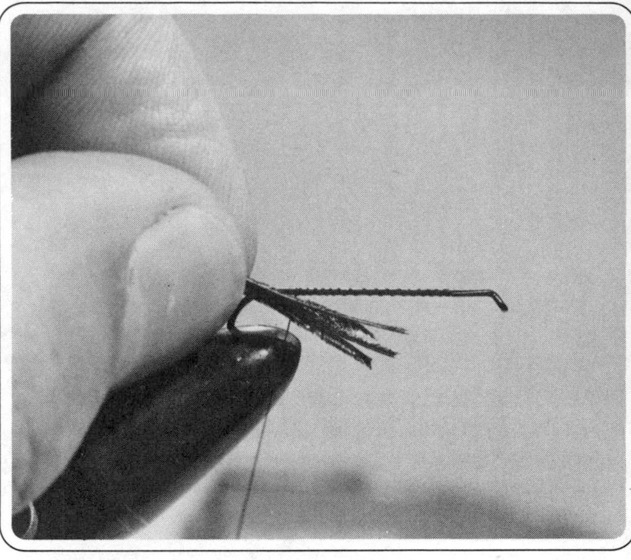

Tying in the herls (above). Note the angle at which they're being held, which will insure that they wind up on the top of the shank. In the lower photo, the tail length is being gauged. Photos by John Merwin.

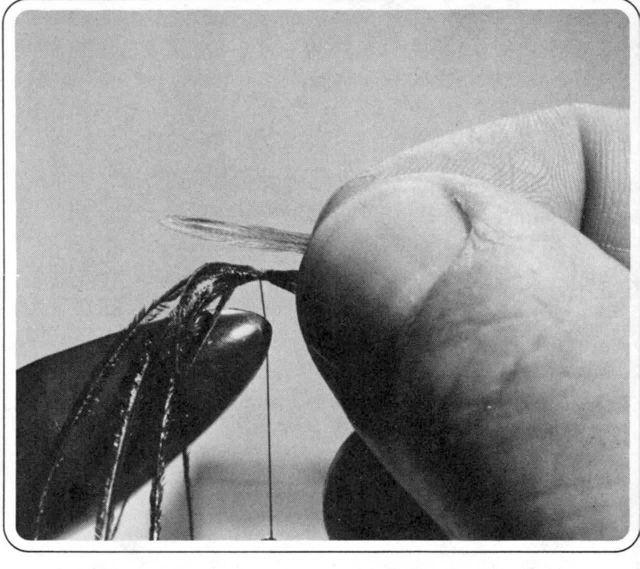

over the hackle tips and toward the rear of the hook. You can now let go of the hackle tips. Check to be certain that they haven't rolled or twisted out of position, then trim the butt ends of the hackle stems as shown.

Twist all four strands of herl simultaneously around the tying thread in a counterclockwise direction. The thread at this point will be hanging down from the hook under tension maintained by the weight of the bobbin. When the herls have been twisted for most of their length, grasp the herl butts and the thread together with your right hand. Wrap the body in close even turns to the right to a point 1/8" behind the hook eye. (That's where the thread was tied in when you first started this fly.)

When you reach that point, hold the thread and herl butts together and extending straight down from the hook. With your left thumb and forefinger, reach be-

The tails have been tied in (above) and the herls are being twisted around the tying thread. In the lower photo, the body has been wound and the herls are being tied off.

In the upper photo, the tip of the hackle is being tied in. The lower photo shows the completely prepared hackle after having been tied in as described in the accompanying text.

hind and under the hook and grasp the tying thread, while still holding the herl butts in your right hand. The thread and herl must separate from each other under tension, so pull them gently away from each other. When this separation has been achieved, pull firmly on the herl butts with your right hand, and at the same time, take one full turn of thread with your left hand over the herls where the body ends. Now the peacock ends are locked in, but you'll need three more turns of thread to make them secure.

Now you need a medium blue-dun rooster hackle. Pick one in which the length of the fibers one third of the way from the butt to the tip is approximately two-thirds of the fly's body length. Holding the feather firmly near the middle, strip the fibers from the lower third of the stem (toward the butt). Then grasp it by the tip and gently stroke the remaining fibers toward the butt so they stand out from the central stem. Be sure to do this gently to avoid tearing these fibers from the central stem.

Tie in the tip of the hackle as shown, with the shiny side of the feather facing the eye of the hook. The hackle tip should be tied in where the body ends, or about 1/8" back from the eye. Two turns of thread around the hackle tip will hold it securely while you trim the excess tip. Make some additional turns of thread, each butting the previous, to within 1/16" of the hook eye. Attach the hackle pliers to the butt of the hackle stem, and then pull on the feather slightly with the pliers to put the hackle under tension. When you wind the hackle around the hook, the hackle feather should be oriented in such a way that the hackle fibers will be perpendicular to the hook shank, and *not* parallel to it. Before you start to wind, and when you've

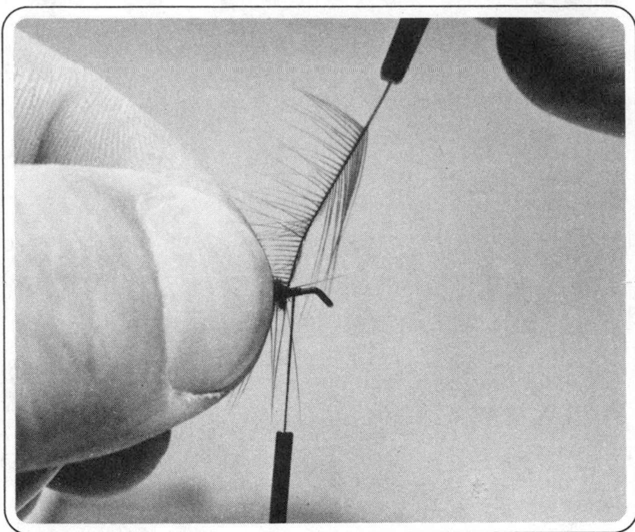

As the hackle is wound, the fibers are stroked to the rear (in both upper and lower photos).

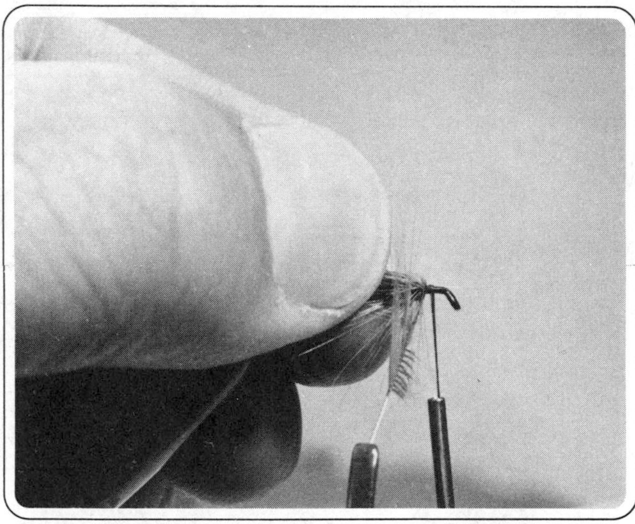

The lower photo shows the finished fly immediately after the whip-finish knot has been tied and before the excess thread has been trimmed.

first put some tension on the feather, you can see whether or not this will be the case. If it's not, you can correct it by simply rotating the hackle pliers to change the orientation of the whole feather.

With a moderate amount of tension, make one full turn of hackle around the hook shank at the point at which the hackle tip was tied in. With your left hand, firmly stroke the hackle fibers back along the body. At the same time, use your right hand to make another complete turn of hackle. The second turn should be just to the right of, but immediately up against, the first. Stroke all the fibers to the left again with the left hand. Repeat the process until at least three full turns of hackle have been accomplished; each must be neatly next to, and not on top of, the previous.

Now hold the hackle stem firmly out from the hook shank with the hackle pliers, and using your left hand, make three tight, close turns of thread over the feather at the point at which it leaves the hook shank as shown in the photo. Cut the excess hackle very close to the turns of thread. Now tie a whip-finish knot as previously instructed. Apply a coating of head cement to the exposed thread at the fly's head, being careful not to plug the eye of the hook with cement. The fly is finished.

Special Tying Techniques

SOME OF THE METHODS just used in tying this fly are really basic lessons and deserve some amplification.

•A complete layer of tying thread was placed over the bare hook shank before any materials were tied in. This layer of thread is much less slippery than the bare metal and thus prevents the tying materials from sliding around the shank and eventually loosening.

•The tails were tied in *after* the peacock herl was secured to the hook shank. Normally, most tiers will tie in the tails first. The method I've illustrated, however, demands that the herl be bound in securely and also makes certain that the first turn of the body material (herl) will cover the last turn of thread that was made to the left. Thus the common fault of exposed thread at the tails of flies is avoided.

•Twisting the peacock herl in a counterclockwise direction around the tying thread not only reinforces the fragile herls, but also forces the entire mass to tighten as it is wound around the hook shank. If the herls had been twisted clockwise around the thread, they would loosen as the body was subsequently wound.

•Holding the turns of hackle back with the left hand while subsequent turns are being applied forces the hackle to ultimately lie back over the body at an angle of about 20 degrees from vertical, thus conforming to the general shape of the natural insect.

These are finished examples of the patterns for which tying instructions are given by Ted Niemeyer on pages 110 to 120.

Fly plates photographed by Don Gray.

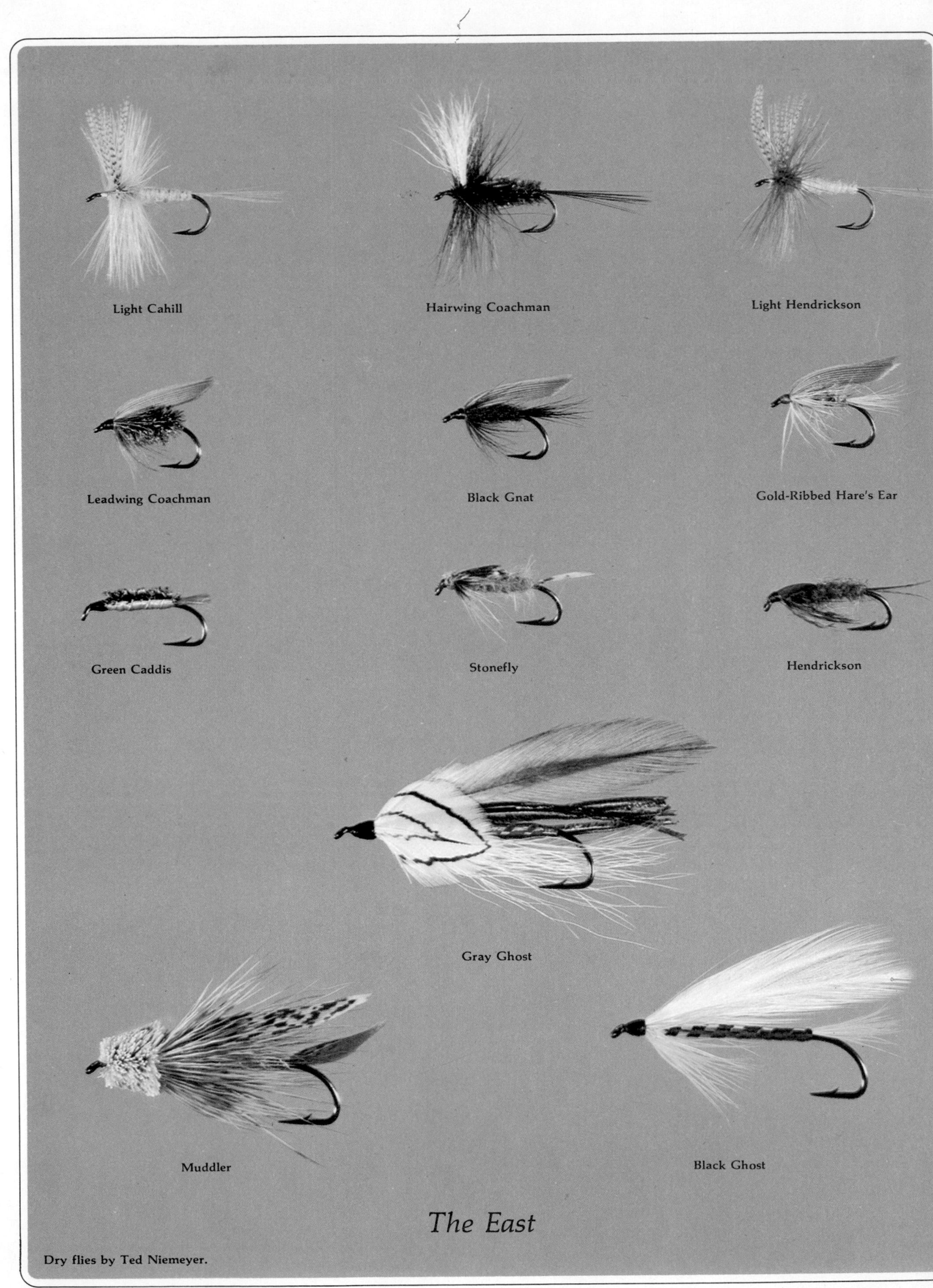

The East

Dry flies by Ted Niemeyer.

Plate 18

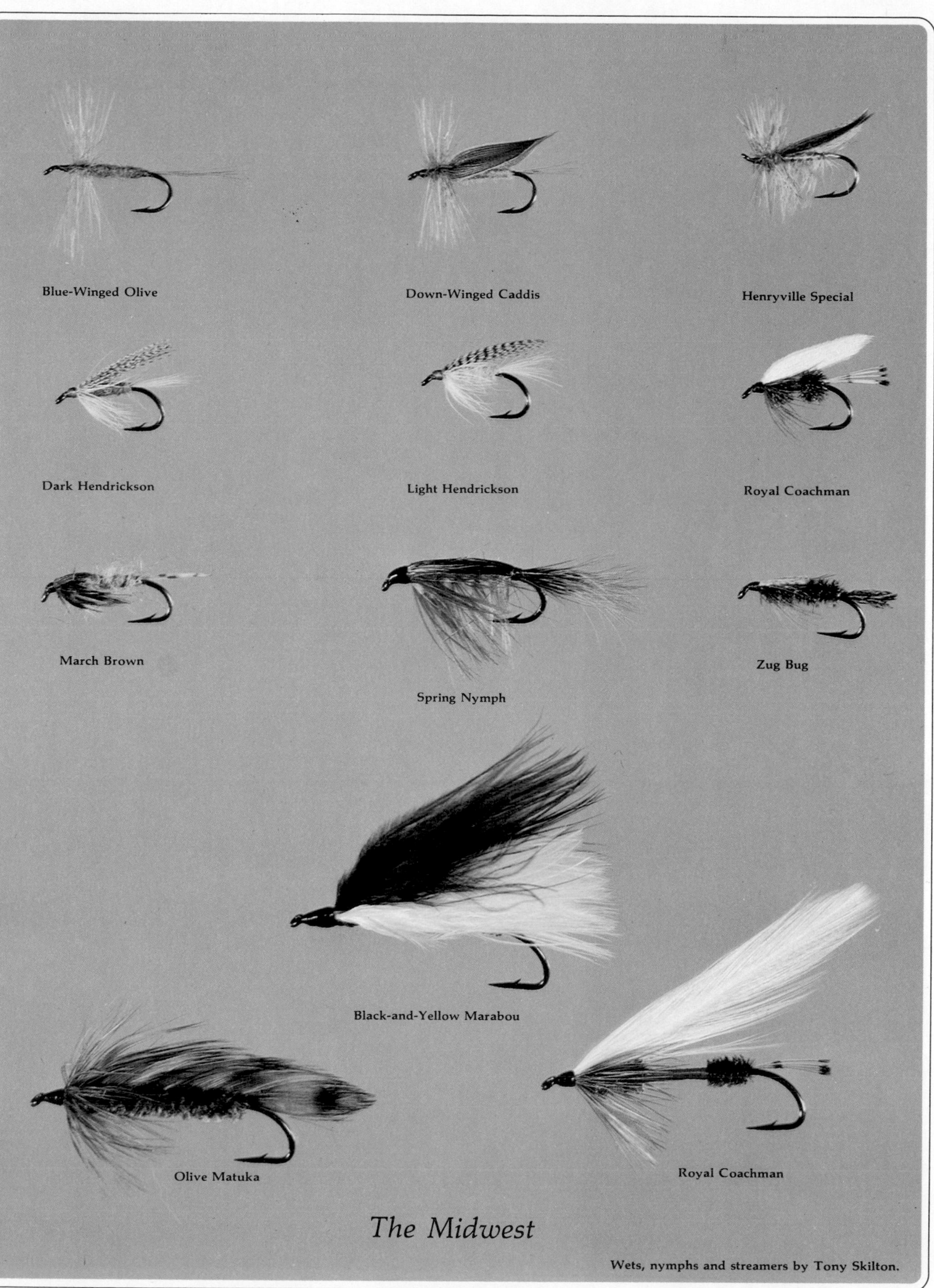

The Midwest

Wets, nymphs and streamers by Tony Skilton.

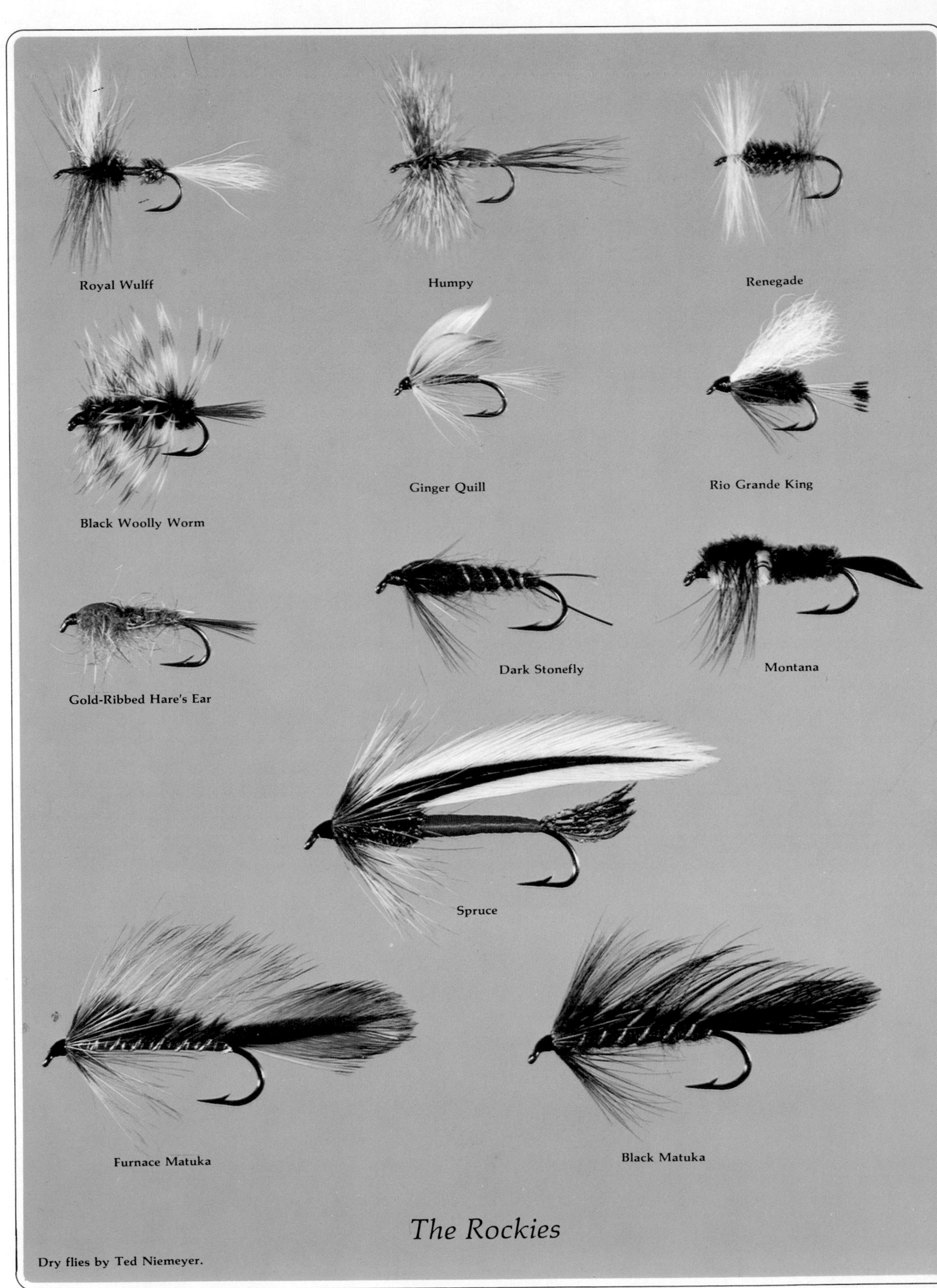

The Rockies

Dry flies by Ted Niemeyer.

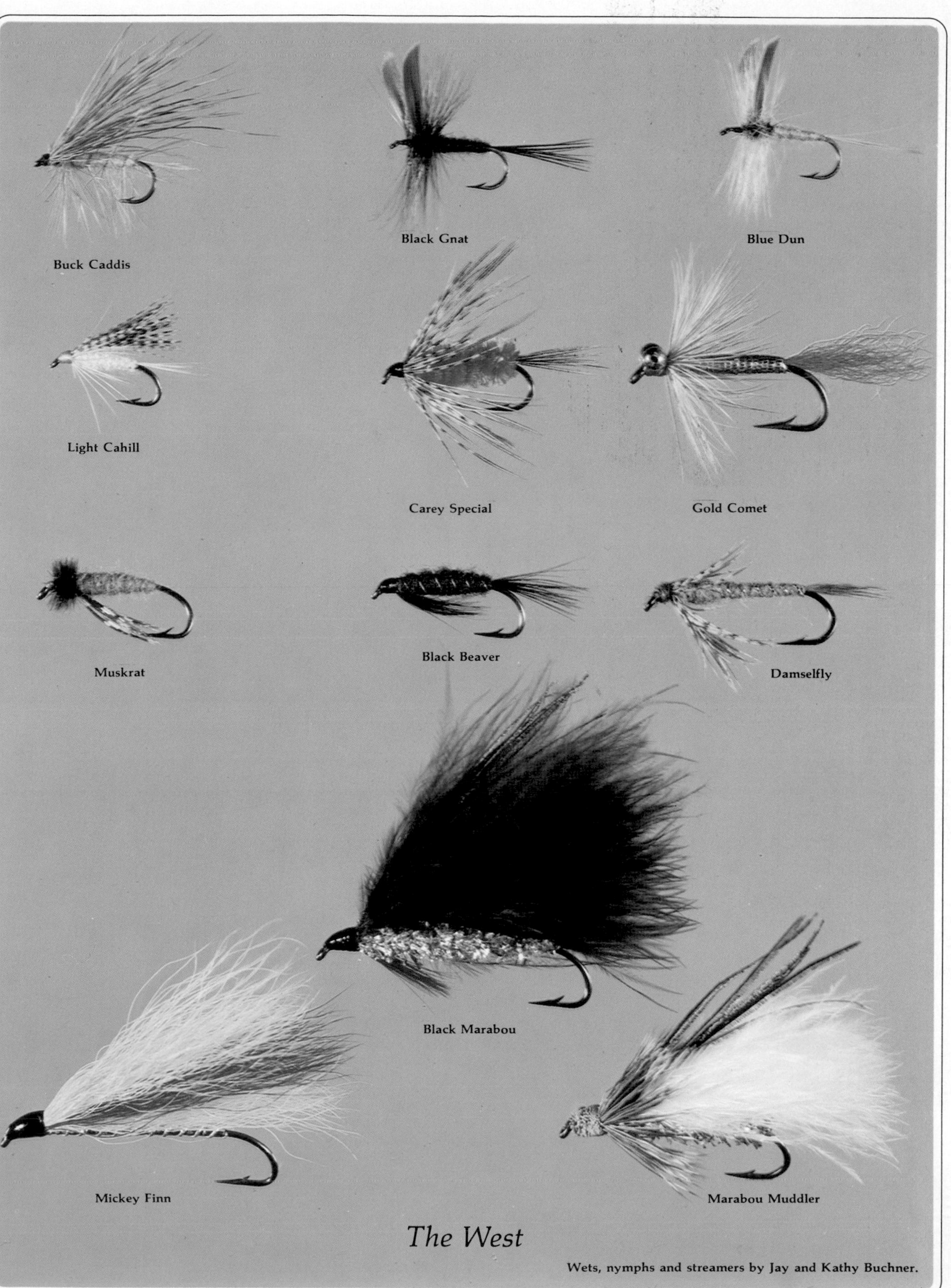

The West

Wets, nymphs and streamers by Jay and Kathy Buchner.

Plate 22

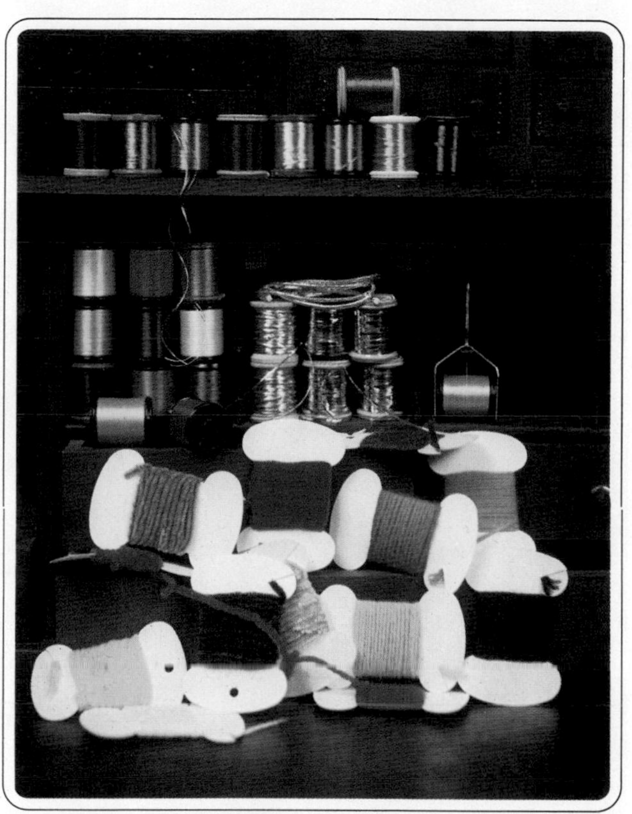

These photos represent most of the basic fly-tying materials described by Eric Leiser in his section on materials starting on page 102. Photos on these pages by John Merwin.

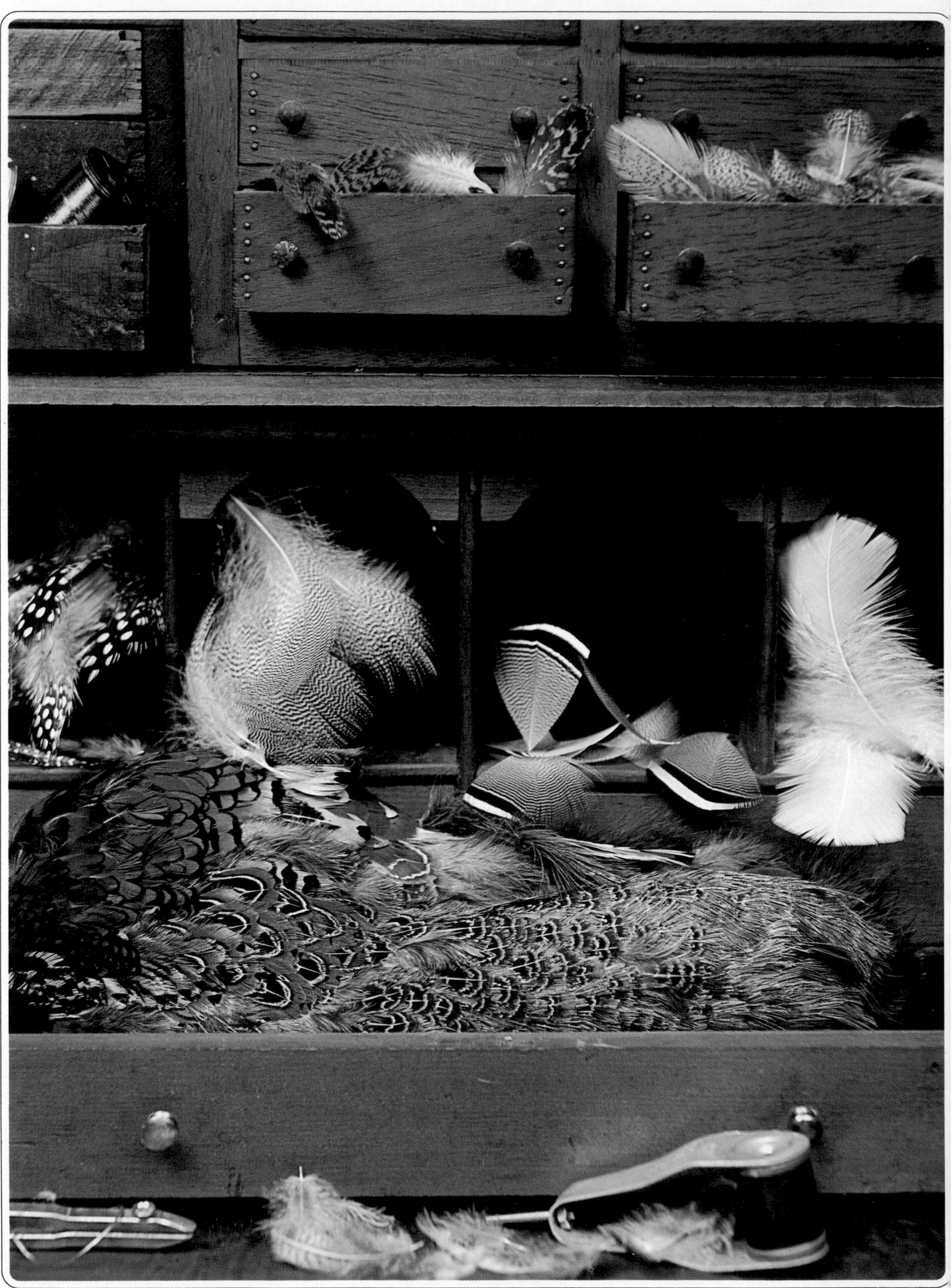

Plate 24

Tying the Black-Nose Dace

OUR SECOND FLY SELECTION introduces the use of tinsel and a favorite hairwing. The Black-Nose Dace represents a baitfish that is eagerly sought by trout in many parts of the country. A great many anglers swear by this pattern and will use nothing else in the spring and fall.

Set before you the following materials, all of which have been described earlier:

HOOK:	Mustad 9671, #8.
TAIL:	Bright red wool yarn.
BODY:	Flat silver mylar tinsel, medium width.
WING:	Brown, black and white bucktail.
THREAD:	Black Herb Howard Prewaxed Nylon.

Select and set before you a short section of bright red wool; a two-inch length should be sufficient. Next, cut 6-8 inches of tinsel from the spool. Select some bucktail in three colors: black, white and natural brown. Art Flick, the originator of this pattern, suggests natural polar bear, black bear and brown bucktail, but polar bear is generally not available, and we must find a substitute. You'll find that white bucktail will work well. I especially like the use of black bear in any pattern because of its sheen and action in the water, and you may wish to use it if black bucktail is not available.

Secure the hook in the vise and apply the tying thread to the hook shank as previously instructed. A complete layer of thread covers the hook shank and ends where the hook bend starts. Hold the section of red wool directly on top of the hook shank and take one complete revolution of the tying thread to hold the wool. It does not matter how far to the left the wool extends at this time, since we'll cut it to proper length as a tail later. With open but even revolutions of the tying thread taken toward the right, bind the wool to the top of the hook shank to within 3/16-inch of the hook eye. Cut the excess wool at a 45-degree angle. Holding the body tinsel at a 45-degree angle (left to right) across the top of the hook shank, take five tight revolutions of the tying thread to bind the end of the tinsel down.

In close, firm revolutions, wind the tinsel down the hook shank to the bend of the hook, covering all the tying thread and wool on the hook shank. Check the last operation for a smooth-looking surface on the body, and have confidence that when you start back up the body with the tinsel, you'll cover the body fully. No gaps should be seen. Return the tinsel up the hook shank with close firm turns. When you reach the point at which the tying thread bound down the tinsel (where you started the body), unwind the five turns of the tying thread and expose the original end of the tinsel. Cut

The upper photo shows the tying thread being wound back up over the red wool after the wool has been tied in. In the lower photo, the tinsel has been started down the body.

In the lower photo, the tinsel has been wound back up the body. The thread that first held the tinsel at the head of the fly is about to be unwound, allowing the returning tinsel to bind itself down.

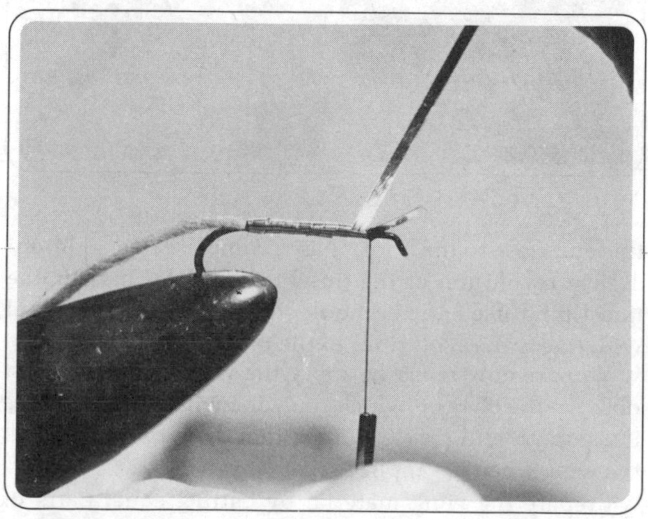

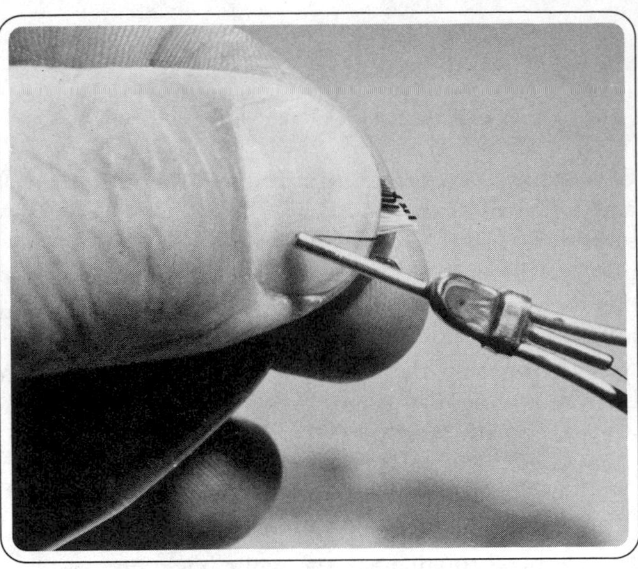

Brown, black and white bucktail sections have been stacked together and are now being judged for length. In the lower photo, the hair butts are being cut at an angle, which will ultimately produce a neat, cone-shaped head.

These are photographs of the bundling procedure described in the text. The hair is being held in position with the left hand while a turn of thread is taken around the hair butts, but not around the hook shank at the same time. In the lower photo, the turn has been completed and the hair is about to be slid down to the hook shank.

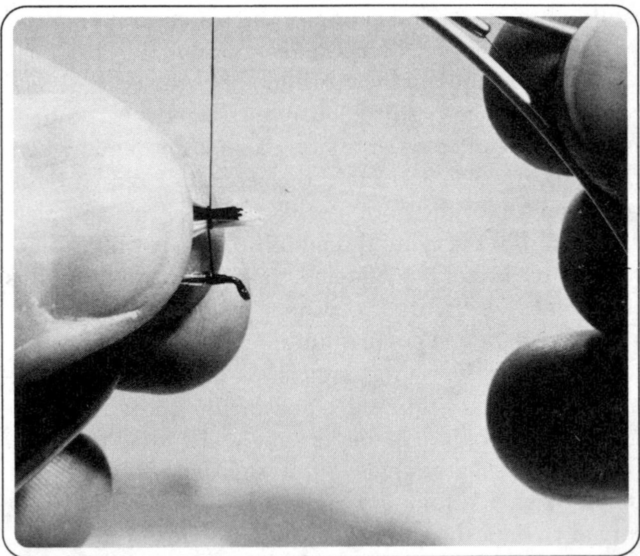

this end close to the hook. Next, complete one additional firm revolution of the tinsel to the right, making the tinsel bind itself to the hook shank. Secure the tinsel with five firm revolutions of the tying thread.

You are now ready to apply the wing material. First observe the base on which the wing will sit. Make sure it's smooth and free of lumps that may twist or offset the wing when it's applied.

Prepare the wing material by cutting equal parts of natural brown and white hair from a bucktail. As you cut these components, use the accompanying photos as a gauge for the length and amount of hair. When a section has been cut, you can set it *gently* on the table—in which case the hair bunch won't become separated—and go on to the next. The amount of black hair used should be about one half that of the white. The total mass of hair (all three colors) should not exceed the diameter of a wooden kitchen match when compressed.

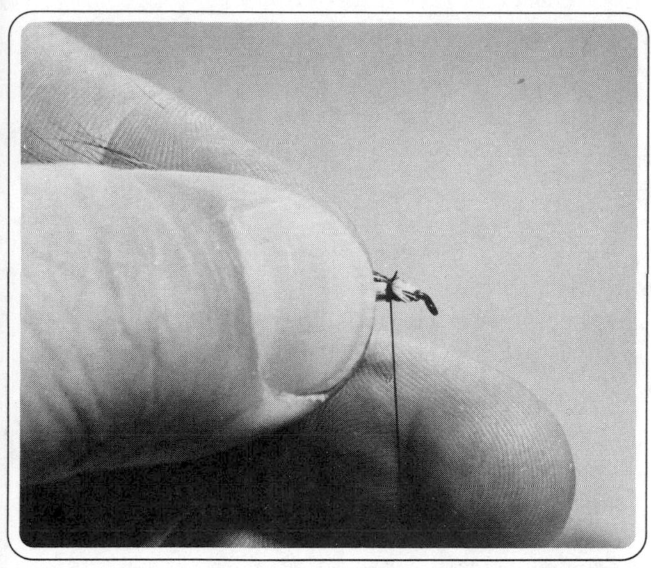

The hair has been slid down to the hook shank and a couple of additional turns of thread have been taken. Note that the thread hasn't yet gone down onto the cut ends of the hair. In the lower photo, cement is being applied to the finished head of the fly.

Pick up the white bunch, remove any errant fibers, and hold the bunch between the thumb and forefinger of your left hand. Then pick up the black bunch and hold it on top of the white so that your thumb and forefinger are holding them simultaneously. Then put the brown bunch on top of the other two. Compress the bunches together gently.

Hold the hair mass firmly in the fingers of the left hand and position the hair over the hook shank but not directly on it. If the length is judged to be correct, then cut the hair butts on a 60-degree angle precisely where they are to be lowered to the hook shank. Apply a small amount of thinned Ambroid cement to the cut ends and hold the hair in this position for a few moments until the cement starts to harden and becomes tacky.

The next manipulation is very important and should be studied with increased concentration. Holding the hair in position above the hook, bring the tying thread up and make one complete revolution around the hair *only*, at a point *just* to the left of the cut ends. Make sure that this turn of tying thread does not slip down on the cut ends of the hair.

Keep upward pressure on the tying thread, and in one continuous motion, slide the hair down to the hook shank, keeping a firm grip on the hair all the while with the left hand. The hair should now be held firmly on the top of the hook shank by your left hand. Pull firmly with the tying thread, and while still keeping a firm hold with the left hand, bind the hair in with four tight turns of the tying thread. Release the left hand slowly and check the wing for position. Return the left hand to pressure and hold the wing. Complete the head with tight, even turns of tying thread to the right. Make a smooth, tight head and then whip-finish.

Return to the tail material and cut the excess red wool, taking care that proportion is correct.

Special Tying Techniques

Let's take a closer look at some of the important manipulations found in tying the Black-Nose Dace:

•We eliminated a potentially serious lump at the head when we secured our tinsel the first time and then removed the five turns of thread later. This provided a smooth base for the wing.

•The loop made around the hair before it was positioned on the hook shank insures that the wing will sit directly on top of the hook and will not twist. If we had desired a flared wing, we would not have done this.

•The application of a small amount of Ambroid cement to the wing butt will help you as a beginner to hold all of the hair in a tight, well-formed wing. As you become more proficient in your tying, you probably will eliminate this practice.

•I cut the tailing material last since it's best to check the wing size first. If the wing is slightly longer than I would like, then the tail is cut slightly longer than normal. If the wing is a little shorter than I normally like, I can cut the tail short.

Tying the Adams

I HAVE HEARD IT SAID MANY TIMES: "If I only had one dry fly to use on any trout stream, I would choose the Adams." If you haven't adopted this philosophy, then tie a few Adams drys in a variety of sizes and head for the nearest trout water. No, don't take any other flies along—you'll probably find that you'll score well without them!

Set before you the following materials:

HOOK:	Mustad 94840, #12.
TAIL:	Grizzly and red-game hackles.
BODY:	Muskrat fur.
WING:	Grizzly hackles.
HACKLE:	Grizzly and red-game hackles.

Secure the hook in your vise and fasten the tying thread behind the eye at a point one-quarter of the distance from the hook eye to the bend. This is the point at which the wings are to be tied in. Trim the bases of two small, matched grizzly hackle-tips and hold them directly on top of the hook shank, hackle tips extending over the eye. Take two firm revolutions of the tying thread over their bases and let go with the left hand. With the fingers of the right hand, push the wings to a vertical position and check the wing height (see photo).

Assuming that you have judged the wings to be of the proper dimension, take two more secure turns of tying thread over their bases. Cut off the excess wing stems. Continue the tying thread to the bend of the hook. At this point, we'll position the tail of our fly.

Mix equal amounts of stiff grizzly and red-game hackle for tailing. A total of about eight fibers is sufficient. Hold these fibers firmly in the fingers of the left hand, and with firm revolutions of the tying thread, secure the tail fibers in position.

It should be noted that when the tail material is placed exactly on top of the hook shank and thread is wound over it, the tail tends to slide very slightly to the far side of the hook. Hold the tail fibers slightly to the *near* side of the hook shank, with the butts angled about five degrees toward your chest. The natural rotation of the material and thread then puts the tail directly on top of the hook shank. This simple procedure will follow you throughout all your tying, whether it be a #28 dry fly or a big 2/0 salmon pattern. Your ability to handle this simple technique will become very evident in all your results.

Continue the turns of tying thread forward over the tailing material until you have reached the butts of the wings. Cut the tail material off precisely where the butts of the wings were cut.

Apply a small amount of wax (if needed) to the tying thread and dub a small amount of muskrat fur to the waxed section. The dubbing should taper from a very thin point to only a slightly larger diameter; just enough fur to cover the tying thread is enough.

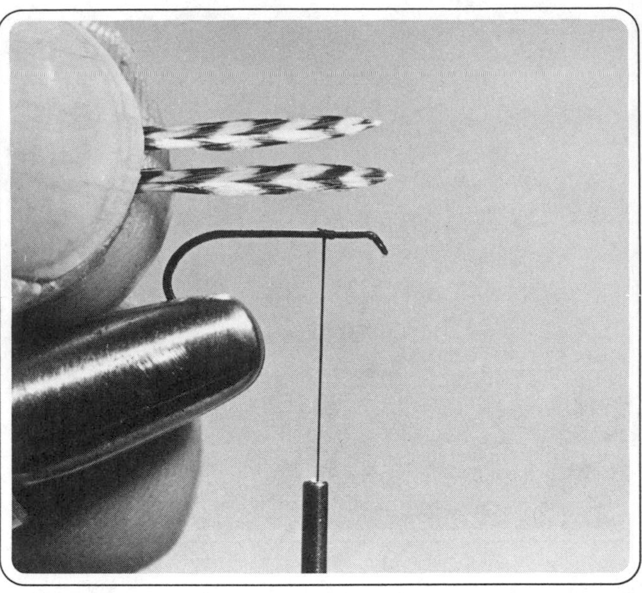

In the upper photo, grizzly hackle tips to be used for the wings are being held and judged for length before tying in. Below, the hackle tips have been tied in and are being pushed upright for a further evaluation.

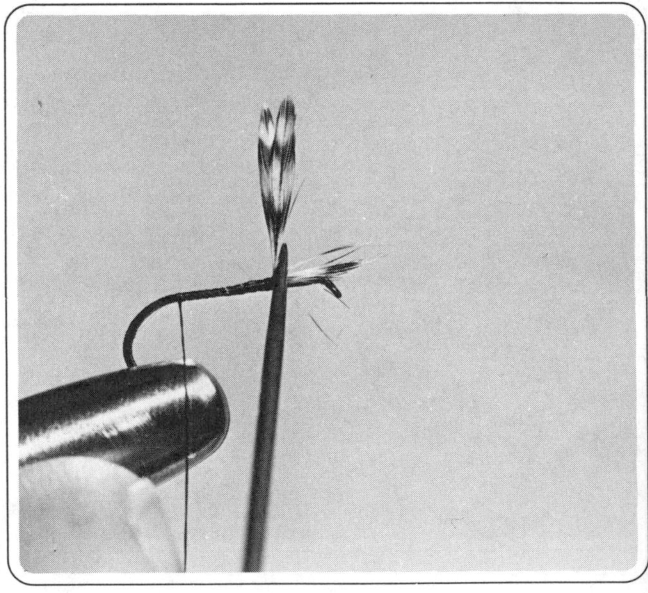

To obtain the fur for dubbing, pluck or cut some of the soft underfur from the piece of muskrat you set out before starting to tie. Remove the stiff guard hairs from the underfur and discard them. Take small amounts of fur between your right thumb and index finger. Spin them onto the thread by holding the fur

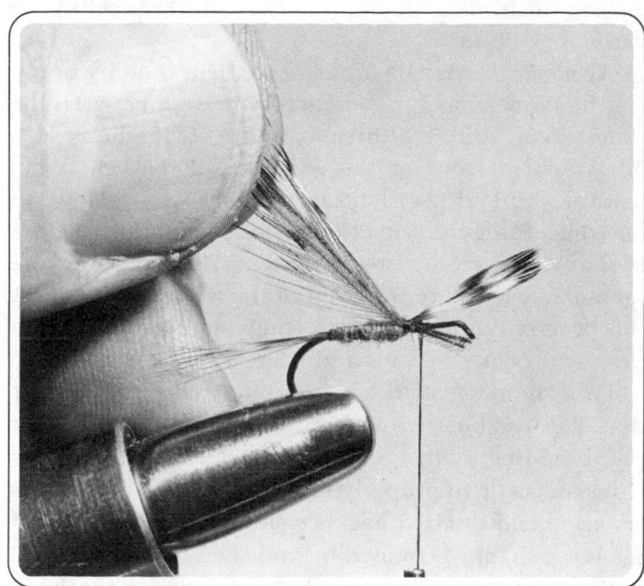

The hackle-fiber tail has been tied in and the excess is being trimmed. Note that the cut is being made at the same point at which the stems of the wing hackles were trimmed. The lower photo shows the dubbed body prior to being wound.

Two hackles tied in and about to be wound. Note the fibers remaining on their ends after trimming, which will help to hold them in position. In the lower photo, both hackles have been wound and the second is being tied off.

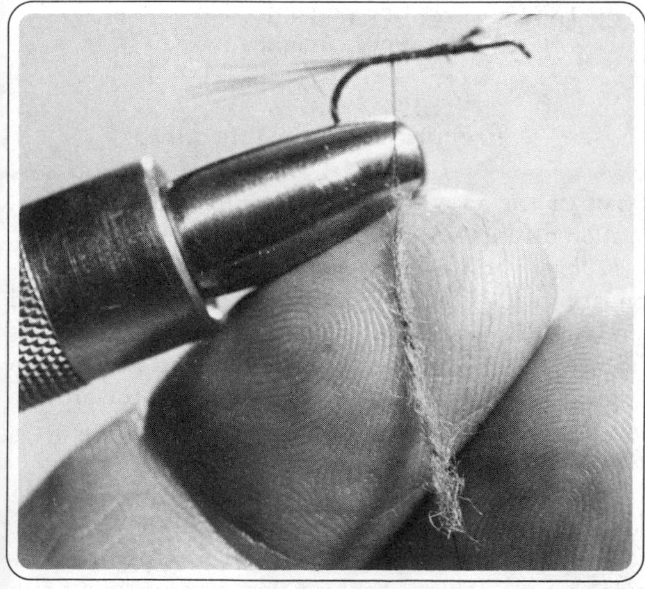

and thread together between your thumb and index finger and rolling them. The object is to produce a neatly tapered "noodle" of fur around the thread. A word of caution: Be careful not to use too much.

Our tying thread is positioned at the wing base now, so we must take additional turns of the thread to the left. Attempt to plan these revolutions so the first turn of dubbing will start *precisely* at the bend of the hook where the tail was first secured. Then carefully wind the dubbing forward in tight, even turns, leaving *no* gaps or lumps as you go. Stop and do it over if it does not look perfect to your eye. Stop the dubbing about 1/16 inch to the left of the wing position. Pluck any excess dubbing material from the thread.

With the fingers of the left hand pull the hackle-tip wings to a vertical position. Take three tight turns against the front of the wing stems to force them into a vertical position.

We next spread them into a V configuration by drawing the tying thread in a crisscross pattern between the stems. Start with the thread coming off the hook at a point just in front of the wing. Pull the near wing toward you and take half a turn over and behind the far wing. Bring the tying thread under and up to the left of the near wing. Grasp the far wing and pass the tying thread across and to the front of the wing base. Repeat this process twice more. The wings should now be in a fine semispent position, and we're ready for hackling.

Trim the bases of the grizzly and red-game hackles that you've chosen for this fly with scissors. Don't *pull* base fibers off, because you need the fine-clipped stubs of hackle to properly secure the stems to the hook shank. Hold the two hackle stems on the near side of the hook shank, 1/16 inch behind the wing base and at a 45-degree angle down and slightly under the hook shank. Three firm revolutions of the tying thread will secure the hackle stems so the hackle butts can be trimmed close to the shank.

We now want to position our tying thread just in front of the wings. Most tiers will simply take one or two turns of thread to get there. This leaves a very insecure and uneven base over which to wind the hackle. The result is what is so frequently seen—hackle that goes in every conceivable direction and looks like a comedy routine. To avoid this, wind the turns of thread to the right in very tight, even turns, being careful to fill any voids as you go. Four or five complete turns are usually enough.

With the hackle pliers, grasp the tip of the hackle nearest you, and with firm, evenly spaced turns, wind it forward, ending with at least two full revolutions in *front* of the wing base. Three tight turns of thread over the hackle-tip will secure it. Trim the excess close. Take two additional turns of thread to the right, forming a smooth base for the finishing turns of the second hackle.

Start the first turn of the second hackle to the left of where the first hackle was started. I frequently pull all of the first hackle toward the right, which allows the first turn of the second hackle to come close against it, holding everything in a vertical plane. Continue the turns of the second hackle evenly toward the right, ending with at least one complete turn of hackle in front of where the first hackle was tied off. Three tight turns of the tying thread over the hackle-tip will hold it so the excess can be trimmed. Put firm pressure on the tying thread and with the nail of the right thumb on top of the hook shank, apply pressure against the whole mass, pushing to the left. This act will compress the hackle and insure sufficient space for the whip-finish knot. Tie the finishing knot and repeat the thumbnail procedure once more before cutting the thread free.

Tying the Ephemerella Nymph

WE'VE NOW COME TO A PATTERN that will, at first glance, seem extremely complicated to tie. There aren't, however, any tying tricks utilized in this pattern that you haven't encountered in tying the previous three. This fly is generally representative of a wide variety of mayfly nymphs. It's an extremely realistic imitation, yet one which still has considerable life in the water because of the softness of the goose-down dubbing that's used for its body.

The preparation of the materials for this nymph will be as important as the actual tying. Reverse, if you will, your thinking of how the finished fly might look, and think instead of how all the components will look when spread out before you. Here's what you'll need:

HOOK:	Mustad 9675, #12.
TAIL:	Three tapered porcupine quills, about 1/32" thick at their bases.
BODY:	Black floss for the underbody; two brass pins; Canada goose breast down.
RIBBING:	Quill stripped from Canada goose secondary feather.
WING CASE:	Dark mallard breast feather.
LEGS:	Six tapered porcupine quills, about 1/24" thick at their bases.
ANTENNAE:	Two fine porcupine hairs.
EYES:	Two fine porcupine hairs.

Preparation of Materials

SOME OF THE ABOVE MATERIALS require additional preparation before we start the process of tying our nymph.

Ribbing is obtained by soaking a Canada goose secondary feather in hot, soapy water overnight and stripping the hard quill surface (center stem) off the feather. Simply nick the upper tip of the stem with a razor, grasp the nicked tip and pull hard toward the butt of the feather. The center stem will part, leaving you with a beautiful solid quill.

For the *wing case*, pull the fluff off the base of a mallard breast feather and cut square across the tip of the feather so that it won't roll over when it is set convex-side up on a table. Apply a thin coat of satin-finish Valspar (varnish) to the convex side. Set the feather aside to dry.

Flatten each porcupine quill (to be used for the *legs*) by compressing each one with your thumbnail (drawn down the length of the quill). Tie a simple overhand knot ¼ inch from the quill tip. Complete all six quills alike.

To make the *eyes*, tie a simple overhand knot in a porcupine hair, and trim one end of the hair close to

The tails have been tied in (above) and wound along the body to help give it shape. Below, the floss underbody has been wound and the pins are being cut.

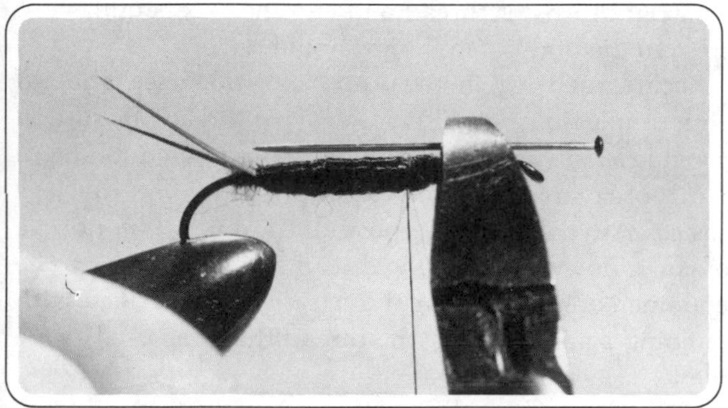

In the lower photo, cut pins have been tied in on either side of the body. The quill for ribbing has also been tied in and the body is ready for dubbing.

The entire body has been dubbed (above) and the ribbing has been started. Below are shown a pair of the quills to be used for legs; one already has the overhand knot.

The lower photo shows all the legs after tying in. Their bases are about to be covered with dubbing.

the knot. You'll be left holding a long hair with a knot at its end. Dip this knot in black lacquer and allow to dry. Apply two additional black lacquer dippings. When you are sure the lacquer is dry, apply three dippings in clear Valspar varnish, allowing a drying period between each application. I usually do 50 eyes at a time to avoid tedious work down the line.

Tying the Fly

PLACE THE HOOK firmly in your vise and complete one layer of the tying thread from the eye to the bend of hook; varnish the layer of tying thread. Take a very small quantity of goose down, dub it on the tying thread, and wind a small ball of dubbing at the bend.

Tie in the three porcupine quills as tails using figure-eight turns of thread to spread and elevate the tails to the proper position (see photo). Wind thread over the butts of porcupine to help build a body base as you return the tying thread to within 1/8 inch of the eye.

Tie in a long section of black floss and commence forming a base for the abdomen and thorax. Tie off the floss when the proper body shape is formed. Keep the body rather thin as there is much more to be added.

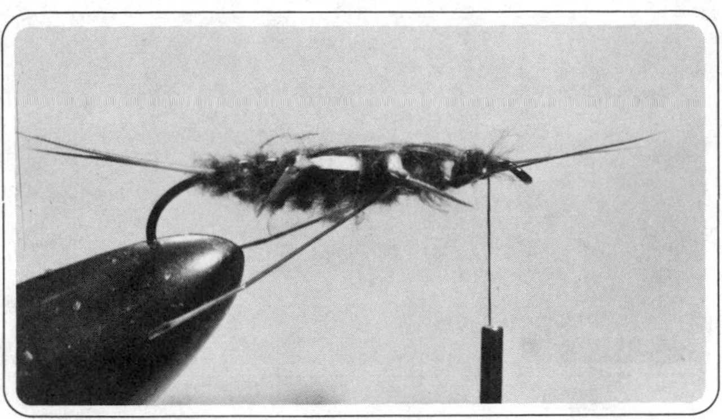

The upper photo shows the antennae after tying in. Below, cement is being applied over the leg bases before the wing case is added.

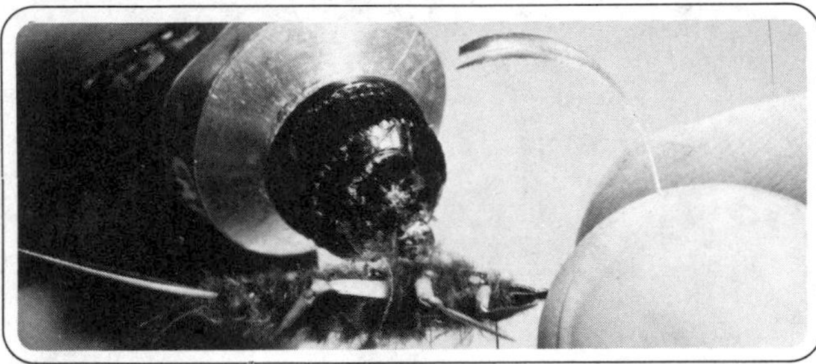

The lower photo shows the eyes having been tied in with figure-eight thread wraps. Now the stalks will be pulled to bring the eyes into position.

The lower photo is a side view of the finished fly. A top view is provided in color plate 17.

Next are the two brass pins, points toward tail, and head cut off ¼ inch from hook eye. Position these pins on each side of the hook shank and slightly below the shank's center of gravity. The fly will turn upside down when fished if this is not done. When thread is wrapped over the pins, you should press the tips of the pins tightly at the tail to form a cigar-shaped taper when viewed from above. Secure the pins with numerous turns of the tying thread. Coat entire body with varnish.

Return the tying thread to the tail position and tie in the small tip of the stripped goose quill, dull side facing you.

Dub generous portions of the goose down to your waxed tying thread and form a solid, evenly dubbed body up to the head. Return the tying thread to the thorax area. Wind the stripped goose quill in open but even turns to the thorax area. Secure the quill with ten very tight turns of thread and clip the excess quill very close to the body. No bump should remain.

Secure each leg in its proper position (see photos) with simple figure-eight turns of tying thread. Be sure to provide a firm and wide base of goose-down dubbing in the thorax area to make the application of the legs easier. After the legs are positioned, dub a *thin* noodle of goose down on the tying thread and wind back to the abdomen area. Now the thorax area will be filled with dubbing again to cover the thread that was used to tie the legs.

Trim the mallard breast feather to the shape of the Ephemerella-nymph wing case, and coat its underside with a small amount of any waterproof adhesive. Secure butt end of feather 1/16 inch behind hook eye.

Lay each antenna fiber along hook shank, extending beyond the hook eye. Secure with tight turns of thread. Dub a small quantity of dark goose down on the tying thread and form a small nymph head.

Return the tying thread to 1/8 inch behind the hook eye and secure the near-side eye. Do this by holding the butt end of the hair (the eye is on tip end) across the top of and perpendicular to the hook shank, much the same as you did for the legs. The far-side eye will be secured in the same manner. Figure-eight turns of thread hold them firmly.

Pull on each eye butt until the ball of the eye has been drawn into its proper position. Bend the stems back 90 degrees over the hook shank and lock the stems down with three tight turns of the tying thread. Clip off the excess butts.

Dub a small quantity of dark goose down on the thread and form a full nymph head. Pass this dubbing behind the eyes as well as in front, covering any exposed turns of tying thread. One turn of dubbing firmly under the antennae will spread them into position. Whip-finish, and then press the head with the thumbnail as was done with the Adams dry fly. Clip off the excess tying thread and the nymph is finished.

Selected Regional Fly Patterns

THE QUESTION OF WHAT FLY patterns to tie or buy is always a puzzle for beginner and expert anglers alike. There are thousands and thousands of fly patterns from which to choose and, at some point, every angler has to pick a few with which to start.

To give you some direction in this area, the editors and field staff of FLY FISHERMAN magazine surveyed 36 well-known fly shops around the country, asking the owners to tell us what were their best-selling patterns in four categories: dry, wet, nymph and streamer. Our inquires were made on the following regional basis: East, Midwest, Rocky Mountains and West.

Based on the information they supplied, it almost seems that we could expect to do well anywhere in the country with an Adams dry, a Gold-Ribbed Hare's Ear (wet or nymph), and a Muddler Minnow; these three patterns dominated everyone's list. But differences in regional fly hatches, traditions and waters contribute to differences in regional fly selections, and so shortly you'll see the results of our survey: the three most popular drys, wets, nymphs and streamers in each of the four regions covered.

All of those patterns are included in the color plates accompanying this section and pattern descriptions are in this section as well. Because we wished to include as many flies as possible within this section, duplicate patterns (those listed for more than one region) were not included in more than one color plate. When this occurred, we took the fourth or fifth most-popular pattern from a given region and included it in that region's color plate of flies, giving you a total of 48 different patterns, plus the four that Ted Niemeyer has already shown you how to tie.

Here then, on a regional basis, are what we found to be America's most-popular fly patterns:

Plate 18: The East

Dry Flies

Light Cahill

HOOK: Mustad 94840.
THREAD: White.
TAIL: Pale ginger cock-hackle fibers.
BODY: Cream colored fox fur dubbing.
WING: Wood-duck flank.
HACKLE: Pale ginger cock hackle.

Hairwing Coachman

HOOK: Mustad 94840.
THREAD: Black.
TAIL: Natural reddish-brown cock-hackle fibers.
BODY: Peacock herl.
WING: White calf-tail hair.
HACKLE: Natural red-brown cock hackles.

Light Hendrickson

HOOK: Mustad 94840.
THREAD: Black.
TAIL: Blue dun hackle fibers.
BODY: Pale urine-burned (pink) fox fur.
WING: Wood duck.
HACKLE: Blue dun.

Wet Flies

Leadwing Coachman

HOOK: Mustad 3906.
TAG: Flat gold tinsel.
THREAD: Black.
TAIL: None.
BODY: Peacock herl.
WING: Dark gray duck quill.
HACKLE: Dark red-brown.

Black Gnat

HOOK: Mustad 3906.
THREAD: Black.
TAIL: None.
BODY: Black chenille.
WING: Gray duck quill.
HACKLE: Black cock or hen.

Gold-Ribbed Hare's Ear

HOOK: Mustad 3906.
THREAD: Black.
TAIL: Brown hackle fibers.
BODY: Hare's-ear fur dubbing ribbed with flat gold tinsel.
WING: Light gray duck quill.
HACKLE: Pick out dubbing at throat to resemble hackle. (Some versions include hackle in any of a number of subdued shades.)

Nymphs

Green Caddis

HOOK: Mustad 9672.
THREAD: Black.
TAIL: Green floss.
BODY: Green floss.
OVERBODY: Peacock herl.
RIBBING: Fine gold wire.

Stonefly

HOOK: Mustad 9672.
THREAD: Brown.
TAIL: Mottled turkey.
BODY: Natural brown rabbit.
WING CASE: Mottled turkey.
HACKLE: Furnace hen hackle.
HEAD: Dubbed rabbit.

Hendrickson

HOOK: Mustad 9672.
THREAD: Black.
TAIL: Wood-duck fibers.
BODY: Blend of tan and gray fox fur and claret seal fur ribbed with olive tying silk or fine gold wire.
WINGCASE: Dark gray duck quill tied over thorax.
LEGS: Brown partridge hackle.

Streamers

Muddler

HOOK: Mustad 79580.
THREAD: Black.
TAIL: A strip of speckled brown turkey quill feather.
BODY: Flat gold tinsel.
WING: Sparse black bear hair with a strip of speckled brown turkey quill feather at either side.
HEAD: Brown deerhair, spun and clipped; tips of first bunch are left to form a collar.

Gray Ghost

HOOK: Mustad 9575.
THREAD: Black.
BODY: Orange silk floss ribbed with flat silver tinsel.
WING: A long golden pheasant crest tied directly over body about 1 inch longer than hook. Over this are 2 gray saddle hackles about an inch-and-a-half longer

than hook; 2 short hackles of the same color are tied in about 1/3 the length of the first pair of hackles, over which are 5 or 6 strands of green peacock herl about the same length as the longest saddle hackles.

HACKLE: A small bunch of white bucktail tied under the body extending full length of the wing. A small golden pheasant crest feather tied about ½ the length of the sides underneath the white bucktail.

SIDES: Silver pheasant feather about 2/3 hook length.

CHEEKS: Jungle cock extending over ½ length of side feathers (now usually omitted).

HEAD: Black lacquer.

Black Ghost

HOOK: Mustad 9575.

THREAD: Black.

TAIL: Lemon yellow hackle fibers.

BODY: Black silk floss dressed full, ribbed with flat silver tinsel.

WING: 4 white saddle hackles about an inch longer than hook.

CHEEKS: Jungle cock about ¼ length of wing (now usually omitted).

HACKLE: Lemon yellow put on before the wing.

HEAD: Black lacquer.

Plate 19: The Midwest

Dry Flies

Blue-Winged Olive

HOOK: Mustad 94840.

THREAD: Black.

TAIL: Blue dun cock hackle fibers.

BODY: Medium olive dubbing.

WING: Dark blue-dun hackle tips.

HACKLE: Blue dun cock hackle.

Down-Winged Caddis

HOOK: Mustad 94840.

THREAD: Black.

TAIL: Blue-dun hackle fibers.

BODY: Gray muskrat dubbing.

WING: Gray duck-quill segments tied downwing-style.

HACKLE: Blue dun.

(This pattern is tied in many styles and colors, of which this one is representative.)

Henryville Special

HOOK: Mustad 94840.

THREAD: Black.

TAIL: None.

BODY: Green floss palmered with grizzly cock hackle.

WING: Gray duck-quill segments tied over smaller slip of wood duck.

HACKLE: Mixed brown and grizzly cock hackle.

Wet Flies

Dark Hendrickson

HOOK: Mustad 3906.

THREAD: Black.

TAIL: Wood-duck fibers.

BODY: Brownish-gray fox fur dubbing.

WING: Wood-duck flank.

HACKLE: Dark rusty dun.

Light Hendrickson

HOOK: Mustad 3906.

THREAD: White.

TAIL: Wood-duck fibers.

BODY: Fawn-colored fox fur dubbing.

WING: Wood-duck flank.

HACKLE: Natural blue dun cock or hen.

Royal Coachman

HOOK: Mustad 3906.

THREAD: Black.

TAIL: Golden pheasant tippets.

BODY: Peacock herl, scarlet floss, peacock herl; each 1/3 shank length.

WING: White duck quill.

HACKLE: Brown hen hackle.

Nymphs

March Brown

HOOK: Mustad 9672.

THREAD: Black.

TAIL: 3 strands from a cock pheasant center tail feather.

BODY: Seal fur dyed amber mixed with a small amount of tan fur from red fox and ribbed with a single strand of brown embroidery cotton.

WINGCASE: From short side feathers of cock pheasant tail (tied over thorax).

HACKLE: Brown partridge.

HEAD: Brown lacquer.

Spring Nymph

HOOK: Mustad 9672.

THREAD: Black.

BODY: Yellow chenille palmered with brown hackle.

TAIL: Red fox-squirrel tail.

OVERBODY: Red fox-squirrel tail.

Zug Bug

HOOK: Mustad 9672.

THREAD: Black.

TAIL: 3 strands of green peacock sword.

BODY: Peacock herl ribbed with silver oval tinsel. Lead wire may be used if weight is desired.

WINGCASE: Mallard flank cut short, extending over forward one fourth of body.

HACKLE: Long, soft brown hen hackle.

HEAD: Black lacquer.

Streamers

Olive Matuka

HOOK: Mustad 79580.

THREAD: Black.

BODY: Olive fur or wool dubbing.

RIBBING: Fine gold tinsel.

WING: 4-6 grizzly hackles dyed olive.

Black-and-Yellow Marabou

HOOK: Mustad 79580.

THREAD: Black.

BODY: Gold tinsel.

RIBBING: Oval gold tinsel.

WING: Black marabou over yellow marabou.

Royal Coachman

HOOK: Mustad 9575.

THREAD: Black.

TAIL: A bunch of golden pheasant tippet fibers.

BUTT: Green peacock herl.

BODY: Red silk floss with a shoulder of green peacock herl same size as butt.

HACKLE: Sparse brown hackle put on before wing.

WING: 4 white saddle hackles about 1/3 longer than hook.

HEAD: Black lacquer.

Plate 20: The Rockies

Dry Flies

Royal Wulff

HOOK: Mustad 94840.

THREAD: Black.

TAIL: White calf tail.

BODY: Peacock herl, scarlet floss, peacock herl; each 1/3 body length.

WING: White calf tail.

HACKLE: Coachman brown.

Humpy

HOOK: Mustad 94840.

THREAD: Black.

TAIL: Deerhair.

BODY: Underbody of deerhair butts, some tips of which form tail. Balance is brought forward and tied as wings.

WING: Deerhair.

HACKLE: Brown and grizzly mixed.

Renegade

HOOK: Mustad 94840.

THREAD: Black.

TAG: Silver Tinsel.

TAIL: None.

BODY: Peacock herl.

WING: None.

HACKLE: White at hook bend, brown at eye.

Wet Flies

Black Woolly Worm

HOOK: Mustad 9671.
THREAD: Black.
TAIL: Red hackle fibers.
BODY: Black chenille.
HACKLE: Grizzly, palmered.

Ginger Quill

HOOK: Mustad 3906.
THREAD: Black.
TAIL: Ginger hackle fibers.
BODY: 2 stripped peacock quills.
WING: Gray duck quill sections.
HACKLE: Ginger.

Rio Grande King

HOOK: Mustad 3906.
THREAD: Black.
TAIL: Golden pheasant tippets.
TAG: Flat gold tinsel.
BODY: Black chenille.
WING: White calf tail.
HACKLE: Brown.

Nymphs

Gold-Ribbed Hare's Ear

HOOK: Mustad 3906B.
THREAD: Black.
TAIL: Brown hackle fibers.
BODY: Hare's ear dubbing.
RIB: Fine gold wire.
WINGCASE: Dark duck quill.
THORAX: Hare's-ear dubbing tied full and picked out to represent legs.

Dark Stonefly

HOOK: Mustad 79580.
THREAD: Black.
TAIL: Dyed black monofilament tied around small ball of dubbing.
BODY: Black fur or synthetic dubbing.
RIB: Silver oval tinsel.
WINGCASE: Goose quill or duck quill.
THORAX: Black dubbing.
HACKLE: Black.

Montana

HOOK: Mustad 9672.
THREAD: Black.
TAIL: Section of black duck quill.
BODY: Black chenille.
THORAX: Yellow chenille.
WINGCASE: Black chenille.
HACKLE: Black, wrapped 3 or 4 turns through thorax.

Streamers

Spruce

HOOK: Mustad 3665A.
THREAD: Black.
TAIL: 4-8 fibers peacock sword.
BODY: Red floss, peacock herl; each ½ shank length.
WING: 4 badger saddle hackles.
HACKLE: Badger tied back.

Black Matuka

HOOK: Mustad 79580 or 38941.
THREAD: Black.
BODY: Black dubbing.
RIB: Silver oval tinsel.
WING: 4-6 black neck hackles.
HACKLE: Black tied back.

Furnace Matuka

HOOK: Mustad 79580 or 38941.
THREAD: Black.
BODY: Gold tinsel (Gold dubbing can be substituted).
RIB: Gold oval tinsel.
WING: 4-6 furnace hackles.
HACKLE: Furnace.

Plate 21: The West

Dry Flies

Buck Caddis

HOOK: Mustad 94840.
THREAD: Black.
TAIL: Ginger cock-hackle fibers.
BODY: Yellow floss, palmered with ginger cock hackle.
WING: Deerhair, tied downwing and flared.
HACKLE: Ginger cock hackle, tied under wing.

Black Gnat

HOOK: Mustad 94840.
THREAD: Black.
TAIL: Black cock-hackle fibers.
BODY: Black chenille or fur dubbing.
WING: Slips of medium-gray duck quill.
HACKLE: Black cock hackles.

Blue Dun

HOOK: Mustad 94840.
THREAD: Black.
TAIL: Medium blue dun hackle fibers.
BODY: Medium gray muskrat dubbing.
WING: Gray mallard quill sections.
HACKLE: Medium blue dun.

Wet Flies

Light Cahill

HOOK: Mustad 3906.
THREAD: Cream.
TAIL: Light ginger hackle fibers.
BODY: Cream fur.
WING: Wood duck or imitation.
HACKLE: Light ginger.

Carey Special

HOOK: Mustad 9672.
THREAD: Black.
TAIL: Pheasant rump fibers.
BODY: Almost any body material (chenille, floss, wool, herl).
HACKLE: Pheasant rump feather, tied back long.

Gold Comet

HOOK: Eagle Claw 1197B.
THREAD: Orange.
TAIL: Orange calf tail.
BODY: Gold oval tinsel over tapered yellow floss.
HACKLE: Yellow and hot-orange mixed.
EYES: Brass bead chain.

Nymphs

Muskrat

HOOK: Mustad 3906B.
THREAD: Gray.
BODY: Muskrat.
THROAT: Guinea fibers.
HEAD: Black ostrich herl.

Black Beaver

HOOK: Mustad 3906B.
THREAD: Black.
TAIL: Black hackle fibers.
BODY: Black beaver.
RIB: Copper wire.
THROAT: Black hackle fibers.

Damselfly Nymph

HOOK: Mustad 79580.
THREAD: Olive.
TAIL: Marabou fibers from feather base.
BODY: Olive dubbing.
RIB: Gold oval tinsel.
WINGCASE: Duck quill.
THORAX: Olive dubbing.
HACKLE: Partridge.

Streamers

Mickey Finn

HOOK: Mustad 3665A.
THREAD: Black.
BODY: Flat silver tinsel (medium).
RIB: Fine oval silver tinsel.
WING: Small clump of yellow bucktail, small clump of red bucktail, medium clump of yellow bucktail.

Black Marabou Streamer

HOOK: Mustad 3665A.
THREAD: Black.
TAIL: Red hackle fibers.
BODY: Silver tinsel chenille.
THROAT: Red hackle fibers.
WING: Black Marabou.
TOPPING: 4-6 strands peacock herl.

Marabou Muddler

HOOK: Mustad 79580, 38941 or 3665A.
THREAD: Black monocord, size A.
BODY: Tinsel chenille, gold or silver.
WING: White marabou, with 4-6 strands of peacock herl topping.
HEAD: Deerhair spun and clipped.

Illustration by John Pimlott

There are possibly a few more things we could tell you in this next spread of pages that might very well tell you a bit more about how to catch fish on the fly rod. But, at least until it gets into your hands, it's still our book—and we think it is also important to know why you should want to fly-fish. For most of us, the joys of fly-angling reach even beyond the esthetics of the act itself, back into the centuries and to the dim roots of our historical past. Man has always known of baited hooks, forked spears and snaring nets—in fact, we can say with truth and without frivolity that Christ Himself was one of the first recorded "ghillies," for it was He who directed His fellow fishermen to cast their nets from the other side of their boat. But, of course, He was feeding the multitudes, and we're certain that He would find satisfaction in knowing that, since His time, man has also fished to feed his soul. And nowhere, to our knowledge, has this story of angling man been so well recounted in such a brief space than on the pages to follow. The multi-faceted Ernie Schwiebert, who could have written any chapter of this book, has directed his efforts to recording the "laying on of hands" that has carried the fly-fishing tradition, with all its glories and delightful inanities, to the present state of the art. Accept this stewardship—with anticipation and obligation.

Chapter 11

The History and Lore of Fly-Fishing

From Genesis through Revelations

ERNEST SCHWIEBERT

THE LITTLE FISHING HOUSE is still there. Its weathered masonry and stone-arched Renaissance doorway and sculptured quoins are stained with time and three centuries of the English climate. It stands in a circle of trees, echoing the fashionable landscape planning of the late seventeenth century. The fishing house is simple, yet its cruciform plan is nothing less than Palladian in design, demonstrating that its builder was a British country gentleman of remarkable cultivation and taste.

There are heavy shutters and leaded windows that witnessed Izaak Walton on the fishing house pool. The slates are dark with moss on its steep, pyramid-shaped roof. Its slopes are capped with a sphere and a tiny trout-shaped weathervane.

Its builder was Charles Cotton of Beresford Hall. Its sandstone steps are worn with the boots and brogues of almost three hundred seasons. The simple iron-grate fireplace is flanked by staghorn trophies. Yellow buttercups and cornflowers fill the meadow that reaches less than a hundred feet to the river. It is a place that seems suspended in time. There is a circular sandstone table set on a pillarlike base, where fishermen could sit and study the Dove for rising trout. It is not difficult to think of Cotton sitting there, dressing a delicate Dun with wings of mallard and a dubbing of mole on yellow buttonhole silk. Both Walton and Cotton must have rested there, talking and tying flies and horsehair leaders and sharing a cold pitcher of ale from the springhouse.

The fishing house at Beresford is perhaps the oldest shrine of our sport. Both Beresford Hall itself and the Sopwell Nunnery, where Dame Juliana Berners compiled her *Treatyse of Fysshynge wyth an Angle* in the fifteenth century, lie in tree-covered ruins. Nothing is known of the fishing shrines of the third century, when Claudianus Aelianus wrote of fly-fishing in Macedonia, let alone of the Chinese roots of fly-fishing in the Chou Dynasty.

The earliest references to fishing as sport probably lie in descriptions of Chinese prehistory found in *The Book of Things*, with passages on silken lines and hooks and thornwood rods. Recent evidence, in a scholarly series of British volumes titled *The History of Chinese Science*, indicates that fly-fishing had its genesis more than 2,300 years ago during the Chou Dynasty. Until Joseph Needham published his unique studies of China, it was widely agreed that the roots of our sport lay in the rivers of Macedonia in the third century. Needham has also offered proof that fishing reels evolved in China before the twelfth century, and it seems likely that spaghetti and gunpowder were not the only things brought back by Marco Polo.

However, the beginnings of fly-fishing in southern Europe perhaps lie in the writings of Plutarch, and his descriptions of fishing along the Nile in his *Life of Antonius* are not his only concern for the sport. Plutarch was apparently an angler, since his essays include references to lines of horsehair. His advice concerns the selection of pale white or grayish hairs to deceive the fish, and he concludes that the hairs of a mare's tail are too weakened by urine for fishing.

Plutarch was followed by Pliny the Elder, since fishing played a considerable role in the remarkable *Historia Naturalis*, which Pliny completed in the first century. His masterpiece of natural history consists of thirty-seven books. Pliny was the first to mention trout and salmon in the mountains of Italy, Spain, Macedonia and the Dalmation Coast.

Dame Juliana Berners

About the middle of the fifteenth century, the first comprehensive monograph on sport fishing was written in the cloisters of an English nunnery at Sopwell.

It was a remarkable folio about the sport, totally without precedent in English or any other language, and its title was simply *The Treatyse of Fysshynge wyth an Angle*. It clearly represents the full-blown birth of fly-fishing literature as such and was obviously written by an angler with considerable experience on British rivers. It is attributed to Dame Juliana Berners.

It has been more than five centuries since Dame Juliana assembled her unique monograph on angling, and the modern reader is both surprised and charmed. The folio is a mixture of technique, fishing equipment, descriptions of the fish themselves, and the philosophy of angling. It is surprisingly complete and expressed in a remarkably Chaucerian mood.

Although the recommendations for tackle in *The Treatyse* are woefully outdated, given the headlong pace of our technology, so are the chapters on tackle in such recent authors as Ritz and Bergman and Hewitt.

Berners describes rods jointed into three sections, with hollow butts fashioned of well-seasoned hazel, willow and aspen. The butt section was joined to the middle section with a ferrule; and such middle joints were often hazelwood. The tips were usually blackthorn, meddlar, juniper or crabtree connected with the splice-wrap still found on some British salmon rods of greenheart and split-cane today. The knowledgeable reader cannot help being startled by the fact that three-piece rods, the concept of the ferrule, and the genesis of hollow construction in the work of makers like Winston and Powell are more than five centuries old.

Berners also suggested that the wood should be harvested in the winter between Candlemas and Michaelmas, predating the convictions of master rod makers like the late Everett Garrison, who refused to build rods except during the dry winter months. The folio also recommends that the wood should be straightened in a heated oven, not unlike our modern heat-tempering and straightening, and allowed to cool and season for another month. After its curing was complete, the butt material was seated firmly against a heavy wooden template. Its pith core was seared out and tapered with a red-hot iron mandrel. The hollow center was gradually enlarged with a series of mandrels until it was complete, and then the butt section was allowed to cool for forty-eight hours, while clamped to its forming template. Finally it was unfastened and smoke-dried while hanging from the roof beams. The middle and top sections were also carefully seasoned and cured, and Dame Juliana recommended a slender tip-piece of supple blackthorn.

Dame Juliana recommended that the line be attached to the rod at the spliced joint between the tip and middle sections and strung through a ring-guide at its blackthorn tip. Such a system had a cushioning effect when the rod was stressed, and in case of a fracture, the line was still securely fastened.

There were also recipes for dyeing horsehair yellow, sepia, olive, dull reddish brown, gray and straw color. These formulas were copied almost word for word in *The Compleat Angler* more than 150 years later. Instructions were included for the weaving of dyed horsehairs into fishing lines, with various specifications for different species of fish.

Berners included instructions for snelling the hooks with horsehair wrapped with buttonhole silk to their eyeless shanks. The fly patterns given in the final pages of *The Treatyse of Fysshynge* demonstrate a gradual evolution from their beginnings in China and Macedonia. Berners keyed her flies to corresponding hatches and months, and their dressings were outlined in such an offhand manner that it seems they were widely known on the English rivers.

Reading her descriptions of the water and its holding lies, the modern angler is invariably startled by the validity of her observations five centuries ago. Berners advised that a skillful fisherman would keep back from the river as much as possible, and perhaps behind a streamside willow, entirely concealed from the trout. There is also advice against letting the shadow of the angler or his rod flicker above the trout, and Berners adds that once it has been frightened a fish will seldom rise again. Her *Treatyse of Fysshynge* also offered strong opinions on the best weather for fishing, mixed with suggestions for reading a river to understand its secrets. Reading these parts of the manuscript more than five centuries after they were written is intriguing and offers more evidence of truth in the old French proverb that the more anything changes, the more it remains the same. Berners clearly outlines the basic premises of stream tactics as completely as they are spelled out in the books of writers like Hewitt and Bergman and Brooks at midcentury, and her folio concludes with a brief sermon advocating a reverence for both the rivers and their fish.

Izaak Walton and the Classical Age

ITS PAGES ARE RICHLY filled with charming moods and observations, and like all great literature *The Compleat Angler* creates a unique universe in itself. Its poetic images include descriptions of swift-flowing riffles and the silken currents of the deeper pools, eddying musically under the roots of their sheltering trees. Walton writes about the beech-leaf patterns flickering kaleidescopically on his rivers and the April smells of the awakening earth, with a silver rain and the first wildflowers in the water meadows and sheltered places.

There were a number of fishing books published between Berners and Walton. The first was *The Arte of Angling*, a mysterious little monograph published in 1577 and discovered by Otto von Kienbusch. The next was a slim volume titled *A Booke of Fishing with Hooke and Line*, which Leonard Mascall wrote in 1590. Its observations on fly-fishing were merely echoes of Berners and her twelve flies. The second book to follow *The Arte of Angling* was called *Certaine Experiments Concerning Fish and Fruite*, written by John Taverner and published in 1600.

Next came *The Secrets of Angling*. Its author was the celebrated John Dennys, and it was a long didactic poem filled with the worship of nature and the joys of fishing. Gervase Markham was the author of *The Pleasures of Princes*, which included an extensive discourse on fishing and was published in 1614. While it has considerable historical interest, Markham was relatively infamous for his ready use of earlier fishing sources, openly paraphrasing Mascall in many passages. Thomas Barker published his book, *The Art of Angling*, in 1651, only two years before Walton.

Although there are obvious overtones of Berners found in Walton, we cannot be certain if the author of *The Compleat Angler* had seen *The Treatyse of Fysshynge*, since he makes no reference to its existence either. Yet these two books of the fifteenth and sixteenth centuries, along with the five writers that followed the Kienbusch manuscript, are the wellspring of information and literary form that lead inexorably to Walton.

It is impossible to praise either Walton or his *Compleat Angler* too highly, since it has since become the

Izaak Walton. Illustrations by George Shortmeier.

best-known single book on sport in the English language. Its author was sixty years old when the Marriott edition was first printed in London. Walton has endeared himself forever to the angling fraternity, for *The Compleat Angler* holds not only a discourse on fish and fishing, but also a richly pastoral philosophy of life.

Its importance in angling literature lies both in its technical precedents and its singular qualities of character. The literary quality of Walton is difficult to fault, and its technical knowledge was a compendium for its time, although there was little fresh information on fly-fishing in the edition that appeared in 1653.

Walton himself lives in his prose, wise and watchful, always seeking a perfect equilibrium between tactics, technique, and sensory enjoyment. His words explain his world perfectly and help us in our search for harmony in the cacophony of our century. Walton's love of fishing is always interwoven with a love of books, the rhythms of the seasons, and the matchless English countryside.

The first edition of Walton consisted of thirteen brief chapters, which partly concealed their exposition in descriptive passages, story line, and the device of dialogue. Viator is a hunter who meets Piscator, a fisherman, and remains for several days of fishing, wandering along the stream, and rambling conversations. There is some fishing and much fishing talk, in about the ratio that still exists on most rivers today, and a description of the valley.

The conversation is largely dominated by Piscator and his discourses on fish and fishing technique, placing considerable importance on the antiquity of his sport.

Some of these exchanges are started spontaneously by Piscator, but most are explanations in response to questions posed during his dialogues with Viator. Both characters evolve the story line and thematic content of *The Compleat Angler* entirely within the dialogue structure. The pace of these dialogues is varied with a counterpoint of minor characters such as the dairy woman and her milkmaid daughter, wandering huntsmen, the wife of the innkeeper, and other anglers met along the stream. Such contrapuntal structures are varied still more with a cornucopia of poems, rambling anecdotes, and fragments of song.

The pastoral landscapes of seventeenth-century England live again in Walton and his *Compleat Angler*, with all the rich brushwork in the paintings of Constable. Walton's prose is filled with both beauty and exposition. Through his pages we meet fishermen like Sir Henry Wotton, the poet and provost of Eton College, and the almost-legendary poet John Donne, who was both a fine angler and the vicar of Saint Dunstan's near Walton's house in Fleet Street. Walton is filled with soft breezes riffling the surface of his rivers, guttering in the summer mornings, and the busy marketplaces of the villages and towns. Walton fishes to take a brace of trout for supper, asks his readers to watch a silvery shower of rain falling softly through the morning sunlight and to smell the sweetness of the earth. There is the coolness of spreading beeches beside the river, the melody of bird-music in their branches, and spring lambs happily at play in the grass. Walton loved poetry and song almost as well as angling, and at one point Piscator and Viator search out a herdswoman and her daughter to have them sing the familiar songs of Christopher Marlowe and Sir Walter Raleigh.

The stature of Walton does not lie in the fishing methods he outlined, or merely in the qualities of literary structure and form so widely praised in *The Compleat Angler*, but in its pastoral moods and themes of contemplative sport. Walton was obviously a master fisherman in terms of tactics and equipment, but his true genius lies in his understanding that fishing is infinitely more than catching fish and in his singular ability to express that philosophy.

Charles Cotton and the Roots of Modern Fly-Fishing

It was Charles Cotton who built the little Renaissance fishing house at Beresford on the Dove and had his initials intertwined with the older Walton's in the keystone of its arched doorway. Letters between Walton and Cotton survive into our time and indicate a remarkable bond of friendship between them, in spite of the difference in their ages. Cotton loved his river and its fly hatches and often sat at his stone table outside the house, watching its trout and grayling porpoising softly to its fluttering mayflies and sedges.

There were certainly scraps of laughter, since Cotton was justly famous for his ribaldry, pornographic verses and spontaneous wit. Although the pious Walton undoubtedly flushed at times, he must have laughed heartily too, since this fishing companion of poets and bishops was certainly no tight-lipped puritan.

Charles Cotton

Cotton enters the history of fly-fishing and its literature in 1676, in the sixth edition of *The Compleat Angler*. Walton decided to include a treatise titled "Being Instructions How to Angle for a Trout or Grayling in a Clear Stream," and its author was his young friend of Beresford Hall. Cotton prepared this appendix in only ten days, yet its obvious competence and knowledge and its list of original fly patterns have permanently enshrined Cotton as the father of modern fly-fishing.

The expository skill that Cotton displayed in condensing so much information into the structural form of *The Compleat Angler* is remarkable. Its comprehensive treatment of fly-fishing had codified everything that had evolved since Aelianus and the Chou Dynasty, and Cotton had added a surprising amount of fresh knowledge, too.

Fly-fishing is filled with a number of basic truths, and Cotton was the first to articulate several of them. Although his knowledge of aquatic biology was rudimentary, and totally in error concerning some fly hatches, Cotton knew far more about stream entomology than other writers in his time. Cotton erroneously believed that mayflies and stoneflies hatched from caddis creepers, yet these passages from his poem "Wonders of the Peake" demonstrate that Cotton knew about the nymphal forms in his river:

The silver Dove! How pleasant is that name!
Runs through a vale high-crested cliffs o'ershade
By her fair progress much more pleasant made;
But with so swift a torrent in her course
As spurs the nymph, flies from her native source
To seek what's there deny'd, the sun's warm beams,
And to embrace Trent's proud swelling streams.

Cotton firmly believed in the philosophy of matching the hatch, and his "Being Instructions How to Angle for Trout and Grayling" outlined a series of sixty-five original fly patterns for the entire spectrum of the season. Cotton fished his simple wet flies across and downstream, sometimes dapping them over a fish from the streamside alders, but he also advocated fishing upstream with the direction of a strong surface-riffling wind. The combination of knowledge, meticulous detail, sound theory, and outright wisdom of Cotton's instructions in fly-dressing is striking, since it is almost three centuries old. His counsel on fly-tying is virtually as modern as the thoughts of writers like Stewart and Skues and Leisenring, and Cotton's advice on fishing his imitations is timeless. He argued that a fisherman who could not take a trout of twenty inches on a two-strand horsehair did not deserve the name of angler, and with his recommendation of fishing a fine hair tippet with long casts — our first example of the classic axiom on fishing fine and far-off — Charles Cotton entered our pantheon of fly-fishing immortals with the principal rule of taking selective fish.

Several other fishing writers published important books late in the seventeenth century. The books of Richard Franck, Col. Robert Venables, Francois Fortin, and James Chetham all appeared in these years.

Colonel Robert Venables' *Experienced Angler* (1662) was a first-rate book on fly-fishing. Venables was the first to observe that selective trout take some time to adjust to feeding on a changing fly hatch, that they rise best relatively late in a single hatching cycle, and that selective fish often reject other flies that are also on the water. Venables also speculated about multiple hatches in the course of a single day and was the first writer to advocate upstream presentation, discussing the tactical differences in fishing upstream or down in surprisingly modern terms. The *Experienced Angler* explores the difficulties of working against the current and understood that a fisherman working upstream could approach his quarry more closely than a colleague fishing down. Venables also included surprisingly modern observations about having the fly drift naturally to the fish, having it cover the fish before it can see the horsehair tippet, and the casting problems involved in such presentation. Venables concluded his discussion of upstream fishing in his *Experienced Angler* in favor of upstream tactics on small streams and downstream to cover bigger water — and his wisdom precedes both Stewart and the rise of the upstream school by almost two hundred years. Venables was also the first writer to mention silkworm gut in the place of horsehair tippets and tells us that he first observed the material in use on stringed musical instruments.

James Chetham published his *Angler's Vade Mecum* at Smedley in 1681, borrowing most of his fly patterns from Cotton. However, Chetham was a professional fly dresser and included several original patterns from the swift rivers of Lancastershire. Many of his patterns are remarkably good imitations of emerging duns, and his dressings include classics like the Grannom, March Brown, and the venerable Blue Dun. Chetham is a curious mixture of plagiarism, shrewd wisdom, and originality combined with a strange belief in witchcraft and the occult — his little *Vade Mecum* also recommends ointments made from cadavers and powdered skulls for his baits.

Robert Howlett started the eighteenth century with his *Angler's Sure Guide* in 1706. Its author was a skilled wet-fly man who fished downstream with multiple-fly casts. Like other writers of his time, Howlett borrowed freely from his colleagues, but his *Angler's Sure Guide* is filled with observations that make it worth reading.

Richard Brookes and his book, *The Art of Angling*, come next in 1740. His work is a minor prelude to the Bowlkers, who exploded into angling history only seven years later, but Brookes is important enough to rank with the best half-dozen works of his century. His book might have stood higher in the literature of angling if the Bowlker masterpiece, *The Art of Angling*, the fourth British work to bear that title, had not appeared in 1747.

Charles Cotton richly deserves his place in history as the father of modern fly-fishing, but it was probably the writings of Richard and Charles Bowlker which began modern fly-dressing.

Many other angling books were written in the eighteenth century, but few had merit in any literary sense. Yet the Bowlkers assembled several editions of their *Art of Angling*, and their work dominated both their own century and several subsequent generations of British anglers.

The younger Bowlker, Charles, rewrote *The Art of Angling* in 1780, and his edition became the enormously successful book that dominated discussions of tactics and streamcraft and fly-dressing. Bowlker was simple and direct, not unlike Bergman in our century, although Bowlker had a rich knowledge of aquatic hatches that Bergman lacked. The principal importance of Bowlker was that he displayed no hesitation in disposing of earlier fly-tying techniques from Berners through Chetham, listing many of their patterns as flies of limited application, and then outlining his thirty-odd patterns. His list included surprisingly modern versions of flies such as the Blue Dun, which Chetham had earlier described in a no-hackle dressing, and the classic Little Iron Blue. Other standard patterns that were codified in Bowlker include the Cowdung, Yellow Sally, Grannom, Black Gnat, Whirling Dun, March Brown, and Welshman's Button.

George Scotcher published his *Fly Fisher's Legacy* at the threshold of the nineteenth century. It was the first attempt to depict the aquatic insects in color. George Bainbridge appeared with his *Fly Fisher's Guide* at Liverpool in 1816, which contained five color plates of British fly hatches. Two years later, William Carroll contributed his *Angler's Vade Mecum*, which was published at Edinburgh. It included many color plates, but their color and draftsmanship were rather poor. Yet these three volumes were a prelude to our modern work in imitative fly-dressing and aquatic entomology.

However, when Alfred Ronalds published his *Fly-Fisher's Entomology* in 1836, the fly-fishing world had its first book about stream insects and matching the hatch.

Alfred Ronalds was a major benchmark in the entire literature and tradition of angling. His beautiful *Fly-Fisher's Entomology* married the scientific method to trout-fishing theory. It was utterly original in its content and research, and the color work achieved with its exquisite copper plates remains equal to our best modern lithography. Ronalds was clearly the prototype of the angling writer schooled in both entomology and his paint boxes, and his work became a yardstick for future work in fly hatches.

His diagrams of stream character, and its effect on both holding and feeding places, were the first to appear in a fishing book. His complex drawings on the refraction of light entering the river, and its effects on the vision of a fish, remain utterly unique today. The diagrams on refraction in *The Fly-Fisher's Entomology* have never been equaled or surpassed, except perhaps in the remarkably complex studies performed by Colonel Harding in his book, *The Flyfisher and the Trout's Point of View*, which was published almost a full century later.

John Younger wrote his *River Angling for Salmon and Trout* in 1840. His techniques of fishing soft-hackled flies of grouse and partridge, which are superb imitations of hatching sedges, are both simple and remarkably effective methods. Younger believed in casting directly across-stream, or slightly downstream, depending on the current speed. He allowed his flies to swing naturally, letting the current give them life.

George Philip Rigney Pulman started his dry-fly experiments in these same years, and they first emerged in 1841. The dry-fly method did not originate with Pulman but was worked out first on the Hampshire chalkstreams. Hugh Sheringham tells us that men who attended Winchester College about 1845 were already familiar with the floating fly.

Pulman published his second edition of the *Vade Mecum of Fly-Fishing* in 1846, and its third printing appeared at midcentury. Pulman observed in his first edition that the trout on his favorite Dorsetshire streams were often found taking natural flies on the surface. Logic compelled him to suggest that imitations designed to float might prove the best solution for such fish. Pulman understood that these trout were poised and waiting for surface foods and that a conventional wet fly might swing below them, failing to attract their interest.

Pulman further observes that not only is a good imitation of the hatching fly needed, but also its behavior on the water should be suggested. His dry-fly philosophy is codified as a complete edifice, from foundations to cornices and ridge-beams. It understands that a specific dry-fly fish must be rising to the surface and that a floating artificial must match the natural's color, configuration and size. It must be tied to float and cock itself perfectly on the current. It must arrive softly above the rising fish without alarming them or interrupting their feeding rhythms. Pulman also understood that the dry fly must float naturally to a feeding trout and arrive without any trace of drag.

William Blacker contributed his book *The Art of Fly-Making* in 1855, and his technique of forming the wings from matched feather sections of opposite wing-quills would later prove important in tying upright-wing dry flies. William Stewart added his *Practical Angler* in 1857, another of the principal benchmarks in fly-fishing.

Stewart was widely acknowledged as the finest trout fisherman in Scotland, and his *Practical Angler* has remained in print for more than a century. His circle of disciples fished the watershed of the Tweed, particularly on tributaries such as the Teviot and Whitadder. It is simple to understand the character of Stewart and his writings after a brief odyssey through his Scottish border country of ruined abbeys, forests and barren moors. It is a countryside drained by tumbling little rivers such as the Galla at Packhorse Bridge, and it holds a hedgerow landscape where the Lammermuirs slope gracefully toward the sea at Cockburnspath.

Stewart attempted to demonstrate that his wet-fly method was most productive on smaller rivers when an upstream presentation was employed, because the trout are more easily approached from behind. Wet-fly men have always experienced the most luck when their rivers were high or slightly discolored with rain, indicating that their downstream methods were most effective when veiled with spatewater. But upstream wet flies were deadly at low water too, even on the small Scottish burns. Stewart understood that his method always approached a fish from behind, since they lie facing the current, and that a hooked fish is always played in water already fished. The downstream method renders the angler visible to the trout, and a hooked fish invariably carries the fight into unfished places with the current. The upstream method also has a higher percentage of hooked fish, since the strike draws the fly back into the trout's jaws instead of away from its mouth. The upstream technique permits a skilled angler to imitate insects that ride the current without fluttering or swimming. Stewart also understood that there are insects best imitated with a teasing downstream swing of the flies, and a skilled angler who understands his stream entomology will use both methods, depending on fly-hatch behavior. With this mix of skills, the nineteenth-century angler could kill fish under most conditions, including wary trout in low, clear water. It was obvious and simple, like all major innovations once they are completed, but before Stewart and his *Practical Angler*, no writer had proved his case so clearly and finally.

Halford, Skues and the Scientific School

GIANT SPRINGS WELL UP from fissures in the chalkdown geology of Hampshire and Wiltshire, flowing past beds of watercress and pale butter-colored gravel and *ranunculus*. There are weirs and millraces and buttercup fields of fat dairy cattle. Medieval inns with intricate half-timbered gables still house both travelers and anglers. It is a world filled with a sense of history.

Salisbury Cathedral rises across its Wiltshire River bottoms, its slender tower almost fragile-looking above the village greens and rooftops of the town.

Several miles farther east lies the somber Winchester Cathedral, the visible echoes of centuries in its brooding Romanesque and Gothic stonework. Its chapels and chambers include the tomb of Izaak Walton, and its older stonework vaults are clumsy and dark beside the soaring chapter house and high stained-glass spaces of Salisbury. It is a unique and tranquil world.

Its chalkstreams flow crystalline and smooth through rich growths of pondweed, chara, water celery, cress, ribbonweed, and starwort. Nitella and water buttercups and dropwort are rooted deep into the chalky silts that are the secret of these fly-rich British rivers. The principal chalkstreams are found in Wiltshire and Hampshire on the south coast of England, and these counties are drained by several rivers. Perhaps the best known are the Itchen, Test, and the Salisbury Avon. Slightly less famous are rivers like the Frome, Kennet, and several tributaries of the Avon and Test—gentle little rivers such as the Wylye, Nadder, Coln, Lambourne, and the lyric Bourne.

Master anglers are both shaped and polished by their rivers, and the demanding character of the chalkstreams has produced a galaxy of skilled anglers over the past two centuries. The shy trout of these difficult rivers

G. E. M. Skues.

provided the challenge that perfected the skills of fly-fishing giants like Francis Francis, George Selwyn Marryat, Lord Edward Grey of Fallodon, Frederic Halford, George Edward MacKenzie Skues, and a host of brilliant anglers who followed them—Phelps, Mottram, Moseley, Hills, Dunne, Harding, Wilson and Sawyer.

The dry-fly method evolved quickly on these south-country chalkstreams in a circle of exceptionally talented minds. Its center was unmistakably George Selwyn Marryat, who was widely acclaimed as the finest fisherman in England late in the nineteenth century. Henry Hall was a brilliant engineer whose work with forged light-wire hooks made Halford's fly patterns possible. William Coggeshall conceived the tapered oil-finished silk lines for dry-fly work. But the disciplined mind that recorded and codified the full spectrum of the dry-fly method was the famous Frederic Maurice Halford.

Halford outlined a dry-fly philosophy in his *Floating Flies and How to Dress Them* in 1886, and his book held nothing less than the seeds of revolution. It established Halford as the principal fishing writer on the chalkstreams, as well as the chief theoretician of the emerging dry-fly method. His work stemmed from a highly disciplined intelligence and strong opinions, and his influence led to the serious investigation of fly hatches throughout the British Isles, as well as the philosophy of matching the hatch.

Halford successfully displaced centuries of wet-fly practice with *Floating Flies and How to Dress Them,* and his *Dry-Fly Fishing in Theory and Practice* enriched and embellished the ground he had freshly broken. These are probably his best books. Halford is still less dogmatic in their pages, which are filled with pleasant anecdotes and observations expressed in a simple style. Although he was intensively studying the fly hatches along the Itchen and Test, there were still a few patterns in his lists that did not imitate specific flies. Most of the exposition and theory in *Floating Flies* and *Dry-Fly Fishing* remain as valid today, particularly on still currents and selective trout, as they were a century ago on the Hampshire chalkstreams.

Dry-Fly Entomology was published in 1897, and although it was another benchmark in both matching the hatch and the codification of dry-fly theory, it was not without several flaws. Halford was obviously a great angler, but his subject almost demanded formal training in aquatic biology. The book treats a surprisingly limited palette of fly hatches, which are not always taxonomically identified, and omits colored plates of the natural flies. Such failings cannot easily be explained, since the literature of angling was already filled with remarkable color lithography of both flies and aquatic insects. Ronalds' *Fly-Fisher's Entomology* had clearly established a standard sixty-odd years earlier that Halford and his *Dry-Fly Entomology* simply failed to meet.

Modern Development of the Dry Fly appeared thirteen years later in 1910, and it was also a relative disappointment. It might have become Halford's masterpiece had it only included color plates that equaled the copper lithography in Ronalds' watercolors of 1836. However, Halford did collect data on the chalkstream fly hatches with impressive discipline and detail.

His final manuscript was *The Dry-Fly Man's Handbook,* published at London in 1913, and it too was a surprising disappointment. It fell short of his earlier books, and his reputation was perhaps considerably reduced after its publication. Its character is deeply flawed by dogmatism and its stream of ex cathedra arguments. Throughout his fly-fishing career, Halford had found the wet-fly method unsuited to his temperament, even in his early years on the Wandle. Toward the end of his life, the high priest of dry-fly fishing did not just dislike the wet fly—he bitterly adopted a posture of outright hostility toward wet-fly fishermen and wanted the sunken fly banned on the chalkstreams.

Yet it is possible to forget the sad pomposity of Halford's last books, with their narrow-minded and faulty logic, knowing that he also produced a monumental body of work. His books began a revolution in fly-fishing. He played a major role in the evolution of dry-fly design and construction, and he taught his colleagues to collect stream insects and dress flies to imitate them.

Other writers explored fly-fishing in these years, and perhaps the most charming was *The Book of the Dry Fly,* which George Dewar published in 1897. Its first edition included color plates of naturals and their imitations, while the second printing added a number of watercolors painted along the Lodden, Itchen, Test, Wye, Whitewater, and other south-country streams. Dewar was a quiet voice of reason in the bitter quarrels over dry-fly dogmatics.

George Edward MacKenzie Skues was a skilled barrister who divided his life between the practice of law in London and his beloved Abbots Barton water on the Itchen. Skues was a bachelor, and it gave him ample time for his sport.

Although the new philosophy of the dry fly was reaching its zenith on the British rivers, Skues was blessed with a penetrating intelligence that would not accept fresh dogmatics or discard old truths. Skues refused to jettison the rich tradition and skills of the wet-fly method simply because the dry fly had become fashionable.

Skues remained a chalkstream fisherman all his life, and he continued to explore fresh alternatives to the dry fly on those waters. His studies were first published in the remarkable *Minor Tactics of the Chalk Stream,* which Skues assembled in 1910. The book was based upon incisive observations and logic, his deeply rooted distrust of dogmatic opinions, a comprehensive knowledge of the literature and tradition of fly-fishing, and a remarkable volume of original thought. *Minor Tactics* made an eloquent case for employing wet-fly methods in the chalkstreams, although it aroused a highly vocal chorus of Halford disciples, and its arguments were so convincingly articulated that the principles found in *Minor Tactics* have never been refuted. It easily parried the foolish argument that only the dry-fly method was sufficiently sporting and difficult to be worthy of the chalkstream angler.

Skues understood that even the most free-rising chalkstream trout take 85 percent to 90 percent of their diet in nymphal and pupal forms. His *Minor Tactics* rejected the notion that he should feel guilty for fishing his delicate nymphs to a rising fish on waters that Halford and his disciples had consecrated to the dry-fly method. The book precipitated years of arguments in London and along the famous south-country rivers. The feud between the nymph and the dry fly reached its climax in a famous encounter at the Flyfishers' Club of London, when the aging Halford and a curia of admiring followers cornered Skues in the foyer.

"Young man," Halford began testily. "You cannot fish the Itchen in the manner you describe in your book!"

"But I've done it," Skues replied softly.

Skues began his work in a posture of complementing the dry fly with his nymph fishing, but his articles in several British sporting journals generated such wrath from the dry-fly purists that Skues quickly found himself outside the pale of accepted doctrine. It was a climate not unlike the political animosity that engulfed the religious reformers of the sixteenth century. His exceptional success made Skues a legend in his own time, and his willingness to adapt himself to the moods and rhythms of the river made him consistently successful. His principal transgression perhaps lay in easily outfishing his dry-fly rivals, and that undeniable fact was utterly unforgivable on the club beats of the Itchen and Test.

The nymph-fishing work first published in *Minor Tactics of the Chalk Stream* was subsequently expanded in 1921, with the introduction of Skues' classic *The Way of a Trout with a Fly*. It was unmistakably his masterpiece, and his fertile mind was permitted to hopscotch freely over the full scope of chalkstream fishing with his palette of wet flies, dry flies and nymphs. The book included watercolors on dressing his nymphs, and Skues' polished doctrine of imitation and fishing his nymphal patterns.

When his experiments with his methods were codified in *Nymph Fishing for Chalk Stream Trout* in 1939, it was curiously the only book that Skues actually conceived in book form, since his earlier work collected pieces that Skues had contributed to *The Field* and the privately published *Flyfishers' Club Journal*. When the book was published, Skues was already in his eighties and rich with the fullness of his chalkstream years.

Skues died at the ripe age of ninety in 1949, almost forty years after his encounter with Halford in the foyer of the Flyfishers' Club. Since the Halford books published in our century tended to diminish his reputation, Skues has gradually emerged as the principal modern writer on trout fishing. Longevity certainly played a role in his reputation, since he fished for trout across eighty-three years of his life. Skues possessed superb powers of observation and an intelligence sharpened in the disciplines of jurisprudence. His passion for fly-fishing was perfectly married with both a remarkable mind and a facility for lucid prose. Skues' writing was prolific and intensely personal, with a pleasant humor in virtually everything he wrote. His books taught gently, with deductions made from a richly varied personal experience, and his turn of mind was so stamped with originality that Skues often explored points that had never been touched by earlier writers. The sole touch of tragedy in his remarkable life perhaps lies in the fact that a group of mindless dry-fly zealots succeeded in banishing this exceptional old man and his nymph-fishing from the Abbots Barton water just a few years before his death.

J. C. Mottram, a skilled and famous British surgeon, also focused his dexterity and powers of perception on the problems of fly-fishing. His observations flowed from a rich inventory of experience and creativity and insights. His fishing ranged from the chalkstreams of south-country Britain to the salmon rivers of Scotland and Norway, where he fished with the celebrated T. T. Phelps. Their collaboration on the classic Laerdal in dry-fly experiments on its sea-run trout is recorded in Phelps' little book *Fishing Dreams*. Mottram explored a number of original themes on fly-dressing and the sensory behavior of fish and the relationships between fly structure and the surface film. His fishing studies were assembled in his intriguing little volume titled *Fly-Fishing: Some New Arts and Mysteries*, which Mottram published in 1916.

Martin Moseley was a skilled entomologist whose interest in fly-fishing came through his uncle, the half-legendary Frederic Halford himself. Moseley painstakingly prepared a handbook of British fly hatches designed to be carried on the stream, and his *Dry-Fly Fisherman's Entomology* finally appeared in 1921, after being delayed by the First World War. His work had been intended to provide the color plates omitted earlier in Halford's *Dry-Fly Entomology*, but Moseley was bitterly unhappy about the amateurish hand-tinted watercolors in his little book. It is tragic that his publishers failed to grasp the fact that his handbook was almost totally dependent on the character and quality of its illustrations.

Major John Waller Hills sought refuge from the bitter wounds suffered in Flanders by fishing the chalkstreams. His thoughtful and unusually perceptive *History of Fly-Fishing for Trout* was published in 1921, and his pastoral respite from the First World War was retold in *A Summer on the Test* three years later. Hills is within the first rank of fly-fishing authors, and his books on chalkstream sport are an impressive display of knowledge and experience, written in a prose that is both lucid and filled with charm.

J. W. Dunne published his fine little *Sunshine and the Dry Fly* in 1924, and it remains an intriguing and challenging book today. Dunne made a number of striking observations on the relationships between fly structure, silhouette, light pattern in the film, translucency, opacity, and color mix in fly-dressing. His book is a fascinating prelude to the work of American writers like Marinaro and Swisher and Richards.

Eric Taverner published his comprehensive *Trout Fishing from All Angles* in 1929, and it still serves as the encyclopedia of trout theory and technique in the United Kingdom. Except for its discussions of trout and their riseforms, and its insights into the problems of managing a fishery, it is not an unusually original book, although it did codify the best of fly-fishing theory from Bowlker to Halford and Skues.

The essence of trout fishing, and the lyric quality of both trout country and the fish themselves, is seldom found in books on fish and fish techniques and fly hatches. Harold Plunkett-Greene published his remarkable book *Where the Bright Waters Meet* in 1929, and its Waltonian moods were perhaps the most poetic evocation of trout fishing since Lord Edward Grey of Fallodon and his little book, *Fly-Fishing*, written at the close of the nineteenth century. Plunkett-Greene should be on the bookshelves of any thoughtful angler, beside the warmly written *Golden Days* by Romilly Fedden. *Where the Bright Waters Meet* is both a fishing book and a log of English village life in those unspoiled years before the summer of 1914.

Colonel E. W. Harding, another retired British officer, published a little-known book titled *The Fly-Fisher and the Trout's Point of View* in 1931. It is a particularly noteworthy book, although perhaps too complex for a large audience. Harding is virtually unique in his exploration of trout and their senses, and the relationship between such perceptions and turbidity, solar transmission and subaquatic refraction, optical problems, the unique light patterns of both insect types and fly-dressings in the surface meniscus, and an intriguing labyrinth of factors that Harding identified in terms of the trout's response to both fly hatches and his imitations. His impact on several major American writers is both extensive and obvious, and books like *A Modern Dry-Fly Code*, *Selective Trout*, and *Matching the Hatch* owe Harding an immense debt.

John Waller Hills published his intriguing book, *Riverkeeper* in 1934, and although it is largely a biography of the famous William Lunn, it is also a superb book about fishing. Lunn was a keeper from 1887 to 1931, starting a line of hereditary keepers at the Houghton Club on the Test that lives today in Michael Lunn of Stockbridge. The book is filled with William Lunn's unique experiments in river management, the transplanting and augmentation of fly hatches, and fisheries biology. Lunn was also a skilled and innovative fly dresser and author of several well known patterns like the Caperer, which anticipated the caddisfly theories of Leonard Wright and his *Fishing the Dry Fly as a Living Insect* by almost fifty years.

Skues died at midcentury, and since his death a growing number of his disciples have joined the ranks of major fishing writers. Perhaps the best known is Frank Sawyer from Wiltshire. Sawyer's fame undoubtedly comes from the effusive praise of Charles Ritz in Ritz's book, *A Flyfisher's Life*, a charming book that has been read around the world. However, it was Wilson Stephens who made Sawyer a living legend in England by editing his notes and papers into *The Keeper of the Stream*, an idyllic book published in 1952. It covers the cycle of the entire year and its effects on the rhythms of the river, and it reveals this Wiltshire keeper as a man with a striking knowledge of ecology and a considerable touch of the poet. Sawyer published his second book six years later, *Nymphs and the Trout*, and it codified the style of minute nymph fishing that Sawyer worked out on his Neatheravon beats above Salisbury.

J. R. Harris's *Angler's Entomology* (1952) added much fresh information to the cumulative studies of Ronalds, Halford, Dewar, Moseley, Skues and Sawyer. This book is a compendium of original research, particularly throughout the beautiful loughs and rivers of his native Ireland. Harris includes observations on the behavior and morphology of the fly hatches, their emergence periods, and pinpointing their distribution and range. He treats the principal mayflies and stoneflies and sedges and also covers the many craneflies, damselflies, dragonflies, crustaceans, midges, ants and tiny reed smuts.

Commander C. F. Walker published his book *Chalk Stream Flies* in this same period. Apart from the pioneer work of Halford, this is the only book dealing exclusively with the slow-water hatches in the south of England. It contains four color plates and augments the work of the earlier studies on aquatic insects. Walker completed his *Lake Flies and Their Imitations* in 1960, and it is still a sound book on the entomology of loch fishing in the United Kingdom.

Major Oliver Kite is the most recent British writer to explore the Skues tradition with his *Nymph Fishing in Practice* in 1963. Kite made a number of valuable observations on chalkstream nymph fishing, and acknowledged his intellectual debt to Skues and Sawyer. His book clearly attempts to correlate the imitative nymphs developed for the chalkstreams with techniques of manipulation designed to suggest the subaquatic movements of the naturals.

John Goddard is an exceptional young British angler, who presently wears the mantle of a tradition that begins with the fly-hatch studies of Ronalds and Halford. *Trout Flies of Stillwater* first demonstrated Goddard's skills, and his subsequent *Trout Fly Recognition* confirmed his promise when it was published in 1966. It includes color photographs of virtually all of the British fly hatches and has quickly become the standard work on the British aquatic species.

The proliferation of large impoundments throughout the British Isles since the Second World War has changed their fishing. Trout planted in these reservoirs have thrived, making the sport available to large numbers of fishermen who might never have had access to the famous beats of the British streams. Both C. F. Walker and John Goddard have explored the entomology of these impoundments, and the young British fishing writer Brian Clarke explored their beginnings in his recent book, *The Pursuit of Stillwater Trout*, 1975.

It should be understood that during the years that followed the books of Ronalds and Pulman and Stewart, the first American fishing writers were beginning to explore the challenge of our continent. Our fly-fishing heritage reaches back beyond the Civil War to the books of George Washington Bethune and Frank Forester and Robert Barnwell Roosevelt.

Our heritage is a logical extension of its British and European genesis, and its evolution is a history of adapting English theory to the singular conditions of American waters. The principal figures in that evolution were unmistakably Thaddeus Norris of Philadelphia, and the frail, tubercular Theodore Gordon, who jealously husbanded his health and his knowledge of fly-dressing beside a pot-bellied stove at the Anson Knight farmhouse in the Catskills.

The Evolution of American Fly-Fishing

Our fishing literature was slow to develop, and more than 200 years passed before American writers began to contribute to angling theory and practice. The Schuylkill Fishing Company was founded in 1732, and in its later years, its members journeyed deep into the Pennsylvania mountains to fish for brook trout. There is a small monument at the headwaters of a spring creek in the Susquehanna country that attests to fishing expeditions beyond Harrisburg and Williamsport.

Reverend Joseph Seccombe published his charming *Discourse Uttered in Part at Ammauskeeg Falls in Fishing Season* in 1739, and his thesis that even Puritan doctrine should not find Sunday fishing offensive must have relieved a few troubled consciences.

Writing in *The American Fly Fisher*, the publication of the Museum of American Fly Fishing, Austin Hogan tells us that the first written evidence of our sport occurred in about 1775. Lieutenant Colonel John Enys served with the British 29th Regiment of Foot, which was stationed in Canada, and fished salmon at the mouth of the Saranac in 1787.

During the half-century that followed, the principal American fishing writers devoted themselves to journals such as the *Farmer's, Mechanic's & Sportsman's Magazine*, the highly successful *American Turf Register & Sporting Magazine*, the poetically named *Spirit of the Times*, and the celebrated magazine *Forest & Stream*. The roster included William Porter, George Washington Bethune, Charles Lanman, General George Gibson, Adirondack Murray and Henry W. Herbert, who wrote extensively under the pseudonym of Frank Forester.

Thaddeus Norris of Philadelphia wrote the first major American fishing book. His trout fishing began on the Broadheads and reached out to embrace both the British rivers where fly-fishing first approached its status as art leavened with science and the rivers of the American and Canadian frontier. Perhaps it is necessary to grasp the fact that Thaddeus Norris was both our Walton and our Cotton in a single angler. The elegant calligraphy of his signature is found in a fading register at Henryville House as early as 1851, and the gentle Brodheads played a considerable role in shaping his life as a fly fisherman. The character of the river also permeates his *American Angler's Book*, published in 1864. It was the first American attempt to capture the sweep of our continent, from the small-mouth rivers of the southern Appalachians to the wilderness of Quebec. Norris also fished for the grayling and brook trout of the Michigan country before its primeval forests were destroyed.

Norris also experimented with floating flies before Theodore Gordon and his Neversink genesis. Norris described his exploratory tactics in 1864, using two flies kept dry with false-casting and settled softly on the currents of the Willowemoc, and these dry-fly tactics were almost twenty-five years before Gordon and the Golden Age of the Catskills.

Genio Scott and William H. H. Murray both emerged as major American fishing writers in 1869. Scott contributed *Fishing in American Waters*, which contained considerable fly-rod material. Adirondack Murray was more a storyteller in the mold of Porter and Herbert, and his *Adventures in the Wilderness* was the prologue of a highly successful career.

William Cowper Prime published *I Go A-Fishing* in 1873. He was the bellwether for a remarkable parade

. . . Thaddeus Norris was both our Walton and our Cotton in a single angler.

of Princeton-educated anglers that included the celebrated Henry Van Dyke, Edward Ringwood Hewitt, Otto Von Kienbusch, Victor Coty, Eugene Connett, Manning Barr, Dudley Mills, Henry Davis, Russell MacGregor, Philip Nash, Frederic Barbour, Sidney Stone, and the lyric fishing writer Dana Storrs Lamb. Prime was quite famous in his time, and his books provided fireside fishing for an entire generation of American anglers.

Henry Van Dyke was a remarkable Princeton scholar who taught both religion and literature at the university. His charming books are considered classics now, particularly *Fisherman's Luck* and *Little Rivers*, which were published just before the close of the century.

Theodore Gordon remains something of a mystery. His letters tell us that he worked as a bookkeeper and bank teller and sold securities, but when he fell on hard times, Gordon disappeared into the Catskills. During these years, he apparently developed his fanatical devotion to trout fishing and taught himself how to dress flies. It is still not certain where Gordon learned that skill. Roy Steenrod received most of Gordon's books after his death at Bradley in 1914, and among those volumes was a well-thumbed copy of Ronalds' classic *Flyfisher's Entomology*, which has a fine color plate illustrating each step in dressing a wet fly. It is possible that Gordon learned the basic secrets of fly-making from these instructions. Gordon tells us in his notes and letters that he learned about dry flies from Halford's *Floating Flies and How to Dress Them* and from subsequent correspondence with Halford himself.

Gordon imported dry-fly tackle and materials and hooks from England about 1889, and Halford sent Gordon a complete series of his imitative dry-fly patterns the following year. These flies were subsequently willed to his protégé, Roy Steenrod, and the historic envelope is presently at The Angler's Club of New York.

Gordon's health failed badly about 1900, forcing him to abandon Manhattan for Haverstraw, several miles north along the Hudson. He moved to the Catskills permanently about five years later. During the last three years of his life, Gordon lived at the old Anson Knight farmhouse near Bradley. Before his health finally collapsed, Gordon fished extensively on all of the famous Catskill rivers, but in those final years he seldom ventured far from his quarters in the Knight place.

It is tragic that Gordon did not live to complete the book that was found half-finished among his effects at the Knight farmhouse. His relatives foolishly burned that partly completed manuscript in fear of his tuberculosis, but his other writings were preserved in *The Complete Fly Fisherman: The Notes and Letters of Theodore Gordon*, which John MacDonald assembled in 1947. Gordon's work clearly demonstrates how much was lost when he failed to complete his book, and his life ended on a melancholy note. Gordon was virtually a hermit at his death, and there is sadness in the Dickens-like images of the frail Catskill fly dresser working beside his pot-bellied stove.

The death of Theodore Gordon in 1915 dropped the curtain on the prelude to American fly-fishing, and more than any other figure, Gordon and his writings were the philosophical bridge between the British fly-fishing heritage and our American beginnings.

Emlyn Gill published his *Practical Dry-Fly Fishing* in 1912. It was a relatively minor work, but it was perhaps the first exposition of the American philosophy of fishing the water. Gill advocated casting a dry fly in likely looking places, or covering a pool with a checkerboard pattern of casts, making sure its trout would see the fly. It was a stream tactic totally unlike the British method, with its emphasis on casting only to rising trout, and Gill's haphazard methods still dominate American dry-fly tactics more than a half-century later.

George Michel Lucien LaBranche was an impeccably groomed and tailored young stockbroker who published his widely acclaimed book *The Dry Fly and Fast Water* in 1914. LaBranche helped to codify the American technique of fishing the water into a full-blown philosophy, and his lucid prose quickly became the bible for the emerging generation of American anglers.

LaBranche fully deserved his acclaim as the writer who consciously modified British chalkstream theory to the swift rivers of the Catskills and Appalachians. His *Dry Fly and Fast Water* took shape primarily on the Beaverkill, Willowemoc and Brodheads, where LaBranche owned a cottage below Canadensis. LaBranche cut quite a dashing character with his graceful casting, striped silk tie, soft-brimmed British fishing hat, and the Burberry shooting coat with its Norfolk tailoring. The lovely etching executed by Gordon Stevenson along the Neversink has captured that elegance forever, from the custom waders and three-ounce Leonard to the perfectly trimmed regimental moustache.

Louis Rhead was the first American writer to attempt the Halford-like correlation between our trout flies and the fly hatches of our waters. His book *American Trout Stream Insects* was published in 1916 and was largely based upon flies collected along the Beaverkill. Like Scotcher and Bainbridge and Carroll, Rhead unfortunately used only popular names of his own invention rather than the discipline of scientific nomenclature, and his entomological drawings were poor. It is virtually impossible to identify the species that he collected in the Catskills, and both his work and his flies have little more than historical interest today.

Illustration by Roy Lewando, Jr.

Edward Ringwood Hewitt made his debut with the book, *Telling on the Trout*, in 1926. Hewitt subsequently wrote several important books on fly-fishing, and he truly deserves his reputation as a technician and creative fly dresser. His famous Big Bend stretch of the

Neversink, with its home camp and hatchery and laboratory, was the setting for a lifetime spent experimenting with the problems of fish culture, trout-fishing techniques, fly-dressing, and methods of fisheries management. Such research ultimately led to books like *Better Trout Streams*, which outlined his theories for stream improvement and fisheries management.

Hewitt's tireless experiments on the river led to the development of dry-fly Spiders and Bivisibles and Hewitt Skaters, with their unusually long, stiff-fibered hackles. Hewitt compiled his *Handbook of Fly Fishing* in 1933 and the following year published his paper-bound book, *Nymph Fly Fishing*. It was the first American book to discuss Skues' revolutionary nymph-fishing methods, which had been introduced in 1910. Hewitt concluded his long and celebrated career with *A Trout and Salmon Fisherman for Seventy-Five Years* in 1948.

Although the Depression years prove a surprisingly rich lode of fly-fishing books, and Hewitt himself published three in that decade, it was the work of Knight, Jennings and Bergman that has stood the judgment of the forty-odd years that have followed.

John Alden Knight did not write about his collaboration with Hewitt in nymph fishing until his book *The Modern Angler* was published in 1936. Their experiments on the Neversink had started five years earlier. It was his first book and included the first public mention of Everett Garrison and his split-cane genius, but the Depression years denied *The Modern Angler* the wide audience it deserved. Knight followed it with his *Theory and Technique of Fresh Water Angling* in 1940, and his *Field Book of Fresh Water Angling* at the close of the Second World War.

Preston Jennings published the classic *A Book of Trout Flies* in its limited Derrydale edition in 1935. It was the first American work on fly-fishing entomology to include accurate identification of the insects. Like the appearance of Alfred Ronalds and his *Fly-Fisher's Entomology* in 1836, the writings of Jennings set a standard of excellence that has measured all subsequent American work on fly hatches. Its illustrations were drawn and painted by Alma Froderstrom, and their elegance was clearly in the character of Ronalds' exquisite watercolors.

The celebrated Ray Bergman published *Just Fishing* in 1932, and with his popularity as a fishing editor of a major outdoor magazine, it sold steadily through twelve printings. It was a book filled with both promise and considerable charm, in many ways Bergman's best work, and its beginnings were followed by the popular *Trout* in 1938. It has been our best comprehensive book on trout fishing since it was first published. *Trout* quickly exhausted eight printings in only six years, its chapters filled with an engaging offhand vernacular that awakened echoes of similar experiences in each of its readers. Its prose was structured in deceptively simple anecdotes that taught without didactic overtones. Bergman led his audience through his early adventures with the wet-fly method and bait-fishing, which he never completely abandoned, and explored the dry fly and the newer nymph-fishing methods. Other chapters covered streamers and bucktails and experiences with fly patterns under many conditions on widespread rivers. Its warmly personal narrative quality dominated its field long after its tackle and technical recommendations, and many of its fly patterns were rendered obsolete by new methods and materials.

James Leisenring emerged with his little classic, *The Art of Tying the Wet Fly*, in 1941. Its publication was lost in relative obscurity, since our explosive entry into the Second World War postponed our interest in angling books. Leisenring was an unsophisticated Pennsylvania toolmaker whose heavy accent betrayed ancestry in the German Palatinate, but his skilled hands and mind were as precise as the finely machined objects that came from his shop.

Charles Wetzel was better known than Leisenring and was a member of the Angler's Club of New York when his book *Practical Fly Fishing* was published in 1943. Although his book added to our knowledge of American fly hatches, its illustrations were poorly drawn and did not attempt to depict the color of the natural aquatic insects or their imitations.

The years that followed the Second World War were richly productive in fly-fishing books. Art Flick completed his slender *Streamside Guide to Naturals and Their Imitations* in 1947, publishing years of research into the fly hatches of his beloved Schoharie. Flick came to dress imitative flies as exquisitely as the best of his tutors, masters like Preston Jennings and Leslie Thompson and Chip Stauffer. It was Thompson and the late Raymond Camp, the fishing editor of *The New York Times*, who badgered Flick into writing his *Streamside Guide*. The fly-fishing world is in their debt.

Vincent Marinaro published his strikingly original *A Modern Dry-Fly Code* in 1950. Its pages are filled with fresh insights into the behavior of hard-fished trout, as well as sophisticated concepts of fly-dressing. British writers like Mottram and Dunne and Harding had explored similar theories and concepts, but Marinaro found concrete applications for these theories in fishing the difficult trout of Big Springs and Letort Spring Run in central Pennsylvania. His brilliant jassid-type imitations of leafhoppers and beetles and his thorax-style dry flies make *A Modern Dry-Fly Code* one of the principal books in American fly-fishing. Alvin Grove also published his *Lure and Lore of Trout Fishing* in 1950, and it was acclaimed in the writings of the late Arnold Gingrich as another of the best fishing books in our history.

John Atherton wrote *The Fly and the Fish* in that same vintage year—a rich mixture of technical skills, creative speculation, and poetic insights. Atherton's illustrations and prose are filled with lyric overtones, not unlike *A River Never Sleeps* and the other books of Roderick Haig-Brown. Atherton's fly patterns and streamside skills were excellent, and his book perfectly evokes the river music of the Neversink and his beloved Battenkill.

Another excellent book appeared just after midcentury, and its studies in nymph fishing were singularly appropriate in a year that witnessed the death of Leisenring. Ray Ovington was the author of *How to Take Trout on Wet Flies and Nymphs*, although its most original content described the innovative fly patterns and nymphing techniques of Edward Sens. His work was remarkably good, and Sens was another skilled fly tier who closely studied the nymphs and pupal life of the Catskill rivers. Sens conceived the first caddis pupal imitations, and like his other mayfly nymphs, they have become standard patterns in many shops.

When William Blades published his comprehensive *Fishing Flies and Fly Tying* in 1952, it quickly became the standard work on American fly-dressing. Blades was the father of highly lifelike dressings, complete with their trimmed wings and hackle-stem legs and wingpads. Blades and his book hold a special place in my library, since he was the master who polished my boyhood skills at the close of the Second World War.

A. J. McClane followed the legendary Ted Trueblood as the fishing editor of *Field & Stream* and, after several years of exciting work in its pages, published *The Practical Fly Fisherman* in 1953. It is clearly the best trout-fishing book since Bergman, its pages filled with creative observations on flies and fly-casting and tackle, mixed with first-rate studies in stream tactics. Its chapters on nymphs and nymph fishing and distance casting are particularly fine, and McClane has a touch of the poet, too. His book, *The American Angler*, followed in 1954, and both of his early books are so finely crafted and based upon such widespread experience that the remarkable scope and expertise of *McClane's Standard Fishing Encyclopedia* should have come as little surprise in 1965.

The late Joseph Brooks published his *Complete Book of Fly Fishing* in 1958, and its chapters were firmly based on wide angling experience throughout the world. It contained considerable material on trout fishing, although his earlier books, *Salt Water Fly Fishing* and *Greatest Fishing* and *Bass Bug Fishing*, covered many other species. His final work, titled simply *Trout Fishing*, was published in 1972. Although he wrote ten angling books, the content and character of *Trout Fishing* suggest that his best writing might still have been ahead. His death robbed us of both his warm fellowship and his vast knowledge of our sport.

Charles Fox published *This Wonderful World of Trout* in 1961, triggering a major new cycle of important American fishing books. Fox collaborated with Vincent Marinaro in many of the experiments that led to *A Modern Dry-Fly Code*, and their tenure on Letort Spring Run has already become legend. Fox wrote a subsequent book titled *Rising Trout* six years later, and its pages are filled with both anecdotes and wisdom from the limestone streams, fly-dressing theory, experiments with wild-fish genetics, stream entomology, enhancement of trout cover and spawning beds, and the transplanting of fly hatches. Their work with imitating ants and leafhoppers and other terrestrial insects is justly famous, and from fishing with them over their difficult fish, their reputation for fishing skill is as richly deserved. The collaboration of Marinaro and Fox seems destined to match the legend of Halford and Marryat a century ago on the British chalkstreams.

The colorful Polly Rosborough lives in a simple house above Agency Lake, not far from Chiloquin in southern Oregon. Rosborough is one of the finest fly dressers alive, and he demonstrated considerable knowledge of the fly life in his Williamson country in his *Fishing and Tying the Fuzzy Nymphs*, which was published in 1969. His list of original fly patterns includes imitations of several mayfly and stonefly nymphs, mixed with several caddis worms and midge larvae. There were also a few general patterns like the Fledermaus and Casual Dress and Nondescript, along with damselflies and freshwater shrimps. Rosborough likes hatching nymphs, and uses marabou fibers to suggest embryonic wings, as well as the breathing tail-gills of damselfly nymphs.

Selective Trout quickly established its authors — Doug Swisher and Carl Richards — as major fishing writers when it was published in 1971. It is perhaps best known for its fresh insights into dressing the no-hackle fly, but it is a cornucopia of other concepts, and it greatly expanded the knowledge of fly hatches found in my own *Matching the Hatch* sixteen years before. It is particularly valuable in its coverage of aquatic flies in the Midwest and Rocky Mountains. *Selective Trout* also places considerable emphasis on emerging nymphs and spinner falls, recommending patterns that use hen hackles to suggest both embryonic wings and the transparent spentwings of mayfly spinners. There were also nymphs dressed entirely of fur, quill-bodied midge pupae, as well as soft-hackle and Sens-type hatching sedges. But perhaps their most intriguing studies were with the wiggle-nymph patterns, a creative adaptation of the articulated salmon flies, and the hinged stonefly nymphs in the work of William Blades. *Selective Trout* is unmistakably part of an evolution in fly-dressing theory that reaches back through Marinaro and Harding and Dunne, to the nineteenth-century work of Halford and Marryat.

My own book, *Nymphs*, was published in 1973, exactly a year after *Selective Trout* reached its surprisingly large audience. *Nymphs* also attracted a remarkable readership, considering its focus on nymphs and its omission of dry-fly material. *Nymphs* consists of largely original nymph patterns, and the book was intended to provide American fly fishermen with a relatively complete guide to our aquatic insects and crustaceans.

Swisher and Richards followed *Selective Trout* with *Fly Fishing Strategy* in 1975. It was wide-ranging in its scope, concerned with casting techniques designed to manipulate the fly properly, fresh concepts in emerging flies and the problems of solving multiple hatches. Their earlier work with backswimmers, sowbugs, freshwater shrimps, damselflies, burrowing nymphs, caddis larvae and pupae, the tiny pupal forms of midges and wiggle-nymphs is explored further. But the most important concept found in *Fly Fishing Strategy* is perhaps the stillborn fly. Although its fly-dressing problems still remain only partly solved, the stillborn fly is clearly a significant step in the evolution of fly-fishing.

Robert Boyle and Dave Whitlock also published their *Fly-Tyer's Almanac* in 1975, and it was filled with fresh thinking about flies and fly-dressing. It includes flies tied to imitate leeches, midge larvae and pupae, including latex larval artificials and a wiggle-nymph imitation of an emerging damselfly. Robert Nastasi and Al Caucci introduced their beautiful book, *Hatches*, that same year. Although *Hatches* is consciously limited to American mayfly species, its color photography alone makes it important on any angling shelf.

The following year, Charles Brooks published his *Nymph Fishing for Larger Trout*, and its comprehensive treatment of nymph-fishing tactics makes it invaluable to American anglers. Brooks had published *The Trout and the Stream* in 1974, and its chapters outlined his preoccupation with heavy water and big trout, although it also includes a perceptive portrait of spring-creek conditions on the Upper Madison and Firehole. Gary LaFontaine also published his book, *The Challenge of the Trout*, in 1976, and it is filled with interesting speculations and insights, particularly in its studies of emerging sedges.

Larry Solomon and Eric Leiser completed *The Caddis and the Angler* early in 1977, starting the disciplined study of our American sedges and their behavior. Although their book sidestepped the taxonomy of species, it is still the first American work to explore the important *Trichoptera* flies.

During the years since midcentury, we have witnessed an American renaissance in fly-fishing books that is virtually unique in the history of the sport, and the technological spirit of change that permeates our society also has its echoes in our sport. Fly lines of polyvinylchloride, graphite rods, and polyamide nylons are obvious examples of such change. But fly-fishing entomology has evolved rapidly in recent years, too. British aquatic hatches have finally been completely catalogued with the work of Harris and Goddard, yet it has taken almost 150 years to match the flies of the British Isles, since Ronalds' *Fly-Fisher's Entomology* was published in 1836.

THOUGHTS OF SUCH EXPLOSIVE GROWTH and change lead a contemplative fisherman to explore his literary genesis. The perspective of time makes us understand that the essence of fly-fishing and the lyric quality of both trout country and the fish themselves is seldom found in books on fish and fishing techniques and fly hatches.

Roderick Haig-Brown, a transplanted British writer, has explored the Waltonian moods of fishing in books such as *Fisherman's Spring* and *Measure of the Year* and *Return to the River*. His classic was perhaps the poetically titled *A River Never Sleeps*, first printed in 1946. It perfectly captured his wild British Columbia rivers, and in its pages we can experience his steelhead fishing on the rain-swollen Campbell and Nimpkish.

American writers have explored similar themes since the books of Thaddeus Norris and George Washington Bethune just before the Civil War. Paul Hyde Bonner included several classic stories of fly-fishing in his book *The Glorious Mornings*, and Dana Storrs Lamb entranced his circle of faithful readers with *Where the Pools are Bright and Deep*, after a creelful of smaller classics published in limited editions. The late Arnold Gingrich was another fine writer, and *The Well-Tempered Angler* is filled with the echoes of the Turnwood years on the Beaverkill, the alpine fishing at Mariazell in Austria, the lava-filled rivers of Iceland, and the misty barrens at Ballynahinch in Connemara. Nick Lyons has also touched the essence of trout fishing in books like *Fishing Widows* and *The Seasonable Angler*. But our most lyric fishing writer was clearly Ben Hur Lampman. His books, *Where Would You Go?* and *A Leaf from French Eddy*, were assembled after his death from his newspaper work in Oregon, and there are no better tickets to the poetry of fishing.

Arnold Gingrich observed years ago, with his rod leaning against a vintage Bentley along the Brodheads, that fishing was really the least important thing about fishing. Some of its peripheral riches are obvious: the rich tradition and history of the sport, the darting choreography of swallows in a fly hatch, the mute ballet of fly lines working in the rain, the bright palette of color and tinsel in our fly boxes, and the lazy dimple of a trout over straw-yellow gravel.

Poets are perhaps the voices that best capture the character of trout and trout country, and such places are a world worthy of their skills. Fishing images are found in the work of such disparate poets as John Donne and William Butler Yeats and Ezra Pound, but perhaps the most evocative images lie in the well-known "Pied Beauty" by Gerard Manley Hopkins:

> Glory be to God for dappled things—
>   For skies as couple-color as a brinded cow;
> For rose-moles all in stipple
>   Upon trout that swim.

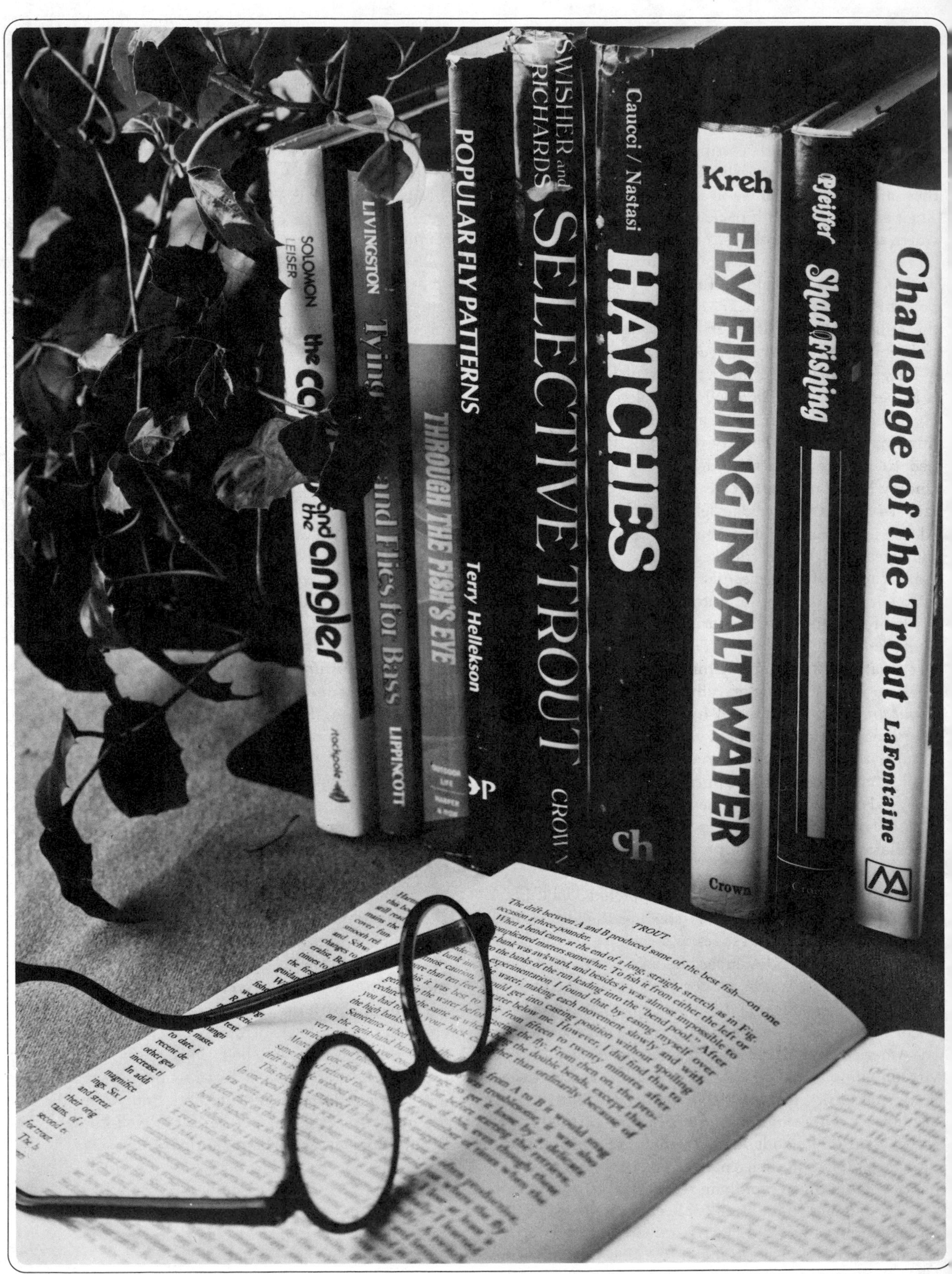

Photo by Don Gray.

Without suggesting that there's not enough enticement and instruction in this book to hook you fatally for life, we feel obligated to disclose that the literature of angling, and especially fly-fishing, is the most extensive of any outdoor sport. You'll probably find this out quickly enough, so we want you to be able to say that you first "read about it here."

A recent FLY FISHERMAN *magazine reader survey indicated that, in the year past, the readers had bought and read 3.5 books on fly-fishing (more than a few publishers are still wondering which book it was that was only half-read!). Not that fly fishers are necessarily a reclusive, bookish lot given to arm-chair adventuring, but rather that the freshwater fishing seasons do come to an end, either through elemental dictate or legislative edict. The withdrawal symptoms of the winter months are painful to see, and it is much better for anglers to sublimate their cravings with a literary fix rather than resort to hidden bottles or common street-pushers.*

You will soon find that angling books offer some four centuries of solace—you learn that for nearly 400 years fly rodders have suffered the same ignominies, crushing defeats, soaring successes and myriad delights astream that you have unknowingly shared. For there has been an almost mystical "laying on of hands" from one angler to another over the span of years, and much of it can be found in books. At the beginning, you will probably want practical, how-to books, but you will begin to reach out for books which tell you, as the late dean of American fly-fishing, Esquire *founder Arnold Gingrich so simply expressed it, that "there is more to fishing than the fish."*

Chapter 12

Building a Fly-Fishing Library

Read All About It!

NICK LYONS

BEFORE YOU'VE BEEN FLY-FISHING very long, you'll discover that there is a world beyond all those Quill Gordons and cane rods, roll casts and nail knots and *Tricorythodes*. Sooner or later, and probably the former, you'll discover that no sport has a vaster, more diversified literature. And once you discover the full dimensions of this, you may well want to throw up your hands in bewildered dismay—"There can't be *this* much to read!"—"*Must* I read it all to be a good fly fisherman?"—"Where do I begin?"

There *is* that much available to read—a couple of thousand volumes of it—but you need not read any of it to be a good fly fisherman. In fact, most fish-writing is probably a luxury, an extravagance. The way to learn to fish, of course, is to fish; writing about the outdoors only rarely reaches the level of what can be called literature; and reading about fishing is, for most of us, a poor substitute for the thing itself. G. E. M. Skues, the noted British innovator and author, offered still a further warning; he suggested that some writing had actually *spoiled* his fishing. "I think of all the sport I have probably missed in the past by believing the authorities," he wrote, "instead of finding out for myself about the behavior of trout." There is no substitute for "finding out for yourself."

Still, a couple of billion words have managed to get themselves written—and read—about fly-fishing, several hundred thousand of them by Mr. Skues, incidentally (and very good ones, indeed), and the flow continues monthly, with articles and books tumbling off the presses like new-minted coins. The best of these record and advance the state of the art, provide a common language for fly fishermen countrywide, and convey practical information, theory, and pure pleasure.

Books "are for nothing but to inspire," said Ralph Waldo Emerson, and the best use of fly-fishing books is that they inspire our own practice and speculation. Contrary to learned opinion, you *can* be a superb fly fisherman without having read Berners, Walton, Gordon, Marinaro, and a host of other luminaries past and present — what you *cannot* be is a fly fisher well-read in the lore and traditions of fly-fishing. So if you want — for any number of good and simple reasons — to be well read, you'll want to start a collection of fly-fishing books. You'll also want to know where to begin, and how to still retain enough money to buy that new fly line.

Some people suggest starting at the beginning, with Dame Juliana Berners, the fifteenth-century nun who wrote *A Treatise on Fishing with an Angle*, or with Izaak Walton's *Compleat Angler*. Not me. We live in the present and have immediate needs; though eventually — and hopefully — these needs will include some knowledge of the traditions that add depth and scope to fly-fishing. There has, however, been enough written on American fly-fishing in the past thirty years to warrant starting there. First collect what you can use; collect what gives you pleasure to read — and necessary instruction. Collecting "collector's items," a separate and distinct pleasure — and often a profitable game — can come later, and probably will.

WHEN I VISIT A NEW MUSEUM, I like to make a quick tour of its rooms to see and feel its scope before looking closely at individual paintings. Similarly, I would recommend that you first buy a good *general* book on fly-fishing, or the particular brand you do. *Trout* by Ray Bergman (Knopf) remains a basic broad-based view of trout fishing and is heavily slanted toward fly-fishing; Joe Brooks's *Trout Fishing* (Outdoor Life/Harper & Row) is a newer and very fine book with a solid fly-fishing focus; and A. J. McClane's *The Practical Fly Fisherman* (Prentice-Hall) a superior third, with more emphasis on technique. Arnold Gingrich's *The Fishing in Print* (Winchester) will give you the best overview of the classic literature of angling, from its origins to the present day, with teasing selections, pithy commentary, and Gingrich's penchant for ranking authors; and my own *Fisherman's Bounty* (Crown) contains a liberal selection of what I consider the best fishing stories and lore (it's been remaindered, is available at an exceptionally low price, and I get no more royalties on it).

Harmon Henkin's two books, *Fly Fishing Tackle* and *The Fisherman's Catalog* (both Lippincott) will introduce you to the span of fly-rodding equipment available to you and sources for best buys; Henkin is an addict in both fields, and his books have the true addict's passion and idiosyncrasy. It's hard to characterize Charles Ritz's *A Fly Fisher's Life* (Crown) or Alvin R. Grove's *The Lure and Lore of Trout Fishing* (Freshet), but both will serve as fine, knowledgeable books with which to start — and you will find that *they* grow as you grow more deeply involved in the life or lore of fly-fishing. In all such books you can find leads to other favorites and "road maps" around the fly-fishing world.

Having started with these, you should begin to seek those books which will expand your knowledge of individual specialties. If you are interested in improving your casting, try the excellent *Fly Casting with Lefty Kreh* (Lippincott); if you are doing more Western fishing, or want to, try Charles Brooks' *The Trout and the Stream* (Crown), which gives a thorough picture of fly-fishing opportunities in the West Yellowstone area; for salmon, try Lee Wulff's classic *The Atlantic Salmon* (Barnes); and for saltwater fishing, Lefty Kreh's *Fly Fishing in Salt Water* (Crown). Mark Sosin and Lefty Kreh have written a helpful little book called *Practical Fishing Knots* (Crown) if yours aren't holding, and Eric Leiser's *Fly-Tying Materials* (Crown) will tell you almost everything you want to know about procuring, preserving, and using the many materials available for tying flies.

Fly-tying and entomology are perhaps the broadest — and most confusing — areas for the serious buyer of fly-fishing books; there are dozens of books in these fields, many of them excellent. I would be hard-pressed to rank those books by Poul Jorgensen, Edson Leonard, Ken Bay, Art Flick, Helen Shaw, Robert Boyle and Dave Whitlock, Eric Leiser, and John Veniard. The best guideline again is *need*. If you are a beginning fly tier, Ken Bay's *How to Tie Freshwater Flies* (Winchester) is one of the best. Poul Jorgensen's *Modern Fly Dressings for the Practical Angler* (Winchester) can show you intermediate and advanced steps, and *Art Flick's Master Fly-Tying Guide* (Crown) puts a batch of the nation's best tiers on display, telling how they tie their favorite patterns. And for an updated view of the most recent developments, the Boyle-Whitlock *Fly-Tyer's Almanac* (Crown) is exceptionally helpful.

Some study of entomology, handmaiden to all efforts at imitating the insects on which trout feed, is essential for successful fly-fishing. Many years ago I found Art Flick's little *Streamside Guide to Naturals and Their Imitations* (Crown) to be the best introduction to "entomological thinking" — it is concise, down-to-earth, practical, and sufficiently limited in scope not to drive you immediately back to worms. Thereafter, according to how deep you are prepared to wade, there are a host of valuable books: Preston Jennings' *A Book of Trout Flies* (Crown), the first important American entomological study of trout-stream insects; Ernest Schwiebert's *Matching the Hatch* (Macmillan), written when the author was in his early twenties, is an important and extremely helpful book, as is his newer *Nymphs* (Winchester); Doug Swisher and Carl Richards' *Selective Trout* (Crown), which popularized the no-hackle fly and brought a new flexibility into the practice of hatch-matching; Caucci and Nastasi's *Hatches* (Comparahatch), an exhaustive recent study; Larry Solomon and Eric Leiser's *The Caddis and the Angler* (Stackpole), the first systematic attempt to deal with this mportant aquatic insect; and Charles Brooks's *Nymph Fishing for Larger Trout* (Crown), which has more emphasis, actually, on methods than on entomology.

Then on to more subtle and theoretical books, like Vincent C. Marinaro's superb *A Modern Dry-Fly Code* Crown) and his penetrating new study of riseforms ınd trout behavior, *In the Ring of the Rise* (Crown); George M. L. LaBranche's *The Dry Fly and Fast Water* Van Cortlandt); *The Complete Fly Fisherman: The Notes and Letters of Theodore Gordon* (Scribner's), edited by John McDonald. These will surely lead you back to Frederic Halford's *Dry Fly Fishing in Theory and Practice* (1889) and G. E. M. Skues' *The Way of a Trout with a Fly* (1921), the older English theorists, who will show you quite how complex and sophisticated the sport can be, if you care to make it so. Some other important older books include: Alfred Ronald's *The Fly-Fisher's Entomology* (1836); W. C. Stewart, *The Practical Angler* (1857); Sir Edward Grey, *Fly Fishing* 1899); William Scrope, *Days and Nights of Salmon Fishing on the Tweed* (1843); Edward R. Hewitt, *A Trout and Salmon Fisherman for Seventy-five Years* 1950); John McDonald, *The Origins of Angling* (the Dame Juliana Berners book, with a fine introduction and scholarly apparatus, 1963). Walton remains reading, especially in the editions that contain Charles Cotton's technical material, for a score of unsurpassed nd memorable passages if not for his silly milkmaids.

AND THEN YOU ENTER THE MOST DIFFICULT — yet to me sweetest — area of all: that which aspires to be literature. It will teach you very little about how to cast or how to imitate a hatch, but it will surely hint at the true soul of angling. For stories and narrative I would recommend William Humphrey's superb *The Spawning Run* (Knopf), Norman Maclean's little gem, *A River Runs Through It* (University of Chicago), any book by Roderick L. Haig-Brown, but especially *A River Never Sleeps* (Crown), Howard T. Walden 2d's *The Last Pool — Upstream and Down* and *Big Stony* (Crown), Steve Raymond's moving *The Year of the Angler* (Winchester), Russell Chatham's *The Angler's Coast* (Doubleday), Sparse Grey Hackle's *Fishless Days, Angling Nights*, the gentle works of Dana Lamb, and Robert Traver's *Trout Madness* (St. Martin's) and *Trout Magic* Crown). Ed Zern's earlier *To Hell with Fishing* (Appleton-Century) and his more recent *A Fine Kettle of Fish Stories* (Winchester) remain my favorite angling humor.

These are my *first* suggestions if you are starting from scratch, and the list is already becoming formidable; if you are not starting, pick up the litany where it suits you — or better, poke around for yourself. I don't mean to legislate or pronounce or preach, merely to suggest — merely to provide a brief tour of the museum according to my lights. You don't get tested, with five hundred short-answer questions, by the High Priests of the Holy Fly, before you're allowed to fish a fly; it's simply an enduring pleasure to know some of the best that's been thought and imagined about your sport. As Gingrich once said: good books often make the best companions to carry inside you while fishing.

Where do you acquire such books?

The new ones you can buy by joining one of the outdoor-oriented book clubs (though you will be required to purchase a certain number of titles each year); FLY FISHERMAN magazine has begun to sell books, and you will have, through them, a good screening mechanism; most good fishing-tackle mail-order houses or retail shops now carry books, some at a discount; these include Dan Bailey's, Bud Lilly's, The Rivergate, Fly Fisherman's Bookcase (the most complete list), Hackle and Tackle, Fireside Angler, Angler's Art, and a raft of others. If your local book store does not have a current title — and they are more and more becoming mere hucksters of best-sellers — they can order any book still in print and usually get it for you within a week or so. And a number of publishing firms, particularly Stoeger Publishing, are now buying up rights to the best fly-fishing titles and bringing them out in handsome paperback editions for about $5.95. If you're looking purely for the information or pleasure, and not for a collector's item, you'll find these paperbacks a marvelous boon — and at a great savings.

If a book is not in print you have two options and two radically different price situations. Some books may have been remaindered — that is, sold in bulk to stores at a fraction of their retail cost, after a publisher has decided to discontinue publication and liquidate his stock. Many stores now have a remainder section and some stores, like Marboro and Barnes & Noble, specialize in what is euphemistically called "publishers' overstock." This is an excellent source of fine, mint-condition books at extraordinarily low prices. I know of one man who, many years ago, bought ten copies of the original edition of Marinaro's *A Modern Dry Fly Code* on such a table for a buck apiece; they are now worth well over $100 each. The recent boom in fly-fishing books has inevitably led to especially large remainder stocks — and stores with such tables should be checked regularly. Only a week ago, I picked up a dozen copies of one of *my* old books at $1.00 each — which at least *I* found a great bargain!

If a book is no longer in print and all of the remainder stock is gone, you'll have to rummage through used-book stores or go to one of the rare book dealers. Five good, reliable dealers are:

Angler's and Shooter's Bookshelf
Goshen, Conn. 06756

(Their two-part catalog, available yearly for several dollars, is the most exhaustive in the field—and a collector's item as well as guide to current prices.)

Sporting Book Service
Box 18
Rancocas, N.J. 08073

Charles Daly Collection
36 Golf Lane
Ridgefield, Conn. 06877

Crossroads of Sport
5 East 47th Street
New York, N.Y. 10017

Morris Heller
RD #1
Swan Lake, N.Y. 12783

Most of these dealers, and others like them throughout the country, will also search for a particular book you might want—for a small extra fee. If the book is old and scarce (perhaps because a small number were printed) you may have to pay a stiff price for it. Any book with the imprint "Derrydale Press," which flourished in the 1930's and early 1940's is valuable; these volumes, published by Eugene V. Connett, are handsome, uniquely designed books on various aspects of fishing and hunting—and all were published in limited editions. Depending upon the condition of the book—and whether it is signed by the author—Derrydale editions can be worth up to several hundred dollars or more. Many of them were numbered, as well—and the lower numbers are of the most value. In fact, any limited edition—with the total number printed and the individual book number listed on one of the early pages—is probably a treasure. And even if it isn't numbered, it may be one of a small printing; it pays to learn the publishing history of important books.

A good dealer's catalog, such as that put out by the Angler's and Shooter's Bookshelf, is your best guide to the approximate current value of a book—though in most cases you will be seeing a price at the higher end of the price range. Still, any good old fly-fishing book can only grow scarcer and more valuable. With more and more people entering the sport and the old stock limited, supply and demand are sure to keep prices rising.

Part of the pleasure, for me at least, of collecting is to find an exceptionally good buy, and for this I like to haunt old thrift shops, Salvation Army book racks and other places where estates are bought (and not ex amined too closely). I've found several dozen excellen old angling books—by John Taintor Foote (whos hilarious *The Wedding Gift* is one of my favorites) Henry Van Dyke (the Princeton professor of theolog whose *Little Rivers* is charming), Leslie P. Thompso (whose *Fishing in New England*, a limited edition pro duced by Connett for Van Nostrand, is a gem of book), and others—in such places, usually for only few dollars each, or less. One saleswoman in a Nev York Salvation Army shop actually apologized to m for charging $3.00 for a Derrydale edition—because was "so beautifully bound." I swallowed my guilt an stole it for her price, *before* she had a chance to reduc the price to further absurdity, which she was on th verge of doing; I knew the book was worth comfort ably more than $200. Any large city will have dozens c shops like that, but small towns in "fish country" ofte have them, too, and on several rained-out trout trip I have poked around and picked up an interesting ol book or two. It's good to remember that most *genera* used-book dealers do not know the special value c angling books.

So. If you're going to collect these books for the sak of collecting—which can be lots more fun than collect ing match covers or Bavarian mugs or old china, sinc it's directly related to a sport you love—get some sens of how much a book is worth from one of the dealers learn the names of those authors who are most collec tible, and strive to specialize a bit—perhaps in the dr fly or in books on rods or nymphs or the literature c the sport, so you have a chance of collecting all that available on a particular subject. Completeness bring special joy to all collectors. Remember: signed volume are always more valuable; numbered and signed ed tions are even more so; and the basic condition of book—its binding and page quality—is always cru cial. Buying from a reliable dealer will assure you c good quality—and even if the price is high you can b consoled by the knowledge that it will surely be sti higher next year. But don't forget to rummage aroun the thrift shops, used-book outlets, even country estat sales and auctions; they can often provide exceptiona buys.

But the best reason to collect fly-fishing books, fc my money, remains personal use and pleasure, not ir vestment. The off-season can be quite long, and it one of the many added joys available to fly fisherme that there *is* such a vast literature—as deliciously d verse as it is potentially bewildering, and as practic for understanding the soul of angling as it is a poor sul stitute for the thing itself.

In your fly-fishing library you can explore rivers yc will never fish, debunk theories and practices that w surely affect next season's fishing, and fish memorably in someone else's waders.

Photo by Don Gray.

Photo by R. Valentine Atkinson

Chapter 13

Casting About

ART LEE

FISHING THE FLY RODDER'S "SPHERE OF AFFLUENCE"

THE WORLD OF THE FLY RODDER is bigger than it has ever been. Not just because of his increased time, expendable income and personal mobility — or even because of the increasingly enlightened conservation and stocking policies of the various state and federal fish-and-game departments. The real expansion of the fly angler's "sphere of affluence" has come from his realization that *fishing with the fly rod* means just that — it's a *way of angling*, the best way, most of us think, and not just for trout.

As you've heard throughout this book, the fly rod is an amazingly efficient instrument and certainly the most most satisfying way of taking fish. The trout's general availability to a large proportion of the country's anglers, coupled with its selectivity (not only in its feeding habits, but in the lovely places it tends to inhabit), make it a prime target for the fly.

But there are other fish in the stream and in the pond, as well as in the ocean. We would hate to have to rate them. There are sections of the country where the smallmouth bass offers more challenge and action than his trout neighbors, and he has a big brother at home in any state that can beat up most trout you've ever met — the explosive, surface-busting largemouth.

And how do you rate the ubiquitous bluegill and his panfish sibling? Most fly anglers can walk to the nearest panfish pond, and some of them run. It's relaxed fishing — until the little popper-buggers strike — and some fly fishers' warmest memories reach back to a warm evening on a nearby farm pond, playing tug-of-war with those colorful little flat-bodies.

Not to mention, of course, the seasonal shad runs in the coastal waters, fighting steelhead, West Coast salmon and their nouveau-riche relatives who have moved into the Great Lakes, the coho — and perhaps the ultimate, the Atlantic salmon.

And finally, fly-fishing's fourth dimension — salt water. The flats of the Florida Keys and beyond. The bays, river mouths, and the brackish backwaters of our East, West and Gulf coasts. And even the oceans beyond. Now we're talking tarpon, skittish bonefish. We're fishing on another scale for schooling striped bass and bluefish, anything that moves into the shallows or feeds near the ocean's surface.

We know 99 ways of driving anglers crazy — on any given day in any given place in this God-given world of the fly fisherman. We've been there, we've had contact with these carriers of "paranoia piscatoris" and the case is terminal. We feel that such high misery deserves company. So, wherever you are, wherever you'll be traveling — come on in! The water's fine . . . and the fishing's even better!

Let's Go Casting About . . .

ON THE NEXT FEW PAGES — and few is 30 — we will make an attempt, and fail miserably, to touch upon the actual fly-fishing opportunities that exist in every state in the Union, and even beyond. Fly fishing knows few boundaries.

We certainly cannot discuss each river or lake, even the major ones. We will do some name-dropping, some stream-hopping, some tale-topping, and we'll point you in the right direction. We can't tell you which bridge to wade under along the East's Battenkill in early June, or just where along Michigan's Au Sable you can hike in some 300 yards above the Anonymous Club's waters for dusk-feeding browns, or even the exact spot just outside Livingston, Montana, that monstrous rainbows do violence to exquisitely manicured dry flies in September.

We don't even do *that* in our regular monthly coverage in the "Stream Watcher's Log" section of FLY FISHERMAN magazine each issue — but we commend to you this regular and more-detailed coverage by five field editors and some 40 stream-reporters. It's the best general coverage for fly-fishermen-only there is — and even there we just dent the surface. You'll have to deliver the splash of the take yourself. We do suggest that you take advantage of the frequently detailed and up-to-date information available from the various state fish and game commissions, a list of which reposes on pages 238-239 of this book.

Meanwhile, to get you moving we introduce FLY FISHERMAN Field Editor Art Lee, who, from his own extensive experience and expertise and with an assist from his field-editor colleagues, will take you casting about the country, region by region and state by state, until your head will spin but your heart will be fishing with the fly rod. It's the only way to go!

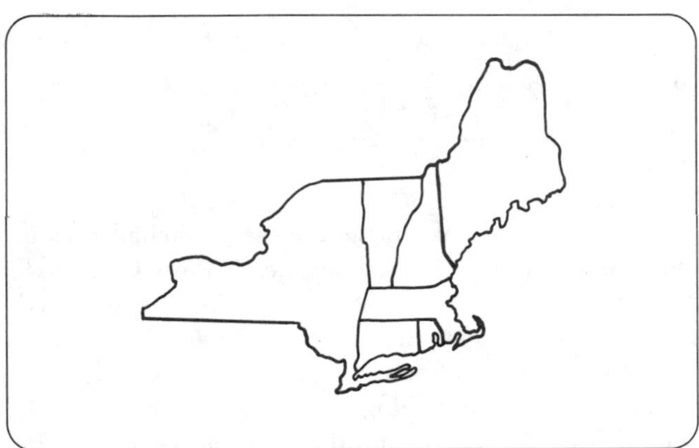

The Northeast

DESPITE A REPUTATION for skyscrapers and a teeming megalopolis, the Northeastern states — Maine, New Hampshire, Vermont, Massachusetts, Rhode Island, Connecticut and New York — boast vast areas of natural beauty and widely varied topography. Also true, though not widely known, is that the region hosts the nation's most numerous and diverse assortment of freshwater fish, many of traditional or awakening interest to fly fishermen.

Among them, brown, brook, rainbow and lake trout, as well as several hybrid species introduced in recent years; Atlantic, coho, chinook, and landlocked salmon; large- and smallmouth bass; walleye; panfish, such as black crappie, bluegill, rock bass, yellow and white perch; the toothy predators, muskellunge, northern pike, two kinds of pickerel, and a mean, mixed breed called "norlunge" that promises exciting angling on streamer flies in years to come.

While the numerous saltwater species abundant along the region's 500 miles of Atlantic coast, ranging from bluefish to bluefin tuna, are covered elsewhere in this volume, worth considering for freshwater sport are prolific spawning runs of anadromous striped bass and shad, both species fair game to a well-presented fly.

American fly-fishing was born in the Northeast, the result of much-publicized correspondence between New World anglers and those scholarly practitioners who remained entangled in their roots across the sea. Thus, Northeastern fly-fishing tends more toward tradition than elsewhere, perhaps inadvertently prepetuating the mistaken impression or myth that the region's true quality angling is to be found only on the Battenkill, Beaverkill or Ausable. While these are unquestionably fine waters, to a region blessed with so many magnificent and fertile fisheries, they amount to no more than three sparkling raindrops in a gentle summer shower.

The Northeast is generally rugged country, draining many mountain ranges — the Longfellow Mountains of Maine, the White Mountains of New Hampshire, the Green Mountains of Vermont, the Berkshires of western Massachusetts and the Adirondacks and Catskills of New York. Only Rhode Island and Connecticut are not "much more up and down than sideways." Long-ago land upheavals and creeping, gouging glaciers left a legacy of countless miles of cuts for rivers and streams, and deep scars for lakes and ponds — all essential for good fishing.

A glance at an atlas tells the story. Maine has almost as much water as land; New York, 15,000 miles of quality trout streams. Vast expanses of two Great Lakes, Ontario and Erie, lie within the region, as well as several of the nation's mightiest rivers — the St. John, the Penobscot, the Connecticut, the Hudson and the Delaware. All are alive, and if not well, improving. Hard to believe, perhaps, for those exposed only to the South Bronx burning on the nightly news, but true. The

Northeast has perhaps the richest angling resources in the country, perhaps the world.

Dense Northeastern population can be viewed with mixed emotions, because although few would deny that out of it is born awesome environmental problems, particularly pollution, or that the "quiet places" become increasingly difficult to find each year, it can be argued with equal conviction that swelling population prompted the network of highways and roads that serve to make easy weekend outings out of onetime two-week trips. Further, fly fishermen are inevitably learning that the political clout of numbers can shore up pioneering concepts such as "special regulations," a conservation technique that one day will surely become the backbone of all quality fly-fishing.

Not that the region is without its quiet places still. Hundreds of square miles of Aroostook, Piscataquis, Somerset and Franklin counties in Maine are among the most rugged and remote in the land, theoretical townships laid out on maps only as sections of timber with names like R1-L3. Now that's remote. Driving north toward Van Buren on Highway 1, you will travel many miles between signs of civilization, not a crossroad or a fast-food joint in sight, only spruce and tea-colored streams and beaver ponds that smell like speckled trout. Remote also describes the Northeast Kingdom of New Hampshire and Vermont and much of the Adirondack Park region in upper New York State (the largest state park, by the way, in America). You can see exactly what Winslow Homer saw when he paddled and portaged the Moose River country more than a century ago. It hasn't changed one bit.

For the single-minded angler or the one with wanderlust, the Northeast may be his *movable feast*. For where else could you hope to fish a Green Drake hatch on Monday and Tuesday and be just an easy two-hour's drive from a Wednesday Broadway matinee? Here is a taste, state by state, of what the region has to offer.

Maine

Dubbed the Down East State, Maine's 33,000 square miles are populated by fewer than a million people, most of them rugged individualists ready with old-time Yankee wit and wisdom. Except for Alaska, Maine is our northernmost state, which, coupled with immense, sparsely inhabited areas, inspires superb fly-fishing for coldwater species, notably landlocked salmon, brook trout (called "speckled trout" or "squaretails" by the natives), rainbow trout and smallmouth bass. Some experienced smallmouth anglers maintain the state's lakes and ponds offer the finest surface fishing for the species in America. Maine also boasts the only consequential U.S. runs of Atlantic salmon, "King of Gamefish," those in late spring, summer and early fall up rivers "restored" by sustained and determined conservation efforts for the past twenty years.

Because of its latitude, spring comes late to Maine waters. Many are iced in until after some popular hatches on well-known waters, such as those in the Catskills of New York, have come and gone. The state's cool climate, however, offers generally dependable seasons, its rivers maintaining stable flows and fish, free of debilitating dog days. Angling plays an integral role in Maine's economy, and visiting fly fishermen will happily note that up-to-date conditions for rivers, lakes and ponds, even in the remotest sections, receive outstanding newspaper coverage on virtually a daily basis. Travelers will also find a thriving and disciplined angling resort and outfitting business can take much of the strain from planning adventures off the beaten track.

Although questionable timbering practices damaged some angling resources in the past, the paper companies, which are the heart of the state's economy, and the conservationists have appeared to compromise in recent years, presenting a brighter angling picture than just one generation ago. Huge company holdings are now open to public fishing on a limited basis under very

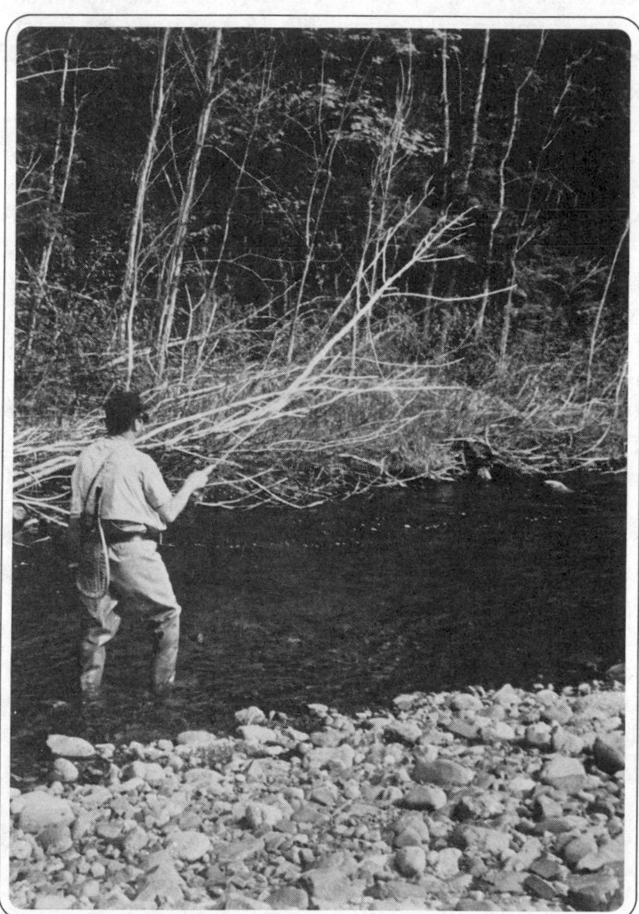

Brook trout fishing on a tributary of the Kennebec River in Maine. Photo by Kris Lee.

strict rules, a boon to those who seek the wilderness experience. On these waters and most others across the state, fly fishermen will find that relatively little in-depth study of the hatches has been made, leaving a wide-open field for the more erudite to explore, and, perhaps, to someday share in print.

Maine romantically carries you back in time with flies such as the Paramachene Belle (a Maine creation), Montreal, Red Ibis, and the Professor. All work remarkably well on Down East waters. Streamers like the Mickey Finn (another Maine original) and Gray Ghost also take cooperative brookies, rainbows and landlocked salmon, often in terrific numbers. Landlocks are probably the state's number-one prize. Rated best waters include Eagle Lake Outlet, Aroostook County; Matagamon Lake Outlet, Penobscot County; West Branch Penobscot River (below Ripogenus), Piscataquis County; Grand Lake Stream and the St. Croix River at East Grand Lake, both in Washington County; Kennebago River, Oxford County; and the Crooked River, Cumberland County. No doubt among the finest landlocked salmon streams anywhere is the Moose River above Moosehead Lake, Somerset County. Moosehead, the largest lake in Maine, is also renowned for smallmouth bass bugging, particularly when the fish arrive on shallow spawning beds in late May or early June.

At the risk of being proved wrong a thousand times by the fickleness of fish, it might be fair to advertise that Maine trout, primarily brookies and rainbows (browns have been introduced in some waters with great success) are less sophisticated than those of streams elsewhere, where fishing pressure gives them honorary Ph.D.'s. Because miles of Down East streams don't see a single fly per season, there are also some really big fish squirreled away. A chance for eight-pound brook trout tends to make things interesting. Choice dry flies for trout and salmon are the Black Gnat, White Wulff, Wulff Coachman, Irresistible and Rat-Faced MacDougall, but that may only be because they're the ones given most river time. Among select trout fishing waters are the Kennebec River, between Solon and Bingham, and the Megallaway and Rapid rivers in the Rangeley Lakes district.

New Hampshire

The Granite State's 9,600 square miles include some of the most beautiful scenery and finest coldwater fishing in the U.S. Located between Maine and Vermont, it is distinguished by mountains climbing to 5,000 feet and spacious belts of verdant forest, dotted with crystal ponds and deep, blue lakes and cut by about 3,500 miles of rivers and streams that abound in trout and landlocked salmon. It should also be added that visiting anglers are sure of a warm welcome.

Fly fishermen have an excellent shot at a "four-bagger" — brown trout, brookie, rainbow and salmon — on New Hampshire's length of the famed Connecticut River, easily one of the finest big-water trout fisheries in America. The Connecticut, like most of the 180-mile-long state's water, peaks in late May and June when you can look for excellent Hendrickson and caddis hatches. Also important to note, however, is that New Hampshire management policy extends trout fishing season into October when the entire state goes "fly-fishing-only — no-kill." Fly rodders who like big water should also be interested in the Androscoggin River, between Errol and Milan, a long stretch that gives up numerous browns in the seven-pound class each season. Top flies on these jewels, as well as waters throughout the state, include the Hornberg (wet and dry), Wulff dries, the Tellico and big stonefly nymphs, and wet flies in various shades of gray and brown, notably the Alder and the Hare's Ear.

Other fine New Hampshire streams are the Baker River near Plymouth, not too heavily fished, the Ammonoosuc near Littleton, where you might take advantage of inevitable swarming black flies in June and fish midges in sizes 26-28, and the Contoocook River in the southern part of the state.

Stillwater anglers should take a crack at Lake Winnipesaukee, a beauty and the state's largest, particularly in the spring and fall near the mouths of streams. Some fine trout and salmon are taken by patient and mobile anglers who rent boats or carry them along. The lake also boasts outstanding smallmouth bass fishing in its bays and coves. The best time for surface popping is definitely late May when scrappers in the four- to five-pound range can be expected on the spawning beds.

Vermont

Probably no area better exemplifies New England to visiting fly fishermen than the Green Mountain State, home of the Battenkill, the White, the Mad, the Lamoille and Dog rivers, and host to volumes of angling lore. Sturdy sugar maples, clapboard houses, rolling fields, mountains, stone walls, gravel lanes and homespun hospitality all seem as natural and unspoiled in this setting as light breezes, clear skies, hatching mayflies and standing on the riverbank swapping lies.

Much of Vermont has forgotten time, or, rather, has remembered well what is best about the past. To be a fly fisherman in Vermont means more than to fish. It is a fulfilling and renewing experience. Not that excuses need be made for the quality of angling. The Battenkill, for instance, may be the finest wild trout fishery in the East, and certainly when you consider both its class trout and predictable, ample hatches, the famous stream must rank among the most rewarding

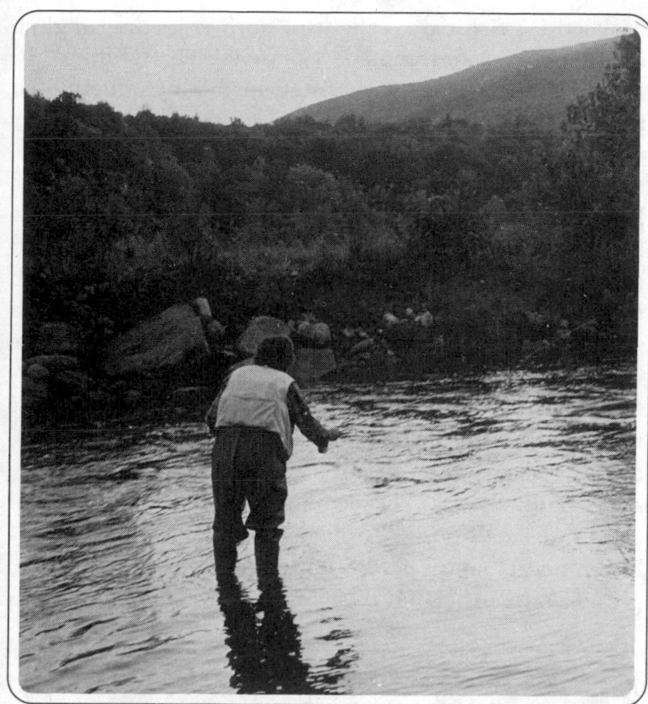

An inviting run on Vermont's Battenkill. Photo by James C. Woods.

fly-fishing challenges anywhere, the kind you'll never forget.

Most of the state, because of a thriving winter ski trade, is accessible by good road, making Vermont wonderful to meander through, to stop here and there at roadside inns, to spend a night or just tip a glass, to regain perspective on what life is supposed to be all about. Except for stretches along the Connecticut which fish akin to those of neighboring New Hampshire, Vermont is not a big-water state. In fact, much enjoyable angling will be found on small mountain streams and brooks, tributaries of better-known waters.

Vermont is not a state of small fish, though. Mile for mile, the Battenkill, particularly in its deep, slow-moving stretches between Manchester and Arlington, boasts as many five-pound browns in the shade of its banks as you'll find anywhere. To land them, though, is another thing, and you can plan to slap a boodle of Muddlers, Spuddlers and Sculpins where they lurk for each one you might hook.

Those after real trophy brown trout may want to trek into the state's Northeast Kingdom to the Black River, a feeder of Lake Memphremagog. Rich in yarns of booze runners during Prohibition, the lake has also managed to distill a fancy tribe of trout to 20 pounds. Not well known or publicized, each fall they migrate up the Black to spawn and will take big, scruffy nymphs and streamer flies enticingly presented. Even when you come away empty, however, the thrill of having cast beneath a canopy of color against a backdrop of flaming New England hills will be a memory nothing can ever take from you, like your fondest dream fulfilled.

Massachusetts

For a locale not renowned for freshwater fly-fishing, the Bay State can claim a lot of it, including a rare opportunity for the East to try your luck at "salty trout." Without venturing into the brine well covered elsewhere in this book, these sea-run rainbows and brown trout, ranging up to six pounds, take on real interest to most fly rodders when they bid the Atlantic good-bye and begin to ascend numerous Massachusetts coastal streams in April. Fisheries managers are gleeful over how well their runs are doing since being introduced more than a decade ago and hasten to advise that these are really "catchable" fish, since they don't migrate to spawn but to follow great schools of young herring, called "sperling," upon which they feed. A streamer, locally known as the Silverside, is effective on such streams as Scorton Creek near Sandwich, the Quashnet River near Falmouth, and the Mashpee River at Mashpee. The Mashpee is particularly noted for its big browns.

Pond fishing for trout is surprisingly popular in eastern Massachusetts, where saltwater angling is the staple. Most notable are Lout Pond near Plymouth and Hamblin Pond, Barnstable, on Cape Cod. What shouldn't be overlooked, however, is that many of these ponds are also ripe with small- and largemouth bass, panfish and pickerel. Experienced anglers say the pickerel, which often reach near-record size, don't get nearly the attention they should from fly rodders.

Farther west, three streams, the Deerfield River near Charlemont, Swift River in Belchertown, and Ware River at Ware, come highly recommended for trout. The Swift, by the way, a tailwater fishery behind the gigantic Quabbin Reservoir, has one of the few "fly-fishing-only" stretches in the state. What Massachusetts lacks in "special regs," however, it more than compensates for in fostering opportunity. For in the Bay State there is no closed season on most species.

Rhode Island

There are about 200 square miles of fresh water in the nation's smallest state, approximately 16 percent of its total area. Unfortunately, most of this water is in private hands. While saltwater fly rodding is Rhode Island's real bright spot, those who like their angling "sweet" are hanging tough against pollution and overdevelopment in what already is overwhelmingly an urban state. When you don't have much, however, you tend to be proud of what you've got. That feeling comes through emphatically when you talk with the small knot of trout fishing fly rodders of little Rhody.

While numerous ponds along the coast have been stocked with trout and also fish well for small- and largemouth bass, pickerel and panfish, the best public brown and rainbow trout fishing the state offers is in the Wood River Watershed, consisting of about a hundred miles of stream, all near Interstate 95. The area boasts excellent Hendrickson hatches around Memorial Day, worthy of special mention because they look like no other Hendricksons reported anywhere. The only way to match the hatch is to tie flies with black hackles and tails. "Don't knock it," a Rhode Island angler quipped in classic Yankee fashion. "Saves a helluva lot of dough on prime blue-dun capes."

Connecticut

One look at a map of the Constitution State shows its 5,000-square-mile area is dotted with ponds and lakes, both natural and manmade. Although not mountainous, Connecticut is not all flatlands, either. Rather, much of it is gently rolling hills that form watersheds for scores of streams and rivers.

While the state is largely urban and suburban, Connecticut conservationists have worked hard during the last decade to motivate responsible public officials to turn pollution problems around, and the record indicates the efforts are paying off. An excellent example of interest to fly fishermen is the Willimantic River, once badly polluted by factories in Stafford Springs. Now it provides good fishing for brown trout up to four pounds. The real class stretch of trout stream in the state, however, is surely the Housatonic River near Cornwall. Caddis are the staple of the brown trout's diet, and larva, pupa, wet and dry imitations are favored by local anglers, although most larger fish, including an occasional eight-pounder, are taken on bucktails or streamers. Another fine trout stream is the Farmington River near Riverton and the People's State Forest.

The state is bisected by the lower reaches of its namesake, the Connecticut River, which, while in an industrialized area, still offers good angling within easy reach of population centers. Besides resident pickerel, northern pike, largemouth bass and panfish, the river hosts excellent runs of shad each year beginning in April. When you challenge the Connecticut, you are tackling very big water, often impossible to fish without a boat. Numerous public and private launching sites are available, however. Fly fishermen interested in warm-water species should also try the scores of ponds and lakes that abound in both game- and panfish.

New York

Some 18,241,266 people live in the Empire State, about 18 million more than in Wyoming, another state renowned for fishing. In light of such statistics, angling in New York is nothing short of awesome. Think of it: All the freshwater species listed in the introduction to this region, as well as fine saltwater fishing; vast reaches of two Great Lakes, teeming now with trout and salmon; mighty rivers, the Hudson and its main tributary, the Mohawk; the broad St. Lawrence of Thousand Islands fame, one of the elite musky fisheries in America and perhaps the most underrated for small- and largemouth bass; the wild Niagara and the turbulent Delaware, a great wild trout river by anybody's standards. And the lakes — prolific Champlain; historic Lake George; Sacandaga Lake, perennial keeper of national records for northern pike; Oneida Lake and its famous walleyes; the six Finger Lakes, home of 15-pound rainbow trout; and Chautauqua Lake, teeming with big muskies. All this, and such storied streams as the Beaverkill, Willowemoc, its share of the Battenkill, and the Ausable, proud waters that have been the very ink to write so much angling history. It would take volumes to even touch on all the fishing in New York State; such volumes have, in fact, already been written.

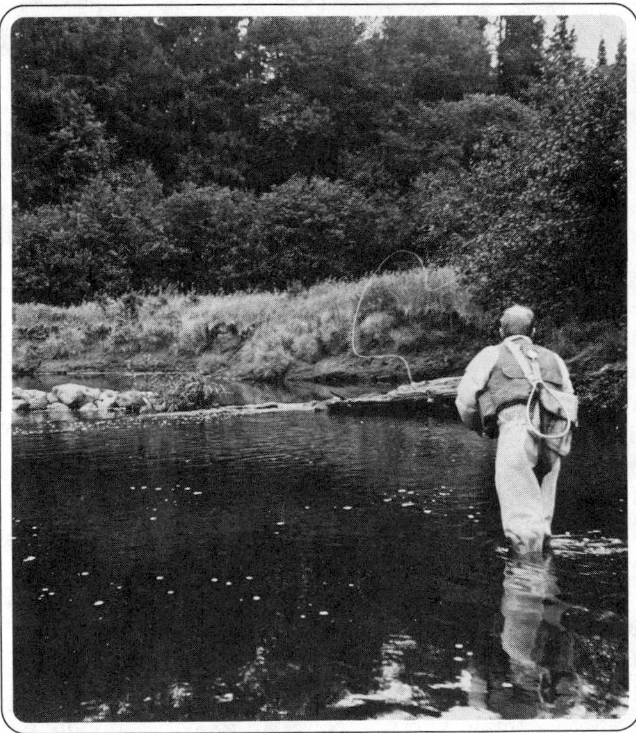

Flat water on New York's Ausable River. Photo by Kris Lee.

First-time touring fly fishermen may be staggered by it all, the marked contrasts between big cities, their highlife and lowlife, and towering Adirondack peaks, a plateau of sun-drenched vineyards, the southern tier, countless rolling Berkshire foothills, the forested Catskill mountainsides. Long Island visitors are often shocked to see the grids of prosperous potato farms just an hour's drive beyond Kennedy or LaGuardia airports, chaotic centers dispatching humanity to the far corners of the world. (Yes, even Long Island has good trout fishing, as Arnold Gingrich loved to tell.)

Under the stewardship of Henry Diamond, environmental conservation commissioner in the late 1960's, New York began an ambitious and aggressive campaign to upgrade the quality of declining water resources, a multi-billion-dollar job still not complete. To improve fishing, dozens of remote Adirondack ponds have been reclaimed and stocked by air with brook trout. New sewage disposal plants have cleaned up the Hudson River to a degree that migrating striped bass are caught on flies as far upstream as Troy. Despite vocal opposition, a vast Adirondack Park was established by the State Legislature, much of it *forever wild*. Within its boundaries are such renowned streams as the East and West Branch Ausable River, the North and South Branch Saranac, the Bouquet River and the upper Hudson. Throughout the region anglers may fish trout to their taste, be it on busy "trophy trout" waters or at the end of demanding pack-ins. If trout and landlocked salmon are not your thing, many Adirondack residents will advise you that their underexploited smallmouth bass fishery may be the best in the nation, particularly in late spring and early fall.

So varied is the topography and climate of the Empire State, a fly fisherman could well go mad just trying to bounce around to keep up with its hatches. Hendricksons, for example, begin coming off the Beaverkill in early May. A week later look for them on Schoharie Creek, two weeks later on the Battenkill. Then, just about the time you're out of flies, word will arrive you can find the hatch again on the brandy-colored pools of the Ausable's West Branch. Follow it there, but don't tarry too long or you're certain to miss the Green Drake back there on the Beaverkill.

Worthy of special mention is the main stem Delaware, a 17-mile big-water stretch between Hancock and Calicoon on the Pennsylvania border. A decade-long fight has finally handed dam water release control to conservation authorities, substantially improving an already superb trout fishery. Three-pound rainbows that take you 150 yards into backing are more common than not, and along with the potential for gigantic browns, occasional 16-inch brook trout may be taken by a few lucky anglers. The fishing is difficult but best with dry flies, and local experts are prone to say "any pattern works — as long as it's an Adams."

Of about 70,000 miles of flowing water in New York, some 15,000 miles harbor trout — rivers and streams of glorious hatches, Quill Gordon, Hendrickson, March Brown, Gray Fox, Light Cahill and Blue-Winged Olive. It is also a state of great innovators and famous tiers of today and of days gone by — Art Flick, the Dettes and the Darbees, Ray Bergman, Reub Cross and Roy Steenrod. To read many New York waters is literally reading angling lore, back to the legendary Theodore Gordon, who got the whole thing started for us. But so long as fly-fishing is an ever-evolving thing, it will be safe to say if there's an idea whose time has come, it's apt to be tried on a New York river first.

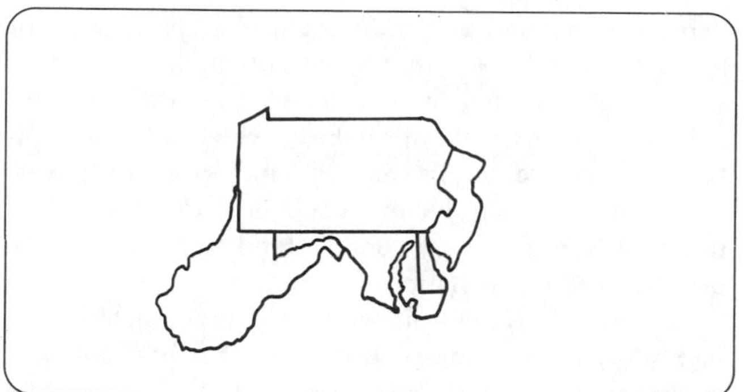

Middle Atlantic

HAD THIS BOOK BEEN COMPILED fifty years ago, of the Middle Atlantic States — New Jersey, Pennsylvania, Delaware, Maryland and West Virginia — probably only Pennsylvania would have garnered more than a cursory coverage. Fly-fishing then still had not come of age. Today, however, against a backdrop of contrasting life-styles and landscapes, from industrialized coastal lowlands to the rough tongue of the Appalachian Mountain chain, this entire region serves to illustrate how far imagination and innovation have brought the art along.

Although there was no so-called "master plan," the principal challenge was to reach viable compromise between economy and ecology, while finding a comfortable niche for fly rodders among spinners, plug casters, bait fishermen and trollers. It meant balancing the practical reality of commerce and sprawl with the spiritual necessity for places to forget it all. To great measure the challenge has been met.

While uniting to stem encroachment and pollution on favorite spots, Middle Atlantic fly fishermen were among the first to look beyond those hallowed waters and the fish traditionally considered their bailiwick to new horizons and dimensions in the sport. Revolutionary fibers, first glass and now graphite, tough to withstand the rigors of salt and light enough to flog farm ponds all day, certainly won their first converts in this region. Torpedo-taper lines were legitimized, while inventive hands fussed over new bugs, poppers and streamer flies, never satisfied until they'd done the job. Even monofilament was given most exacting tests, for until tippets could be developed fine as single strands of maiden's hair, even limestone water stacked with trout remained just another enigma. With heartfelt thanks for its important contribution to us all, here is some of what the Middle Atlantic region has to offer.

New Jersey

ON THE FACE OF IT, New Jersey, a relatively small, densely populated and industrialized state, might not appear to overflow with angling potential. Per capita, in fact, the Garden State probably has the most fly fishermen of any state in the East, which tends to heap terrific pressure on its limited cold-water resources. Crowding also may have a good deal to do with the fact that New Jersey fly rodders tend to be among the best traveled in the nation.

At home, however, anglers constitute a sizable and highly organized conservation force that has managed in recent years to stabilize the quality of most state streams before it was too late. Although these waters take a powerful pounding each spring, fly fishermen can find "blue-ribbon" brown trout angling on several streams, most notably Big Flat Brook near Layton, which boasts hatches comparable to those in the Catskills of New York. Another excellent stream is the South Branch of the Raritan River between Clifton and Califon, particularly a stretch known as the Ken Lockwood Gorge.

Garden State fly fishermen have a choice between limestone (upstream) or freestone (downstream) on the Musconetcong ("Musky") River, with the breakoff point between the two near Hampton. The upstream flat-water stretches boast a fine *Isonychia* hatch in May.

While New Jersey has no major lakes, there are a substantial number of small ones, ponds and manmade reservoirs, most of which harbor good populations of large- and smallmouth bass, pickerel and panfish. Top choice for surface largemouths is probably the eastern shore of Round Valley Reservoir, off Interstate 78, near White House Station. There is a state boat-launching site on the lake.

Pennsylvania

THE CUMBERLAND VALLEY and its fabled limestoners first cast Keystone State fly-fishing to national attention. Unforgiving browns and brook trout of these meandering meadow streams, cold, clean and fertile, offered American anglers, even those who believed they'd seen it all, a novel challenge. Big names began to gather on the banks from all across the country, and although many of them were humbled then as now, the publicity generated by their labors soon made it clear that Pennsylvania angling would become a state of mind.

Pennsylvania's famed Letort. Photo by Kris Lee.

Not that an inner circle of Pennsylvania fly rodders wasn't already well aware of the superlative angling with which the state is so well endowed. Into three big rivers, the Susquehanna, Allegheny and the Delaware, abundant water flows, draining two major mountain ranges. Throughout these watersheds could be found browns, brookies and rainbow trout, large- and smallmouth bass, musky, pike and pickerel, all terrific gamefish. Its awakening before the angling world at large, however, may not have come a minute too soon. Even as the ink dried for the "sporting books," Pennsylvania fisheries were feeling the strain of burgeoning population, industrialization and, worst of all, coal mining. It's been said, "A secret place has no friends," and so the *discovery* of Pennsylvania turned out to be auspicious. Along with its new popularity, there evolved a fisheries policy among the most enlightened in the nation. Pennsylvania can claim the first serious attempts to arrest the devastation of strip mining, while resource managers with public support pioneered the concept of "fish for fun." Today, Pennsylvania is *living* proof that where sound judgment prevails, everybody wins.

Central to the story is the legend of the Letort, a little limestoner in Carlisle, which has become a mecca for discriminating fly fishermen in search of the ultimate challenge, smart fish on small flies and fine tippets. The Letort, however, is not the only limestone stream of note. Big Spring near Newville, the Yellow Breeches, Boiling Springs, Falling Spring Run near Chambersburg, and Penn's Creek near Weikert, the biggest of them all, are among the finest anywhere. But then, the entire story of fly-fishing in the Keystone State is not chiseled in limestone, either.

The Brodhead, which rises in the Poconos and flows into the Delaware River near East Stroudsburg, has often been immortalized, both on canvas and in print. It is also important to recall that Pennsylvania claims one bank of the big Delaware for 139 miles, including, by the way, that 17-mile stretch of incomparable trout water so often attributed to New York alone.

The main ridge of the Appalachian Mountain chain bisects the state, flanked to the west by the noble Alleghenies. Though lesser known, the western portion of the state also provides some interesting fly-fishing. Among the best waters is Laurel Hill Creek above Ligonier. An Adams is the favorite fly. Wild-trout enthusiasts should have a go at the Youghiogheny River, where one of the outfitters in Ohiopyle can take you to the big ones.

Far to the west in the state, salmon enthusiasts gather each spring on Elk Creek to meet migrating Pacifics that follow smelt from Lake Erie up into the stream. Big rainbows also run and, pound for pound, put up the strongest fight. When it comes to a test against hard-fighting fish, however, Pennsylvania's great musky fishing may be fly-fishing's number-one "sleeper." Because so much trout fishing is available, few anglers have doped out the secret to hooking this tiger on a fly, despite substantial emphasis placed on muskies by the state fisheries bureau. Muskellunge can now be found in numerous lakes and reservoirs across the state, as well as big river systems including the Susquehanna, Allegheny and lower Delaware. Someday before long, this open field may present fly rodders a challenge equal to taking 20-inch trout on 8x tippets and size 28 flies.

Delaware

More than 260 people per square mile live in the country's second smallest state (2,000 square miles), which doesn't leave a lot of room for freshwater fish. Because of its location on Delaware Bay at the mouth of its namesake river, most of the state's prime fly-fishing is reserved for salt and brackish water. That, however, is a story told elsewhere in this book. The First State does have about 50 freshwater ponds that hold largemouth bass, pickerel, white and yellow perch, as well as the fledgling fly fisher's favorite, the sunfish. All take flies readily if sought around snags, over weed beds and in shallows. A few trout are also stocked in Delaware ponds each season.

Shad enter the bay in great numbers in the spring on their way to the big Delaware River, but a few also ascend such streams as the Murderkill at Bowers, the Mispillion, which empties into the bay at Mispillion Light, and the Indian River near Millsboro.

Maryland

So varied is the topography of the Old Line State that, despite a relatively limited area, it is rich in fish and fishing. Rolling farmlands give way to the fringes of the Appalachian range where the state borders West Virginia, while in the eastern zone coastal lowlands sweep out to meet Chesapeake Bay, into which numerous tidal streams and rivers flow. Rivers rich in history traverse the state, the Potomac to the south, the Patapsco and Gunpowder in the central region, and the magnificent Susquehanna in the east. Thus, considering there are also numerous ponds, lakes and reservoirs, the growing number of Maryland fly fishermen finds itself with a virtually unlimited shopping list of sport—brown, brook and rainbow trout, large- and smallmouth bass, pickerel, panfish including yellow perch and black crappie, as well as bountiful runs of anadromous hickory and true shad, and striped bass, locally called "rockfish."

Popping for largemouth bass can bring trophy-size rewards in shallow areas of the Megothy, Gunpowder, Bush, Seneca, Middle, West and South rivers, along with dozens of ponds and lakes on the Eastern shore. Fine fly-fishing for smallmouth bass is also available on the Susquehanna and Potomac rivers, where an August white miller hatch is nothing short of spectacular.

Hickory shad, the smaller of the two varieties, begin their migrations from salt water in early April and are followed by true shad up the Susquehanna, Patuxent and Potomac rivers, as well as numerous smaller streams and creeks, about a month later. "Rockfish" between one pound and twenty pounds ascend virtually all tidal rivers in good years, but the favorites of fly rodders remain the Potomac and Susquehanna, where the fish seem to be ready takers once the schools are hunted up. To be most effective, however, it is often essential to have a boat.

Excellent trout fishing and the rare chance to glimpse a black bear or bobcat highlight the Savage River and Savage River Reservoir in the state forest near New Germany. While hatches are sparse, Black Gnats and Mosquitoes do well on the browns and rainbows, as do large sculpins fished deep. Other good bets for year-round trout fishing include the Youghiogheny River, also near New Germany, and Big Hunting Creek, Thurmont, an easy two-hour drive from the nation's capital.

West Virginia

West Virginia is blessed with ruggedly beautiful scenery, dense forest shading tumbling mountain streams, plump pools below glistening, terraced waterfalls. Winding roads seem to roam no place in particular. When you fish there, it's easy to feel comfortable and detached. Nice country to forget your troubles in.

Dominated by highlands, the backbone of the Appalachian chain and the Allegheny Plateau, there was a time when the state could claim one of the most abundant wild-brook-trout fisheries in the land. Acid drainage, however, from another resource, coal, did a job on that, and for many years it was all fly fishermen could do to keep ahead of spreading degradation. Strides by the state Water Resources Board to stem drainage of coal washery wastes into streams, coupled with an aggressive and efficient hatchery program, however, have apparently turned the situation around.

Today, West Virginia has year-round trout fishing, with an added advantage of early hatches because of moderate temperatures. Among its many fine trout fisheries is the Elk River, thirty miles of varied water in the south-central region of the state. Browns, brook trout, rainbows, along with a hybrid strain known locally as the "golden," are heavily stocked, and while weekend pressure is rather tough, comparative solitude can be expected throughout the week.

Some claim West Virginia's rocky stretches of the Potomac River offer the best smallmouth-bass fishing in the country. Not so well known, however, is that the South Branch of the Potomac near the Virginia border boasts 36 miles of outstanding trout fishing, including the pool that produced the state record in 1968, a 16-pounder. This water produces many holdover browns and some large native brookies to a foot long.

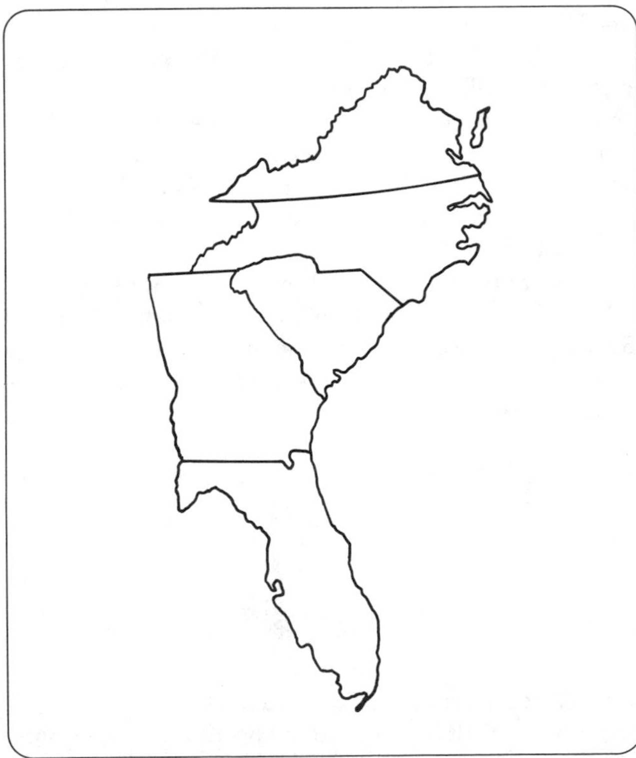

The Southeast

MANY LONGTIME RESIDENTS of this 241,894-square-mile region—Virginia, North Carolina, South Carolina, Georgia, and Florida—still rise to the tune of "Dixie." Except for the Atlantic and Gulf coasts of Florida and other pockets along the way, there remains token suspicion that a fly rod is the utensil of carpetbaggers and eccentrics. Nor do many anglers from traditional fly-fishing states fully appreciate southeastern potential for fine trout fisheries in western Virginia, North Carolina and Georgia, abundant smallmouth bass, and enormous largemouths prowling weedy shallows of seemingly endless ponds and lakes. The Southeast is a fertile land and thus has lots of water.

It is probably fair to say this is still the heartland of bait casting, spinning and the old cane pole, each with its own colorful tradition. More and more, however, visiting fly fishermen are discovering it is also welcome turf with splendid hospitality, where once accepted, nothing is too much trouble to assist new-found friends. Why, occasionally, a fly rodder may even be taught there's more sport to bait casting than "chuck and chance it."

The Southeast is a fly fisherman's "target of opportunity," a place to cast to fish that have never seen a fly, a place to make new friends. Here is some of what this region has to offer.

Virginia

IT WOULD BE WORTH TRAVELING BACK to "ol' Virginny" just to read the sign posts and say the names of streams aloud. Lush forest plays tricky games with broken sunlight on little Blue Ridge Mountain creeks with handles like the Bull Pasture River, Crab Run and Ramsey's Draft. With names such as those, who could care if there were fish at all? It's a bonus, to be sure, that they are full of small, native brook trout. Anglers who love fly-fishing just for the sake of it, could find no better place.

Most popular, certainly, of the mountain streams among "Old Dominion" fly fishermen (who also number notables on "R & R" from the trials of governing) is the Rapidan River near Madison, which tumbles through beautiful Shenandoah National Park. Strictly for hip boots, it, too, is a pleasant throwback to a time when most fly boxes carried the Montreal, Black Gnat, Grizzly King and Parmachene Belle. These flies, little drys and ants also work well on another favorite, Big Run, in the southern sector of the park.

A mixed bag of smallmouth bass and brown trout highlight the action on the North and South Forks of the scenic Shenandoah River near Front Royal, while on the historic Rappahannock River and its tributaries it is fun to pick your way through the rocky pools and pockets, casting poppers to spunky smallmouth bass. The Rappahannock also boasts excellent spring runs of both hickory and true shad that seem to love fluorescent flies.

In the eastern Piedmont area, scores of lakes and ponds offer exciting largemouth bass fly rodding from early spring to late fall. Among the best is Lake Anna near Mineral, where several good boat liveries are located. A good time for surface-popping Lake Anna, along with most other Virginia lakes, is May when the fish come off their spawning beds hungry enough to eat a boat.

North Carolina

WHEN THE LEGENDARY "COUNTRY LAWYER," Senator Sam Ervin, decided to bid Capitol Hill goodbye, among the last things he confided to the press was that he had an itch to "go on home and catch up on some neglected fishin'." What may be our sport's best-kept secret, now as then, is that the Great Smoky Mountains that gave us Senator Sam also rate among the top trout-fishing regions in all the U.S.

The Tarheel State enjoys the East's heaviest annual rainfall which, when coupled with the gradual slope away from the state's western mountains toward the central Piedmont plateau and coastal lowlands, provides a natural drainage through systems of rivers, streams and big and little basins to form countless ponds and lakes. Thus, visiting anglers can rely on ideal waters for brown, brook and rainbow trout in the high country, giving way to smallmouth bass as temperatures rise and finally largemouth bass that find lakes, ponds and reservoirs ideal for their numbers and growth. Fine largemouth fishing, incidentally, continues all the way to the brackish water on the coast.

Perhaps because much trout water is in private hands, the state's upland fishing remains relatively unknown, underpublicized and vastly underrated. Among the ideal streams open to the public, however, are the Davidson and South Mills rivers, both of which course through the Pisgah National Forest between Asheville and Brevard. One advantage of these and other North Carolina streams is early hatches prompted by the state's moderate climate. Another outstanding trout fishery is the Nantahala River in the Standing Indian Wildlife Management Area of the Nantahala National Forest near Franklin.

Beautiful rivers holding smallmouth bass include the North Fork of the New River near the Tennessee border, the South Fork below Laurel Springs, and the Yadkin River and Elks Creek, both near Ferguson. Big rivers of the Piedmont are often turbid due to hydroelectric power impoundments, but the impoundments themselves, such as Rhodhiss Lake near Granite Falls and Lake Hickory near Stoney Point, two in the Catawba River system, produce largemouth bass in the 10-pound class from their bushy shorelines. Nor should bass buggers bypass thousands of farm ponds ranging in area from less than one-half acre to ten acres. Most are well stocked by the U.S. Fish and Wildlife Service. In the extreme east, try the brackish stretches where the Currituck River flows into Currituck Sound. It's a good place when you're armed with 1/0 largemouth streamers, and you can launch a boat at the Poplar Branch ramp.

South Carolina

ALTHOUGH THERE ARE ABOUT 200 MILES of good rainbow trout fishing in western portions of the Palmetto State, the most appealing story to fly fishermen should be vast reaches of some of the nation's truly ambitious reservoirs. "Headline news" seldom reported to fly rodders is 100,000-acre Lake Marion, an impoundment on the Santee River in the east-central portion of the state. Marion hosts a magnificent population of landlocked striped bass, called "rockfish" by local anglers. While trolling, spinning and bait-casting remain the most popular techniques to catch these fish (which run to 50 pounds), it must be remembered that South Carolina is not traditionally considered a fly fisherman's state, and so the field should be pretty much wide open.

Lake Marion also has excellent stocks of largemouth bass, as does Lake Moultrie (60,000 acres), connected downstream by a seven-mile channel, or canal. Other large impoundments with fine largemouth angling are Lake Murray (50,000 acres) and Lake Greenwood (11,800 acres), both on the Saluda River. Below Lake Murray is a 12-mile tailwater fishery for rainbow and brown trout, which occasionally turns up fish in the near-20-inch class to savvy fly rodders.

The state's western trout streams are largely stocked with rainbows, although some browns and a few brookies are also planted. Among those waters to try are the Chatooga and Chouga rivers, both near Walhalla. A 13-pound brown was taken from the Chouga several years ago.

Georgia

WAY DOWN UPON THE SUWANNEE RIVER, or others in middle and south Georgia — the Flint, Satilla, Alapaha, Altamaha, Canoochee and Ogeechee — a leisurely float by fly fishermen can turn up superb angling for largemouth bass, pickerel and panfish to rival any in the nation. And all this in a state also blessed with one of the most captivating, if eerie, swamps in the world, the Okefenokee, seemingly endless miles of majestic cypress with long, gray beards of Spanish moss. Too few fly rodders take advantage of Georgia's angling potential or of its ideal year-round fishing climate.

The state has 3,500 miles of such warm-water streams, but that's not half the story. Seventeen major reservoirs also cover some 300,000 acres; there are 40,000 smaller lakes and ponds, not to mention about 700 miles of trout water, much of it supporting wild fish. Besides three trout species and well-known "hawgs" up to 15 pounds, Georgia can also claim good populations of smallmouth, white and redeye bass, anadromous stripers, walleye, and panfish, labeled "bream" in the South and pronounced "brim," for which a fly rod is the ideal tool. The national record for pickerel, incidentally, was taken in southern Georgia.

In the northern region, TVA reservoirs, such as Blue Ridge, Nottely and Chatuge, all offer excellent bass bugging for those with boats, as do power company impoundments including Burton, Seed and Rabun, which also hold heavy trout. In the central region, Georgia shares shores of Barlett's Ferry, Goat Rock and Lake Oliver with Alabama, while gigantic Clark Hill Reservoir lies on the South Carolina line. In the southern portion, try 45,000-acre Walter F. George Reservoir (known locally as Lake Eufaula) and 37,500-acre Lake Seminole to "hang a hawg" in the 15-pound class.

While numerous small trout streams are located upstate, probably the most popular big water for rainbows is 30 miles of tailwater below Lake Lanier, near Atlanta. It makes a beautiful float.

Florida

THERE ARE SPOTS IN THE SUNSHINE STATE where a fly rodder could cast one direction into fresh water, the other into salt. For example, from the dam at the tail of 5,000-acre Deer Point Lake near Panama City, a bass bug fished one way might hook a lunker largemouth. A dropped backcast, however, might put you into tarpon. The same thing might happen in the J. Ding Darling Bird Sanctuary on Sanibel Island off Fort Meyers. Such are the trials of Florida angling.

Bass-bugging the cypress stumps in Florida. Photo by Lefty Kreh.

So productive are Florida waters, it is virtually impossible to write a piece without remarking that the state is a saltwater fly rodder's paradise. That is handled well elsewhere in this volume, however, so it becomes most pertinent here to point out that Florida also boasts some 58,000 square miles of freshwater lakes, rivers, canals and receding ponds, locally called sloughs. A look at a state map really tells the tale. There's water, water everywhere.

Although the entire peninsula is almost flat, it is by no means monotonous to look at. The state is about 450 miles long, a good day's drive for anyone, and while the north looks much like Georgia with grand oaks and cyprus hung with Spanish moss, it is not until south of vast seas of saw grass that you truly encounter what we fondly, if wrongly, refer to as the "tropics." Florida is subtropical. Much of the freshwater fishing is, in fact, in the northern two-thirds of the state, but from Lake Okeechobee south spreads one of the last true wildernesses in our nation, the mysterious Everglades.

It shouldn't be news to anyone that Florida is famous for largemouth bass. Largemouth waters number some 30,000, lending credibility to the old saw, "If it's wet, you can bet there's bass in it." Besides its abundance of fish, Florida is also renowned for their size. "Hawgs" from five to eight pounds barely spur a yawn, and although most monsters, frankly, are caught by bait casters, hanging one of 15 pounds on a streamer or popper should never be counted out. If it can be done anywhere, shallow Florida lakes are ideal.

Fishing, of course, is a year-round pursuit. Among the best waters in the northern region are Lakes Talquin, Jackson, Iamonia and Miccosukee, with fish most cooperative from October to June. Another nearby hot spot, the Dead lakes, fishes exceptionally well with fly-rod poppers. In the southeast, Lake George, Little Lake George and Lake Crescent are known to live up to their collective nickname of "Bass Capital" of the country.

Angling is big business in Florida, a natural extension of the tourist trade. Wherever you go, there are boats for rent, launching sites and guiding services advertised. Although the fly rod has become a common sight on saltwater flats, however, it is important to remember Florida freshwater fishing remains largely the province of plug casters and spin fishermen. Before hiring a guide, be sure he is familiar with fly-fishing, or there are likely to be some unfortunate misunderstandings.

Guides are particularly helpful when you tackle Florida's rivers for bass or the coastal waters for snook, sea-trout, ladyfish and tarpon. They serve not only to take you to the fish, but as interpreters when you find it necessary to pronounce the names. Among the most productive rivers are the Chipola, Apalachicola, Caloosahatchee, Oklawaha, Withlacoochee, Chassahowtza, Suwannee and Homosassa, where it is rumored that bass developed largemouths only so they can tell each other where they live.

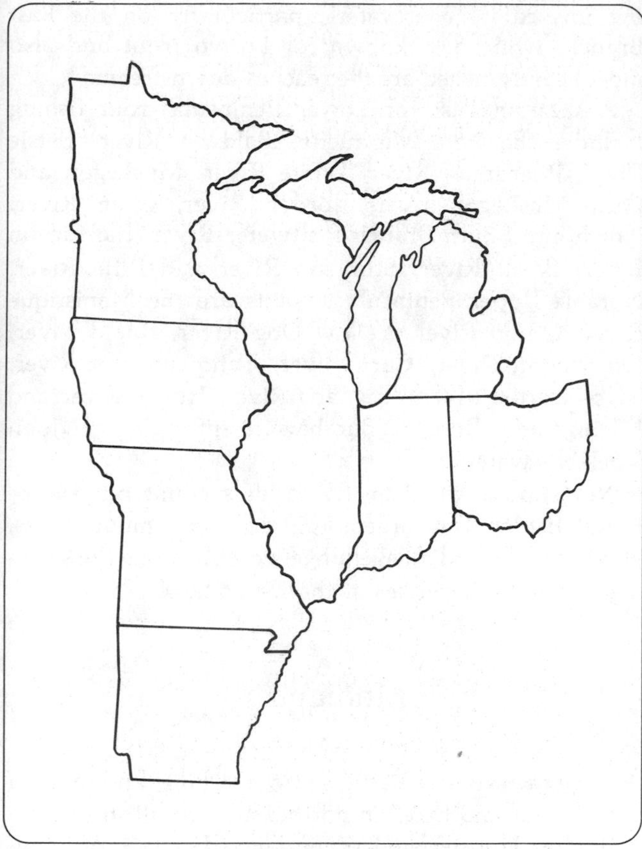

Midwest

THE CATSKILLS AND FLY-FISHING were once considered synonymous by anglers with names like Hendrickson and, oh yes, Sparse Grey Hackle. Although the Midwest, Rocky Mountains and the Pacific Coast could always claim their share of fly rodders, to great measure it was a regional thing, based on local participation. Most publicity for the sport was generated from the East and focused on itself. Few but the pros and the most adventurous (and well-to-do) traveled very far to fish, and those who did travel were as apt as not to make their pilgrimages to, you guessed it, the Beaverkill. Not until the post-war period of improved communications, stepped-up mobility, and maybe most important, relatively general affluence did most fly fishermen really begin to look around.

The Midwest, a vast and varied region of forest land and open plain, revolutionized the fly-fishing map, which should come as no great surprise when you consider that it possesses about one-seventh of all the world's fresh water (Michigan alone has borders on four of the five Great Lakes.) The "Heartland of America," because of its diversity of conditions, also served to diffuse attention of fly fishermen to species other than trout and salmon, notably smallmouth bass and northern pike, as well as to give us some new names with new ideas, Schwiebert, Swisher, Richards and Traver. The region also deposited one bit of mass confusion. Where is the Au Sable, anyway? Nowhere near the Ausable; bet on that.

For purposes of fly-fishing only, and with a special tip of the hat to the fabulous White River in Arkansas, we will say the Midwest is comprised of the following states: Ohio, Michigan, Indiana, Illinois, Wisconsin, Iowa, Minnesota, Missouri and Arkansas. With that out of the way, it's fair to conclude that what follows is the best, state by state, *our* Midwest has to offer.

Ohio

ALTHOUGH THE BUCKEYE STATE prides itself on "liberalized fishing," that is, no closed seasons and few limits, dense population, industrial pollution and acid runoff from extensive mining have tended to make management of quality angling a major problem. A point of fact, for instance, is that the state has little trout fishing, except for that on waters protected by exclusive clubs, which, by the way, remains superb. Thus, what public trout water there is, such as the Mad River in the southeast of the state, takes a terrific pounding.

Two-thirds of Ohio's northern boundary borders Lake Erie, which remains quite a fish factory despite fears a decade ago it was "dying." Based on Erie stocks, Ohio anglers share the coho, chinook and steelhead fever, a pleasant malady often reaching epidemic proportions. For Buckeye fly rodders, however, the problem is the runs are limited to a few streams — the Chagrin, Conneout and Huron rivers — so, without sufficient cold-water action elsewhere to disperse the competition, when the fish start coming, it can be tough enough to find a spot to stand, let alone one to make a backcast.

Ohio has many lakes, ranging in size from Lake Pymatuning (15,500 acres) down to one-eighth-acre farm ponds. Most hold fish including large- and smallmouth bass, muskellunge, northern pike, and panfish, notably yellow perch, which are excellent fly-rod fare. Fine smallmouth bass and yellow perch fishing can be found off the scores of islands in the Port Clinton-Sandusky area of Lake Erie. Smallmouths also take well on the upper Huron and Vermilion rivers in May. Among top lakes for largemouths and muskies are Lake Clendening, Beach City Lake, Leesville Lake and Piedmont Lake. A 55-pound musky, the state record, came from Leesville Lake.

Michigan

THE BEWITCHING CALL OF THE LOON echoing through a conifer forest is somehow symbolic of Michigan and its angling riches. Just the mention of Michigan, with its two peninsulas touching four Great Lakes, should conjure up essential images of our sport nothing less than spiritual — Hemingway's immortal stories, plentiful hatches, light spring rains and cloudless summer night skies.

Once Michigan's natural resources were thought limitless. As vast areas were logged, the grayling disappeared forever, and commercial fishermen depleted Great Lakes stocks. As population swelled bringing with it inevitable pollution, the state had to learn the hard way and then, in turn, teach the rest of us just how presumptuous and costly that belief could be. Because Michigan had so much to lose, it had so far to go to bring it back, and although it can never be the same again, thanks to enlightened management and aggressive public support, today the state can claim fisheries to rival the finest in the land. It was here in 1959, an important year to note, that a small group of dedicated angler-conservationists conceived an organization they called Trout Unlimited, now so important to our sport.

Michigan has so many fly-fishing possibilities that dozens of lifetimes would be required to sample them all. Internationally famous are coho and chinook salmon, and even more important to fly rodders, steelhead trout, which grow huge on alewives in the Great Lakes before making annual migrations up numerous Michigan rivers and streams. Since "nothing succeeds like success," the economic base stemming from these fisheries, which draw anglers from across the nation, has provided impetus for one of the most progressive and responsive programs in the world. Contemporary fly rodders are probably more familiar with Michigan steelheading than that of the West Coast — where it has been a traditional pursuit for a century.

Steelhead have also served to substantially lengthen the Michigan fly-fishing season. Although spring and fall are most popular, even in the dead of winter fly anglers await steelhead up to 25 pounds, occasionally even larger. Among the best-known steelhead fisheries are the Muskegon River from the Croton Dam downstream, the Pere Marquette, which flows into Lake Michigan at Ludington, the Big Manistee from the Tippy Dam downstream, the St. Joseph River in the state's southwest region, and from the renowned Au Sable up to the Foote Dam.

The Au Sable is also the state's best-known trout stream. Like New York's Beaverkill or the Yellowstone of Montana, the Au Sable annually attracts thousands of anglers from across the country to fish its copious hatches. Long gone are the days when its name was misspelled or mispronounced by anglers who could identify only the Ausable of Adirondack fame and legend. Now equally revered, the Au Sable, which has four branches (East, South and North Branches, plus the Main Stream), rises in the state's central highlands and flows all the way to Lake Huron at Oscoda. A scenic and varied stream, it offers excellent brook-trout fishing toward its headwaters, particularly on the East Branch, while best known for brown trout and also most heavily fished are the reaches downstream.

A shopping list for Lower Peninsula trout fishing includes the Pere Marquette, Baldwin River, Betsie River, Boardman River, White River, Muskegon and Little Muskegon rivers, Jordon River, Clam River, North and South Branch Pentwater River, the Pigeon River, Black River, Sturgeon River and Rifle River. Notable Upper Peninsula streams are the Manistique River, Onion River, Yellow Dog River, Rapid River, Ontonagon River, Carp River, Tahquamenon River, Two-Hearted River, Escanaba River, Huron River and Michigamme River. (But beware infringing on John Voelker's waters!)

Nor should Michigan fly rodders count out exceptional fishing for largemouth and smallmouth bass, northern pike and muskellunge, notably along the seemingly endless shorelines of the Great Lakes.

Indiana

Although Indiana has little trout fishing, and most of that is "put and take" in northeastern smallish streams and lakes, Hoosier anglers can take advantage of abundant largemouth, smallmouth, white bass (locally called "silvers") and panfish in eighteen different watersheds, each with hundreds of miles of rivers and numerous ponds and lakes.

In some cases even obviously negative aspects of strip-mining coal have been turned around by flooding abandoned mine pits to provide excellent bass fishing. Less than perfect, perhaps, but something nonetheless. On a per acre of water basis, however, Indiana, which is situated in the industrial heart of the country, has serious environmental problems that in many places preclude real quality angling.

The best fly-fishing will be found on several popular smallmouth rivers, including the Tippecanoe, which flows southwest from Lake Tippecanoe to the Wabash River. Shallow and fast moving, the river offers a choice of good wading or floating for scrappy smallmouths that hit surface poppers. Other fine, shallow smallmouth streams are the St. Joseph and Kankakee rivers, both near South Bend, a major population center. The Kankakee is also known for northern pike.

Although they do provide some bass bugging, two of the state's major rivers, the Wabash and White, are badly polluted, leading many Indiana anglers to favor lakes. In the northeast there are dozens of small lakes and ponds that offer good bass fishing. Indianapolis fishermen have their choice of three large reservoirs that serve their city — Bloomington, Geist and Morse. For size of bass, Yellow Wood Lake in the Yellow Wood State Forest, Brown County, promises the best shot.

Two examples of well-known Eastern trout waters: above, the Ausable in New York's Adirondacks, photographed by John Merwin. Below, the Letort in Pennsylvania, photographed by Mark Sosin.

Plate 26

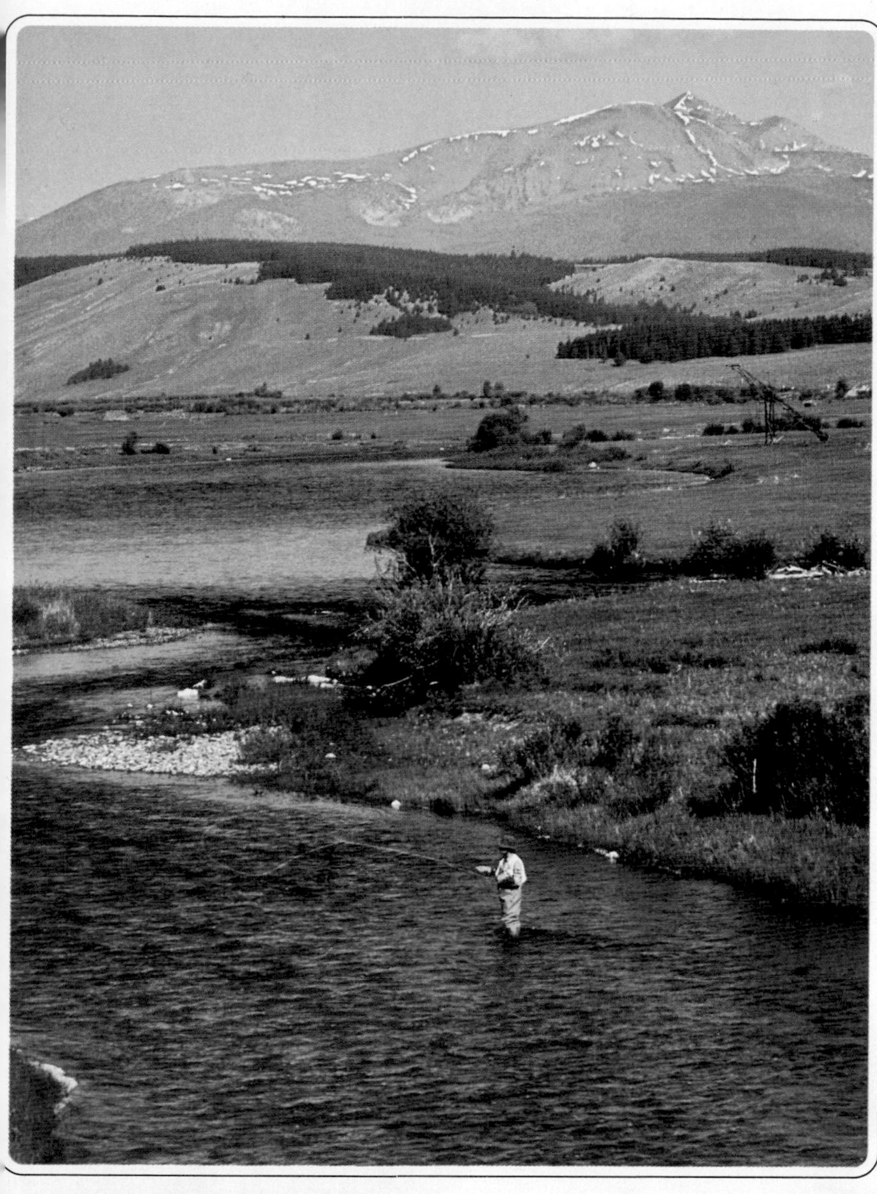

At the far left is shown a typical stretch of Michigan's famous Au Sable River, photographed by Leland Day. At the immediate left is shown the headwaters of Montana's Big Hole River, photographed by Jonathan T. Wright.

Shown above is the Gibbon River in Yellowstone National Park, photographed by Alexander Lowry. Below is Oregon's Deschutes River, being run in a drift boat, and photographed by Ron Cordes. The following four pages of antique and classic fly-fishing gear were taken by Don Gray at the Museum of American Fly-Fishing. The final color plate in this section is of a collection of paraphernalia from a 19th century rod-building shop.

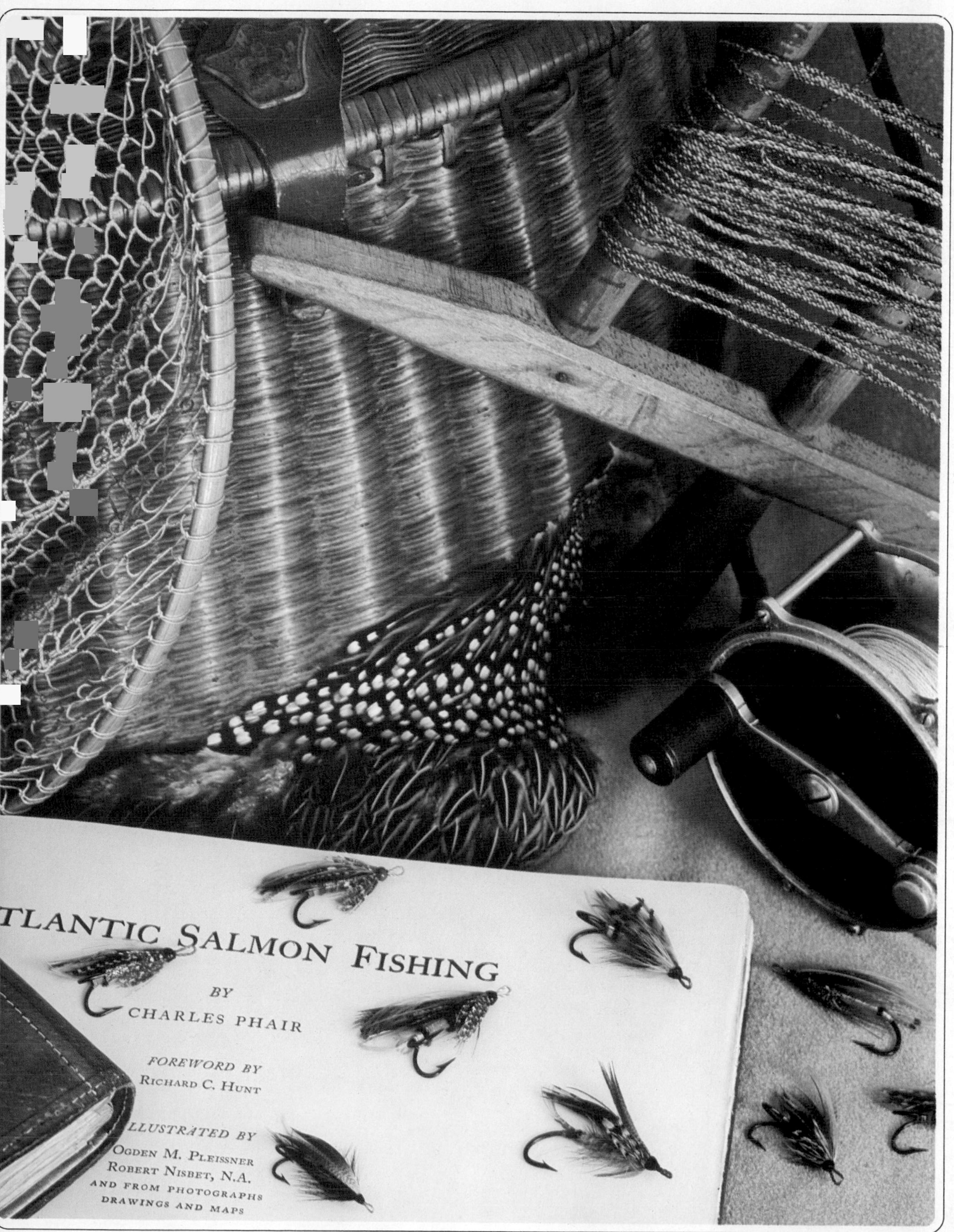
TLANTIC SALMON FISHING
BY
CHARLES PHAIR
FOREWORD BY
RICHARD C. HUNT
LLUSTRATED BY
OGDEN M. PLEISSNER
ROBERT NISBET, N.A.
AND FROM PHOTOGRAPHS
DRAWINGS AND MAPS

Plate 29

Plate 30

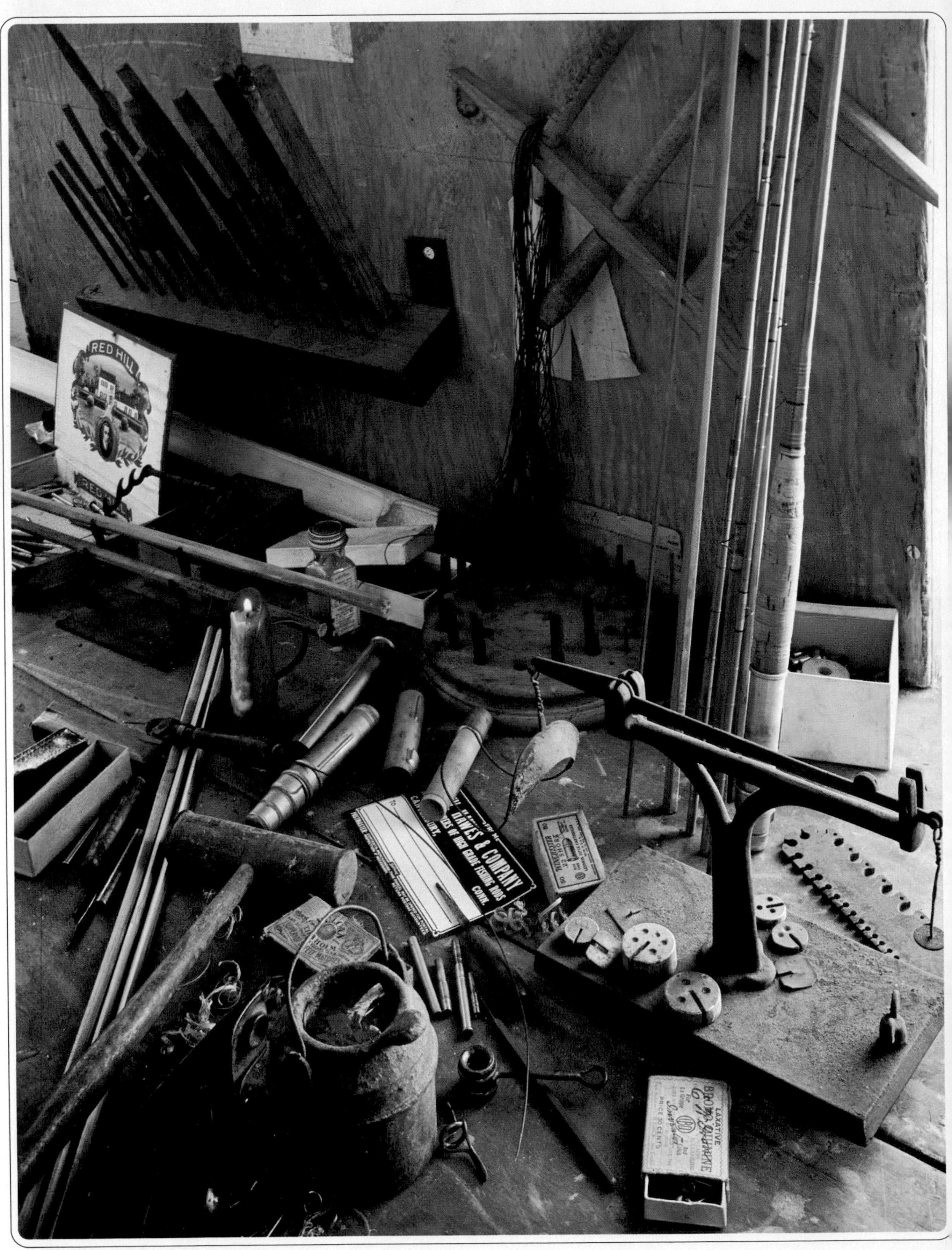
RED HILL
DAWES & COMPANY
OF HIGH GRADE FISHING RODS
CONN.
LAXATIVE
BROMO QUININE
PRICE 30 CENTS

Plate 32

Illinois

Numerous problems, notably big cities, widespread industrialization and awesome suburban sprawl, minimize fly fishing in the Prairie State, home for more than 11 million people. Rugged winters that often cause substantial fish-kills also make it tough for both fish and angler. For those willing to scout around, however, there is fly-fishing to be found, if little of it is for the traditional favorite, trout.

Illinois has no mountains and few hills, which doesn't help the cause of trout fishing, and because many sophisticated anglers live in the state, what little such water exists is usually terribly crowded. Probably the best stream trout-fishing the state offers will be found on the Apple River in the Apple River Canyon State Park near Warren, while stillwater anglers should try Coleta Pond near Coleta.

The Mississippi River constitutes the entire western border of Illinois, and from July through October its shallow sloughs and backwaters are perfect for surface popping largemouth bass. Bass up to 10 pounds can also be taken on the surface of 1,000-acre Little Grassy Lake near Marion, a veritable jungle of sunken trees and stumps. Smallmouth anglers will find good sport on numerous waters including the Kankakee River near Kankakee, the Kishwaukee River near Belvidere, and the Du Page River near Plainfield.

It's worth noting for Chicago residents that, although Illinois has no streams to attract spawning runs, coho and chinook salmon up to 20 pounds and some large brown trout frequent the waters of Lake Michigan just off the Windy City from early March to mid-May.

Wisconsin

While Wisconsin hasn't received the ink other states have—New York, Vermont, Pennsylvania, Michigan and Montana—the Badger State ranks high on a national scale for fly-fishing opportunities. About the same size as Illinois, its neighbor to the south, Wisconsin must contend with only about one-third the population. And Wisconsin can also claim some 500 miles of shoreline on Lakes Superior and Huron, with plentiful streams for spawning steelhead and thousands of miles of spring-fed rivers teeming with brown, brook and rainbow trout. Does Wisconsin have any ponds or lakes? Look at a map of the northeastern corner and wonder how anyone has dry feet.

Of Wisconsin's 1,400 trout streams, the Bois Brule River, a big stream ideal for float trips flowing into Lake Superior near the Minnesota border, is unquestionably the state's most famous, both for migrating steelhead and resident populations of rainbows and brook trout. State forest lines most of its length, this river of contrasts, quiet spring-fed upstream stretches holding mostly brookies, brawling rapids full of rainbows downstream. Steelhead fishing on the Bois Brule is best from late March or early April through May. (The Bois Brule, incidentally, should not be confused with another fine stream, called only the Brule, which is located along the Michigan border near Nelma.)

Two other good steelhead waters less familiar to anglers are the Flag River, where the hot spots center on the town of Fort Wayne, and the Cranberry River downstream of the twin bridges near Herbster. Both streams are smaller than the Bois Brule, making it easier to spot fish.

Those interested only in resident trout have about 8,000 miles of streams to choose from. Two good ones with fly-fishing-only stretches are the upper Wolf River near Langlade County, and the Peshigo River, Forest and Marinette counties. The Prairie River near Gleason gave up the state record for brook trout but is also acclaimed for browns. The Prairie hosts a very heavy Sulphur hatch from mid-May into June. Another fine river, known for big fish and deep, sandy downstream stretches, is the Mecan near Wautoma. Nor will you go wrong with the North Branch of the Popple near the town of Popple River, in May and June.

Other outstanding streams, all of which boast excellent Hendrickson hatches, include the Tomorrow River near Wapaca, the Willow River near Red Granite, and the Pine River near Poy Sippee. The Pine has a particularly challenging meadow stretch below the town of Wild Roser with crystal water and camouflage for the angler in short supply. Besides streams, hundreds of ponds and lakes hold trout, but for effective fly-fishing it's best to hit them in the spring and fall when the fish work near the top.

No rundown on Wisconsin fishing could be complete without mentioning the mean and solitary predator that stalks many of the state's large waters, muskellunge. Although it is widely known that even plugcasters often work many hours between strikes, you'll never hear a soul complain that each fish isn't worth the work or waiting. A prosperous tourist industry surrounds Wisconsin musky fishing. For a fly rodder's best hope to hook this trophy, it may take an experienced guide to show the way. Among the most popular spots for musky are the Chippewa and Flambeau flowages, about 1,700 acres each.

Iowa

The state's biggest business, agriculture, has broadcast some good news and some bad news for Iowa anglers. The good news—there are literally thousands of shallow farm ponds packed with largemouth bass, easy to hook on surface poppers. The bad news—accepted agricultural practice has included dredging and channelizing many streams, which turns them into little more than warm-water ditches. Only individual taste, unfortunately, can decide if the trade-off has been worth it.

The Hawkeye State's northeastern sector was blessed with some rich limestone deposits that offer some trout fishing, but most area waters, especially tributaries of the Maquoketa, Wapsipinicon, Iowa and Cedar rivers, prove far more productive for smallmouth bass than trout.

Iowa has some 50 major lakes totaling about 45,000 acres, centering on Dickinson, Emmet and Palo Alto counties, known locally as the "Iowa Greater Lakes Region." The state's largest, Spirit Lake (5,684 acres), hosts excellent numbers of northern pike, small- and largemouth bass. Other top lakes include Okoboki Lake (3,939 acres), the state's deepest at about 130 feet, and Clear Lake (3,643 acres). Clear Lake is known for outstanding northern pike angling. For all the fishing lakes provide, however, none of it touches the hundreds of miles of shoreline bass-bugging potential offered by the Mississippi and Missouri rivers, which make up Iowa's eastern and western borders, respectively. The Mississippi is particularly productive from the northern border with Minnesota south to Dubuque.

Minnesota

It's difficult to write about the North Star State, largest east of the Mississippi River (84,068 square miles), without sounding like a promotional brochure. Streams of interest to fly fishermen? Visitors will find 15,000 miles of them. Lakes? Dare you try to count them. The motto claiming "10,000 Lakes" is actually vastly understated. Minnesota has 14,215 lakes, in fact, totaling about two million acres of water, another million acres if you count the state's share of Lake Superior. Scenery? Gorgeous and varied, with expansive forests of pine, fir and spruce in the north, a rich belt of oak and maple in the central region and flat farmland to the west. Minnesota owns more fresh water than any state in the Union, but for some reason it has remained vastly underrated.

What kind of fish are we talking about? The answer is, if it can survive in a cool to moderate climate, you'll find it in Minnesota. The state abounds in rainbow, brook and brown trout, big steelhead, coho and chinook runs from Lake Superior, lake trout, even kamloops, large- and smallmouth bass, pickerel, northern pike up to 40 pounds, muskellunge, walleye, and of course, plenty of panfish. Fishing potential is staggering. A young man could launch a canoe, paddle and portage a lifetime, and not make it back to where he began, even if he never stopped to make one cast.

The first river to study might be Minnesota's Brule, not to be confused with Michigan's two Brules already mentioned. Like Michigan's Bois Brule, Minnesota's Brule flows into Lake Superior and boasts outstanding steelhead runs that peak in May. Because the river flows through the Magney State Park, there are numerous easy-access points for visiting anglers. Another top steelhead stream offering fly-fishing for 60 miles is the Knife River, about 20 miles north of Duluth. The Knife has an exceptionally long season that begins with the first warm weather as early as March and continues until June. When spawning is completed, the steelhead also take readily as they migrate back downstream.

For those interested only in resident trout, the Straight River near Park Rapids is an excellent bet. The Straight has deep runs and undercut banks and is considered particularly good for night fishing. Minnesota anglers also tout the White River near Elba, an easy stream to wade that holds good browns, Hay Creek upstream of the Walking Trail Bridge, and Crooked Creek near Hinckley. Those who seek brookies and rainbows from stillwater should try Trout Lake near Grand Marais or Gindstone Lake near Pine City.

Smallmouth bass buggers have more than enough water to choose from, notably the St. Croix River on the Wisconsin border and the Mississippi River between Minneapolis and Brainerd. Among top smallmouth lakes are Lake Rainy and Lake Brule near Ely. Baswood Lake nearby is noted for fly-rod popping. Northern pike fishermen should take a whack at Ball Club Lake or Winnibigoshish Lake, both near Bena. The latter is also known for muskies. Other top Minnesota musky waters include the headwaters of the Mississippi River, Cass and Leech lakes, near Walker.

Missouri

From the clear, cool streams of the Ozark highlands to the warm shallow lakes and bayous of the southern delta lowlands, Missouri boasts real quality angling, particularly for those enamored with leisurely float trips. The Show Me State has 20,000 miles of streams ideal for floats of one day to a week, each through scenery that somehow seems unique. While much of the attention of fly fishermen has been paid of late to the state's trout fishing, many know relatively little of the virtually endless miles of beautiful smallmouth water, much of it perfect for surface popping. Among the best are the Gasconade River, the Meramec, the Bourbeuse, the Big River, the Black, the upper St. Francis River, the Eleven Point, the Current, Jack's Fork, the Huzzah, the Courtois, Big Piney, the Elk, the James River and the Niangua.

Of greatest interest to trout fishermen, though, should be that the North Fork of the White River near West Plains or Gainsville fishes as well for browns as its now-famous cousin, the White River of Arkansas. A stream of remarkable clarity often requiring fine tippets to meet the challenge, no angler could ask for a more fulfilling experience than to float it between the Hammond's Camp Access and Blair Bridge, a distance of about eight miles. Another excellent discovery for rainbows and browns is the Meramec River near Scott's Ford. The Meramec has the added attraction to sporting-minded anglers of a 16-inch-minimum size limit.

The famous Current River flows entirely within the Ozark National Scenic Riverways area and holds a good population of browns, particularly in a six-mile stretch from the Montauk State Park to the Cedar Grove Access. Among other Missouri trout streams to check out are Capps Creek near Cedar City, the Niangua River below Bennett Springs, Dry Creek near Johnson Ford, Roubidoux Creek near Pulaski City, and the Eleven Point Creek near Turner's Mills.

Missouri anglers should also look into Lake Taneycomo near Branson, a cold-water reservoir reputed to offer some of the best trophy rainbow trout fishing in the Midwest. In September large rainbows migrate to the Shepherd of the Hills Hatchery where the big lake is wadable.

Arkansas

Whether you call Arkansas the Wonder State or the Land of Opportunity, you should get no argument from fly fishermen, particularly those who have fished the famed White River. Since the river was dammed to form 87-mile-long Bull Shoals Lake in 1951, the water below the impoundment has provided spectacular fly-rodding for trophy brown and rainbow trout. A stretch of about 60 miles feels the effect of bottom-release water that comes out at 52 degrees year-round. There is no closed season, of course. Anglers are attracted from across the nation to try their hand at the White's lunkers. Four-pounders are common. Seventeen-pounders are taken. That's the sort of trout dreams are made of.

The White offers the bonus of being ideal for floats, and there are numerous outfitters and guides along both banks from Bull Shoals Lake downstream. Such a float takes you through magnificent scenery, ledges and lush forests, over some of the clearest water you'll ever see. The river doesn't move fast, but it is extremely wide, a hundred yards in places. Thus, if you are wading and the river begins to rise, get to the nearest shore on the double, no matter which shore you entered the river from. Passing canoeists are more than pleased to give a stranded angler a lift to the opposite bank. The White, however, is not the state's only fine trout fishery. Other good bets are the North Fork River at McClellan's Landing, the Little Missouri River near Murphysboro, which receives only light fishing pressure, and the Little Red River near Heber Springs.

For some of the country's finest smallmouth bass angling, the Buffalo River, which eventually flows into the colder waters of the White, combines scenic beauty and four- to six-pound deep-bellied, fighting "brownies" (as the Ozarkers call them) to offer what many aficionados think is the finest fly-rod angling in the Midwest. A great combination, especially in hot weather, is a float down the Buffalo to its confluence with the air-conditioned White River, switching to big trout upstream.

Visiting anglers shouldn't forget that Arkansas also boasts incredible lake fishing for largemouth bass. Bull Shoals Lake holds "hawgs" up to 15 pounds, while the Norfolk Reservoir near Mountain Home has a nice shoreline for surface popping. Another spot to keep in mind is the 40,000-acre Lake Ouachita near Hot Springs.

Fly-casting to black bass on a Texas lake. Photo by Russell Tinsley.

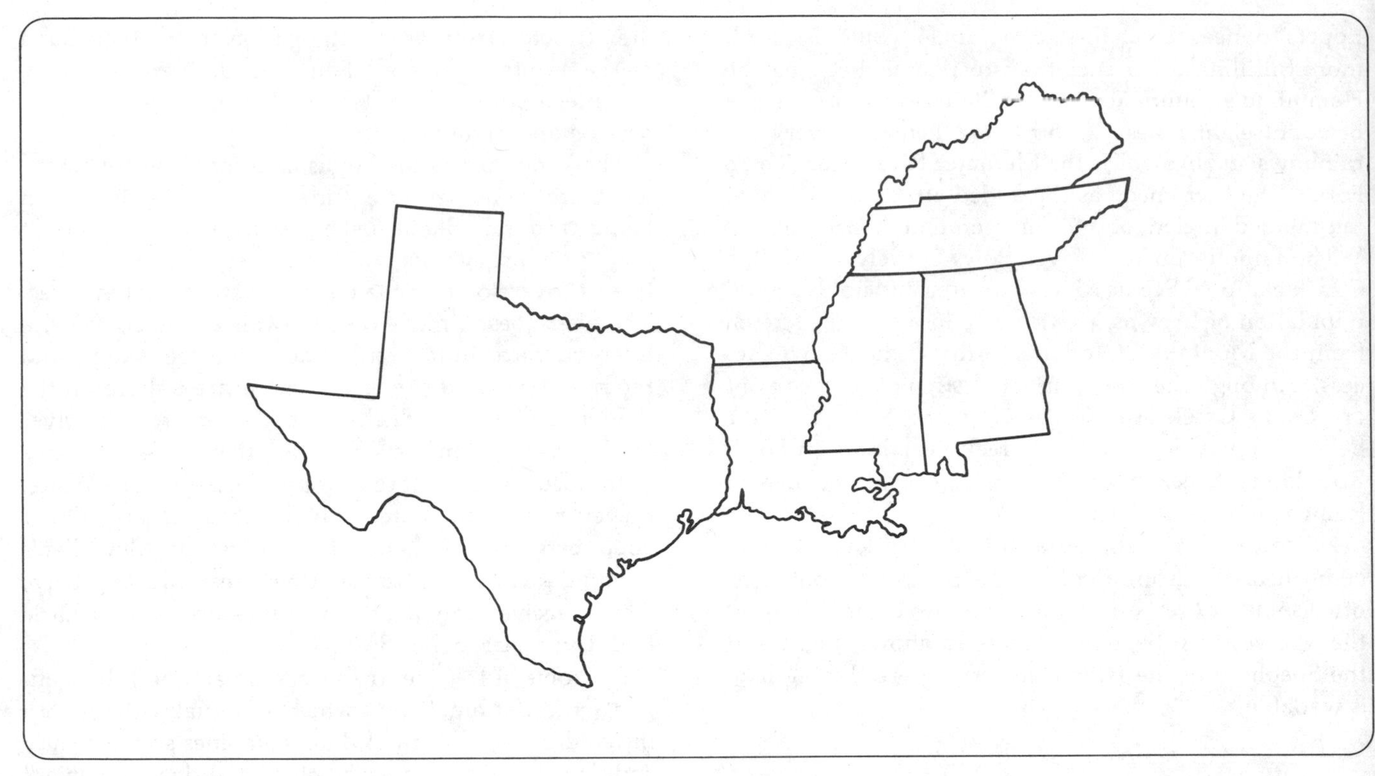

The Deep South and Gulf States

THIS REGION — Kentucky, Tennessee, Alabama, Mississippi, Louisiana and Texas — offers an immense and diverse angling bonanza. (Texans will tell you, even if you never ask, that the Lone Star State is about as big as the entire Northeast.) There are relatively few trout, true, compared to cooler climes, but what adventurous fly rodders will find is an abundance of gorgeous and varied scenery in a climate ideal both for angling and for growing lunker warmwater fish. With deference to the region's thousands of miles of quality flowing water, and leaving for coverage elsewhere the outstanding saltwater fly-fishing from Gulf Port, Alabama, to Brownsville, Texas, it should be said flat out that the Deep South and Gulf states offer the finest warmwater fly-fishing of any section of the U.S.

The best largemouth bass angling in America is located here, much of it on lakes with hundreds of miles of weedy and brush-cluttered shallows. Just the impoundments, among the most ambitious water-taming projects in the world, would take volumes to cover. Excellent smallmouth fisheries in both lakes and streams abound, as do the opportunities to take on the spotted bass. Even runs of anadromous striped bass to 60 pounds can be found. All this on big and little waters, the mighty Mississippi, the TVA lakes, and the seemingly endless bayou country that affords the authentic romantic an insight into what much of the earth must have looked like millions of years ago. Here on a state by state basis is some of what you can expect to find.

Kentucky

ALTHOUGH DUBBED THE BLUEGRASS STATE for its rolling central pasturelands, it is the lesser-known Cumberland Mountains to the east and the swampy lowlands to the west that are really most significant to Kentucky fishermen. The state boasts some 13,000 miles of flowing water, substantial amounts of it impounded to form about a dozen large lakes. Bottom release of cold tailwater from impoundment dams in several cases now provides excellent rainbow trout fishing where there was little or none before. Cold water below 100-mile-long Cumberland Lake on the Cumberland River, for instance, offers 28 miles of excellent fly-fishing along the wooded shores downstream to Burkesville. Other excellent tailwater trout fisheries include the Nolin River in the Mamouth Cave National Park and the Buckhorn River near Hazard.

Largemouth and smallmouth bass fishing, however, certainly rate the state's top challenge for fly rodders. Kentucky Lake, for example, formed by a TVA dam across the Tennessee River at Gilbertsville, has almost 2,500 miles of shorelines for excellent surface popping. At about 134,000 acres, it is one of the largest impoundments in the world. Anglers who tire of the trout fishing below should try Cumberland Lake (50,000 acres), which spreads to 1,250 miles of shoreline alive with large- and smallmouths, plus great numbers of spotted bass. Six- to eight-pound largemouths are common in Dewey Lake east of Prestonburg, while a top spot for smallmouth fly rodders is Buckhorn Reservoir.

Floating for days without seeing another human being highlights smallmouth bass fishing on the Cumberland River's upper reaches, while Elkhorn Creek east of Lexington has long been a favorite with fly fishermen who want to wade. Those seeking an unusual combination of smallmouth bass and limestone water might take a shot at Slate Creek on the fringes of the famed bluegrass country. Although there are dozens of smaller rivers and streams to choose from, visiting anglers shouldn't pass up bass bugging in the backwaters along the Ohio River, which makes up the state's northwestern boundary.

Tennessee

It's always tempting when writing of Tennessee fishing in general to lead with "The Great Lakes of the South," those twenty-two monsters impounded during the heyday of the Tennessee Valley Authority. When the subject is fly-fishing, however, the Volunteer State's fine brown and rainbow trout fishing take top billing. In some instances, of course, when you get into one, you also cover the other. Many TVA impoundments are, in fact, fine trout fisheries themselves, while the coldwater releases from their dams provide outstanding trout fishing downstream.

Wautauga Lake, for example, on the Holston River near the Virginia border, holds large rainbows throughout a season lengthened by the state's moderate climate. Then in the fall, rainbows migrate up Doe Creek, a tributary, where 10-pounders are taken regularly. The tailwater below Dale Hollow Reservoir in the north central region once turned up a 26-pound brown, and while fish like that can't be called common, this water does offer substantial numbers of both browns and rainbows that respond readily to the flies of visiting anglers. Other notable tailwater trout fisheries are located below Wilbur Lake, Daniel Boone Lake, Fort Patrick Henry Lake, all on the Holston River, and below Norris Lake on the Clinch River.

Rainbows and browns up to five pounds are plentiful in undammed streams such as the Little Tennessee and Hiawassee Rivers, both near the North Carolina border, where anglers should take advantage of early hatches and extremely long seasons, often beginning as early as February. The Great Smoky Mountains National Park and Tellico Wildlife Management areas boast fine streams such as the Little River and Abrams Creek in the park and the Tellico River and Citico Creek in the management area.

A state of forested beauty, Tennessee offers splendid largemouth, smallmouth and spotted bass fishing on hundreds of thousands of acres of water. Although largemouths probably outnumber smallmouths, the state's rivers are famous for big bronzebacks, often in the seven- to nine-pound class. Among select streams to bug them up are the Elk River, the Upper Duck River, the Collins River and the Buffalo River. The Powell and Clinch rivers above Norris Lake are also superb smallmouth fisheries. With all these big waters around, fly rodders should not forget that Tennessee also boasts some 55,000 farm ponds that are particularly productive from March through November.

Mississippi

Although the vast majority of Magnolia State anglers swear by casting rods or bait fishing, the possibilities for fly rod bass and crappie-popping are almost endless in Mississippi. The willows and cypress-lined shorelines of Granada, Sardis, Enid and Arkabutta reservoirs in the Delta Lakes region, for instance, couldn't be better suited to the technique. The same is true of the Strong River and Limestone Creek in the state's central region.

Although more than two-million people live in Mississippi, there remain vast, wild areas of sandy hills and pine forest. Most awesome, however, are the bayous of the south, which not only provide beautiful, if somewhat eerie, scenery, but also a climate ideal for year-round angling. Nowhere is better than Yucatan Lake, a wonder for bass, or such streams as the Chickasawhay River, Red Creek or the Leaf River, all in the southeastern sector.

Coverage of this state must include mention of the mighty river that forms the eastern boundary, the Mississippi. It would be impossible, however, to even touch on the thousands of backwaters and eddies, innumerable ponds and lakes that lie along the river's course. Suffice it to say that those in the know or those who know the right person could spend a lifetime on the terrific largemouth and crappie fly-rodding of this water.

Alabama

Can you believe that through the Heart of Dixie flows one of the great river systems in the world, 1,700 miles classified as navigable, thirty impoundments totaling some 430,000 acres, superb fly-fishing for trophy smallmouth bass, plentiful runs of striped bass topping 60 pounds, and even rainbow trout up to 10 pounds? Yes, Alabama has it all, 50 rivers, 250 streams, 21,000 lakes and ponds, plus a climate just about ideal for year-round angling.

One of the best spots is the Black Warrior River, which drains the north-central zone from the Tennessee

River to Demopoles. Visiting anglers can try excellent bass fishing on the river, but of particular interest to fly rodders will be Lewis Smith Lake, a 21,000-acre impoundment on the Sipsey River, a Black Warrior tributary that is chock full of rainbows. Trout have also been introduced into Lewis and Inland lakes in the northeastern sector of the state.

The shallowness of much Alabama water, coupled with weedy or brush-cluttered bottoms, means ideal fly-rod bass fishing. Two impoundments on the Tennessee River, which flows about 200 miles through the state's northern region, are particularly noted for smallmouth — Wilson and Pickwick lakes. Numerous camps cater to anglers in search of six- to eight-pound bronzebacks. Other fertile impoundments in the chain include Guntersville and Wheeler Lakes.

The Tallapoosa River, notably through a narrows near Tallassee, boasts runs of striped bass reaching 60 pounds. Although not as well known, stripers move between three impoundments on the river, Lakes Martin, Yates and Thurlow, during its 125-mile course southwest from the Georgia line. The lakes also offer fine largemouth bass fishing. Striper runs should also lure you to the Chattahoochee River up to the Columbus Dam near Phenix City. The best time to hit them is June.

For those pleased by meandering through swampy waters while casting for largemouths, the Mobile River Delta, made up of the Mobile and Tensow rivers in the southwestern region, is perfect. Here, visiting anglers couple leisurely fishing with photographing cypress forests heavy with hoary Spanish moss.

Louisiana

ALTHOUGH FLY-RODDING in the Pelican State has never attained national prominence, nowhere in the Deep South are local advocates more enthusiastic. Well they should be, because nowhere is a fly rod better suited to warmwater fishing than on Louisiana's seemingly infinite waters. Salt water aside, Louisiana, the land of old world hospitality, is truly a visiting angler's paradise.

Boasting year-round angling potential, Louisiana has four-million acres of water, including some of the world's finest largemouth bass fishing amid thousands of backwater ponds on the flood plains of the Mississippi, Red and Black and Atchafalaya rivers. Two of the best are the Spring Bayou Backwater and Pearl River Backwater, both ideal for fly-rod popping. Nor should bass fishermen pass up numerous fine lakes such as Toledo Reservoir and Caddo Lake, both at the Texas border, Cross Lake near Shreveport, Lake Bistineau near Ringgold, and Lake Verret, between Grand Lake and Napoleonville. Wherever you fish, notably around settlements with exotic French names, don't plan to come away losing any weight. Louisiana also offers some of the most sumptuous table fare in America.

While salt water is not covered in this chapter, it should be noted that as anglers move inland, fresh- and salt water species often mingle. Traveling the bayous, for instance, it is common to hook largemouths and sea trout in the same water on the same flies. For those who tire of the almost tropical look of the coastal and bayou landscape, some of the small, swift inland rivers and streams, full of both largemouth and spotted bass, will actually remind you of northern trout streams. Streamers and poppers fish exceptionally well on them throughout the year.

Texas

THOSE WHO THINK of the Lone Star State as dry, crammed with rattlesnakes, herds of noisy cattle and more oil derricks than trees should cruise the shoreline of Lake Caddo in the Cypress River Basin as the sun comes up some morning. The 40,000-acre lake will be slick as glass, its surface broken only by rolling bass and swirling alligators. (That's right, alligators.) Weathered cypress butts stand throughout the shallows, and the water at their roots just smells of largemouth bass. The banks look like verdant jungle, and all around the boat are acres of lily pads. Any bass-bugger might think he'd died and gone to heaven.

In fact, it's true that much of Texas is arid and sparsely settled. Texas is so big, however (267,000 square miles), that it can well afford to give a lot of land away to tumbleweed and cactus. If the state's angling suffers a particular lack, it is that there are so many big ranches that much good water is private. All you can do is ask and hope Texans are as neighborly as advertised.

This state, of course, does nothing in a small way. Take, for example, Toledo Bend Reservoir, one of the most popular largemouth lakes in the country. It has more than 181,000 acres to explore. Although smaller by far, Lake Murvaul (3,800 acres) in Panola County, can claim so many eight-pound "hawgs," catching one produces little more than yawns. Another fine bass fishery is Lake O'Pines, above Lake Caddo along Cypress Creek, while in the Sulphur River Basin, Lake Texarkana (20,300 acres), full of stumps and downed trees, is absolutely ideal for fly-rod popping.

Nor should anglers forget that the state is virtually rimmed by rivers, the Red to the north, Sabine on the east, and the Rio Grande, which forms the U.S. border with Mexico. All hold excellent populations of bass and panfish. In the Trinity River below Fort Worth, white bass (locally called "sandies") are so plentiful that daily catches of a hundred are common. The same is true of the Texoma Reservoir on the Oklahoma border, where white bass fishing is best in February and March.

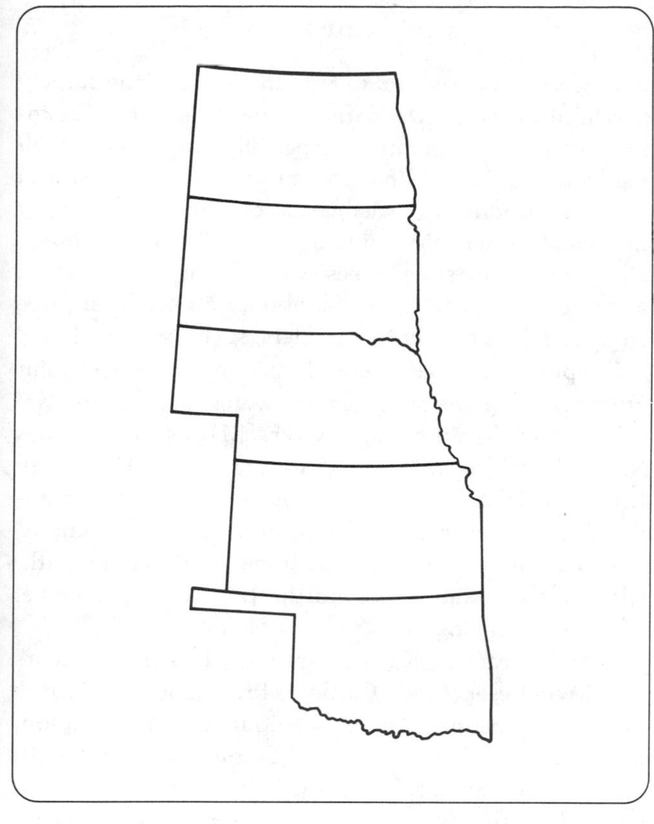

The Great Plains

To say the country's flatlands — the states of North and South Dakota, Nebraska, Kansas and Oklahoma — are a fly rodder's Utopia would be untrue, but it would be untrue also to maintain the region has nothing to offer the fly fisherman.

Summers usually tend to be very hot, and winters are often severe in this region. Violent and sudden storms are common, and winds are often high. All this brings periods of very high or low water, difficult casting conditions at times for fly rodders and perhaps worst of all, severe fish-kills. To effectively handle the region, up-to-the-minute reports from reliable sources are a must.

North Dakota

If it's true some states are happily afflicted with "trout fever," a similar malady certainly affects Sioux State anglers where northern pike are concerned. North Dakota pays the same kind of attention to pike propagation and management that states such as Pennsylvania, Michigan and Montana reserve for their trout. The "Pike Capital of the United States" is what North Dakota now calls itself with pride and substantial evidence to back it up.

Cornerstone of North Dakota's fishing is the 200-mile-long Garrison Reservoir, an impoundment on the Missouri River, which hosts incredible populations of pike along its more than 1,500 miles of shorelines. Much of the water is shallow enough for those with the know-how to lure this big predator to the right streamer. Because no one has "written the book" on fly-rod pike fishing yet, it's still a matter of search and experimentation, but those who have mastered the art claim the rewards are terrific. Anglers not interested in pike will find the huge lake holds good numbers of rainbow trout to five pounds, especially the reaches near Riverdale. In all, twenty-six species of fish, including largemouth bass, have found a home in the lake's 300,000 acres of water.

Garrison Reservoir, because it's so big, represents a substantial portion of North Dakota's best fishing, especially when you consider its numerous feeder streams that provide perfect habitat for pike and other species. The Little Missouri River, for instance, which flows through the Theodore Roosevelt National Memorial Park in the Badlands, is a favorite for floaters, as well as sightseers. Another hot spot is Tobacco Garden Creek above Waterford City. An exciting tailwater fishery for pike on the Missouri between Garrison and the head of Lake Oahe is also worth a try. Other top pike and bass fisheries include Lake Ashtabula (5,400 acres) on the Sheyenne River in the east, Jamestown Reservoir (1,200 acres) on the Janus River near Jamestown, and Lake Darling (14,000 acres) on the Souris River northwest of Minot.

South Dakota

Historians and novelists have already immortalized the southwest region of the Coyote State, known as the Black Hills. Names like Spearfish, Bear Butte, Buffalo Gap, Blue Bell and Hell Canyon, not to mention General Custer, must reawaken images of Indian war parties on pinto ponies, files of horse soldiers and grizzled adventurers seeking to survive in a rugged, lawless land.

While the landscape varies from plains in the east, the Missouri River lowlands in the central sector and finally those at once famous and infamous Badlands of buttes and fossil beds awaiting aspiring paleontologists, it's the Black Hills that hold the greatest fascination to fly rodders. A good jumping-off place for rainbow trout is Spearfish Canyon south of Cheyenne Crossing. Rainbows are also plentiful in Rapid Creek near Rockford, a good brook trout fishery upstream. Other exciting Black Hills trout waters include Redwater Creek, Box Creek, Elder Creek, Beaver Creek, Elk Creek and Little Spearfish Creek.

Many South Dakota lakes also hold rainbows and browns including Pactola Reservoir near Rapid City, noted for trout up to 20 pounds, Sheridan Lake near Hill City, a fine bass lake as well, and Sylvan and Center lakes, both located amid the inspiring scenery of the Custer State Park. Rapid Creek, incidentally, both above and below Pactola Reservoir, offers outstanding stream trout fishing. Nor when touring South Dakota lakes should fly fishermen neglect northern pike opportunities in Fort Randall Reservoir (80,000 acres) between Pickstown and Chamberlain, or monstrous Lake Oahe, an impoundment of 376,000 acres on the Missouri River, from Pierre to the North Dakota border.

Nebraska

PERHAPS SO MANY PEOPLE are turned on by the "oceans of wheat" that they overlook the fact that Nebraska is also one of the most underexploited states for fly-rodding in the nation. Of the Cornhusker State's 77,000-square-mile area, much is sown in grain, for sure, but 3,300 lakes, 11,000 miles of rivers and streams, including about 30 cool, clear trout streams in the western panhandle region alone, isn't bad anywhere, particularly in a state more renowned for rye than rainbows.

The Sand Hills region produces the most dependable all-round trout fishing on tributaries of the Niobrara and Loup rivers, specifically Long Pine Creek, part of the Niobrara system, which is superb. Other top streams are Plum Creek near Ainsworth, Coon Creek near Bassett, and Schlagel Creek on the fringes of the Valentine Refuge. The headwaters of the Snake River in Cherry County also offer respectable trout fishing. Farther north in the Pine Ridge area, a long list of challenging small streams includes Monroe Creek, Sowbelly Creek, Hat Creek, Soldier Creek, the White River, Dead Horse Creek, Big and Little Bordeaux Creeks, Beaver Creek and White Clay Creek.

The North Platte River watershed near Scott's Bluff promises outstanding brown trout fishing on small streams, notably Lawrence Fork, Greenwood, Red Willow, Wild Horse, Strucken Hole, Nine Mile, Sheep, Spotted Tail and Winter creeks. In the same region, Lake McConoughy (35,000 acres) heads a list of fisheries that provide excellent angling for several species, including trout and bass. McConoughy hosts both browns and rainbows, the latter also caught by fly rodders when they ascend the North Platte River above the lake each spring. Otter Creek, which enters McConoughy on the northwest shore, boasts a late-winter rainbow run but holds browns year-round.

Other attractive Nebraska lakes include Lewis and Clark Lake near Yankton, and Harlan County Reservoir on the Kansas border near Alma, a state record holder for brown and brook trout, smallmouth and white bass. While these lakes are open to public fishing, visiting anglers should note that many smaller Nebraska waters are private and require permission to be fished.

Kansas

BETTER KNOWN FOR THE GUN than the rod, the largely agricultural Sunflower State nevertheless has definite fly-angling potential, especially for largemouth bass and panfish. Although Kansas has no big natural lakes, unproductive streams have been improved by man-made reservoirs running to 2,500 acres. Thirty-eight so-called state lakes were designated, which although small (the largest is about 350 acres) are free from activities that bother anglers, such as waterskiing.

Popping for largemouths is promising in the Flint Hills region of the southeast on waters such as the Neosko River, Cottonwood River, Marais des Lygnes River, Verdigris River, Fall River, Elk River, Caney River and Walnut River. The state has also taken advantage of a bad situation in the area by flooding countless strip-mine pits, stocking them with largemouth, spotted and white bass, northern pike and crappie, while encouraging construction of farm ponds.

Other attractive Kansas largemouth angling occurs on Kirwin Reservoir on the north branch Solomon River below Phillipsburg where five-pounders are common, and Webster Reservoir on the Solomon River's south branch near Stockton. State lakes best for bass include Rooks County State Lake near Stockton, Leavenworth County State Lake near Topeka and Kansas City, Cowley County State Lake near Arkansas City, and Woodson County State Lake near Yates Center.

Oklahoma

FLY FISHERMEN HAVE READ substantial publicity recently on establishment of marginal trout fishing on a few waters in the Sooner State. Although this is certainly worthy of note, an unfortunate side effect has proved to be that Oklahoma's fantastic fly-rodding potential for bass is taking a back seat. There are fourteen federally owned lakes in Oklahoma, totaling some 350,000 acres, virtually all of them waters excellent for bass fishing. City lakes add 200,000 acres, as do farm ponds. Oklahoma has numerous rivers and about 700 flood-control lakes. Considering the high-quality boat-launching and camping facilities available, coupled with a climate attuned to year-round angling, the state is looking increasingly better to anglers.

Not only is Oklahoma a state of big water, but it's one of big bass, with lunkers in the eight- to ten-pound class. From mid-March through June, when the fish come off shallow spawning beds, is the ideal time for fly-rod poppers. Find lunker largemouths along shorelines of such waters as Eufaula Reservoir (102,000 acres) from Dow north to Hitchita, Lake Texoma (95,000 acres), an impoundment on the Red River along the Texas border, and an enormous string of big lakes in the northeast including Lake o' the Cherokees, Lake

Hudson, Lake Spavinaw and Fort Gibson Reservoir. In the northwest, Canton Reservoir (7,700 acres) is a good bet.

For those interested in limited trout fishing, rainbows have been stocked in several lakes and streams, mostly on a put and take basis, notably Carl Etling Lake in the Black Mesa country near the Colorado state line. A tailwater trout fishery exists on the Tenkiller River, a tributary of the Illinois River, below Tenkiller Reservoir, while a resident population of browns has established itself in the Blue River in southeastern Oklahoma.

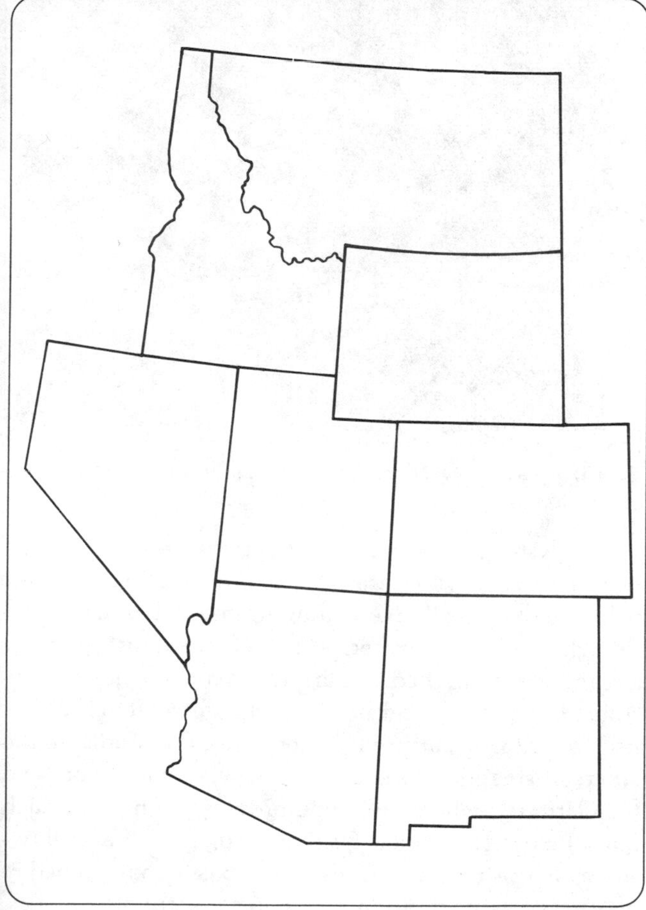

The Rocky Mountains

NO SUPERLATIVE SERVES ADEQUATELY to describe the Rockies—they must be seen. A generation ago, few fly rodders from outside the region got the chance. To fish Western rivers was a dream, sustained by reading outdoor-magazine stories and panting over the pretty pictures. Along the Rocky Mountain rivers in those days a single parked car suggested "overcrowding," and any Western angler worth his salt would simply shake his fist and move along to other "less congested" spots.

There are more highly touted rivers and streams in the Rocky Mountain states today than anywhere in America. As most fly rodders are aware of the Beaverkill, the Ausable and Au Sable, the Letort and the Battenkill, even when they haven't fished them, who also hasn't heard of the Madison, Yellowstone, the Green, the Firehole or Silver Creek to name a few? While "name" streams get more ink, dozens of others, from small meadow creeks snaking through oxbows to big brawling rivers, fish altogether as well and with far less pressure.

Montana

THEY CALLED IT THE TREASURE STATE, more for its gold, silver and copper deposits than for the arm-long cutthroats the early settlers found, but long after most mother lodes went bust, Montana remained as rich as ever in a resource for which fly rodders might forego such worldly riches—trout. After all, who'd want to bother striking it rich unless it was to subsidize Montana fishing trips? Of foremost interest to anglers is the western third of the state, a 50,000-square-mile area that even includes a little nugget of Yellowstone National Park, a true treasure straddling the Continental Divide on the Wyoming border.

Montana abounds in public angling. Much water is also in the hands of private ranches and clubs and few exceptions are allowed to the "Posted" signs. Asking never hurts, however, but private interests cannot bar floating through.

Among the best public fisheries are the upper Clarks Fork in the Deer Lodge district, which offers challenging fishing for big browns that fancy slowly moving water and undercut banks, and farther down, the lower Clarks Fork of the Missoula Valley, where the flow is filled out with water from the Blackfoot and Bitterroot rivers and boasts rainbows to eight pounds. The Beaverhead River below Clark Canyon Dam is often overlooked by visiting fishermen, although sculpin imitations take big trout there. Armstrong and Nelson spring creeks, both near Livingston—an excellent jumping-off place, by the way, to tackle the Yellowstone—are two challenging streams for rainbows and browns sipping tiny insects. Both are in private hands but may be fished for a reasonable daily fee. The Missouri River from Hotter Dam to Great Falls fishes well throughout the season but is particularly active beginning in September, when its massive browns forsake the banks and head for center current. Nor should anglers pass up the marvelous Big Hole River from Divide to Melrose, Big Spring Creek near Lewiston, the Kootenai River near Libby, or the Flathead River and Flathead Lake, both near Kalispell.

In general, Montana has short seasons compared to those in less rugged climates. Angling is "iffy" before snow runoff in late spring, as is fall fishing. Weather patterns are the thing. The most dependable period for dramatic mayfly, caddis and stonefly hatches is summer.

Idaho

MORE THAN 12 MILLION TROUT are taken each season in the Gem State, about 17 for every man, woman and child living in this beautiful state. Idaho abounds in productive waters for rainbows, cutthroats, browns, brookies, and Dolly Vardens, each of significant interest to visiting fly rodders. Although it lies far inland from the Pacific, Idaho also hosts substantial runs of strong chinook salmon and steelhead trout. All this amid gorgeous scenery, dramatic panoramas of the Bitterroots on the Montana border, and the Grand Tetons farther south. Influenced by the climate of Washington and Oregon to the west, Idaho is the greenest of Rocky Mountain states.

Perhaps the state's best-known stream is Silver Creek of Lemhi County, in recent years reputed "the Letort of the Rockies." A broad, challenging spring creek with great moss growths, deep channels and banks of overhanging grass, Silver Creek is a must for all fly rodders who seek big trout on small flies and fine leaders. Also famous since the opening of Railroad Ranch to public fishing is the Henrys Fork of the Snake, which meanders below the Island Park Reservoir, itself an exceptional opportunity for rainbow and cutthroat trout fishing. Other spring creeks to try include Riley Creek, the Malad River and Niagra Springs, all in the Twin Falls area, and Thousand Springs near Hagerman. Riley Creek, incidentally, is referred to as "a miniature Silver Creek."

Seasons on spring creeks are considered to span mid-May through October. The summer months, July and August, attract most anglers to Idaho's freestone waters, lakes and reservoirs. The Salmon River, which boasts runs of steelhead and chinooks below Riggins, fishes well for rainbow trout to 10 pounds from Clayton to its headwaters, as does the Snake River in the Twin Falls-Boise area. Fine Snake River tributaries include Box Canyon Creek and Crystal Springs. In the Sun Valley area, the Big Wood River is an outstanding freestoner of varying fast and slow stretches.

Wyoming

IN THE EQUALITY STATE'S northwest corner is located most of Yellowstone National Park, some two-million acres where Lee Wulff, who has influenced so many fly fishermen, has said, "I saw the fishing of the future . . . superb, available to everyone, and . . . free." Park management, noted Lee, has fulfilled his wistful dream that "a good gamefish is too valuable to be caught only once." Yet, with all it offers, Yellowstone is only one small sector of this vast state (98,000 square miles), so rich in angling a writer might take the plunge and declare it's *the best of the best.*

Armstrong's Spring Creek in Montana. Photo by Dave Engerbretson.

Yellowstone Park is a national treasure, where some of America's finest cutthroat, rainbow and brown trout fishing is free to all. No fishing license is required. Although alive with water, some of the most popular streams easily reached by park roads include the Yellowstone, both above and below vast Yellowstone Lake—itself a fantastic cutthroat fishery, and the Madison, the ethereal, steaming Firehole, the Lewis and Lemar, and the Gardiner, where awesome browns are hooked each fall. Below the famed Fishing Bridge on the Yellowstone, a special-regulations area exists that someday may serve as inspiration for the entire country.

Another mecca for visiting fly rodders is Jackson Hole, a railhead which by cooperation and careful planning has become at once a center for outdoor recreation and Western culture. The nearby Snake River is a favorite for float trips, although its lower reaches don't clear of snow runoff until as late as August. Jackson also boasts excellent guides to introduce visitors to innumerable streams like the upper Gros Ventre and Hoback rivers. The most wonderful "armchair" float in the state, however, must be that below Alcova Dam on the North Platte River, which turns up fine rainbows all season and awesome browns in the fall. Nor should fly rodders forget the Wind River, which passes through the Wind River Indian Reservation west of Riverton, reopened to fee fishing in 1976.

If a major problem exists for anglers in Wyoming, it is the amount of water closed to the public by ranchers "tired," as they say, "of being pushed around by slobs who don't know enough to close a gate or pick up paper." A classic example is the Green River near Pinedale, one of the finest rainbow and brown trout fisheries in the state. Although the Wyoming Bureau of Land Management has acquired some fishing accesses, the bulk of water can be fished only by floating.

Wyoming, like Montana, has short seasons, relative to warmer regions. In a single day at these high altitudes an angler can be fried, frozen and almost blown off the face of the earth.

Nevada

If Lady Luck deserts you at the tables, don't "take to the bridge." Go fishing. Why, even when there's still some money left, but you want to contemplate your *system*, a respite with a rod may prove just the thing.

A map illustrates well enough that of Nevada's 110,000 square miles, most angling centers in a region of the High Sierra near the California border—except, of course, for giant Lake Mead near Las Vegas and the Colorado River below Hoover Dam where fly-fishing for rainbows is challenging in swift currents through Black Canyon. Lake Mead, incidentally, is full of largemouth bass best taken on poppers in the spring when they move into shallows to spawn.

Lake Tahoe, which Nevada touches for about 100 miles, hosts good numbers of hefty cutthroats, browns and rainbows in cool, clear water. Better for the fly rodder, however, is the Truckee River, Lake Tahoe's natural outlet, which supports many miles of outstanding trout fishing all the way, in fact, to the heart of Reno. And Pyramid Lake north of Reno once claimed the world-record cutthroat, a 41-pounder taken in 1941.

Utah

Utah angling is a paradox—so many resources dammed and dredged to death, yet a dependable producer of among the biggest brown trout taken in America each season. It's no wonder they call this the Beehive State. But imagine what it might be like if only it were left alone.

Nevertheless, Utah, the setting for some of the great wonders of nature—Monument Valley, Zion Canyon, Cathedral Valley, Bryce Canyon and, of course, the Great Salt Lake—will show visiting anglers some mighty fish, not the least of which are trophy browns from some 30 miles of tailwater below Flaming Gorge Dam on the Green River.

To beat the bulldozers, the Uinta Mountains, ranging to 13,000 feet, are a good bet. Guides headquarter in Minor Lake and are a necessity, since pack horse is the only way to reach high-country lakes brimming with cutthroats, brookies, arctic grayling and even golden trout. Nor should fly rodders pass up Uinta Mountain streams, including Henrys Fork and Rock Creek on the north slope and the Uinta River and Lake Fork on the south slope.

Colorado

The Centennial State ranks high nationally among fly rodders. The western half of the state, site of more high mountain peaks than anywhere in the Rockies, is of primary importance to fly fishermen, although excellent warmwater angling can be found in the eastern prairie country. Because it's a state of narrow valleys, Colorado streams tend to be narrower and more turbulent than elsewhere in the region, but high mountain meadows also host scores of small streams, and the high country abounds in small, crystal-clear lakes, too.

The Frying Pan and Roaring Fork rivers in the Aspen area below Basalt are among the most famous Colorado streams for brown and rainbow trout. Because each year Aspen becomes a busier tourist attraction, pressure, particularly on weekends during the summer months, can be heavy. About 70 miles of quality fly-rodding, including some wonderful meadow stretches, can be found below the Granby Dam on the Colorado River. The Brown's Canyon area is notably beautiful and productive. Two other exquisite Colorado streams include the Blue River between the Dillon Dam and the Colorado River at Kremmling, and the Eagle River near Dotsoro, perhaps the most underrated of the state's trout fisheries.

In the Colorado Springs-Denver area, the Arkansas River from Leadville to the Pueblo Reservoir holds browns to 15 pounds. It fishes well between February and April, as well as during the traditional prime-time summer months. The South Platte River from South Park to Waterton is another outstanding brown trout stream with a long season. Nor should anglers pass up such smaller waters as Tarryhall Creek, Chalk Creek, Beaver Creek and Lost Creek.

Excellent fly-rod trout fishing is available on numerous Colorado reservoirs, including the Antero Reservoir near Hartsel, Eleven-Mile Reservoir near Lake George, Blue Mesa Reservoir near Gunnison, and Taylor Reservoir west of Ten Camp.

Arizona

Wonders, both natural and man-made, attract multitudes of tourists to Arizona each year—the Grand Canyon, the Painted Desert, the Petrified Forest and, of course, Boulder Dam, to name just a few. Another wonder is why so very few are even aware of the fly-fishing potential in the nation's sixth largest state. Perhaps because so much of Arizona is desert, attractive to those seeking a dry climate for one reason or another. All but overlooked are about 1,000 miles of trout water flowing through the Grand Canyon State, some of it beneath the cathedrallike walls of that inspiring example of nature's artistry.

The Colorado River loops into Arizona from the tail of Lake Powell, and just below Glen Canyon Dam begins miles of rainbow trout water, amid the splendor of the Grand Canyon National Park. Farther down-river on the Nevada border, the Colorado is impounded again by Hoover Dam to produce massive Lake Mead, a fine fishery for both trout and bass. Below Hoover Dam, heading south toward Lake Mohave, there is more great trout fishing, and even in the tailwaters of Mohave's Davis Dam, you remain in trout country.

New Mexico

MEETING A FELLOW FLY RODDER from the Land of Enchantment who wears an unearthly smirk shouldn't make you want to search his garden for locoweed or peyote. He just knows something you probably don't. One of fly-fishing's best-kept secrets must be that New Mexico, location for nine-million acres of national forest, plus five-million more in the public domain, ranks with some of the best areas in America for rainbows, browns, brookies and cutthroat trout (not to mention smallmouth or largemouth bass).

Rainbows and browns to 15 pounds inhabit an 80-mile stretch of powerful river on the Rio Grande beginning at the Colorado border. These fish are known for an inordinate fighting capacity, assisted undoubtedly by the wild rushes of flows through fabulous gorges. The upper 50 miles are meat for anglers who love to hike, because road access is available only at a few spots where bridges happen to cross the river. Farther east, the San Juan River below the Navajo Dam commonly turns up rainbows between 4 and 12 pounds, particularly to big streamers.

One of New Mexico's most spectacular areas is the Sangre de Cristo mountain range where peaks tower to 17,000 feet, a region boasting both fine stream fishing and the Latir Lakes. Latir Creek, among others, is great for trout, as is the Red River, a wild trout fishery about 20 miles south. Among other lovely New Mexico streams are the Rio Pueblo and the Santa Barbara River in the Carson National Forest. Hondo Creek near Taos offers fine rainbows, while the Chama River from El Vado Lake upstream is a dandy, with the added attraction of the Brazos River, its main tributary, an all-wild trout fishery. The upper Pecos River is another hot spot, along with the nearby Mora Fork.

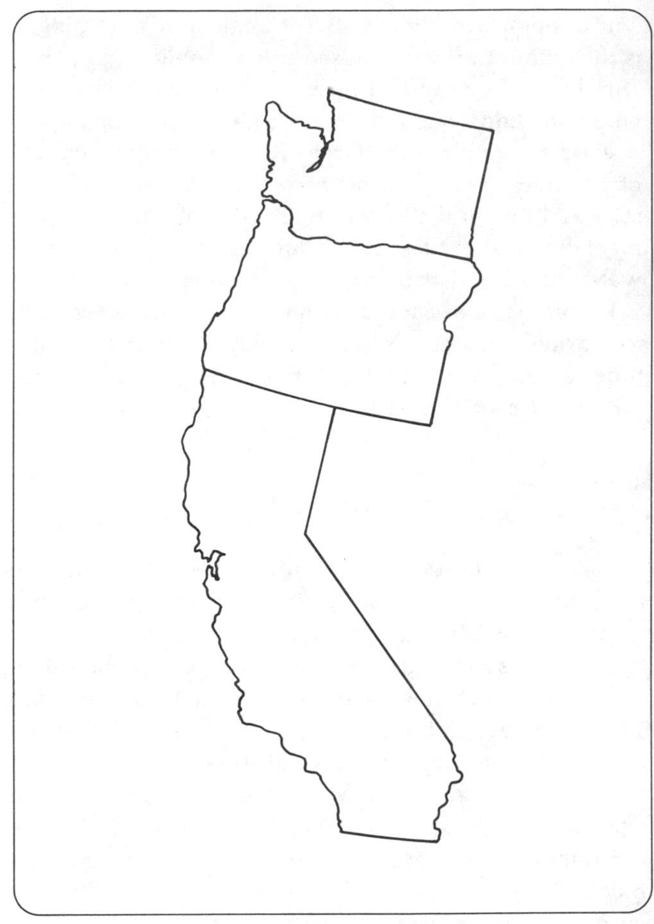

The Far West

THE "FAR WEST" totals nearly 1,000,000 square miles, a figure tough to comprehend until you reflect that it represents more than one-quarter of the nation's real estate.

It's also the region to boast the world's only continuous 12-month cycle of anadromous fish migration—which includes steelhead trout, chinook, coho, cutthroat trout, striped bass and shad. This cornucopia alone should suffice to turn on the most jaded angler.

So here, in its vastness and complexity, is what to look for in the fly-angler's Far West.

Washington

THE EVERGREEN STATE has two schools of fly-rodding—steelhead anglers and "all others." These sea-run rainbows, often reaching 20 pounds, have captivated fly fishermen to a point that may have abandoned more traditional delicate tackle and technique altogether. To be a "steelheader" is akin to being an Atlantic salmon fisherman in the East, perhaps even more exclusive, since Americans who fish in the Atlantic are generally trout fishermen limited to one or two salmon trips per season. For the Washington steelheader, his game is right there year-round.

The state of Washington is beautiful country, a land of rugged loggers and, of course, stately Mount Rainier. Several mountain ranges dominate the landscape, the largest being the monumental Cascade Range. Washington boasts about 150 winter and 30 summer steelhead streams, of which several are located in beautiful Olympic National Park—the Queets, Hoh, and Quinault rivers. The state's salmon and steelheading is generally divided into three areas, the Olympic Peninsula, the Puget Sound region and the Columbia River drainage.

Probably the best known for summer steelheading, which is of greatest interest to fly fishermen, is the Skagit River, near Burlington, with especially productive stretches located above Rockport and at confluences of the Skagit and the Cascade River and Bacon Creek. Another notable steelhead stream, which also hosts late-summer runs of cutthroats and coho salmon, is the Stillaguamish River near Sylvania. Its north fork has a fly-fishing-only stretch. Also recommended are the Toutle River near Castle Rock, and its tributary, the Green River.

Other Washington rivers for "steelies" include, the Cowlitz, Skykomish, Snake, Columbia, Washougal, Puyallup, Snoqualmie, Pilchuck, Sol Duc, Sammamish, Sauk, Grand Ronde and the Wind. The Wenatchee River, which joins Columbia below Lake Entiat, offers 55 miles of steelhead, cutthroat and Dolly Varden angling along with its tributaries, Icicle Creek, the Chiwawa River and Noron Creek. Nor should anglers forget that many of these streams offer excellent opportunities for resident trout.

Washington's best trout fishing, however, is generally found in lakes and ponds, numbering about 6,000 in all. Among the top are 70 "seep lakes," so-called because they were formed by runoff from major impoundments. Notable are, Quincy Lake, Burke Lake, Warden Lake, Corral Lake, Heart Lake, Blythe Lake, Upper Hampton Lake, Windmill Lake, and Goldeneye Lake, with convenient jumping-off places at Othello and Moses Lake.

Oregon

About 15,000 miles of flowing water, teeming with a mixed bag of anadromous fish, including steelhead, chinook and coho salmon, striped bass and shad (both introduced into Western waters), plus a population of resident trout of bragging size in hundreds of streams and high mountain lakes, highlight fly-rodding in the Beaver State. Names of rivers like the Rogue, the Umpqua and the Deschutes have become altogether as well known to savvy steelheaders in recent years as the Beaverkill, Au Sable and Yellowstone have been for generations of more traditional anglers. Oregon, it's fair to say, is the nation's "steelheading capitol."

With a climate much milder than might be thought for its latitude, Oregon provides year-round fly-fishing for migrating species, including some inspiring summer steelheading. The Deschutes, for instance, one of many Columbia River tributaries, shows visiting anglers both outstanding summer steelhead fishing and plenty of opportunity to hook big native rainbow trout. Ideal for the latter is the area of Warm Springs and Gateway, which can be approached only from the east bank without a permit issued by the Warm Springs Indian Reservation. Deschutes tributaries, such as the Metolius River near Bend and the Crooked River near Prineville, produce wonderful hatches, including the famed salmon-fly hatch in June. Another superlative example of steelhead and resident rainbow angling occurs on the McKenzie River near Springfield, a tributary of the Willamette River. The Umpqua, which enters salt water at Reedsport, remains productive for steelhead. Inland, the North Branch Umpqua has a fly-fishing-only stretch above Rock Creek. The renowned Rogue River, which flows into the Pacific at Gold Beach, continues to be a fine steelhead stream, as are the Sieletz River above Kernville and the Trask, Wilson and Nehalem rivers, all in the extreme northwestern part of the state near Portland.

Pacific salmon, including coho and chinook, enter numerous river systems with suitable access, notably the Columbia, the Willamette, the Rogue and the Umpqua. Striped bass, a recent boon to fly rodders, give plenty of sport on the Coos River above Empire, on the Umpqua from Reedsport to Winchester, and on the Coquille River above Brandon. Best time for stripers is June through October. Shad run the Coos in May and June, as well as the Umpqua, the Sandy and the Lower Willamette.

The state also has hundreds of high mountain lakes, providing ideal hiking and camping opportunities. Hosmer Lake, Crane Prairie Reservoir, Davis Lake and Wickiup Reservoir in the Deschutes River system are particularly productive for rainbows and landlocked Atlantic salmon. Fly rodders interested in largemouth bass, an increasingly popular gamefish in Oregon, shouldn't pass up Takenitch Lake near Florence, or Ten Mile Lake near Reedsport.

California

Golden State fisheries management is a complicated affair—perhaps the reason that California employs more biologists than any other state. Fly rodders should note that California is the nation's most populous state, home for 20,000,000 people, nearly two million more than New York State. California, however, is three times larger than New York, although New York has substantially more fresh water per acre. California freshwater angling is almost totally dependent on weather, and specifically the depth of the previous winter's high-country snowpack. In California water is a valuable commodity, both for human consumption and for irrigation. Seasons, therefore, range in quality from outstanding to not-so-good, depending upon how much water nature provides initially each year and how it's doled out later.

All this emphasizes the necessity for establishing reliable angling contacts before planning California fishing trips. Given good conditions, however, anglers can expect quality fishing for rainbows and browns on the Upper Sacramento River between Dunsmuir and

A nice trout from Hat Creek, California. Photo by Valentine Atkinson.

Lake Shasta, while another good spot is the picturesque McCloud River, especially the stretch near Lady Bug Creek. The Lower Sacramento, by the way, has excellent spring runs of shad below Keswick Dam, as well as steelhead, salmon and striped bass through December. Choice striper fly-rodding is available at tributary mouths.

Three top California trout fisheries are the Pit River, Fall River and Hat Creek, all in the Redding area. While the Pit is very swift, the latter two streams are spring-fed and have outstanding slow stretches which turn up trophies in the six-pound class. Other attractive possibilities for trout include the Truckee River, a Lake Tahoe feeder on the Nevada border, the South Fork of the Kings River in the Cedar Grove area, the Upper Klamath River near the Oregon border, and the West Walker and Merced rivers, both within Yosemite National Park. Lake Tahoe, incidently, is a fine rainbow and cutthroat fishery. Among good steelhead, shad and striper waters are the Yuba, American and Feather rivers.

California has scores of high mountain lakes where adventurous fly rodders don't mind hiking to locate some superb trout fishing, including the rare opportunity to try their luck on the wary native goldens. Most of these waters are small and fragile resources, however, maintained as much by angler cooperation as by official management.

Also, because there are so many impoundments in California, quality lake fishing for several species, including trout and bass, lies within easy reach. Pyramid Lake, for instance, near the Nevada border, is excellent for cutthroats, along with Eagle Lake, Boca Lake and Stampede Lake. Lake Shasta is a fine bass fishery, especially in Centimundi Bay, Bridge Bay, and Bailey Cove where fly-rodding is notably effective. Berryessa Lake and Clear Lake, northeast of San Francisco, hold largemouth to six pounds, as does Success Lake near Porterville.

Alaska

AT 536,400 SQUARE MILES total area, Alaska is more than twice the size of Texas, representing a full one-fifth of U.S. territory. Yet it has fewer residents than Wyoming—qualifications, along with its arctic and sub-arctic location, to make it one of the finest cold-water fisheries in the world and a fly rodder's paradise. Although more and more roads traverse the nation's last frontier each year, this remains a land of outfitter and seaplane, not country for the neophyte to be wandering alone. It gives plenty, but it's also demanding. To fish Alaska effectively, more than any other region covered in this section, reliable information is *essential.*

To cover even a small percentage of Alaskan fisheries for rainbows, Dolly Varden, Arctic grayling, char, steelhead, coho and chinook salmon, whitefish, and the unusual sheefish, a supreme acrobat, would require a full volume. A good bet is to write the Alaskan Department of Fish and Game in Juneau for its *Alaskan Sport Fishing Guide*, which fills the bill admirably. It should be noted, however, the prime months are July and August, although fishing is available from May through October, depending on the season. Remember, though, only a crazy man would visit Alaska anytime without woolies, down-filled outerwear and mosquito netting. Lacking the latter protection, the insects might just pick you up and carry you away.

Against the backdrop of gorgeous mountain scenery, some great fisheries include the Fortymile River, a gem for grayling near Eagle. You'll find spectacular lake fishing for rainbows on Deadman Lake at mile 1,251 of the Alaskan highway. North of Fairbanks, try the trout fishing of the Chatanika River, the Washington River, and Tatalina River. On the Kenai Peninsula, one of the most popular areas for sportsmen, incredible fly-rodding for steelhead and coho and chinook salmon is available on the Kenai River, although you'll undoubtedly have to share the water at times with those furry fellow fishermen, the Alaskan brown bears.

Fly-Fishing in Canada

JIM ENGER

NEARLY EVERY MAJOR SPECIES of coldwater gamefish that will take a fly is found in Canada, which makes this country especially attractive to fly fishermen. Canadian waters hold brook trout, browns, rainbows (and their ocean-run relatives, the steelhead), cutthroats, char, grayling, lake trout, the major Pacific salmon (chinook, coho and sockeye), landlocked salmon and, of course, the princely Atlantic salmon.

Fly fishermen, particularly U.S. anglers, are generally interested in three main regions of Canada: The steelhead, salmon and trout waters of the Pacific West; the trout, bass and pike waters of Ontario; and the brook trout and Atlantic salmon streams of Quebec and Labrador.

The province of British Columbia is best known for its steelhead and salmon rivers, which are among the best in the world. The Thompson River, flowing into the Fraser at Lytton, has become famous. It has fishing from early fall until April or May.

The Vedder in the lower region of the province has good fishing from mid-winter through April. The Coquihalla and the Silver near Hope get summer steelhead.

In the northern region of the province, perhaps the most famous stream is the Kispiox. Plenty of 20-pound-plus steelhead have been caught in the Kispiox, as well as a few fish over 30 pounds. The Kispiox is east of Prince Rupert and can be reached via Route 16. Other good rivers in this area are the Bulkley, Morice and the Copper.

The area around the city of Kamloops at the junction of Routes 5 and 1, as you might guess from its name, offers excellent fishing for rainbows.

Cutthroat trout are found throughout British Columbia, both sea-run and resident fish. Some brown and brook trout are to be found, but these fish offer limited possibilities for fly fishermen in British Columbia.

Ontario

THE PROVINCE OF ONTARIO provides excellent fly-fishing for both warm- and coldwater species. The Algoma district is a first-class wilderness area, yet readily accessible and, for that reason, is probably the area visited in Canada by more American anglers than any other. It's possible to get into some parts of the Algoma by car; more remote areas are served by numerous bushplane operations, many of them located in the Sault St. Marie.

Brook trout are found throughout the province. In streams in the southern reaches of the province, such as those that flow into Lake Superior, brookies do not generally run large in size. However, in the more northerly regions, particularly in the streams flowing into Hudson and James bays, fly fishermen can expect brookies in the three- to five-pound range. Some of the top streams in this area are the Albany, the Sutton, the Severn and the Winisk.

The Algonquin Provincial Park north of Lake Ontario near the Quebec/Ontario border offers excellent brook trout fishing and is less than a day's drive from Toronto. Lake Nippigon above Fort William is also noted for its brook trout fishing.

Smallmouth bass are also widely scattered throughout the province and, especially in the Algoma region, provide excellent opportunities for fly fishermen.

Quebec-Labrador

THE QUEBEC-LABRADOR REGION of Canada is best known for its char, brook trout and Atlantic salmon fishing. In Quebec, brook trout fishermen often concentrate on the Lake St. John region. The Mistassini River flows into Lake St. John, and has excellent brook trout fishing. The Broadback, north of the Mistassini and flowing into Lower James Bay, is an extraordinary brook trout river.

In Labrador, perhaps the best known area is the Mininipi Lake region, including the Mininipi River. Brook trout in the three- to five-pound class are common. Atlantic salmon fishing in either Quebec or Labrador requires careful planning. Many of Quebec's best salmon streams are held privately by clubs such as those on the Moise, Grand Cascapedia, Matapedia and Restigouche.

Salmon rights that are not held by clubs are usually leased to camp operators. Anglers have access to these rivers on a fee basis. Weekly rates average between $500 and $1,500, depending upon the nature of the leaseholder's operation. Several operators have leased water on the streams in the Ungava Bay region, northeast of Hudson Bay. The three best streams in this area are the George, Whale and Koksoak. This area is in the subarctic region of Canada and has generally superb fishing. Salmon average in the 12- to 14-pound class on all of these rivers, but can go as high as 25 pounds.

A few Canadian Atlantic salmon streams are open to public fishing, two of which are the Matane and the Little Cascapedia.

Canadian fly-rodding often means wilderness fishing, and fly rodders contemplating trips to remote parts of Canada should plan carefully with their outfitter or camp operator. To the U.S. angler used to an occasional mosquito, black flies can be a tremendous problem during the summer and early-fall months in many regions of Canada.

Further information on fly-fishing in a particular province may be obtained by writing to the regulatory agency of that province. Those addresses appear on page 239.

Fly-Fishing the Tropics

MARK SOSIN

Biscayne Bay, Miami

FEW VISITORS TO MIAMI realize that Biscayne Bay, that brilliantly hued body of water separating Miami from Miami Beach, harbors some of the best bonefishing in Florida and it's all within sight of the Miami skyline. The South Bay is the prime choice and you can find fish on the flats whenever the water temperature is above 70 degrees.

The flats of Biscayne Bay hold other species. Sharks are abundant, especially during the warmer months, and they are an excellent target for the fly fisherman. There's a tendency to ignore the shark, but in shallow water, it can be a tough adversary and difficult fish to hook. Casts must be close to the shark's eye (remember the fish is moving) and the presentation must be delicate.

Along the edges of the flats as well as in the shallows, there are hordes of barracuda during the colder months and enough to keep you busy at other times of the year. They are particularly difficult to fool with a fly. A most successful pattern is an extra-long streamer tied from Fishair, about 10 inches long. Bucktails and multiwing streamers also work at times, but you can't believe how sophisticated a barracuda can be until you cast to one.

The deeper cuts and channels of Biscayne Bay hold a variety of fish throughout the year. In the colder months, bluefish will enter the bay, and there are trout almost year round. The trout are in residence in perhaps six to 10 feet of water where there are grass beds. Jack crevalle prowl the channels, ladyfish are always present, mackerel come into the bay in the winter, and snook are around the pilings and bridge supports at night.

The 10,000 Islands and the Everglades

UNLESS YOU KNOW THIS AREA, you should have a guide to fish this country. From January through March, snook are in the back bays and creeks and can be taken on top water poppers as well as streamer flies. When the weather turns very cold, the fish will be in deep holes. Towards April, some snook will show along the outside islands.

The first part of the year finds redfish cruising the oyster bars, outside points, and channel edges. Sea trout fishing can be good and it will peak by April. During the winter, guides from Islamorada run into Everglades Park and fish for snook on the flats, as well as redfish and sea trout. When the weather warms for a few days and water temperatures on the flats climb to 75 degrees, tarpon may show on some of the shallows. They'll remain until the temperature drops and then disappear.

Deeper channels hold mackerel, bluefish, jacks, and other denizens during the winter and early spring. Cobia will be around markers or other structures in the water.

As the weather warms toward May and June, snook fishing is at its peak with much of the action at night. Tarpon fishing improves steadily and will peak by late May or early June. Spring tarpon sport starts in the backcountry on the fringes of the Park and throughout the myriad islands that lead through the southwest coast of Florida.

By summer, most of the snook and tarpon activity has slowed, although occasional fish can be taken any time of the year. There are always smaller tarpon in the 10,000 islands, but the big migratory push of May and June is over. Redfishing builds toward a peak in September and October and then the schools spread out in November and December, working into the creeks when a cold snap hits.

Florida Keys—Islamorada

TARPON AND BONEFISH constitute the premier fly fishing in this area. Although both of these species are present throughout the year, the main tarpon thrust starts in March or April and continues through July. Fish will also appear earlier if water temperatures on the flats warm up. With the exception of the spring and early summer tarpon run, the majority of the resident tarpon are not big. There are a few heavyweights around into the fall, but if you want plenty of 100-pound class tarpon, try April, May, and June.

The first tarpon come into the backcountry and fishing holds there for the initial part of the season. By May, the fish have started to push into the ocean side and, although fish are caught along Buchanan Bank through July, excellent fishing can occur in the ocean. Interestingly, the backcountry fish will have more of a greenish cast, while the ocean fish take on a bluish hue across the edges of the back.

Bonefishing is year-round sport, with peak periods in the spring and fall. It's the same deal with water temperature—if it's too hot in the summer, the fish will only be on the flats early and late in the day. In the cooler periods of the year, bonefish will hurry to deep water when temperatures on the flats drop below about 70 degrees.

The extensive flats in the Islamorada area hold sharks, barracuda, jacks, the elusive permit, and, in the spring, you can sometimes find mutton snappers. It's exciting country to fish, because just looking in the water can be thrilling and boat rides at high speeds over this skinny water are always remembered.

Florida Keys—Marathon

FISHING AT MARATHON is similar to that in Islamorada. There are some excellent tarpon spots in the Marathon backcountry and right in front on the ocean side. The fish start in the Gulf and work around to the Ocean by May or early June. Again, when the weather is warm, the tarpon show. By July or August, the main body of fish have moved out and there are stragglers through September.

Fishing for permit can be good out of Marathon. One prime area is on the edge of the Gulf at Contents and Sawyers keys. Catching a permit on fly is difficult, and it is often a matter of luck in finding a cooperative fish.

During the coldest part of the winter, the backcountry west of Marathon becomes a haven for big barracuda. Not only are there plenty of fish, but some of those monsters will scare you. That's the place for a long, Fishair fly worked across the top of the water.

Bonefishing is excellent in the Marathon area, with most of the activity on the ocean side and back out by the Harbor Keys and the Contents. The outer Gulf Keys, down to the Snipes and Barracudas, have plenty of bonefish and there are some spots closer to the bridges that also produce.

Florida Keys—Key West

IF THEY WERE LIMITED to a single area to fish in southern Florida, most local experts would unquestionably settle on Key West. It has always been underrated in terms of publicity, but the fishing can be excellent. Tarpon are almost always in the harbor and big fish move on the flats any time there is warm weather, from January through July or August. Some skippers can find tarpon through October, but not in the numbers that are there in the spring.

To find bonefish, you have to travel back up the Gulf side to the Snipe and Barracuda keys, but Key West has plenty of permit working toward the west, with the area around Boca Grande prime. You can also find plenty of permit right around the harbor.

During the cold part of the winter, Key West is the jumping off point for reef fishing. Schools of balao and other baitfish congregate over the myriad of reefs and a mixed bag zeros in on the feast. You'll find jacks, grouper, snapper, kingfish, mackerel, and other denizens. In November, acres of big jacks move through the Gulf side and can be a fly fisherman's bonanza.

The wrecks surrounding Key West are legendary, but they are almost impossible to find unless you have someone show you where they are. These wrecks harbor cobia, amberjack, barracuda, and even permit. The technique is to use chum or to swish hookless teasers made from dead fish across the surface. If you have live bait for teasers, it's that much better. Once the predator is worked up, you simply substitute the fly for the live bait.

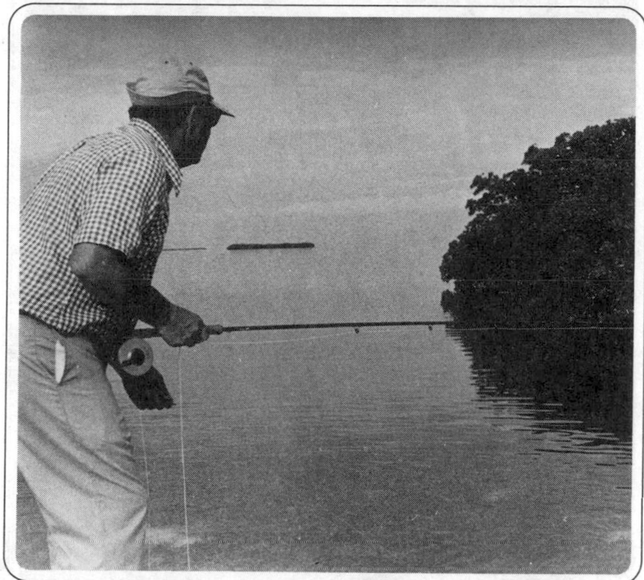

Casting to snook under the mangroves. Photo by Mark Sosin.

Bermuda

DURING JUNE, JULY, AND AUGUST, Bermuda offers some of the most fantastic offshore fly fishing found anywhere in the world. That's the time when chumming operations for Allison tuna, blackfins, and a host of other species is in full swing and it's worth the price of admission to see it and participate. In most cases, you'll be fishing the fly dead in the chum slick, but you usually pick your quarry first and then work on a specific fish. The whole vista unfolds before you and you wait until the fish is properly chummed before casting the fly.

Bahamas

THE BAHAMAS ARE NOTED primarily for bonefishing. With miles and miles of flats, Deep Water Cay offers excellent bonefishing. During the winter, weather patterns and water temperature determine if the fish will be on the flats. With the exception of a few cold snaps, bonefish and some permit are present year-round.

Walker's Cay produces a mixed bag for the fly fisherman, on the reefs as well as the flats. Barracuda are present during the winter, and there are usually bonefish on the flats at all times.

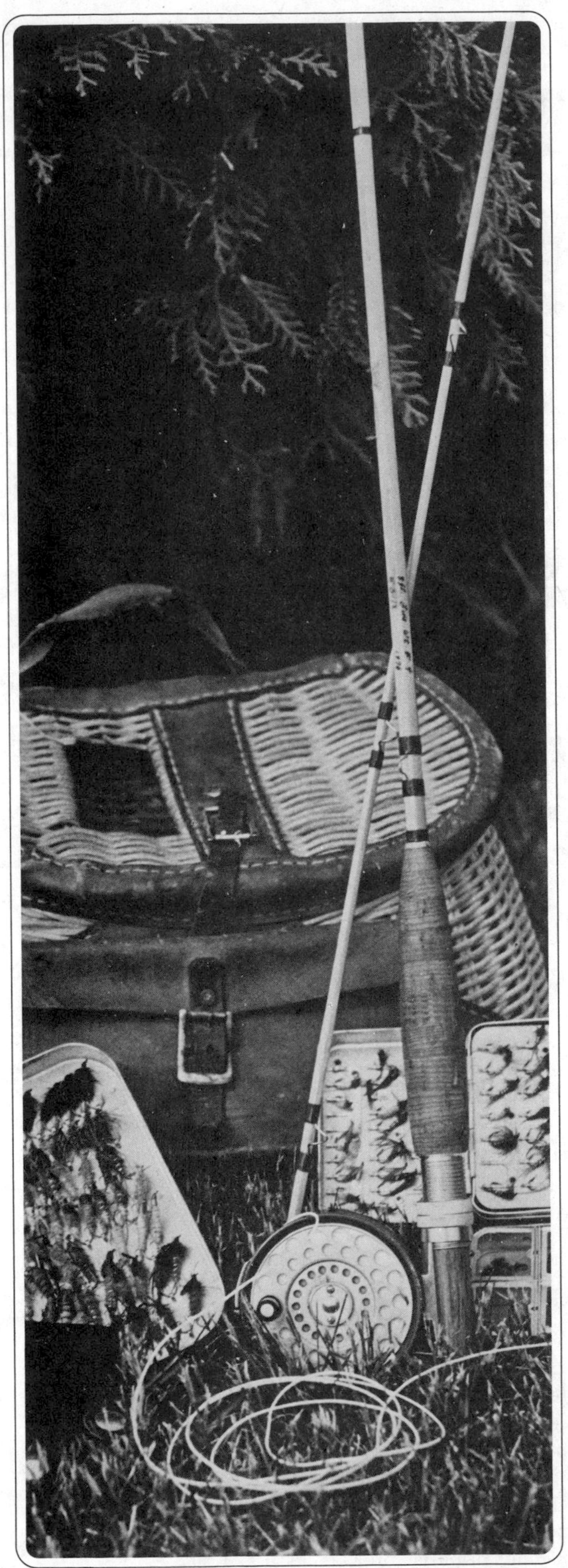

Photo by Dave Engerbretson.

In the next 58 pages, we will dangle before you unspeakable enticements—an almost total listing of the myriad rods, reels, lines and accessory equipment available to American fly anglers. In each section we have briefly described the company or supplier, then listed the basic varieties of rod, reel or other item of equipment appropriate to that section—including general descriptions and, when available, 1978 prices or price ranges. We have also selected representative photographs to illustrate different styles or types of equipment.

In the case of suppliers of more than one basic item of equipment, we have included the company description in the first section, with the firm name being repeated in later sections covering other equipment supplied by that firm. (All listings in these sections have been made at no charge to the manufacturer.)

In no case have we attempted to evaluate equipment. Especially in the case of rods and reels, this would be such a personal and subjective opinion that in most cases we would rather discuss religion, politics or the relative merits of our children. Price is certainly not a criterion in itself. There are perfectly good rods, reels and lines available that would be capable of out-performing many of their users—the entire outfit costing about $50-$60.

You will soon learn to cherish your streamside companion's bamboo rod, covet your neighbor's bench-made fly reel and leer wantonly at a passing angler's imported fly boxes overflowing with patterns you will instinctively know that you can't catch a fish without.

You will not need further counsel from us, and we will not give it. In fact, we decline all legal responsibility as accomplices in any further felonies you may commit.

Chapter 14

Fly-Tackle Directory

COMPILED BY CRAIG WOODS

Although we have earlier explained that the act of casting a fly is one of *chain reaction*, with no link of the chain separable from the others, the key link beyond the caster himself has to be the fly rod. For it is, both literally and figuratively, the angler's "joy stick," the instrument which the caster sets in motion and which, afterward, does most of the work.

If you are a fly fisherman of some experience, you will probably know as much about the mystical process of selecting a rod as you want us to tell you. But, if you are just beginning, we can suggest a few tips.

For many, *price* will and should enter into the choice of a fly rod. First rods always remain in the affections, but usually, after the first season, in the closet. For $25-$35, you can buy a rod which is better than you can use at first.

Amazing things have been done in recent years with *fiberglass* to give fly rods the delicacy and lightness they need and deserve. They also take nice finishes, and are, with reasonable use, indestructible.

It seems that it was only yesterday that *graphite* rods were introduced to the market. It took some time to learn just how to use the new material in rod design, but development has been rapid in the past few years. Graphite has the quick recovery of bamboo, much of the relative indestructibility of fiberglass, and a lightness unequalled by any other material. For the beginner or for the more experienced angler, graphite is a balm to unused muscles.

Bamboo, of course, is the highest achievement of the rodmaker's art, and nearly every fly fisherman, eventually if not now, wants to own one—many have more than one, perhaps six, and fish with nothing else!

Glass is lively, bamboo is lovely, and graphite is light.

The price range of quality glass rods can run from $25 to $100—above this for custom work. Graphite is presently running in the area of $60 to as high as $250 or more. Bamboo, occasionally found for under $100, is more usually in the $125-$400 price range (even more for custom work beyond the normal high craftsmanship expected of these lovely creations).

For the beginner, a friend or acquaintance who is an *experienced fly rodder* is probably the best guide you could find in selecting that first rod. Failing this, we can certainly suggest a visit to a *quality tackle shop* in your area. First, however, see how much fly-fishing tackle the store carries—this will be an indication of its staff's experience in purveying such equipment. Check for broad selections of flies, lines and reels as an indication of their interest and clientele.

Beyond this there are many first-rate *mail-order operations* advertising catalogs—good sources for solid information and good buys if you have no good tackle store near you. Many of these, as well as manufacturers themselves, are listed in the Appendix of this book, and, of course, regularly in the pages of *Fly Fisherman* magazine.

Fly Rods

Fiberglass Rods

Algonquin Fishing Tackle

Algonquin manufactures fiberglass and graphite rods for spinning, casting, trolling and fly-fishing. Other products include spinning and casting reels and spinning lures. Algonquin is a division of the Grew Corporation and is located in Toronto, Canada.

Model: *Imperial Fiberglass (4 models)*. Length: *7½'-9' (1 model with butt extension)*. Weight: *n.a.* No. pieces: 2. Reel seat: *double-locking metal*. Rec. line: *#6-9*. Price: *n.a.*

Model: *Black Stag*. Length: *8½'*. Weight: *n.a.* No. pieces: 2. Reel seat: *down-locking metal*. Rec. line: *#8*. Price: *n.a.*

Model: *Cherry.* Length: *8½'.* Weight: *n.a.* No. pieces: *2.* Reel seat: *double-locking metal.* Rec. line: *#8.* Price: *n.a.*

Model: *Brown Stag.* Length: *8½'.* Weight: *n.a.* No. pieces: *2.* Reel seat: *down-locking metal.* Rec. line: *#8.* Price: *n.a.*

Model: *Algonquin Tubular.* Length: *8½'.* Weight: *n.a.* No. pieces: *2.* Reel seat: *down-locking metal.* Rec. line: *#8.* Price: *n.a.*

Model: *Expert Fiberglass (7 models).* Length: *7½'-9' (2 models with butt extension).* Weight: *3 oz.-n.a.* No. pieces: *2.* Reel seat: *down-locking metal.* Rec. line: *#6-10.* Price: *n.a.*

American Import Co.

THE AMERICAN IMPORT COMPANY offers a broad range of outdoor and general sports equipment under the L. M. Dickson name. L. M. Dickson angling products include rods, reels, clothing and accessories for most types of fishing, with an emphasis on spin- and bait-casting items. American Import is located in San Francisco, California.

Model: *L. M. Dickson Premier Fiberglass (4 models).* Length: *7'-8½'.* Weight: *n.a.* No. pieces: *2.* Reel seat: *down-locking metal.* Rec. line: *n.a.* Price: *n.a.*

Model: *L. M. Dickson Gold Medal (2 models).* Length: *7½'-8'.* Weight: *n.a.* No. pieces: *2.* Reel seat: *locking.* Rec. line: *n.a.* Price: *n.a.*

Model: *L. M. Dickson Telescopic (2 models, one spin-fly).* Length: *7'.* Weight: *n.a.* No. pieces: *1 (telescopic).* Reel seat: *locking metal.* Rec. line: *n.a.* Price: *n.a.*

Angler's World

ANGLER'S WORLD CARRIES a full line of high-quality, high-price fly-fishing tackle from fiberglass, graphite and bamboo rods to leaders, flies and accessories. Angler's World is a companion store to Hunting World of New York, founded by Bob Lee in 1965 as an outlet to market the varied products he encountered in his travels with Lee Expeditions Ltd.

Model: *International Seven.* Length: *7'.* Weight: *2-3/4 oz.* No. pieces: *2.* Reel seat: *down-locking anodized aluminum.* Rec. line: *#5.* Price: *$75.*

Model: *International Eight.* Length: *8'.* Weight: *3-3/4 oz.* No. pieces: *2.* Reel seat: *down-locking anodized aluminum.* Rec. line: *#6, 7.* Price: *$75.*

Model: *International Nine.* Length: *9' (plus removable butt extension).* Weight: *5 oz.* Reel seat: *down-locking anodized aluminum.* Rec. line: *#9.* Price: *$85.*

Prices (and price ranges) listed in this directory are the manufacturer's suggested retail prices as of late 1977, and they are subject to change without notice. Please consult pp. 233-235 for addresses of manufacturers from whom up-to-date price information may be obtained, or check with your local fly-tackle dealer.

Model: *International 8/4 Pak.* Length: *8'.* Weight: *4 oz.* No. pieces: *4.* Reel seat: *down-locking anodized aluminum.* Rec. line: *#8.* Price: *$80.*

Model: *Elite Single Six.* Length: *6'.* Weight: *1-3/8 oz.* No. pieces: *1.* Reel seat: *cork with sliding rings and walnut butt cap.* Rec. line: *#4.* Price: *$100.*

Model: *Elite Sixty Eight.* Length: *6'8".* Weight: *1-13/16 oz.* No. pieces: *2.* Reel seat: *cork with sliding rings and walnut butt cap.* Rec. line: *#5, 6.* Price: *$110.*

Model: *Elite Eight.* Length: *8'.* Weight: *2-3/8 oz.* No. pieces: *2.* Reel seat: *up-locking walnut and aluminum with walnut butt cap.* Rec. line: *#8.* Price: *$125.*

Model: *Magnum Elite Nine.* Length: *9' (plus 2" and 5" removable butt extensions).* Weight: *5 oz.* No. pieces: *2.* Reel seat: *up-locking walnut and aluminum.* Rec. line: *#9.* Price: *$165.*

Berkley & Co.

BERKLEY BEDELL BEGAN TYING bluegill flies for use in the several lakes around Spirit Lake, Iowa, in the late 1930's. He developed a small tackle-shop business that eventually moved into the production of plastic-coated steel leaders, and then monofilament nylon lines. Berkley & Company has become well known in the tackle industry for its knotless tapers, and in 1950 Berkley & Company began making rods for all angling uses. In the 1970's, while retaining a broad-based manufacture of angling products, Berkley began to place an emphasis on fly-fishing products, including rods, lines and reels.

Model: *Para/Metric (5 models).* Length: *6'3"-8½'.* Weight: *n.a.* No. pieces: *n.a.* Reel seat: *n.a.* Rec. line: *#5-8.* Price: *n.a.*

R. W. Bianco Custom Fishing Tackle

BIANCO PRODUCES over 100 models of fiberglass and graphite rods including bait, spinning, worm, trolling and casting models as well as fly-rod models. Bob Bianco is a second-generation rodmaker, and his blanks incorporate tapers of his own design and are manufactured according to his specifications. The Bianco Company is located in San Diego, California.

Model: *Bianco Fiberglass (10 models).* Length: *6'-9'.* Weight: *n.a.* No. pieces: *2.* Reel seat: *aluminum.* Rec. line: *#3-10.* Price: *$70-$100.*

Model: *Bianco Fiberglass Backpacking (3 fly, 2 spin-fly models).* Length: *7'-8'.* Weight: *n.a.* No. pieces: *4.* Reel seat: *n.a.* Rec. line: *#4-7.* Price: *$70-$80.*

Browning

THE BROWNING NAME is familiar to many sportsmen for the Browning shotguns, rifles, pistols and archery equipment, as well as a full line of clothing and accessories. Angling products from Browning include a line of graphite and fiberglass fly rods and two fly reels. Browning is located in Morgan, Utah.

Model: *Silaflex (8 models).* Length: *6'-9'.* Weight: *1.9 oz. to 5.6 oz.* No. pieces: *2.* Reel seat: *down-locking anodized metal and cork.* Rec. line: *#5-11.* Price: *$44.95-$62.95.*

Model: *Silaflex II (3 models).* Length: *7½', 8', 8½'.* Weight: *2-3/5 oz. to 3½ oz.* No. pieces: *2.* Reel seat: *down-locking metal.* Rec. line: *#5-8.* Price: *$23.95.*

F. M. Claudio Rod Co.

FERD CLAUDIO MAKES CUSTOM FIBERGLASS rods in a full range of lengths and actions, and his experience as a rodmaker spans more than 20 years. Located in San Francisco, Claudio grew up within close distance of the famous San Francisco Golden Gate Angling and Casting Club, and his knowledge of rods and rod actions is gleaned and complemented by the information imparted to him by the masters that belonged to the club, for which he eventually served as president.

Model: *Ferdinand Claudio Trout Rod (9 models).* Length: *7'-8'9".* Weight: *n.a.* No. pieces: *2.* Reel seat: *up-locking aluminum and wood.* Rec. line: *DT5, 6, WF8.* Price: *$90.*

Model: *Ferdinand Claudio Steelhead and Salmon Rod (4 models).* Length: *8'9"-9'.* Weight: *n.a.* No. pieces: *2.* Reel seat: *up-locking aluminum and wood.* Rec. line: *WF8-WF11.* Price: *$90.*

Cortland Line Company

THE CORTLAND NAME IS WELL KNOWN to fly fishermen. Although the company produces products for all types of fishing, most of their products center around fly-fishing. The "444" series of top-quality fly lines is familiar to many anglers, as are the fiberglass and graphite rods that Cortland produces. Other products include a broad selection of accessories and terminal tackle. Cortland is located in Cortland, New York, and many anglers are familiar with this company through the Cortland Pro Shops—an extensive network of tackle shops with expertise in fly-fishing.

Model: *FR-2000 Series (7 models).* Length: *6½'-9'.* Weight: *3 oz. to 6 oz.* No. pieces: *2.* Reel seat: *down-locking metal.* Rec. line: *#5-9.* Price: *$33.*

Model: *Leon Chandler Signature (7 models).* Length: *7½'-9'.* Weight: *3¼ oz. to 4½ oz.* No. pieces: *2.* Reel seat: *locking rosewood.* Rec. line: *n.a.* Price: *$70.*

Prices (and price ranges) listed in this directory are the manufacturer's suggested retail prices as of late 1977, and they are subject to change without notice. *Please consult pp. 233-235 for addresses of manufacturers from whom up-to-date price information may be obtained,* *or check with your local fly-tackle dealer.*

Daiwa Corp.

DAIWA SPECIALIZES in precision-engineered spinning and casting reels, and this firm also produces graphite and fiberglass rods. Fly-fishing products include a series of fly reels and several models of graphite and fiberglass fly rods. Daiwa's only products are rods and reels, and it is located in Gardena, California.

Model: *V.I.P. Series (5 models).* Length: *7'-9'.* Weight: *n.a.* No. pieces: *2.* Reel seat: *down-locking anodized aluminum with double rings.* Rec. line: *#5-8, 11, 12.* Price: *n.a.*

Model: *Regal Spin-Fly.* Length: *6½'.* Weight: *n.a.* No. pieces: *6.* Reel seat: *locking anodized aluminum.* Rec. line: *n.a.* Price: *n.a.*

Model: *Regal Series (5 models).* Length: *7'-8½'.* Weight: *n.a.* No. pieces: *2.* Reel seat: *locking anodized aluminum.* Rec. line: *#5-8.* Price: *n.a.*

Model: *1345.* Length: *8'.* Weight: *n.a.* No. pieces: *2.* Reel seat: *down-locking anodized aluminum.* Rec. line: *#7, 8.* Price: *n.a.*

Ee-da-how Custom Rods

EE-DA-HOW PRODUCES CUSTOM fiberglass and graphite fly rods, and its only other products are hand-tied flies. The proprietor is L. C. "Bob" Burnham, and the shop is located in Appleton, Wisconsin.

Model: *Ee-da-how 6', 7', 7½'.* Weight: *2-1/8 oz. to 2-7/8 oz.* No. pieces: *2.* Reel seat: *down-locking anodized aluminum.* Rec. line: *#4-6.* Price: *$50.*

Model: *Ee-da-how 8', 8½'.* Weight: *3-1/8 oz., 3-3/8 oz.* No. pieces: *2.* Reel seat: *down-locking anodized aluminum.* Rec. line: *#5-8.* Price: *$55.*

Model: *Ee-da-how 9'.* Length: *9'.* Weight: *3-7/8 oz.* No. pieces: *2.* Reel seat: *down-locking anodized aluminum.* Rec. line: *#8-10.* Price: *$60.*

Model: *Ee-da-how 7½' Pack Rod.* Length: *7½'.* Weight: *3-1/8 oz.* No. pieces: *4.* Reel seat: *down-locking anodized aluminum.* Rec. line: *#6.* Price: *$60.*

Fenwick

FENWICK MANUFACTURES fiberglass and graphite fishing rods and blanks for spinning, casting, trolling and fly-fishing. It has been a leader in the development of fiberglass and graphite rods, and among the company's "firsts" is the introduction of the fiberglass ferrule to rodmaking over 15 years ago. Other products include big-water lures, fishing-wire products and a selection of rod-building components. Fenwick is located in Westminster, California.

Model: *Fenwick Fiberglass (13 models)*. Length: *6'-9'*. Weight: *2-1/8 oz. to 5 oz.* No. pieces: *2.* Reel seat: *down-locking anodized aluminum with double rings.* Rec. line: *#5-10.* Price: *$46-$64.*

Model: *Voyageur.* Length: *7½'.* Weight: *3 oz.* No. pieces: *4.* Reel seat: *down-locking anodized aluminum with double rings.* Rec. line: *#6.* Price: *n.a.*

Model: *Voyageur.* Length: *8½'.* Weight: *3½ oz.* No. pieces: *5.* Reel seat: *down-locking anodized aluminum with double rings.* Rec. line: *#6.* Price: *n.a.*

Model: *Voyageur Spin-Fly (2 models).* Length: *7', 7½'.* Weight: *4-3/4 oz., 4-7/8 oz.* No. pieces: *4(7'), 5(7½').* Reel seat: *reversible locking anodized aluminum.* Price: *n.a.*

J. Kennedy Fisher Inc.

FISHER BEGAN MANUFACTURING fishing tackle in 1922. The Fisher Company, located in Los Angeles, California, supplies many major rod manufacturers with graphite and fiberglass blanks, as well as producing blanks and finished rods of their own. Other Fisher products include graphite golf shafts and industrial fiberglass tubing; Fisher products carry the "3-Jays" trademark.

Model: *8250-3F.* Length: *6', 7½'.* Weight: *n.a.* No. pieces: *2.* Reel seat: *aluminum.* Rec. line: *#3.* Price: *$39.25.*

Model: *8250-4F, 8250-45F.* Length: *6', 7½'.* Weight: *n.a.* No. pieces: *2.* Reel seat: *aluminum.* Rec. line: *#4, 5.* Price: *$39.25.*

Model: *8250-5F.* Length: *7', 8'.* Weight: *n.a.* No. pieces: *2.* Reel seat: *aluminum.* Rec. line: *#5.* Price: *$39.25.*

Model: *8250-6F, 8250-67F.* Length: *8', 9'.* Weight: *n.a.* No. pieces: *2.* Reel seat: *aluminum.* Rec. line: *#6, 7.* Price: *$39.25.*

Model: *8250-8F, 8250-9F, 8250-10F.* Length: *8½', 9'.* Weight: *n.a.* No. pieces: *2.* Reel seat: *aluminum.* Rec. line: *#8, 9, 10.* Price: *$41.75.*

Model: *8250-11F, 8250-12F.* Length: *9'.* Weight: *n.a.* No. pieces: *2.* Reel seat: *aluminum.* Rec. line: *#11, 12.* Price: *$45.95.*

Model: *8250-13F.* Length: *9'.* Weight: *n.a.* No. pieces: *2.* Reel seat: *aluminum.* Rec. line: *#13.* Price: *$47.60.*

Model: *8254-5F, 8254-6F Pack Rods.* Length: *7', 8'.* Weight: *n.a.* No. pieces: *4.* Reel seat: *aluminum.* Rec. line: *#5, 6.* Price: *$51.75.*

Model: *8254-5SF Spin-Fly.* Length: *7'.* Weight: *n.a.* No. pieces: *4.* Reel seat: *cork with sliding rings.* Rec. line: *#5.* Price: *$51.75.*

Fly Fisherman's Bookcase and Tackle Service

FLY FISHERMAN'S BOOKCASE AND TACKLE SERVICE, owned and operated by Sam Melner, offers a fiberglass rod, the River Rat model, in a full range of lengths and actions, and they also offer a graphite model called the FFB Custom Graphite. Sam Melner's "Bookcase" is well known among anglers as a prime mail-order source for quality fly-fishing tackle from major manufacturers. The Fly Fisherman's Bookcase and Tackle Service is located in Eugene, Oregon.

Model: *RR70, RR75.* Length: *7', 7½'.* Weight: *2.85 oz., 3.4 oz.* No. pieces: *2.* Reel seat: *down-locking metal.* Rec. line: *#5-7.* Price: *$31.90.*

Model: *RR80, RR85.* Length: *8', 8½'.* Weight: *3½ oz., 3-3/4 oz.* No. pieces: *2.* Reel seat: *down-locking metal.* Rec. line: *#7-9.* Price: *$33.50.*

Model: *RR90.* Length: *9'.* Weight: *4 oz.* No. pieces: *2.* Reel seat: *down-locking metal.* Rec. line: *#9.* Price: *$34.95.*

The Garcia Corp.

GARCIA IS BEST KNOWN in the angling world for its Garcia-Mitchell spinning reels. However, Garcia offers a full range of spinning, trolling and casting tackle, including electronic fish-finding aids, as well as fly reels, fiberglass fly rods, fly lines and the recently introduced series of graphite fly rods. The Garcia Corporation is located in Teaneck, New Jersey, and was founded in 1946.

Model: *Americana (8 models).* Length: *6'-9' (9' model has 6" removable butt extension).* Weight: *2 oz. to 4-3/4 oz.* No. pieces: *2 (6' model is one piece).* Reel seat: *cork with sliding rings (6' model), down-locking metal.* Rec. line: *#5-10.* Price: *$30-$50.*

Model: *Avocado (2 models).* Length: *8', 8½'.* Weight: *4-7/10 oz., 4½ oz.* No. pieces: *2.* Reel seat: *down-locking metal.* Rec. line: *#6, 8, 9.* Price: *$22-$31.*

Model: *Silver (3 models).* Length: *7'3"-8½'.* Weight: *3½ oz. to 5-7/10 oz.* No. pieces: *2.* Reel seat: *down-locking metal.* Rec. line: *#6, 7.* Price: *$15-$24.*

James Heddon's Sons

THE HEDDON NAME IS KNOWN to fly fishermen as a one-time mass producer of quality split-cane rods. The current Heddon line of fishing tackle includes graphite and fiberglass rods for spinning, casting and fly-fishing, as well as a line of reels. Other products include spinning lures. James Heddon's Sons, located in Dowagiac, Michigan, is a division of Victor Comptometer Corporation.

Model: *Legacy (4 models).* Length: *7½ '-9'.* Weight: *n.a.* No. pieces: *2.* Reel seat: *down-locking metal.* Rec. line: *#6, 7, 8.* Price: *$32.*

Model: *Galaxy 6026.* Length: *8'.* Weight: *n.a.* No. pieces: *2.* Reel seat: *down-locking metal.* Rec. line: *#7, 8.* Price: *$26.*

Model: *Slick Stick 5028.* Length: *8½'.* Weight: *n.a.* No. pieces: *2.* Reel seat: *down-locking metal.* Rec. line: *#8.* Price: *$23.*

Model: *Brown Pal 4828.* Length: *8½'.* Weight: *n.a.* No. pieces: *2.* Reel seat: *down-locking metal.* Rec. line: *#8.* Price: *$19.*

Model: *Green Pal 4728.* Length: *8½'.* Weight: *n.a.* No. pieces: *2.* Reel seat: *down-locking metal.* Rec. line: *#8.* Price: *$18.*

Model: *Starcast 4428.* Length: *8'3".* Weight: *n.a.* No. pieces: *2.* Reel seat: *up-locking metal.* Rec. line: *#7.* Price: *$14.50.*

Wrapping fiberglass cloth around a tapered steel mandrel, one of several steps in fiberglass rodmaking. Photo by Dale Clemens.

Herter's Inc.

HERTER'S WAS FOUNDED in 1893 and has become almost a household word for generations of sportsmen. Herter's, which is an importer, exporter and manufacturer of outdoor equipment, carries virtually all items of use to hunters, fishermen and outdoorsmen, and is best known as a mail-order house offering tackle and equipment at reasonable costs. Herter's has stores in Minnesota, Wisconsin, South Dakota and Washington.

Model: *600HE Spin-Fly Pack Rod.* Length: *6'10".* Weight: *n.a.* No. pieces: *5.* Reel seat: *up-locking metal.* Rec. line: *n.a.* Price: *$18.27.*

Model: *RB6Y2F.* Length: *8'.* Weight: *5-3/4 oz.* No. pieces: *2.* Reel seat: *down-locking metal.* Rec. line: *#6.* Price: *$18.57.*

Model: *RB6Y4F.* Length: *8½'.* Weight: *6½ oz.* No. pieces: *2.* Reel seat: *down-locking metal.* Rec. line: *#7.* Price: *$18.77.*

Model: *105HE.* Length: *8½'.* Weight: *6½ oz.* No pieces: *2.* Reel seat: *down-locking metal.* Rec. line: *#7.* Price: *$11.97.*

Model: *RFSC6.* Length: *6'.* Weight: *2 oz.* No. pieces: *2.* Reel seat: *cork with sliding rings.* Rec. line: *#5.* Price: *$19.27.*

Model: *RFSC7.* Length: *6'8".* Weight: *2-1/8 oz.* No. pieces: *2.* Reel seat: *cork with sliding rings.* Rec. line: *#6.* Price: *$19.27.*

Model: *108P Spin-Fly Pack Rod (2 models).* Length: *6'3", 8'.* Weight: *n.a.* No. pieces: *7.* Reel seat: *down-locking metal.* Rec. line: *#7.* Price: *$41.77.*

Prices (and price ranges) listed in this directory are the manufacturer's suggested retail prices as of late 1977, and they are subject to change without notice. Please consult pp. 233-235 for addresses of manufacturers from whom up-to-date price information may be obtained, or check with your local fly-tackle dealer.

Kodiak Corporation

LOCATED IN BESSEMER, MICHIGAN, the Kodiak Corporation produces only one product, tubular and solid fiberglass fishing rods. Most of their production includes spinning, casting and trolling rods, but their line also features several fly-rod models.

Model: *9301.* Length: *8½'.* Weight: *n.a.* No. pieces: *2.* Reel seat: *down-locking metal.* Rec. line: *n.a.* Price: *$26-$30.*

Model: *6301 (4 models).* Length: *7½'-8½'.* Weight: *n.a.* No. pieces: *2.* Rec. line: *n.a.* Reel seat: *down-locking metal.* Price: *$16-$19.*

Model: *6301M.* Length: *8½'.* Weight: *n.a.* No. pieces: *2.* Reel seat: *down-locking metal.* Rec. line: *n.a.* Price: *$17-$20.*

Model: *3301 (2 models).* Length: *8', 8½'.* Weight: *n.a.* No. pieces: *2.* Reel seat: *down-locking anodized aluminum.* Rec. line: *n.a.* Price: *$14-$17.*

Model: *2301 (3 models).* Length: *8'-9'.* Weight: *n.a.* No. pieces: *2.* Reel seat: *down-locking aluminum.* Rec. line: *n.a.* Price: *$12-$15.*

Lamiglas Inc.

LAMIGLAS HAS BEEN MANUFACTURING rods and blanks for over 25 years. The company has been a pioneer in the development of graphite as a rod-building material, and its fiberglass and graphite blanks are sold to many major rodmakers throughout the country. Lamiglas makes rods for spinning, casting, surf-casting, trolling and fly-fishing. Lamiglas is located in Woodland, Washington.

Model: *"S"-Glass Fly Rods (3 models).* Length: *8', 8½', 9' (8½' and 9' have butt extension).* Weight: *4 oz. to 4-5/8 oz.* No. pieces: *2.* Reel seat: *up-locking split cork and metal.* Rec. line: *#6-8.* Price: *$65.*

Model: *"S"-Glass Pack Rod.* Length: *8'.* Weight: *4 oz.* No. pieces: *5.* Reel seat: *up-locking split cork and metal.* Rec. line: *#7.* Price: *$55.*

Model: *"S"-Glass Spin-Fly.* Length: *7½'.* Weight: *3-5/8 oz.* No. pieces: *5.* Reel seat: *up-locking split cork and metal plus sliding rings.* Rec. line: *#6.* Price: *$55.*

Model: *Telescopic Pack Rods (2 models, one spin-fly).* Length: *7½', 8½'.* Weight: *n.a.* No. pieces: *n.a.* Reel seat: *n.a.* Rec. line: *n.a.* Price: *$38.95.*

Model: *Glass Ferruled Pack Rods (2 models, one spin-fly).* Length: *8', 8½'.* Weight: *n.a.* No. pieces: *5.* Reel seat: *n.a.* Rec. line: *n.a.* Price: *$39.95.*

H. L. Leonard Rod Inc.

THE FIRST FISHING ROD built by Hiram Lewis Leonard was made of ash and lancewood, in Bangor, Maine, in 1871. Soon after, Leonard began to work with split-bamboo fly rods, and by the time the company moved to its present location in Central Valley, New York, in 1881, the Leonard bamboo fly rod was already becoming recognized as among the finest fly rods made. Hiram Leonard is credited with refining the construction processes of six-strip bamboo fly rods to a degree that has set the standard of cane-rod excellence. Early apprentices of Hiram Leonard include rodmakers who later produced excellent rods under their own names: E. F. Payne, Fred Thomas, E. W. Edwards, and H. W. Hawes. Today Leonard Rod continues to make quality bamboo rods, and its line is supplemented by a graphite series and a fiberglass series of fly rods. Other Leonard products include fly lines, waders, and accessories.

Model: *Leonard Glass Fibre (5 models, one 7' spin-fly).* Length: *7'-8½' (8½' model avail. with 3" detachable butt extension).* Weight: *2-3/8 oz. to 4-3/8 oz.* No. pieces: *2 (7', 8½' models), 3 (7½', 8' models).* Reel seat: *cork with nickel-silver butt cap and aluminum sliding ring (7' models), up-locking wood (7½', 8' models), locking metal (8½' model).* Rec. line: *#4-6, 8.* Price: *$80-$95.*

Martin Reel Co.

THE FIRST AUTOMATIC MARTIN FLY REEL was patented by Herman W. Martin in 1884. The Martin Reel Company, although it now offers a broad range of fly-fishing, spinning and casting tackle, is still best known for its reels. Most of Martin's products are designed for fly-fishing, and its line of fly reels includes a selection of automatic, single- and multiple-action models. The Martin Reel Company is located in Mohawk, New York.

Model: *Portage 3-666.* Length: *6½'.* Weight: *4½ oz.* No. pieces: *6.* Reel seat: *down-locking metal.* Rec. line: *#7.* Price: *n.a.*

Model: *Portage 31-666 Spin-Fly.* Length: *6½'.* Weight: *6 oz.* No. pieces: *6.* Reel seat: *sliding rings for spin, down-locking metal for fly.* Rec. line: *#6, 7.* Price: *n.a.*

Model: *Bass Pro 73-434, 73-437.* Length: *7', 8½'.* Weight: *5½ oz.* No. pieces: *2.* Reel seat: *down-locking metal.* Rec. line: *#10.* Price: *n.a.*

Model: *Blue Chip Series (4 models).* Length: *7'-8½'.* Weight: *4¼ oz.-5 oz.* No. pieces: *2.* Reel seat: *down-locking metal.* Rec. line: *#5-8.* Price: *n.a.*

Model: *Fly Wate Series (5 models).* Length: *7'-9'.* Weight: *3¼ oz.-n.a.* No. pieces: *2.* Reel seat: *down-locking metal.* Rec. line: *#5-9.* Price: *n.a.*

Model: *Tuffy Series (3 models).* Length: *7½'-8½'.* Weight: *3¼ oz.-4¼ oz.* No. pieces: *2.* Reel seat: *down-locking metal.* Rec. line: *#7, 8.* Price: *n.a.*

O. L. M. International Corp.

O. L. M. INTERNATIONAL, of the Olympic Fishing Tackle Corporation of Japan, offers a full line of fishing products, specializing in spinning, casting and trolling rods and reels and accessories. Fly-fishing products include graphite and fiberglass rods, fly reels, accessories and waders. O.L.M. International is located in Burlingame, California.

Model: *7180-FG.* Length: *8'.* Weight: *n.a.* No. pieces: *2.* Reel seat: *down-locking aluminum.* Rec. line: *#7, 8.* Price: *n.a.*

Model: *3000 Series (2 models).* Length: *8', 8½'.* Weight: *n.a.* No. pieces: *2.* Reel seat: *down-locking aluminum.* Rec. line: *#7, 8.* Price: *n.a.*

Model: *2000 Series (3 models).* Length: *7½'-8½'.* Weight: *n.a.* No. pieces: *2.* Reel seat: *down-locking metal.* Rec. line: *#7, 8.* Price: *n.a.*

Model: *2570-X Spin-Fly.* Length: *7'.* Weight: *n.a.* No. pieces: *4.* Reel seat: *down-locking metal.* Rec. line: *n.a.* Price: *n.a.*

Model: *1180.* Length: *8'.* Weight: *n.a.* No. pieces: *2.* Reel seat: *down-locking aluminum.* Rec. line: *#8.* Price: *n.a.*

The Orvis Co.

ORVIS WAS FOUNDED in 1856 by Charles F. Orvis. Since that time the company has been one of the industry's leaders in the manufacture of quality fly-fishing equipment. Orvis markets a complete line of fly-fishing tackle and accessories, as well as tackle for spinning, specializing in high-quality items. Orvis is located in Manchester, Vermont, and though its business is primarily mail-order, Orvis also operates a large retail store.

Model: *Fullflex A (4 models).* Length: *7'-8½'.* Weight: *2-3/4 oz.-3-3/4 oz.* No. pieces: *2.* Reel seat: *down-locking cork.* Rec. line: *#5-8.* Price: *$67.50-$72.*

Model: *Fullflex A Spin-Fly Pack Rod.* Length: *7'.* Weight: *3-1/8 oz.* No. pieces: *4.* Reel seat: *cork with sliding rings.* Rec. line: *#6.* Price: *$69.50.*

Model: *Fullflex A II (4 models).* Length: *7'-8½'.* Weight: *3 oz.-4 oz.* No. pieces: *2.* Reel seat: *down-locking metal.* Rec. line: *#5-8.* Price: *$46.50-$49.50.*

Model: *Fullflex A II Spin-Fly Camper.* Length: *7'.* Weight: *3-3/8 oz.* No. pieces: *4.* Reel seat: *cork with sliding rings.* Rec. line: *#6.* Price: *$49.50.*

Model: *Golden Eagle (8 models).* Length: *6½'-9'.* Weight: *1-7/8 oz.-7 oz.* No. pieces: *2.* Reel seat: *cork with sliding rings, down-locking walnut or down-locking chromed metal.* Rec. line: *#4-11.* Price: *$89-$105.*

Russ Peak

RUSS PEAK FLY RODS ARE KNOWN and sought after throughout the world, and the demand far exceeds the supply. Peak made his first commercial bamboo rod in 1942, and he changed his efforts to the production of fiberglass rods in the early 1950's. It has been the superlative quality of his fiberglass models that have earned him the greatest fame. Peak rods are produced in fiberglass, graphite and graphite-and-glass models, and each rod is entirely handmade by Peak. They are made in a wide range of lengths and actions, and prices range from about $150 to over $600. Peak rods are produced in different grades, of which the most popular is the Zenith Grade, priced between $250 and $300 for most models.

Due to the overwhelming demand and the custom-crafted nature of the product, no model descriptions follow. (Russ Peak will provide product information upon request. Serious inquiries only.)

Pflueger

WELL KNOWN TO THE FLY FISHERMAN for their line of Medalist reels, Pflueger's current selection of fly reels is broad and they also manufacture fly rods in graphite, fiberglass, and in a graphite-and-fiberglass combination. Most of their line, however, centers around spinning and casting products. Other products include electric motors and accessories. Pfleuger is located in Columbia, South Carolina.

Model: *Pflueger Fiberglass (4 models).* Length: *7½ ', 8'.* Weight: *n.a.* No. pieces: *2.* Reel seat: *down-locking metal.* Rec. line: *n.a.* Price: *n.a.*

Powell Rod Co.

E. C. POWELL MADE HIS FIRST bamboo rod for his own use around 1910 in Red Bluff, California. Circa 1920, after a demand for Powell rods developed, E. C. moved to Marysville, California, where he developed machinery for the production of quality bamboo rods. E. C. Powell obtained the first patent given for bamboo-rod construction — on the semi-hollow construction, where a cedar or cork insert is placed between nodes. The present owner of Powell Rod Company, E. C.'s son, Walton, began working for his father in 1922 at the age of seven, and he began his own plant in 1948. The Powell Rod Company, now located in Chico, includes both Walton Powell's and his father's plants, and the range of rods includes custom graphite, fiberglass and bamboo models.

Model: *Fiberglass Dry Fly (9 models).* Length: *6'-8½'.* Weight: *n.a.* No. pieces: *2.* Reel seat: *up-locking machined anodized aluminum.* Rec. line: *#3-8.* Price: *$45, $65 (with extra tip).*

Model: *Fiberglass Steelhead and Saltwater (4 models).* Length: *8½'-9' (one model with 2" butt extension, one model with 6" butt extension, other length butt extensions avail. on request).* Weight: *n.a.* No. pieces: *2.* Reel seat: *up-locking machined anodized aluminum with two locking rings.* Rec. line: *#7-12.* Price: *$45, $65 (with extra tip), add $12.50 for butt extension.*

Model: *Tarpon.* Length: *9' (plus 6" butt extension).* Weight: *n.a.* No. pieces: *2.* Reel seat: *up-locking machined anodized aluminum with two locking rings.* Rec. line: *#10-13.* Price: *$75, $100 (with extra tip).*

Prices (and price ranges) listed in this directory are the manufacturer's suggested retail prices as of late 1977, and they are subject to change without notice. Please consult pp. 233-235 for addresses of manufacturers from whom up-to-date price information may be obtained, or check with your local fly-tackle dealer.

Ryobi America Corp.

RYOBI AMERICA OF RYOBI LTD., a world-leading Japanese die-casting and mechanical products manufacturer, produces rods and reels for spinning, casting, trolling and fly-fishing. Ryobi concentrates on the production of precision-engineered spinning and casting reels, and its fly-fishing line is limited, including several models of fiberglass fly rods and two fly reels. Ryobi America is located in Elk Grove Village, Illinois.

Model: *Ryobi Fiberglass (4 models).* Length: *7½'-9'.* Weight: *3.9 oz. to 5 oz.* No. pieces: *2.* Reel seat: *down-locking metal.* Rec. line: *#6-8.* Price: *n.a.*

St. Andrews Ltd.

ST. ANDREWS GRAPHITE and fiberglass fly rods are made by John Pinto of Ike's Fly Shop, Oak Park, Michigan. Ike's Fly Shop, a retail, wholesale, import, export and manufacturing tackle firm specializing in fly-fishing products, began making these rods in 1969.

Model: *St. Andrews Ltd. Fiberglass (20 models).* Length: *6'-9'.* Weight: *1½ oz. to 5-1/8 oz.* No. pieces: *2.* Reel seat: *down-locking anodized aluminum.* Rec. line: *#3-10.* Price: *n.a.*

St. Croix Corp.

ST. CROIX WAS FOUNDED in 1948, and it manufactures tackle for spinning, casting and fly-fishing. The major part of the company's production centers around spinning and casting rods and reels, although numerous fly-rod models are available. St. Croix is located in Minneapolis, Minnesota.

Model: *1900 Series (2 models).* Length: *8', 8½'.* Weight: *n.a.* No. pieces: *2.* Reel seat: *up-locking metal with hood and double lock nuts.* Rec. line: *#6-8.* Price: *$34.95-$39.95.*

Model: *1200 Series (2 models).* Length: *8', 8½'.* Weight: *n.a.* No. pieces: *2.* Reel seat: *up-locking metal.* Rec. line: *#6-8.* Price: *$34.95-$39.95.*

Model: *900 Series, 09FF-80ML.* Length: *8'.* Weight: *n.a.* No. pieces: *2.* Reel seat: *up-locking metal.* Rec. line: *#6, 7.* Price: *$34.95-$39.95.*

Model: *2900 Series (8 models).* Length: *6½'-9'.* Weight: *2 oz. to 6-3/4 oz.* No. pieces: *2.* Reel seat: *cork with hood and sliding ring (6½ ', 7' models), down-locking metal with double lock nuts (all other models).* Rec. line: *#5-11.* Price: *$34.95-$39.95.*

Sceptre

SCEPTRE FIBERGLASS BLANKS are produced in Alnwick, England, and the final rod assembly is carried out by the Constable Rod Works, Bromley, England. These rods are produced exclusively for Anglersmail of Cleveland, Ohio, the U.S. agent for Sceptre rods and blanks.

Model: *Series I (5 models).* Length: *6'3"-8'.* Weight: *2¼ oz.-2-3/4 oz.* No. pieces: *2.* Reel seat: *cork with hood and sliding ring.* Rec. line: *#3½ -5.* Price: *$52.50-$59.50.*

Model: *Series II (2 models).* Length: *8½', 9'.* Weight: *3-15/16 oz., 4¼ oz.* No. pieces: *2.* Reel seat: *cork with hood and sliding ring.* Rec. line: *#6-9.* Price: *$54.50.*

Model: *8' Pack Rod.* Length: *8'.* Weight: *3 oz.* No. pieces: *4.* Reel seat: *cork with hood and sliding ring.* Rec. line: *#4, 4½ , 5, 6.* Price: *$59.50.*

Model: *8½' Pack Rod.* Length: *8½'.* Weight: *4¼ oz.* No. pieces: *4.* Reel seat: *cork with hood and sliding ring.* Rec. line: *#6, 7, 8.* Price: *$59.50.*

Scientific Anglers

SCIENTIFIC ANGLERS WAS FORMED in 1945 by Leon P. Martuch and Clare Harris. The first products of the company were a silicone fly dressing and a rod case. In 1955 Martuch and Harris introduced the Air Cel and Wet Cel fly lines—revolutionary lines that utilized a tapered plastic coating over a level braided core, and Scientific Anglers patented machinery to mass produce quality lines. Leon L. Martuch took over active management of the company from his father in 1962, and in the late 60's, and working with Jon Tarantino, rods and reels were introduced and the concept of System-balanced equipment was founded. Scientific Anglers' System rods, reels and lines, made specifically to balance properly at a chosen weight, simplified tackle selection for many fly fishermen. In 1973 Scientific Anglers was purchased by the 3M Company, and the company is located in Midland, Michigan.

Model: *System 4.* Length: *7'2".* Weight: *n.a.* No. pieces: *2.* Reel seat: *down-locking anodized aluminum.* Rec. line: *#4.* Price: *$95.*

Model: *System 5.* Length: *7'7".* Weight: *n.a.* No. pieces: *2.* Reel seat: *down-locking anodized aluminum.* Rec. line: *#5.* Price: *$95.*

Model: *System 6.* Length: *8'1".* Weight: *n.a.* No. pieces: *2.* Reel seat: *down-locking anodized aluminum.* Rec. line: *#6.* Price: *$95.*

Model: *System 7.* Length: *8'5".* Weight: *n.a.* No. pieces: *2.* Reel seat: *down-locking anodized aluminum.* Rec. line: *#7.* Price: *$95.*

Model: *System 8.* Length: *8'8" (plus optional 2" or 5" butt extension).* Weight: *n.a.* No. pieces: *2.* Reel seat: *down-locking anodized aluminum.* Rec. line: *#8.* Price: *$95, $100 (with butt extension).*

Model: *System 9.* Length: *8'11" (plus optional 2" or 5" butt extension).* Weight: *n.a.* No. pieces: *2.* Reel seat: *down-locking anodized aluminum.* Rec. line: *#9.* Price: *$95, $100 (with butt extension).*

Model: *System 10.* Length: *9'1" (plus optional 2" or 5" butt extension).* Weight: *n.a.* No. pieces: *2.* Reel seat: *down-locking anodized aluminum.* Rec. line: *#10.* Price: *$95, $100 (with butt extension).*

Model: *System 11.* Length: *9'3" (plus optional 2" or 5" butt extension).* Weight: *n.a.* No. pieces: *2.* Reel seat: *down-locking anodized aluminum.* Rec. line: *#11.* Price: *$95, $100 (with butt extension).*

Model: *System 6 Pack Rod.* Length: *8'1".* Weight: *n.a.* No. pieces: *5.* Reel seat: *down-locking anodized aluminum.* Rec. line: *#6.* Price: *n.a.*

Scott PowR-Ply Co.

SCOTT POWR-PLY MAKES FLY RODS in fiberglass and graphite. Rodmaker Harry Wilson is among the most knowledgeable fiberglass fly-rod craftsmen, and he began the company in 1971, supplying rods to Abercrombie & Fitch. The company was incorporated in 1974, and it is located in San Francisco, California.

Model: *Very Light Trout Rod (5 models).* Length: *6'-8'.* Weight: *1-5/8 oz. to 3 oz.* No. pieces: *2.* Reel seat: *cork with hood and sliding ring.* Rec. line: *#2-DT4F.* Price: *$90-$97.50.*

Model: *Light Trout Rod (4 models).* Length: *7'-8'4".* Weight: *2-3/8 oz. to 3-3/8 oz.* No. pieces: *2.* Reel seat: *cork with hood and sliding ring.* Rec. line: *WF5F, DT5F.* Price: *$90-$97.50.*

Model: *Medium Trout Rod (3 models).* Length: *8', 8½'.* Weight: *3-7/8 oz. to 4-3/8 oz.* No. pieces: *2.* Reel seat: *up-locking metal.* Rec. line: *WF6F, DT6F, WF7F.* Price: *$90-$97.50.*

Model: *Multi-Piece Trout Rods (5 models).* Length: *7'-8½'.* Weight: *2½ oz. to 4½ oz.* No. pieces: *5.* Reel seat: *cork with hood and sliding ring, cork with sliding rings.* Rec. line: *WF4F-WF7F.* Price: *$90-$97.50.*

Model: *Steelhead Rod (3 models).* Length: *8'9"-9'3".* Weight: *5 oz. to 5-3/4 oz.* Reel seat: *up-locking metal.* Rec. line: *ST9S-ST11S.* Price: *$90-$97.50.*

Model: *Bass and Saltwater Rods (5 models).* Length: *8'-9' (all models except one have fixed 1½" butt extension).* Weight: *4-1/8 oz. to 5-7/8 oz.* No. pieces: *2.* Reel seat: *up-locking metal.* Rec. line: *WF7F-WF11, ST9-ST10.* Price: *$90-$97.50.*

Shakespeare Company

THE SHAKESPEARE COMPANY was founded in 1896 in Kalamazoo, Michigan, by William Shakespeare, a watchmaker and jeweler (not the dramatist!). Shakespeare decided he could improve his bait-casting reel; he did so with the invention of the level-wind mechanism, the first workable system for winding line evenly over a reel spool.

In 1946 the Shakespeare Company introduced the first tubular fiberglass rod to the angling market. It was called the Wonderod Rod, and its production was made possible by Shakespeare's development of the patented Howald Process. This process is named after its originator, Dr. Arthur M. Howald, and it involves the construction of a rod with a continuous fiberglass inner spiral and an outer layer of parallel fiberglass fiber from butt to tip.

In addition to a broad range of tackle and rods for most types of angling, Shakespeare offers the fly fisherman rods constructed of fiberglass and graphite.

Model: *BWF1100.* Length: *9' (plus 2½" butt extension).* Weight: *6½ oz.* No. pieces: *2.* Reel seat: *down-locking black anodized aluminum.* Rec. line: *#10.* Price: *n.a.*

Model: *FY1100.* Length: *8½'.* Weight: *4½ oz.* No. pieces: *2.* Reel seat: *down-locking black anodized aluminum.* Rec. line: *#8.* Price: *n.a.*

Model: *FY900 (2 models).* Length: *7½', 8½'.* Weight: *3½ oz., 4½ oz.* No. pieces: *2.* Reel seat: *down-locking black anodized aluminum.* Rec. line: *#5, 8.* Price: *n.a.*

Model: *FY900L.* Length: *8'.* Weight: *3.8 oz.* No. pieces: *2.* Reel seat: *down-locking black anodized aluminum.* Rec. line: *#6.* Price: *n.a.*

Model: *FY900B.* Length: *8'.* Weight: *4 oz.* No. pieces: *2.* Reel seat: *down-locking black anodized aluminum.* Rec. line: *#8.* Price: *n.a.*

Model: *FY900B 9'.* Length: *9'.* Weight: *4.7 oz.* No. pieces: *2.* Reel seat: *down-locking black anodized aluminum.* Rec. line: *#9.* Price: *n.a.*

Model: *FY900BW 9'.* Length: *9' (plus 2½" butt extension).* Weight: *6½ oz.* No. pieces: *2.* Reel seat: *down-locking black anodized aluminum with two locking rings.* Rec. line: *#11.* Price: *n.a.*

Model: *FY200 (3 models).* Length: *7½'-8½'.* Weight: *3.7 oz.-4.1 oz.* No. pieces: *2.* Reel seat: *down-locking black anodized aluminum.* Rec. line: *#6-8.* Price: *n.a.*

Model: *FY160.* Length: *8½'.* Weight: *4 oz.* No. pieces: *2.* Reel seat: *down-locking polished aluminum.* Rec. line: *#8.* Price: *n.a.*

Model: *FY170.* Length: *8'.* Weight: *4 oz.* No. pieces: *2.* Reel seat: *down-locking black anodized aluminum.* Rec. line: *#6.* Price: *n.a.*

Timberline Rods

TIMBERLINE RODS of North Conway, New Hampshire, is just entering its fourth year, but the quality of Timberline fiberglass and graphite fly rods is already becoming well known—not solely in New England, but throughout the country.

Timberline has built most of its reputation on its line of Backpacker Rods—four-piece pack rods (now available in two-piece models). Timberline also offers a separate line of two- and four-piece custom fiberglass and graphite rods, as well as fly-spin models and a limited number of spinning rods. Although Timberline also carries fly reels and lines, it is primarily a fly-rod company specializing in its own line of finished fly rods and offering a line of blanks and rod-building components from major manufacturers.

Model: *Backpacker Presidential.* Length: *6'.* Weight: *2.4 oz.* No. pieces: *4.* Reel seat: *down-locking metal.* Rec. line: *#5, 6.* Price: *$42.50.*

Model: *Backpacker Yellowstone.* Length: *7'.* Weight: *3 oz.* No. pieces: *4.* Reel seat: *down-locking metal.* Rec. line: *#5, 6.* Price: *$42.50.*

Model: *Backpacker Sierra Spin-Fly.* Length: *7'.* Weight: *3.4 oz.* No. pieces: *4.* Reel seat: *cork with sliding rings.* Rec. line: *#6.* Price: *$42.50.*

Model: *Backpacker Appalachian Spin-Fly.* Length: *6'.* Weight: *2½ oz.* No. pieces: *4.* Reel seat: *cork with sliding rings.* Rec. line: *#5.* Price: *$42.50.*

Model: *Backpacker Two Piece.* Length: *6', 7'.* Weight: *n.a.* No. pieces: *2.* Reel seat: *down-locking metal.* Rec. line: *#5, 6.* Price: *$45.*

Model: *Backpacker Two Piece Spin-Fly.* Length: *7'.* Weight: *n.a.* No. pieces: *2.* Rec. line: *#5, 6.* Price: *$45.*

Prices (and price ranges) listed in this directory are the manufacturer's suggested retail prices as of late 1977, and they are subject to change without notice. Please consult pp. 233-235 for addresses of manufacturers from whom up-to-date price information may be obtained, or check with your local fly-tackle dealer.

Model: *Lightweight (4 models).* Length: *6½'-8'.* Weight: *n.a.* No. pieces: *2.* Reel seat: *cork with hood and sliding ring.* Rec. line: *#3-5.* Price: *$65-$70.*

Model: *Medium Weight (4 models).* Length: *8'-9'.* Weight: *n.a.* No. pieces: *2.* Reel seat: *locking rosewood.* Rec. line: *#6-8.* Price: *$72-$78.*

Model: *Timberline 9' Fiberglass (2 models).* Length: *9' (plus 3" removable butt extension).* Weight: *n.a.* No. pieces: *2.* Reel seat: *locking metal.* Rec. line: *#8-10.* Price: *$85.*

Model: *Timberline Spin-Fly Fiberglass.* Length: *7½'.* Weight: *n.a.* No. pieces: *2.* Reel seat: *cork with sliding rings.* Rec. line: *#5.* Price: *$60.*

Wrapping cellophane around the steel mandrel and fiberglass cloth. The assembly is heat cured after this step—the cellophane applies pressure to help maintain shape of the blank. Photo by Dale Clemens.

Trimarc

TRIMARC'S ONLY PRODUCTS are telescopic fiberglass fishing rods and poles for spinning, casting, trolling and fly-fishing. The company was founded in 1970 by Jim McKeown. Trimarc is a division of Phoenix International Sales Ltd. and is located in Hillside, Illinois.

Model: *FQ7553, FQ8063.* Length: *7½', 8'.* Weight: *3½ oz.* No. pieces: *1 (telescopic).* Reel seat: *down-locking anodized aluminum.* Rec. line: *#6-8.* Price: *$15-$20.*

Uslan Rod Company

FOR MANY FLY FISHERMEN the name Uslan is readily associated with bamboo fly rods of five-strip construction. Jim

Uslan began making five-strip cane rods in about 1931 after working previously in six-strip processes. He learned the basics of the five-strip rod from rod designer Robert Crompton. Uslan first began to make rods in numbers for commercial sale in 1945 when he moved from Spencer, Iowa, to Spring Valley, New York. The Uslan Company has also become well known for their nickel-silver ferrules, and Everett Garrison is among the rodmakers to whom these ferrules have been supplied. The Uslan Company is currently located in North Miami Beach, Florida, and their fly-rod line includes fiberglass and graphite models, as well as the five-strip cane models.

Model: *Uslan Glass Rod (8 models).* Length: *6'-9'.* Weight: *n.a.* No. pieces: *2.* Reel seat: *locking cork (#5-7 line rods), locking anodized aluminum (#8-10 line rods).* Rec. line: *#5-10.* Price: *$75.*

Model: *Uslan Special Tarpon, Sail or Marlin.* Length: *9' (plus 2" butt extension).* Weight: *n.a.* No. pieces: *2.* Reel seat: *up-locking metal.* Rec. line: *#12-15.* Price: *$125.10.*

Wanigas Rod Co.

WANIGAS, THE ANAGRAMMATIC ROD COMPANY located in Saginaw, Michigan, produces custom fiberglass, graphite and bamboo rods. Although there are numerous spinning-rod models in the Wanigas line, fly-rod production is the major concern. Other products include custom flies, and tackle items from major manufacturers. Art Neumann, who founded Wanigas in 1946, has been a rodmaker for 39 years.

Model: *Wanigas Ausable (7 models).* Length: *6'-9' (9' model with butt extension).* Weight: *n.a.* No. pieces: *2.* Reel seat: *locking cork.* Rec. line: *#4-9.* Price: *$70-$80.*

Model: *Wanigas Pere Marquette (7 models).* Length: *6½'-9' (9' models with butt extension).* No. pieces: *2.* Weight: *n.a.* Reel seat: *locking metal.* Rec. line: *#4-11.* Price: *$57.50-$65.*

Model: *Wanigas Pere Marquette Spin-Fly Pack.* Length: *7'.* Weight: *n.a.* No. pieces: *4.* Reel seat: *locking.* Rec. line: *#6.* Price: *$60.*

Webley & Scott Ltd.

WEBLEY & SCOTT IS WELL KNOWN to many sportsmen as a producer of military, police and sporting arms, including pistols, rifles and shotguns. The firm was formed in 1897 by the merger of two gun-making firms, P. Webley & Sons and W. & C. Scott & Sons. Webley & Scott has recently expanded their product line to include fishing equipment, and their fishing products are fiberglass spinning, casting, boat and fly rods and fly lines. The company is a member of the Harris & Sheldon Group and is located in Birmingham, England. A U.S. distributor for Webley & Scott fishing products has not yet been announced.

Model: *Stream Fly Rod (7 models).* Length: *6½'-9'.* Weight: *n.a. to 4-3/4 oz.* No. pieces: *2.* Reel seat: *up-locking metal.* Rec. line: *#4-7.* Price: *n.a.*

Model: *Lake Fly Rod.* Length: *9'3".* Weight: *4-3/4 oz.* No. pieces: *2.* Reel seat: *up-locking black nylon.* Rec. line: *#7, 8.* Price: *n.a.*

Model: *Glen Fly Rod (2-handed salmon, 2 models).* Length: *12½', 14'.* Weight: *14¼ oz., 15-3/4 oz.* No. pieces: *3.* Reel seat: *down-locking metal.* Rec. line: *#9, 10.* Price: *n.a.*

R. L. Winston Rod Co.

THE WINSTON ROD COMPANY began making fly rods in San Francisco in 1929, when the West Rod Company was taken over by Robert Winther and Lew Stoner. The present name of the company is a contraction of the original name of the firm begun in 1929, the Winther-Stoner Manufacturing Company, because their rods were often referred to as "Winstons." In 1938 the R. L. Winston Company developed the first fluted-hollow bamboo fly rods, originally for use as tournament-casting models. Today the company is owned by Tom Morgan and located in Twin Bridges, Montana. Products include fly rods in fiberglass, graphite and bamboo, and several rod-building items.

Model: *Stalker (9 models).* Length: *6½'-8½'.* Weight: *1-2/3 oz. to 2-7/8 oz.* No. pieces: *2.* Reel seat: *all cork with German-silver hood and sliding ring.* Rec. line: *#2-4.* Price: *$95.*

Model: *Trout Rod (15 models).* Length: *5½'-9'.* Weight: *1-5/8 oz. to 4¼ oz.* No. pieces: *2.* Reel seat: *all cork with German-silver hood and sliding ring, or locking rosewood.* Rec. line: *#5-7.* Price: *$95.*

Model: *Steelhead, Salmon, Bass and Light Saltwater Rods (6 models).* Length: *8'9"-9' (plus optional removable butt extension).* Weight: *4½ oz. to 5-5/8 oz.* No. pieces: *2.* Reel seat: *locking rosewood or locking anodized aluminum.* Rec. line: *WF8-WF11, ST9-ST12.* Price: *$100.*

Model: *Heavy Saltwater Rod (2 models).* Length: *9'.* Weight: *6 oz., 7½ oz.* No. pieces: *2.* Reel seat: *locking anodized aluminum.* Rec. line: *WF11-WF13.* Price: *$100-$110.*

Model: *3-Piece Travel Rod (2 models).* Length: *7½', 8'.* Weight: *2½ oz. to 3-3/8 oz.* No. pieces: *3.* Reel seat: *cork and sliding rings (7½'), locking wood (8').* Rec. line: *#5, 6.* Price: *$97.50.*

Model: *4-Piece Travel Rod (3 models).* Length: *8'-8½'.* Weight: *3¼ oz. to 5 oz.* No. pieces: *4.* Reel seat: *locking wood.* Rec. line: *#5, 6, 8.* Price: *$97.50.*

Wright & McGill

THE EAGLE CLAW BRAND of fishing tackle, products of the Wright & McGill Company of Denver, Colorado, has roots that extend back to the renowned Granger bamboo rods. Eagle Claw presently makes rods in graphite and fiberglass, and its complete line, which also includes reels and hooks, centers around products for spinning, casting and trolling, while still offering numerous items for fly-fishing.

Model: *Water Seal (6 models).* Length: *6½'-8½'.* Weight: *n.a.* No. pieces: *2.* Reel seat: *internal-thread locking.* Rec. line: *#4-7.* Price: *$69.*

Model: *Featherlight FLFU225.* Length: *6', 6½', 7'.* Weight: *n.a.* No. pieces: *2.* Reel seat: *external-thread locking.* Rec. line: *#6.* Price: *$27.*

Model: *Trailmaster 4 (4 models).* Length: *6½', 7½'.* Weight: *n.a.* No. pieces: *4.* Reel seat: *fixed double-nut locking.* Rec. line: *#7.* Price: *$44.*

Model: *Trailmaster 6 (3 models).* Length: *6'9".* Weight: *n.a.* No. pieces: *6.* Reel seat: *fixed double-nut locking.* Rec. line: *#7.* Price: *$46-$54.*

Model: *Sweetheart (4 models).* Length: *7½'-9'.* Weight: *n.a.* No. pieces: *2.* Reel seat: *internal-thread locking.* Rec. line: *#7.* Price: *$34.*

Model: *Starfire (3 models).* Length: *7½'-8½'.* Weight: *n.a.* No. pieces: *2.* Reel seat: *internal-thread locking.* Rec. line: *#7.* Price: *$27.*

Model: *Denco Super II (5 models).* Length: *7'-9'.* Weight: *n.a.* No. pieces: *2.* Reel seat: *external-thread locking.* Rec. line: *#6, 7, 9.* Price: *$22.*

Model: *Jerry McKinnis.* Length: *8'.* Weight: *n.a.* No. pieces: *2.* Reel seat: *internal-thread locking.* Rec. line: *#7.* Price: *$30.*

Graphite Rods

Algonquin Fishing Tackle

Model: *Expert Graphite (14 models).* Length: *7½'-10½' (4 models with butt extension).* Weight: *n.a.* No. pieces: *2.* Reel seat: *down-locking metal.* Rec. line: *#5-11.* Price: *n.a.*

Model: *Imperial Graphite (5 models).* Length: *8'-10½' (2 models with butt extension).* Weight: *n.a.* No. pieces: *2.* Reel seat: *down-locking metal.* Rec. line: *#6-9.* Price: *n.a.*

American Import

Model: *L. M. Dickson Premier Graphite (5 models).* Length: *7'-9'.* Weight: *n.a.* No. pieces: *2.* Reel seat: *up-locking cork.* Rec. line: *n.a.* Price: *n.a.*

Angler's World

Model: *Graphite Seven.* Length: *7'.* Weight: *1-7/8 oz.* No. pieces: *2.* Reel seat: *cork with sliding rings and walnut butt cap.* Rec. line: *#4.* Price: *$155.*

Model: *Graphite Eighty-Six.* Length: *8½'.* Weight: *3 oz.* No. pieces: *2.* Reel seat: *up-locking walnut and aluminum with walnut butt cap.* Rec. line: *#7.* Price: *$175.*

Prices (and price ranges) listed in this directory are the manufacturer's suggested retail prices as of late 1977, and they are subject to change without notice. Please consult pp. 233-235 for addresses of manufacturers from whom up-to-date price information may be obtained, or check with your local fly-tackle dealer.

Model: *Graphite Nine.* Length: *9' (plus 2" and 5" removable butt extensions).* Weight: *4 oz.* No. pieces: *2.* Reel seat: *up-locking walnut and aluminum.* Rec. line: *#10.* Price: *$210.*

Berkley & Co.

Model: *Berkley Graphite (5 models).* Length: *7'-9'.* Weight: *n.a.* No. pieces: *n.a.* Reel seat: *n.a.* Rec. line: *#5-9.* Price: *n.a.*

R. W. Bianco

Model: *Bianco Graphite (13 models).* Length: *7'-10' (3 models with fighting butt).* Weight: *n.a.* No. pieces: *2.* Reel seat: *rosewood.* Rec. line: *#4-12.* Price: *$125-$180.*

Browning

Model: *Browning Graphite (3 models).* Length: *8', 8½', 9½'.* Weight: *2½ oz. to 3.3 oz.* No. pieces: *2.* Reel seat: *down-locking metal and cork.* Rec. line: *#5-8.* Price: *$97.50-$99.95.*

Chaplin Tackle Co.

CHAPLIN TACKLE IS LOCATED in Raytown, Missouri, and it specializes in several items of custom tackle for the fly fisherman. Products include custom graphite rods and wood landing nets for trout.

Model: *Chaplin Tackle Graphite Fly Rod.* Length, weight, no. pieces, rec. line: *your specification.* Reel seat: *down-locking wood and metal (your specification of wood).* Price: *$50 and up.*

Lew Childre & Sons

CHILDRE SPECIALIZES IN SPINNING and casting rods and reels, and rod-building components. The Childre/Fuji line of Speed Team products is well known to many anglers, and the company has just recently introduced a graphite fly-rod model to their line of Speed Stick rods. Childre & Sons is located in Foley, Alabama.

Model: *Speed Stick (4 models).* Length: *7'-8½'.* Weight: *n.a.* No. pieces: *2.* Reel seat: *n.a.* Rec. line: *n.a.* Price: *n.a.*

Cortland Line Company

Model: *Black Diamond (7 models).* Length: *7½'-9'.* Weight: *2-1/8 oz. to 3-7/8 oz.* No. pieces: *2.* Reel seat: *down-locking anodized aluminum and wood.* Rec. line: *#4-10.* Price: *$140-$150.*

Daiwa Corp.

Model: *Graphite Series (6 models).* Length: *7½'-8½'.* Weight: *n.a.* No. pieces: *2.* Reel seat: *down-locking anodized aluminum with two locking rings.* Rec. line: *#6-8.* Price: *n.a.*

Doc's Rod Co.

DOC'S ROD COMPANY IS LOCATED in Chicago, Illinois, and its only product is graphite rods. These rods are offered at reasonable prices on a mail-order basis.

Model: *Doc's Rod Graphite (5 models).* Length: *7'-9'.* Weight: *n.a.* No. pieces: *2.* Reel seat: *n.a.* Rec. line: *#4-8.* Price: *$49.99-$69.99.*

Ee-da-how Custom Rods

Model: *Ee-da-how 7'.* Length: *7'.* Weight: *2 oz.* No. pieces: *2.* Reel seat: *down-locking anodized aluminum.* Rec. line: *#3-5.* Price: *$110.*

Model: *Ee-da-how 7½'.* Length: *7½'.* Weight: *2-1/8 oz.* No. pieces: *2.* Reel seat: *down-locking anodized aluminum.* Rec. line: *#3-6.* Price: *$115.*

Model: *Ee-da-how 7'10".* Length: *7'10".* Weight: *2-3/8 oz.* No. pieces: *2.* Reel seat: *down-locking anodized aluminum.* Rec. line: *#4, 5.* Price: *$140.*

Model: *Ee-da-how 8'.* Length: *8'.* Weight: *2-5/8 oz.* No. pieces: *2.* Reel seat: *down-locking anodized aluminum.* Rec. line: *#4-7.* Price: *$120.*

Model: *Ee-da-how 8'3".* Length: *8'3".* Weight: *2-7/8 oz.* No. pieces: *2.* Reel seat: *down-locking anodized aluminum.* Rec. line: *#5.* Price: *$140.*

Model: *Ee-da-how 8½'.* Length: *8½'.* Weight: *3 oz.* No. pieces: *2.* Reel seat: *down-locking anodized aluminum.* Rec. line: *#5-8.* Price: *$130.*

Model: *Ee-da-how 9'.* Length: *9'.* Weight: *3-5/8 oz.* No. pieces: *2.* Reel seat: *down-locking anodized aluminum.* Rec. line: *#6-9.* Price: *$130.*

Model: *Ee-da-how 9½'.* Length: *9½'.* Weight: *4-3/8 oz.* No. pieces: *2.* Reel seat: *down-locking anodized aluminum.* Rec. line: *#6-10.* Price: *$150.*

Model: *Ee-da-how 10'.* Length: *10'.* Weight: *4-3/4 oz.* No. pieces: *2.* Reel seat: *down-locking anodized aluminum.* Rec. line: *#10.* Price: *$155.*

Model: *Ee-da-how 8' Pack Rod.* Length: *8'.* Weight: *2-7/8 oz.* No. pieces: *4.* Reel seat: *down-locking anodized aluminum.* Rec. line: *#6.* Price: *$135.*

Al Ellis Rod Co.

AL ELLIS BEGAN MAKING RODS in 1938, and he has custom built many fly rods for well-known fly fishermen in the United States and abroad. He has also built rods for the Paul H. Young Company, Abercrombie & Fitch and Hank Roberts. His current line includes only graphite models. The company is located in Phoenix, Arizona.

Model: *Limited Edition Stream Dream (4 models).* Length: *7'-8'8".* Weight: *2 oz. to 2½ oz.* No. pieces: *2.* Reel seat: *cork with sliding rings or locking anodized aluminum.* Rec. line: *#4-6.* Price: *$96.50-$125.50.*

Model: *Limited Edition Special Nymph.* Length: *8'8".* Weight: *2¼ oz.* No. pieces: *2.* Reel seat: *cork with sliding rings or locking anodized aluminum.* Rec. line: *#3, 4.* Price: *$125.50.*

Model: *Limited Edition Wet or Dry (3 models).* Length: *7'5"-8'5".* Weight: *2¼ oz. to 3 oz.* No. pieces: *2.* Reel seat: *cork with sliding rings or locking anodized aluminum.* Rec. line: *#5-7.* Price: *$96.50-$110.50.*

Model: *Limited Edition Salmon, Bass, Steelhead (6 models).* Length: *8'5"-11'.* Weight: *3 oz. to 4 oz.* No. pieces: *2.* Reel seat: *cork with sliding rings or locking anodized aluminum.* Rec. line: *#9-12.* Price: *$110.50-$115.50.*

Model: *Limited Edition Saltwater Power (5 models).* Length: *9'-11'.* Weight: *3½ oz. to 4 oz.* No. pieces: *2.* Reel seat: *cork with sliding rings or locking anodized aluminum.* Rec. line: *#8-12.* Price: *$125.50-$151.50.*

Model: *Limited Edition Pack Rods (3 models).* Length: *7'5"-8'8".* Weight: *2 oz. to 2½ oz.* No. pieces: *4.* Reel seat: *cork with sliding rings or locking anodized aluminum.* Rec. line: *#3-6.* Price: *$110.50-$125.50.*

Model: *Very Limited Edition Dry Fly & Nymph (3 models).* Length: *8'-8'10".* Weight: *n.a.* No. pieces: *2.* Reel seat: *your choice: locking cork, cork with nickel-silver sliding rings, locking rosewood, walnut or ebony, aluminum with hood and sliding ring, cork with brass hood and brass sliding ring.* Rec. line: *#4, 5.* Price: *$150-$165.*

Model: *Very Limited Edition Wet or Dry (4 models).* Length: *8'4"-9'3".* Weight: *n.a.* No. pieces: *2.* Reel seat: *your choice: locking cork, cork with nickel-silver sliding rings, locking rosewood, walnut or ebony, aluminum with hood and sliding ring, cork with brass hood and brass sliding ring.* Rec. line: *#6, 7.* Price: *$150-$165.*

Model: *Very Limited Edition Wet Fly & Streamer.* Length: *8'9".* Weight: *n.a.* No. pieces: *2.* Reel seat: *your choice: locking cork, cork with nickel-silver sliding rings, locking rosewood, walnut or ebony, aluminum with hood and sliding ring, cork with brass hood and brass sliding ring.* Rec. line: *#8.* Price: *$165.*

Model: *Very Limited Edition Salmon & Steelhead (2 models).* Length: *9'4", 9'5".* Weight: *n.a.* No. pieces: *2.* Reel seat: *your choice: locking cork, cork with nickel-silver sliding rings, locking rosewood, walnut or ebony, aluminum with hood and sliding ring, cork with brass hood and sliding ring.* Rec. line: *#9, 10.* Price: *$165.*

Model: *Very Limited Edition Saltwater Power (4 models).* Length: *8'7"-9'5".* Weight: *n.a.* No. pieces: *2.* Reel seat: *your choice: locking cork, cork with nickel-silver sliding rings, locking rosewood, walnut or ebony, aluminum with hood and sliding ring, cork with brass hood and brass sliding ring.* Rec. line: *#10, 11.* Price: *$165.*

Fenwick

Model: *HMG Graphite Fly Rod (20 models).* Length: *6'3"-14' (6 models have removable 6" butt extension, 1 model has fixed 2" butt extension).* Weight: *1-7/8 oz. to 11-5/8 oz.* No. pieces: *2, 3 (models 10½' and over).* Reel seat: *up-locking cork (#4-8 line rods), locking anodized aluminum with double rings (#9-12 line rods).* Rec. line: *#4-12.* Price: *$119-$317.*

Model: *Voyageur.* Length: *8'.* Weight: *3 oz.* No. pieces: *4.* Reel seat: *down-locking anodized aluminum.* Rec. line: *#6.* Price: *n.a.*

Model: *Voyageur Spin-Fly.* Length: *7'.* Weight: *4 oz.* No. pieces: *4.* Reel seat: *reversible locking anodized aluminum.* Rec. line: *#6.* Price: *n.a.*

J. Kennedy Fisher

Model: *20290, 20296.* Length: *7½', 8'.* Weight: *n.a.* No. pieces: *2.* Reel seat: *locking aluminum.* Rec. line: *#3, 4.* Price: *$99.95.*

Prices (and price ranges) listed in this directory are the manufacturer's suggested retail prices as of late 1977, and they are subject to change without notice. Please consult pp. 233-235 for addresses of manufacturers from whom up-to-date price information may be obtained, or check with your local fly-tackle dealer.

Model: *20390, 20396, 20302, 20308.* Length: *7½', 8', 8½', 9'.* Weight: *n.a.* No. pieces: *2.* Reel seat: *locking aluminum.* Rec. line: *#4, 5.* Price: *$99.95.*

Model: *20490, 20496, 20402, 20408.* Length: *7½', 8', 8½', 9'.* Weight: *n.a.* No. pieces: *2.* Reel seat: *locking aluminum.* Rec. line: *#5, 6.* Price: *$99.95.*

Model: *20596, 20502, 20508.* Length: *8', 8½', 9'.* Weight: *n.a.* No. pieces: *2.* Reel seat: *locking aluminum.* Rec. line: *#6, 7.* Price: *$99.95.*

Model: *20696, 20602, 20608.* Length: *8', 8½', 9'.* Weight: *n.a.* No. pieces: *2.* Reel seat: *locking aluminum.* Rec. line: *#7, 8.* Price: *$99.95.*

Model: *21008.* Length: *9'.* Weight: *n.a.* No. pieces: *2.* Reel seat: *locking aluminum.* Rec. line: *#9, 10.* Price: *$99.95.*

Model: *21008FB.* Length: *9' (plus 6" removable butt extension).* Weight: *n.a.* No. pieces: *2.* Reel seat: *locking aluminum.* Rec. line: *#9, 10.* Price: *$109.95.*

Model: *21014FB, 21020FB, 21026FB.* Length: *9½', 10', 10½' (plus 6" removable butt extension).* Weight: *n.a.* No. pieces: *2.* Reel seat: *locking aluminum.* Rec. line: *#9, 10.* Price: *$133.95.*

Model: *40396.* Length: *8'.* Weight: *n.a.* No. pieces: *4.* Reel seat: *locking aluminum.* Rec. line: *#4, 5.* Price: *$124.95.*

Model: *40496.* Length: *8'.* Weight: *n.a.* No. pieces: *4.* Reel seat: *locking aluminum.* Rec. line: *#5, 6.* Price: *$124.95.*

Model: *40596.* Length: *8'.* Weight: *n.a.* No. pieces: *4.* Reel seat: *locking aluminum.* Rec. line: *#6, 7.* Price: *$124.95.*

Model: *21308FB.* Length: *9' (plus 2" removable butt extension).* Weight: *n.a.* No. pieces: *2.* Reel seat: *locking aluminum.* Rec. line: *#12, 13.* Price: *$116.95.*

Model: *21508FB.* Length: *9' (plus 2" removable butt extension).* Weight: *n.a.* No. pieces: *2.* Reel seat: *locking aluminum.* Rec. line: *#13, 14.* Price: *$124.95.*

Model: *21408T Super Strong Butt.* Length: *9' (plus 2" removable butt extension).* Weight: *n.a.* No. pieces: *2.* Reel seat: *locking aluminum.* Rec. line: *#12, 13.* Price: *$134.95.*

Model: *40590 Spin-Fly.* Length: *7½'.* Weight: *n.a.* No. pieces: *4.* Reel seat: *cork with sliding rings.* Rec. line: *#6, 7.* Price: *$124.95.*

Fly Fisherman's Bookcase and Tackle Service

Model: *FFB Custom Graphite.* Length, weight, no. pieces, reel seat, rec. line: *your specification.* Price: *n.a.*

The Garcia Corp.

Model: *Garcia 100 Plus (3 models).* Length: *7½'-8½'.* Weight: *2-7/8 oz. to 4 oz.* No. pieces: *2.* Reel seat: *down-locking metal.* Rec. line: *#4-8.* Price: *$78.*

James Heddon's Sons

Model: *Graphite 8024, 8026.* Length: *7½', 8'.* Weight: *n.a.* No. pieces: *2.* Reel seat: *down-locking metal.* Rec. line: *#5-7.* Price: *$65.*

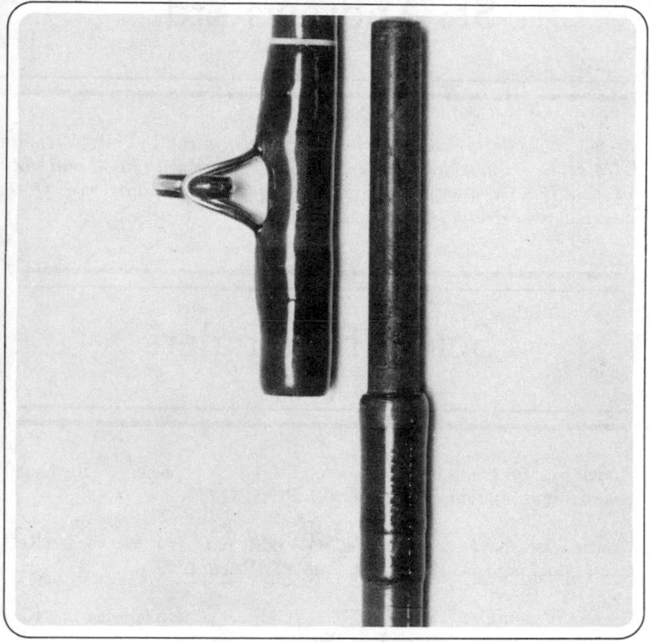

An example of the internal ferrule used in the construction of many graphite rods. Photo courtesy of Scott PowR-Ply.

Herter's Inc.

Model: *RB6G80.* Length: *8'.* Weight: *3 oz.* No. pieces: *2.* Reel seat: *up-locking metal and cork.* Rec. line: *#7.* Price: *$59.97.*

Lamiglas Inc.

Model: *Graphite Spin-Fly Backpacker Rod.* Length: *7'.* Weight: *3½ oz.* No. pieces: *4.* Reel seat: *up-locking split cork and metal plus sliding rings.* Rec. line: *#5.* Price: *$160.*

Model: *Graphite 8½', 9' (8 models).* Length: *8½', 9' (plus butt extension).* Weight: *3½ oz. to 4¼ oz.* No. pieces: *2.* Reel seat: *up-locking split cork and metal.* Rec. line: *#5-9.* Price: *$137-$144.*

Model: *Graphite 9½', 10', 10½'.* Length: *9½', 10', 10½' (plus butt extension).* Weight: *4-9/16 oz. to 5-7/8 oz.* No. pieces: *2.* Reel seat: *up-locking split cork and metal.* Rec. line: *#8, 9.* Price: *$152-$165.*

Model: *Tarpon Fly Rod (2 models).* Length: *9' (plus 3" butt extension).* Weight: *6½ oz., 6-3/4 oz.* No. pieces: *2.* Reel seat: *up-locking split cork and metal.* Rec. line: *#11-13.* Price: *$165, $170.*

H. L. Leonard Rod Inc.

Model: *Golden Shadow Lightweight Line (6 models).* Length: *5'-8'.* Weight: *3/4 oz. to 2¼ oz.* No. pieces: *2 (5' model is one pc.).* Reel seat: *n.a.* Rec. line: *#3, 4.* Price: *$165-$195.*

Model: *Golden Shadow Medium Weight Line (9 models).* Length: *7½'-9'.* Weight: *2 oz. to 3-1/8 oz.* No. pieces: *2.* Reel seat: *n.a.* Rec. line: *#5-7.* Price: *$195.*

Model: *Golden Shadow Heavy Weight Line (4 models).* Length: *8½'-10'.* Weight: *3½ oz. to 4-3/4 oz.* No. pieces: *2 (10' model is 3 pc.).* Reel seat: *n.a.* Rec. line: *#8-10.* Price: *$220-$240.*

O. L. M. International Corp.

Model: *9000 Series (5 models).* Length: *7'-9'.* Weight: *n.a.* No. pieces: *2.* Reel seat: *down-locking anodized aluminum.* Rec. line: *#6-8, 10.* Price: *n.a.*

The Orvis Co.

Model: *5-by-5 Graphite.* Length: *5'.* Weight: *1-1/8 oz.* No. pieces: *1.* Reel seat: *all cork with sliding rings.* Rec. line: *#5.* Price: *$135.*

Model: *Graphite Flea.* Length: *6½'.* Weight: *1-3/8 oz.* No. pieces: *2.* Reel seat: *cork with sliding rings.* Rec. line: *#4.* Price: *$155.*

Model: *Rocky Mountain Graphite.* Length: *6½'.* Weight: *2 oz.* No. pieces: *3.* Reel seat: *locking cork.* Rec. line: *#6.* Price: *$165.*

Model: *Graphite Spin-Fly (2 models).* Length: *7', 8½'.* Weight: *2 oz., 2-3/4 oz.* No. pieces: *2.* Reel seat: *cork with sliding rings.* Rec. line: *#5, 8.* Price: *$155, $170.*

Model: *Graphite Otter (2 models).* Length: *7'.* Weight: *1-5/8 oz., 2 oz.* No. pieces: *2.* Reel seat: *cork with sliding rings.* Rec. line: *#5.* Price: *$155.*

Model: *Graphite II (5 models).* Length: *7'-8½'.* Weight: *2-5/8 oz.-3-1/8 oz.* No. pieces: *2.* Reel seat: *down-locking black metal.* Rec. line: *#5-8.* Price: *$125-$140.*

Model: *Graphite Trout (4 models).* Length: *7½', 8'.* Weight: *1-3/4 oz. to 2¼ oz.* No. pieces: *2.* Reel seat: *cork with sliding rings, cork locking.* Rec. line: *#6.* Price: *$155.*

Model: *Graphite Far-and-Fine.* Length: *7'9".* Weight: *2-1/8 oz.* No. pieces: *2.* Reel seat: *locking cork.* Rec. line: *#5.* Price: *$155.*

Model: *Graphite All Rounder.* Length: *8'3".* Weight: *2½ oz.* No. pieces: *2.* Reel seat: *locking cork.* Rec. line: *#7.* Price: *$170.*

Model: *Graphite Limestone Special.* Length: *8½'.* Weight: *2-5/8 oz.* No. pieces: *2.* Reel seat: *locking cork.* Rec. line: *#6.* Price: *$170.*

Model: *Graphite Powerhouse.* Length: *8½'.* Weight: *2-7/8 oz.* No. pieces: *2.* Reel seat: *down-locking walnut.* Rec. line: *#8.* Price: *$170.*

Model: *Graphite Shooting Star (3 models).* Length: *8½', 9', 9½' (plus 2" or 6" butt extension).* Weight: *4 oz., 4¼ oz., 4½ oz.* No. pieces: *2.* Reel seat: *down-locking metal.* Rec. line: *#8, 9, 10.* Price: *$190.*

Model: *Graphite S/S/S.* Length: *8'9" (plus 2" or 6" butt extension).* Weight: *4 oz.* No. pieces: *2.* Reel seat: *down-locking metal.* Rec. line: *#10* Price: *$185.*

Model: *9-by-9 Graphite.* Length: *9'.* Weight: *3-1/8 oz.* No. pieces: *2.* Reel seat: *down-locking walnut.* Rec. line: *#9.* Price: *$170.*

Model: *Graphite Tarpon.* Length: *9½' (plus 2" butt extension).* Weight: *6-1/8 oz.* No. pieces: *2.* Reel seat: *down-locking chrome-plated brass.* Rec. line: *#11.* Price: *$195.*

Model: *Graphite Spring Creek.* Length: *9'3".* Weight: *2-3/4 oz.* No. pieces: *2.* Reel seat: *down-locking cork.* Rec. line: *#5.* Price: *$170.*

Model: *Graphite Presentation.* Length: *9½'.* Weight: *3-5/8 oz.* No. pieces: *2.* Reel seat: *down-locking walnut.* Rec. line: *#8.* Price: *$170.*

Model: *Graphite Ultimate.* Length: *10½'.* Weight: *3-7/8 oz.* No. pieces: *3.* Reel seat: *down-locking walnut.* Rec. line: *#6.* Price: *$180.*

Model: *Graphite Salmon (2 models).* Length: *10' (plus 2" or 6" butt extension).* Weight: *4-5/8 oz., 4-7/8 oz.* No. pieces: *2, 3.* Reel seat: *down-locking metal.* Rec. line: *#9, 10.* Price: *$195, $205.*

Model: *Graphite Two-Handed Salmon.* Length: *13½'.* Weight: *9¼ oz.* No. pieces: *3.* Reel seat: *down-locking cork.* Rec. line: *#10.* Price: *$250.*

Pflueger

Model: *Pflueger Graphite (4 models).* Length: *7½ '-9'.* Weight: *n.a.* No. pieces: *2.* Reel seat: *cork with sliding rings.* Rec. line: *n.a.* Price: *n.a.*

Model: *1480, 1486 (graphite/fiberglass).* Length: *8', 8½'.* Weight: *n.a.* No. pieces: *2.* Reel seat: *down-locking metal.* Rec. line: *n.a.* Price: *n.a.*

Powell Rod Co.

Model: *Signature.* Length: *6'-10'.* Weight: *n.a.* No. pieces: *your specification.* Reel seat: *up-locking machined anodized aluminum or up-locking wood (your choice of wood).* Rec. line: *your specification.* Price: *$90 (models up to but not including 9½' length, $130 with extra tip), $100 (models 9½' and over, $140 with extra tip), add $10 for wood reel seat.*

Model: *Silver Signature.* Length: *6'-10'.* Weight: *n.a.* No. pieces: *your specification.* Reel seat: *up-locking machined aluminum or up-locking wood.* Rec. line: *your specification.* Price: *$115 (models up to but not including 9½' length, $160 with extra tip), $125 (models 9½' and over, $170 with extra tip), add $10 for wood reel seat.*

Prices (and price ranges) listed in this directory are the manufacturer's suggested retail prices as of late 1977, and they are subject to change without notice. Please consult pp. 233-235 for addresses of manufacturers from whom up-to-date price information may be obtained, or check with your local fly-tackle dealer.

St. Andrews Ltd.

Model: *St. Andrews Ltd. Graphite (5 models).* Length: *7'-9'.* Weight: *1-1/8 oz. to 3½ oz.* No. pieces: *2.* Reel seat: *cork with hood and sliding ring (7', 7½' models), down-locking anodized aluminum (8'-9' models).* Rec. line: *#4-10.* Price: *n.a.*

Scientific Anglers

Model: *System G4.* Length: *8'.* Weight: *n.a.* No. pieces: *2.* Reel seat: *up-locking rosewood.* Rec. line: *#4.* Price: *$225.*

Model: *System G5.* Length: *8'4".* Weight: *n.a.* No. pieces: *2.* Reel seat: *up-locking rosewood.* Rec. line: *#5.* Price: *$225.*

Model: *System G6.* Length: *8'7".* Weight: *n.a.* No. pieces: *2.* Reel seat: *up-locking rosewood.* Rec. line: *#6.* Price: *$225.*

Model: *System G7.* Length: *8'8".* Weight: *n.a.* No. pieces: *2.* Reel seat: *up-locking rosewood.* Rec. line: *#7.* Price: *$225.*

Model: *System G8.* Length: *8'9" (plus optional 2" or 5" butt extension).* Weight: *n.a.* No. pieces: *2.* Reel seat: *n.a.* Rec. line: *#8.* Price: *$225, $230 (with butt extension).*

Model: *System G9.* Length: *9'4" (plus optional 2" or 5" butt extension).* Weight: *n.a.* No. pieces: *2.* Reel seat: *n.a.* Rec. line: *#9.* Price: *$225, $230 (with butt extension).*

Model: *System G10.* Length: *9'5" (plus optional 2" or 5" butt extension).* Weight: *n.a.* No. pieces: *2.* Reel seat: *n.a.* Rec. line: *#10.* Price: *$225, $230 (with butt extension).*

Scott PowR-Ply Co.

Model: *G85-4.* Length: *8½'.* Weight: *2 oz.* No. pieces: *2.* Reel seat *cork with hood and sliding ring.* Rec. line: *#4.* Price: *$165 and up.*

Model: *G90-4.* Length: *9'.* Weight: *2¼ oz.* No. pieces: *2.* Reel seat *cork with hood and sliding ring.* Rec. line: *#4.* Price: *$165 and up.*

Model: *G85-5.* Length: *8½'.* Weight: *2-1/8 oz.* No. pieces: *2.* Ree seat: *cork with hood and sliding ring.* Rec. line: *#5.* Price: *$165 and up.*

Model: *G95-8.* Length: *9½'.* Weight: *3½ oz.* No. pieces: *2.* Reel sea *up-locking metal and cork.* Rec. line: *#8.* Price: *$165 and up.*

Model: *G95-9*. Length: *9½'*. Weight: *3-7/8 oz*. No. pieces: *2*. Reel seat: *up-locking metal and cork*. Rec. line: *#9*. Price: *$165 and up*.

Model: *G95-10*. Length: *9½' (plus 1½" fixed fighting butt)*. Weight: *4-3/4 oz*. No. pieces: *2*. Reel seat: *up-locking metal*. Rec. line: *#10*. Price: *$165 and up*.

Model: *G95-12*. Length: *9½' (plus 1½" fixed fighting butt)*. Weight: *5 oz*. No. pieces: *2*. Reel seat: *up-locking metal*. Rec. line: *#12*. Price: *$165 and up*.

Model: *G90-7*. Length: *9'*. Weight: *3¼ oz*. No. pieces: *2*. Reel seat: *split-cork and metal*. Rec. line: *#7*. Price: *$165 and up*.

Model: *Long Rod Series*. Length: *10'*. Weight: *n.a.* No. pieces: *2*. Reel seat: *custom designed*. Rec. line: *#5-9*. Price: *$165 and up*.

Model: *Long Rod Series (2 models)*. Length: *11', 12'*. Weight: *n.a.* No. pieces: *3*. Reel seat: *custom designed*. Rec. line: *#5-9*. Price: *$165 and up*.

Shakespeare Company

Model: *FY1000 7½'*. Length: *7½'*. Weight: *2½ oz*. No. pieces: *2*. Reel seat: *down-locking black anodized aluminum*. Rec. line: *#5*. Price: *n.a.*

Model: *FY1000 8'*. Length: *8'*. Weight: *2.8 oz*. No. pieces: *2*. Reel seat: *down-locking black anodized aluminum*. Rec. line: *#6*. Price: *n.a.*

Model: *FY1001 8'*. Length: *8'*. Weight: *3.2 oz*. No. pieces: *2*. Reel seat: *down-locking black anodized aluminum*. Rec. line: *#7*. Price: *n.a.*

Model: *FY1000 8½'*. Length: *8½'*. Weight: *4 oz*. No. pieces: *2*. Reel seat: *down-locking black anodized aluminum with two locking rings*. Rec. line: *#8*. Price: *n.a.*

Model: *FY1000 9'*. Length: *9' (2½" butt extension avail.)*. Weight: *4.2 oz*. No. pieces: *2*. Reel seat: *down-locking black anodized aluminum with two locking rings*. Rec. line: *#9*. Price: *n.a.*

Model: *FY1001 9'*. Length: *9' (plus 2½" butt extension)*. Weight: *4.8 oz*. No. pieces: *2*. Reel seat: *down-locking black anodized aluminum with two locking rings*. Rec. line: *#10*. Price: *n.a.*

Skyline Industries

SKYLINE INDUSTRIES MANUFACTURES graphite fishing rods and blanks. Their line includes eight models, of which one is a fly-rod model. Skyline is located in Fort Worth, Texas.

Model: *Skyline Graphite Fly Rod (3 models)*. Length: *8'*. Weight: *n.a.* No. pieces: *2*. Reel seat: *down-locking anodized aluminum with two locking rings*. Rec. line: *#5-8*. Price: *n.a.*

Thomas & Thomas

THOMAS & THOMAS OF Turner's Falls, Massachusetts, began as a part-time business in 1969, and until 1975 their only product was bamboo fly rods. Today the company offers graphite and fiberglass fly rods, as well as the bamboo models; they also handle fly reels, angling accessories and fly-tying tools. The emphasis remains on high-quality split-cane rods, with a limited production of about 250 bamboo rods a year.

Model: *Special Dry Fly*. Length: *8'*. Weight: *2-3/8 oz*. No. pieces: *2*. Reel seat: *walnut with hood and sliding ring*. Rec. line: *#4, 4½, 5*. Price: *$225*.

Model: *Trout (5 models)*. Length: *7'-9'*. Weight: *n.a.* No. pieces: *2*. Reel seat: *n.a.* Rec. line: *#4-6*. Price: *$165-$185*.

Model: *Salmon (5 models)*. Length: *8½'-10½'*. Weight: *n.a.* No. pieces: *2*. Reel seat: *n.a.* Rec. line: *#7-11*. Price: *$190-$200*.

Timberline Rods

Model: *Timberline Graphite 8½', 9' (4 models)*. Length: *8½', 9'*. Weight: *n.a.* No. pieces: *2*. Reel seat: *locking rosewood*. Rec. line: *#6-8*. Price: *$150-$153*.

Model: *Timberline Graphite 9'*. Length: *9' (plus 3" removable butt extension)*. Weight: *n.a.* Reel seat: *locking metal*. No. pieces: *2*. Rec. line: *#9, 10*. Price: *$160*.

Model: *Timberline Graphite Pack Rod (2 models)*. Length: *8'*. Weight: *n.a.* No. pieces: *4*. Reel seat: *cork with sliding rings*. Rec. line: *#4-7*. Price: *$145*.

Model: *Timberline Graphite Spin-Fly Pack Rod*. Length: *7½'*. Weight: *n.a.* No. pieces: *4*. Reel seat: *cork with sliding rings*. Rec. line: *#6, 7*. Price: *$125*.

Model: *Ultra-light Graphite (2 models)*. Length: *7½', 8'*. Weight: *n.a.* No. pieces: *2*. Reel seat: *cork with hood and sliding ring*. Rec. line: *#4, 5*. Price: *$135-$138*.

Model: *Timberline Graphite 8½', 9'*. Length: *8½', 9'*. Weight: *n.a.* No. pieces: *2*. Reel seat: *locking cork*. Rec. line: *#4, 5*. Price: *$145-$148*.

Model: *Timberline Lightweight Graphite Trout Rod (3 models)*. Length: *7½'-8½'*. Weight: *n.a.* No. pieces: *2*. Reel seat: *locking cork*. Rec. line: *#5, 6*. Price: *$140-$145*.

Uslan Rod Company

Model: *Uslan Graphite (10 models)*. Length: *7'11"-9'4" (3 models with 2" or 5" butt extension)*. Weight: *n.a.* No. pieces: *2*. Reel seat: *locking cork or rosewood (#4-10 line rods), locking anodized metal (#8-10 line rods with butt extension)*. Rec. line: *#4-10*. Price: *$195, $200 (with butt extension)*.

Wanigas Rod Co.

Model: *Wanigas Manistee (10 models)*. Length: *7'-9' (9' models with butt extension)*. Weight: *n.a.* No. pieces: *2*. Reel seat: *locking cork*. Rec. line: *#4-10*. Price: *$100-$125*.

Weir & Son

WEIR & SON WAS FOUNDED in 1925, and the company has produced fine split-bamboo rods for three generations. Weir & Son has recently expanded its line to include a graphite series of rods. The only other products of the firm are custom-tied Atlantic salmon flies. Weir & Son is located in Los Gatos, California.

Model: *Black Hawk (14 models).* Length: *7½'-10'.* Weight: *2-3/4 oz.-6¼ oz.* No. pieces: *2.* Reel seat: *locking aluminium and wood.* Rec. line: *#3-10.* Price: *$175 (down-locking reel seat), $185 (up-locking reel seat).*

R. L. Winston Rod Co.

Model: *Steelhead, Atlantic Salmon, Bass and Light Saltwater Rod (4 models).* Length: *9', 10' (plus optional removable butt extension).* Weight: *3½ oz. to 4-3/8 oz.* No. pieces: *2.* Reel seat: *locking walnut or machined bakelite.* Rec. line: *WF8-WF10, ST9-ST11.* Price: *$195, $225 (10', WF10 rod).*

Model: *Light Trout Rod (7 models).* Length: *7½'-9'.* Weight: *1-7/8 oz. to 2-3/4 oz.* No. pieces: *2.* Reel seat: *all cork with German-silver hood and sliding ring or locking walnut.* Rec. line: *#4, 5.* Price: *$175.*

Model: *Trout Rod (5 models).* Length: *8'-9'.* Weight: *2½ oz. to 3¼ oz.* No. pieces: *2.* Reel seat: *locking walnut.* Rec. line: *#6, 7.* Price: *$185.*

Model: *Saltwater Rod.* Length: *9' (plus optional removable butt extension).* Weight: *4¼ oz.* No. pieces: *2.* Reel seat: *locking anodized aluminum.* Rec. line: *WF11.* Price: *$200.*

Wright & McGill

Model: *Blue Diamond (10 models).* Length: *7'-9'.* Weight: *n.a.* No. pieces: *2.* Reel seat: *internal-thread locking.* Rec. line: *#4-10.* Price: *$155-$161.*

Bamboo Rods

Angler's World

Model: *Impercane 99.* Length: *8'3".* Weight: *4½ oz.* No. pieces: *2.* Reel seat: *down-locking cork and metal.* Rec. line: *#5, 6.* Price: *$210 (plus $60 for extra tip).*

Model: *Impercane 101.* Length: *8'5".* Weight: *4¼ oz.* No. pieces: *2.* Reel seat: *down-locking cork and metal.* Rec. line: *#5, 6.* Price: *$225 (plus $60 for extra tip).*

Model: *Impercane 104.* Length: *8'8".* Weight: *5 oz.* No. pieces: *2.* Reel seat: *down-locking cork and metal.* Rec. line: *#5, 6.* Price: *$210 (plus $60 for extra tip).*

Model: *Impercane 84.* Length: *7'.* Weight: *3¼ oz.* No. pieces: *2.* Reel seat: *cork with hood and sliding ring.* Rec. line: *#5.* Price: *$185 (plus $60 for extra tip).*

Prices (and price ranges) listed in this directory are the manufacturer's suggested retail prices as of late 1977, and they are subject to change without notice. Please consult pp. 233-235 for addresses of manufacturers from whom up-to-date price information may be obtained, or check with your local fly-tackle dealer.

Model: *Impercane 90.* Length: *7½ '.* Weight: *4 oz.* No. pieces: *2.* Reel seat: *cork with hood and sliding ring.* Rec. line: *#5.* Price: *$185 (plus $60 for extra tip).*

Model: *Impercane Midge 70.* Length: *5'10".* Weight: *1-5/8 oz.* No. pieces: *1.* Reel seat: *cork with hood and sliding ring.* Rec. line: *#6.* Price: *$165 (plus $60 for extra tip).*

Model: *Impercane Midge 72.* Length: *6'.* Weight: *1-7/8 oz.* No. pieces: *2.* Reel seat: *cork with hood and sliding ring.* Rec. line: *#6.* Price: *$165 (plus $60 for extra tip).*

Model: *Deluxe Sixty Six.* Length: *6½'.* Weight: *2-1/8 oz.* No. pieces: *2 (plus extra tip).* Reel seat: *wood with hood and down-sliding ring.* Rec. line: *DT4.* Price: *$550.*

Model: *Deluxe Seven.* Length: *7'.* Weight: *2½ oz.* No. pieces: *2 (plus extra tip).* Reel seat: *wood with hood and down-sliding ring.* Rec. line: *#5.* Price: *$550.*

Model: *Deluxe Eight.* Length: *8'.* Weight: *4 oz.* No. pieces: *2 (plus extra tip).* Reel seat: *wood with hood and down-sliding ring.* Rec. line: *#6.* Price: *$575.*

Model: *Deluxe Salmo Salar Twelve (two-handed).* Length: *12'.* Weight: *15 oz.* No. pieces: *3 (plus extra tip).* Reel seat: *down-locking metal and wood.* Rec. line: *DT9, 10.* Price: *$850.*

Model: *Salmo Supreme Nine.* Length: *9' (plus 2" and 5" removable butt extensions).* Weight: *6¼ oz.* No. pieces: *3 (plus extra tip).* Reel seat: *up-locking aluminum and walnut.* Rec. line: *DT9, WF9.* Price: *$695.*

Model: *Impercane Twelve-Six (two-handed).* Length: *12½'.* Weight: *16 oz.* No. pieces: *3 (plus extra tip).* Reel seat: *cork with down-sliding ring.* Rec. line: *#9.* Price: *$495.*

Model: *Impercane Nine.* Length: *9' (plus removable 6" butt extension).* Weight: *6-3/4 oz.* No. pieces: *2.* Reel seat: *down-locking metal.* Rec. line: *#7, 8.* Price: *$245 ($370 with extra tip).*

Dennis Bailey

DENNIS BAILEY, who founded the Coventry and Birmingham Schools of Casting, located in Coventry, England, is well known in that country as an angler, rodmaker and a pioneer in angling education. He has invented equipment and techniques to allow disabled persons to fish, and proceeds from his rodmaking are used to finance this work. Bailey's background includes experience in mechanical engineering, metallurgy and research and development in the application of glass and graphite reinforced plastics—although as a rodmaker he works exclusively in cane. Bailey completely handcrafts his rods himself, and they are distributed in the United States by the Bamboo Rod in Weston, Vermont.

Model: *Dennis Bailey Custom Fly Rod (6 models).* Length: *7'-9½' (other lengths avail. on request).* Weight: *3½ oz. to 6 oz.* No. pieces: *2 (plus extra tip).* Reel seat: *up-locking metal and oak with hexagonal locking nut.* Rec. line: *your choice.* Price: *$700.*

The Carlson Rod Co.

THE CARLSON ROD COMPANY, founded in 1957 and located in Greenville, New Hampshire, acquired the Thomas Rod Company of Bangor, Maine, in 1958. Sam Carlson notes that he planned to complement the Thomas line with his own rods of four-strip bamboo construction. Increased demand for the "Carlson 4," however, and the limited production capacity of the Carlson shop (Sam makes the rods and his wife does the rod winding) allowed time only for the production of the Carlson four-strip rods, which remain the primary product of the company. Sam Carlson began making rods with E. W. Edwards & Sons in Mt. Carmel, Connecticut, in 1920.

Model: *Two-piece Trout Rods (4-strip construction, 3 models).* Length: *7', 7½', 8'.* Weight: *n.a.* No. pieces: *2 (plus extra tip).* Reel seat: *your specification: all cork with sliding ring and butt cap, all cork up-sliding, walnut down-locking, walnut up-locking, walnut and down-sliding ring.* Rec. line: *#4-9.* Price: *$295.*

Model: *Three-Piece Trout Rod (4-strip construction, 4 models).* Length: *7½', 8', 8½', 9'.* Weight: *n.a.* No. pieces: *3 (plus extra tip).* Reel seat: *your specification: all cork with sliding ring and butt cap, all cork up-sliding, walnut down-locking, walnut up-locking, walnut and down-sliding ring.* Rec. line: *#4-9.* Price: *$315.*

Model: *Three-Piece Salmon Rod (4-strip construction, 2 models).* Length: *8½', 9' (plus butt extension).* Weight: *n.a.* No. pieces: *3 (plus extra tip).* Reel seat: *your specification: walnut up-locking, down-locking, or sliding ring.* Rec. line: *n.a.* Price: *$340.*

Constable

CONSTABLE SPLIT-BAMBOO fly rods are made at the Constable Rod Works in Bromley, England, by Clifford Constable. The rods are handcrafted, and most of the machinery and fittings are produced by Constable Rod Works as well. The U.S. agent for these rods and blanks is Anglersmail of Cleveland, Ohio, a firm that has worked with Constable to design the American-oriented series of rods it handles.

Model: *R. H. Woods 6'9".* Length: *6'9".* Weight: *2-7/8 oz.* No. pieces: *2.* Reel seat: *cork with hood and sliding ring.* Rec. line: *DT4F.* Price: *$109.50.*

Model: *R. H. Woods 6'9" Classic.* Length: *6'9".* Weight: *2-7/8 oz.* No. pieces: *2 (plus extra tip).* Reel seat: *cork with hood and sliding ring.* Rec. line: *DT4F.* Price: *$139.50.*

Model: *R. H. Woods 7½ '.* Length: *7½ '.* Weight: *3-7/8 oz.* No. pieces: *2.* Reel seat: *cork with hood and sliding ring.* Rec. line: *DT5F.* Price: *$109.50.*

Model: *R. H. Woods 7½ ' Classic.* Length: *7½ '.* Weight: *3-7/8 oz.* No. pieces: *2 (plus extra tip).* Reel seat: *cork with hood and sliding ring.* Rec. line: *DT5F.* Price: *$139.50.*

Model: *R. H. Woods Dual.* Length: *6' or 6'9".* Weight: *n.a.* No. pieces: *2 (plus interchangeable butt section).* Reel seat: *cork with hood and sliding ring.* Rec. line: *DT4F (6'9" model), DT3½ (6' model).* Price: *$129.50 (one tip), $169.50 (extra tip).*

Model: *R. H. Woods 82.* Length: *8'2".* Weight: *4½ oz.* No. pieces: *2 (plus extra tip).* Reel seat: *cork with hood and sliding ring.* Rec. line: *#5, 6.* Price: *$114.50 (one tip), $144.50 (extra tip).*

Model: *Dart.* Length: *5'9".* Weight: *2½ oz.* No. pieces: *2.* Reel seat: *cork with sliding rings.* Rec. line: *#4, 4½, 5.* Price: *$99.50.*

Model: *Empress.* Length: *8'.* Weight: *3-5/8 oz.* No. pieces: *2.* Reel seat: *cork with hood and sliding ring.* Rec. line: *DT4F, DT4½ F.* Price: *$109.50 (one tip), $139.50 (extra tip).*

Hardy Brothers

FOR OVER A HUNDRED YEARS the firm of Hardy Brothers, Alnwick, England, has been manufacturing fishing tackle. The reputation of this company is worldwide, and it is synonomous with top-quality fly-fishing tackle. Hardy produces a full range of tackle for the fly fisherman, and the name is well known to American anglers for their fly reels, rods and angling accessories. Harrington and Richardson Inc., Gardner, Massachusetts, is the exclusive U.S. distributor of Hardy products.

Model: *Palakona Cane Fly Rod (7 models).* Length: *6'-8'9".* Weight: *n.a.* No. pieces: *2 (plus extra tip).* Reel seat: *n.a.* Rec. line: *#5-9.* Price: *$240-$275.*

Herter's Inc.

Model: *St. Albans.* Length: *8'.* Weight: *4-3/4 oz.* No. pieces: *2.* Reel seat: *down-locking metal.* Rec. line: *#5, 6.* Price: *$72.97 (plus $23.47 per extra tip).*

Model: *St. Albans.* Length: *9'.* Weight: *7 oz.* No. pieces: *3.* Reel seat: *down-locking metal.* Rec. line: *#7.* Price: *$79.97 (plus $23.47 per extra tip).*

Model: *Deluxe Impregnated.* Length: *8'.* Weight: *5½ oz.* No. pieces: *3.* Reel seat: *down-locking metal.* Rec. line: *#5, 6.* Price: *$14.97 (plus $4.69 per extra tip).*

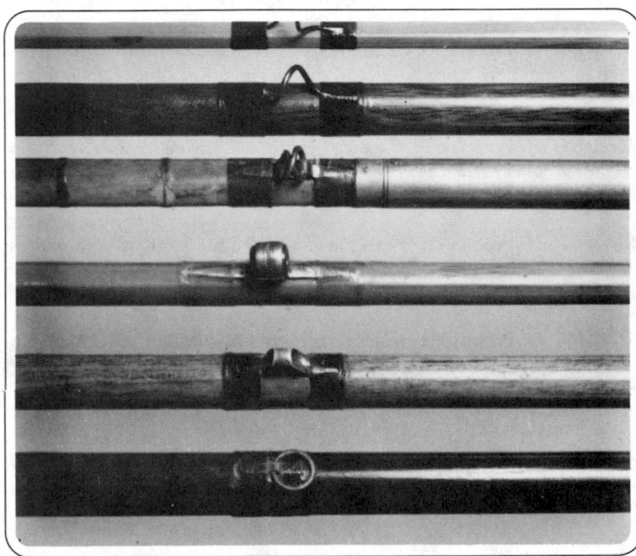

Variations of fly-rod guides from the early 1800's through the present. From top: 1973 snake guide, circa 1910 English snake guide, double-twist guide, circa 1905 agate butt guide, tunnel guide, ring guide typical of type used from 1800 to 1900. Photo courtesy of The Museum of American Fly Fishing.

G. H. Howells Rod Co.

HOWELLS BAMBOO RODS, made by Gary Howells, feature fluted-hollow butts on all models except the #3-line rods, and all models are constructed and finished to exacting standards. Howells, located in Richmond, California, produces only 75 rods a year, and delivery after an order averages nine months. Gary Howells' experience as a rodmaker includes over 27 years, and he worked for the R. L. Winston Rod Company before building rods under his own name. The G. H. Howells Rod Company was founded in 1970, and its only product is bamboo rods.

Prices (and price ranges) listed in this directory are the manufacturer's suggested retail prices as of late 1977, and they are subject to change without notice. Please consult pp. 233-235 for addresses of manufacturers from whom up-to-date price information may be obtained, or check with your local fly-tackle dealer.

Model. *#3 Line Rod (1 models).* Length: *6'3"-7'3".* Weight: *2 oz.-2-3/8 oz.* No. pieces: *2 (plus extra tip).* Reel seat: *your specification.* Rec. line: *#3.* Price: *$325.*

Model: *#4 Line Rod (4 models, fluted-hollow butt construction).* Length: *6½'-8'.* Weight: *2-3/8 oz.-3-5/8 oz.* No. pieces: *2 (plus extra tip).* Reel seat: *your specification.* Rec. line: *#4.* Price: *$325.*

Model: *#5 Line Rod (8 models, fluted-hollow butt construction).* Length: *7'-8½'.* Weight: *2-5/8 oz.-4 oz.* No. pieces: *2 (plus extra tip).* Reel seat: *your specification.* Rec. line: *#5.* Price: *$325.*

Model: *#6 Line Rod (4 models, fluted-hollow butt construction).* Length: *7½'-8½'.* Weight: *3-3/8 oz.-4-3/8 oz.* No. pieces: *2 (plus extra tip).* Reel seat: *your specification.* Rec. line: *#6.* Price: *$325.*

Model: *#7 Line Rod (4 models, fluted-hollow butt construction).* Length: *8'-8'9".* Weight: *4¼ oz.-4-5/8 oz.* No. pieces: *2 (plus extra tip).* Reel seat: *your specification.* Rec. line: *#7.* Price: *$325.*

H. L. Leonard Rod Inc.

Model: *Classic 50 Series (3 models).* Length: *8'.* Weight: *3-5/8 oz. to 4-5/8 oz.* No. pieces: *3 (plus extra tip).* Reel seat: *n.a.* Rec. line: *#4-6.* Price: *n.a.*

Model: *Yellowstone Series (4 models).* Length: *7'-8½'.* Weight: *3¼ oz. to 5-1/8 oz.* No. pieces: *2 (plus extra tip).* Reel seat: *up-locking mahogany.* Rec. line: *#5-8.* Price: *$425.*

Model: *Ausable Series (4 models).* Length: *7'-8½'.* Weight: *3-1/8 oz. to 4-5/8 oz.* No. pieces: *2 (plus extra tip).* Reel seat: *down-locking mahogany with nickel-silver butt cap.* Rec. line: *#4-7.* Price: *$425.*

Model: *Letort Series (4 models).* Length: *7'-8½'.* Weight: *2-5/8 oz. to 3-7/8 oz.* No. pieces: *2 (plus extra tip).* Reel seat: *cork with nickel-silver hood and sliding ring (7', 7½' models), locking cork (8', 8½' models).* Rec. line: *#3-6.* Price: *$425.*

Model: *Duracane Western Series (5 models).* Length: *7'-9'.* Weight: *2-7/8 oz. to 5½ oz.* No. pieces: *2 (plus extra tip).* Reel seat: *up-locking walnut.* Rec. line: *#5-9.* Price: *$295.*

Model: *Duracane Standard Series (5 models).* Length: *7'-9'.* Weight: *2-5/8 oz. to 5-1/8 oz.* No. pieces: *2 (plus extra tip).* Reel seat: *down-locking walnut.* Rec. line: *#4-8.* Price: *$295.*

Model: *Duracane Midge Series (5 models).* Length: *7'-8½'.* Weight: *2-3/8 oz. to 4-1/8 oz.* No. pieces: *2 (plus extra tip).* Reel seat: *cork with nickel-silver butt cap and sliding ring (7', 7½' models), locking cork (8', 8½' models).* Rec. line: *#3-6.* Price: *$295.*

Model: *Duracane Dry Fly Salmon Series (2 models).* Length: *8½', 9' (plus 3" detachable butt extension).* Weight: *5¼ oz., 5-5/8 oz.* No. pieces: *2 (plus extra tip).* Reel seat: *up-locking walnut.* Rec. line: *#8, 9.* Price: *$320.*

Gus Nevros

SPLIT-BAMBOO RODS are the only rods that Gus Nevros builds, and they are handcrafted on tools of his own design.

Nevros rods have been offered for sale to the public for two years, handled exclusively by Fireside Angler of Melville, New York. Nevros has been making rods for over ten years.

Model: *Six-strip 6'5", 8'3".* Length: *6'5", 8'3".* Weight: *2¼ oz., 3-3/4 oz.* No. pieces: *2 (plus extra tip).* Reel seat: *locking rosewood and aluminum.* Rec. line: *#4.* Price: *$480.*

Model: *Six-strip 7'7".* Length: *7'7".* Weight: *3¼ oz.* No. pieces: *2 (plus extra tip).* Reel seat: *locking rosewood and aluminum.* Rec. line: *#5.* Price: *$480.*

Model: *Six-strip 8'.* Length: *8'.* Weight: *3-3/4 oz.* No. pieces: *2 (plus extra tip).* Reel seat: *locking rosewood and aluminum.* Rec. line: *#6.* Price: *$480.*

Model: *Six-strip 8'9".* Length: *8'9".* Weight: *5 oz.* No. pieces: *2 (plus extra tip).* Reel seat: *locking rosewood and aluminum.* Rec. line: *#8,9.* Price: *$480.*

Model: *Five-strip 7'3".* Length: *7'3".* Weight: *3 oz.* No. pieces: *2 (plus extra tip).* Reel seat: *locking rosewood and aluminum.* Rec. line: *#8,9.* Price: *$480.*

Model: *Five-strip 8'9".* Length: *8'9".* Weight: *4 oz.* No. pieces: *2 (plus extra tip).* Reel seat: *locking rosewood and aluminum.* Rec. line: *#8,9.* Price: *$480.*

The Orvis Co.

Model: *Wes Jordan (2 models).* Length: *7½', 8'.* Weight: *3-7/8 oz., 4-3/8 oz.* No. pieces: *2 (plus extra tip).* Reel seat: *down-locking wood and metal.* Rec. line: *WF6F, WF8F.* Price: *$345, $360.*

Model: *Battenkill (8 models).* Length: *6½'-8½'.* Weight: *2-7/8 oz.-4-3/4 oz.* No. pieces: *2 (6 models), 3 (2 models).* Reel seat: *down-locking wood.* Rec. line: *#6, 8.* Price: *$173-$280.*

Model: *Madison (6 models).* Length: *6½'-8½'.* Weight: *2½ oz.-4-3/8 oz.* No. pieces: *2.* Reel seat: *down-locking cork.* Rec. line: *#6, 8.* Price: *$143-$164.*

Model: *Orvis Flea.* Length: *6½'.* Weight: *2 oz.* No. pieces: *2.* Reel seat: *n.a.* Rec. line: *#4.* Price: *$164 ($226 with extra tip).*

Model: *MCL Flea, MCL 7/3, MCL Midge, MCL Nymph, MCL Limestone Special.* Length: *6½'-8½'.* Weight: *2-3/8 oz.-4-1/8 oz.* No. pieces: *2.* Reel seat: *down-locking cork.* Rec. line: *#3-6.* Price: *$143-$164.*

Model: *Orvis 7/3.* Length: *7'.* Weight: *2-3/8 oz.* No. pieces: *2 (plus extra tip).* Reel seat: *cork with sliding rings.* Rec. line: *#3.* Price: *$242.*

Model: *Orvis 7/4.* Length: *7'.* Weight: *2-3/4 oz.* No. pieces: *3 (plus extra tip).* Reel seat: *n.a.* Rec. line: *#4.* Price: *$280.*

Model: *Orvis Midge.* Length: *7½'.* Weight: *3-5/8 oz.* No. pieces: *2.* Reel seat: *n.a.* Rec. line: *#5.* Price: *$189 ($242 with extra tip).*

Model: *Orvis Midge/Nymph.* Length: *7½'/7'9".* Weight: *3-5/8 oz.* No. pieces: *2 (with 2 interchangeable tips).* Reel seat: *n.a.* Rec. line: *#4, 5.* Price: *$242.*

Model: *Orvis Nymph.* Length: *7'9".* Weight: *3-5/8 oz.* No. pieces: *2 (plus extra tip).* Reel seat: *down-locking walnut.* Rec. line: *#4.* Price: *$242.*

Model: *Classic.* Length: *8'.* Weight: *4-1/8 oz.* No. pieces: *3 (plus extra tip).* Reel seat: *butternut with black-anodized hood and down-sliding ring.* Rec. line: *#6.* Price: *this special limited-edition rod is avail. only in presentation kit including line, reel and mahogany case, $675, or leather case, $600.*

Model: *Orvis Limestone Special.* Length: *8½'.* Weight: *4½ oz.* No. pieces: *2 (plus extra tip).* Reel seat: *down-locking wood.* Rec. line: *#6.* Price: *$257.*

Model: *Orvis Green Heart (greenheart wood construction).* Length: *8'.* Weight: *5¼ oz.* No. pieces: *3 (plus extra tip).* Reel seat: *butternut with hood and down-sliding ring.* Rec. line: *#6.* Price: *$350.*

Partridge of Redditch

PARTRIDGE OF REDDITCH is an English rodmaking firm. The Golden Shadow split-cane fly rods are bench-crafted in England, with actions and tapers designed for American anglers. Partridge rods, blanks and angling accessories are distributed in the U.S. by Thomas & Thomas of Turners Falls, Massachusetts.

Model: *Golden Shadow (4 models).* Length: *6½'-8'.* Weight: *n.a.* No. pieces: *2.* Reel seat: *down-locking rosewood.* Rec. line: *#4-6.* Price: *$125 ($155 with extra tip).*

E. F. Payne Rod Company

THE PAYNE ROD COMPANY IS ONE OF the oldest and most distinguished bamboo fly-rod manufacturers in the United States. Established in 1898, its founder, Edward Fletcher Payne, worked as a rodmaker for Hiram Leonard, and Edward's son, James Arthur Payne, began working with his father in 1908 and made rods until his death in 1968. The same tools and special procedures employed by Ed and Jim Payne are used by today's rodmakers at Payne. The Payne Company is located in Highland Mills, New York.

Model: *Payne Two-Piece Fly Rod (10 models).* Length: *6'-8½'.* Weight: *1-5/8 oz. to 4-3/4 oz.* No. pieces: *2 (plus extra tip).* Reel seat: *your choice: up-locking or down-locking Spanish cedar and aluminum, cork with sliding rings, cork with hood and sliding ring.* Rec. line: *#3-7.* Price: *$575.*

Model: *Payne Three-Piece Fly Rod (8 models).* Length: *7½'-8½'.* Weight: *3½ oz. to 5¼ oz.* No. pieces: *3 (plus extra tip).* Reel seat: *your choice: up-locking or down-locking Spanish cedar and aluminum, cork with sliding rings, cork with hood and sliding ring.* Rec. line: *#5-7.* Price: *$595.*

Model: *Payne Parabolic (3 models).* Length: *7'1", 7'9" (2 7'9" models).* Weight: *2-7/8 oz. to 4¼ oz.* No. pieces: *2 (plus extra tip).* Reel seat: *cork with hood and sliding ring.* Rec. line: *#3-7.* Price: *$575.*

Model: *Payne Bass Bug Rod.* Length: *9'.* Weight: *6½ oz. to 6-5/8 oz.* No. pieces: *3 (plus extra tip).* Reel seat: *up-locking or down-locking Spanish cedar and aluminum.* Rec. line: *n.a.* Price: *n.a.*

Model: *Payne Streamer Fly Rod (2 models).* Length: *8'3", 9'.* Weight: *5-5/8 oz. to 6¼ oz.* No. pieces: *3 (plus extra tip).* Reel seat: *up-locking* or *down-locking Spanish cedar and aluminum*. Rec. line: *n.a.* Price: *n.a.*

Model: *Payno Circular Bend Trout Rod.* Length: *8'.* Weight: *3-5/8 oz. to 4-1/8 oz.* No. pieces: *3 (plus extra tip).* Reel seat: *slide panel.* Rec. line: *n.a.* Price: *n.a.*

Pezon et Michel

PEZON ET MICHEL PRODUCES fly, casting and trolling rods in fiberglass, graphite and bamboo, as well as a full line of fly-fishing tackle and accessories. Located in Amboise, France, this company has been known as a manufacturer of superior quality split-bamboo fly rods for over forty years. Pezon et Michel products are offered in the U.S. by Stoeger Industries, South Hackensack, New Jersey.

Model: *Parabolic Mirage Riccardi.* Length: *6½'.* Weight: *2-11/16 oz.* No. pieces: *2 (plus extra tip).* Reel seat: *all cork with sliding rings.* Rec. line: *#4.* Price: *$350.*

Model: *Parabolic Super Royale (4 models).* Length: *6'10"-8'3".* Weight: *3-3/4 oz. to 4-13/16 oz.* No. pieces: *2 (plus extra tip).* Reel seat: *down-locking walnut.* Rec. line: *#5.* Price: *$300.*

Model: *Parabolic Royale (4 models).* Length: *6'10"-8'3".* Weight: *3 oz. to 4-3/8 oz.* No. pieces: *2.* Reel seat: *cork with hood and sliding ring, locking metal.* Rec. line: *#5.* Price: *$200.*

Model: *Speedcast Riccardi I.* Length: *7'7½".* Weight: *4 oz.* No. pieces: *2 (plus extra tip).* Reel seat: *n.a.* Rec. line: *#5, 6.* Price: *$300.*

Model: *Speedcast Riccardi II.* Length: *7'11½".* Weight: *4-1/8 oz.* No. pieces: *2 (plus extra tip).* Reel seat: *n.a.* Rec. line: *#6.* Price: *$300.*

Model: *Colorado Pate.* Length: *7'7".* Weight: *3-7/8 oz.* No. pieces: *2 (plus extra tip).* Reel seat: *n.a.* Rec. line: *#5.* Price: *$300.*

Model: *Fario Club Ritz.* Length: *8'5".* Weight: *5-5/16 oz.* No. pieces: *2 (plus extra tip).* Reel seat: *n.a.* Rec. line: *#6.* Price: *$300.*

Model: *Parabolic Ritz.* Length: *8'2".* Weight: *5-3/4 oz.* No. pieces: *2 (plus extra tip).* Reel seat: *n.a.* Rec. line: *#5.* Price: *$250.*

Powell Rod Co.

Model: *Signature.* Length, weight, no. pieces: *your specification.* Reel seat: *up-locking machined anodized aluminum or up-locking wood.* Rec. line: *your specification.* Price: *$250.*

Model: *Golden Signature.* Length, weight, no. pieces: *your specification.* Reel seat: *up-locking machined anodized aluminum or up-locking wood.* Rec. line: *your specification.* Price: *$400.*

Prices (and price ranges) listed in this directory are the manufacturer's suggested retail prices as of late 1977, and they are subject to change without notice. Please consult pp. 233-235 for addresses of manufacturers from whom up-to-date price information may be obtained, or check with your local fly-tackle dealer.

J. S. Sharpes

SHARPES MAKES HANDCRAFTED split-bamboo rods and blanks. These quality cane rods are well known in England, and their introduction to the U.S. market is comparatively recent. The Scottie Series is designed for American anglers in cooperation with Anglersmail of Cleveland, Ohio, that serves as U.S. agent for the firm, which is located in Aberdeen, Scotland.

Model: *Scottie (6 models).* Length: *6'-8½'.* Weight: *2 oz.-4-3/4 oz.* No. pieces: *2.* Reel seat: *cork with hood and sliding ring.* Rec. line: *#4-7.* Price: *$109.50-$125 (extra tip available at extra cost).*

R. W. Summers Co.

BOB SUMMERS' ROD-BUILDING experience began with an after-school job in 1956 with the Paul H. Young Company in Traverse City, Michigan. Summers worked with Paul Young, Sr., and stayed on with the company after Young's death. In about 1975 he left the company and began producing rods under his own name. In addition to making rods, Summers also does refinishing and repairs on rods of any make. His only products are bamboo rods. His shop is located in Traverse City, Michigan.

Model: *Midge (3 models).* Length: *6'2", 6'4", 6½'.* Weight: *n.a.* No. pieces: *2 (plus extra tip).* Reel seat: *cork with sliding rings.* Rec. line: *#3, 4.* Price: *$250 (avail. with 1 tip for $190).*

Model: *75.* Length: *7'.* Weight: *n.a.* No. pieces: *2 (plus extra tip).* Reel seat: *cork with sliding rings or locking.* Rec. line: *#5.* Price: *$260 (cork reel seat), $275 (locking reel seat), avail. with one tip for $195, $210.*

Model: *735.* Length: *7'3".* Weight: *n.a.* No. pieces: *2 (plus extra tip).* Reel seat: *cork with sliding rings or locking.* Rec. line: *#4, 5.* Price: *$260 (cork reel seat), $275 (locking reel seat), avail. with 1 tip for $195, $210.*

Model: *275.* Length: *7½'.* Weight: *n.a.* No. pieces: *2 (plus extra tip).* Reel seat: *cork with sliding rings or locking.* Rec. line: *#4.* Price: *$260 (cork reel seat), $275 (locking reel seat), avail. with 1 tip for $195, $210.*

Model: *856.* Length: *8'.* Weight: *n.a.* No. pieces: *2 (plus extra tip).* Reel seat: *cork with hood and sliding ring or locking.* Rec. line: *#5, 6.* Price: *$275 (cork reel seat), $290 (locking reel seat), avail. with 1 tip for $205, $220.*

Thomas & Thomas

Model: *Classic (7 models).* Length: *6½'-8'.* Weight: *2-1/8 oz. to 4 oz.* No. pieces: *2.* Reel seat: *walnut with hood and sliding ring (#3, 4 line rods); up-locking walnut (#5, 6 line rods).* Rec. line: *#3-6.* Price: *$225 ($295 with extra tip).*

Model: *Individualist Trout (44 different models).* Length: *6'-9'.* Weight: *n.a.* No. pieces: *2 or 3 (plus extra tip).* Reel seat: *walnut with hood and sliding ring (#3, 4 line rods); up-locking walnut (#5 line rods and above.* Rec. line: *#3-8.* Price: *$425 (2 pc.), $450 (3 pc.).*

Model: *Individualist Salmon (10 different models).* Length: *8'-10' (choice of fixed or removable butt extension).* Weight: *n.a.* No. pieces: *2 or 3 (plus extra tip).* Reel seat: *up-locking walnut.* Rec. line: *#6-9.* Price: *$500.*

Model: *Individualist Salmon (double-handed, 6 different models).* Length: *12'-14'.* Weight: *n.a.* No. pieces: *3 or 4.* Reel seat: *up-locking walnut.* Rec. line: *#9-12.* Price: *$700 (3 pc.), $775 (4 pc.).*

Model: *Individualist Sans Pareil.* Length: *6'-10'.* Weight: *n.a.* No. pieces: *1.* Reel seat: *walnut with hood and sliding ring (#2-4 line rods); up-locking walnut (#5 and above).* Rec. line: *your specification.* Price: *$350-$1100 (depending on length).*

Model: *Individualist Sans Pareil Custom Built.* Length, weight, no. pieces, reel seat, rec. line: *your specification.* Price: *n.a.*

Model: *Special Trouter (4 models).* Length: *6½'-8'.* Weight: *2 oz. to 3-3/4 oz.* No. pieces: *2 (plus extra tip).* Reel seat: *cork with hood and sliding ring.* Rec. line: *#3-6.* Price: *$195.*

Uslan Rod Company

Model: *Uslan Split Bamboo (5-strip construction, 7 models).* Length: *7'-9'.* Weight: *2¼ oz. to 6½ oz.* No. pieces: *2 (one model 3 pc., all with extra tip).* Reel seat: *n.a.* Rec. line: *#4-10.* Price: *$225-$250.*

Wanigas Rod Co.

Model: *Wanigas Supreme (7 models).* Length: *5½'-8'.* Weight: *1½ oz. to 4 oz.* No. pieces: *2 (plus extra tip).* Reel seat: *cork with sliding rings or locking.* Rec. line: *#4-6.* Price: *$300.*

Model: *Wanigas Special (3 models).* Length: *7'-8'.* Weight: *3 oz. to 4 oz.* No. pieces: *2 (plus extra tip).* Reel seat: *locking cork.* Rec. line: *#4-6.* Price: *$150.*

Marcus Warwick

SPLIT-BAMBOO FLY RODS by Marcus Warwick are manufactured in Uppingham, England. The models available in the United States were developed from specifications provided by Ike's Fly Shop of Oak Park, Michigan, and the rods are designed for American anglers. All marketing rights in the United States are held by Ike's.

Model: *Marcus Warwick (hollow-butt construction, 5 models).* Length: *6½'-8½'.* Weight: *n.a.* No. pieces: *n.a.* Reel seat: *rosewood locking.* Rec. line: *#4-6.* Price: *n.a.*

Weir & Son

Model: *LW/M603.* Length: *6'.* Weight: *1¼ oz.* No. pieces: *2 (plus extra tip).* Reel seat: *all cork with hood and sliding ring.* Rec. line: *L2.* Price: *$275.*

Model: *D603.* Length: *6'.* Weight: *1-3/4 oz.* No. pieces: *2 (plus extra tip).* Reel seat: *all cork with hood and sliding ring.* Rec. line: *DT3F, WF4F.* Price: *$275.*

Model: *LW/M763.* Length: *7½'.* Weight: *2½ oz.* No. pieces: *2 (plus extra tip).* Reel seat: *all cork with hood and sliding ring.* Rec. line: *DT3F, WF4F.* Price: *$275.*

Model: *LW/M803.* Length: *8'.* Weight: *3-3/4 oz.* No. pieces: *2 (plus extra tip).* Reel seat: *all cork with hood and sliding ring.* Rec. line: *DT4F, WF5F.* Price: *$275.*

Model: *M761, M762, M763.* Length: *7½'.* Weight: *3-3/4 oz.* No. pieces: *2 (plus extra tip).* Reel seat: *locking aluminum and wood, wood and sliding ring or all cork with hood and sliding ring.* Rec. line: *DT5F, WF6F.* Price: *$275-$300 (depending on reel seat).*

Model: *M801, M802, M803.* Length: *8'.* Weight: *4 oz.* No. pieces: *2 (plus extra tip).* Reel seat: *locking aluminum and wood, wood and sliding ring or all cork with hood and sliding ring.* Rec. line: *DT6F, WF7F.* Price: *$275-$300 (depending on reel seat).*

Model: *HW/M701, HW/M702, HW/M703.* Length: *7'.* Weight: *3¼ oz.* No. pieces: *2 (plus extra tip).* Reel seat: *locking aluminum and wood, wood and sliding ring or cork with hood and sliding ring.* Rec. line: *DT5F, WF6F.* Price: *$275-$300 (depending on reel seat).*

Model: *HW/M761, HW/M762, HW/M763.* Length: *7½'.* Weight: *4-1/8 oz.* No. pieces: *2 (plus extra tip).* Reel seat: *locking aluminum and wood, wood and sliding ring or all cork with hood and sliding ring.* Rec. line: *DT6F, WF7F.* Price: *$275-$300 (depending on reel seat).*

Model: *D661, D662, D663.* Length: *6½'.* Weight: *2-3/8 oz.* No. pieces: *2 (plus extra tip).* Reel seat: *locking aluminum and wood, wood and sliding ring or all cork with hood and sliding ring.* Rec. line: *DT3F, WF4F.* Price: *$275-$300 (depending on reel seat).*

Model: *D701, D702, D703.* Length: *7'.* Weight: *3 oz.* No. pieces: *2 (plus extra tip).* Reel seat: *locking aluminum and wood, wood and sliding ring or all cork with hood and sliding ring.* Rec. line: *DT3F, WF4F.* Price: *$275-$300 (depending on reel seat).*

Model: *D761, D762, D763.* Length: *7½'.* Weight: *3-7/8 oz.* No. pieces: *2 (plus extra tip).* Reel seat: *locking aluminum and wood, wood and sliding ring or all cork with hood and sliding ring.* Rec. line: *DT5F, WF6F.* Price: *$275-$300 (depending on reel seat).*

Model: *D801, D802, D803.* Length: *8'.* Weight: *4-1/8 oz.* No. pieces: *2 (plus extra tip).* Reel seat: *locking aluminum and wood, wood and sliding ring or all cork with hood and sliding ring.* Rec. line: *DT6F, WF7F.* Price: *$275-$300 (depending on reel seat).*

Model: *D861, D862, D863.* Length: *8½'.* Weight: *4½ oz.* No. pieces: *2 (plus extra tip).* Reel seat: *locking aluminum and wood, wood and sliding ring or all cork with hood and sliding ring.* Rec. line: *DT7F, WF8F.* Price: *$275-$300 (depending on reel seat).*

Model: *Special Rod-Bass Bug.* Length: *9'.* Weight: *5¼ oz.* No. pieces: *2 (plus extra tip).* Reel seat: *n.a.* Rec. line: *#8, 9.* Price: *$365.*

Model: *Special Rod.* Length: *9'.* Weight: *5-1/8 oz.* No. pieces: *2 (plus extra tip).* Reel seat: *n.a.* Rec. line: *280 grain shooting head.* Price: *$365.*

Model: *Special Rod.* Length: *9'.* Weight: *5-5/8 oz.* No. pieces: *2 (plus extra tip).* Reel seat: *n.a.* Rec. line: *300-600 grain shooting head.* Price: *$365.*

Model: *Special Rod.* Length: *9½'.* Weight: *6½ oz.* No. pieces: *2 (plus extra tip).* Reel seat: *n.a.* Rec. line: *DT9F, WF10F.* Price: *$365.*

Model: *Citation Rod.* Length, weight: *your specification.* No. pieces: *n.a.* Reel seat: *locking aluminum and hand-rubbed ebony.* Rec. line: *your specification.* Price: *$950.*

R. L. Winston Rod Co.

Model: *Light Trout Rod (11 models).* Length: *5½'-8'.* Weight: *1-3/4 oz. to 3-1/8 oz.* No. pieces: *2 (plus extra tip).* Reel seat: *all cork with German-silver hood and sliding ring.* Rec. line: *#3, 4.* Price: *$350.*

Model: *Trout Rod (11 models, fluted hollow construction).* Length: *6½'-9'.* Weight: *2-3/4 oz. to 5 oz.* No. pieces: *2 (plus extra tip).* Reel seat: *all cork with German-silver hood and sliding ring, locking teak or machined bakelite.* Rec. line: *#5-7.* Price: *$350.*

Model: *Steelhead and Atlantic Salmon Rod (7 models, fluted hollow construction).* Length: *8'9"-9½'.* Weight: *4-7/8 oz. to 6 oz.* No. pieces: *2 (plus extra tip).* Reel seat: *milled bakelite or locking teak.* Rec. line: *WF8-WF10, ST9-ST11.* Price: *$350.*

Paul H. Young Co.

PAUL YOUNG BEGAN MAKING split-bamboo fly rods around 1900, and since that time his rods have earned the reputation of being among the best American bamboo fly rods. The company was incorporated in 1946, when Jack Young joined his father in the business. The Paul Young Company, located in Traverse City, Michigan, is now run by Jack Young.

Model: *Midge.* Length: *6'3".* Weight: *1-3/4 oz.* No. pieces: *2.* Reel seat: *cork with sliding rings.* Rec. line: *#4.* Price: *$235 ($325 with extra tip).*

Model: *Driggs.* Length: *7'2".* Weight: *2-7/8 oz.* No. pieces: *2.* Reel seat: *cork with sliding rings.* Rec. line: *#4.* Price: *$235 ($325 with extra tip).*

Model: *Perfectionist.* Length: *7½'.* Weight: *2½ oz.* No. pieces: *2.* Reel seat: *n.a.* Rec. line: *#4.* Price: *$235 ($325 with extra tip).*

Model: *Martha-Marie.* Length: *7½'.* Weight: *3½ oz.* No. pieces: *2.* Reel seat: *cork with sliding rings or locking.* Rec. line: *#5.* Price: *$235 ($325 with extra tip).*

Model: *Parabolic 15.* Length: *8'.* Weight: *3-3/4 oz. to 4 oz.* No. pieces: *2.* Reel seat: *cork with sliding rings or cork locking.* Rec. line: *#5.* Price: *$245 ($335 with extra tip).*

Model: *Boat Rod.* Length: *8'.* Weight: *4¼ oz. to 4½ oz.* No. pieces: *2.* Reel seat: *locking.* Rec. line: *#6.* Price: *$245 ($335 with extra tip).*

Model: *Texan.* Length: *8½'.* Weight: *4.85 oz.* No. pieces: *2.* Reel seat: *locking.* Rec. line: *#6.* Price: *$255 ($345 with extra tip).*

Model: *Texas General.* Length: *8½'.* Weight: *5½ oz.* No. pieces: *2.* Reel seat: *n.a.* Rec. line: *#7.* Price: *$255 ($345 with extra tip).*

Model: *Parabolic 17.* Length: *8½'.* Weight: *5.4 oz.* No. pieces: *2.* Reel seat: *locking.* Rec. line: *#8.* Price: *$255 ($345 with extra tip).*

Model: *Bob Doerr.* Length: *9'.* Weight: *6 oz.* No. pieces: *2.* Reel seat: *locking.* Rec. line: *#8, 9.* Price: *$265 ($355 with extra tip).*

Model: *Florida Special.* Length: *9' (plus 2" fixed butt extension).* Weight: *6.65 oz. to 6-3/4 oz.* No. pieces: *2.* Reel seat: *n.a.* Rec. line: *#9.* Price: *$265 ($355 with extra tip).*

Model: *Powerhouse.* Length: *9½' (plus 2" fixed butt extension).* Weight: *7.15 oz. to 7¼ oz.* No. pieces: *n.a.* Reel seat: *n.a.* Rec. line: *#10.* Price: *$265 ($355 with extra tip).*

Evaluating a Rod's Recovery Rate

REGARDLESS OF THE MATERIAL from which a rod is made, and regardless of its cost, it must be able to cast a fly line. An important consideration in selecting a fly rod is to choose one that has a good recovery rate; one, in other words, which throws a minimum number of shock waves in the line.

When you apply the power stroke to a fly rod, you create a pendulum effect. How well the rod handles this effect determines its recovery rate. The rod tip responds to power by dipping in one direction and then over-recovering in the other. The tip continues to go back and forth in diminishing arcs until it comes to rest. Usually, the first dip will be the longest.

There are two measures in this action that are significant: the length of each movement (from the static position), and the frequency of movements (number of strokes the tip makes before it comes to rest). A fly rod with a good recovery rate will immediately minimize both of these factors after the power stroke is applied.

When the fly line leaves the tip of the rod, it reflects any subsequent movement of the tip as shock waves. Every time the tip moves up and down while recovering from the power stroke, the line moves up and down and waves are created in the line. The fly itself will not move until the line has straightened, and a good portion of all fly-casting effort is expended in simply straightening the line. Thus, the more shock waves in the fly line, the more difficult it is to straighten, and power spent in straightening the line could be more directly applied to moving the fly to its target.

Determining the recovery rate of a fly rod is not difficult if you know what to look for. When a rod is cast you will be able to see the shock waves created by the tip fluctuation on the backcast. (They also take place on the forward cast but may be more difficult to spot.) There should not be more than two modest shock waves in the line. If you are inside a store and don't have the opportunity to cast a rod, hold the rod parallel to the floor with the butt at your belt buckle and both hands on the cork grip. Snap the rod sharply once from side to side or downward, and watch it recover, checking the number and distance of the fluctuations of the tip. Ideally, a rod should register one major vibration and then dampen severely before the second one with the balance of movements involving a few minor vibrations. MARK SOSIN

THEORETICALLY, FLY REELS can be looked upon as the least important link in the fly-casting chain of events. A place to store unused line. However, this has led to some misconceptions and actual trouble for many beginning anglers, especially when they play their first fish with their line hand instead of winding excess line in and playing the fish directly from the reel.

This becomes especially serious when the angler moves on—sometimes with stark suddenness—to larger fish and longer and faster runs. No, the fly reel deserves serious consideration.

For general trout fishing, the best reel is the single-action type with an effective drag-set (with or without the "click" mechanism). "Single-action" indicates one rotation of the reel-spool for each rotation of the reel handle. There are now several models of "multiplying reels" on the market which are geared to allow a faster retrieve of excess fly line—useful in big waters and for big fish. (In the following product descriptions, models are single-action unless otherwise noted.)

An important consideration in selecting a reel is to make certain additional spools can be interchanged. The broad and useful range of fly lines today requires the quick interchangeability of lines, most commonly from floating to sinking lines; extra spools with the lines ready for use are no longer a luxury but a necessity.

While there is a certain advantage to "matching" the reel size and weight to the rod carrying it, the prime factor in reel selection is that of matching the reel to the *line* to be used with that rod. Most reel manufacturers offer a variety of reel sizes to accommodate the line-weight to be used (as well as taper type). A #4-5 line (details on this elsewhere) can be carried on a quite small (3" diameter) reel—with the added consideration of taper, because a double-taper line will take up more room on the spool than a forward taper of equal weight.

You will also want to add "backing line" at the reel-end of the fly line. Not only does this extra line allow you to handle far-ranging fish, but it also effectively widens the spool-core diameter and thus minimizes the coiling and kinking effect of the narrow spool core on the line when the inner portions are stripped from the reel.

You will find that some reels cannot be used with the handle on either side—these will be for right-hand use only. Many are interchangeable, however, and this should be a consideration, because a right-handed caster must switch hands to play a fish if he's using a right-hand reel-handle. However, if left-handed operation of the handle is clumsy, the non-switching advantage is somewhat nullified.

As you will find in the directory, there are also many special-purpose or heavy-duty reels for saltwater gamefish, salmon, steelhead and other large fish. Such listings will primarily be of advantage to the more experienced angler.

Fly Reels

Aladdin Laboratories

THE ALADDIN COMPANY manufactures Perrine automatic fly reels and accessories. E. B. Perrine (rhymes with "line") invented the first free-stripping, long-spring automatic fly reel in the late 20's, and the company remains one of the best-known manufacturers of automatic reels. Other Perrine products include the well-known Perrine fly boxes. Aladdin is located in Minneapolis, Minnesota.

Model: *No. 51 Automatic.* Size: *n.a.* Capacity: *all line sizes through WF9F.* Weight: *8-3/4 oz.* Features: *free-stripping horizontal-mount automatic, blue and gold color.* Price: *n.a.*

Model: *No. 57 Automatic.* Size: *n.a.* Capacity: *all line sizes through WF9F.* Weight: *9 oz.* Features: *free-stripping, vertical-mount automatic, green and gold color.* Price: *n.a.*

Model: *No. 50 Automatic.* Size: *n.a.* Capacity: *all line sizes through WF9F.* Weight: *8-7/8 oz.* Features: *free-stripping automatic with snubbing brake, brown and gold color.* Price: *n.a.*

Model: *No. 81 Automatic.* Size: *n.a.* Capacity: *all line sizes through WF10F.* Weight: *8-7/8 oz.* Features: *free-stripping, horizontal-mount automatic, blue and gold color.* Price: *n.a.*

Model: *No. 87 Automatic.* Size: *n.a.* Capacity: *all line sizes through WF10F.* Weight: *9-1/8 oz.* Features: *free-stripping, vertical-mount automatic, green and gold color.* Price: *n.a.*

Model: *No. 80 Automatic.* Size: *n.a.* Capacity: *all line sizes through WF10F.* Weight: *9 oz.* Features: *free-stripping automatic with snubbing brake, brown and gold color.* Price: *n.a.*

American Import

Model: *L. M. Dickson Skeleton Type Flyweight.* Size: *2-3/8" spool diam.* Capacity: *n.a.* Weight: *3-3/4 oz.* Features: *black steel frame.* Price: *n.a.*

Model: *L. M. Dickson 205 Fly Reel.* Size: *2-7/8" spool diam.* Capacity: *n.a.* Weight: *4½ oz.* Features: *black-anodized frame, aluminum spool.* Price: *n.a.*

Model: *L. M. Dickson Kentfield Automatic.* Size: *2-3/4" spool diam.* Capacity: *n.a.* Weight: *9½ oz.* Features: *green-anodized finish, free-stripping, vertical mount, folding trigger.* Price: *n.a.*

Model: *L. M. Dickson Featherweight.* Size: *2¼" spool diam.* Capacity: *n.a.* Weight: *3-7/8 oz.* Features: *metallic bronze-brown color.* Price: *n.a.*

Model: *L. M. Dickson Lightweight.* Size: *2-3/4" spool diam.* Capacity: *n.a.* Weight: *6 oz.* Features: *adjustable drag, metallic bronze-brown color, chromed line guard.* Price: *n.a.*

Model: *L. M. Dickson Heavyweight.* Size: *4" spool diam.* Capacity: *n.a.* Weight: *10½ oz.* Features: *adjustable drag, metallic bronze-brown color, chromed rim and line guard.* Price: *n.a.*

Angler's World

Model: *Angler's World Custom-Built Bogdan 1X.* Size: *1-3/8" spool width.* Capacity: *WF9 plus 200 yds. 20 lb. test Dacron backing.* Weight: *11 oz.* Features: *frame and spool machined from solid aluminum alloy, double-shoe brake system, 2:1 retrieve ratio.* Price: *$210.*

Model: *Angler's World Custom-Built Bogdan 2X.* Size: *1-3/16" spool width.* Capacity: *WF10 plus 200 yds. 20 lb. test Dacron backing.* Weight: *13¼ oz.* Features: *frame and spool machined from solid aluminum alloy, double-shoe brake system, 2:1 retrieve ratio.* Price: *$220.*

Model: *Angler's World Custom-Built Bogdan 3X.* Size: *1-3/8" spool width.* Capacity: *WF10 plus 300 yds. 20 lb. test Dacron backing.* Features: *frame and spool machined from solid aluminum alloy, double-shoe brake system, 2:1 retrieve ratio.* Price: *$230.*

S. E. Bogdan

STANLEY BOGDAN BEGAN MAKING saltwater and salmon fly reels in 1944. His products are entirely handcrafted, and their high quality places them among the finest fly reels made. Bogdan is currently expanding his line to include more trout reels than in the past. Stephen Bogdan joined his father in the business about three years ago, and the shop is located in Nashua, New Hampshire.

Prices (and price ranges) listed in this directory are the manufacturer's suggested retail prices as of late 1977, and they are subject to change without notice. Please consult pp. 233-235 for addresses of manufacturers from whom up-to-date price information may be obtained, or check with your local fly-tackle dealer.

Model: *No. 00.* Size: *3¼" frame diam., 2-3/4" spool diam., 1-5/32" spool width.* Capacity: *WF9F plus 100 yds. 20-lb. test backing.* Weight: *10 oz.* Features: *gold-anodized frame, black-anodized side plate, 2:1 retrieve ratio, avail. in single action with perforated side-plate and spool.* Price: *$205, $195 (single action), ($35-40, extra spool: 2:1 retrieve ratio reels only).*

Model: *No. 0.* Size: *3¼" frame diam., 2-3/4" spool diam., 1-3/8" spool width.* Capacity: *WF9F plus 200 yds. 20-lb. test backing.* Weight: *11 oz.* Features: *gold-anodized frame, black-anodized side plate, 2:1 retrieve ratio, avail. in single action with perforated side plate and spool.* Price: *$210, $200 (single action), ($35-40, extra spool: 2:1 retrieve ratio reels only).*

Model: *No. 150.* Size: *3½" frame diam., 3" spool diam., 1-3/8" spool width.* Capacity: *WF10F plus 250 yds. 20-lb. test backing.* Weight: *12 oz.* Features: *gold-anodized frame, black-anodized side plate, 2:1 retrieve ratio, avail. in single action with perforated side plate and spool.* Price: *$210, $200 (single action), ($35-$40, extra spool: 2:1 retrieve ratio reels only).*

Model: *No. 1.* Size: *3-3/4" frame diam., 3-1/4" spool diam., 1-3/16" spool width.* Capacity: *WF10F plus 200 yds. 20-lb. test backing.* Weight: *13 oz.* Features: *gold-anodized frame, black-anodized side plate, 2:1 retrieve ratio, avail. in single action with perforated side plate and spool.* Price: *$220, $210 (single action), extra spool: $35-$40, 2:1 retrieve ratio reels only).*

Model: *No. 2.* Size: *3-3/4" frame diam., 3¼" spool diam., 1-3/8" spool width.* Capacity: *WF11F plus 300 yds. 20-lb. test backing.* Weight: *14 oz.* Features: *gold-anodized frame, black-anodized side plate, 2:1 retrieve ratio, avail. in single action with perforated side plate and spool.* Price: *$225, $215 (single action), (extra spool: $35-$40, 2:1 retrieve ratio reels only).*

Model: *No. 100M.* Size: *3½" frame diam., 3" spool diam., 1-5/32" spool width.* Capacity: *WF9F plus 150 yds. 20-lb. test backing.* Weight: *11 oz.* Features: *gold-anodized frame, black-anodized side plate, 2:1 retrieve ratio, avail. in single action with perforated side plate and spool.* Price: *$210, $200 (single action), (extra spool: $35-$40, 2:1 retrieve ratio reels only).*

Model: *No. 300M.* Size: *3-3/4" frame diam., 3¼" spool diam., 1-5/8" spool width.* Capacity: *WF12F plus 300 yds. 36-lb. test backing.* Weight: *15 oz.* Features: *gold-anodized frame, black-anodized side plate, 2:1 retrieve ratio, avail. in single action with perforated side plate and spool.* Price: *$230, $220 (single action), (extra spool: $35-$40, 2:1 retrieve ratio reels only).*

Model: *Trout.* Size: *3¼" frame diam., 2-3/4" spool diam., 11/16" spool width.* Capacity: *WF5F plus 50 yds. 12-lb. test backing.* Weight: *5 oz.* Features: *perforated side plate and spool, single action.* Price: *$160.*

Model: *Steelhead.* Size: *3¼" frame diam., 2-3/4" spool diam., 1-5/32" spool width.* Capacity: *WF6F plus 100 yds. 20-lb. test backing.* Features: *perforated side plate and spool, single action.* Price: *$170.*

Browning

Model: *Lightweight Fly'R-4.* Size: *n.a.* Capacity: *DT5F plus 25 yds. 15-lb.-test braided backing.* Weight: *4 oz.* Features: *quick take-apart spool, right- or left-hand wind.* Price: *$12.95 (extra spool: $3.50).*

Model: *Medium Weight Fly'R-5.* Size: *n.a.* Capacity: *DT6F plus 50 yds. 15-lb.-test braided backing.* Weight: *5 oz.* Features: *quick take-apart spool, right- or left-hand wind.* Price: *n.a. (extra spool: $3.95).*

Cortland Line Company

Model: *Crown Rim Control Small.* Size: *3¼" spool diam.* Capacity: *WF6F plus 90 yds. 20-lb.-test backing.* Weight: *n.a.* Features: *rim-control drag, right- or left-hand wind.* Price: *$15.95 (extra spool: $6).*

Model: *Crown Rim Control Medium.* Size: *3½" spool diam.* Capacity: *WF7F plus 120 yds. 20-lb.-test backing.* Weight: *n.a.* Features: *rim-control drag, right- or left-hand wind.* Price: *$16.95 (extra spool: $6.50).*

Model: *Crown Rim Control Large.* Size: *3-5/8" spool diam.* Capacity: *WF8F plus 170 yds. 20-lb.-test backing.* Weight: *n.a.* Features: *rim-control drag, right- or left-hand wind.* Price: *$17.95 (extra spool: $7).*

J. Lee Cuddy Associates

J. Lee Cuddy of Miami, Florida, is primarily a distributor of rod-building components and accessories from major manufacturers, although they carry several products of their own design and manufacture, including the John Emery Fly Reel. John Emery is a rod designer and associate of J. Lee Cuddy Associates.

Model: *John Emery Fly Reel.* Size: *3-7/8" spool diam., 1-3/16" spool width.* Capacity: *WF13F plus 450-600 yds. 30-lb.-test backing.* Weight: *13-7/8 oz.* Features: *machined from single piece of aluminum alloy bar-stock, hard-coat black-anodized finish, flanged spool for palming drag, cork and aluminum drag disks, right- or left-hand models avail.* Price: *$300.*

Daiwa Corp.

Model: *731.* Size: *n.a.* Capacity: *#6, 7 line.* Weight: *5.3 oz.* Features: *quick-release spool, 4-point drag setting, right- or left-hand wind.* Price: *n.a.*

Model: *732.* Size: *n.a.* Capacity: *#7, 8 line.* Weight: *6.3 oz.* Features: *quick-release spool, 4-point drag setting plus skirted spool for thumb drag, right- or left-hand wind.* Price: *n.a.*

Model: *734.* Size: *n.a.* Capacity: *#8, 9 line.* Weight: *7 oz.* Features: *quick-release spool, 4-point drag setting plus skirted spool for thumb drag, right- or left-hand wind.* Price: *n.a.*

Feurer Brothers Inc.

Feurer Brothers is a Swiss watchmaking firm, located in North White Plains, New York, that has applied the tradition of Swiss craftsmanship to the manufacture of FB fishing reels. Their only angling products are reels, and their selection includes spinning and casting reels, as well as fly-fishing models.

Model: *Taurus.* Size: *n.a.* Capacity: *WF11 plus 250 yds. backing.* Weight: *12 oz.* Features: *can be set for right hand, left hand or off, adjustable drag.* Price: *$95.*

Model: *Gemini I.* Size: *2-7/8" spool diam.* Capacity: *50 yds. #3 or 4 line.* Weight: *5½ oz.* Features: *non-corrosive enamel finish, lightweight aluminum spool and housing, click pawl, quick take-apart.* Price: *$13.50.*

Model: *Gemini II.* Size: *3½ " spool diam.* Capacity: *50 yds. #5 or 6 line.* Weight: *6½ oz.* Features: *non-corrosive enamel finish, lightweight aluminum spool and housing, click pawl, quick take-apart.* Price: *$16.25.*

The Garcia Corp.

Model: *GK-40.* Size: *n.a.* Capacity: *DT4.* Weight: *4 oz.* Features: *adjustable drag, quick spool release, chromed line guard, ventilated alloy spool.* Price: *n.a.*

Model: *GK-42.* Size: *n.a.* Capacity: *DT6 plus 50 yds. backing.* Weight: *4½ oz.* Features: *adjustable drag, quick spool release, chromed line guard, ventilated alloy spool.* Price: *n.a.*

Model: *GK-44.* Size: *n.a.* Capacity: *DT6 plus 100 yds. backing.* Weight: *5 oz.* Features: *adjustable drag, quick spool release, chromed line guard, ventilated alloy spool.* Price: *n.a.*

Model: *GK-52 Automatic.* Size: *n.a.* Capacity: *DT6.* Weight: *9-3/4 oz.* Features: *tension-release knob, trigger lock, vertical-mount automatic.* Price: *n.a.*

Hardy Brothers

Model: *Perfect (3 models).* Size: *3-1/8", 3-3/8", 3-5/8" spool diam.* Capacity: *n.a.* Weight: *n.a.* Features: *aluminum alloy construction, ball-bearing mechanism.* Price: *$85, $90, $95.*

Model: *Flyweight.* Size: *2" spool diam.* Capacity: *#4 line.* Weight: *2 oz.* Features: *ultra-light construction.* Price: *$57.50.*

Model: *Husky.* Size: *3-5/8" spool diam.* Capacity: *#9 line.* Weight: *7-3/4 oz.* Features: *wide-range brake mechanism, also avail. as Multiplier with 1-3/4:1 retrieve ratio and right- or left-hand wind.* Price: *$78.50, $96.50 (Husky Multiplier).*

Model: *Featherweight.* Size: *2-7/8" spool diam.* Capacity: *#5 line.* Weight: *3 oz.* Features: *super-light construction, also avail. as Multiplier with 1-3/4:1 retrieve ratio and right- or left-hand wind.* Price: *$62.50, $72.50 (Featherweight Multiplier).*

Model: *L.R.H. Lightweight.* Size: *3-3/16" spool diam.* Capacity: *#6 line.* Weight: *3-3/4 oz.* Features: *also avail. as Multiplier with 1-3/4:1 retrieve ratio and right- or left-hand wind.* Price: *$64.50, $75 (L.R.H. Lightweight Multiplier).*

Model: *Princess.* Size: *3½" spool diam.* Capacity: *#7 line.* Weight: *4-3/4 oz.* Features: *also avail. as Multiplier with 1-3/4:1 gear ratio and right- or left-hand wind.* Price: *$67, $77.50 (Princess Multiplier).*

Model: *Zenith.* Size: *3-5/8" spool diam.* Capacity: *#9 line.* Weight: *6½ oz.* Features: *also avail. as Multiplier with 1-3/4:1 gear ratio and right- or left-hand wind.* Price: *$72.50, $82.50 (Zenith Multiplier).*

Model: *Saint Aidan.* Size: *3-3/4" spool diam.* Capacity: *#8 line.* Weight: *6 oz.* Features: *contracted spool for rapid wind-in.* Price: *$68.50.*

H. Hart Tackle Corp.

H. HART TACKLE HAS BEEN in business for four years, and their line of products is limited to the production of big-game fly reels. Although they manufacture numerous models for other firms, two years ago they began offering the Marquessa and the Umpqua models under their own name. H. Hart Tackle is located in Melville, New York.

Model: *Umpqua.* Size: *3-3/8" spool diam.* Capacity: *WF9 plus 200 yds. 20-lb. test backing.* Weight: *8-3/4 oz.* Features: *right- or left-hand wind, 8-surface 2-position floating drag system, anti-reverse and coil spring and split-pawl activate for fast lock up, needle-bearing retrieve.* Price: *$190.*

Model: *Marquessa.* Size: *3-3/4" spool diam.* Capacity: *WF11 plus 200 yds. 20-lb. test backing.* Weight: *12½ oz.* Features: *right- or left-hand wind, 8-surface 2-position floating drag system, anti-reverse and coil spring and split-pawl activate for fast lock up, needle-bearing retrieve.* Price: *$190.*

James Heddon's Sons

Model: *755 Single Action.* Size: *n.a.* Capacity: *#6-8 line.* Weight: *4 oz.* Features: *right- or left-hand wind, click drag, quick-change spool.* Price: *$8.*

Model: *320A Single Action.* Size: *n.a.* Capacity: *#6-9 line.* Weight: *4½ oz.* Features: *right- or left-hand wind, click drag, quick-change spool.* Price: *$12.*

Model: *310A Single Action.* Size: *n.a.* Capacity: *#6-8 line.* Weight: *4 oz.* Features: *right- or left-hand wind, click drag, quick-change spool.* Price: *$11.*

Model: *300A Single Action.* Size: *n.a.* Capacity: *#5, 6 line.* Weight: *3½ oz.* Features: *right- or left-hand wind, click drag, quick-change spool.* Price: *$10.*

Model: *11 Automatic.* Size: *n.a.* Capacity: *#6-9 line.* Weight: *9.4 oz.* Features: *vertical-mount automatic, fold-away trigger.* Price: *$19.*

Model: *5 Automatic.* Size: *n.a.* Capacity: *#6-8 line.* Weight: *9.1 oz.* Features: *horizontal-mount automatic, fold-away trigger.* Price *$16.*

Herter's Inc.

Model: *International 314.* Size: *13/16" pillar, 3¼' plate.* Capacity: *n.a.* Weight: *5¼ oz.* Features: *aluminum frame, two-way click, quick take-apart.* Price: *$7.97 (extra spool $2.37).*

Model: *International 358.* Size: *13/16" pillar, 3-5/8" plate.* Capacity: *n.a.* Weight: *6 oz.* Features: *aluminum frame, two-way click, quick take-apart.* Price: *$8.07 (extra spool $2.37).*

Model: *703A Automatic.* Size: *2-7/8" spool diam., 7/8" spool width.* Capacity: *n.a.* Weight: *11½ oz.* Features: *anodized aluminum case, all other parts hand-polished and chrome-plated.* Price: *$9.17.*

Martin Reel Co.

Model: *Fast Retrieve 72.* Size: *n.a.* Capacity: *WF9F plus 150 yds. 18-lb. test braided Dacron backing.* Weight: *9¼ oz.* Features: *3:1 retrieve ratio, floating Teflon disk drag, right- or left-hand wind, on-off click, quick release spool.* Price: *n.a.*

Model: *Blue Chip 70.* Size: *n.a.* Capacity: *WF9F plus 150 yds. 18-lb. test braided Dacron backing.* Weight: *8 oz.* Features: *floating Teflon disk drag, right- or left-hand wind, on-off click, quick-release spool.* Price: *n.a.*

Model: *Blue Chip 71.* Size: *n.a.* Capacity: *WF9F plus 200 yds. 18-lb. test braided Dacron backing.* Weight: *9 oz.* Features: *floating Teflon disk drag, right- or left-hand wind, on-off click, quick-release spool.* Price: *n.a.*

Model: *Multiple Action 68.* Size: *n.a.* Capacity: *WF9F plus 150 yds. 18-lb. test braided Dacron backing.* Weight: *7 oz.* Features: *3:1 retrieve ratio, right- or left-hand wind, on-off click, quick-release spool.* Price: *n.a.*

Model: *Light Weight 67-A.* Size: *n.a.* Capacity: *WF9F plus backing.* Weight: *5½ oz.* Features: *adjustable drag, right- or left-hand wind, quick-release spool.* Price: *n.a.*

Model: *Ultra-Light MG-7.* Size: *3-5/16" diam.* Capacity: *DT8F, WF9F plus backing.* Weight: *4 oz.* Features: *adjustable drag, right- or left-hand wind, quick-release spool.* Price: *n.a.*

Model: *Tuffy 60.* Size: *n.a.* Capacity: *DT6F.* Weight: *3½ oz.* Features: *on-off click drag.* Price: *n.a.*

Model: *Tuffy 61.* Size: *n a.* Capacity: *WF8F.* Weight: *3-3/4 oz.* Features: *right- or left-hand wind.* Price: *n.a.*

Model: *Tuffy 62.* Size: *n.a.* Capacity: *DT6F.* Weight: *3½ oz.* Features: *on-off click drag, quick-change spool, right- or left-hand wind.* Price: *n.a.*

Model: *Tuffy 63.* Size: *n.a.* Capacity: *WF8F.* Weight: *3-3/4 oz.* Features: *on-off click drag, right- or left-hand wind, quick-release spool.* Price: *n.a.*

Model: *Tuffy 64.* Size: *n.a.* Capacity: *WF9F plus 150 yds. 18-lb. test braided Dacron backing.* Weight: *6¼ oz.* Features: *adjustable drag, on-off click, right- or left-hand wind, quick-release spool.* Price: *n.a.*

Model: *Tuffy 65.* Size: *n.a.* Capacity: *WF9F plus 130 yds. 18-lb. test braided Dacron backing.* Weight: *5 oz.* Features: *on-off click drag, right- or left-hand wind, quick-release spool.* Price: *n.a.*

Model: *Tuffy 66.* Size: *n.a.* Capacity: *WF9F plus 130 yds. 18-lb. test braided Dacron backing.* Weight: *5½ oz.* Features: *on-off click drag, right- or left-hand wind, quick-release spool, twin hardened plated line guides.* Price: *n.a.*

Model: *Blue Chip 83 Automatic.* Size: *n.a.* Capacity: *DT8F, WF8F* Weight: *9¼ oz.* Features: *vertical mount, push-button tension release, adjustable trigger, silent wind.* Price: *n.a.*

Model: *Fly Wate 49 Automatic.* Size: *n.a.* Capacity: *DT8F, WF8F.* Weight: *9¼ oz.* Features: *vertical mount, push-button tension release, adjustable trigger, silent wind, free stripping.* Price: *n.a.*

Model: *Fly Wate 39 Automatic.* Size: *n.a.* Capacity: *DT8F, WF8F.* Weight: *9¼ oz.* Features: *horizontal mount, push-button tension release, adjustable trigger, silent wind, free stripping.* Price: *n.a.*

Model: *Fly Wate 48 Automatic.* Size: *n.a.* Capacity: *DT6F.* Weight: *9 oz.* Features: *vertical mount, push-button tension release, adjustable trigger, silent wind, free stripping.* Price: *n.a.*

Model: *Fly Wate 38G Automatic.* Size: *n.a.* Capacity: *DT6F.* Weight: *8-3/4 oz.* Features: *horizontal mount, push-button tension release, adjustable trigger, silent wind, free stripping.* Price: *n.a.*

Model: *Tuffy 81 Automatic.* Size: *n.a.* Capacity: *DT8F, WF8F.* Weight: *9 oz.* Features: *vertical mount, adjustable trigger, free stripping, click wind.* Price: *n.a.*

Model: *Tuffy 8 Automatic.* Size: *n.a.* Capacity: *DT6F.* Weight: *n.a.* Features: *vertical mount, adjustable trigger, free stripping, click wind.* Price: *n.a.*

Model: *Tuffy 94 Automatic.* Size: *n.a.* Capacity: *DT6F.* Weight: *8-3/4 oz.* Features: *horizontal mount, adjustable trigger, free stripping, click wind.* Price: *n.a.*

Model: *Martin 6 Automatic.* Size: *n.a.* Capacity: *DT6F.* Weight: *9¼ oz.* Features: *vertical mount, open construction, adjustable trigger, free stripping, click wind.* Price: *n.a.*

Model: *Trol-o-matic 35A Automatic.* Size: *n.a.* Capacity: *WF9F plus 150 yds. 18-lb. test braided Dacron backing.* Weight: *15-3/4 oz.* Features: *vertical mount, adjustable trigger, free stripping.* Price: *n.a.*

Model: *Sovereign 23 AXL Automatic.* Size: *n.a.* Capacity: *DT6F.* Weight: *10 oz.* Features: *vertical mount, adjustable trigger, free stripping, right- or left-hand wind.* Price: *n.a.*

O. L. M. International Corp.

Model: *9300.* Size: *n.a.* Capacity: *30 yds. L5F.* Weight: *2.7 oz.* Features: *graphite construction, quick take-apart spool, right- or left-hand wind, click drag.* Price: *n.a.*

Model: *9320.* Size: *n.a.* Capacity: *40 yds. L7F.* Weight: *3.4 oz.* Features: *graphite construction, quick take-apart spool, right- or left-hand wind, click drag.* Price: *n.a.*

Model: *4300.* Size: *n.a.* Capacity: *30 yds. L5F.* Weight: *3½ oz.* Features: *aluminum-alloy one-piece frame, quick take-apart spool, right- or left-hand wind.* Price: *n.a.*

Model: *4310.* Size: *n.a.* Capacity: *35 yds. L6F.* Weight: *4 oz.* Features: *aluminum-alloy one-piece construction, quick take-apart spool, right- or left-hand wind.* Price: *n.a.*

Model: *4320.* Size: *n.a.* Capacity: *40 yds. L7F.* Weight: *5 oz.* Features: *aluminum-alloy one-piece construction, quick take-apart spool, right- or left-hand wind.* Price: *n.a.*

Model: *4340.* Size: *n.a.* Capacity: *60 yds. WF10F.* Weight: *6 oz.* Features: *aluminum-alloy one-piece construction, quick take-apart spool, right- or left-hand wind.* Price: *n.a.*

Model: *420.* Size: *n.a.* Capacity: *40 yds. L6F.* Weight: *6.3 oz.* Features: *adjustable drag, quick take-apart spool, right- or left-hand wind.* Price: *n.a.*

Model: *440.* Size: *n.a.* Capacity: *50 yds. L8F.* Weight: *7.1 oz.* Features: *adjustable drag, quick take-apart spool, right- or left-hand wind.* Price: *n.a.*

Model: *450.* Size: *n.a.* Capacity: *40 yds. L6F.* Weight: *3.8 oz.* Features: *adjustable drag, quick take-apart spool, right- or left-hand wind.* Price: *n.a.*

Model: *460.* Size: *n.a.* Capacity: *70 yds. WF10F.* Weight: *9.8 oz.* Features: *adjustable drag, quick take-apart spool, right- or left-hand wind.* Price: *n.a.*

Model: *470.* Size: *n.a.* Capacity: *50 yds. L8F.* Weight: *5.7 oz.* Features: *adjustable drag, quick take-apart spool, right- or left-hand wind.* Price: *n.a.*

Model: *480 Automatic.* Size: *n.a.* Capacity: *40 yds. L6F.* Weight: *9½ oz.* Features: *free-stripping vertical-mount automatic, folding trigger.* Price: *n.a.*

Early American fly reels: above a Follett, derived from the wire Billinghurst below. The Billinghurst was the first fly reel to receive an American patent. Photo courtesy of The Museum of American Fly Fishing.

The Orvis Co.

Model: *CFO II.* Size: *2-9/16" spool diam.* Capacity: *DT3F, WF4F.* Weight: *2 oz.* Features: *one-side frame, right- or left-hand wind, quick take-apart spool.* Price: *$72.50 (extra spool: $26.50).*

Prices (and price ranges) listed in this directory are the manufacturer's suggested retail prices as of late 1977, and they are subject to change without notice. Please consult pp. 233-235 for addresses of manufacturers from whom up-to-date price information may be obtained, or check with your local fly-tackle dealer.

Model: *CFO III.* Size: *3" spool diam.* Capacity: *WF6F plus 50 yds. backing.* Weight: *3 oz.* Features: *adjustable drag, one-side frame, quick take-apart spool, right- or left-hand wind, avail. as Multiplier with 1-2/3:1 retrieve ratio (4 oz.).* Price: *$74.50 ($76.50 with line guard, 3¼ oz., extra spool: $27.50), $84.75 (CFO III Multiplier, extra spool: $19.75).*

Model: *CFO IV.* Size: *3-3/16" spool diam.* Capacity: *WF8F plus 50 yds. backing.* Weight: *3½ oz.* Features: *adjustable drag, one-side frame, quick take-apart spool, right- or left-hand wind, line guard, avail. as Multiplier with 1-2/3:1 retrieve ratio (4-3/4 oz.).* Price: *$79.50 (extra spool: $28.50), $87.25 (CFO IV Multiplier, extra spool: $20.75).*

Model: *CFO V.* Size: *3-7/16" spool diam.* Capacity: *WF10F plus 150 yds. backing.* Weight: *4¼ oz.* Features: *adjustable drag, one-side frame, quick take-apart spool, right- or left-hand wind, line guard, avail. as Multiplier with 1-2/3:1 retrieve ratio (5¼ oz.).* Price: *$82.50 (extra spool: $29.50), $89.75 (CFO V Multiplier, extra spool: $21.75).*

Model: *Battenkill III.* Size: *3¼" spool diam.* Capacity: *WF5F plus 100 yds. 20-lb. test Dacron backing.* Weight: *3½ oz.* Features: *magnesium alloy construction.* Price: *$47.50 (extra spool: $21).*

Model: *Battenkill IV.* Size: *3-5/8" spool diam.* Capacity: *WF7F plus 125 yds. backing.* Features: *magnesium alloy construction.* Price: *$49.50 (extra spool: $23).*

Model: *Battenkill V.* Size: *3-7/8" spool diam.* Capacity: *WF9F plus 200 yds. backing.* Weight: *4-3/4 oz.* Features: *magnesium alloy construction.* Price: *$52.50 (extra spool: $25).*

Model: *Madison 4/5.* Size: *3" spool diam.* Capacity: *WF4F, WF5F.* Weight: *4 oz.* Features: *quick take-apart spool.* Price: *$25.75 (extra spool: $8.75).*

Model: *Madison 6/7.* Size: *3¼" spool diam.* Capacity: *WF6F, WF7F plus backing.* Weight: *5¼ oz.* Features: *adjustable drag, quick take-apart spool.* Price: *$27.75 (extra spool: $9.50).*

Model: *Madison 8.* Size: *3-5/8" spool diam.* Capacity: *WF8F plus 150 yds. backing.* Weight: *6 oz.* Features: *adjustable drag, quick take-apart spool.* Price: *$29.75 (extra spool: $9.75).*

Model: *Madison 9.* Size: *3-5/8" spool diam.* Capacity: *WF9F plus 200 yds. backing.* Weight: *6-3/4 oz.* Features: *adjustable drag, quick take-apart spool.* Price: *$30.75 (extra spool: $10.50).*

Model: *Large Saltwater and Salmon.* Size: *3-3/4" spool diam.* Capacity: *400 yds. WF11F.* Weight: *13 oz.* Features: *8-surface 2-position drag system, needle-bearing retrieve, roller line guard.* Price: *$200.*

Model: *Medium Saltwater and Salmon.* Size: *3-3/8" spool diam.* Capacity: *200 yds. DT9.* Weight: *9 oz.* Features: *8-surface 2-position drag system, needle-bearing retrieve, roller line guard.* Price: *$190.*

Model: *Orvis Lord I.* Size: *3½" spool diam., 4/5" width.* Capacity: *WF7F plus 150 yds. 20-lb.-test Dacron backing.* Weight: *7 oz.* Features: *2.14:1 retrieve ratio, stainless-steel, anodized aluminum, bronze and nickel-plated aluminum construction, anti-reverse mechanism, 3-position drag system.* Price: *$215.*

Model: *Orvis Lord II.* Size: *4" spool diam., 1" width.* Capacity: *WF9F plus 300 yds. 20-lb.-test Dacron backing.* Weight: *8-1/10 oz.* Features: *2.14:1 retrieve ratio, stainless-steel, anodized aluminum, bronze and nickel-plated aluminum construction, anti-reverse mechanism, 3-position drag system.* Price: *$227.50.*

Prices (and price ranges) listed in this directory are the manufacturer's suggested retail prices as of late 1977, and they are subject to change without notice. Please consult pp. 233-235 for addresses of manufacturers from whom up-to-date price information may be obtained, or check with your local fly-tackle dealer.

Pflueger

Model: *Medalist 1494½.* Size: *1" (pillar), 3¼" (plate).* Capacity: *50 yds. L7.* Weight: *6 oz.* Features: *cast aluminum frame, take-apart spool release, adjustable drag, right- or left-hand wind.* Price: *n.a.*

Model: *Medalist 1495.* Size: *13/16" (pillar), 3-5/8" (plate).* Capacity: *50 yds. L7.* Weight: *6 oz.* Features: *cast aluminum frame, take-apart spool release, adjustable drag, right- or left-hand wind.* Price: *n.a.*

Model: *Medalist 1495½.* Size: *1" (pillar), 3-5/8" (plate).* Capacity: *60 yds. L7.* Weight: *6-3/4 oz.* Features: *cast aluminum frame, take-apart spool release, adjustable drag, right- or left-hand wind.* Price: *n.a.*

Model: *Medalist 1498.* Size: *1" (pillar), 4" (plate).* Capacity: *80 yds. L7.* Weight: *6-7/8 oz.* Features: *cast aluminum frame, take-apart spool release, adjustable drag, right- or left-hand wind.* Price: *n.a.*

Model: *Supreme 577.* Size: *n.a.* Capacity: *all line sizes plus 250 yds. 15-lb. test mono backing.* Weight: *10½ oz.* Features: *single action, recessed drag, nylon bearings, aluminum spool, corrosion resistant finish, line-strip control lever to bypass drag.* Price: *n.a.*

Model: *Supreme 578.* Size: *n.a.* Capacity: *all line sizes plus 300 yds. 15-lb. test mono backing.* Weight: *12½ oz.* Features: *single action, recess drag, nylon bearings, aluminum spool, corrosion resistant finish, line-strip control lever to bypass drag.* Price: *n.a.*

Model: *1554.* Size: *n.a.* Capacity: *L7 plus 75 yds. 15-lb. test backing* Weight: *5 oz.* Features: *perforated spool, aluminum frame.* Price: *n.a.*

Model: *576.* Size: *n.a.* Capacity: *all line sizes.* Weight: *4½ oz.* Features: *metal frame, aluminum spool.* Price: *n.a.*

Model: *1534.* Size: *n.a.* Capacity: *40 yds. L7.* Weight: *4 oz.* Features: *adjustable sliding click, push-button take-apart spool.* Price: *n.a.*

Model: *1535.* Size: *n.a.* Capacity: *all line sizes.* Weight: *6 oz.* Features: *adjustable drag.* Price: *n.a.*

Model: *Medalist 1492.* Size: *13/16" (pillar), 2-7/8" (plate).* Capacity: *25 yds. L7.* Weight: *4 oz.* Features: *cast aluminum frame, take-apart spool release, adjustable drag.* Price: *n.a.*

Model: *Medalist 1492½.* Size: *1" (pillar), 2-7/8" (plate).* Capacity: *30 yds. L7.* Weight: *4½ oz.* Features: *cast aluminum frame, take-apart spool release, adjustable drag.* Price: *n.a.*

Model: *Medalist 1494.* Size: *13/16" (pillar), 3¼" (plate).* Capacity: *40 yds. L7.* Weight: *5 oz.* Features: *cast aluminum frame, take-apart spool release, adjustable drag, right- or left-hand wind.* Price: *n.a.*

Pezon et Michel

Model: *Super Parabolic Type 76.* Size: *n.a.* Capacity: *DT4 plus 74 yds. backing.* Weight: *3½ oz.* Features: *lightweight alloy construction, right- or left-hand wind, adjustable drag, line guard, raised rim for hand drag.* Price: *$75.*

Model: *Super Parabolic Type 83.* Capacity: *DT5 plus 74 yds. backing* Weight: *4-1/14 oz.* Features: *lightweight alloy construction, right or left-hand wind, adjustable drag, line guard, raised rim for hand drag.* Price: *$75.*

Quick Corp.

QUICK SPECIALIZES IN SPINNING and casting reels and rods, but they also produce three models of a fly reel. Other products include Damyl monofilament line. The corporation's main plant is located in West Germany, and Quick Corporation of America is located in Costa Mesa, California. Quick has been making reels for over 50 years.

Model: *Quick 25.* Size: *3½" housing diam., 1-3/16" width.* Capacity: *DT5 plus 50 yds. 20-lb.-test backing.* Weight: *4½ oz.* Features: *n.a.* Price: *$17-$20.*

Model: *Quick 45.* Size: *3½" housing diam., 1-3/16" width.* Capacity: *DT5 plus 50 yds. 20-lb.-test backing.* Weight: *6 oz.* Features: *quick-change spool.* Price: *$20-$25.*

Model: *Quick 55.* Size: *3½" housing diam., 1¼" width.* Capacity: *DT6 plus 50 yds. 30-lb.-test backing.* Features: *quick-change spool.* Price: *$20-$25.*

Ryobi America Corp.

Model: *FLY 455.* Size: *n.a.* Capacity: *70 yds. WF10F.* Weight: *7 oz.* Features: *adjustable drag, quick take-apart spool, right- or left-hand wind.* Price: *n.a.*

Model: *FLY 355.* Size: *n.a.* Capacity: *50 yds. L8F.* Weight: *5.7 oz.* Features: *adjustable drag, quick take-apart spool, right- or left-hand wind.* Price: *n.a.*

St. Croix Corp.

Model: *#29 Automatic.* Size: *n.a.* Capacity: *DT7F.* Weight: *9½ oz.* Features: *vertical mount, folding line-trigger.* Price: *n.a.*

Model: *#330 Single Action.* Size: *n.a.* Capacity: *DT7F.* Weight: *5 oz.* Features: *adjustable drag, push-button take-apart spool.* Price: *n.a.*

Model: *#47 Single Action Salmon.* Size: *n.a.* Capacity: *DT9F plus 50 yds. backing.* Weight: *10 oz.* Features: *adjustable drag, push-button spool release.* Price: *n.a.*

Scientific Anglers

Model: *System 4.* Size: *2-3/4" diam.* Capacity: *#4 line plus backing.* Weight: *3½ oz.* Features: *right- or left-hand wind, adjustable one-directional click drag, spring latch for spool change.* Price: *$62 (extra spool $27).*

Model: *System 5.* Size: *3" diam.* Capacity: *#5 line plus backing.* Weight: *3-3/4 oz.* Features: *right- or left-hand wind, adjustable one-directional click drag, spring.* Price: *$63 (extra spool $27).*

Model: *System 6.* Size: *3¼" diam.* Capacity: *#6 line plus backing.* Weight: *4¼ oz.* Features: *right- or left-hand wind, adjustable one-directional click drag, spring latch for spool change.* Price: *$64 (extra spool $28).*

Model: *System 7.* Size: *3-7/16" diam.* Capacity: *#7 line plus backing.* Weight: *4½ oz.* Features: *right- or left-hand wind, adjustable one-directional click drag, spring latch for spool change.* Price: *$65 (extra spool $28).*

Model: *System 8.* Size: *3-5/8" diam.* Capacity: *#8 line plus backing.* Weight: *5-3/4 oz.* Features: *right- or left-hand wind, adjustable one-directional click drag, spring latch for spool change.* Price: *$66 (extra spool $28).*

Model: *System 9.* Size: *3-3/4" diam.* Capacity: *#9 line plus backing.* Weight: *6¼ oz.* Features: *right- or left-hand wind, adjustable one-directional click drag, spring latch for spool change, plus special corrosion resistant components for saltwater use.* Price: *$71 (extra spool $29).*

Model: *System 10.* Size: *3-7/8" diam.* Capacity: *#10 line plus backing.* Weight: *7½ oz.* Features: *right- or left-hand wind, adjustable one-directional click drag, spring latch for spool change, plus special corrosion resistant components for saltwater use.* Price: *$72 (extra spool $29).*

Model: *System 11.* Size: *4" diam.* Capacity: *#11 line plus backing.* Weight: *8 oz.* Features: *right- or left-hand wind, adjustable one-directional click drag, spring latch for spool change, plus special corrosion resistant components for saltwater use.* Price: *$73 (extra spool $29).*

Seamaster Corp.

THE FIRST SEAMASTER REEL was made in 1955 by Bob McChristian, Jr. Since then Seamaster reels have earned a position among the premier saltwater fly reels. The line of Seamaster products is currently being expanded to include fly rods, saltwater flies, rod-building components and other accessories. Seamaster is operated by McChristian and Jim Lopez, and the company is located in Coral Gables, Florida.

Model: *Mark I.* Size: *n.a.* Capacity: *WF7F plus 300 yds. 20-lb.-test Micron backing.* Weight: *6 oz.* Features: *stainless-steel ball-bearing mounted drag, gold-anodized and Blachstone finish.* Price: *$170.*

Model: *Mark II.* Size: *n.a.* Capacity: *WF9F plus 200 yds. 20-lb.-test Micron backing.* Weight: *8 oz.* Features: *stainless-steel ball-bearing mounted drag, gold-anodized and Blachstone finish.* Price: *$185.*

Model: *Mark III.* Size: *n.a.* Capacity: *WF11F plus 1000 ft. 20-lb.-test Micron backing.* Weight: *10 oz.* Features: *stainless-steel ball-bearing mounted drag, gold-anodized and Blachstone finish.* Price: *$200.*

Model: *Mark IV.* Size: *n.a.* Capacity: *WF13F plus 600 yds. 30-lb.-test Micron backing.* Weight: *13 oz.* Features: *stainless-steel ball-bearing mounted drag, gold-anodized and Blachstone finish.* Price: *$250.*

Model: *Salmon.* Size: *n.a.* Capacity: *WF9F plus 200 yds. 20-lb.-test Micron backing.* Weight: *8 oz.* Features: *anti-reverse, stainless-steel, naval brass and bar-stock construction, gold-anodized and Blachstone finish, right- or left-hand model avail.* Price: *$185.*

Model: *Tarpon.* Size: *n.a.* Capacity: *WF11F plus 1000 ft. 20-lb.-test Micron backing.* Weight: *12 oz.* Features: *anti-reverse, stainless-*

steel, naval brass and bar-stock construction, gold-anodized and Blachstone finish, right- or left-hand models avail. Price: $200.

Model: *Marlin.* Size: *n.a.* Capacity: *30 ft. ST11S plus 2000 ft. 20-lb.-test Micron backing.* Weight: *14 oz.* Features: *anti-reverse, stainless-steel, naval brass and bar-stock construction, gold-anodized and Blachstone finish.* Price: *$215.*

Seaway Importing Co.

SEAWAY CARRIES A BROAD RANGE of outdoor-oriented equipment, including spinning reels and fly reels. Most of this company's line, however, centers around raingear, boots and outdoor accessories. Seaway is a division of U.S. Industries Inc. and is located in Niles, Illinois.

Model: *Seaway Fly Reel.* Size: *n.a.* Capacity: *30 yds. #9 line plus 50 yds. backing.* Weight: *n.a.* Features: *adjustable drag, on-off click button.* Price: *n.a.*

Model: *Seaway Automatic.* Size: *n.a.* Capacity: *30 yds. #7 line plus 50 yds. backing.* Weight: *n.a.* Features: *vertical-mount automatic, spring-loaded line retrieve.* Price: *n.a.*

Shakespeare Company

Model: *1898 Purist.* Size: *3½" spool diam.* Capacity: *any size line plus 200 yds. 20-lb.-test braided backing.* Weight: *13 oz.* Features: *adjustable drag, warning click, quick take-apart spool.* Price: *n.a.*

Model: *7590 President II.* Size: *2-5/8" spool diam.* Capacity: *DT7, DT8.* Weight: *2.8 oz.* Features: *aluminum and magnesium composite construction, exposed rim for drag control.* Price: *n.a.*

Model: *7593 Purist.* Size: *2-3/16" spool diam.* Capacity: *L6.* Weight: *4½ oz.* Features: *n.a.* Price: *n.a.*

Model: *7594 Purist.* Size: *2-11/16" spool diam.* Capacity: *L7.* Weight: *4.9 oz.* Features: *n.a.* Price: *n.a.*

Model: *7595 Purist.* Size: *2-11/16" spool diam.* Capacity: *L8.* Weight: *5.6 oz.* Features: *n.a.* Price: *n.a.*

Model: *7596 Purist.* Size: *3-1/16" spool diam.* Capacity: *L11.* Weight: *5.6 oz.* Features: *n.a.* Price: *n.a.*

Model: *7597 Purist.* Size: *3-1/16" spool diam.* Capacity: *L12.* Weight: *6.4 oz.* Features: *n.a.* Price: *n.a.*

Model: *1890 Purist.* Size: *3-1/8" spool diam.* Capacity: *n.a.* Weight: *3.8 oz.* Features: *ultra-light construction, audible click or silent operation.* Price: *n.a.*

Prices (and price ranges) listed in this directory are the manufacturer's suggested retail prices as of late 1977, and they are subject to change without notice. Please consult pp. 233-235 for addresses of manufacturers from whom up-to-date price information may be obtained, or check with your local fly-tackle dealer.

Model: *2530 Purist.* Size: *2½" spool diam.* Capacity: *L7.* Weight: *4.9 oz.* Features: *built-in selective drag.* Price: *n.a.*

Model: *2531 Purist.* Size: *3" spool diam.* Capacity. *L11.* Weight: *5¼ oz.* Features: *adjustable drag.* Price: *n.a.*

Model: *1827 Tru-Art Automatic.* Size: *n.a.* Capacity: *#6 line.* Weight: *9.4 oz.* Features: *vertical-mount automatic, fold-away trigger.* Price: *n.a.*

Model: *1824 OK Automatic.* Size: *n.a.* Capacity: *#6 line.* Weight: *8.9 oz.* Features: *vertical-mount automatic, fold-away trigger.* Price: *n.a.*

Model: *1837 Tru-Art Automatic.* Size: *n.a.* Capacity: *#6 line.* Weight: *9 oz.* Features: *horizontal-mount automatic, fold-away trigger.* Price: *n.a.*

Model: *1822 OK Automatic.* Size: *n.a.* Capacity: *#6 line.* Weight: *8½ oz.* Features: *horizontal-mount automatic, fold-away trigger.* Price: *n.a.*

Thomas & Thomas

Model: *Classic 275.* Size: *2-3/4" spool diam.* Capacity: *DT3-5, WF4-6* Weight: *4½ oz.* Features: *right- or left-hand wind, adjustable drag aluminum, stainless-steel and brass construction.* Price: *$90.*

Model: *Classic 300.* Size: *3" spool diam.* Capacity: *DT4-6, WF5-7* Weight: *5 oz.* Features: *right- or left-hand wind, adjustable drag aluminum, stainless-steel and brass construction.* Price: *$90.*

Model: *Classic 325.* Size: *3¼" spool diam.* Capacity: *DT5-7, WF6-8* Weight: *5½ oz.* Features: *right- or left-hand wind, adjustable drag aluminum, stainless-steel and brass construction.* Price: *$90.*

Tycoon/Fin-Nor Corp.

TYCOON/FIN-NOR BEGAN producing reels in 1935. Since that time it has become known as one of the premier producers of handcrafted, heavy-duty reels for spinning and trolling, as well as fly-fishing. Other Fin/Nor products include fiberglass trolling and spinning rods, rod components, Dacron and monofilament lines, and angling accessories. Tycoon/Fin-Nor is located in Miami, Florida.

Model: *Fin-Nor #2 Standard.* Size: *3½" spool diam.* Capacity: *#9 line plus 200 yds. 15-lb.-test backing.* Weight: *9 oz.* Features: *large diameter brake disk, adjustable drag, one-piece aluminum bar-stock frame and spool, right- or left-hand models avail.* Price: *$175 (extra spool: $60).*

Model: *Fin-Nor #2 Anti-Reverse.* Size: *3-1/8" spool diam.* Capacity: *#9 line plus 200 yds. 15-lb.-test backing.* Weight: *8 oz.* Features: *large diam. brake disk with adjustable drag, one-piece aluminum bar stock frame and spool, right- or left-hand models avail., inset double handle with anti-reverse.* Price: *$190.*

Model: *Fin-Nor #3 Standard.* Size: *4" spool diam.* Capacity: *#9 line plus 250 yds. 20-lb.-test backing.* Weight: *12 oz.* Features: *large diam. disk brake with adjustable drag, one-piece aluminum bar-stock frame and spool, right- or left-hand models avail.* Price: *$190 (extra spool: $65).*

Model: *Fin-Nor #3 Anti-Reverse.* Size: *3½" spool diam.* Capacity: *#10 line plus 250 yds. 20-lb.-test backing.* Weight: *11 oz.* Features: *large diam. brake disk with adjustable drag, one-piece aluminum bar-stock frame and spool, right- or left-hand models avail., inset double handle with anti-reverse.* Price: *$195.*

Val-Craft Inc.

The Valentine fly reel, a product of Valentine Tool & Stamping Inc., producers of precision stamping products, was developed by the company's fly-fishing president, Charles Valentine, in the late 1960's. It was first produced in 1972, and in 1976 two new sizes of the reel were introduced. Valentine Tool & Stamping was incorporated in 1954, and Val-Craft is located in Chartley, Massachusetts.

Model: *Valentine 400.* Size: *4" spool diam.* Capacity: *WF11F plus 300 yds. 20-lb.-test backing.* Weight: *9½ oz.* Features: *quick take-apart spool, Teflon drag, anodized-aluminum construction, 1½:1 retrieve ratio.* Price: *$75 (extra spool: $14.50).*

Model: *Valentine 375.* Size: *3-3/4" spool diam.* Capacity: *WF9F plus 200 yds. 20-lb.-test backing.* Weight: *9 oz.* Features: *quick take-apart spool, Teflon drag, anodized-aluminum construction, 1½:1 retrieve ratio.* Price: *$68 (extra spool: $13.50).*

Model: *Valentine 350.* Size: *3½" spool diam.* Capacity: *WF7F plus 150 yds. 20-lb.-test backing.* Weight: *7½ oz.* Features: *quick take-apart spool, Teflon drag, anodized-aluminum construction, 1½:1 retrieve ratio.* Price: *$60 (extra spool: $12.60).*

Wright & McGill

Model: *EC-10.* Size: *n.a.* Capacity: *30 yds. #5 line.* Weight: *3½ oz.* Features: *adjustable drag, latch-release spool.* Price: *$15.*

Model: *EC-11.* Size: *n.a.* Capacity: *30 yds. #7 line.* Weight: *4 oz.* Features: *adjustable drag, latch-release spool.* Price: *$15.*

Model: *EC-12.* Size: *n.a.* Capacity: *30 yds. #8 line.* Weight: *4½ oz.* Features: *adjustable drag, latch-release spool.* Price: *$15.*

Model: *EC-14.* Size: *n.a.* Capacity: *30 yds. #8 line.* Weight: *4-7/8 oz.* Features: *adjustable drag, latch-release spool.* Price: *$18.*

Model: *ECD Automatic.* Size: *n.a.* Capacity: *30 yds. #7 line.* Weight: *9 oz.* Features: *aluminum construction, slip clutch, multiple gearing, 3-position spring clamp.* Price: *$21.*

Zebco

Zebco, a division of the Brunswick Corporation, makes spinning and casting reels as its primary products, but it also produces fiberglass spinning and casting rods. Its only fly-fishing products are the recently introduced Cardinal fly reels. Zebco is located in Tulsa, Oklahoma.

Model: *Cardinal 156.* Size: *2-7/8" spool diam.* Capacity: *WF5, 6, DT5, 6 plus 55 yds. backing.* Weight: *3.9 oz.* Features: *wide-span drag adjustment, right- or left-hand wind, quick-release spool.* Price: *n.a.*

Model: *Cardinal 178.* Size: *3¼" spool diam.* Capacity: *WF7, 8, DT7, 8.* Weight: *5.3 oz.* Features: *wide-span drag adjustment, right- or left-hand wind, quick release spool.* Price: *n.a.*

A selection of fly reels, 1860 to the present. Photo courtesy of The Museum of American Fly Fishing.

ANGLERS JUST MOVING INTO FLY-FISHING cannot totally appreciate the miracle of the modern fly line. While the traditional silk lines were delightful to cast under ideal conditions, they needed constant dressing with various exotic preparations, had to be dried out at the end of the day (they sometimes *ended* the day for the angler), and they became gummy and tacky with prolonged storage.

With the coming of the modern fly line in the 1950's, fly anglers were freed of their bondage. Lines would last for years with normal use, they needed little or no dressing, and they were available in various tapers and densities. These lines were built around a level braided core, usually of nylon, and a plastic coating was added under heat-controlled conditions, with the thickness of the coating varying with the design requirements of the line. Control of the density was also available to the manufacturer, so that a line could sink (at various rates, and in varying sements of its length), float, or either (in similar fashion to the line-dressing aspect of the old silk lines).

One of the greatest resulting gains, however, was the fact that carefully controlled line diameters and tapers allowed the fly lines to be accurately classified by weight (the weight of the *forward 30 feet* of the line head). In the case of silk lines — various in their braiding styles and source of silk — the only convention available was line *diameter*. This was often misleading and confusing — letters of the alphabet were assigned to various line diameters, and tapers were indicated by such mystical designations as "HEH" or "GAF." Anglers thought it meant more than it did.

Now, the weight of the forward 30 feet of fly line — the normal amount of line one would have in the air when loading up the fly rod -- could be assigned a number. This number could then be matched to the recommendation of the manufacturer of any given fly rod: e.g., a rod designated by the maker to respond most optimally with a 6-weight line would carry such a designation toward its butt-end. Technically, this indicated a 30-foot line weight of 152-168 grains, that specific rod's critical weight. There is, however, some room for leeway in such recommendations, and an experienced caster can handle a fairly wide range of line weights on any given rod. (Line tapers are now designated by DT, double taper; WF, weight-forward taper; and L, level, or untapered.)

The other development, however, is the wide range of sinking lines now on the market, giving the fly-rodder more versatility in his fishing. Lines can be made of various densities to sink slowly, fast or extra-fast, and these can be obtained in styles in which only the line tip sinks, the full 30-foot head sinks, or in which the entire line sinks.

Even more specialized lines now exist, as will be indicated in the following directory of line manufacturers.

Fly Lines

Angler's World

Model: *Angler's World Premium Floating Fly Line.* Tapers avail.: *DT, WF, long-belly WF.* Length(yds.): *n.a.* Color(s): *n.a.* Sizes avail.: *DT3-11, WF4-11, long-belly WF5-10.* Price: *$21.*

Model: *Angler's World Premium Sinking Fly Line.* Tapers avail.: *long-belly WF, ST.* Length(yds.): *n.a.* Color(s): *n.a.* Sizes avail.: *long-belly WF5-10, ST8-11.* Price: *$21 (long-belly WF), $23 (ST).*

Model: *Angler's World Premium Floating-Sinking Fly Line.* Tapers avail.: *WF, long-belly WF.* Length(yds.): *n.a.* Color(s): *n.a.* Sizes avail.: *WF5-10, long-belly WF5-10.* Price: *$21 (WF), $23 (long-belly WF).*

Model: *Angler's World Premium Slow-Sinking Fly Line.* Tapers avail.: *DT.* Length(yds.): *n.a.* Color(s): *n.a.* Sizes avail.: *DT5-7.* Price: *$21.*

L. L. Bean

L. L. BEAN WAS FOUNDED in 1912 by Leon Leonwood Bean — his first and only product at that time was his original Maine Hunting Shoe. From those origins the company has grown to be one of the best-known outdoorsmen's outfitters in the world. Located in Freeport, Maine, Bean's products include hunting and fishing clothing, footwear, raingear and accessories. Bean carries angling products from major manufacturers, but also offers a fly line and several accessories of their own.

Model: *Bean's Double L Floating.* Tapers avail.: *L, DT, WF, SW.* Length(yds.): *25(L), 30(DT), 35(WF), 35(SW).* Color(s): *amber.* Sizes avail.: *L5-8, DT5-8, WF7-9, SW9-11.* Price: *$2.60-$8.25.*

Model: *Bean's Double L Sinking.* Tapers avail.: *L, DT, WF.* Length (yds.): *25(L), 30(DT), 35(WF).* Color(s): *mahogany.* Sizes avail: *L5-8, DT5-8, WF6-9.* Price: *$2.50-$7.75.*

Berkley & Co.

Model: *Specialist Floating.* Tapers avail.: *DT, WF, Blunt-Tip WF.* Length(yds.): *n.a.* Color(s): *n.a.* Sizes avail.: *DT3-10, WF4-10, Blunt-Tip WF7-11.* Price: *n.a.*

Model: *Specialist Floating-Sinking.* Tapers avail.: *WF.* Length(yds.): *n.a. (first 10' sinking).* Color(s): *n.a.* Sizes avail.: *WF5-10.* Price: *n.a.*

Model: *Specialist Sinking.* Tapers avail.: *DT, WF, ST.* Length(yds.): *n.a.* Color(s): *n.a.* Sizes avail.: *DT5-10, WF6-10, ST7-11.* Price: *n.a.*

Bevin-Wilcox Line Co.

Bevin-Wilcox is a division of Brownell & Company of Moodus, Connecticut, and it manufactures lines primarily for spinning, bait-casting, trolling and saltwater use, but their product selection includes two fly lines. Other products include cord and seine twine.

Model: *Neversink Floating.* Tapers avail.: *L, DT, WF.* Length(yds): *25(L), 30(DT), 35(WF).* Color(s): *dark green, amber.* Sizes avail.: *L5-8, DT5-7, WF5, 7, 9.* Price: *n.a.*

Model: *Salmon River Floating.* Tapers avail.: *L, DT.* Length(yds): *25(L), 30(DT).* Color(s): *light green.* Sizes avail.: *L5-7, DT4-6.* Price: *n.a.*

Cortland Line Company

Model: *333 Floating.* Tapers avail.: *DT, WF, L.* Length(yds.): *30(DT), 35(WF), 25(L).* Color(s): *mist-green, white, yellow.* Sizes avail.: *DT4-10, WF5-11, L3-9.* Price: *$16(DT), $17(WF), $4.25-$6(L).*

Model: *333 Sinking.* Tapers avail.: *L, DT, WF, ST.* Length(yds.): *25(L), 30(DT), 35(WF), 10(ST).* Color(s): *dark green.* Sizes avail.: *L4-9, DT5-9, WF5-11, ST6-11.* Price: *$4.50-$6(L), $16(DT), $17(WF), $8.50(ST).*

Model: *333 Sink Tip.* Tapers avail.: *WF.* Length(yds.): *35 (first 10' extra-fast-sinking).* Color(s): *light green with dark-green tip.* Sizes avail.: *WF5-11.* Price: *$18.*

Model: *333 Saltwater Floating.* Tapers avail.: *WF.* Length(yds.): *35.* Color(s): *white.* Sizes avail.: *WF7-11.* Price: *$17.*

Model: *Fairplay Floating.* Tapers avail.: *L, DT, WF.* Length(yds.): *25(L), 30(DT), 35(WF).* Color(s): *russet, aqua.* Sizes avail.: *L5-9, DT5-9, WF6-8.* Price: *$2.20-$2.75(L), $7.50(DT), $8(WF).*

Model: *444 Floating.* Tapers avail.: *DT, WF, Bug, SW.* Color(s): *peach.* Length(yds.): *30(DT), 35(WF, Bug, SW).* Sizes avail.: *DT3-10, WF4-11, Bug 7-10, SW8-11.* Price: *$17.50(DT), $18.50(WF, Bug, SW).*

Model: *444 Sinking.* Tapers avail.: *DT, WF.* Length(yds.): *30(DT), 35(WF).* Colors: *n.a.* Sizes avail.: *DT5-9, WF5-11 (each line avail. in medium-, fast- or extra-fast-sinking densities).* Price: $16.50(DT), $18.50(WF).

Model: *444 Sink-Tip.* Tapers avail.: *DT, WF.* Length(yds.): *30(DT), 35(WF), (first 10' fast-sinking).* Color(s): *peach with darker sinking section.* Sizes avail.: *DT5-9, WF5-11.* Price: *$19.50.*

Model: *444 Sink-Hed.* Tapers avail.: *WF.* Length(yds.): *35 (first 30' fast-sinking).* Color(s): *peach with darker sinking section.* Sizes avail.: *WF6-11.* Price: *$19.50.*

Model: *444 Sinking Shooting Taper.* Tapers avail.: *ST.* Length(yds.): *10.* Color(s): *n.a.* Sizes avail.: *ST9-11 (avail. in medium-, fast- or extra-fast-sinking densities).* Price: *$9.*

Model: *444 Floating Shooting Taper.* Tapers avail.: *ST.* Length(yds.): *10.* Color(s): *n.a.* Sizes avail.: *ST9-11.* Price: *$9.*

Model: *444 Slow-Sink Tip.* Tapers avail.: *WF.* Length(yds.): *35 (first 10' slow-sinking).* Color(s): *n.a.* Sizes avail.: *WF4-9.* Price: *n.a.*

Model: *Cortland Lead-Core.* Tapers avail.: *n.a.* Length(yds.): *sold in desired lengths.* Color(s): *n.a.* Sizes avail.: *13 grains-per-foot throughout.* Price: *n.a.*

Model: *444 Nymph-Tip Floating.* Tapers avail.: *WF.* Length(yds.): *35.* Color(s): *peach with fluorescent-red strike indicator.* Sizes avail.: *WF4-9.* Price: *$19.50.*

Model: *444 Tournament Floating.* Tapers avail.: *DT, WF.* Length (yds.): *30(DT), 30(WF).* Color(s): *ultra-visible red.* Sizes avail.: *DT5-9, WF5-9.* Price: *$18.50.*

The Garcia Corp.

Model: *Long Belly Floating.* Tapers avail.: *Long Belly Taper.* Length (yds.): *30.* Color(s): *ivory, aqua, gray.* Sizes avail.: *#5-10.* Price: *n.a.*

Model: *Long Belly Sinking.* Tapers avail.: *Long Belly Taper.* Length (yds.): *30.* Color(s): *ivory, aqua, gray.* Sizes avail.: *#5-10.* Price: *n.a.*

Model: *Long Belly Sink Tip.* Tapers avail.: *Long Belly Taper.* Length (yds.): *30.* Color(s): *ivory, aqua, gray.* Sizes avail.: *#5-10.* Price: *n.a.*

Model: *Kingfisher Floating.* Tapers avail.: *L, DT, WF.* Length(yds.): *30.* Color(s): *n.a.* Sizes avail.: *L4-8, DT4-7, WF5-9.* Price: *n.a.*

The Gladding Corp.

Gladding has been manufacturing fishing tackle since 1816, and its current line of products includes fishing lines for almost all uses. Many fly fishermen are acquainted with

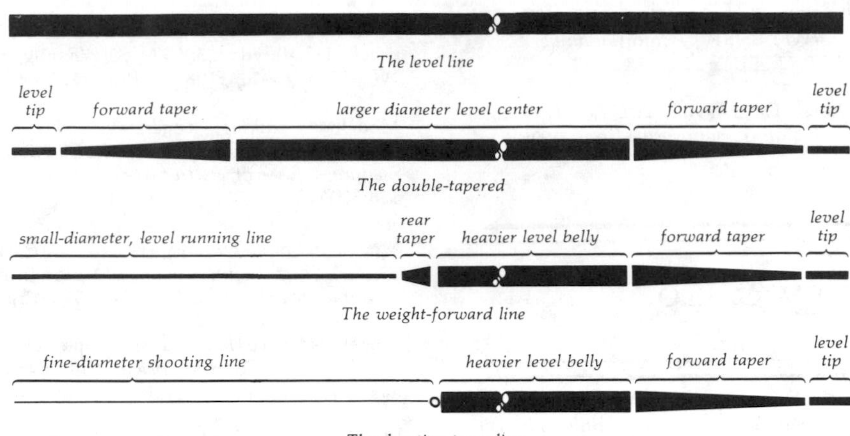

Gladding's broad range of fly lines, as well as their monofilament and Dacron lines. The Fishing Line Division of Gladding Corporation is located in South Otselic, New York.

Model: *Super Aerofloat Floating.* Tapers avail.: *L, DT, WF, SW, ST.* Length(yds.): *25(L), 30(DT), 35(WF), 40(SW), 11(ST).* Color(s): *white.* Sizes avail.: *L3-9, DT5-9, WF6-10, SW9-11, ST9, 10.* Price: *n.a.*

Model: *Super Aqua-Sink Sinking.* Tapers avail.: *L, DT, WF, ST.* Length(yds.): *25(L), 30(DT) 35(WF), 11(ST).* Color(s): *dark green.*

Model: *Magistrate Floating.* Tapers avail.: *L, DT, WF.* Length(yds.): *25(L), 30(DT), 35(WF).* Color(s): *green.* Sizes avail.: *L1-5, DT5, 7, WF6, 7.* Price: *n.a.*

Model: *Ideal Floating.* Tapers avail.: *L.* Length(yds.): *25.* Color(s): *dark green.* Sizes avail.: *L3-7.* Price: *n.a.*

Model: *Super Floating.* Tapers avail.: *L, DT.* Length(yds.): *25(L), 30(DT).* Color(s): *light green.* Sizes avail.: *L5-7, DT5-7.* Price: *n.a.*

Model: *Salmon Taper Sinking.* Tapers avail.: *WF.* Length(yds.): *40 plus 200 backing.* Color(s): *different bright color every 10'.* Sizes avail.: *WF9-12.* Price: *n.a.*

Model: *Aqua-Sink Tip (first 10' fast-sinking).* Tapers avail.: *WF.* Length(yds.): *35.* Color(s): *dark green.* Sizes avail.: *WF5-12.* Price: *n.a.*

Gudebrod

GUDEBROD MANUFACTURES LINES for all kinds of fishing, specializing in casting and spinning products and rod-building tools, materials and components. Fly-fishing products include fly lines, fly-line backing, fly-tying threads, and rod-building materials and components. Other products include spinning lures and accessories. Gudebrod is also the exclusive U.S. distributor for the English Masterline fly lines. Gudebrod is located in Philadelphia, Pennsylvania.

Model: *Hi-Spot Floater.* Tapers avail.: *L, DT.* Length(yds.): *24(L), 27(DT).* Color(s): *green, amber.* Sizes avail.: *L4-8, DT5-7.* Price: *n.a.*

Model: *G-5 Floater.* Tapers avail.: *L, DT, WF, SW.* Length(yds.): *24(L), 27(DT, WF, SW).* Color(s): *green, white (SW in white only).* Sizes avail.: *L4-10, DT4-10, WF5-10, SW8-11.* Price: *n.a.*

Model: *Sink-R'-Dacron.* Tapers avail.: *L, DT, WF.* Length(yds.): *24(L), 27(DT, WF).* Color(s): *walnut brown.* Sizes avail.: *L6-10, DT6-10, WF7-10.* Price: *n.a.*

Model: *Masterline Chancellor Floating.* Tapers avail.: *DT, WF.* Length(yds.): *30(DT4-9, WF4-8), 35 (DT10, 11, WF9-11).* Color(s): *green or white.* Sizes avail.: *DT4-11, WF4-11.* Price: *$17.50 (30-yd. lines), $18.50 (35-yd. lines).*

Model: *Masterline Chancellor Sinking.* Tapers avail.: *DT, WF.* Length (yds.): *30(DT4-9), WF4-8, 35(DT10, 11, WF9-11).* Color(s): *gray.* Sizes avail.: *DT4-11, WF4-11.* Price: *$17.50 (30-yd. lines), $18.50 (35-yd. lines).*

Model: *Masterline Chalkstream Floating.* Tapers avail.: *DT.* Length (yds.): *30.* Color(s): *chalk gray.* Sizes avail.: *DT3-8.* Price: *$25.*

Model: *Masterline Chalkstream Floating with Sinking Tip.* Tapers avail.: *DT, WF.* Length(yds.): *30(DT6-9, WF6-8), 35(DT10, 11, WF9).* Color(s): *hot orange with black sinking-tip section.* Sizes avail.: *DT6-11, WF6-9.* Price: *$30.*

Model: *Masterline Chalkstream Very-Fast-Sinking Lead-Cored.* Tapers avail.: *DT, WF.* Length(yds.): *30(DT5-9, WF6-8), 35(DT10, 11, WF9).* Color(s): *charcoal.* Sizes avail.: *DT5-11, WF6-9.* Price: *$30.*

Herter's Inc.

Model: *Guide Floating.* Tapers avail.: *L, DT, WF.* Length(yds.): *25(L), 30(DT, WF).* Color(s): *green.* Sizes avail.: *L4-7, DT4-7, WF6-8.* Price: *$2.95(L), $6.95(DT), $7.95(WF).*

Model: *Masterweave Floating.* Tapers avail.: *L, DT, WF.* Length (yds.): *25(L), 30(DT), 35(WF).* Color(s): *green, tan.* Sizes avail.: *L5-7, DT5-7, 9, WF7-9.* Price: *$1.77(L), $2.89(DT, WF).*

Model: *Masterweave Sinking.* Tapers avail.: *L, DT, WF.* Length (yds.): *25(L), 30(DT), 35(WF).* Color(s): *dark brown.* Sizes avail.: *L8, 9, DT5, 6, 8, WF9, 10.* Price: *$1.77(L), $2.89(DT, WF).*

King-Eider Silk Lines

KING-EIDER SILK LINES were manufactured by Cumberland (Aylestone) Ltd. of Leicester, England. The Cumberland silk lines were sold under the Kingfisher name throughout the world, except in the U.S., where the name King-Eider was used. The factory closed down in 1975, and the lines listed below are among the last lines manufactured by Cumberland. These lines are offered by Norton S. Remmer of Worcester, Massachusetts.

Model: *King Eider Silk Fly Line.* Tapers avail.: *DT.* Length(yds.): *30.* Color(s): *green.* Sizes avail.: *#5, 7.* Price: *$45 ea. (the stock is the last 40 lines manufactured by Cumberland (Aylestone) Ltd. of Leicester, England, 5 #5 lines and 35 #7 lines).*

H. L. Leonard Rod Inc.

Model: *Leonard Floating.* Tapers avail.: *DT, WF.* Length(yds.): *n.a.* Color(s): *n.a.* Sizes avail.: *DT3-8, WF4-10.* Price: *$18.50.*

Model: *Leonard Sinking.* Tapers avail.: *WF.* Length(yds.): *n.a.* Color(s): *n.a.* Sizes avail.: *WF5-10.* Price: *$18.50.*

Model: *Leonard Floating-Sinking.* Tapers avail.: *WF.* Length(yds.): *n.a.* Color(s): *n.a.* Sizes avail.: *WF5-10.* Price: *$19.95.*

The Orvis Co.

Model: *Orvis Floating.* Tapers avail.: *WF, DT, Bass Bug/Saltwater.* Length(yds.): *30 (WF, DT), 35 (Bass Bug/Saltwater).* Color(s): *pale green, dark gray (WF only), pale green with blaze orange strike indicator (WF only), n.a. (Bass Bug/Saltwater).* Sizes avail.: *WF3-11, DT3-10, Bass Bug/Saltwater 8-11.* Price: *$17.50-$18.50.*

Model: *Orvis Fast Sinking.* Tapers avail.: *WF.* Length(yds.): *30.* Color(s): *dark green.* Sizes avail.: *WF5-9.* Price: *$17.50.*

Model: *Orvis Shooting Head Line.* Tapers avail.: *ST.* Length(yds.): *43-1/3.* Color(s): *light green running line, dark green shooting head.* Sizes avail.: *ST8-11.* Price: *$19.50.*

Model: *Intermediate Weight.* Tapers avail.: *DT, WF.* Length(yds.): *30.* Color(s): *amber.* Sizes avail.: *DT4-10, WF4-12.* Price: *$18.50.*

Pezon et Michel

Model: *Super Parabolic Floating.* Tapers avail.: *DT, WF.* Length (yds.): *30(DT), 35(WF).* Color(s): *n.a.* Sizes avail.: *DT4-9, WF4-11.* Price: *$16(DT), $17(WF).*

Model: *Super Parabolic Sinking.* Tapers avail.: *DT, WF.* Length (yds.): *30(DT), 35(WF).* Color(s): *n.a.* Sizes avail.: *DT6, 7, WF6-11.* Price: *$18(DT), $19(WF).*

Martin Reel Co.

Model: *Sovereign Floating.* Tapers avail.: *L, DT, WF.* Length(yds.): *25(L), 30(DT), 35(WF).* Color(s): *white.* Sizes avail.: *L6-8, DT5-8, WF6-9.* Price: *n.a.*

Model: *Sovereign Saltwater Floating.* Tapers avail.: *WF.* Length (yds.): *35.* Color(s): *white.* Sizes avail.: *WF8, 10.* Price: *n.a.*

Model: *Sovereign Sinking.* Tapers avail.: *DT, WF.* Length(yds.): *30(DT), 35(WF).* Color(s): *dark blue-green.* Sizes avail.: *DT6-8, WF8, 9.* Price: *n.a.*

Scientific Anglers

Model: *Wet Cel Wet Head Floating/Sinking (first 30' fast sinking).* Tapers avail.: *WF.* Length(yds.): *27-1/3.* Color(s): *two-tone green.* Sizes avail.: *WF7-12.* Price: *$19-$23.*

Model: *Wet Cel I Slow-Sinking.* Tapers avail.: *DT, WF, L, ST.* Length (yds.): *27-1/3 (DT, WF), 24 (L).* Color(s): *medium green.* Sizes avail.: *DT5-10, WF5-10, L5-11, ST6-11.* Price: *$16-$20 ($10, ST 30' coil).*

Model: *Wet Cel II Fast-Sinking.* Tapers avail.: *DT, ST, WF, L.* Length (yds.): *27-1/3 (DT, WF), 24 (L).* Color(s): *dark green.* Sizes avail.: *DT4-12, WF4-12, L4-11, ST6-11.* Price: *$5.50-$21 ($10, ST 30' coil).*

Model: *Wet Cel Hi-D Extra-Fast-Sinking.* Tapers avail.: *DT, WF, ST.* Length(yds.): *27-1/3.* Color(s): *greenish-black.* Sizes avail.: *DT7-10, WF7-10, ST7-11.* Price: *$19-$22 ($11, ST 30' coil).*

Model: *Wet Cel Hi-Speed Hi-D Super-Fast-Sinking.* Tapers avail.: *ST, WF.* Length(yds.): *27-1/3.* Color(s): *greenish-black.* Sizes avail.: *ST7-15, WF6-13.* Price: *$22-$23 ($12, ST 30' coil).*

Model: *Air Cel Fisherman Intermediate Depth.* Tapers avail.: *DT, WF, L.* Length(yds.): *27-1/3 (DT, WF), 24 (L).* Color(s): *kelly green.* Sizes avail.: *DT5-10, WF6-12, L5-9.* Price: *$5.50-$23.*

Model: *Air Cel Supreme Floating.* Tapers avail.: *DT, WF, SW.* Length (yds.): *27-1/3.* Color(s): *ivory, mahogany, fluorescent orange, non-glare gray (SW only).* Sizes avail.: *DT3-11, WF4-10, SW8-12.* Price: *$20-$25.*

Prices (and price ranges) listed in this directory are the manufacturer's suggested retail prices as of late 1977, and they are subject to change without notice. Please consult pp. 233-235 for addresses of manufacturers from whom up-to-date price information may be obtained, or check with your local fly-tackle dealer.

Model: *Air Cel Floating.* Tapers avail.: *DT, ST, L, WF, Bass Bug.* Length(yds.): *27-1/3 (DT, WF, Bass Bug), 24 (L), 10 (ST).* Color(s): *white (ST), white, light green, dark brown (DT, WF, L), light green, fluorescent orange (Bass Bug).* Sizes avail.: *DT4-9, L1-9, ST6-11, WF5-9, Bass Bug 6-9.* Price: *$5-$18.*

Model: *Air Cel Wet Tip Floating/Sinking (first 10' fast-sinking).* Tapers avail.: *DT, WF.* Length(yds.): *27-1/3.* Color(s): *two-tone green.* Sizes avail.: *DT4-8, WF5-10.* Price: *$18-$21.*

Model: *Air Cel Wet Tip Hi-D Floating/Sinking (first 10' extra-fast-sinking).* Tapers avail.: *WF, SW, Bass Bug.* Length(yds.): *27-1/3.* Color(s): *yellow/dark green.* Sizes avail.: *WF5-10, SW11-13, Bass Bug 8-10.* Price: *$19-$26.*

Model: *Air Cel Wet Belly Hi-D Floating/Sinking (first 20' extra-fast-sinking).* Tapers avail.: *WF.* Length(yds.): *27-1/3.* Color(s): *yellow/dark green.* Sizes avail.: *WF7-11.* Price: *$20-$23.*

Model: *Wet Cel Wet Head Hi-D Floating/Sinking (first 20' extra-fast-sinking).* Tapers avail.: *WF.* Length(yds.): *27-1/3.* Color(s): *yellow/dark green.* Sizes avail.: *WF7-11.* Price: *$20-$23.*

Model: *Air Cel Variweight I.* Tapers avail.: *DT (different weight on each end).* Length(yds.): *24.* Color(s): *high-visibility orange.* Sizes avail.: *n.a.* Price: *$13.*

Model: *Air Cel Variweight II.* Tapers avail.: *L (different weight on each end).* Length(yds.): *24.* Color(s): *high-visibility green.* Sizes avail.: *n.a.* Price: *$13.*

Shakespeare Company

Model: *4300 Purist Floating.* Tapers avail.: *L, DT, WF.* Length(yds.): *25(L), 30(DT, WF5-WF9), 40(WF10, 11).* Color(s): *white.* Sizes avail.: *L4-9, DT5-9, WF5-11.* Price: *n.a.*

Model: *4332 Presidential Sinking.* Tapers avail.: *L, DT, WF.* Length (yds.): *25(L), 30(DT, WF6-10), 40(WF11).* Color(s): *deep green.* Sizes avail.: *L6-9, DT6-9, WF6-11.* Price: *n.a.*

Model: *4335 Presidential Floating.* Tapers avail.: *L, DT, WF.* Length (yds.): *25(L), 30(DT, WF5-9), 40(WF10).* Color(s): *natural green.* Sizes avail.: *L4-9, DT4-9, WF5-10.* Price: *n.a.*

Sunset Line & Twine Co.

SUNSET WAS FOUNDED in 1932 in San Francisco and moved to its present facility in Petaluma, California, in 1940. Sunset manufactures fishing lines for all types of angling, as well as lines for fly-fishing. Among the "firsts" for this firm are the manufacture of shooting-tapers for fly fishing. Other products include hardware products and cords and lines for industry.

Prices (and price ranges) listed in this directory are the manufacturer's suggested retail prices as of late 1977, and they are subject to change without notice. Please consult pp. 233-235 for addresses of manufacturers from whom up-to-date price information may be obtained, or check with your local fly-tackle dealer.

Model: *Formula Ultimate Dry Fly.* Tapers avail.: *DT.* Length: *n.a.* Color(s): *n.a.* Sizes avail.: *DT3-8.* Price: *$25.*

Model: *Formula Floating.* Tapers avail.: *DT, WF, Shooting Head.* Length(yds.): *n.a.* Color(s): *n.a.* Sizes avail.: *DT4-9, WF4-10, Shooting Head 5-11.* Price: *$18.50 (DT, WF), $9 (Shooting Head).*

Model: *Formula Medium Sinking.* Tapers avail.: *DT, WF, Shooting Head.* Length(yds.): *n.a.* Color(s): *n.a.* Sizes avail.: *DT4-9, WF4-10, Shooting Head 5-11.* Price: *$18.50 (DT, WF), $9 (Shooting Head).*

Model: *Formula Extra Fast Sinking.* Tapers avail.: *DT, WF, Shooting Head.* Length(yds.): *n.a.* Color(s): *n.a.* Sizes avail.: *DT5-9, WF5-10, Shooting Head 5-11.* Price: *$18.50 (DT, WF), $9 (Shooting Head).*

Model: *Cannonball Lead-Core Shooting Head.* Tapers avail.: *n.a.* Length(yds.): *n.a.* Color(s): *n.a.* Sizes avail.: *500-grain-plus weight.* Price: *n.a.*

U. S. Line Co. Inc.

U. S. LINE PRODUCES fishing lines and accessories for all angling uses. Fly-fishing products include fly lines, backing, monofilament and several creels and vests. U. S. Line is located in Westfield, Massachusetts, and its wholly owned subsidiary company, Universal Vise, manufactures fly-tying tools and vises and supplies fly-tying materials.

Model: *U.S. Professor Sinking.* Tapers avail.: *L, DT, WF.* Length (yds.): *25(L), 30(DT), 35(WF).* Color(s): *dark gray.* Sizes avail.: *L3-8, DT6-9, WF6-10.* Price: *n.a.*

Model: *U. S. Westfield Floating.* Tapers avail.: *L, DT, WF.* Length (yds.): *25(L), 30(DT), 35(WF).* Color(s): *steel green.* Sizes avail.: *L3-9, DT5-9, WF6-10.* Price: *n.a.*

Model: *U. S. Westfield Sinking Tip.* Tapers avail.: *WF.* Length(yds.): *n.a. (first 10' sinking).* Color(s): *steel green with darker sinking tip.* Sizes avail.: *WF6-10.* Price: *n.a.*

Model: *U. S. Queen of Waters Floating.* Tapers avail.: *L, DT, WF.* Length(yds.): *25(L), 30(DT), 35(WF).* Color(s): *white.* Sizes avail.: *L5-9, DT4-9, WF4-10.* Price: *n.a.*

Model: *U. S. Royal Trout Floating.* Tapers avail.: *L, DT, WF.* Length (yds.): *25(L), 30(DT), 35(WF).* Color(s): *green.* Sizes avail.: *L3, 6, 7, DT6, 7, WF7.* Price: *n.a.*

Model: *Green River Sinking.* Tapers avail.: *n.a.* Length(yds.): *25.* Color(s): *light tan.* Sizes avail.: *n.a.* Price: *n.a.*

Webley & Scott Ltd.

Model: *Webley Floating.* Tapers avail.: *DT, WF.* Length(yds.): *n.a.* Color(s): *n.a.* Sizes avail.: *DT4-9, WF5-10.* Price: *n.a.*

Model: *Webley Sinking.* Tapers avail.: *DT, WF.* Length(yds.): *n.a.* Color(s): *n.a.* Sizes avail.: *DT4-9, WF5-10.* Price: *n.a.*

Leaders are the last link, before the fly, in the "long arm" of the fly fisherman. As in the case of rods, reels and lines, your choice of leader should be dictated by the type of fishing you plan to do. Leaders are generally measured in two dimensions—length and strength. Leaders are now made of monofilament, but before the development of nylon, silkworm gut was used. Gut leaders had to be soaked in water before use to make them supple enough for fly-casting, and their strength was usually measured by the number of times the gut had been drawn through a series of sequentially smaller holes to form its diameter. A tippet of gut might be drawn five times—or 5x. This designation has been carried over into monofilament as a measure of diameter. But diameter doesn't always give the angler an idea of breaking strength, so monofilament is also designated with a pounds-tested-at-for-breaking, or simply "pounds-test." Many monofilaments also have their diameter stated in inches. The angler should simply be aware that the "x" designation measures diameter, not strength. The length of most leaders is usually between six and 15 feet, and the taper may be produced by knotting diminishing diameters of monofilament together, or it may be imparted to the monofilament itself in manufacture. Whether you choose a knotless or a knotted leader is largely a matter of personal preference—either one holds as well.

Leaders usually incorporate a stiff, large-diameter (up to .023") butt section, with suppleness and lightness gradually imparted through the taper, which may be as fine as .003". Because the knots used to tie on a tippet that has been lost or broken are generally the same as those used to construct a leader, most anglers have the ability to make their own leaders. While the price of a leader is almost always less than $2.00, many anglers prefer to "roll their own," and complete leader kits are included in this section.

Also included in this section are shooting-lines and backing. Shooting-line is attached to the back of a 30-foot shooting-taper line, and the availability of a variety of shooting-lines—floating, sinking, or of monofilament—is growing to match the increasing use of shooting-taper lines. Backing is available in a wide variety of strengths, suitable for use in different situations.

Leaders

Leaders

Angler's World Knotted Tru-Turn Leaders. *Compound taper, 7½'-12', 6x (1 lb. test)-0x (5 lb. test) tippet sizes.* Price: *$.70-$1.*

Angler's World Knotless Tru-Turn Leaders. *Compound taper, 7½'-12', 6x (1½ lb. test)-0x(7 lb. test) tippet.* Price: *$.65-$.95.*

Angler's World Knotless Special Salmon, Bass and Saltwater Leaders. *Compound taper, 9'-12', 8/5-6/5, 12-15 lb. test tippets.* Price: *$1.25.*

Dan Bailey Platlon Tapered Leaders. *Knotted, 7½'-12', 1x to 6x tippet size.* Price: *$.75-$1.*

Dan Bailey French Nylon Tapered Leaders. *Knotted, 9'-12', 0x to 6x tippet size.* Price: *$1-$1.25.*

Bean's Knotless Leaders. *7½', 9', 10-lb.-test to 1-3/4-lb.-test tippet size, camouflage color.* Price: *$1.60-$1.65.*

Berkley Qwik-Sink Knotless Leaders. *7½', 9', 0x-6x tippet size.* Price: *n.a.*

Berkley Heavy Taper Knotless Leaders. *7½', 9', 6/5-4x tippet size.* Price: *n.a.*

Berkley Specialist Knotless Leaders. *Flat butt section, 9', 0x-6x tippet size.* Price: *n.a.*

Berkley Not-A-Knot Knotless Leaders. *6', 7½', 9', 0x-6x tippet size.* Price: *n.a.*

Cortland 333 Knotless Tapered Leaders. *Mist-blue color, 1½-lb.-test to 6-lb.-test tippet size, 7½'-9'; bass/salmon models, 9', 8-lb.-test to 13-lb.-test tippet size, mist-blue color.* Price: *$.65-$.95.*

Cortland 444 Twin-Tip Tapered Leaders. *2-pc. leaders to be knotted by angler, 10', 8/5 to 6x tippet size.* Price: *$1-$1.25.*

Cortland Crown Knotless Tapered Leaders. *7½'-12', trout leader tippet size 1x-6x; bass/salmon leader, 9', 0x, 8/5, 6/5 tippet size.* Price: *$.60-$.90.*

Cortland Crown Sinking Tapered Leaders. *7½'-9', 1x-5x tippet size.* Price: *$.60-$.75.*

Creative Sports Knotless Tapered Leaders. *Compound taper, 7½', 9', 12', 0x to 6x tippet size.* Price: *$.85-$.95.*

Garcia Knotless Tapered Leaders. *7½', 9', 0x(8-lb. test) to 6x(1½-lb. test) tippet size.* Price: *n.a.*

Gladding Gladyl Salmon Leader. *·9', 6/5-8/5 tippet, clear color.* Price: *n.a.*

Gladding Clearon Knotless Tapered Nylon Leader. *7½'-9', 6x-0x tippet, clear color.* Price: *n.a.*

Gladding Gladyl Knotless Tapered Leader. *6'-9', 5x-0x tippet, clear color.* Price: *n.a.*

Gladding-South Bend Knotless Tapered Leader. *7½ '-9', 8- to 2.1-lb. test tippets.* Price: *n.a.*

Hackle & Tackle Custom Knotted Leaders. *7½'-12', 0x(10-lb.) to 7x(1-lb.) tippet size.* Price: *$.70-$1.*

Hackle & Tackle Wet Fly and Dropper Leader. *Knotted, 7½', 1x(8-lb.) to 4x(4-lb.) tippet size, clips for attaching flies.* Price: *$.90.*

Herter's Leaders. *Knotless 6'-9' (4x-0x tippet size), flat-butt knotless 9' (1-3/4 lb. test to 6 lb. test tippet size).* Price: *$1.10-$2.50 (per set of 3).*

Hille Leaders. *Knotted, 6'-12', 1x to 5x tippet sizes, camouflage color.* Price: *$.50-$.90.*

Hille's Knotless Leaders. *6'-9', 1x to 5x tippet sizes, camouflage color.* Price: *$.40-$.60.*

Leonard Knotless Leaders. *6'-12', 6x to 9/5 tippet size.* Price: *$.70-$1.25.*

Leonard Knotted Leaders. *7½'-12', 7x to 17-lb.-test tippet size.* Price: *$.80-$1.10.*

Mason Knotless Tapered Leaders. *6'-12', 6x-9/5 tippet sizes, gray or mist color.* Price: *n.a.*

Mason Balanced Leaders. *Knotted, hand-tied, 6'-12', 5x-0x tippet size, mist color.* Price: *n.a.*

Martin Sovereign Knotless Leaders. *7½', 9' 6x(1-3/4 lb.) to 0x(6 lb.) tippet size.* Price: *n.a.*

Orvis Special Knotted Leaders. *9', 12', 4x(3 lb.) to 7x(1 lb.) tippet size.* Price: *$.85, $1.10.*

Orvis Two-Knot Leaders. *7½'-12', 0x(6 lb.) to 6x(1¼ lb.) tippet size.* Price: *$.70-$1.10.*

Orvis Knotted Leaders. *7½'-12', 0x(6 lb.) to 7x(1 lb.) tippet size.* Price: *$.70-$1.10.*

Orvis Standard Compound Taper Salmon and Saltwater Leader. *Knotted, 7½'-12', 6 lb. to 18-3/4 lb. tippet size.* Price: *$.70-$1.*

Orvis Bass Bug Leaders. *Knotless, 9', 6 lb. to 12 lb. tippet size.* Price: *$.85-$1.10.*

Orvis Compound Taper Wet Fly Leaders. *Knotted, 7½', 9', 3½ lb. to 6 lb. tippet size, leader with clips for attaching fly and dropper.* Price: *$.85-$1.10.*

Pezon et Michel Parabolic and Super Parabolic Leaders. *Knotted, 9', knotless, 7½'.* Price: *$1.49, $1.99.*

U.S. Knotless Tapered Leaders. *7½'-12', 10-lb. to 1-3/4-lb.-test tippet size, brown, brown-and-mist colors.* Price: *n.a.*

Universal Vise Sink Leader. *Knotless, 7½'-9', 5x-00x tippet sizes, etched green nylon.* Price: *$1.50 (for 3).*

Wanigas Leaders. *Knotted, 7½'-12½', 6x-7x tippet size.* Price: *$1-$1.50.*

Leader Material

Angler's World Ultra-Soft Tippet Material. *5x-6/5, 2 lb.-15 lb. test, 10-20 yd. spools.* Price: *$.25.*

Berkley Trilene Tippet Material. *1-lb. to 40-lb.-test.* Price: *n.a.*

Cortland Nylorfi Tippet Material. *French-made monofilament, 1x (9.4-lb.-test) to 8x(1.1-lb.-test) sizes, 27.4-yd. spool.* Price: *$1.*

E. I. du Pont de Nemours & Co. Stren Leader Material. *Monofilament avail. in various spool sizes, clear-blue, golden, orange colors.* Price: *n.a.*

Gladding Leader Material. *Gladyl leader material, 1.2-lb. to 25.7-lb. test.* Price: *n.a.*

Gladding Leader Material. *Monofilament leader material, 1-lb. to 25-lb. test.* Price: *n.a.*

Herter's Leader Material. *Available in full range of sizes and quantities, clear and mist-blue.* Price: *$.82 (per 3 20 yd. spools).*

Leonard Leader Material. *Tippet material: .003" diam. to .015" diam.; butt material: .017" diam. to .028" diam.* Price: *$.75-$1.*

Mason Leader Material. *Soft- and hard-type nylon monofilament, 1-lb. test to 200-lb. test, avail. in assorted lengths, packaged, on wheels or in dispensers.* Price: *n.a.*

Mason Tippets. *22" and 44" lengths, 6x-0x size.* Price: *n.a.*

Maxima Chameleon Monofilament Leader Material. *Leader wheels, 1-lb. to 40-lb. test, 17 yds. and 27 yds. per spool.* Price: *n.a.*

Orvis Tippet Material. *8x(3/4 lb.) to 1x(5½ lb.), 25-yd. spools (2x only in 15-yd. spool).* Price: *$.70 per spool.*

Pezon et Michel Kroic Nylon Leader Material. *.8-lb test to 36-lb. test, 25-yd. spools.* Price: *$.85-$1.50.*

Pezon et Michel Kroic GT Nylon Leader Material. *.65-lb. test to 32-lb. test, 25- or 100-yd. spools.* Price: *$1.50-$5.*

Shakespeare Leader Material. *Blue and clear monofilament, assorted spool sizes, 2-lb. to 50-lb. test.* Price: *n.a.*

Universal Vise Sinking Tippet Material. *Etched green nylon, 6x-00x* Price: *$.50 (per 30' spool).*

U. S. Leader Material. *2-lb. to 60-lb. test, 10-yd. to 20-yd. spool.* Price: *n.a.*

Leader Kits

Hille Leader Tying Kits. *2 models: freshwater and saltwater, 12 spools, 2-lb. to 22-lb.-test (freshwater), and 5-lb. to 32-lb.-test (saltwater).* Price: *$5.95.*

Mason Leader Tie Kit. *3 models: freshwater, saltwater and super-soft, 12 spools, 2-lb. test to 22-lb. test (freshwater), 5-lb. test to 32-lb. test (saltwater), 2-lb. test to 40-lb. test (super-soft).* Price: *n.a.*

Maxima Leader Tying Kits. *12 spools Chameleon monofilament in assorted strengths, instructions.* Price: *n.a.*

Orvis Leader Tie Kit. *20 spools of monofilament plus instructions.* Price: *$10.95.*

Backing and Shooting-Lines

Angler's World Fly Line Backing. *Braided dacron, 12 lb.-30 lb. test, 100 yd. spool.* Price: *$3.50-$4.20.*

Berkley Specialist Backing. *18-lb.-test braided Dacron.* Price: *n.a.*

Cortland 333 Floating Running Line. *Braided nylon with floating finish, mist-green color, 100' coil.* Price: *$5.50.*

Cortland 333 Fly Line Backing. *Braided 18-lb.-test Dacron, sand color, 50-yd. spool.* Price: *$1.70.*

Cortland Micron Braided Backing. *White color, 50-yd. spool.* Price: *$2.25-$2.50 (1200-yd. spool: $34-$40).*

Cortland Cobra Flat Monofilament Shooting Line. *Mist or bright-red color, 12-lb. test to 30-lb. test, 50-yd. spool.* Price: *$1.60-$2.30*

Gladding Backing. *Tri-bac fly line backing, braided Dacron, 20-lb. test.* Price: *n.a.*

Gudebrod Dacron Backing. *50-yd., 1200-yd. spools, 15-, 20-, 30-lb. test.* Price: *n.a.*

Kaufmann's Green Dot Backing. *Braided Dacron, 15-, 20-, 30-lb. test, 100-yd. spool.* Price: *$3.25.*

Martin Sovereign Backing. *Braided Dacron, 18-lb. test,* Price: *n.a.*

Mason Backing. *Braided Dacron, 10-lb. test to 120-lb. test.* Price: *n.a.*

Orvis Freshwater Backing. *20-lb. test, 50-yd. to 1000-yd. spools, braided Dacron.* Price: *$1.50-$25.*

Orvis Salmon/Saltwater Backing. *Braided Dacron, 30-lb. test, 100-yd. to 200-yd. spools.* Price: *$3-$6.25.*

Scientific Anglers Air Cel Floating Shooting Line. *Light green, fluorescent-orange colors, 100' coil.* Price: *$7.*

Shakespeare Backing. *Braided dacron and monofilament backing, 12-lb. to 30-lb. test.* Price: *n.a.*

Sunset Line & Twine Amnesia Shooting Line. *Line for backing shooting tapers and lead heads, 15-lb. test to 40-lb. test.* Price: *n.a.*

Tycoon/Fin-Nor Backing. *Dacron backing, 20-lb. to 130-lb. test, 1000-yd. spools.* Price: *$35-$90.*

U. S. Fly Line Backing. *Braided Dacron or nylon, 18-lb. to 30-lb. test, tan, black-stripe colors.* Price: *n.a.*

Boots and Waders

Chest-High Waders

Angler's World Men's Waders. *Ankle-fit boots, felt soles and heels, suspenders.* Price: *$70.*

Angler's World Tall Men's Waders. *Ankle-fit boots, felt soles and heels, suspenders.* Price: *$80.*

Angler's World Ladies' Waders. *Ankle-fit boots, felt soles and heels, suspenders.* Price: *$70.*

Bean's Stockingfoot Wader. *Seamless construction, gum rubber, for use with wading shoes, suspenders, deep brown color.* Price: *$24.50.*

Converse Wadewell Waders. *Fabric inside and outside with rubber between, drawstring top, suspender buttons, belt loops, inside pocket, sponge cushion insoles, avail. cleated or with felt soles, women's cleated model avail.* Price: *n.a.*

Converse Rod & Reel Wader. *Rubber outside, cloth inside, inside pocket, belt loops, suspender buttons, sponge-cushion insoles, insulated model avail.* Price: *n.a.*

Converse Nylon Waders. *Felt or cleated soles, two-ply nylon construction, inside pocket, drawstring top, suspender buttons, belt loops, steel-shank sole.* Price: *n.a.*

Converse Cleated Sole Waders. *Fabric-surface nylon, inside pocket, belt loops, women's model avail.* Price: *n.a.*

Converse Nylon Stockingfoot Wader. *Fabric-surface nylon, belt loops, for use with wading shoes.* Price: *n.a.*

L. M. Dickson Stockingfoot Waders. *Elastic suspenders, light-brown color.* Price: *n.a.*

Herter's Hudson Bay Waders. *Insulated or uninsulated, steel-shank arch support, inside pocket.* Price: *$57.97 (insulated), $50.97 (uninsulated).*

Herter's Guide Association Waders. *Insulated, inside leg harness.* Price: *$26.95.*

Herter's Bacrene Plastic Waders. *Fold into 6"x8" package, for use with wading shoes.* Price: *$4.47.*

Herter's Hudson Bay Latex Waders. *For use with wading shoes, one piece, no seam.* Price: *$23.97.*

Hille Stockingfoot Waders. *Waist-high, heavy-gauge vinyl, suspenders, elastic waist, brush-brown color.* Price: *$13.95.*

Leonard Waders. *Fully vulcanized nylon weave, belt loops, suspender buttons, drawstring top, inside pocket, steel-shank boot, cushioned insole, polysynthetic sole material, green color.* Price: *$58.50.*

Marathon Over-the-Shoe Waders. *For use over shoes.* Price: *n.a.*

Marathon Stockingfoot Waders. *For use with wading shoes.* Price: *n.a.*

Marathon Waders. *Ankle-fit boots, felt-sole and insulated models avail.* Price: *n.a.*

Nelson Nesco Vinyl Stockingfoot Waders. *For use with wading shoes, suspenders, marsh-brown color.* Price: *n.a.*

Nelson Nesco Nylon Waders. *Drawstring top, inside pocket, suspender buttons, steel-shank sole.* Price: *n.a.*

Nelson Nesco Double-Faced Nylon Waders. *Nylon inside and outside with rubber between, inside pocket, steel-shank sole, cushioned soles, green color.* Price: *n.a.*

Nelson Nesco Vulcanized Wader. *Steel-shank sole, drawstring top, inside pocket, suspender buttons, insulated model avail.* Price: *n.a.*

OLM Nylon Waders. *Dark green nylon, silicone oil finish, inside pocket, steel shank, drawstring, insulated or uninsulated.* Price: *n.a.*

OLM Waders. *Dark green multi-ply rubber between layers of nylon, inside pocket, steel shank, outside buttons for suspenders, insulated or uninsulated.* Price: *n.a.*

OLM Vinyl Stockingfoot Waders. Price: *n.a.*

O'Neill Wader. *Neoprene dry-suit wader for use with wading shoes.* Price: *n.a.*

Orvis Deluxe Waders. *Nylon uppers, woven felt soles, inside pocket, drawstring, suspender buttons, belt loops.* Price: *$89.50, $98.50 (felt soles with aluminum studs).*

Orvis Waders. *3-ply construction, inside pocket, drawstring, belt loops, steel shank in boot, 7½ lbs.* Price: *$61.75 (felt soles), $72.75 (felt soles with aluminum studs), $52.75 (rubber soles), $61.75 (ladies' felt soles).*

Orvis Latex Stockingfoot Waders. *For use with wading shoes, inside pocket, adjustable elastic shoulder straps.* Price: *$33, $48 (heavy gauge, 50% thicker).*

Orvis Economical Waders. *2-ply (nylon-rubber) construction, inside pocket, belt loops, dark green color.* Price: *$33.95 (rubber soles), $47.95 (felt soles).*

Ranger Chestwader Waders. *Rubber construction, belt loops.* Price: *n.a.*

Royal Red Ball Dryfoot Stockingfoot Waders. *One-piece vinyl construction, elastic waist, inside pouch, for use with wading shoes, marsh-brown color.* Price: *$9.*

Royal Red Ball Cahill and Diana Waders. *Inside-outside pouch, suspender buttons, insulated models avail., dark-brown color.* Price: *$70-$75 (men's Cahill), $75 (women's Diana, uninsulated model only).*

Royal Red Ball Stream King Waders. *Drawstring top, inside pocket, insulated model avail., marsh-brown color.* Price: *n.a.*

Fritz von Schlegell Waders. *Rubber laminated between layers of nylon, non-slip Wadesafe soles, belt loops.* Price: *$42.75.*

Fritz von Schlegell Lightweight Waders. *Single-layer rubber-backed nylon, non-slip Wadesafe soles, forest-green color.* Price: *$33.50.*

Seal-Dri Waders (Wichita Canvas Supply). *Pure latex, no-seams, lightweight, stretchable, for use with wading shoes.* Price: *$40 ($58 Super Seal-Dri, 50% thicker).*

Seaway Stockingfoot Waders. *Vinyl with reinforced seams, for use with wading shoes, green color.* Price: *n.a.*

Seaway Double-Ply Nylon Waders. *Nylon outer, rubber inner, steel-shank sole, inside pocket, green color.* Price: *n.a.*

Seaway Nylon Waders. *Nylon outer, rubber inner, steel-shank sole, green color.* Price: *n.a.*

Seaway Rubber Waders. *Steel-shank arch, drawstring top, inside pocket, insulated model avail., marsh-brown color.* Price: *n.a.*

Seaway Insulated Nylon Waders. *Nylon outer and inner with rubber between, steel-shank sole, drawstring top, inside pocket, brown or green color.* Price: *n.a.*

Seaway Deluxe Oxford Nylon Waders. *Oxford nylon outer, nylon inner with rubber between, steel-shank sole, drawstring top, inside pocket, belt loops, green color.* Price: *n.a.*

Seaway Deluxe Canvas Waders. *Canvas inner and outer with rubber between, drawstring top, inside pocket, belt loops, natural color.* Price: *n.a.*

World Famous Rubber Boot-Foot Wader. *Double-ply construction, inside pocket, steel-shank soles, drawstring-closing top, marsh-brown color, insulated model available.* Price: *n.a.*

World Famous Deluxe Triple-Ply Canvas Wader. *Cotton to rubber to cotton construction, steel-shank soles, inside pocket, drawstring top and belt loops, tan color.* Price: *n.a.*

World Famous Nylon Wader. *Nylon outer, rubber inner, steel-shank soles, inside pocket, drawstring top.* Price: *n.a.*

World Famous Deluxe Nylon Boot-Foot Wader. *Triple-ply: nylon to rubber to nylon construction, steel-shank soles, detachable outer hanging pocket, drawstring top, green color.* Price: *n.a.*

World Famous Stockingfoot Nylon Wader. *Heavy-gauge vinyl, elastic suspenders, reinforced seams.* Price: *n.a.*

Hip Boots

Angler's World Hip Boots. *2 models: men's and ladies', knee harness, belt straps.* Price: *$60.*

Bean's Insulated Sporting Boot. *Hip boots, knee harness, belt strap, olive-drab color.* Price: *$29.75.*

Bean's Regular Sporting Boot. *Hip boots, knee harness, belt strap, olive-drab color.* Price: *$23.*

Bean's Ankle-Fitting Sporting Boot. *Hip boots, knee harness, belt strap, trim fitting through ankle area, olive-drab color.* Price: *$24.75.*

Converse Wadewell Hip Boots. *Cleated or felt soles, sponge-cushion insoles, drawstring tops, belt straps.* Price: *n.a.*

Converse Rod & Reel Hip Boots. *Rubber surface with fabric inside, cleated crepe sole, adjustable belt straps, knee harness, sponge-cushion insole, insulated model avail., women's uninsulated model avail.* Price: *n.a.*

Converse Nylon Hip Boots. *Knee harness, belt strap, steel-shank sole, avail. with felt or cleated sole, women's cleated-sole model avail.* Price: *n.a.*

Herter's Hudson Bay Hip Boots. *Insulated or uninsulated, steel-shank arch support, olive-drab color.* Price: *$33.97 (insulated), $24.97 (uninsulated).*

Herter's Guide Association Hip Boots. *Insulated, steel shanks, olive-green color.* Price: *$21.95.*

Marathon Ankle-Fit Hippers. *Inside harness, drawstring top, rubberized-nylon uppers, belt straps, felt-sole and insulated models avail.* Price: *n.a.*

Marathon 28-20 Hippers. *Inside harness, drawstring top, rubberized-nylon uppers, belt straps, for use over shoes.* Price: *n.a.*

Marathon Stockingfoot Hippers. *Belt straps, drawstring top, for use with wading shoes.* Price: *n.a.*

Nelson Nesco Extra-Duty Nylon Hip Boots. *Knee harness, hip straps, steel-shank soles, olive-drab color.* Price: *n.a.*

Nelson Nesco Rubber Hip Boots. *Steel-shank sole, knee harness, hip straps, cushioned inner sole, insulated or uninsulated, boys' and ladies' models avail.* Price: *n.a.*

OLM Hip Boots. *Dark green nylon outside, molded soles with steel shank, insulated or uninsulated.* Price: *n.a.*

Orvis Hippers. *3-ply construction, knee-harness, belt straps, boot with steel shank.* Price: *$52.75 (felt soles), $62.75 (felt soles with aluminum studs), $45.75 (rubber soles), $52.75 (ladies' felt soles).*

Ranger Hipwader Hip Boots. *Leg harness, belt straps, rubber construction.* Price: *n.a.*

Ranger Fisherman Hip Boots. *Leg harness, belt straps, steel-shank sole, cushioned insole, rubber construction, brown color.* Price: *n.a.*

Ranger Angler Hip Boots. *Leg harness, belt straps, steel-shank sole, cushioned insole, carpeted outer sole, brown color.* Price: *n.a.*

Ranger Flycaster Hip Boots. *Leg harness, belt straps, cushioned insole, steel-shank sole, rubber construction, brown color.* Price: *n.a.*

Ranger Mallard Hip Boots. *Leg harness, belt straps, cushioned insole, steel-shank sole, insulated, brown color.* Price: *n.a.*

Royal Red Ball Swiftwater Hip Boots. *Inside knee harness, adjustable belt straps, insulated model avail., dark brown color.* Price: *$50-$55.*

Royal Red Ball Nimrod Hip Boots. *Knee harness, adjustable belt straps, adjustable top straps, insulated model avail., marsh-brown color.* Price: *n.a.*

Fritz von Schlegell Lightweight Travel Hippers. *Single-layer rubber-backed nylon, non-slip Wadesafe soles, forest-green color.* Price: *$24.75.*

Fritz von Schlegell Hippers. *Rubber laminated between layers of nylon, non-slip Wadesafe soles.* Price: *$34.25.*

Seaway Hip Boots. *Nylon outer lined with rubber, knee harness, hip straps, steel-shank sole, green color.* Price: *n.a.*

Seaway Deluxe Rubber Hip Boots. *Knee harness, hip straps, steel-shank sole, insulated model avail., marsh-brown color.* Price: *n.a.*

Seaway Insulated Nylon Hip Boots. *Nylon outer and inner with rubber between, insulated, knee harness, hip straps, steel-shank sole, felt-sole model avail., brown or green color.* Price: *n.a.*

World Famous Nylon Boot-Foot Hip Boots. *Nylon outside, rubber inside, steel-shank soles, knee harness, adjustable hip strap, green color.* Price: *n.a.*

World Famous Women's Hip Boots. *Double-ply construction, steel-shank soles, knee harness, adjustable hip strap, marsh-brown color.* Price: *n.a.*

World Famous Boot-Foot Hip Boots. *Double-ply construction, steel-shank soles, knee harness, adjustable hip strap, insulated model available, marsh-brown color.* Price: *n.a.*

Wading Shoes and Accessories

Angler's World Wader Belt. *All elastic, adjustable.* Price: *$4.95.*

Angler's World Wader Suspenders. *Adjustable, leather button tabs, front snap loops.* Price: *$5.95.*

Angler's World Wading Staffs. *2 models: hazelwood, 57" long and ash, 54" long.* Price: *$85 (hazelwood), $15 (ash).*

Dan Bailey Super Stream Cleats. *Aluminum bars attached to sole of rubber overshoe sandals, stretches to slip over wader or boot foot.* Price: *$27.50.*

Bean's Felt-Sole Wading Shoe. *Canvas uppers, inside toe box, olive-green color.* Price: *$23.75.*

Bean's Felt Sole Kit. *Wool felt soles, cement, buffer.* Price: *$6.75.*

Converse Lakestream Felt-Sole Wading Sandals. *Take-up straps.* Price: *n.a.*

Converse Wader Suspenders. *36" Y-type strap, rust-resistant clasps, adjustable elastic.* Price: *n.a.*

Converse Lakestream Wading Shoes. *Cleated-rubber or felt-sole models, for use with stockingfoot waders.* Price: *n.a.*

Converse Universal Repair Kit. *One tube special cement plus five 4½"x9" patches repair material.* Price: *n.a.*

Converse Felt-Sole Replacement Kit. *One pair soles, roughening scraper, one tube cement.* Price: *n.a.*

Prices (and price ranges) listed in this directory are the manufacturer's suggested retail prices as of late 1977, and they are subject to change without notice. Please consult pp. 233-235 for addresses of manufacturers from whom up-to-date price information may be obtained, or check with your local fly-tackle dealer.

Creative Sports Wading Shoes. *Poly-felt soles, leather uppers, speed laces, extra wide.* Price: *$42.50.*

L. M. Dickson Wader Suspender. *Adjustable cotton, rust proof metal hardware.* Price: *n.a.*

L. M. Dickson Wire Boot Hanger. Price: *n.a.*

L. M. Dickson Wall-Type Boot Hanger. Price: *n.a.*

Fly-Tyer's Carry-All Folstaff Wading Staffs. *Folding staff fits in leather case when not in use, cork grip, carbide tip, 3 models: Regular, ½" diam. shaft, 45" long; Long, ½" diam. shaft, 54" long; Super, 3/4" diam. shaft, 50" long.* Price: *$19.95 (Regular), $20.95 (Long), $29.95 (Super).*

Korkers Wading Sandals. *Flexible sandal for use over wading boot or sneakers, steel-studded soles.* Price: *$19.95.*

Marathon Wader Suspenders. *Elastic webbing, leather loops.* Price: *n.a.*

Marathon Wader Belt. *Elastic webbing, easy-latch buckle.* Price: *n.a.*

Minute Mend Repair Adhesive. *Sealing wax-type adhesive.* Price: *$1.98.*

Nelson Nesco Boot Hanger. *Steel construction, for one pair boots.* Price: *n.a.*

Nelson Nesco Wader Suspenders. *Elastic backstraps, metal clasps.* Price: *n.a.*

Orvis Wading Staff. *Walnut-stained white ash, 53½" long, stainless-steel cup tip.* Price: *$13.60.*

Orvis Wading Sandals. *Elastic toe-strap, nylon heel-strap, ½" woven crepe-core sole.* Price: *$13.25.*

Orvis Felt Insoles. *1/8" thick for boots or waders.* Price: *$2 (per pair).*

Orvis Wader Belt. *47", cotton webbing.* Price: *$3.85.*

Orvis Felt Liners. *Felt boot-style insert for use with waders or hip boots.* Price: *$9.75.*

Orvis Emergency Repair Stick. *Apply to waders like sealing wax.* Price: *$2.25.*

Orvis Wader Repair Kit. *Rubber cement, repair material, abrasive for preparing boot.* Price: *$2.95.*

Orvis Wader Suspenders. *Adjustable H-back style.* Price: *$7.50.*

Orvis Wading Shoe. *Full bellows tongue, leather construction.* Price: *$61 (felt sole), $67.50 (felt soles with aluminum studs).*

Royal Red Ball Lunker Wading Shoes. *2 models: polyester-mesh or Tuff-Guard uppers, for use with stockingfoot waders or as boat shoe, ankle-high padded vinyl cuff, foam tricot lining.* Price: *$25,*

Fritz von Schlegell Wadesafe Resole Kit. *Polypropylene soles.* Price: *$6.25.*

Seaway Wader Suspenders. *2 models: cotton-web and elastic (Regular) or stainless steel, leather and elastic (Deluxe), tan color (Regular), green color (Deluxe).* Price: *n.a.*

Seaway Boot Hanger. *Formed steel frame for one pair boots.* Price: *n.a.*

Sportsman's Felt Co. Wading Sole Kits. *Wool-felt soles in gray or white, 2 pc. (heel and sole), or 1 pc. (contour-flex fit).* Price: *n.a.*

Pete Test's Compleat Angler Woven Nylon Felt Sole Kit. *Soles, 4-oz. tube cement, application brush, abrasive for preparing boot.* Price: *$8.50.*

Pete Test's Compleat Angler Wader Patch Kit. *2-oz. tube silicone adhesive, abrasive paper, nylon reinforcing material.* Price: *$3.50.*

Pete Test's Compleat Angler Waterproof Cement. *4-oz. tube.* Price *$2.50.*

Vandy's Dri-But Never Slip Sole Conditioning Kit. *Black diamond grit cured to boot soles for traction. One kit conditions two pairs wading gear.* Price: *$10.*

World Famous Wader Suspenders. *Cotton webbing with elastic stretch section, double snaps, olive-drab color.* Price: *n.a.*

World Famous Deluxe Nylon Wader Suspenders. *Elasticized nylon with rubber attachments, olive-drab color.* Price: *n.a.*

World Famous Metal Boot Hanger. *Fits all waders.* Price: *n.a.*

Fly-Fishing Accessories

Fly Boxes

Bonnand of France Series 8 Fly Boxes (M. Sharf & Co.). *3 models, transparent pale-green ABS construction, brass hinge, models avail. in different compartment styles, 6.6"x4"x1.2".* Price: *n.a.*

Angler's World Flexible Clear Plastic Fly Boxes. *Stainless-steel hinges, different compartment styles, 9 models: 4¼"x3-1/8"x1-1/8" to 13"x 6½"x1½".* Price: *$2.50-$15.*

Bonnand of France Series 10 Fly Boxes (M. Sharf & Co.). *Transparent pale-green ABS construction, brass hinge, 15 compartments, 9.6" 5-3/4"x1.6".* Price: *n.a.*

Bonnand of France Series 3 Fly Boxes (M. Sharf & Co.). *4 models poly-styrene construction with clear lid, brass hinge, models avail. with compartments, magnetic floors, clips, 3½"x2½"x3/4".* Price: *n.a.*

Bonnand of France Series 6 Fly Boxes (M. Sharf & Co.). *3 models transparent pale-green ABS construction, brass hinge, models avail. in different compartment styles, magnetic bars, 5.9"x3.7"x1.2".* Price: *n.a.*

Cortland Fly Boxes. *Unbreakable transparent Tenite with stainless-steel hinges, deep-green carpetlike material lining bottom, 7 models and compartment styles from 4-3/16"x3"x1-1/8" (6 compartments) to 12-3/4"x6-3/8"x1-7/16" (18 compartments).* Price: *$2.50-$10.*

L. M. Dickson Fly Box. *Plastic with 13 clips, 6"x3-7/8", aqua color.* Price: *n.a.*

L. M. Dickson Dial Fly Box. *Round plastic box, 6 compartments, 4-3/4" diam., cork-lined bottom, chromed belt clip.* Price: *n.a.*

L. M. Dickson Clear Plastic Fly Box. *6 compartments, 3"x1"x1".* Price: *n.a.*

Fly-Rite Fly Box. *Polypropylene box with permanent hinges, polyethylene-foam ridges inserted to hold flies, 7"x3"x1", 11 rows of foam ridges.* Price: *n.a.*

Fly-Safe Fly Box (Martin Reel Co.). *Patented clips hold flies upright without damage, holds 72 flies, ventilated anodized aluminum, 6¼"x 4"x1-1/8".* Price: *n.a.*

Herter's Polypropylene Fly Boxes. *11 models with different compartment styles, 4-5/8"x3"x1-1/8" to 13-1/8"x9"x2-5/16", yellow color.* Price: *$.52-$3.69.*

Herter's Crystal-Clear Boxes. *6 models with compartments, 2-3/4"x 4½"x1" to 6¼"x10½"x1-3/4".* Price: *$1.21-$7.89.*

Herter's Magnetic Fly Cases. *Magnetic insert on one side, 4 coil clips and 3 rows of ten clips on the other.* Price: *$5.27 (6"x3-3/4"x1¼"). $3.57 (3-3/4"x2-3/4"x7/8").*

Herter's Clip Duraluminum Fly Cases. *3 models: 60 clips (3-3/4"x 2-3/4"x7/8"), 140 clips (6"x3-3/4"x7/8"), 140 clips (6"x3-3/4"x1¼").* Price: *$2.79-$4.17.*

Martin Model 660 Fly Box. *3-3/4"x4¼"x1¼", ABS construction, 6 compartments with lid that holds sample fly, 4 oz.* Price: *n.a.*

OLM Dial Fly Box. *Circular box with compartments, 4-3/4" diam.* Price: *n.a.*

Orvis Streamer Books. *Leather zippered case with shearling liners, 2 sizes: 5-3/4"x3-3/4"x½", 7¼"x3-3/4"x½".* Price: *$6.95, $8.95.*

Orvis Rangeley Fly Books. *Canvas cover, sheepskin lining, single snap closing, 2 sizes: 4½"x2½" (closed), 6"x3" (closed).* Price: *$2.20, $4.*

Orvis Workhorse Fly Boxes. *6 models, 7/8"x3¼"x7½" to 8¼"x4-1/8"x 1-1/8", various compartment styles avail., blue and clear or tan and clear plastic.* Price: *$2.50-$3.50.*

Perrine No. 90, 92, 96, 97, 60, 66 Fly Boxes. *2-3/4"x3-3/4"x7/8" to 3-3/4"x6"x1¼" with different combinations of clips and coils, ventilated anodized aluminum.* Price: *n.a.*

Perrine No. 91 Dry Fly Box. *3-3/4"x6"x1½" with 10 compartments, 3 rows of 10 clips, 3 coil clips, ventilated anodized aluminum.* Price: *n.a.*

Perrine No. 98 Fly Box. *3-3/4"x6"x1-3/8" with polypropylene insert and clips, ventilated anodized aluminum.* Price: *n.a.*

Perrine No. 99 Fly Box. *3-3/4"x6"x1¼" with 5 plastic-lined compartments, 7 coil clips, ventilated anodized aluminum.* Price: *n.a.*

Perrine No. 69 Magnetic Fly Box. *2-3/4"x3-3/4"x1-1/8" with 3 rows of 10 clips and magnetic insert, ventilated anodized aluminum.* Price: *n.a.*

Perrine No. 101 Magnetic Fly Box. *3-3/4"x6"x1¼" with 4 coil clips, 3 rows of 10 clips, magnetic insert, ventilated anodized aluminum.* Price: *n.a.*

Perrine No. 95 Salmon Fly Box. *3-3/4"x6"x1¼" with 16 rows of 5 clips, ventilated anodized aluminum.* Price: *n.a.*

Perrine No. 100 Fly Box. *3-3/4"x6"x1-3/8" with individual plastic-lined compartments with lids, ventilated anodized aluminum.* Price: *n.a.*

Plano Molding Utility Boxes. *Transparent styrene plastic with hinged plastic covers, different compartment styles, 11 models, 4-5/8"x2-7/8" x1" to 11"x7¼"x1-3/4", single compartment to 18 compartments.* Price: *n.a.*

Richardson Chest Fly Box. *Custom-built aluminum fly box, 3-tray (24 oz.), 4-tray (28 oz.), 5-tray (32 oz.) models, avail. with foam liners on top and bottom of trays, straps for carrying criss-cross angler's back, flex-light, fly spray, Bausch & Lomb magnifying glass avail. installed on box, brown wood-grain, green wood-grain, moss green or black color.* Price: *n.a.*

Sampo Utility Boxes. *Stainless-steel hinges, avail. in assorted sizes and compartment styles, 11 models, 4"x3"x1" to 8¼"x4¼"x1-1/8", 3 compartments to 18 compartments.* Price: *n.a.*

Scientific Anglers Fly File. *3-3/4"x6"x1" plastic floating box, rust-proof, flies gripped by plastic inserts, colors: orange, yellow or blue.* Price: *$4.*

U. S. Line Polystyrene Utility Boxes. *6 models: 4-5/8"x2¼"x1-1/8" (4 compartments) to 8¼"x5"x1¼" (18 compartments).* Price: *n.a.*

Universal Vise Midge Fly Box. *Metal with clear plastic top, 6 compartments.* Price: *$1.*

Universal Vise Floating Fly Boxes. *Plastic with foam lining, 2 sizes: 10¼"x4½" and 7¼"x3½".* Price: *$1.75 (small), $2.50 (large).*

Vlchek Fly Boxes. *40 models, opaque polypropylene and clear plastic, 4-5/8"x3"x1-1/8" to 13-1/8"x9"x2-5/16", various compartment styles, plastic hinges.* Price: *$.75-$5.10.*

Richard Wheatley Clip Boxes (M. Sharf & Co.). *14 models: 3½"x 2-3/8"x3/4" to 6"x3½"x1-1/8" for trout wet flies, salmon flies, salt-water flies, models avail. with swing leaves, washable contents tablet, aluminum alloy with stainless-steel clips.* Price: *n.a.*

Richard Wheatley Compartment Boxes (M. Sharf & Co.). *9 models: 3½"x2-3/8"x1" (6 compartments, 24 clips) to 6"x3½"x1½" (32 compartments), aluminum alloy, each compartment with individual transparent spring lid, models avail. with foam drying pad, washable contents tablet, clips on one side of box.* Price: *n.a.*

Richard Wheatley Ventilated Boxes (M. Sharf & Co.). *7 models: 3½" x2-3/8"x3/4" to 6"x3½"x1-1/8", models avail. with clips, compartments, coil springs, magnetic floor, foam drying pad.* Price: *n.a.*

Richard Wheatley Magnetic Boxes (M. Sharf & Co.). *2 models: 3½" x2-3/8"x1" and 6"x3½"x1-1/8", aluminum alloy, plastic magnetic bars.* Price: *n.a.*

Wheatley Kilroy Fly Boxes (M: Sharf & Co.). *3 models: 4"x2-3/8"x1" to 6"x3½"x1¼", models avail. with coil springs, salmon-fly gauge in lid, fitted with tweezers and triangular carborundum stone.* Price: *n.a.*

Nets

Angler's World Model Deluxe Trout Net. *Hand-laminated maple and mahogany with walnut handle, 2 models: standard, 20½"x9½", 6 oz., and large, 22½"x10½", 7½ oz.* Price: *$40 (standard), $45 (large).*

Angler's World Dee and Vee Nets. *Telescopic aluminum frame, 19" closed, 32" extended, 18"x14" mouth, 22" deep. Dee is D-shaped, Vee is triangular.* Price: *$38 (Dee), $58 (Vee).*

Bean's Collapsible Landing Net. *30" nylon net, 16"x18" net bow folds for storage inside 29" aluminum handle.* Price: *$8.30.*

Bean's Wood Frame Trout Net. *Oak and black walnut veneer, swiveling solid-brass lanyard attachment, 24" deep nylon net bag, 23" overall, 10"x15" bow, 8 oz.* Price: *$17.50.*

Cascade Lakes Landing Nets. *Mahogany and ash construction with choice of mahogany or cherry handle, nylon bag, French snap, 2 models: 8½"x13" opening, 9½"x15" opening.* Price: *$26.95, $27.95.*

Cascade Lakes Landing Net Kits. *Laminated ash frame, cherry handle, nylon bag, French snap, swivel provided to be finished by angler, 3 models: 7½"x13" opening, 8½"x15" opening, 6"x11" opening.* Price: *$17.95-$18.95 (also avail. assembled, $24.95-$26.95).*

Chaplin Tackle Co. Trout Net. *2 models: Monogram and Presentation Grade, hand-made from walnut and blond woods, hand-tied fly inlaid in handle, Presentation Grade inscribed with owner's name and includes choice of woods, 14"x13" mouth, 23" long, 16 oz.* Price: *$50 (Monogram), $65 (Presentation Grade).*

L. M. Dickson Landing Nets. *2 models: 10½"x12" and 17" overall, 12½"x15" and 20" overall, aluminum frame, cotton net, elastic cord.* Price: *n.a.*

Isaac Franklin Co. Landing Nets. *Models for fresh- and saltwater use, replacement net bags.* Price: *n.a.*

Herter's Stow-A-Way Net. *Aluminum frame, nylon bag, handle locks into position.* Price: *$8.97 (23"x20" bag), $11.97 (27"x21" bag).*

Herter's LF6A2, LF6A3 Landing Nets. *Aluminum construction, "nylocable" bag material.* Price: *$4.77 (LF6A2, 38" long, 24" deep bag), $5.37 (48" long, 36" deep bag).*

Herter's LF6A6 Floating Landing Net. *Aluminum, 20" length, 24" deep bag, neoprene cord, plastic handle.* Price: *$3.27.*

Herter's LB3H1 Folding Net. *10 oz., 18"x1½" folded, 30"x11½" open, 20" deep bag.* Price: *$4.97.*

Herter's Model LF6A4 Extension Net. *Aluminum, net size 20"x23", 48" long closed, 73" long extended.* Price: *$6.87.*

OLM Trout Net. *Aluminum frame, 9"x11".* Price: *n.a.*

Orvis Landing Net. *Cherry wood frame, 15½"x8½".* Price: *$47.50.*

Orvis Wood Frame Landing Net. *Ash, mahogany, and butternut, 2 sizes: medium, 20" long, 9"x12½" opening; large: 23" long, 10"x14" opening.* Price: *$34.50 (medium), $37.50 (large).*

Orvis North Fork Pocket Net. *11 oz., 9" long folded, locks open to 8"x13" opening, stainless steel and anodized aluminum.* Price: *$37.35.*

J. F. Pepper Co. Nets. *Full range of models for fresh- and saltwater fishing.* Price: *n.a.*

St. Croix F795 Trout Landing Net. *9"x11" tubular aluminum frame, 5" rubber grip with elastic cord.* Price: *n.a.*

Prices (and price ranges) listed in this directory are the manufacturer's suggested retail prices as of late 1977, and they are subject to change without notice. Please consult pp. 233-235 for addresses of manufacturers from whom up-to-date price information may be obtained, or check with your local fly-tackle dealer.

Thomas & Thomas Impregnated Trout Net. *Laminated ash-and-mahogany frame, walnut handle, available in 17" or 20" model.* Price: *$36.*

U. S. Line Wood Handled Trout Net. *7" handle, 15"x10" hoop, 20" bag.* Price: *n.a.*

U. S. Line Trout Net. *Heavy aluminum frame, elastic cord, non-slip handle, cotton net, 4 sizes.* Price: *n.a.*

U. S. Line Replacement Net Bags. *Minnow- or regular-mesh size, black cotton, 8 sizes.* Price: *n.a.*

Fly and Line Dressings

Cascade Lakes Dry Fly Floatant. *Silicone-formula floatant, pump spray, 1 oz. bottle.* Price: *$1.95.*

Cortland Dry-Ur-Fly. *Dries and cleans flies when flies are immersed in solution.* Price: *$1.50.*

Cortland Dry Fly Spray. *2-oz. can, aerosal spray waterproofs dry flies.* Price: *$1.50.*

Cortland Fly Line Cleaner. Price: *$1.*

Fireside Angler Dunk. *Sinks fly or tippet, absorbant capillary action, squeeze bottle with suede wiper for leader application.* Price: *$1.45.*

Fireside Angler Dry and Clean. *Granulated application to dry and clean flies, squeeze bottle with flip-open spout.* Price: *$1.45.*

Garcia Silicote Dry Fly Dressing. *Liquid silicone, ½-oz. bottle.* Price: *n.a.*

Garcia Fly Line Cleaner and Dresser. *3/8-oz. tube.* Price: *n.a.*

Gherke's Gink Fly Floatant (Fly Fisherman's Bookcase and Tackle Service). *Soft cream compound may also be used as line dressing.* Price *$1.10.*

Gudebrod Silicone Dry Fly Dressing. *1-oz. bottle.* Price: *n.a.*

Gudebrod Fly Line Dressing. *Cleans and dresses line.* Price: *n.a.*

Kaufmann's Float High Super Fly Floatant. *Cream floatant.* Price: *$1.25.*

Laggie's Fish Catching Co. Hi & Dry Floatant. *Liquid formula floatant, avail. with leader pin-on holder.* Price: *$1.50 ($3.75 with holder)*

Laggie's Fish Catching Co. Fast-Sink Leader Coating. *Lead compounc in flexible bonding agent, 1 oz.* Price: *$2.50.*

Orvis Fly Line Cleaner. *2-3/4" diam. container.* Price: *$1.85.*

Orvis Dry-N-Float. *Powder formula cleans and dries flies, 1-oz. squeeze bottle.* Price: *$3.35.*

Orvis Leader Sink. *Cleans and sinks leader, 1 oz. bottle.* Price: *$2.25.*

Orvis Aerosol Fly Spray. *Silicone formula fly floatant, 2-oz. can.* Price: *$3.10.*

Pezon et Michel Fly Line Cleaner. *Silicone paste.* Price: *$2.*

Hank Roberts Drifly Spray. *Aerosol silicone floatant, 2-oz can.* Price: *n.a.*

Scientific Anglers Fly Line Conditioner. *Impregnated disposable towlette cleans and conditions line.* Price: *$1 (4 disposable packets).*

Seidel's 600 Leader Sink. *Sinks flies and leaders, 1¼-oz. polyethylene vest-pocket-size bottle.* Price: *$1.75.*

Seidel's 700 Dry Fly Spray. *Silicone formula, avail. in 1¼-oz. squeeze bottle or 2-oz. aerosol aluminum can.* Price: *$2.*

Seidel's 800 Dry Fly Powder. *Powdered silicone.* Price: *$1.75.*

U. S. Line Dry Fly Spray. *2-oz. can silicone aerosol.* Price: *n.a.*

U.S. Line Fli-Restore. *Silicone and powder.* Price: *n.a.*

U. S. Line Flyline Cleaner & Lubricant. Price: *n.a.*

Wanigas Flyline Dressing. Price: *$1.50.*

Wanigas Dry Fly Dressing. *Liquid solution, 1 oz. bottle.* Price: *$1.50.*

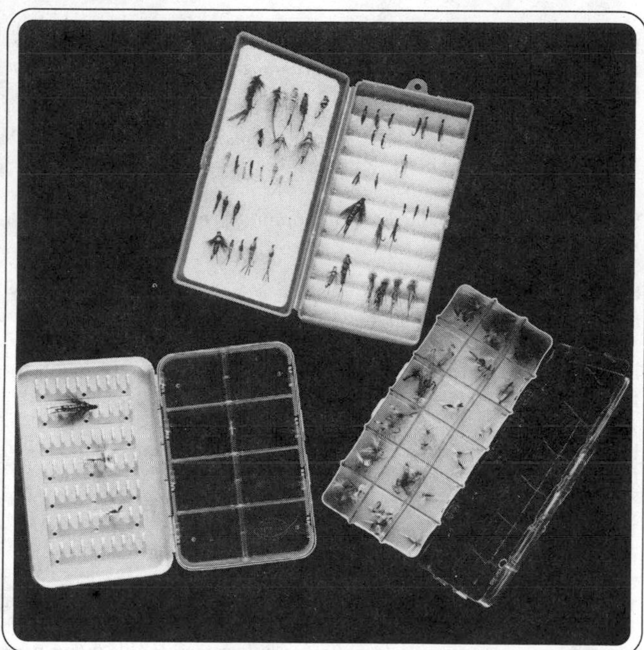

Examples of fly boxes, including, on left an anodized, ventilated aluminum model, center a polypropylene box with polyethylene foam inserts to hold flies and, at right, an all-plastic model. Photo by Don Gray.

Vests, Shirts and Jackets

America's Cup Flotation Vest. *U.S.C.G. approved.* Price: *n.a.*

Angler's World Compleat Angler's Vest. *Hand-tailored lightweight silicone-treated gabardine, 9 outside pockets, 12 inside pockets, detachable ventilated creel, nylon zippers, 2 D-rings, detachable lambskin fly patch.* Price: *$75.*

Angler's World Angler's Life Vest. *U.S.C.G. approved, 4 pockets, nylon zipper.* Price: *$35.*

Dan Bailey T.H.E. Vest. *2 models: Regular and Shortie, extra-large arm holes, 3 D-rings, rod holder, epaulet, 14 pockets (12 pockets, Shortie), Velcro and rust-resistant closures, tan-and-brown color.* Price: *$37.95 (Regular), $34.95 (Shortie).*

Dan Bailey T.H.E. Dan Bailey Vest. *2 large outside zipper pockets, 2 large inside zipper pockets, 8 additional pockets plus large rear bellows pocket with side zipper, 2 D-rings, rod holder, tan color.* Price: *$29.95.*

Dan Bailey T.H.E. Blue Denim Vest. *Blue denim construction, 7 zipper- or snap-closing pockets, 3 D-rings.* Price: *$20.95.*

Dan Bailey T.H.E. Blue Denim Bib. *Blue denim, 7 Velcro- or zipper-closing front pockets, 2 D-rings.* Price: *$18.95.*

Bean's Tackle Pack Vest. *10 pockets, 2 sheepskin fly patches, landing-net ring, rod holder, detachable mesh creel, tan color.* Price: *$31.*

Bean's Mesh Tackle Pack. *Nylon mesh, 6 pockets, 2 sheepskin fly patches, green color.* Price: *$23.*

Bean's Fisherman Vest. *Cotton, 4 front pockets, large rear bellows-type pocket, 2 inside pockets, 1 large utility pocket, rod holder, sheepskin fly patch, olive color.* Price: *$16.75.*

Columbia Sportswear Steelheader Vest. *100% cotton duck, 8 velcro-closing front bellows pockets, 2 inside splash-proof pockets, rear cargo pocket, rod-holding lanyard, zipper-closing front, khaki color.* Price: *n.a.*

Columbia Sportswear Floater Vest. *8 front cargo pockets zipper- and velcro-closing, rear cargo pouch, deep moss-green color.* Price: *n.a.*

Columbia Sportswear North Umpqua Vest. *4 zippered pockets, 4 velcro pockets, inside and rear bellows pocket, dark moss-green color.* Price: *n.a.*

Columbia Sportswear Furnace Creek Vest. *100% nylon-mesh body, 6 nylon-coated cargo pockets, dark forest-green color.* Price: *n.a.*

Columbia Sportswear Deschutes Vest. *10 velcro- and zipper-closing pockets, rear pouch, dark tan color.* Price: *n.a.*

Columbia Sportswear Kalama Vest. *Designed short for wading deep, 15 pockets, rear cargo pouch, deep moss-green color.* Price: *n.a.*

L. M. Dickson F012 Vest. *Cotton poplin, fly patch, 4 pockets, zipper front, green color.* Price: *n.a.*

L. M. Dickson Spun-Rayon Rubberized Vest. *Fly patch, 6 pockets with snaps, large back pocket, vinyl license holder.* Price: *n.a.*

L. M. Dickson Y31/T Vest. *Cotton poplin, tan color, suede shoulder trim, 10 pockets, large zippered back pocket, 3 loops, detachable creel, zippered front.* Price: *n.a.*

L. M. Dickson 7-3/T Vest. *Tan color, cotton poplin, 6 Velcro-closing pockets, fly patch, zippered detachable creel, plastic license holder, zipper front.* Price: *n.a.*

Fly-Tyer's Carry-All Hippak. *8 waterproof nylon pockets with elastic tops, 4 D-rings, nylon-web belt, tan cordura waterproof nylon shell.* Price: *$21.95.*

Herter's Chambray Fishing Shirt. *4 large pockets, epaulets, sheepskin patch, medium-blue or light-rust color.* Price: *$12.97.*

Herter's Hudson Bay Fishing Jacket. *8 pockets, sheepskin patch, sand-tan color.* Price: *$15.97.*

Leonard Catskill Vest. *23 pockets, 3 D-rings, fleece patch, rod holder, oversize tippet-spool pockets, forest-green color.* Price: *$45.95.*

Leonard Shorty Vest. *Inside pockets, 2 outside side-zippered pockets, rear pocket, 2 high front pockets, nylon-zippered front, 2 D-rings, forest-green color.* Price: *$29.95.*

Leonard Catskill Flotation Vest. *8 pockets plus rear cargo pouch, nylon-zipper and Velcro closures, 2 D-rings, fleece patch, rod holder, Ensolite flotation material, U.S.C.G. approved, forest-green color.* Price: *$56.*

Nelson Nesco Fishing Vest. *Cotton poplin, 4 front pockets with snap closures, button-down front, fly patch, net ring, rod holder.* Price: *n.a.*

Nelson Nesco Cotton Fishing Vest. *Cotton sateen, zipper front, 6 pockets, 2 fly patches, rod holder.* Price: *n.a.*

Nelson Nesco Cotton Fishing Vest With Creel. *Zip-off creel, zipper front, 12 pockets, fly patches, rod holder.* Price: *n.a.*

Nelson Nesco Deluxe Cotton Fishing Vest. *10 pockets, fly patches, zipper front, zipper back pouch, rod holder.* Price: *n.a.*

OLM Deluxe Vest. *Lamb's wool fly patch, 6 front pockets, large rear pocket, D-ring for landing net, tan or mist-green color.* Price: *n.a.*

OLM Select Vest. *Non-slip suede shoulder lining, suede trim on shoulders, 12 bellows-style pockets plus large rear pocket, tan or mist-green color.* Price: *n.a.*

OLM Master Vest. *Non-slip suede shoulder lining, suede shoulder strap, 9 pockets, plus large rear pocket, nylon-lined mesh creel, D-ring for net, tan or mist-green color.* Price: *n.a.*

OLM Fishing Vest. *12 bellows-style pockets plus large rear pocket, nylon-lined mesh creel, tan or mist-green color.* Price: *n.a.*

Orvis Tac-L-Pak Jacket. *Silicone treated, 20 pockets, tan color.* Price: *$56.*

Orvis Deluxe Tac-L-Pak. *65% Dacron, 35% cotton, 19 zipper- and Velcro-closing compartments, tabs for detachable articreel, rod holder, fleece patches, tan or green color.* Price: *$46.50.*

Orvis Standard Tac-L-Pak. *13 Velcro- and zipper-closing pockets plus rear pouch, 100% cotton, tan or green color.* Price: *$29.50.*

Orvis Warm Weather Tac-L-Pak. *Nylon-mesh construction, 8 Velcro-closing pockets plus rear storage pouch, fleece patch.* Price: *$34.*

Orvis Flotation Vest. *U.S.C.G. approved, 4 front pockets, cargo pouch, 2 fleece patches.* Price: *$38.50.*

Orvis Shorty Wader Vest. *65% polyester, 35% cotton, fleece patch, 9 Velcro- and zipper-closing pockets plus rear cargo pocket, olive-green color.* Price: *$27.50.*

Orvis Simplicity Vest. *2 fleece patches, 6 pockets plus rear pouch with snap closure.* Price: *$13.95.*

Orvis Insulated Fishing Jacket. *Silicone treated, 9 pockets, 8 oz. polarguard insulation.* Price: *$65.*

Orvis French Fishing Coat. *100% cotton poplin, hood, detachable cape, 10 pockets.* Price: *$9.95.*

Orvis Fishing Shirt. *4 pockets, fleece patch, tan poplin.* Price: *$21.95.*

Hank Roberts Personal Vest. *20 Velcro- and zipper-closing pockets, Velcro-attached fly patch, polyester and cotton, soft-green color.* Price: *$42.50.*

Hank Roberts Shorty Vest. *4" shorter than Personal Vest for use with waders, 20 Velcro- and zipper-closing pockets, Velcro-attached fly patch, polyester and cotton, soft-green color.* Price: *$42.50.*

Hank Roberts Steelhead Vest. *100% cotton, Velcro-closing pockets, forest-green color.* Price: *$26.95.*

Hank Roberts Angler's Shirt. *100% cotton, 5 Velcro-closing pockets, Velcro-attached sheepskin patch, tan color.* Price: *$26.95.*

Fritz von Schlegell Fishing Vest. *15 Velcro-closing pockets, rod holder, D-rings, hooks for arctic-type creel, light green or desert-sand color.* Price: *$29.95 (arctic-type creel: $8.95).*

Fritz von Schlegell Shirt-Jac. *5 pockets plus large rear pocket, D-ring, epaulettes, rod holder.* Price: *$19.95.*

Seaway Fishing Vest. *100% cotton poplin, 5 front pockets, fly patch, rod holder.* Price: *n.a.*

Seaway Deluxe Fishing Vest. *Cotton sateen, vinyl-lined creel, 12 front pockets, fly patch, rod holder.* Price: *n.a.*

Dick Surette's Angler's Vest. *Pullover style, large pockets, nylon zippers, dark olive color.* Price: *$19.95.*

U. S. Line Fishing Vests. *3 models, 5, 8 or 12 pockets, rear pocket, fly patches, light-green poplin or light-tan sateen.* Price: *n.a.*

World Famous Fishing Vest. *Water-repellent cotton poplin, button-down front, fly patch, 4 pockets, rod holder, tan color.* Price: *n.a.*

World Famous Custom Fishing Vest. *Water-repellent cotton poplin, zipper front, zipper back pouch, 2 fly patches, 14 outer bellows pockets, 4 inner pockets, rod holder, license holder, detachable nylon-mesh creel, tan color.* Price: *n.a.*

World Famous Deluxe Fishing Vest. *Water repellent, 60% cotton, 40% polyester, zipper front, 12 bellows pockets, 2 fly patches, rod holder, detachable nylon-mesh creel, green color.* Price: *n.a.*

Fly-Tying Tools

Vises

Cahill House Catskill Vise. *Table-clamp mount, adjustable height, black finish, cam-operated jaws.* Price: *$29.95.*

Fly Fisherman's Bookcase and Tackle Service Anywhere Vise. *Sunrise India's AA vise adapted to bolt into metal base eliminating need for clamp-style mount, clamp mount also supplied.* Price: *$17.95.*

Herter's Model 18T Vise. *Stands 4½" above table top, table clamp has 1-3/8" clearance, lever-action jaws, handles 1/0-#22 hooks, overall 6"x½".* Price: *$2.17.*

Herter's Model T9C Vise. *Clamp mount, adjustable height, handles 2/0-#22 hooks.* Price: *$10.47.*

Herter's Model T9GLH Vise. *Material-holder mounts on pedestal, handles 2/0-#22 hooks.* Price: *$9.77.*

Herter's Model TA6 Vise. *Clamp mount, handles 2/0-#22 hooks, base socket allows vise to be turned in any direction.* Price: *$12.97.*

Herter's Model T11 Vise. *Lever-and-cross-bolt jaws, handles 2/0-#22 hooks, clamp mount, jaws 6" from table top.* Price: *$5.17.*

Herter's Model T3D, T4D Vises. *Jaws with screw knob, clamp mount, height from table top 8½ " (T3D), 6½ " (T4D).* Price: *$9.67 (T3D), $9.87 (T4D).*

Hille's Deluxe Vise. *Cam jaws, holds any hook size, right- or left-hand use, table-clamp mount, chrome plated.* Price: *$16.10.*

Hille Super A Vise. *Chrome finish, clamp mount.* Price: *$12.75.*

Hille Special Vise. *Wing-nut jaws, adjustable height, right- or left-hand use, table-clamp mount, chrome finish.* Price: *$5.85.*

Hille Beginner Vise. *Tempered steel, black finish, wing-nut jaws.* Price: *$2.65.*

HMH Model Premium Vise. *Rotary or stationary use, jaw-attitude adjustment, 3 interchangeable heads (midge, medium, magnum) handles 6/0-#32 hooks, avail. with pedestal brass base or C-clamp mount.* Price: *$95 (9" standrod and C-clamp), $102.50 (6" standrod and pedestal).*

HMH Model Standard Vise. *3 interchangeable heads (midge, medium, magnum), handles 6/0-#32 hooks, avail. with brass pedestal base or C-clamp mount.* Price: *$75 (9" standrod and C-clamp), $82.50 (6" standrod and pedestal).*

Orvis Fly-Tying Vise. *Blacked steel, jaw rotates 360°, table clamp mount, height 8" above table, adjustable jaw angle, handles 1/0-#28 hooks, replacement parts avail.* Price: *$43.50.*

Orvis 2-in-1 Vise. *Table clamp mount, interchangeable jaws to handle 3/0-#28 hooks.* Price: *$26.75.*

Orvis Presentation Vise. *360° jaw rotation, jaws offset at 60° angle, 2 interchangeable jaws to handle hooks from 5/0 to #28, material clip, bobbin cradle, stainless-steel, polished-brass and aluminum construction, jaws are hardened industrial tool steel.* Price: *$149.95.*

Phelps Flies Co. Xuron Vise. *Carbon-steel head, handles 4/0-#28 hooks, head mounted on sharply angled stem, stem mounted in ball joint.* Price: *$39.95.*

Price's Angler's Corner Price Vise. *Table-clamp adjustable to 3-3/4" spread, rotating jaws may be tilted in any direction.* Price: *$59.95.*

Tackle Craft Supreme Tyer's Vise. *Chrome-plated, plastic-covered jaw, table-clamp mount, handles 7/0-#28 hooks.* Price: *$19.95.*

Thompson Ultra Vise. *Adjustable collet angle, adjustable collar, steel throat, C-clamp mount.* Price: *$28.*

Thompson Special Ultra Vise. *Slightly offset shank allows jaws and collet to be adjusted in a vertical attitude, C-clamp mount.* Price: *$32.*

Thompson A Vise. *Tempered-steel collet, hardened-steel throat, double-cam jaws, adjustable height, right- or left-hand use, C-clamp or pedestal mount.* Price: *$23 (avail. in No-Glare Pro model for $25).*

Thompson Midge Jaws. *Collet for use with #18-32 hooks.* Price: *$9 (for Thompson A, Ultra or Pro Vise), $12 (fitted to other vise).*

Thompson B Vise. *Threaded hand-nut closing collet, C-clamp mount, avail. in 9" height or 4½" height.* Price: *$17.*

Thompson C Vise. *Threaded hand-nut closing collet, C-clamp mount, hardened-steel working parts.* Price: *$14.*

Thompson F Vise. *Lever-closing cam jaws, C-clamp mount.* Price: *$14.*

Thompson H Vise. *Cam lever-closing jaws, case-hardened strip-steel construction, C-clamp mount.* Price: *$3.*

Turrall Cadet Vise (M. Sharf & Co.). *Jaws operated by large knurled nut, 5 oz.* Price: *n.a.*

Turrall Precision Lever Vise (M. Sharf & Co.). *Sheffield-steel jaws, handles 5/0-#28 hooks, satin-chrome finish, replacement parts avail., 8 oz.* Price: *n.a.*

Turrall Quadrant Vise (M. Sharf & Co.). *Sheffield-steel jaws, handles 5/0-#28 hooks, jaw rotates 360°, replacement parts avail., 8 oz.* Price: *n.a.*

Universal 2 Rotating Vise. *Reversible chuck for right- or left-hand use, rotating jaws.* Price: *$10.95.*

Universal Streamside Vise. *Threaded shaft to screw into log or tree.* Price: *$5.95.*

Universal Stationary Vise. *Table clamp, adjustable height.* Price: *$5.95.*

Universal Economy Vise. *Table-clamp mount.* Price: *$1.95.*

Veniard Hand Vise (M. Sharf & Co.). *Collet-type jaws, finger loop, 2.1 oz.* Price: *n.a.*

Veniard Midge Vise (M. Sharf & Co.). *Swan-type neck adjustable to any angle or height, collet-type jaws, handles up to #28 hooks, 8½ oz.* Price: *n.a.*

Veniard Aston Beginner's Vise (M. Sharf & Co.). *Collet-type jaws, handles hooks to #1, 8-3/4 oz.* Price: *n.a.*

Veniard Salmo Deluxe Vise (M. Sharf & Co.). *Oven-baked black enamel base, chrome-plated head and stem, handles hooks to 6/0, 17½ oz.* Price: *n.a.*

Bobbins

Herter's T42B Bobbin. *Chrome-plated brass tube, extra-long thread-tube.* Price: *$1.57.*

Herter's TK63 Bobbin. *Tenite shell covers vertically held spool.* Price: *$2.87.*

Herter's TK72 Bobbin. *Chrome-plated steel.* Price: *$1.77.*

Hille Bobbin. *4½" long, chrome plated.* Price: *$3.10.*

Matarelli Bobbin. *Stainless steel, 2 models with different length thread tubes, holds any size spool.* Price: *$4.50.*

Matarelli Midge Bobbin. *Stainless steel, holds sewing-machine spool, small diam. thread tube for close control of small threads on small flies.* Price: *$5.75 (spool not included).*

Orvis 2-in-1 Bobbin. *Stainless steel, flared tube.* Price: *$4.20.*

Orvis Bobbin. *Stainless steel, 3½" long.* Price: *$4.75.*

Sunrise India Bobbins. *6 models: standard, standard with collar, fine tube with collar, plate bobbin, plastic with large spool, plastic with small spool.* Price: *n.a.*

Tackle Craft Deluxe Fly-Tying Bobbin. *Fits any spool, spring steel with seamless brass chromed tube, threader included.* Price: *$2.75.*

Thomas & Thomas Floss Bobbin. *3-3/4" long, stainless steel and brass, large diameter thread-tube.* Price: *$4.75.*

Thomas & Thomas Streamer Bobbin. *4½" long, stainless steel and brass, long thread-tube for large flies.* Price: *$4.75.*

Thomas & Thomas Midge Bobbin. *3-3/4" long, stainless steel and brass, fine-diameter thread-tube.* Price: *$4.75.*

Thomas & Thomas Standard Bobbin. *3-3/4" long, stainless steel and brass.* Price: *$4.75.*

Thompson Spring-Wire Bobbin. *Offset thread-tube, adjusts to any size spool.* Price: *$4.*

Thompson Jiffy Bobbin. *Adjustable thread tension, 2½" or 4" tube lengths.* Price: *$4.50.*

Thompson Open-Side Bobbin. *Adjustable tension, accommodates any size spool.* Price: *$5.50.*

Universal Metal Bobbin. *Steel construction, thread tension applied with fingers.* Price: *$2.75.*

Universal Vise Material Bobbin. *Metal construction, for use with floss, wool, mylar.* Price: *$.75.*

Universal Vise Bobbin. *Adaptable to different size spools.* Price: *$3.25.*

Hackle Pliers

Herter's TA1C1 Hackle Pliers. *Nickel-plated steel construction, one jaw side rubber pad, other grooved brass.* Price: *$.97.*

Herter's TA1A, TA1B English Hackle Pliers. *Hand-polished stainless-steel, rubber finger-grip sleeves.* Price: *$1.97 (TA1A, standard size), $1.67 (TA1B, trout size).*

Hille Hackle Pliers. *English-style, white bronze, 3 sizes, 3", 2½", 1-7/8" long.* Price: *$2-$2.15.*

Orvis E-Z Hook Hackle Pliers. *Hooking device to grasp and wind hackles.* Price: *$1.60.*

Orvis Hackle Pliers. *Stainless steel, 3 models: long nose, short nose, midget.* Price: *$2.50-$3.*

Sunrise India Hackle Pliers. *9 models: large, medium, small sizes; Sunrise, Swiss, English, midge styles.* Price: *n.a.*

M. Sharf & Co. Hackle Pliers. *2 sizes: small and medium, stainless-steel spring tension, one jaw side with rubber sleeve.* Price: *n.a.*

Thompson English Type Hackle Pliers. *Spring tension, stainless steel.* Price: *$5.*

Thompson Non-Skid Hackle Pliers. *Tempered tool steel, corrogated rubber pads on jaws.* Price: *$1.40.*

Thompson Duplex Hackle Pliers. *Tempered tool steel, toothed metal pad on one side jaw, soft rubber on other.* Price: *$1.75.*

Prices (and price ranges) listed in this directory are the manufacturer's suggested retail prices as of late 1977, and they are subject to change without notice. Please consult pp. 233-235 for addresses of manufacturers from whom up-to-date price information may be obtained, or check with your local fly-tackle dealer.

Thompson Midget Hackle Pliers. *Hardened and tempered tool steel.* Price: *$1.50.*

Universal Wing and Hackle Pliers. *Holds wings for tying in and hackles for winding.* Price: *$3.25.*

Universal Vise Stainless-Steel Hackle Pliers. *3 sizes: small, large and midget.* Price: *$3.25 (small and large), $1.90 (midget).*

Scissors

Herter's T8S Scissors. *Length 5", cutting edge 1-3/4".* Price: *$3.99.*

Herter's T10S Scissors. *Length 3½", cutting edge 1¼".* Price: *$3.89.*

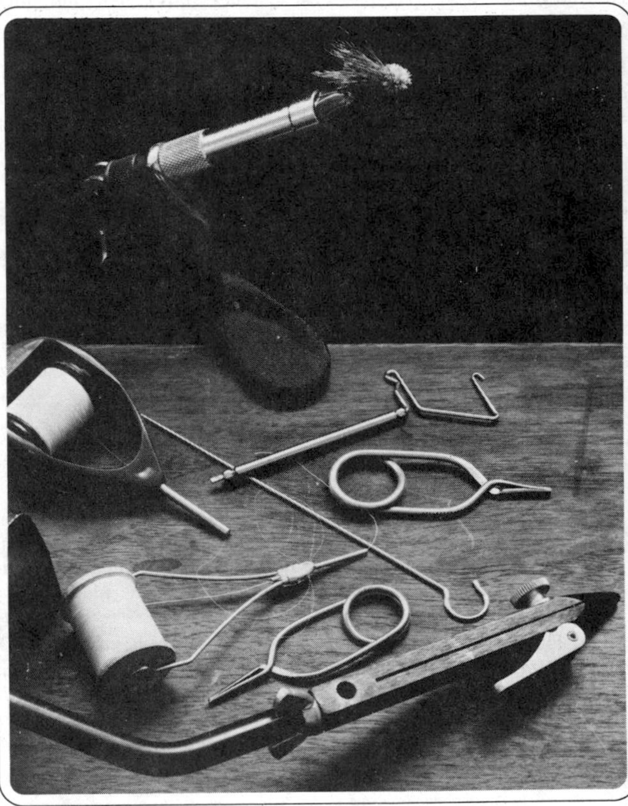

Examples of fly-tying tools: Vises, bobbins, hackle pliers, dubbing needle and whip-finisher. Photo by Don Gray.

Hille Miniature Snips. *Tempered steel, black finish, 4" long, self-opening without pivot.* Price: *$1.85.*

Liberty Organization Fly Tie Scissors. *2 models, 3½" long, large finger holes.* Price: *$5 (nickel plated), $2.50 (chrome plated).*

Orvis Scissors. *2 models: 3-3/4" and 3".* Price: *$4.50.*

M. Sharf & Co. Scissors. *2 models: straight and curved, stainless steel, 4" long, 1" blades.* Price: *n.a.*

Sunrise India Scissors. *12 models: 3"-6", straight or curved, extra fine-point models avail.* Price: *n.a.*

Universal Vise Scissors. *3 models, curved or straight.* Price: *$4-$5.95*

Dubbing Needles and Bodkins

Hille Dubbing Needle. *Polished aluminum, half-hitch hole in base end.* Price: *$1.25.*

Matarelli Dubbing Twister and Needle. *Stainless steel, one end is hook for twisting dubbing material, other end is dubbing needle.* Price: *$2.10.*

M. Sharf & Co. Bodkin. *Steel point, aluminum handle.* Price: *n.a.*

Sunrise India Bodkins. *2 models: large with half-hitch tool, small.* Price: *n.a.*

Thomas & Thomas Brass Dubbing Needle. *6½" long, stainless-steel needle with hexagonal brass handle.* Price: *$2.95.*

Thompson Bodkin. *Aluminum handle, magnetized tempered-steel point.* Price: *$3.*

Universal Vise Half-Hitch Bodkin. *Needle on one end, half-hitch tool on the other.* Price: *$.60.*

Fly-Tying Kits

Ivan Arnold Fly-Tying Kit. *Custom-designed tool kit includes vise, bobbin with extra spool, bobbin rest, bobbin threader, half-hitch tool, carrying box.* Price: *n.a.*

Fly Fisherman's Bookcase and Tackle Service. *Poul Jorgensen streamside fly-tying kit.* Price: *$33.95.*

Hille Fly-Tying Kits. *Material and tool and material kits, 12 models.* Price: *$4.05-$50.*

Herter's Fly-Tying Kits. *15 different models.* Price: *$9.27-$29.47.*

Kaufmann's Fly-Tying Kits. *6 models: American Nymph (materials), All-Purpose (materials), Contemporary Steelhead (materials), Dry Fly (materials), Basic Beginning (materials), and Professional Tool Kit (tools).* Price: *$12.75-$69.95.*

Orvis Fly-Tying Kit. *Tools, materials, two books.* Price: *$62.50.*

Hank Roberts Fly-Tying Kits. *3 models with tools and materials.* Price: *$14.95-$42.95.*

Dick Surette Fly-Tying Kits. *6 models, tools and materials, from beginner to advanced to super.* Price: *$6.95-$86.80.*

Universal Vise Fly-Tying Kits. *7 models, including a series of single-pattern material kits.* Price: *$2-$24.95.*

The Worth Co. Fly-Tying Kit. *Tools and materials.* Price: *$8.*

Whip-Finishers, Other Tools

Charlie's Whipper Whip-Finisher (Charlie Cole). Price: *$1.95.*

D-Boone Enterprises Half-Hitch Tyer. *Plastic half-hitch tool for use on #8-22 hooks.* Price: *$1.25.*

Fly Fisherman's Bookcase and Tackle Service Fly-Tying Bench. *Right- and left-hand models, walnut-stained wood with cork working surface, material and tool holders, magnetic hook-holder.* Price: *$9.50.*

Fly-Tyer's Carry-All Mini-Vac Vise Base. *Vacuum mechanism holds base securely to workboard or nonporous surface, accommodates 3/8" diam. vise shaft.* Price: *n.a.*

Fly-Tyer's Carry-All. *Portable fly-tying work unit, canvas with compartments for materials, white acrylic work board, Mini-Vac Vise Base.* Price: *$55.*

Fly-Tyer's Carry-All Push Pen. *Dispenses lacquer to fly head or body.* Price: *$1.50.*

Herter's TA7 Eyeglass. *2½x magnifying power, headband.* Price: *$1.97.*

Herter's T18 Fly-Tier's Tray. *Fits on shank of vise, 4" square with 4 compartments 1-3/4"x1".* Price: *$2.97.*

Herter's T9M Fly-Tying Mirror. *Clamps to shank of vise, adjustable angle, nickel-plated steel.* Price: *$6.97.*

Herter's T26 Magnifying Glass. *4" diam. with 10" focus, clamps on stand, adjustable angle, 2x magnifying power.* Price: *$18.97.*

Herter's TB6A Wing Maker. *Metal combs regulate wing size, cement fibers, form matching right and left wings.* Price: *$7.79 (includes two comb sizes, $2.17 ea. for extra comb sizes).*

Herter's T31W Winging Pliers. Price: *$1.37.*

Herter's T15T Stand. *Table-top clamp, thread clip, material holder.* Price: *$4.97.*

Herter's TB3A Portable Cabinet. *All steel with 8 clear-plastic drawers, one stainless-steel drawer, 8-1/8"x12½"x6½".* Price: *$9.59.*

Herter's TA2A, TA2B Whip-Finisher. *Chrome-plated brass with knurled handle.* Price: *$1.97 (TA2A), $1.87 (TA2B, small size).*

Herter's T4A Half-Hitch Tool. *Double-ended.* Price: *$1.69.*

Hille Wing-Cutter. *Wood handle, cuts matching right and left wings, plastic cutting board included.* Price: *$5.95.*

Kaufmann's Fly-Tying Desk. *15"x12" board with cork surface, left- or right-hand model, vise rack, tool rack.* Price: *$16.*

Laggie's Fish Catching Co. Stacker. *Aluminum base and tube.* Price: *$1.95.*

Laggie's Fish Catching Co. BT Bobbin Threader S.S. *Wood handle, spring stainless steel.* Price: *$1.*

Chauncey Lively's Spiralator (Fly Fisherman's Bookcase and Tackle Service). *Tool for tying parachute-style hackle independent of hook and attaching it to hook.* Price: *$2.50.*

Matarelli Whip-Finisher. *Stainless steel, right- or left-hand use, may also be used to divide wings on drys.* Price: *$4.75.*

Matarelli Bobbin Threader and Cleaner. *Stainless steel, threader on one end, cleaning needle on the other separated by bead chain for folding to convenient size.* Price: *$2.10.*

Orvis Luxo Magnifying Lamp. *Table-clamp mount, adjustable angle, fluorescent lighting and magnification.* Price: *$88.75.*

Orvis Fly-Tying Desk. *14-3/4"x11½", cork surface, tool rack, 6 magnets, vise rack, right- or left-hand models avail.* Price: *$17.50.*

Orvis Tweezers. *5" long, nickel-plated.* Price: *$5.95.*

M. Sharf & Co. Wing Cutter. *Hardwood handle, stainless-steel blade, cuts wings for #10-16 flies.* Price: *n.a.*

Sunrise India Forceps. *6 models: straight, curved or bent; large and small.* Price: *n.a.*

Sunrise India Hackle Guard. Price: *n.a.*

Sunrise India Half-Hitch Tools. *3 models: small, medium, large holes.* Price: *n.a.*

Sunrise India Hair Tamping Tool. Price: *n.a.*

Sunrise India Hair Stacker. Price: *n.a.*

Sunrise India Fly-Tying Lance. Price: *n.a.*

Sunrise India Whip-Finishers. *5 models: small, large, improved small, improved large, super.* Price: *n.a.*

Sunrise India Material Clip. Price: *n.a.*

Sunrise India Material Spring. Price: *n.a.*

Sunrise India Tweezers. *3 models: straight, curved, larval.* Price: *n.a.*

Sunrise India Dubbing Twisters. *3 models: regular, small, with bodkin.* Price: *n.a.*

Sunrise India Bobbin Threader. Price: *n.a.*

Thomas & Thomas Threader and Cleaner. Price: *$3.95.*

Thomas & Thomas Brass Whip-Finish Tool. *6" long, hexagonal handle, whip-finish tool at one end, half-hitch tool at other.* Price: *$4.75.*

Thomas & Thomas Brass Half-Hitch Tool. Price: *$2.75.*

Thomas & Thomas Brass Dubbing Twister. Price: *$4.75.*

Thompson Junior Waxer. Price: *$10.*

Thompson Clamp Thread Clip. Price: *$7.*

Thompson Material Clip. Price: *$1.50.*

Thompson Whip-Finisher. *Knurled handle, small and standard models.* Price: *$5.50.*

Thompson Hackle Guards. Price: *$3 (for three sizes).*

Thompson Wing Former. *Metal combs shape wings for cutting from feather.* Price: *$18 (with 3 different-size combs, extra comb sizes: $1.50).*

Thompson Aluminum Bobbin Needle. Price: *$18 (includes table rest or rest for use with Thompson A Vise).*

Thompson Apex Bobbin Needle. Price: *$10.*

Universal Vise Hackle Guards. Price: *$2.50.*

Universal Vise Material Clip. Price: *$1.25.*

Universal Vise Material Clip. *Lies flat on vise.* Price: *$.60.*

Universal Vise Whip-Finisher. *Stainless steel.* Price: *$4.50.*

Universal Vise Bobbin Threader. Price: *$.50.*

Hooks

O. Mustad & Son. *Fly-tying hooks.* Price: *n.a.*

Wright & McGill Co. *Fly-tying hooks.* Price: *n.a.*

A. E. Partridge & Sons. *Fly-tying hooks.* Price: *n.a.*

Rod-Building Materials, Components and Tools

Blanks

Bianco Fishing Tackle. *Graphite and Fiberglass blanks; graphite, 2 pc., 7'-10'; fiberglass, 2 pc. and 4 pc., 6'-9'.* Price: *$80-$120 (graphite), $24-$43 (fiberglass).*

Browning. *Graphite and fiberglass blanks; graphite, 2 pc., 8' and 8½'; fiberglass, 2 pc., 6'-9'.* Price: *$48.20 and $53.40 (graphite), $10.75-$21.50 (fiberglass).*

Dale Clemens Custom Tackle. *Fiberglass blanks, 2 pc., 7'-9'.* Price: *$11.78-$17.95.*

Composite Development Corporation Graphite USA. *Graphite blanks, 2, 3, and 4 pc., 6½'-11'.* Price: *$66-$140.*

Cortland Line Co. *Graphite blanks, Black Diamond models, 7-9', 2 pc.* Price: *$70-$76.*

J. Kennedy Fisher. *Graphite and fiberglass blanks. 28 graphite models, 2 and 4 pc., 7½'-10½'; 15 fiberglass models, 2 and 4 pc., 6'-9'.* Price: *$79.95-$105.95 (graphite), $17.50-$32 (fiberglass).*

Herter's, Inc. *Fiberglass blanks, 7'8"-9'.* Price: *$6.87-$9.71.*

E. Hille's Angler's Supply House. *Graphite and fiberglass blanks. Graphite, 7'-9', 2 pc. Fiberglass, 5'-10', 1- and 2-pc. models.* Price: *$50.95-$68 (graphite), $9.55-$22.15 (fiberglass).*

Lamiglas. *Graphite blanks, 2 and 3 pc., 7'-14'; fiberglass blanks, 1, 2 and 5 pc., 7'-9'.* Price: *$60-$190 (graphite), $8.55-$28 (fiberglass).*

Partridge of Redditch (Thomas & Thomas). *Bamboo blanks.* Price *n.a.*

Sceptre. *Fiberglass blanks, 10 models, 2, 3, and 4 pc., 6'3"-9'.* Price: *$16.50-$21.50.*

Scientific Anglers. *Graphite blanks, 10 models, 2 pc., 7'11'-9'4".* Price: *n.a.*

Scott PowR-Ply. *Graphite and fiberglass blanks, 8 graphite models, 2 pc., 8½'-9½'; 25 fiberglass models, 6'-9'3".* Price: *n.a.*

Sharpes. *Scottie bamboo blanks, 5 models, 2 pc. with extra tip, 6½'-8½'.* Price: *$99.50-$109.50.*

Skyline Industries. *Graphite blanks, 2 pc., 8'.* Price: *n.a.*

Wanigas Rod Company. *Graphite and fiberglass blanks; graphite, 2 pc., 7'-9'; fiberglass, 2 pc., 6'-9'.* Price: *$55-$80 (graphite), $22.50-$27.50 (fiberglass).*

R. L. Winston Rod Co. *Fiberglass blanks (31 models), 2 pc., 5½'-9'.* Price: *$32-$35.*

Hardware

Allan Tackle Guides. *Tip-top, stainless steel with chrome or black finish.* Price: *$6.63 per doz.*

Allan Tackle Ferrules. *Nickel-plated, untapered, light wall; chrome-plated, tapered, heavy wall.* Price: *$10.18-$44.52 per doz.*

Childre Fuji Hard Speed Guides. *Diamond-polished aluminum oxide one-foot guides for stripping and intermediate guides, polymer shock insert, tip-tops avail., avail. individually or in sets.* Price: *n.a.*

J. Lee Cuddy Guides. *Tip-top, snake.* Price: *$.25-$.46.*

J. Lee Cuddy Hookkeepers. *Stainless steel.* Price: *$.18.*

Herter's Ferrules and Guides. *Speed ferrules for repair of broken sections. English ferrules, complete guide sets.* Price: *$.30-$1.49.*

Hille Guide Sets. *Tip-top, snake, stripping.* Price: *$1.50-$6.90 (per set, individual guides avail.).*

Hille Hookkeepers. Price: *$.10 ea.*

Hille Winding Checks. *Aluminum.* Price: *$.30 ea.*

Hille Ferrules. *Nickel-silver and aluminum models.* Price: *$.80-$1.80.*

Orvis Winding Checks and Butt Plates. Price: *$1-$1.25.*

Orvis Guides. *Snake, tip-tops.* Price: *$4 (complete set).*

Rodon Winding Checks. *Flexible hard rubber, black or gray, 4 sizes.* Price: *$.30.*

Rodon Hookkeepers. *Stainless steel.* Price: *n.a.*

Uslan Nickel-Silver Ferrules. *Hand-machined, hand-polished finish.* Price: *$7.95 (includes one female and two male parts).*

Varmac Guides. *Snake, tip-top and stripping guides.* Price: *n.a.*

R. L. Winston Guides. *Hard-chrome snake, carbaloy stripping, ceramic stripping, tip-top.* Price: *$.25-$1.25 ea.*

R. L. Winston Winding Checks and Hookkeepers. Price: *$.25, $.05 ea.*

Cork

Dale Clemens Deluxe Custom Grip. *Cigar-shaped cork, inlaid dark rings, 6" long.* Price: *$5.75.*

J. Lee Cuddy Cork. *Rings, sticks, arbors, shaped grips.* Price: *$.08-$6.45.*

Herter's Cork Rings. *All rings ½" thick, sold in varying quantities and diameters.* Price: *$.81-$1.05 (per 14 rings).*

Hille Pre-Formed Grips. Price: *$.35-$.90.*

Hille Cork Rings. *Specie cork.* Price: *$.08-$.12 ea.*

Orvis Cork Grips. *Formed handles, or individual rings.* Price: *$.20 ea. (rings), $2.65 (shaped handle).*

R. L. Winston Cork Rings. *Select cork.* Price: *$.20 ea.*

R. L. Winston Cork Handles. *6', 6½' half-Wells style.* Price: *$2.25-$2.40.*

Reel Seats

Allan Tackle Reel Seats. *Locking aluminum.* Price: *$17.81-$31.80 per doz.*

Cal-Air Aluminum Reel Seats. *4 models, gold, brown or black colors, fixed hood and plug with retaining rings and optional lock ring.* Price: *n.a.*

Dale Clemens Ultimate Reel Seats. *Locking metal, locking cork, locking walnut, nickel-silver rings, hood and sliding ring, teak with hood and sliding ring, removable butt extensions avail.* Price: *$3.95-$11.95.*

J. Lee Cuddy Reel Seats. *Locking aluminum.* Price: *$.85.*

Herter's Reel Seats. *Down-locking metal, 2 sizes.* Price: *$1.89, $2.29.*

Hille Reel Seats. *Locking metal, extension reel seat, wood fillers avail.* Price: *$2.05-$4.85 (wood fillers, $.35 ea.)*

Orvis Reel Seats. *Down-locking metal, cork or basswood.* Price: *$4.25-$21.*

Orvis Butt Extension. *2" or 6" models.* Price: *$8.*

Orvis Sliding Rings. Price: *$2-$3.*

Rodon Reel Seats. *Aluminum locking, skeleton up- or down-locking, models for use with screw-in or push-in fighting butt, rubber plugs and extra lock rings avail., nickel-silver slide bands and hoods, aluminum slide bands and hoods, aluminum parts avail. in dark brown, black or clear anodized colors.* Price: *$1.30-$10.95.*

Rodon Wood Spacers. *For use with skeleton locking reel seats, avail. in rosewood, East Indian rosewood, bubinga, walnut, zebra wood.* Price: *n.a.*

Rodon Aluminum Fly-Rod Butt Plate. *Avail. in anodized black, dark brown or clear.* Price: *$1.25-$1.40.*

Rodon Fighting Butts. *Removable, push in or screw in, screw in avail. in anodized black, dark brown or clear, 2½" or 5" lengths, other lengths avail. on request.* Price: *$4.50-$6.50.*

Sceptre Reel Seats. *Screw-lock aluminum reel seat.* Price: *$4.45, $4.95 (with extra locking ring).*

Uslan Butt Cap and Sliding Ring. *Hand-polished nickel-silver.* Price: *$3.50 (band), $1.75 (butt cap).*

Uslan Reel Seat Assembly. *Locking polished aluminum, nickel-silver butt cap, mahogany filler.* Price: *$11.95.*

Varmac Reel Seats. *Aluminum locking reel seats.* Price: *n.a.*

R. L. Winston Reel Seats. *Aluminum hood and sliding ring, bakelite, small and large wood (walnut, rosewood or teak).* Price: *$5-$20.*

Threads and Wrapping Kits

Gudebrod Butt Wind. *Decorative flat braided-nylon tape for rod butt, 3/32" wide, 3 yds. long.* Price: *n.a.*

Gudebrod Rod-Winding Threads. *Nylon, 50-yd., 1-oz., 4-oz. spools, 00, A, D, E, EE sizes; solid colors, variegated colors, two-tone color, space dyes; silk also avail.* Price: *n.a.*

Gudebrod Rod-Wrapping Kits. *6 spools nylon thread, color preserver, rod varnish, liquid rod cement, 2 brushes, stick ferrule cement, booklet.* Price: *n.a.*

Herter's Fly-Rod Rebuilding Kit. *Guides, 2 spools thread, color preservative, rod finish.* Price: *$2.09.*

Herter's Rod Repair Kit. *Rod finish, color preservative, ferrule cement, 2 spools thread.* Price: *$1.27.*

Hille Rod-Wrapping Thread. *Assorted colors, nylon and silk.* Price: *$.30-$.65 (per 50-yd. spool).*

Orvis Rod-Wrapping Kit. *6 spools size A thread, color preserver, varnish.* Price: *$4.25.*

R. L. Winston Winding Thread. *Size 00 in assorted colors.* Price: *$.35.*

Finishes and Color Preservers

Dale Clemens Crystal Coat Wrapping Finish. *2-part epoxy, 2 oz.* Price: *$3.69.*

Gudebrod Liquid Rod Cement. *Solvent-type adhesive, 1-oz. bottle.* Price: *n.a.*

Gudebrod Cleaning Solvent. *Solvent for cleaning rod brushes, 1-oz. bottle.* Price: *n.a.*

Gudebrod Color Preserver. *1-oz. bottle.* Price: *n.a.*

Gudebrod Glass Rod Varnish. *Self-leveling plastic-resin-base varnish, 1-oz. bottle.* Price: *n.a.*

Gudebrod Hard 'n Fast Rod Finish. *2-part mix for application with natural-hair brush.* Price: *n.a.*

Herter's Rod Finish, Color Preserver and Cane Rod Covering. *1 oz. or 1 pint sizes, rod finish sold in 1 oz. size with hardener.* Price: *$.40-$6.87.*

Prices (and price ranges) listed in this directory are the manufacturer's suggested retail prices as of late 1977, and they are subject to change without notice. Please consult pp. 233-235 for addresses of manufacturers from whom up-to-date price information may be obtained, or check with your local fly-tackle dealer.

Hille Ferrule Cement, Rod Varnish, Color Preservative. Price: *$.40-.75.*

Wanigas Rod Varnish. *Bakelite-base spar, 1 oz. jar.* Price: *$1.25.*

Rod Kits

Backpacker Rod Kits (Timberline Rods). *Complete kits, 2 and 4 pc., 6'-7'.* Price: *$27.50.*

Dale Clemens Custom Tackle. *Fiberglass kits (does not include thread or varnish), 7'-8½', 2 pc.* Price: *$20.18-$21.72.*

Herter's Rod Kits. *Fiberglass and graphite.* Price: *$12.79-$15.34 (fiberglass), $39.97 (graphite 8').*

Hille Rod Kits. *Graphite and fiberglass. Fiberglass 5'-10', 1 and 2 pc., graphite, 7'-9', 2 pc.* Price: *$13.90-$30.80 (fiberglass), $67.05-$85.80 (graphite).*

Lamiglas Rod Kits. *Graphite, 2 pc., 8'-9'; fiberglass, 2 pc., 8'-9'.* Price: *$95-$106 (graphite), $22-$24 (fiberglass).*

The Orvis Co. *Bamboo kits: 19 models, 2 pc., 6½'-8½'. Graphite kits: 29 models, 1, 2 and 3 pc. (7 models with butt extension), 5'-10½'. Fiberglass kits: 18 models, 2-pc. (one 4-pc. model), 6½'-9'.* Price: *$117-$166 (bamboo), $88-$177 (graphite), $28-$77 (fiberglass).*

R. L. Winston Rod Co. *Fiberglass kits, 31 models, 2 pc., 5½'-9'.* Price: *$60-$70.*

Scott PowR-Ply. *Graphite and fiberglass kits.* Price: *n.a.*

Skyline Rod Kits. *Graphite, 2 pc., 8', 3 models.* Price: *n.a.*

Vista Custom Tackle Co. *Fiberglass and graphite kits, 2 and 4 pc., 7'-9'.* Price: *$48-$69 (graphite), $17-$26 (fiberglass).*

Wanigas Rod Kits. *Graphite, 2 pc., 7'-9'; fiberglass, 2 pc., 6'-9'.* Price: *$65-$90 (graphite), $32.50-$42.95 (fiberglass).*

Rod-Building Tools

Dale Clemens Rod Wrapping Jig. *Adjustable thread tension, 3 felt-lined U-supports, mahogany and aluminum construction.* Price: *$37.95.*

Dale Clemens Thread Tension Tool. *2"x5" base may be clamped or screwed to table, adjustable tension, holds 2 spools.* Price: *$11.95.*

Dale Clemens Tension Hardware. *Thread tension device adaptable to existing wrapping jig.* Price: *$4.50.*

Dale Clemens Rod-Building Lathe. *Head assembly with large chuck (2¼" capacity), 1/15 horsepower motor, pulleys (8:1 ratio), variable-speed foot-control.* Price: *$136.*

Dale Clemens Ball Bearing Rod Lathe Support. *Frictionless ball bearings clamp to blank to eliminate vibration.* Price: *$24.95, $47 (pair).*

Dale Clemens Thread Tool and Burnisher. *Eliminates gaps in thread wraps and aids in positioning individual threads, stainless-steel construction.* Price: *$1.60.*

J. Lee Cuddy Rod Supports. *V-grooved, felt-lined, table-clamp mount.* Price: $5.

J. Lee Cuddy Rod-Winding and Rod-Lathe Motor. Price: $16.60.

J. Lee Cuddy Rotisserie Motor. *Revolves rod for application of finish.* Price: $8.50.

J. Lee Cuddy Redwood Rod Winding Jig. *3 rod supports, mounting block for Cuddy rod-winding motor.* Price: $30.

J. Lee Cuddy Foot Speed Pedal. *For use with Cuddy rod-winding motor.* Price: $4.40.

Gudebrod Rod-Building Brushes. *Ox hair, sabeline, camel hair, round and flat handles, ¼"-1" widths.* Price: n.a.

Herter's Sable Brushes. *¼" width.* Price: $2.57.

Herter's Rod-Winding Tool. *Adjustable thread tension.* Price: $4.49.

Herter's Model Perfect Rod Wrapper. *Adjustable thread tension, holds 2 spools thread.* Price: $10.97.

Orvis Rod-Wrapping Stand. *Unassembled wood stand with V grooves and 2 spool mounts.* Price: $24.50.

Pfeiffer's Rod Master. *Wrapping device with adjustable thread tension, roller supports for rod, overall adjustable height, table-clamp mount.* Price: $24.95.

Pfeiffer Rod Rollers. *Plastic rollers, bracket, sold in sets of 4.* Price: $2.50.

Thompson Rod Winder. *Adjustable thread tension, table-clamp mount.* Price: $8.50 (rest for rod: $1.50).

Vista Custom Tackle Rod-Wrapping Jig. *2 models.* Price: $5, $12.95.

Appendix I
Addresses of Tackle Manufacturers

Aladdin Laboratories
620 S. 8th St.
Minneapolis, Minn. 55409

Algonquin Fishing Tackle
Div. of Grew Corp.
6 Bartlett Ave.
Toronto, Ontario
Canada M6H 3E7

Allan Tackle Mfg. Company
325 Duffy Ave.
Hicksville, N.Y. 11802

America's Cup
1443 Potrero Ave.
S. El Monte, Calif. 91733

American Import Company
1167 Mission St.
San Francisco, Calif. 94103

Anglersmail
6497 Pearl Rd.
Cleveland, Ohio 44130

Angler's World
16 E. 53rd St.
New York, N.Y. 10022

Backpacker Rods, see Timberline Rods

Ivan Arnold
P. O. Box 1811
Newport Beach, Calif. 92663

Dan Bailey Flies & Tackle
209 W. Park St., Box 1019
Livingston, Mont. 59047

Dennis Bailey Rods, see The Bamboo Rod (U. S. distributor)

The Bamboo Rod
Rte. 100
Weston, Vt. 05161

L. L. Bean
Main St.
Freeport, Me. 04032

Berkley and Company
Hwys. 9 & 71
Spirit Lake, Iowa 51360

Bevin-Wilcox Line Company
Div. of Brownell & Company
Main St.
Moodus, Conn. 06469

Bianco Fishing Tackle Company
3350 Sports Arena Blvd.
San Diego, Calif. 92110

S. E. Bogdan
33 Friefield St.
Nashua, N.H. 03060

Bonnand of France, see M. Sharf & Co. (U. S. distributor)

Browning
Rte. 1
Morgan, Utah 84050

Cahill House
RD #2
Benton, Pa. 17814

Cal-Air Products Company
737 N. Lake St.
Burbank, Calif. 91502

Carlson Rod Company
Rte. 31, P. O. Box 322
Greenville, N.H. 03048

Cascade Lakes Tackle Company
3 Mill Rd.
Ballston Lake, N.Y. 12019

Chaplin Tackle Company
Box 11552
Raytown, Mo. 64138

Charlie's Whipper
6052 Montgomery Bend
San Jose, Calif. 95134

Lew Childre & Sons
P. O. Box 535
Foley, Ala. 36535

Dale Clemens Custom Tackle
Rte. 2, Box 850
Wescosville, Pa. 18106

Columbia Sportswear
6600 N. Baltimore St.
Portland, Ore. 97203

Composite Development Corp.
7569 Convoy Court
San Diego, Calif. 92111

Constable Rods, see Anglersmail (U. S. distributor)

Converse
55 Fordham Rd.
Wilmington, Mass. 01887

Cortland Line Company
Cortland, N.Y. 13045

Creative Sports Enterprises
P. O. Box 2157
Walnut Creek, Calif. 94595

J. Lee Cuddy Associates
450 N.E. 79th St.
Miami, Fla. 33138

Daiwa Corp.
14011 S. Normandie Ave.
Gardenia, Calif. 90247

D-Boone Enterprises
P. O. Box 8
High Spire, Pa. 17034

Doc's Rod
208 S. Jefferson Ave.
Chicago, Ill. 60606

E. I. du Pont de Nemous & Company
Plastic Products & Resin Dept.
Wilmington, Del. 19898

Eagle Claw, see Wright & McGill

Ee-da-how Custom Rods
613 E. McArthur
Appleton, Wis. 54911

Al Ellis Rod Company
9420 N. 16th St.
Phoenix, Ariz. 85020

Fenwick
Box 723
Westminster, Calif. 92683

Feurer Bros.
77 Lafayette Ave.
North White Plains, N.Y. 10603

Fireside Angler
P. O. Box 823
Melville, N.Y. 11746

J. Kennedy Fisher
6701 11th Ave.
Los Angeles, Calif. 90043

Fly Fisherman's Bookcase & Tackle Service
3890 Stewart Rd.
Eugene, Ore. 97402

Fly-Rite
Box 6101
Flint, Mich. 48508

Fly-Safe Company
8 White St.
Barre, Vt. 05641

Fly-Tyer's Carry-All
Box 299 Village Station
New York, N.Y. 10014

Garcia Corp.
329 Alfred Ave.
Teaneck, N.J. 07666

Gladding Corp.
Fishing Line Division
South Otselic, N.Y. 13155

Gudebrod
12 S. 12th St.
Philadelphia, Pa. 19107

Hackle & Tackle Company
Central Square, N.Y. 13036

Hardy Bros., see Harrington & Richardson (U. S. distributor)

Harrington & Richardson
Industrial Rowe
Gardner, Mass. 01440

H. Hart Tackle Corp.
566 Walt Whitman Rd.
Melville, N.Y. 11746

James Heddon's Sons
414 West St.
Dowagiac, Mich. 49047

Herter's
Rte. 1
Waseca, Minn. 56093

E. Hille
The Angler's Supply House
P. O. Box 996
Williamsport, Pa. 17701

HMH Tools
Valley View Lane
New Boston, N.H. 03070

G. H. Howells Rod Company
655 33rd St.
Richmond, Calif. 94804

Ike's Fly Shop
23461 Norwood
Oak Park, Mich. 48237

Isaac Franklin
630 N. Pulaski St.
Baltimore, Md. 21217

Kaufmann's Streamborn Fly Shop
P. O. Box 23032
Portland, Ore. 97223

King Eider Silk Lines
98 Coolidge Rd.
Worcester, Mass. 01602

Kodiak Corp.
P. O. Box 467
Ironwood, Mich. 49938

Korkers
P. O. Box 166
1924 S. W. G St.
Grants Pass, Ore. 97526

Laggie's Fish Catching Company
7059 Varna Ave.
N. Hollywood, Calif. 91605

Lamiglas
P.O. Box 148
Woodland, Wash. 98674

H. L. Leonard Rod Company
Central Valley, N.Y. 10917

Liberty Organization
P.O. Box 306
Montrose, Calif. 91020

Marathon Rubber Products Company
510 Sherman St.
Wausau, Wis. 54401

Martin Reel Company
30 E. Main St.
P. O. Drawer 8
Mohawk, N.Y. 13407

Mason Tackle Company
Otisville, Mich. 48463

Masterline, see Gudebrod (U. S. distributor)

Frank Matarelli
San Francisco, Calif.

Maxima
Bruce B. Mises
1122 S. Robertson Blvd.
Los Angeles, Calif. 90035

Minute Mend Company
Div. of H & G Enterprises
30160 Maison
St. Clair Shores, Mich. 48082

O. Mustad & Son (USA) Inc.
Box 838, 185 Clark St.
Auburn, N.Y. 13021

Nelson Sales Company
626 Broadway
Kansas City, Mo. 64105

Gus Nevros Rods, see Fireside Angler (distributor)

O. L. M. International Corp.
145 Sylvester St.
S. San Francisco, Calif. 94080

O'Neill Waders, see Creative Sports Enterprises (distributor)

The Orvis Company
Manchester, Vt. 05254

A. E. Partridge and Sons Ltd.
Mount Pleasant
Redditch, Worcestershire B97 4JE
England

E. F. Payne Rod Company
Highland Mills, N.Y. 10930

Russ Peak
21 North Allen Ave.
Pasadena, Calif. 91106

J. F. Pepper Company
RD #1
Lee Center, N.Y. 13363

Perrine, see Aladdin Laboratories

Pezon et Michel, see Stoeger Industries (U. S. distributor)

Pfeiffer's Tackle Crafters
9306 Joey Dr.
Ellicott City, Md. 21043

Pflueger
1801 Main St.
P. O. Box 185
Columbia, S.C. 29202

Phelps Flies Company
42 Ridge St.
Katonah, N.Y. 10536

Plano Molding Company
113 South Center Ave.
Plano, Ill. 60545

Powell Rod Company
1148 W. 8th Ave.
Chico, Calif. 94926

Price's Anglers' Corner
15637 Sherrie Way
P. O. Box 356
LaPine, Ore. 97739

Quick Corp. of America
620 Terminal Way
Costa Mesa, Calif. 92627

Ranger Rubber Company
Div. of Endicott Johnson
1100 E. Main St.
Endicott, N.Y. 13760

Richardson Chest Fly Box
Osceola Mills, Pa. 16666

Hank Roberts Outfitters
1033 Walnut St.
Boulder, Coló. 80302

Rodon Manufacturing Company
123 Sylvan Ave.
Newark, N.J. 07104

Royal Red Ball
8530 Page Ave.
St. Louis, Mo. 63114

Ryobi America Corp.
Ryobi Group
1555 Carmen Dr.
Elk Grove, Ill. 60007

St. Andrews Ltd., see Ike's Fly Shop

St. Croix Corp.
9909 S. Shore Dr.
Minneapolis, Minn. 55441

Sampo
North St.
Barneveld, N.Y. 13304

Sceptre Rods, see Anglersmail

Fritz Von Schlegell
1407 Sante Fe Ave.
Los Angeles, Calif. 90021

Scientific Anglers/3M Company
New Business Ventures/Leisure Time
3M Center
St. Paul, Minn. 55101

Scott PowR-Ply Company
111 Cook St.
San Francisco, Calif. 94118

Seal Dri
Div. of Wichita Canvas Supply
2945 S. Kansas
Wichita, Kan. 67216

Seamaster Corp.
4615 Le Jeune Rd.
Coral Gables, Fla. 33146

Seaway Importing Company
7200 N. Oak Pk. Ave.
Niles, Ill. 60648

T. R. Seidel Company
P. O. Box 268
Arvada, Colo. 80001

Shakespeare Company
Box 246
Columbia, S.C. 29202

M. Sharf & Company
200 McGrath Hwy.
Somerville, Mass. 02143

J. S. Sharpes Rods, see Anglersmail (U. S. distributor)

Skyline Industries
4900 N. E. Parkway
Fort Worth, Tex. 76101

Sportsman's Felt Company
368 Prospect Ave.
Hartford, Conn. 06105

Stoeger Industries
55 Ruta Court
S. Hackensack, N.J. 07606

R. W. Summers
1142 E. 8th St.
Traverse City, Mich. 49684

Sunrise India
233/5 Ach, Jagadish Bose Rd.
Calcutta-20, India

Sunset Line & Twine Company
Petaluma, Calif. 94952

Dick Surette Fly Fishing Shop
Box 686
North Conway, N.H. 03860

Tackle Craft
Chippewa Falls, Wis. 54729

Pete Test's Compleat Angler
P. O. Box 14441
Albuquerque, N.M. 87111

Thomas & Thomas
22 Third St.
Turner's Falls, Mass. 01376

Thompson Tackletools
D. H. Thompson
11 N. Union St.
Elgin, Ill. 60120

Timberline Rods
Box 774 N. Main St.
North Conway, N.H. 03860

Trimarc
High Point Plaza
Hillside, Ill. 60162

Turrall of Devon, see M. Sharf & Co. (U. S. distributor)

Tycoon/Fin-Nor Corp.
29 Essex St.
Maywood, N.J. 07607

U. S. Line Co., Inc.
22 Main St.
Westfield, Mass. 01085

Universal Vise Company
22 Main St.
Westfield, Mass. 01085

Uslan Rod Mfg. & Sales Corp.
18679 W. Dixie Hwy.
N. Miami Beach, Fla. 33160

Valentine Reels

Val-Craft
67 N. Worcester St.
Chartley, Mass. 02712

Vandy's DriBut Never Slip Company
P. O. Drawer 1149
Ceasar Blvd.
Glenwood Springs, Colo. 81601

Varmac Manufacturing Company
4201 Redwood Ave.
Los Angeles, Calif. 90066

Veniard, see M. Sharf & Co. (U. S. distributor)

Vista Custom Tackle
1064 Chambers Court #101
Aurora, Colo. 80011

Vlchek Plastics Company
Middlefield, Ohio 44062

Wanigas Rod Company
4855 Sheridan Rd.
Saginaw, Mich. 48601

Marcus Warwick Rods, see Ike's Fly Shop (U. S. distributor)

Webley & Scott Ltd.
Park Lane
Handsworth, Birmingham
England B21 8LU

Weir & Son
101 W. Main St.
Los Gatos, Calif. 94030

Richard Wheatley Fly Boxes, see M. Sharf & Co. (U. S. distributor)

R. L. Winston Rod Company
Box 248
Twin Bridges, Mont. 59574

Wright & McGill Company
4245 E. 46th St.
Denver, Colo. 80216

World Famous Sales Company
3580 N. Elston Ave.
Chicago, Ill. 60618

The Worth Company
P. O. Box 88
Stevens Point, Wis. 54481

Paul H. Young Company
14039 Peninsula Dr.
Traverse City, Mich. 49684

Zebco
Division of Brunswick Corp.
6101 E. Apache
Tulsa, Okla. 74101

Appendix II
Retail Suppliers of Flies

The Andra Company
P.O. Box 137
Southport, Conn. 06490

Anglersport
5236 Dundas St.
Burlington, Ont.
Canada L7R 3L3

Angling Specialties Company
Box 97
Ancaster, Ont.
Canada L9G 3L3

Dan Bailey Flies & Tackle
209 West Park St.
Livingston, Mont. 59047

Pat Barnes Tackle Shop
West Yellowstone, Mont. 59758

The Battenkill Angler's Nook
Route 313
Shushan, N.Y. 12973

Beaverkill Sportsman
Broad St.
Roscoe, N.Y. 12776

Chuck Billie's
Northern Wildlife
P.O. Box 116
Lake Nebagamon, Wis. 54849

Bodmer's Fly Shop
2400 Naegle Rd.
Colorado Springs, Colo. 90904

Buz's Fly and Tackle Shop
805 West Tulare Ave.
Visalia, Calif. 93277

The Caddis Fly Angling Shop
688 Olive St.
Eugene, Ore. 97401

Cahill House
R.D. 2
Benton, Pa. 17814

Cascade Tackle Company
2425 Diamond Lake Blvd.
Roseburg, Ore. 97470

The Compleat Angler
P.O. Box 6712
Asheville, N.C. 28806

Creative Anglers
P.O. Box 3186
Boulder, Colo. 80807

Mr. and Mrs. Harry Darbee
Roscoe, N.Y. 12776

Doiron Enterprises
R.R. #1, Westfield
Kings County, N.B.
Canada E0G 3J0

Fireside Angler Inc.
P.O. Box 823
Melville, N.Y. 11746

FisHair Inc.
P.O. Box 8367
St. Paul, Minn. 55113

The Fisherman's Fly
941 Chicago Ave.
Evanston, Ill. 60202

Fishin' Fool Fly Shoppe
760 Main Ave. N.
Twin Falls, Idaho 83301

The Fly Factory
P.O. Box 1900
Sparks, Nev. 89431

The Fly Line Inc.
2935 Washington Blvd.
Ogden, Utah 84401

The Flyfisher
315 Columbine St.
Denver, Colo. 80206

Fly Fisherman's Bookcase and
Tackle Service
3890 Stewart Road
Eugene, Ore. 97402

Flyfisher's Paradise
P.O. Box 448
Lemont, Pa. 16851

Fly-Rite
Box 6101
Flint, Mich. 48508

Gapen's World of Fishing Inc.
Hwy. 10
Big Lake, Minn. 55309

Greenwich Sportsman Center
398 Greenwich Ave.
Greenwich, Conn. 06830

Ned Grey's Sierra Tackle
2615 Honolulu Ave.
P.O. Box 338
Montrose, Calif. 91020

Hackle & Tackle Company
Central Square, N.Y. 13036

The Hatch
P.O. Box 5624
Tucson, Ariz. 85705

Henry's Fork Anglers
P.O. Box 487
St. Anthony, Idaho 83445

Jim Hepner's Twin Rivers Tackle Shop
1206 North River Ave.
Sunbury, Pa. 17801

Herter's Inc.
Waseca, Minn. 56093

High Country Flies
Box 1022
Jackson, Wyo. 83001

E. Hille The Angler's Supply House Inc.
P.O. Box 996
Williamsport, Pa. 17701

Hoffman's Fly Shop
Rte. 2, Box 41A
Dauphin, Pa. 17018

Hoffman's Hackle Farm
P.O. Box 130
Warrenton, Ore. 97146

Hook and Hackle Company
Box 1003
Plattsburg, N.Y. 12901

Hunter's Fly Shop
Valley View Lane
New Boston, N.H. 03070

Joe's Tackle Shop
186 Main St.
Warehouse Point, Conn. 06088

Kaufmann's Streamborn Fly Shop
P.O. Box 23032
Portland, Ore. 97223

The Keel Fly Company
Thornapple Village
Ada, Mich. 49301

Laggie's Fish Catching Company
7059 Varna Ave.
North Hollywood, Calif. 91605

Lakefork Flies
P.O. Box 741
Lakefork, Idaho 83635

H. L. Leonard Rod Inc.
P.O. Box 393
Central Valley, N.Y. 10917

Bud Lilly
Trout Shop
Box 698
West Yellowstone, Mont. 59758

John May
33019 West Chicago
Livonia, Mich. 48150

William S. McIntyre
106 White Gate Rd.
Pittsburgh, Pa. 15238

Monson's Custom Tackle
P.O. Box 518
Ephrata, Wash. 98823

Neptune Boat and Tackle Inc.
P.O. Box 267
Wilsonville, Ore. 97070

Ojai Fisherman
218 North Encinal Ave.
Ojai, Calif. 93023

Oliver's Orvis Shop
44 Main St.
Clinton, N.J. 08809

The Orvis Company
Manchester, Vt. 05254

The Orvis Shop Inc.
7710 Cantrell Rd.
Little Rock, Ark. 77207

Park's Fly Shop
Gardiner, Mont. 59030

The Plumlea Angler
1 Swan St.
Biltmore Village
Asheville, N.C. 28803

Poulsen Quality Flies
2605 NE Pacific St.
Portland, Ore. 97232

Price's Angler's Corner
General Delivery
LaPine, Ore. 97739

Rangeley Region Sport Shop
Box 850
Rangeley, Me. 04970

Norton S. Remmer
98 Coolidge Rd.
Worcester, Mass. 01602

The Rivergate
Box 275 (Rte. 9)
Cold Spring, N.Y. 10516

Hank Roberts Outfitters
P.O. Box 171
1033 Walnut St.
Boulder, Colo. 80302

Rod and Reel
P.O. Box 132
Leola, Pa. 17540

Rogers Fly Shop
Box 297
Etowah, N.C. 28729

Raymond C. Rumpf & Son
Ferndale, Pa. 18921

Seamaster Corp.
4615 Le Jeune Rd.
Coral Gables, Fla. 33146

Shannon's Fly & Tackle Shop
Califon, N.J. 07830

Shive's Custom Flies
Box 218
Pagosa Springs, Colo. 81147

Silk Fur & Feathers
P.O. Box 6193
Fort Lauderdale, Fla. 33310

Streamside Anglers
P.O. Box 2158
Missoula, Mont. 59801

Dick Surette Fly Fishing Shop
Box 686
North Conway, N.H. 03860

Al Troth Custom Tied Flies
Box 1307
Dillon, Mont. 59725

Wanigas Rod Company
4855 Sheridan Rd.
Saginaw, Mich. 48601

Weir & Son
101 West Main St.
Los Gatos, Calif. 95030

Wilderness Enterprises
124 East Olympic Blvd.
Los Angeles, Calif. 90015

Woodsan Trout Shop
3394 Lake Elmo Ave.
Lake Elmo, Minn. 55042

The Wo'Zoo Fly Shop
RD 2, Box 192B
Wilkes-Barre, Pa. 18702

Yankee Fly Tyers
Rockland Road
Roscoe, N.Y. 12776

Yellow Breeches Fly Shop
Box 200, Rte. 174
Boiling Springs, Pa. 17007

Appendix III
Fish-and-Game Departments in the United States and Canada

UNITED STATES

Alabama Dept. of Conservation
and Natural Resources
64 N. Union St.
Montgomery, Ala. 36104
(205) 269-7221

Alaska Dept. of Fish and Game
Subport Bldg.
Juneau, Alaska 99801
(907) 465-4100

Arizona Game and Fish Dept.
2222 W. Greenway Rd.
Phoenix, Ariz. 85023
(602) 942-3000

Arkansas Game and Fish
Commission
Game and Fish Bldg.
Little Rock, Ark. 72201
(501) 371-1145

California Dept. of Fish and Game
The Resources Agency
1416 9th St.
Sacramento, Calif. 95814
(916) 445-3535

Colorado Dept. of Natural
Resources
Division of Wildlife
6060 Broadway
Denver, Colo. 80216
(303) 825-1192

Connecticut Dept. of
Environmental Protection
State Office Bldg.
Hartford, Conn. 06115
(203) 566-5460

Delaware Dept. of Natural
Resources and Environmental
Control
Division of Fish and Wildlife
D Street
Dover, Del. 19901
(302) 678-4431

District of Columbia Metropolitan
Police
300 Indiana Ave., NW
Washington, D.C. 20001
(202) 626-2305

Florida Dept. of Natural Resources
620 S. Meridian
Tallahassee, Fla. 32304
(904) 488-2972

Georgia State Game and Fish
Division
Trinity-Washington Bldg.
270 Washington St., SW
Atlanta, Ga. 30334
(404) 656-3500

Guam Dept. of Agriculture
Division of Fish and Wildlife
Agana, Guam 96910
772-6866

Hawaii Dept. of Land and Natural
Resources
Division of Fish and Game
1179 Punchbowl St.
Honolulu, Hawaii 96813
(808) 548-4000

Idaho Fish and Game Dept.
600 S. Walnut, Box 25
Boise, Idaho 83707
(208) 384-3771

Illinois Dept. of Conservation
State Office Bldg.
Springfield, Ill. 62706
(217) 782-6302

Indiana Dept. of Natural
Resources
Division of Fish and Wildlife
608 State Office Bldg.
Indianapolis, Ind. 46204
(317) 633-6344

Iowa State Conservation
Commission
State Office Bldg.
300 4th St.
Des Moines, Iowa 50319
(515) 281-5384

Kansas Forestry, Fish and Game
Commission
Box 1028
Pratt, Kan. 67124
(316) 672-5911

Kentucky Dept. of Fish and
Wildlife Resources
Capitol Plaza Tower
Frankfort, Ky. 40601
(502) 564-3400

Louisiana Wildlife and Fisheries
Commission
P.O. Box 44095
Capitol Station
Baton Rouge, La. 70804

Maine Dept. of Inland Fisheries
and Game
State Office Bldg.
Augusta, Me. 04330
(207) 289-3371

Maryland Fish and Wildlife
Administration
Natural Resources Bldg.
Annapolis, Md. 21401

Massachusetts Dept. of
Environmental Resources
100 Cambridge St.
Boston, Mass. 02202
(617) 727-3151

Michigan Dept. of Natural
Resources
Mason Bldg.
Lansing, Mich. 48926
(517) 373-1220

Minnesota Dept. of Natural
Resources
Division of Game and Fish
301 Centennial Bldg.
658 Cedar St.
St. Paul, Minn. 55101
(612) 296-2894

Mississippi Game and Fish
Commission
Robert E. Lee Office Bldg.
239 N. Lamar St.
P.O. Box 451
Jackson, Miss. 39205

Missouri Dept. of
Conservation
P.O. Box 180
Jefferson City, Mo. 65101
(314) 751-4115

Montana Fish and Game Dept.
Helena, Mont. 59601
(406) 449-3186

Nebraska Game and Parks
Commission
P.O. Box 30370
2200 N. 33rd
Lincoln, Neb. 68503
(402) 464-0641

Nevada Dept. of Fish and Game
Box 10678
Reno, Nev. 89510
(702) 784-6214

New Hampshire Fish and Game Dept.
34 Bridge St.
Concord, N.H. 03301
(603) 271-3421

New Jersey Dept. of
Environmental Protection
Division of Fish, Game, and Shellfisheries
Box 1390
Trenton, N.J. 08625
(609) 292-7348

New Mexico Dept. of Game and Fish
State Capitol
Santa Fe, N.M. 87501
(505) 827-2923

New York Dept. of Environmental
Conservation
Fish and Wildlife Division
50 Wolf Rd.
Albany, N.Y. 12201
(518) 457-5960

North Carolina Wildlife
Resources Commission
325 N. Salisbury St.
Raleigh, N.C. 27611
(919) 829-3391

North Dakota State Game and
Fish Dept.
2121 Lovett Ave.
Bismarck, N.D. 58501
(701) 224-2180

Ohio Dept. of Natural Resources
Division of Wildlife
Fountain Square
Columbus, Ohio 43224
(614) 466-4603

Oklahoma Dept. of Wildlife
Conservation
1801 N. Lincoln
P.O. Box 53465
Oklahoma City, Okla. 73105
(405) 521-3851

Oregon Fish and Wildlife
Commission
Box 3503
Portland, Ore. 97208
(503) 229-6593

Pennsylvania Fish Commission
P.O. Box 1567
Harrisburg, Pa. 17120
(717) 787-3633

Puerto Rico Dept. of Natural
Resources
P.O. Box 11488
San Juan, P.R. 00910

Rhode Island Dept. of Natural
Resources
Division of Fish and Wildlife
83 Park St.
Providence, R.I. 02903
(401) 277-2784

South Carolina Wildlife Resources
Dept.
Box 167
1015 Main St.
Columbia, S.C. 29202
(803) 758-2561

South Dakota Dept. of Game,
Fish and Parks
State Office Bldg.
Pierre, S.D. 57501
(605) 224-3387

Tennessee Wildlife Resources
Agency
Box 40747
Ellington Agricultural Center
Nashville, Tenn. 37220
(605) 741-1431

Texas Parks and Wildlife Dept.
John H. Reagan Bldg.
Austin, Tex. 78701
(512) 475-8074

Utah State Dept. of Natural
Resources
Division of Wildlife Resources
1596 W.N. Temple
Salt Lake City, Utah 84116
(801) 328-5081

Vermont Agency of Environmental
Conservation
Fish and Game Dept.
Montpelier, Vt. 05602
(802) 828-3371

Virginia Commission of Game
and Inland Fisheries
4010 W. Broad St.
Box 11104
Richmond, Va. 23230
(804) 770-4974

Washington Dept. of
Fisheries
115 General Administration Bldg.
Olympia, Wash. 98504
(206) 753-6623

Washington Dept. of Game
600 N. Capitol Way
Olympia, Wash. 98504
(206) 753-5700

West Virginia Dept. of Natural
Resources
1800 Washington St., East
Charleston, W.Va. 25305
(304) 348-2754

Wisconsin Dept. of Natural
Resources
Box 450
Madison, Wis. 53701
(608) 266-2243

Wyoming Game and
Fish Dept.
Box 1589
Cheyenne, Wyo. 82001
(307) 777-7631

CANADA

Alberta Dept. of Recreation,
Parks and Wildlife
Fish and Wildlife Division
9833 109th St.
Edmonton, Alta.
Canada T5K 2E1
(403) 427-6749

British Columbia Dept. of
Recreation and Tourism
Fish and Wildlife Branch
Parliament Bldgs.
Victoria, B.C.
Canada V8V 1X4
(604) 387-6409

Manitoba Dept. of Renewable
Resources and Transportation Services
1495 St. James St.
Winnipeg, Man.
Canada R3H 0W9
(204) 786-9252

New Brunswick Dept. of Natural
Resources
Fish and Wildlife Branch
Centennial Bldg.
Fredericton, N.B.
Canada E3B 5H1
(506) 453-2433

Newfoundland Dept. of Fisheries
Viking Bldg.
Crosbie Rd.
St. John's, Nfld.
Canada A1C 5T7
(709) 737-3707

Nova Scotia Dept. of Fisheries
Howe Bldg.
Halifax, N.S.
Canada B3J 3C4
(902) 424-7653

Ontario Ministry of Natural Resources
Division of Fish and Wildlife
Parliament Bldg.
Toronto, Ont.
Canada M7A 1X5
(416) 965-4704

Prince Edward Island Dept. of
Fisheries
Provincial Administration Bldg.
P.O. Box 2000
Charlottetown, P.E.I.
Canada C1A 7N8
(902) 892-3493

Quebec Dept. of Tourism, Fish
and Game
150 St. Cyrille E.
Quebec City, Que.
Canada G1R 4Y3
(418) 643-2205

Saskatchewan Dept. of Tourism
and Renewable Resources
Fisheries and Wildlife Branch
Financial Bldg.
Regina, Sask.
Canada S4P 2H9
(306) 523-1693

N.W.T. Dept. of Economic
Development
Division of Game Management
Yellowknife, N.W.T.
Canada OXE 1HO
(403) 873-8263

Yukon Territorial Government
Game Branch
Box 2703
Whitehorse, Y.T.
Canada Y1A 2C6
(403) 667-5228